HUMAN SOCIETIES

HUMAN SOCIETIES

AN INTRODUCTION TO MACROSOCIOLOGY   Second Edition

GERHARD LENSKI   **JEAN LENSKI**

McGRAW-HILL BOOK COMPANY

New York   St. Louis   San Francisco   Düsseldorf   Johannesburg   Kuala Lumpur
London   Mexico   Montreal   New Delhi   Panama   Rio de Janeiro   Singapore
Sydney   Toronto

COVER SCULPTURE: "City Square" by Giacometti. Used by permission of Morton G. Neumann.

This book was set in Helvetica Light by Progressive Typographers. The editors were David Edwards, Ronald Kissack, and David Dunham; the designer was Janet Durey Bollow; and the production supervisor was Thomas J. LoPinto. The drawings were done by Edward Malsberg. The printer was The Murray Printing Company; the binder, The Book Press, Inc.

HUMAN SOCIETIES

AN INTRODUCTION TO MACROSOCIOLOGY

1234567890   MUBP   79876543

Library of Congress Cataloging in Publication Data

Lenski, Gerhard Emmanuel, date
  Human societies.

  Includes bibliographical references.
  1. Sociology. 2. Social evolution. I. Lenski,
Jean, joint author. II. Title.
HM51.L357 1974   301   73-8956
ISBN 0-07-037172-5

Contents

Preface

The reception given the first edition of *Human Societies* has been a source of continuing pleasure for both of us. We have particularly enjoyed hearing the reactions of students at a wide variety of institutions, both in this country and abroad. These responses have reinforced our belief that introductory sociology can be intellectually challenging — and relevant to the crises and controversies confronting societies today. But this requires a framework that pulls together the various threads of our discipline; a framework that raises important questions and relates them to research findings; a framework that only a coherent, parsimonious body of theory can provide.

Unfortunately, neither functionalism nor eclecticism has provided this. Courses built on these foundations too easily degenerate into a plethora of definitions, facts, techniques, and scattered hypotheses, with little or nothing to hold them together or justify their place in the course. When such a course succeeds, it says more for the instructor's talents and efforts than it does for the course. Little wonder so many senior faculty over the last several decades have pulled their rank and fled the course — pleading their skills were required elsewhere!

In the preface to the first edition, we noted the criticisms most often directed at the introductory course and argued that an ecological-evolutionary approach would help to overcome them:

1. The course presents a largely static, structural view of society — despite the fact that we are living through a social revolution.
2. The course concentrates on *micro*level phenomena (i.e., social psychology and institutional materials) and neglects the *macro*level (i.e., total societies).
3. The course tends to be ethnocentric, focusing chiefly on American society despite the increasing need to understand other societies.
4. The course overemphasizes the systemic qualities of societies, slighting the crucial processes of social conflict.
5. The course devotes too much attention to terminology, too little to explaining social phenomena.
6. The materials of the course are poorly integrated and do not add up to a coherent and meaningful body of knowledge.
7. The course is not sufficiently challenging, especially for today's students, who are better prepared in the social sciences than their predecessors of twenty years ago.

We believe that the ecological-evolutionary approach deals more effectively with each of these problems. To begin with, it puts social change right where it belongs—at center stage. It automatically focuses on macrolevel phenomena, for it is, after all, societies which are evolving. Moreover, because its approach is comparative, it forces students to consider other societies. It also, inevitably, directs attention to social conflict. Then, evolutionary theory is far more concerned with explanation than with definition. And because it *is* explanatory, it integrates the materials in the field and facilitates the accumulation of knowledge. All of this together, of course, adds up to a much greater challenge for students, and it also brings the introductory course more into line with the newer trends in theory.

There is one other benefit to this approach, and we believe it is a considerable one. The ecological-evolutionary approach provides a remarkably effective vehicle for pulling together not only the scattered materials of sociology, but the basic findings of the other social sciences and biology as well. This is no small contribution in the modern multiversity, where the fragmentation of knowledge has become such a serious impediment to learning. Sociology may never become "the queen of the sciences," as some nineteenth-century sociologists hoped. But the evolutionary approach may yet make it "the integrator of the social sciences."

A comparison of this edition of *Human Societies* with the earlier one will reveal both continuity and change. The basic theoretical framework is the same, though a bit tighter and clearer perhaps. Chapter 4, where we develop the critical argument for technology's unique role in the evolutionary process, has been substantially overhauled, and we think both students and instructors will find the analysis built around Figure 4.3 a significant improvement. We also believe that the treatment of both environment and population has been substantially improved throughout the book.

Another important modification is the expanded application of ecological-evolutionary theory to contemporary problems. In particular, we enlarged our analyses of the environmental crisis and the problems of developing nations, and added a unit on the changing role of women. Also, the chapters on industrial societies now include more detailed comparisons of socialist and nonsocialist nations. All these topics flow naturally from an ecological-evolutionary mode of analysis.

The chief deletion from the original edition was Chapter 3, in which we analyzed the relationship between sociocultural and organic evolution. We have been persuaded that this analysis was more suitable for professional sociologists and graduate students than for introductory students. We hated to see it go and hope you will send some of your brighter, more highly motivated students back to it. At any rate, dropping it enabled us to expand the analysis of the modern industrial era, which we know will meet with general approval.

ACKNOWLEDGMENTS

It is impossible to acknowledge all our intellectual debts, but we must mention the following scholars, whose writings are clearly reflected in these pages: Thomas Malthus, Charles Darwin, Karl Marx, Thorstein Veblen, Max Weber, William Graham Sumner, Albert Keller, William Ogburn, R. H. Tawney, V. Gordon Childe, Ralph Turner, G. G. Simpson, Sir Julian Huxley, Leslie White, Julian Steward, and Amos Hawley. And we ask that the footnotes in this volume be regarded as so many further acknowledgments of indebtedness and appreciation.

A number of scholars were kind enough to provide valuable suggestions and criticisms for either the original edition or this revision. Those to whom we owe a real debt in this connection include Alfred E. Emerson, David Featherman, George Furniss, Walter Goldschmidt, Amos Hawley, Donald Irish, Philip Marcus, Ross Purdy, Norman Storer, and Everett K. Wilson.

To Ronald Kissack, our editor at McGraw-Hill, we both extend our warmest thanks. His able assistance and constant support have been invaluable; his enthusiasm and good humor have made our collaboration a pleasure from the beginning. His combination of attributes are rare indeed.

Finally, we want to acknowledge the skill and care of Mrs. L. H. Snyder in typing the manuscript.

Gerhard Lenski
Jean Lenski

Chapel Hill

Part I
GENERAL INTRODUCTION TO HUMAN SOCIETIES

CHAPTER ONE
Starting Points

The most striking feature of contemporary life is the revolutionary pace of social change. Never before have things changed so fast for so much of mankind. Everything is affected: art, science, religion, morality, education, politics, the economy, family life, even the inner aspects of our lives—nothing has escaped.

There is probably no better indicator of this than our language, for it mirrors the world around us. Words and phrases that only a short time ago were unknown, or had very different meanings, are now integral parts of our speech and our thinking:

> . . . the Pill . . . the Bomb . . . Women's Lib . . . nuclear power . . . strip mining . . . organ transplants . . . moon shots . . . hard rock . . . transistors . . . Medicare . . . napalm . . . swinging . . . tripping . . . data banks . . . black power . . . the population explosion . . . communications satellites . . . genetic engineering . . . the Third World . . . instant replay . . . automation . . . the computer . . . the environmental crisis . . .

This social revolution—for that is what it is—raises urgent questions. What is causing it? Where is it leading? Most important of all, how can we control it, how ensure that it does not culminate some terrible day in an atomic holocaust, an ecological disaster of global proportions, or an Orwellian 1984?

In many ways, we are like travelers in a rocket ship hurtling through space on an unknown trajectory. Even worse, we have only the most limited knowledge of the vehicle—our society—on which our lives depend. Under the circumstances, it is not surprising that people are more concerned today than ever before with the study of human societies.

Sociology is the branch of modern science that specializes in the study of human societies.[1] Its aims and interests are extremely broad. Some sociologists study the subunits that make up societies—such as communities, family groups, political parties, and churches. Others focus on societal processes—processes of urban growth, the political process, the educational process. Still others study various problems that afflict human societies—poverty, for example, or crime, or racial conflict. All these studies contribute to our understanding of the larger picture.

It would be a mistake, of course, to suppose that only sociologists study

---

[1] For a definition of this and other terms, see the Glossary, pp. 492–499.

human societies. They share this interest to a greater or lesser degree with most other social scientists. As a consequence, any analysis of human societies, such as this volume develops, draws on the contributions of scholars in a wide variety of fields, especially anthropology, history, political science, and economics.

The primary purpose of this volume is to introduce you to the results of the modern study of human societies. While no single book can present more than a fraction of the knowledge accumulated by social scientists in the last hundred years or more, we will cover the most basic findings. The more detailed or specialized are left to subsequent books and courses.

Another way of stating the purpose of this volume is to say that it seeks to provide you, the reader, with a comprehensive and meaningful framework for organizing your thinking about human societies. Facts alone are not enough. If they are to be useful, they have to be organized in a meaningful framework. Without that, we have difficulty even remembering what we have learned.

In sociology, as in any large and active field of study, controversy is inevitable. Not all sociologists share the view of human societies presented in this volume. A brief history of sociology is appended at the end of this chapter, partly to provide a historical survey for those who are interested but also to indicate some of the controversies that divide sociologists. Suffice it to say here that sociology is currently in a period of transition. The structural-functional approach to the study of human societies, which dominated the field from the 1930s to the 1960s, is now being challenged by alternative approaches. One of the more promising is the ecological-evolutionary approach, and that is the one on which this volume is based.

HUMAN SOCIETIES: THEIR PLACE IN NATURE

Though human societies are an important and familiar part of the world we live in, their relation to other parts of the world of nature is not always clearly understood. In fact, many people think of them as somehow set apart from the rest of the natural world. While it is true that human societies *are* unique in a number of fundamental ways, it is also true that they share many essential characteristics with other parts of the natural world. Therefore, it is important to establish at the outset the place of man's societies in the natural order and to spell out the consequences of this relationship.

As many scholars have observed, the world of nature is structured much like a system of wheels within wheels, with all the parts ultimately related. Thus, when we examine any object carefully, we find that it is made up of various differentiated parts and that these parts, in turn, are made up of still smaller parts. In the same way, we find that our original object is a unit within some larger, more inclusive system, and that this system is, in turn, part of a still larger and more inclusive system.

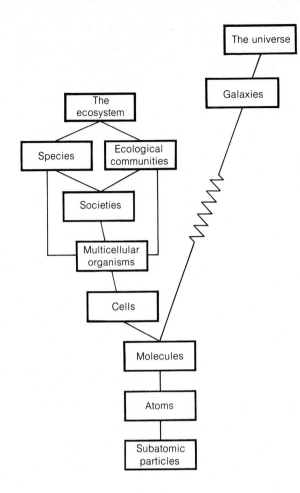

Figure 1.1 The hierarchy of organization.

As a starting point for our analysis of human societies, it is helpful to see where they are located in this complex hierarchy. Figure 1.1 provides a somewhat oversimplified view of the matter. Subatomic particles, such as electrons and protons, form the lowest level in the hierarchy of organization. These are combined in various ways to form atoms, such as carbon and radium. Atoms, in turn, are organized to form molecules, such as water, salt, amino acids, and proteins. Though Figure 1.1 does not show it, molecules constitute more than a single level in the hierarchy, since certain of the simpler molecules, the amino acids, for example, are the building blocks for more complex and more inclusive molecules, such as the proteins.

Once we go beyond the level of molecules, we encounter the important division between living and nonliving things. Since our concern is with human societies, we need not examine all the levels in the hierarchy of nonliving things. Suffice it to note that this hierarchy leads by degrees to the level of the giant galaxies, or star systems, that wheel through space, and it appears to end with the universe itself.

Societies, by contrast, are part of the biotic world, the world of plants and animals. More specifically, they are one of the forms of organization found in that world. From the standpoint of inclusiveness, they are between the level of the multicellular organism and the level of the species. In other words, some species are divided into territorially bounded subunits known as societies, and these societies, in turn, are made up of individual organisms.

As Figure 1.1 suggests, relations among the various levels and types of organizations in the biotic world become rather complex once we go beyond the level of the multicellular organism. For one thing, not all species are divided into societies (as the direct line from organism to species, bypassing the societal level, denotes). For another thing, species and ecological communities are two different, but overlapping, forms of organization on essentially the same level of inclusiveness.[2]

For our purposes, however, these complications are not important. What *is* important is that we begin to think of human societies as a part of the world of nature, especially the biotic world, and that we come to recognize what this has meant in the life of man and his societies.

A DEFINITION OF SOCIETIES

Up to this point, we have discussed societies without actually defining them. We have identified two of their basic characteristics, however. Specifically, we have seen that a society is a territorially distinct organization and that it is made up of animals of a single species. To complete the definition, we must add three further criteria.

First, a society is a form of organization involving *relatively sustained ties of interaction among its members.* Occasional contacts are not enough. Thus, we would not say that the species of wasp known as the mud dauber maintains societies, since interaction among members of this species occurs only for brief intervals at the time of mating and reproduction. On the other hand, the criterion is clearly met in the case of the many varieties of social insects that maintain sustained contacts with others of their kind throughout their lives.

Second, a society is a form of organization involving *a relatively high degree of interdependence among its members.* That is to say, the survival and well-being of each member depend to a great degree on the actions of others. A colony of ants, with its division of labor among workers, soldiers, and queen, provides a good illustration of this.

Third, and finally, a society is a form of organization characterized by *a*

---

[2] The term "ecological community" refers to a population of plants and animals of diverse species that occupy a given territory and are bound together by ties of mutual dependence. Species and ecological communities are placed on the same level of organization in Figure 1.1 since neither subsumes the other. A species usually includes portions of a number of ecological communities and vice versa. The term "ecosystem" refers to the planetwide network of interdependent plant and animal species and ecological communities.

high degree of autonomy. In other words, a society is not subject to the control or regulation of any outside organization to a significant degree. Applying this criterion, we see that the American nation constitutes a society but that the individual families, communities, churches, and other groups found within it do not.

Bringing together the various parts of our definition, we can now say that *a society exists to the degree that a territorially bounded population of animals of a single species maintains ties of association and interdependence and enjoys autonomy.* As this definition indicates, the world of animal organizations cannot be neatly divided into those which are societies and those which are not. Rather, there is a scale or continuum along which organizations are ranged, and between those which obviously are societies and those which obviously are not, there is a gray area of organizations that possess the qualities of a society in varying degrees.

The position of a group on this scale is not immutably fixed. Over a period of time, some groups take on more of the qualities of a society while others lose them. Many American Indian groups could serve as examples. Several hundred years ago, prior to contact with Europeans, these groups were autonomous. The members of a group were bound together by strong ties of interaction and interdependence. Following contact with the Europeans, and later the Americans, these groups gradually lost most of their autonomy and were brought increasingly under foreign control. Eventually, the ties of intragroup interaction and interdependence began to break down as individuals established more and more ties with the surrounding American population. Thus, over the years these groups gradually lost the properties of a society. As such cases illustrate, it is often difficult to say with certainty whether, at a specific point in time, a given population does or does not constitute a society. If this is clearly understood, it will not be a problem.

THE BASIC FUNCTION OF SOCIETIES

There have not always been societies in the biotic world. Rather, they are a form of organization that emerged during the long course of evolutionary history. Some years ago, one writer referred to their appearance as "one of the great steps in evolution" and compared it in importance to the emergence of the cell, the multicellular organism, and the vertebrate system.[3] As he pointed out, society is a form of organization that has evolved, not once, but a number of times, independently and in widely separated animal lines. It is found not only among humans, but also among many species of mammals, birds, fish, and even insects. Furthermore, those species which have developed the societal mode of organization have generally prospered and multiplied.

---

[3] Kingsley Davis, *Human Society* (New York: Macmillan, 1949), p. 27. See also a similar statement by a leading zoologist, Alfred E. Emerson, in "Human Cultural Evolution and Its Relation to Organic Evolution of Insect Societies," in Herbert Barringer et al. (eds.), *Social Change in Developing Areas: A Reinterpretation of Evolutionary Theory* (Cambridge, Mass.: Schenkman, 1965), pp. 50–51.

What function does this form of organization perform that might account for its widespread occurrence? Precisely the same answer emerges from the study of both human societies and other societies: *the societal form of organization is a mode of adaptation whereby certain types of organisms have increased their chances of surviving and multiplying.* In essence, therefore, the societal mode of organization may be thought of as a functional counterpart of other familiar adaptive mechanisms in the animal world, such as speed, strength, bodily weapons and armament, instinctive response sets, intelligence, and so forth.

The importance of this can hardly be exaggerated, since it has far-reaching implications for our whole approach to the study of human societies. Above all, it reminds us once again that the study of human societies cannot be divorced from the study of the rest of the biotic world. More than that, it suggests that we would do well to adopt an evolutionary approach in our study of human societies, since it is only in these terms that adaptive mechanisms can be fully understood. This is not to say that the study of human societies should be swallowed up by the biological sciences, but it does mean that as students of human societies we must have a clear understanding of man's relation to the biotic world and of the ways in which basic biological forces influence human life.

MAN'S THREEFOLD RELATION TO THE BIOTIC WORLD

The nature of man's relation to the biotic world has long been a source of confusion and misunderstanding. Much of the difficulty has been caused by two sharply contrasting views of man. The first view was popularized by some of Charles Darwin's more enthusiastic followers in the nineteenth century. They argued that his work proved that man is essentially an animal and can best be understood if he is studied solely, or largely, in biological terms.

Though this view still has its supporters, most scholars now reject it on the ground that it involves what some have called the "nothing but" fallacy. As George Gaylord Simpson, a leading paleontologist, explained:

> To say that man is nothing but an animal is to deny, by implication, that he has *essential* attributes other than those of all animals. This would be false as applied to any kind of animal; it is not true that a dog, a robin, an oyster, or an ameba is nothing but an animal. As applied to man the "nothing but" fallacy is more serious than in application to any other sort of animal, because man is an entirely new kind of animal in ways altogether fundamental for understanding of his nature. It is important to realize that man is an animal, but it is even more important to realize that the essence of his unique nature lies precisely in those characteristics that are not shared with any other animal.[4]

[4] George Gaylord Simpson, *The Meaning of Evolution* (New Haven, Conn.: Yale, 1951), pp. 283–284. Quoted by permission of Yale University Press.

Figure 1.2a Man shares the need for food, light, and air with all living things.

Figure 1.2b Man shares the societal form of organization with some other species.

Figure 1.2c Religion is unique to man.

In reacting against the excesses of the "nothing but" fallacy, many sociologists and other social scientists in recent decades have backed into the opposite camp. By tending to ignore, or give perfunctory treatment to, the biological bases of human society, they almost seem to have adopted the position of those who deny man's animal heritage. The chief reason for this is probably the failure to see clearly that our choice is not limited to these two opposed positions. There is a third possibility—one that recognizes that man has some qualities that are uniquely his and others that he shares with other forms of life. This position can be summarized in three simple propositions:[5]

1. Man shares some attributes with *all* living things.
2. Man shares some additional attributes with certain other forms of life, but not with all.
3. Man has still other attributes that he does not share with any other form of life.

Once we accept these three propositions, the risks in viewing man and his societies as part of the biotic world become minimal and are far outweighed by the advantages.

The Universals

When we first survey the great diversity of living things, it is easy to suppose there are no universals, no properties common to all. The differences between man and the ameba are immense and obvious. Yet underlying these differences are certain uniformities, and these are tremendously important if we are to develop a meaningful perspective on human societies.

This fundamental unity first became evident in the work of Darwin, more than a century ago. Since then, biological research has served to strengthen Darwin's basic insight. As one biologist recently expressed it:

> The world of living things is [now] seen as far more of a unity than was conceivable a hundred years ago. The post-Darwinian era in research has tended, on the whole, to break down the barriers between phyla and between individual disciplines. The same fundamental principles are [now] seen to be operating to a very large extent throughout the animal and plant kingdoms.[6]

Much the same point was made earlier by Simpson when he wrote:

> The first grand lesson learned from evolution was that of the unity of life. . . . all living things are brothers in the very real, material sense that all have arisen from one source and been developed within the divergent intricacies of one process. Man is part of nature, and he is kin to all life.[7]

---

[5] For a parallel statement about individuals, see Clyde Kluckhohn and Henry Murray, *Personality: In Nature, Society, and Culture,* rev. ed. (New York: Knopf, 1965), p. 53.

[6] W. H. Thorpe, *Learning and Instinct in Animals,* 2d ed. (Cambridge, Mass.: Harvard, 1963), p. 467. Quoted by permission of Harvard University Press.

[7] Simpson, p. 281. Quoted by permission of Yale University Press.

What, then, are these universals that apply to all living things? The following are among the most important relevant to the study of human societies. Other, less relevant ones could easily be added.

1. All living things require food, water, and air to survive.
2. Because of these needs, all living things are involved in intimate interaction with, and are dependent on, their physical and biotic environments.
3. All living things have a capacity for reproduction that, in the long run, exceeds the environment's capacity to sustain.
4. So long as living things reproduce freely, sustenance is in short supply.
5. So long as sustenance is in short supply, there is competition for it.
6. Living things usually reproduce true to kind, but owing to the occurrence of mutation and recombination of genes by means of sexual reproduction, genetic variation can be expected in all large populations.
7. So long as there is competition for sustenance, and differences exist within and between species, a process of natural selection occurs, favoring populations with the following characteristics: high fecundity (i.e., a capacity for high rates of reproduction), strength and offensive weapons, defensive armament, speed, social organization, intelligence (i.e., the capacity to learn), camouflage, the capacity to utilize unusual foods, the capacity to survive in generally unfavorable environments, behavioral flexibility, and genetic flexibility (i.e., a moderate rate of mutation).[8]
8. So long as variation and natural selection occur, there will be organic and behavioral evolution (i.e., a nonrandom, or progressive, development in the directions indicated in item 7 above).

With respect to the last point, it should be noted that no single species could possibly evolve in all these directions simultaneously. Rather, they are alternatives, and some species survive through the development of high rates of reproduction, others through the development of great speed, and still others through the development of powers of learning. Of necessity, there are built-in incompatibilities between many of these solutions to the problems created by competition. For example, great speed and elaborate defensive armament (e.g., the turtle's shell) tend to be incompatible, since the weight of armament necessarily reduces speed. Similarly, high fecundity and high intelligence tend to be incompatible, since large numbers of offspring cannot be cared for by the parents during the prolonged period of maturation that is necessary for the learning potential to be fully realized. Hence, different species follow different evolutionary paths.

---

[8] On the adaptive value of a *moderate* rate of mutation, see W. C. Allee, A. E. Emerson, O. Park, and K. P. Schmidt, *Principles of Animal Ecology* (Philadelphia: Saunders, 1949), pp. 600 and 684.

The list of universals has definite implications for human societies. Because of man's physical needs, every human society is dependent on its environment. However, since man is both omnivorous and highly intelligent, human societies have been able to adapt to almost every kind of terrestrial environment and even, to a limited extent, to marginal marine environments. Human societies, like other populations, have a reproductive capacity that exceeds the environment's capacity to sustain life, and as a consequence food has often been in short supply. Thus, competition for it has been a recurrent feature of human life, both within and between societies. Though the relevance of items 6, 7, and 8 above has been quite limited since the emergence of Homo sapiens, or biologically modern man, a curious, but important, functional equivalent of them has developed. We will examine this shortly (see *Specialties* below).

The Semispecialties

Some years ago, the author and humorist Clarence Day wrote a book entitled *This Simian World.* Speculating about the kind of civilization that might have developed had man evolved in the feline, rather than the simian, or primate, line, he wrote:

> A race of civilized beings descended from the great cats would have been rich in hermits and solitary thinkers. The recluse would not have been stigmatized as peculiar, as he is by us simians. They would not have been a credulous people, or easily religious. False prophets and swindlers would have found few dupes. And what generals they would have made! what consummate politicians!
>
> . . . They would never have become as poised or as placid as, say, super-cows. Yet they would have had less insanity, probably, than we. Monkeys' . . . minds seem precariously balanced, unstable. The great cats are saner. They are intense, they would have needed sanitariums: but fewer asylums. And their asylums would have been not for weakminded souls, but for furies.
>
> They would have been strong at slander. They would have been far more violent than we in their hates, and they would have had fewer friendships. . . .
>
> The super-cat-men would have rated cleanliness higher. Some of us primates have learned to keep ourselves clean, but it's no large proportion; and even the cleanest of us see no grandeur in soap-manufacturing, and we don't look to [manicurists] and plumbers for social prestige. A feline race would have honored such occupations; . . . the rich Vera Pantherbilt would have deigned to dine only with [manicurists].
>
> None but the lowest dregs of such a race would have been lawyers spending their span of life on this mysterious earth studying the long dusty records of dead and gone quarrels. We simians naturally admire a profession

full of wrangle and chatter, but that is a monkeyish way of deciding disputes, not a feline.

It is fair to judge peoples by the rights they will sacrifice most for. Super-cat-men would have been outraged had their right of personal combat been questioned. The simian submits with odd readiness to the loss of this privilege. What outrages him is to make him stop wagging his tongue. He becomes most excited and passionate about the right of free speech, even going so far in his emotion as to declare it is sacred. . . .

In a world of super-cat-men, I suppose there would have been few sailors; and people would have cared less for seaside resorts, or for swimming. . . .

Among them there would have been no anti-vivisection societies:
No Young Cats Christian Associations or Red Cross work:
No vegetarians:
No early closing laws:
Much more hunting and trapping:
No riding to hounds; that's pure simian . . .

They would have had few comedies on their stage; no farces. Cats care little for fun. In the circus, superlative acrobats. No clowns.

In drama and singing they would have surpassed us probably. Even in the stage of arrested development as mere animals, in which we see cats, they wail with a passionate intensity at night in our yards. Imagine how a Caruso descended from such beings would sing.[9]

Fanciful as this is, it points to a basic truth we cannot afford to ignore: *human societies bear the special mark of man's primate ancestry.*

A lot has been written about the significance of this fact for us *as individuals.* From our primate ancestors we inherited such important physical characteristics as our upright posture and flexible arms, our flexible hands with the separated fingers and opposable thumbs, our excellent vision, our year-round sexual readiness, our prolonged period of immaturity, our enlarged cerebrum, and our complex central nervous system. Because of these and other physical features that reflect our primate ancestry, our patterns of action as individuals differ from those of other animals. The further removed other animals are from the primate line, the greater the difference. Thus we have more in common with the primates (and especially the suborder of anthropoids, which includes monkeys and apes as well as man) than with other mammals; more with other mammals than with other vertebrates; and more with other vertebrates than with invertebrates or plants.

For present purposes, however, we are concerned less with the implications of our ancestry for us as individuals than with its implications for *human societies.* For a crucial point emerges here: the societal mode of organization

---

[9] Reprinted with omissions, by permission of Alfred A. Knopf, Inc., from *This Simian World* by Clarence Day. Copyright, 1920, by Clarence Day. Renewed 1948 by Katherine B. Day.

itself is something man inherited, not something he developed on his own. Recent research has made it clear that all anthropoids live in societies.[10] Though it is remotely possible that human and other modern anthropoid societies are independent developments, the weight of evidence is strongly against this. Not only are societies universal in the anthropoid line, they are also, in varying degrees of development, widespread among other mammals. Furthermore, there seems to be an evolutionary progression that culminates in human societies, the most complex of them all. Thus, though evidence for the thesis that man inherited the societal mode of existence is circumstantial, it is compelling.

The close association between mammals and the societal form of organization brings us back to a question we dealt with briefly and in very general terms earlier: what is the function of societies? At that time we limited ourselves to saying that societies are adaptive mechanisms that certain species have adopted, thereby enhancing their chances of surviving and multiplying.

Because societies differ so much from one phylogenetic line to another (e.g., compare insect and mammalian societies), this is as much as can be said in general terms. When we limit our discussion to mammalian societies, however, or better yet to primate societies, we can be much more specific, as was shown recently by two scholars in the important new subdiscipline of primate behavior. At the conclusion of a volume reporting the findings of a number of recent studies, they pointed out that all species of monkeys and apes live in social groups and then posed the question of why this should be so. They concluded that the chief reason is that *the societal mode of organization enhances opportunities for learning.* As they observed, "The group is the locus of knowledge and experience far exceeding that of the individual member. It is in the group that experience is pooled."[11] The same answer could be given in the case of human societies, where, as we shall note in the next section, the opportunities for learning are vastly greater than in other anthropoid societies.

Learning may be defined as *that process which manifests itself by changes in behavior* (*usually adaptive in nature*) *based on prior experience.*[12] As this definition indicates, learning is not an end in itself. Rather, it is a tool that aids men and animals in the attainment of their goals. This is what makes it so important.

The ability to learn enables an organism (or a species) to adapt more quickly to diverse or changing circumstances. Instinct (or what we, today, might call the genetic programming of behavioral responses or response sets) is the

---

[10] See Sherwood L. Washburn and David A. Hamburg, "The Implications of Primate Research," in Irven DeVore (ed.), *Primate Behavior: Field Studies of Monkeys and Apes* (New York: Holt, 1965), p. 612.

[11] Ibid., p. 613.

[12] Thorpe, p. 55. Occasionally learning can be maladaptive for the individual, as in the case of the person who learns to rely on patent medicines or medical quacks rather than on competent practitioners, but this is the exception, not the rule.

only alternative to learning that nature has devised. But because instincts are genetically determined, the process of adaptation is far slower and the outcome, therefore, far less certain.

To contrast learning and instinct in this way may seem to suggest that learned behavior is independent of genetics. However, such is not the case. Though learned behavior is not genetically programmed, the ability to learn has a definite genetic basis. As a consequence, some species have a highly developed capacity for learning, while others have little or none.

The marked capacity for learning evident in mammals is clearly linked with certain genetic peculiarities of this class of animals. For example, it is definitely linked with the advanced development of the brain and central nervous system. Less obvious, but no less important, is the prolonged physical immaturity of mammalian offspring that necessitates prolonged contact between them and adults and greatly increases their opportunities for learning. Thus, even learned behavior has a genetic basis.

The importance of this becomes evident when we compare the various species of mammals. Here we find a pattern indicating a definite evolutionary progression. Among the various orders, the primates are distinctive both genetically and behaviorally. Genetically, they are remarkable in the ways we noted previously. Behaviorally, they are remarkable for the strong social bonds that unite them, as well as for their singular dependence on learned patterns of behavior. For example, studies have shown that among many species of primates, even the sex act must be learned. Both genetically and behaviorally, the differences separating the primates and other mammals are most pronounced in the case of the anthropoids, that part of the primate order which includes man. From this we can only conclude that man belongs to a part of the animal world whose very survival depends on a complex combination of the societal mode of existence and learned forms of behavior.

The Specialties

We do not need the tools of modern science to show us that man is different. We need only to look around us. People build skyscrapers, compose symphonies, set off atomic explosions, philosophize and moralize, travel in outer space, and do a thousand other things that no other animal can do. Such patterns of behavior suggest that genetically man is profoundly different from all other forms of life, since modern biology has shown that usually behavior and genetics are closely linked. The surprising fact is, however, that man is not nearly as distinctive genetically as his behavior suggests. The physical differences that separate him from the other anthropoids are minor compared to the differences separating these anthropoids from most other animals. *Behaviorally,* however, the picture is reversed: apes and monkeys have far more in common with most other animals than with man. It looks as though some critical threshold was crossed when man evolved, with only a few, modest genetic changes opening the way to a major behavioral breakthrough.[13]

The explanation for this curious development lies in man's immense capacity for learning—a capacity far exceeding that of even his closest kin among the anthropoids. This has made it possible for man to develop a unique mode of adaptation to his environment, one that social scientists refer to as *cultural*. Because this cultural mode of adaptation is such a crucial feature of human life, it is important to understand it clearly. The problem is complicated because the word "culture" has been used in a number of different ways. In popular usage, for example, it has long referred to the refinement of taste and manners that results from special training. In the social sciences, however, the term has a much broader meaning.

The classic definition for social scientists was formulated by the pioneer anthropologist E. B. Tylor at the end of the last century. He defined culture as "that complex whole which includes knowledge, belief, art, morals, law, custom, and any other capabilities and habits acquired by man as a member of society."[14] More recently, others have sought to sharpen the definition to take account of our modern understanding of the basic difference that sets man apart from the rest of the animal world. To this end, one contemporary anthropologist defined culture as "an organization of phenomena—acts (patterns of behavior), objects (tools; things made with tools), ideas (belief, knowledge), and sentiments (attitudes, 'values')—*that is dependent upon the use of symbols*."[15] The great virtue of this definition is that it links the concept "culture" to the concept "symbols."

For our purposes, we can simplify and clarify the definition even further. Everything essential is present if we define culture simply as *mankind's symbol systems and all the aspects of human life dependent on them*.[16] This raises the question of what is meant by "symbols" and "symbol systems," which brings us directly to the basis of the breakthrough that sets man apart from all other living things.[17] All mammals are able to communicate with others of their species, but except for man, they are limited to the use of *signals*. Man, however, uses symbols as well as signals.

Both symbols and signals are *vehicles for the transmission of infor-*

---

[13] For a more detailed discussion of this point, see A. L. Kroeber, *Anthropology,* rev. ed. (New York: Harcourt, Brace, 1948), chap. 2, especially pp. 70–71.

[14] E. B. Tylor, *Primitive Culture* (New York: Holt, 1889).

[15] Leslie White, *The Science of Culture* (New York: Grove Press, 1949), pp. 139–140. Emphasis added.

[16] Not only is this definition brief and therefore easy to remember, but also it makes clear that symbols themselves are a part of culture.

[17] For a more extended discussion of this subject, see White, pp. 22–39. See also J. Bronowski and Ursula Bellugi, "Language, Name, and Concept," *Science,* 168 (May 8, 1970), pp. 669–674.

mation. But there is one important difference. The relationship between a signal and its meaning is wholly or largely fixed from the genetic standpoint (i.e., it is a genetically determined response to a particular stimulus). The relationship between a symbol and its meaning, by contrast, is not fixed in this way.

A classic example of a signal is the cry of pain uttered by an injured animal. This cry is largely an involuntary response, and within a single species it is not subject to much variation except in intensity. A member of the group responds instinctively to this sound, or else learns through observation and experience to associate it with the moods and actions of his fellows. He then adjusts his behavior accordingly. Hence, though they lack variety and flexibility, signals are extremely useful in ordering social relations within a group

Not all signals are of such a primitive nature. Anticipatory signals illustrate the ability of certain animals to use signals to anticipate a sequence of events. For example, if one deer in a herd is frightened by an unexpected sound, it is likely to bolt, and this action normally warns others to do the same. Thus, by its action the first animal transmits vital information and saves its fellows from potential harm.

This example illustrates several important characteristics of signals. First, they are not merely responses to experiences but may actually anticipate them. Animals can learn to associate experiences and, by means of signals, communicate essential information. Second, signals are not always vocal in character; in fact, in the animal world most are not. Body movements and glandular secretions are both common methods of signaling, and recent research shows that signaling often involves a combination of several methods. Third, signaling is often involuntary and not necessarily intended to be a method of communication. The animal that bolts when frightened by an unexpected sound may be concerned only with its own safety, but its action serves as a warning to other, less attentive members of the group. Finally, the example illustrates the relatively inflexible character of signals. Though the bolting action of the animal is sometimes a learned response, the range of his possible responses to sudden fright, or any other stimulus, is apparently determined by his genetic heritage and is severely limited.

Symbols, by contrast, because they are not determined genetically, can easily be modified. We see abundant evidence of this in the history of every language, wherein countless symbols have changed while their meanings remained unchanged, and vice versa. There are hundreds of examples of the former in the unrevised version of Chaucer's *Canterbury Tales* or the King James Version of the Bible, and of the latter in the kaleidoscopic world of slang, the very essence of which is the modification of the meanings of traditional symbols.

The genetic independence of symbols can be illustrated in yet another way. When we examine the symbols we currently use, we find that many have a variety of unrelated meanings. For example, consider the sound we designate in our written language by the letter *c*. This single sound may refer to the third letter of the alphabet, the act of perceiving, the jurisdiction of a bishop, or a large body of water. To Spanish-speaking people, the sound means "yes"; to French-speaking people it means "yes," "if," "whether," or "so." Obviously there is no logical connection between these varied meanings, nor is there any genetically determined connection between the meanings and the sound. All of them are simply arbitrary usages that the members of certain societies have adopted.

Because they are not genetically determined, as signals are, symbols can be combined and recombined indefinitely to form *symbol systems* of fantastic complexity, subtlety, and flexibility. As a consequence, *there are no intrinsic limits to the amount or variety of information they can handle.* The only limits are those set by their users' physical limitations (e.g., the number, type, and accuracy of their senses and the efficiency and capacity of their brains and nervous systems). With the aid of a symbol system, even these limitations can be partly overcome. For example, the substitution of written records for human memory greatly increased man's capacity for storing information. Similarly, the invention of tools that supplement man's senses (e.g., microscopes and telephones) greatly increased his capacity for acquiring and transmitting information.

In technologically advanced societies today, the volume of information transmitted from generation to generation has become so great that no single individual can master it. Thus, though individual men and women are the bearers of culture, a culture in its totality is the property of a society.

In the final analysis, the importance of symbols and symbol systems lies not in what they are but in what they have made it possible for man to become. They are the basic tools with which we think, communicate, calculate, plan, build, moralize, and speculate. Art, science, religion, philosophy, technology, politics—these are possible only for symbol users. Because of symbols, life is infinitely richer and more varied for us than for any other species. Symbol systems, in short, have provided mankind with a radically new way of relating and adapting to the biophysical world.

A basic analogue   Once we appreciate how crucial symbol systems have been, we are well on the way to recognizing one of the most important relationships in the biological world: *symbol systems are the functional analogue of genetic systems.*[18] Both are mechanisms that facilitate the behavioral adaptation of populations to their environment through the acquisition, storage, transmission, and use of relevant information.[19] Genetic systems accomplish this by

---

[18] Emerson, "Human Cultural Evolution," p. 58.

[19] Modern studies of genetics, especially studies of deoxyribonucleic acid (DNA) and ribonucleic acid (RNA), have done much to clarify the information-handling function of genetic systems. For a brief summary of this work,

Figure 1.3 Symbol systems are the functional analogue of genetic systems. Both are mechanisms that facilitate the behavioral adaptation of populations to their environments through the acquisition, storage, transmission, and use of information. The figure on the right is a model of the structure of the DNA molecule, the famous double helix.

the slow, and always costly (in terms of lives), method of *organic evolution;* symbol systems accomplish the same thing by the swifter, and usually less costly, method of *sociocultural evolution.* For the first time in evolutionary history, major behavioral changes can occur without corresponding genetic and organic changes. Only the forms of social organization or the culture need change.

see Emerson, pp. 56–58, or René Dubos, *So Human an Animal* (New York: Scribner, 1968), chap. 3. For a discussion of this subject among a group of scientists, see Sol Tax and Charles Callender (eds.), *Evolution after Darwin: The University of Chicago Centennial* (Chicago: University of Chicago Press, 1960), vol. III, pp. 79–86. Note that the only objection to the idea that genetic systems serve an information-handling function comes from Hermann Muller, and he objects solely on the ground of the association of the word "information" with the idea of *conscious* knowledge. In an era of computers, the risk of confusion because of this traditional connotation should be minimal. For early uses of the concept "information" by social scientists, see Kenneth Boulding, *The Image: Knowledge in Life and Society* (Ann Arbor: University of Michigan Press, Ann Arbor Paperbacks, 1961), p. 35, and O. D. Duncan, "Social Organization and the Ecosystem," in R. E. L. Faris (ed.), *Handbook of Modern Sociology* (Chicago: Rand McNally, 1964), pp. 39–45.

To appreciate the significance of this, consider how much more easily a human population can adapt to environmental change than an animal population can. To survive a sharp drop in average annual temperature in its habitat, for example, an animal population must undergo a rigorous process of natural selection that causes the death of large numbers of individuals who lack the genetic capacity to respond properly and sufficiently (e.g., by producing a heavier coat of fur or a thicker layer of subcutaneous fat). Sometimes, there may be no survivors. By contrast, a human population can usually adapt culturally, with little hardship and little loss of life, simply by adopting warmer clothing or building better-insulated housing.

Through the creation of symbol systems, our prehistoric forefathers laid the foundation for a major evolutionary breakthrough—a breakthrough that has enabled their descendants to modify their behavior and achieve progressively more efficient and more rapid adaptations to their environment without recourse to organic evolution. *The nature and consequences of this development will be our primary concern throughout this volume.*

A caution   Although we sometimes refer to symbol systems as mechanisms for the mobilization of information, we must be careful not to think of them or of the culture of which they are a part merely as tools that men manipulate in a calculating, rational way to achieve their goals. This is a dangerous half-truth. In certain respects, culture has the qualities of Frankenstein's monster—that is, once it has been brought into being, it possesses a life of its own and often forces its creators to respond to its demands. To a considerable degree, the members of a society become prisoners in the cultural system they have created.

There are many reasons for this, but the most important is that cultures outlive their creators. Each of us is born into a society with an established culture, and it is only through the mastery of this culture that we are able to satisfy our needs and desires. But while we are trying to master the culture, the culture tends to master us and make us its creatures. To a great degree, it even defines our goals in life and shapes the patterns of our thought.

The problem is further compounded because people often find it difficult, even painful, to unlearn what they have learned. New information can threaten an individual's entire view of life, and it may be easier for him to ignore it than to restructure his thinking. This problem is especially acute among older people; yet they are the very ones who occupy most of the seats of power in society. Hence, elements of culture often persist long after the conditions that gave rise to them have ceased to exist.

We will return to this subject in Chapter 3. For the present, suffice it to say that if culture is to be compared to a tool—and this is legitimate—it is wise not to compare it to a hammer or saw or any other simple tool that can be used and set aside as you wish. Rather, we should compare it to an artificial kidney or to some other marvel of modern medical technology that is, for those who need it, a vital part of the life process—a tool, yes, but a tool that cannot be set aside or manipulated at will to suit the passing whims of its beneficiaries.

EXCURSUS: A BRIEF HISTORY OF SOCIOLOGY

Before going further in our analysis of human societies, it may be well to pause and take a look at sociology itself—its origins and history, its recent trends and current status. This brief excursus will also provide an opportunity to consider the relationship between sociology and the various other social sciences.

Though sociology is a relatively recent addition to the scholarly world, its roots extend at least as far into the past as the writings of Plato and Aristotle. In their day, philosophers were already speculating about their own societies, comparing one with another and trying to understand the forces that shaped them.

The immediate origins of modern sociology, however, lie in two more or less independent developments of the seventeenth and eighteenth centuries. The first of these was the revival of interest in the systematic study of man and society, fostered by writers such as Thomas Hobbes, John Locke, Giambattista Vico, Montesquieu, Jacques Rousseau, Jacques Turgot, the Marquis de Condorcet, David Hume, Adam Ferguson, John Millar, Adam Smith, and Thomas Malthus. Before the eighteenth century ended, these men had established the independence of social theory from theology and had laid many of the basic philosophical foundations of the modern social sciences. Some of them even went so far as to identify the phenomenon of sociocultural evolution—long before Darwin, or even Lamarck—and to formulate explanations for it.[20]

During this same period, other men began making systematic, quantitative studies of various social phenomena. Birth and death rates were an early object of research; later there were studies of class, family income, jury verdicts, election results, and a variety of other phenomena. Sometimes, as in the case of Condorcet, those who were involved in developing theory were also involved in research, though this was not usually the case. By the end of the century, the quantitative tradition was firmly established; and if the ties to theory were still imperfectly developed, a basis had been established for the eventual integration of these two traditions.[21]

The term "sociology" first appeared in the 1830s in the writings of a Frenchman, Auguste Comte. As a result, Comte is often referred to as the founder of modern sociology. This is an undeserved honor, however, since his writings were in an already established tradition and his own distinctive contribution was not that great.

The most famous nineteenth-century sociologist, and the most influential in his own day, was an English scholar, Herbert Spencer. Through his writings, which were widely translated, he brought sociology to the attention of the educated classes throughout the world. Like Comte, Vico, Turgot, Montesquieu, Ferguson, Millar, Condorcet, and others, Spencer was profoundly interested in sociocultural evolution, though he saw it as but one manifestation of a universal cosmic process linking the physical, biotic, and human worlds. Interest in

---

[20] For a good, brief summary of these developments, see Marvin Harris, *The Rise of Anthropological Theory* (New York: Thomas Y. Crowell, 1968), chap. 2.

[21] For a good review of the early history of social research, see Bernard Lecuyer and Anthony R. Oberschall, "Sociology: The Early History of Social Research," in *International Encyclopedia of the Social Sciences* (New York: Macmillan and Free Press, 1968), vol. 15, pp. 36–53.

evolution was further stimulated in that period by the writings of Darwin, Spencer's contemporary.

Another major contributor to the study of human societies in the nineteenth century was Karl Marx. Unlike Spencer, he stood apart from the emerging discipline of sociology, with the result that the relevance of his work to the discipline went unrecognized for many years. With the passage of time, however, this has changed. One reason has been the belated appreciation of the importance of the material base of human life—people's need for food, shelter, and the like, and the techniques for meeting these needs—which most of the other pioneer social scientists neglected or minimized.

Ironically, despite its European origins, sociology found more rapid acceptance in the United States. A number of leading American universities established professorships even before the turn of the century, and by the early decades of the present century, many institutions had established full-fledged departments of sociology. During the period between the two world wars, sociology continued to expand in the United States but failed to do so in Europe, partly because of attacks by totalitarian governments, especially in Germany and Russia, partly because of the greater resistance to change and innovation by the faculties of European universities. As a result, sociology became primarily an American enterprise.

Following World War I, sociology underwent a number of important changes. Under American leadership the discipline became increasingly concerned with contemporary society and, even more narrowly, with contemporary American society. Interest in other societies declined, as did interest in the historical dimension of human life. To a large extent these changes reflected the desire of a new generation of sociologists to make the discipline more scientific. The result was a greatly heightened interest in empirical research, especially studies of local communities and their problems—crime, poverty, divorce, juvenile delinquency, illegitimacy, prostitution, the adjustment problems of immigrants, and so forth.

With this shift in the focus of interest, sociologists gradually abandoned the earlier evolutionary approach. In part, this was because of criticisms leveled against it, but primarily it was because the older approach seemed irrelevant to the concerns of the newer generation. Sociologists were forced to find a substitute for evolutionary theory—some new theoretical approach that could organize the growing, but diffuse, body of sociological knowledge. By the late 1930s, the *structural-functional* approach emerged as the apparent successor to evolutionary theory.

The structural-functional approach to the study of human societies is, in effect, the sociological counterpart of the anatomical and physiological approaches in biology. Like anatomists, structural-functionalists are concerned with the identification and labeling of the many different parts of the things they study and with the structural relations among them (e.g., the structural patterns formed within business organizations, families, etc.). Like physiologists, they are interested in the functions each of the parts performs. For example, just as physiologists are concerned with the functions of organs, such as the liver, heart, and spleen, structural-functionalists are interested in the functions of institutions, such as the family, and of moral rules, such as the taboo against incest.

A Harvard professor named Talcott Parsons was especially instrumental in establishing the structural-functional approach. Building on foundations laid around the turn of the century by Max Weber in Germany and Emile Durkheim in France, Parsons developed a theoretical system that was carried by his students into leading universities throughout the country.

Since World War II, sociology has grown substantially not only in the United States but in Europe, Japan, and Canada, and it has begun to take root in other areas as well.[22] One significant development has been the changing attitude of Communist authorities in Eastern Europe. During the Stalin era and for some time thereafter, sociology was regarded as subversive and was for-

---

[22] See, for example, Charles Modge, "From Small Beginnings," *The Times Literary Supplement*, Apr. 4, 1968, pp. 337ff., on the recent growth of sociology in England.

bidden in most Communist nations. Today, however, restrictions are being removed and interest in the subject is growing.[23] The development of sociology in other countries has reduced the unhealthy concentration of the discipline in the United States that characterized the decades of the 1930s and 1940s.

Another notable development has been the movement of sociology beyond the confines of the academic community. Prior to the 1940s, sociologists were employed almost entirely by universities and colleges. Beginning during World War II and continuing to the present, there has been a growing demand for their services by government, industry, and other kinds of organizations.

Intellectually, too, sociology has made substantial progress. In this respect, two of the more important developments have been the increasing use of quantitative techniques and the revival of evolutionary theory. The first of these was a natural outgrowth of the efforts of sociologists to achieve greater precision in their descriptions of social phenomena and greater rigor in their analyses. This trend was given an enormous boost by the invention of computers, which enable researchers to handle large volumes of data and carry out complex statistical analyses that otherwise would be impossible or prohibitively slow and costly.

The more surprising of the newer trends has been the revival of interest in evolutionary theory. Thirty years ago, evolutionary theory seemed as dead as the dodo. Even a decade ago, the structural-functional approach seemed solidly entrenched as the dominant theoretical orientation. Today, however, it is definitely on the decline. Criticism of this approach increases with each passing year, and even some of those who were leading spokesmen for it only a few years ago have turned to evolutionary theory.[24]

The chief reason for this shift has been a growing recognition that the structural-functional approach does not provide an adequate basis for understanding two crucial aspects of human life—*change* and *conflict*. Though these have been important features of human life in most eras, they have never been more important than in our own day. Recent events—the civil rights struggle, the women's liberation movement, the war in Indochina, the exploration of space, and the continuing technological revolution—have all contributed to the growing dissatisfaction with the structural-functional approach.

The new approach might best be described as *ecological-evolutionary*. As its name suggests, it too has links with two of the basic approaches in the biological sciences. Since the ecological-evolutionary approach is the one used in this volume, its nature will become evident in later chapters. Suffice it to say here that it shares with the evolutionary approach in biology an intense interest in the process of change—especially basic, long-term, developmental, and adaptive change—and in the related processes of competition and conflict. With the ecological approach in biology, it shares an interest in the ties of interdependence within and among populations and in the relations between populations and their environments.[25]

Despite their criticisms of the older approach, proponents of the ecological-evolutionary approach do not ignore structural and functional relations within societies. On the contrary, they recognize them as important. However, the identification and description of these relations is no longer

---

[23] See, for example, Alex Simirenko (ed.), *Soviet Sociology* (Chicago: Quadrangle, 1966), especially pp. 19–35, or Zev Katz, "Sociology in the Soviet Union," *Problems of Communism*, 20 (May–June, 1971), pp. 22–40, on the Soviet Union. Czechoslovakia is an unhappy exception to the general trend; since 1968, the freedom of sociologists there has been severely curtailed.

[24] See especially Talcott Parsons, "Evolutionary Universals in Society," *American Sociological Review*, 29 (1964), pp. 339–357, or *Societies: Evolutionary and Comparative Perspectives* (Englewood Cliffs, N.J.: Prentice-Hall, 1966). See also the work of Robert Bellah and S. N. Eisenstadt.

[25] For a pioneering statement of the newer ecological-evolutionary approach, see Duncan, pp. 36–82.

the sole or primary concern in sociological analysis. Rather, structural and functional relations are studied within the larger and more inclusive framework provided by the ecological and evolutionary perspectives. Thus, we could legitimately label our approach *structural-functional-ecological-evolutionary,* since it incorporates all the essential elements. But for the sake of convenience, it is usually referred to simply as the *evolutionary* approach.

Sociology and the Other Social Sciences

The study of human societies has never been exclusively a sociological concern. All the social sciences have been involved in one way or another. Most of the others, however, have focused on some particular aspect of the subject. Economics and political science limit themselves to a single institutional area. Human geography studies the impact of the physical and biotic environments on societies. Social psychology is concerned with the impact of social organization on the behavior and personality of individuals.

Only sociology and anthropology have been concerned with human societies per se. That is to say, only these two disciplines have interested themselves in the full range of social phenomena, from the family to the nation and from technology to religion. And only these two disciplines have sought to understand societies as entities in their own right.

In matters of research, there has been a fairly well established division of labor between the fields. Sociologists have, for the most part, studied modern industrial societies; anthropologists have concentrated on primitive preliterate societies of both the past and present. This division of labor has made good sense, since the skills needed to study a remote tribe in the mountains of New Guinea are very different from those needed to study a modern industrial society such as our own.

From the standpoint of teaching and the development of theory, however, such a division is far less satisfactory. There are many problems that can be understood only if one takes into account the findings of both disciplines. This is especially true of long-term, evolutionary processes: to ignore the findings of either discipline is likely to result in incomplete or biased interpretations and conclusions. As a consequence, there has been a long tradition of intellectual "borrowing" between sociology and anthropology, and this volume follows in that tradition.

With the revival of evolutionary theory,[26] scholars in these fields have come to recognize that both disciplines were neglecting agrarian societies—those societies which occupy the middle range in the evolutionary scale between primitive preliterate societies and modern industrial societies. In recent years, therefore, both sociologists and anthropologists have begun research in Southeast Asia, the Middle East, and Latin America.

The growing concern with agrarian societies has also led to increased contact between sociologists and historians. Since history is the study of written records of the past, historians have been the experts on agrarian societies of earlier centuries. Much of the older work by historians, with its heavy emphasis on the names and dates of famous men and events, is of limited value for the student of human societies. But that discipline has been changing too, and historians today are increasingly concerned with the basic social patterns and processes that underlie the more dramatic but usually less significant events on which their predecessors focused. As a result, history and sociology are becoming more valuable to each other.

This trend toward interdisciplinary cooperation is evident today in all the social sciences, and even beyond. Scholars are coming to recognize that no discipline is sufficient unto itself. To the degree that any field cuts itself off from the others, it impoverishes itself intellectually. Con-

---

[26] The revival of interest in evolutionary theory is even more pronounced in anthropology and archaeology than in sociology. See, for example, the work of Leslie White, Julian Steward, Walter Goldschmidt, Elman Service, Marshall Sahlins, Robert Carneiro, Marvin Harris, Robert Adams, Robert Braidwood, Grahame Clark, and Stuart Piggott.

versely, to the degree that it enters into communication with other disciplines, it enriches itself and them. This is especially true of such fields as sociology and anthropology, which are concerned with *all* aspects of the life of human societies. Human societies are such fantastically complex phenomena that we need to draw on the resources of every discipline whose work sheds light on the subject. This is why the present volume draws as heavily as it does on research and theory outside sociology. Though this may offend a few disciplinary purists, it is the only responsible course for those whose goal is to understand human societies.

CHAPTER TWO

The Structure and Functioning of Human Societies

Structure and function are two of the most basic concepts in the world of science. Structure refers to the arrangement of the parts of an entity, whether that entity is an atom or a galaxy. As we saw in the last chapter, our universe is organized like a system of wheels within wheels: larger entities are made up of smaller ones, which, in turn, are made up of still smaller ones. The identification of these parts and the study of how they fit together to form structures of various kinds has long been one of science's major concerns. Just as important has been the effort to determine the functions that each part performs, that is, its characteristic activities and the consequences of these activities for the larger entity.

Human societies can be analyzed in structural and functional terms, just like any other object of scientific interest. Like plants and animals, they have an anatomy and physiology that must be understood before the larger and more difficult questions of ecology and evolution are attempted.

Before turning to questions of societal structure and function, however, we must first consider the nature of man himself. For his genetic heritage provides the raw materials his societies have to work with, and it is his needs that they must satisfy. This means that the way human societies are structured and the way they function reflect the more basic and unalterable elements in human nature.

HUMAN NEEDS AND HUMAN NATURE

As we saw in Chapter 1, man stands in a threefold relation to the biotic world. Some of his attributes he shares with all living things, others he shares with his nearer kin in the animal world, still others are uniquely his own. The same is true of man's *needs*. Some are common to all living things, some man shares with a part of the animal kingdom, and some he shares with no other living creature. Each of these needs influences the structure and functioning of human societies.

Elemental Individual Needs

Whatever else people may be, they are animal organisms that depend for survival on the continuing satisfaction of certain basic biological needs. These include the need for light, warmth, oxygen, food, moisture, sleep, and physical safety (i.e., protection against other men, animals, germs, and physical and chemical processes of various kinds). In addition, most humans have a need for sexual gratification that, though not essential to the survival of the individual, is essential to the survival of society.

Some of these needs can be satisfied by individuals with little or no effort, acting entirely on their own. Light and oxygen, for example, are readily available to everyone. With respect to these needs, we live in a Garden of Eden — or did until recently.

The satisfaction of other needs, however, requires effort on our part, and the outcome is much less certain. Even when people make a vigorous effort, there is no guarantee they can satisfy them. For example, there is only a finite quantity of food available at any given time, and the human population, with its infinite capacity for growth, can easily become larger than the current food supply can sustain. When this happens, as it often has, some people's needs go unsatisfied and they die.

A comparable situation exists with respect to the need for safety. Again, there is no guarantee that efforts will be successful. There are many hostile forces that are capable of destroying men, no matter how clever or vigorous they may be.

Because these two needs have been so difficult to satisfy, they have always loomed large in human life. The culture of every society contains a wealth of information relevant to the problems of food production and safety, and many man-hours are invariably spent working on them. What is more, these needs give rise to cooperative activities and thereby lay the foundation for societal organization. In the process, however, they generate a host of derivative needs that become as compelling and demanding as any of our elemental, individual needs.

Derivative Social Needs

It is one of the great ironies of human life, yet also one of its great fascinations and challenges, that in solving one set of problems we so often create others. This has clearly been true in the case of man's reliance on the societal mode of organization. From one standpoint, societal life can be viewed as a means of satisfying certain basic needs. From another standpoint, however, it looms as one of the chief *sources* of mankind's problems and needs. Many of our needs arise only because we live in societies. If Homo sapiens were a solitary species like the mud dauber, we would have far fewer problems and far fewer needs. For societies, once they are formed, develop needs and problems of their own. Certain conditions must be met if the organization is to survive *as an organization*.[1] Sociologists usually refer to these as the *functional requisites* of societies.[2]

---

[1] The survival of its individual members is no guarantee that an organization will survive. If the members of a society are scattered and their social ties broken, the group has been destroyed though every individual survives.

[2] See, for example, D. F. Aberle et al., "The Functional Prerequisites of a Society," *Ethics,* 60 (1950), pp. 100–111, or Talcott Parsons, *The Social System* (Glencoe, Ill.: Free Press, 1951), pp. 26–36.

Figure 2.1 Functional requisites of societies.

a system of communication

a system of production

a system of distribution

a system of defense

a system of member replacement

a system of social control

The first functional requisite of every society is *a system of communication.* This is the *sine qua non* of every social organization, whether animal or human. The members must be able to exchange relevant information. In subhuman societies, communication systems employ signals;[3] in human societies, a mixture of signals and symbols is used. The more complex a society, the more complex its system of communication will be.

A second requisite of societies is *a system of production.* If societies are to survive, they must develop techniques to provide their members with the material necessities of life. While people satisfy some of these needs individually, production is largely a social process in species that have adopted the societal mode of existence. Among insects and other lower animals, production techniques are, for the most part, genetically determined, but among man and other mammalian species, these techniques are usually behavior that the individual learns through participation in the group. Sometimes this learned behavior can be applied by the individual working alone, but more often a cooperative effort is required, as in the case of a pack of wolves running down a deer or a group of men building an automobile.

A third requisite of societies is *a system of distribution.* Whatever is produced must be gotten into the hands of those who will consume it. Producers and consumers are never entirely the same in any society, and in complex societies (i.e., those with considerable specialization in production) there is little overlap between the producers and consumers of a given product. At the very least, producers must transfer a portion of what they produce to children and others who are unable to provide for themselves. Where there is specialization, there must be mechanisms of exchange among the producers themselves. These mechanisms must provide not only for the technical problems of moving goods and services about but also for the potentially explosive social problem of determining who gets how much of what.

---

[3] See, for example, the fascinating work of Karl von Frisch on communication systems among bees, in *Bees: Their Vision, Chemical Senses, and Language* (Ithaca, N.Y.: Cornell, 1950), or "Dialects in the Language of Bees," *Scientific American* (August 1962), pp. 3–7.

A fourth requisite of societies is *a system of defense.* Every society must develop techniques to protect its members, individually and collectively, against hostile forces. No society is completely successful in this: sooner or later, all of us die. What is necessary for a society's survival is simply that enough of its members live long enough, and in good enough health, for the work of the society to be carried on and the next generation raised to adulthood. As this implies, systems of defense include both military and medical components.

Since death is the eventual fate of every individual, a fifth requisite of societies is *a system of member replacement.* Basically, this need is satisfied by biological reproduction, supplemented in some societies by in-migration (either voluntary immigrants, or involuntary captives of war, or slaves purchased outside the society). But simply adding new bodies does not answer a society's need: each individual must acquire certain skills if he is to be a member of the group in the real sense of the term. He must learn its language, and he must become familiar with its rules and customs. As an adult, he must be able to make some contribution, usually economic, to the group. All of this requires a complex learning process that extends over many years, a process known as *socialization.*

Sixth, and finally, societies require *a system of social control.* This need stems from the fact that, although we live in societies, our relations with one another are not adequately regulated by genetic mechanisms. We do, however, have a capacity for *learning* to conduct ourselves in socially responsible ways, and systems of social control develop as a "mechanism" for helping us do it. Analytically, systems of social control can be divided into two parts. First, there must be a system of rules and values to define acceptable conduct and a system of beliefs to provide a rationale, or reason, for these rules and values. Second, there must be a system of rewards and punishments to motivate the individual to act in socially approved ways. As sociologists have long noted, however, no system of social control can operate effectively if sanctions—that is, rewards and punishments—are imposed on the individual only by others. To a large degree, each person must assume responsibility for policing his own conduct. This brings us back to the socialization process, since one of its major objectives is to so mold the individual that he will take the standards and beliefs of his society for his own and govern his behavior accordingly. Though no society is ever completely successful in this, every group must at least approximate it. The only alternative is anarchy and the speedy dissolution of the society.

Derivative Individual Needs and Desires

In one sense, man's needs as an individual are few. We named them earlier: light, warmth, oxygen, food, moisture, sleep, and safety. If these needs are met, the individual can survive. But if *only* these needs are met, the individual will not become a human being in the full sense of the term. He will remain a helpless, animallike creature with few of the skills or qualities of personality we normally associate with humans. This has been well documented in several cases. In one instance, an illegitimate child and her deaf-mute mother were isolated in a dark room for the first six and a half years of the child's life.[4] When they were finally discovered by authorities, the child was unable to speak and could not walk properly; when confronted with strangers, her behavior "was almost that of a wild animal, manifesting much fear and hostility." At first, it was thought that the child was feebleminded, but with intensive training and through association with normal people she became a completely normal child within a two-year period.

Cases such as this serve as reminders that *the qualities that are most distinctively human emerge only as a result of our association with others.* The potential is there in every genetically normal individual; but the potential is *realized* only when the individual shares in the life of society — especially in the crucial early years of life. This is a fact we easily overlook, since few of us ever meet people who have been cut off from society this way.

Involvement in the life of society and exposure to the socialization process equip the individual with the skills that make it possible for him, in his adult years, to satisfy his elemental needs — at least to the degree that the environment permits. At the same time, however, they create or activate in him a whole series of further needs. He becomes a person who is no longer content merely to eat and sleep and have his basic needs satisfied. He is now concerned about such things as his relations with others — whether they like him, whether they respect him, whether they love him, and whether they will do what he wants them to. In other words, he develops the need for affection, for respect, for love, and for power. Not all individuals develop these needs to the same degree. For a variety of reasons that we are only beginning to understand, the intensity of these needs varies considerably from one person to the next, but most of us develop all of them to some degree. When someone does not have these needs, it is usually because of deficiencies in his early socialization experience or because of later experiences that destroyed all hope of their fulfillment.

Many efforts have been made to catalog human needs and desires, but none has been fully satisfactory. Though the following list is incomplete, it suggests something of the diversity of the needs and desires that are generated by our involvement in society. Not all of them are found in every society, and certainly not all are present in every individual, but they do occur with considerable frequency.

The need for love and affection
The need for the respect of others

---

[4] See Kingsley Davis, "Extreme Social Isolation of a Child," *American Journal of Sociology,* 45 (1940), pp. 554–565, and "Final Note on a Case of Extreme Isolation," *American Journal of Sociology,* 52 (1947), pp. 432–437.

The need for self-respect[5]

The need for power (either as a means of satisfying other needs or as
   an end in itself)

The need for material possessions and wealth (either as means or end)

The need for the satisfaction of intellectual curiosity

The need for peace of mind

The need for salvation

The need for aesthetic satisfaction

The need for new experience or variability of experience

The need for creative opportunities

One could easily add to this list, but even this serves as a reminder of the complexity of the human animal and the magnitude and diversity of the demands people make on their societies.

The Nature of Human Nature

Our primary concern throughout this volume is with human societies. However,
as we have seen, the study of human societies cannot be divorced from the
study of human individuals—which brings us to the troublesome, but important,
subject of human nature.

This concept has had a very checkered career in the history of social
thought. Much of the difficulty stems from the uncritical use of the term in earlier
times by many laymen and some social scientists who equated human nature
with the behavioral patterns of their own societies or, perhaps, the Western
world. If the people they knew regarded eating snails as repulsive and infanticide as reprehensible, they assumed that such reactions were simply expressions of "human nature."

Most social scientists quickly came to realize that such attitudes are
not shared by people in all societies and therefore cannot be the expression of
a universal human nature. Rather, they are reflections of the cultures of particular societies. Misgivings about the usefulness of the concept were reinforced as
anthropological studies showed how variable mankind's behavior patterns
actually are. Under the influence of a school of anthropologists known as the
"cultural relativists," it became fashionable to argue that *all* patterns of human
behavior are socially determined.[6] The newborn infant often was likened to a
completely blank slate awaiting the markings of his society.

---

[5] See especially the work of Charles Horton Cooley and George Herbert Mead on this important subject: Cooley's
Human Nature and the Social Order (New York: Scribner, 1922); and Mead's *Mind, Self and Society* (Chicago:
University of Chicago Press, 1934).

[6] See especially Ruth Benedict, *Patterns of Culture* (Boston: Houghton Mifflin, 1934), a volume that did much to
popularize cultural relativism. For a much earlier statement of this view, see John Locke, *An Essay on Human Understanding.*

This view of man was highly attractive to many people for ideological reasons. If there is no such thing as human nature, mankind is infinitely malleable. This means that all man's nasty practices, such as war, crime, exploitation, and cruelty, could be eliminated if only the powers of societies were used correctly. With the right kind of schools, the right kind of government, or the right kind of economy, men could create a new social order in which peace and justice would prevail forever.

In recent years, however, a reaction has set in against this optimistic, relativistic view of man. Events of the twentieth century have cast grave doubts on theories that proclaim the extreme malleability and perfectibility of man. Despite many vigorous efforts to eliminate economic injustice, political tyranny, and war, these evils all remain a part of the human scene.

Psychology and the biological sciences reinforce the lessons of history: their research has shown that the newborn infant is anything but a blank slate. As one writer recently observed: "Like all animals, man enters the world with a primitive value system which seems to be genetically determined, that is, built into the nervous system by the genes. Straight from the womb we like milk, we dislike loud noises, and we dislike falling."[7]

But more than that is involved. Not only do we have certain specific likes and dislikes programmed into our nervous systems at birth, we also have more general, and more basic, behavioral tendencies built in. As new parents quickly discover, every baby comes equipped with imperious needs and a determination to satisfy them without regard to the cost to others.[8] If, later, the child becomes more considerate of those around him, it is not because his interest in satisfying his own needs has diminished. Nor has he become an altruist, loving others as much as he loves himself. Rather, he has learned that maximal satisfaction of his own needs and desires depends on his willingness to take the concerns of others into account to some extent and that enlightened self-interest is more rewarding than unenlightened self-interest.[9] In addition, he may also come to love a few people enough that he is willing to sacrifice his own safety and happiness for theirs, but the number included in this circle tends to be extremely small.

As we have already observed, human needs and desires have an ex-

[7] Kenneth Boulding, *A Primer on Social Dynamics: History as Dialectics and Development* (New York: Free Press, 1970), p. 31.

[8] See, for example, L. Z. Freedman and Anne Roe, "Evolution and Human Behavior," in Anne Roe and George Gaylord Simpson (eds.), *Behavior and Evolution* (New Haven, Conn.: Yale, 1958), pp. 455–479. See also Dennis Wrong, "The Oversocialized Conception of Man in Modern Sociology," *American Sociological Review*, 26 (1961), pp. 183–193.

[9] Elman Service makes a similar point when he speaks of the evolution of culture as "redirecting [man's] selfishness," rather than as overcoming or eliminating it. See *The Hunters* (Englewood Cliffs, N.J.: Prentice-Hall, 1966), p. 32. See also Gerhard Lenski, *Power and Privilege* (New York: McGraw-Hill, 1966), pp. 26–31, for a more detailed treatment of this subject.

pansive character.[10] Once our basic physical requirements are satisfied, new needs and desires are activated—and these may then become as compelling as the more basic ones were. We see this clearly in the desire of people in affluent societies for the latest nonessential consumer goods and in the desire of young people for popularity.

In striving to satisfy their needs and desires, people seem to be governed by an "economizing principle." That is, they use as few of their resources as possible in the effort to satisfy any specific need. This does not surprise us when we realize that few, if any, individuals have enough resources—time, money, energy, strength, etc.—to satisfy fully *all* their needs. Economizing, therefore, is a necessary corollary of their desire to achieve maximal satisfaction.

The sciences of ethology and genetics help us understand the biological basis of these elements of human nature. Comparative studies of animal societies show that individuality tends to be suppressed in insect and other societies in which genetic mechanisms regulate the social life of the group. By contrast, individuality is fairly pronounced in mammalian societies, where social unity depends so much more on learned behavior. Hence, there is a fair degree of intragroup conflict in most mammalian societies, and human societies are no exception. The recent discovery of DNA, RNA, and the genetic code help us see more clearly the ways in which, and the degree to which, these patterns are rooted in the genetic heritages of different species.

Gradually, a new view of human nature is emerging. It is now clear that the term "human nature" cannot refer to most of the specifics of human behavior—how people dress, how they marry, what they eat, and the like. These are merely customs, socially determined and highly variable. When the term is used today, it should be only with reference to basic behavioral tendencies rooted in mankind's common genetic heritage.

Our genes contain the heritage of literally hundreds of millions of years of evolutionary experience—a heritage shaped not only by the interaction of our human ancestors with their environments but also by the interaction of our more remote animal ancestors with their even stranger environments. For example, the salinity of our blood apparently reflects the composition of the ancient seas in which our remote prereptilian ancestors lived.[11] Over the mind-boggling expanse of time since life began on our planet, selective forces have been constantly at work, slowly sifting and sorting genetic materials, providing one heritage for the invertebrates, another for the vertebrates, one for fish, another for

---

[10] For the classic statement of this point, see Thorstein Veblen, *The Theory of the Leisure Class* (New York: Macmillan, 1899). See also A. H. Maslow, *Motivation and Personality* (New York: Harper, 1954), especially chap. 5, or Amos H. Hawley, "Ecology: Human Ecology," in *International Encyclopedia of the Social Sciences* (New York: Macmillan and Free Press, 1968), vol. 4, p. 331.

[11] René Dubos, *So Human an Animal* (New York: Scribner, 1968), p. 76.

mammals, one for felines, another for primates. From all this has emerged modern man's distinctive genetic heritage, which includes among other things (1) his basic biological needs and his physical equipment (eyes, ears, arms, brain, etc.) for satisfying them, (2) a genetically programmed motivation to satisfy them as fully and as economically as possible, (3) a genetically based dependence on sociocultural systems, and (4) a genetically based culture-building potential. As René Dubos, a leading biologist, reminds us, "The past is not dead history; it is the living material out of which man makes himself and builds the future."[12]

As we come to understand this newer view of human nature, we begin to see the tension that is built into the very fabric of human life: man is, at one and the same time, a social animal and an individualistic, self-seeking animal. It is this, above all, which creates the uncertainties in human life, as well as the drama, and it is this which justifies the description of human societies as systems of "antagonistic cooperation."[13]

FIVE BASIC COMPONENTS OF HUMAN SOCIETIES

In trying to cope with the problems of human existence, people have created societies of amazing diversity and complexity. One of sociology's most difficult tasks has been to sort out all the components of human societies and classify them in a meaningful way. So far, no system of classification has found acceptance by all sociologists, though most of them agree that *population, culture,* and *social structure* are three basic elements.

The fivefold classification that follows reflects the influence of earlier work by O. D. Duncan, a sociologist, and Leslie White, an anthropologist.[14] Among its several virtues is, first of all, its simplicity—it is easy to understand and easy to remember. Second, it is more inclusive than either of the older systems. Finally, it is explicitly designed to deal with some of evolutionary theory's most basic problems.

The five basic components of every human society are *population, language, technology, social structure,* and *ideology.* This is actually the basic trinity of population, culture, and social structure, except that culture has been subdivided into its three basic components, language, technology, and ideology.

---

[12] Ibid., p. 270.

[13] William Graham Sumner, *Folkways* (New York: Mentor, 1960, first published 1906), p. 32.

[14] O. D. Duncan, "Social Organization and the Ecosystem," in R. E. L. Faris (ed.), *Handbook of Modern Sociology* (Chicago: Rand McNally, 1964), pp. 36–82, and Leslie White, *The Science of Culture* (New York: Grove Press, 1949), p. 366ff. Indirectly, this system of classification reflects the influence of two pioneer sociologists, Malthus and Marx.

Population

The term "population" refers to *the members of a society considered collectively*. In the study of human societies, there are two aspects of population that are crucial. First, the term refers to Homo sapiens' common genetic heritage, which is a kind of mathematical *constant* in the evolutionary equation (i.e., it is the same for all societies). Second, the term refers to such *variable* properties of populations as size, density, age and sex composition, geographical distribution, and birth and death rates.

With respect to its constant aspect, population is the source of powerful precultural and prerational forces in human life, a heritage from our remote subhuman past. But man's genetic heritage also provides society with the brain and nervous system on which all culture and rationality depend. Population, then, is at one and the same time society's most precious resource and the source of many of its most serious problems.

This paradox is seen most clearly in the newborn infant. He begins life totally self-centered, driven by instinctive biological urges over which he has no control, and knowing nothing of the society of which he has just become a member—nothing of its traditions, its ideals, its needs. Moreover, unless other members of the society devote time, energy, and other resources to caring for him and training him, he never will become a productive member of the group. In short, though he is a resource, he is also a problem.

The variable properties of population are also important. Whether a society is large or small, whether it has an excess of men or women or a balanced sex distribution, whether its members are widely scattered over its territory or concentrated in a few great urban centers, whether its birthrate is high or low—these are all vital elements in the total picture of a society, whether we are describing it, analyzing it, or making predictions about its future.

Language

Every human society requires a system of communication. To some extent, this need is met through the use of signals. For example, we make a face when we taste something bitter, and we cry out when we are badly startled or hurt. But signals are not enough. Even the simplest human society must have a language, that is, *a system of symbols capable of transmitting and storing information.*

The core of every language is a system of spoken sounds that have distinctive meanings attached to them. These meaningful sounds are combined in customary ways that constitute the grammar of the language. Languages differ not only in the sounds they use and the ways they combine them but also in the way experience is divided into the units of meaning we call words.[15] Before we study foreign languages, we have the illusion that they all have an exact counterpart for every word or phrase in our own. But we soon learn otherwise—some words have no exact counterpart in other languages. This can be a source of considerable confusion, as Americans and Russians discovered in talks between President Kennedy and Chairman Khrushchev some years ago.[16] At their meeting in Vienna, Kennedy repeatedly told Khrushchev that he should not *miscalculate* the will and intentions of the American people. Every time this word was translated into Russian, Khrushchev flushed angrily. Kennedy learned later that there is no true Russian equivalent of "miscalculate" and that the translator had fallen back on a Russian expression meaning "inability to count." Thus it seemed to Khrushchev that Kennedy was implying he was too stupid to add two and two! Similarly, Khrushchev used a colloquial Russian expression to state his conviction that the Soviet system would outlast the American. When translated literally, he was quoted as saying, "We will bury you," which in English, where there is no comparable colloquial expression, suggested a deadly threat.

Languages, like other parts of culture, are subject to change. Sounds acquire new meanings, usually by a process of association with traditional meanings. For example, the word "tap" originally meant "something cut out."[17] Later, it came to mean a plug that was cut out of a piece of wood and used to stop up a hole. In time, the word was applied to the stoppers used to control the flow of beer from a keg. Since these "taps" were knocked into place by a light blow, the word came, by extension, to be used with reference to any light blow. In England, the word has also come to be applied to valves or faucets regulating the flow of any liquid (as in the kitchen sink or the bathtub), and, since these taps are threaded on the inside, the instrument used to cut threads on the inside of pipes has also come to be called a tap.

Obviously, there is a large element of chance involved in this process, and it is highly unlikely that the identical pattern would occur in two societies. Even if exactly the same vocabulary is used by two different societies, as when a small group splits off from the parent group to settle in a new territory, it is certain to become differentiated as time goes by unless there is a *very* high degree of communication between the groups' members.[18]

In addition to the spoken language, most societies have what might be

---

[15] Recent research helps us better understand why this is so. Languages are built through a process of inferences about the world, and there is no reason why different groups must draw exactly the same inferences. See J. Bronowski and Ursula Bellugi, "Language, Name, and Concept," *Science,* 168 (May 8, 1970), p. 673.

[16] Fred Blumenthal, "The Man in the Middle of the Peace Talks," *The Washington Post,* July 14, 1968.

[17] These examples are from Charlton Laird's popular and stimulating introduction to linguistics, *The Miracle of Language* (Greenwich, Conn.: Premier Books, 1953), pp. 54ff.

[18] Good examples of this point are the differences that developed between the German and British Saxons and later between the British and Americans. Recent reports suggest similar differences are beginning to appear between East and West Germans.

called an *unspoken* language made up of conventional gestures and facial expressions. These should not be confused with signals, such as the facial grimace we make when we taste something bitter. That is a reflexive movement and biologically determined. Symbols, whether spoken or unspoken, are *socially* determined. A good example of an unspoken symbol is the shrug of the shoulders that Americans and some other peoples use to express indifference, uncertainty, or a lack of relevant information (the meaning intended is usually evident from the context or from other gestures).

Unspoken language is especially effective in communicating emotional reactions, which is one reason many people avoid the telephone when they have an emotionally sensitive message to deliver (e.g., in reporting a death). In a face-to-face situation they can communicate their own feelings more effectively and read the responses of the other person more clearly, because they have a combination of spoken symbols, unspoken symbols, and signals to guide them.

In technologically advanced societies, *writing* is yet a third form of language. The earliest function of the written language was to provide a durable record of contractual agreements between Mesopotamian temple authorities and their business associates.[19] Later, it was used to record royal decrees, sacred traditions, judicial decisions, military triumphs, and other things too important to entrust to human memory or requiring an exact and durable record. Writing also provided a means of communication for people separated by barriers of distance and time and a way to reach large and scattered audiences. Finally it came to be used as a medium of artistic expression and for the purposes of education and entertainment.

After its invention five thousand years ago, the written language gradually gained in use and importance relative to the spoken and unspoken languages. More recently, the trend has been reversed, as the telephone, radio, movies, television, and other electronic devices have largely overcome the ancient barriers of distance and time. This reversal will probably continue, but it is unlikely that the written language will be replaced, any more than it could replace spoken or unspoken language. Each means of communication performs multiple functions, and no single method could prove superior for all of them.

When we first think about language, it seems to be merely a neutral and passive vehicle for exchanging information. But as political leaders, propagandists, advertising men, and others have long recognized, many words have powerful emotional connotations that make rational responses by their hearers difficult. Terms like "racist" and "Communist," for example, have powerful negative associations for most Americans. Therefore, to pin one of these labels on

---

[19] See V. Gordon Childe, *Man Makes Himself* (New York: Mentor, 1951), pp. 144ff.

an individual is to discredit him in the eyes of many people who will respond unthinkingly to the emotional content of the symbol.

The emotional loading built into words is not always negative. Many words have strong *positive* connotations, and these can also be used to manipulate emotions. Kinship terms that can be linked with organizations and individuals are particularly useful in stimulating positive responses. Several examples that come readily to mind are the use of "mother," as in "Mother Russia" or "Mother Church," or "uncle," as applied to the late North Vietnamese leader, "Uncle Ho," or the mythical symbol of this country, "Uncle Sam."

A leading linguist of the last generation, Edward Sapir, went so far as to claim that the "real world," as men understand this term, "is to a large extent unconsciously built upon the language habits of the group" and that because of this, different societies live in different worlds, "not merely the same world with different labels attached."[20] Though most modern scholars would not go this far, they would agree that language is by no means the simple, neutral, passive vehicle for exchanging information that we so often imagine it to be.[21]

Technology

"Technology" refers to *the information, techniques, and tools with which people utilize the material resources of their environment to satisfy their many needs and desires.* In effect, it is a cultural extension of the organic equipment with which we are endowed: our hands, our eyes, our ears, our legs, and all the rest. Like language, it is an essential element in every sociocultural system; without it, most human needs could not be satisfied.

Each set of needs tends to give rise to its own distinctive technology. Thus, we can speak of the technology of production, the technology of defense, the technology of communication, and so forth. In modern, technologically advanced societies, the number and variety of technologies are extremely large; no one person can master them all.

Sometimes it is helpful to speak of a single society as having a number of different technologies or technological systems. Usually, however, we speak of a society's technology in the singular. In part, this is a semantic convenience. But it is also the reflection of an underlying unity. To a considerable degree, the basic elements in the different technologies are shared. If, for example, a society has discovered the techniques of metallurgy in its effort to solve one problem, this information is likely to be applied to other problems before long. In short, in every society there is a common core of information, techniques, and tools that is applied to a wide range of problems.

---

[20] Edward Sapir, *Selected Writings in Language, Culture, and Personality,* ed. David Mandelbaum (Berkeley: University of California Press, 1949), p. 162.

[21] See, for example, Dell Hymes, "Linguistics: The Field," *International Encyclopedia of the Social Sciences* vol. 9, pp. 367–368, or William Bright, "Language: Language and Culture," *International Encyclopedia of the Social Sciences,* vol. 9, p. 22.

For some purposes, a distinction is drawn between technology and science. "Science" is used to refer to the search for general information about the natural world, without regard to its immediate practical uses. "Technology," in contrast, is used to refer to the pursuit of information for specific practical ends and to the application of scientific information to practical problems. This distinction can be quite important in modern industrial societies, where the question often arises as to the relative proportion of the gross national product that should be invested in each of these competing forms of activity. For our present purposes, however, most of science can be subsumed under the more general heading of technology, to avoid adding basic categories we really do not need.

Of the five major components of sociocultural systems, technology is often thought of as the most prosaic, and it has interested social scientists less than any of the others.[22] As we shall see, however, its influence on societal evolution and change has been way out of proportion to the recognition accorded it until fairly recently.

Social Structure

"Social structure" is a rather general term that is used to refer to *any system of relationships among people.* It may, for example, be used to refer to the system of relationships among the members of an entire society. Or it may be applied to any of the various systems of relations found in a group or organization within a society, such as the relations among the members of a family or the members of a labor union. Finally, the term may mean the system of relations within some international or intersocietal organization, such as the Roman Catholic Church. In the present context, however, we are concerned chiefly with the first meaning.

Individuals The two basic building blocks in every social structure are (1) the individuals who enter into social relations with one another and (2) the roles they fill. Little need be said about the former except that the number of individuals involved may be no more than two, as in families and cliques. At the other extreme, a structure may involve millions of individuals, as in the case of large metropolitan communities or modern industrial societies.

Roles The concept "role," as the term suggests, has been borrowed from the theater. In sociology, as in the theater, it refers to *a position which can be filled by an individual and to which distinctive behavioral expectations and requirements are attached.*[23] Thus, just as a person may play the role of Polonius in *Hamlet,* so he may "play" the role of doctor in his community or elder in his church.

---

[22] See, for example, Robert S. Merrill, "Technology: The Study of Technology," *International Encyclopedia of the Social Sciences,* vol. 15, p. 576.

[23] For a more detailed discussion of the important subject of roles, see Ralph Turner, "Role: Sociological Aspects," *International Encyclopedia of the Social Sciences,* vol. 13, pp. 552–557.

The key feature of a role is that it involves a set of behavioral expectations and requirements to which anyone who fills it must adapt. Roles vary greatly in the degree to which these are spelled out. In some the obligations are fuzzy and ill-defined, in others they are clear and precise. In the latter case, when the role is a position in a formal organization (e.g., a church or a governmental agency) and is held in special honor or entitles the incumbent to exercise authority, we speak of it as an *office*. Offices, in other words, are a special type of role.

Despite the fact that a role entails a set of behavioral expectations and requirements, it is possible for these to be changed by the individual who occupies it. This takes effort, however, and incumbents generally find it easier to accept their obligations, or evade them, than to change them. The chance that an individual can make changes varies greatly according to the nature of the role. For example, if it is a role he shares with thousands of others in a large organization (e.g., the role of student in a large state university), it will be much more difficult to change than if it is a unique role in a small and informal organization (e.g., the role of president in a small student club).

As an alternative to changing the obligations associated with a particular role, an individual sometimes has the option of switching to another. For example, if a college student finds the requirements of this role too difficult or too tedious, he can take a job or join the armed services. Some roles, however, usually cannot be changed, as in the case of age, sex, race, or ethnicity. These are known as *ascribed* roles; those which can normally be changed through the effort, or lack of effort, of the individual are *achieved* roles.

Roles serve many functions in societies, but four are of crucial importance. First, roles encourage specialization, which tends to increase the efficiency of human labor. Second, role specialization has an integrative effect: the more people divide up the tasks necessary to their survival and well-being, the more dependent they become on one another. Third, roles function as a mechanism of social control: they harness people's energies to tasks that the group as a whole, or its more powerful members, regard as necessary and desirable. Fourth, roles function as a mechanism for transmitting traditions from one generation to the next: individuals die, or leave the group for other reasons, but roles can persist indefinitely. Unlike humans, they are not mortal. The role of rabbi, for example, has existed for over 2,500 years, contributing immeasurably to the survival of the Jewish group and the preservation of its cultural heritage.

Groups In most societies, the members are divided into a variety of functional units we call groups. These range from small family units and cliques to giant corporate entities of various kinds. In popular usage, the term "group" is sometimes applied rather indiscriminately to any aggregation of people, regardless of their other characteristics. Sociologists, however, limit the term to *those aggregations whose members (1) act together in a common effort to satisfy*

Figure 2.2 Types of human groups.

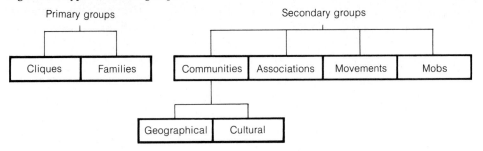

common, or complementary, needs, (2) share common behavioral expectations, and (3) have a sense of common identity.[24]

As this definition suggests, human aggregations differ in the *degree* to which they have the quality of "groupishness." Though some aggregations clearly qualify as groups (e.g., the United Auto Workers) and others just as clearly do not (e.g., all the redheads in the United States), many are on the borderline (e.g., Americans of Irish descent). As this last example reminds us, the degree of "groupishness" of an aggregation is not permanently fixed. Aggregations may take on more of the qualities of a group, or they may lose them: their members may come to work together more closely; develop new, stronger, and more generally shared behavioral expectations; and acquire a stronger sense of common identity; or just the opposite may occur, as in the case of the Irish-Americans during the last hundred years.

Despite the exclusion of aggregations such as redheads, the concept "group" still includes such a wide variety of organizations that it is often necessary to differentiate among them. The most familiar way is by their basic functions. Thus, we differentiate between families, religious groups, educational groups, political groups, and so forth.

Sociologists also differentiate among groups on the basis of their size and the intensity of the social ties among their members. Small groups in which face-to-face relations of a fairly intimate and personal nature are maintained are known as *primary groups.* Larger, more impersonal groups are known as *secondary groups.* Primary groups are of two basic types, *families* and *cliques.* In other words, they are organized around ties of either kinship or friendship. The category of secondary groups also contains two basic types, associations and communities. An *association* is a formally organized secondary group that performs some relatively specialized function or set of functions. Political parties, churches, labor unions, corporations, and governmental agencies are familiar examples. *Communities,* by contrast, are less formally organized and perform a wider range of functions.

---

[24] The term "group" may also be used to refer to a society, as the definition indicates, but in this section we are concerned with the *internal* structure of societies.

Basically, there are two types of communities, geographical and cultural. *Geographical communities* are those whose members are united primarily by ties of spatial proximity, such as neighborhoods, villages, towns, cities, and regions (e.g., the South). *Cultural communities* are those whose members are united by ties of a common cultural tradition, such as racial and ethnic groups. This category may include members of a religious group if they are closely integrated by ties of kinship and marriage and if the group has also developed a distinctive subculture of its own.[25]

As this last example indicates, associations may give rise to communities. And, it should be added, communities may give rise to associations. The emergence of black militant groups is a good example of the latter process. When either of these possibilities is realized, the membership of the community and the membership of the association overlap to a considerable degree. Usually, however, the community is larger, since its membership requirements are less stringent (often membership is automatic by virtue of birth).

In addition to associations and communities, there are several other types of secondary groups, the most important of which are *social and political movements.* These are loose-knit groups that hope to change the existing social order in some way. If such a group is successful in developing a following, a more tightly organized association usually is formed, and this becomes the nucleus of the movement. A good example is the rise and spread of the socialist movement in nineteenth-century Europe, with socialist parties eventually formed in most countries.

Mobs are another type of secondary group. Like movements, they tend to be hostile to the existing social or political order, but, unlike movements, they are very short-lived, localized groups, often violent or threatening violence, and usually much less effective.

Statuses Up to this point in our discussion of social organization, we have considered only the "horizontal" dimension of societies, the functional differences between individuals, roles, and groups. There is a second dimension, however, a *vertical* dimension. Individuals, roles, and groups can be ranked in a variety of ways, such as by income, wealth, education, or other culturally defined standards. This ranking is said to be the *status* of the unit in the society. The term "status" may be used to refer either to a ranking based on a *specific* criterion (such as income) or to the *overall* ranking of the unit. Sociologists are especially concerned with statuses that reflect the power, privilege, or prestige of units, since these are extremely important in the structure and functioning of societies.

Usually the various statuses of a unit are fairly consistent. People who

---

[25] See, for example, Gerhard Lenski, *The Religious Factor* (Garden City, N.Y.: Doubleday, 1961), pp. 17–19 and 301–302.

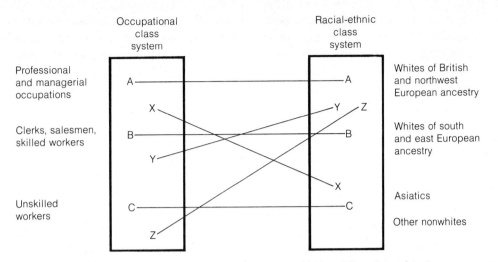

Status combinations A, B, and C are consistent; combinations X, Y, and Z are inconsistent.

Figure 2.3 Consistent and inconsistent statuses in contemporary American society.

are wealthy and well educated, for example, also tend to be powerful and to enjoy considerable prestige There are exceptions, however, and these are often interesting and important. A leader of the Mafia, for example, may enjoy great power and wealth in the community at large but have little prestige except in the Mafia itself. A person, a role, or a group exhibiting such characteristics is said to have *inconsistent status.*

The status of a unit often changes with the passage of time. When this occurs, we say that the unit is *upwardly mobile* or *downwardly mobile.* For example, when an individual is promoted, he is upwardly mobile; when a family fortune is gradually dissipated, the family is downwardly mobile.

Classes Like "status," the term "class" is used in two different, though related, ways. Sometimes it refers to an aggregation or group of people whose *overall* status is fairly similar. In this case, we usually speak of upper, middle, and lower classes; or we may divide the hierarchy more narrowly into upper-middle, lower-middle, and so on.

The term "class" is also frequently applied to an aggregation or group of people who stand in a similar position with respect to *some specific resource,* such as wealth, education, occupation, or anything else that affects their access to power, privilege, or prestige. Used in this way, the term is applicable to the nobility and peasantry of the past as well as to the rich and poor today. Similarly, one may speak of a propertied class, a managerial class, a working class, or a governing class. Generally, this usage of the term "class" is the more precise and unambiguous.

One question that naturally arises at this point is whether classes are groups. The answer is both yes and no. Many times, classes are simply human aggregates whose members, though in a similar position with respect to some resource, lack a sense of common identity and common behavioral expectations and do not act together to satisfy their common, or complementary, needs. For example, this is true of office workers, an occupational class in our society. On the other hand, American blacks, a racial-ethnic class, have long been a cultural community with a strong sense of common identity.

Taken together, all the classes of a given type (e.g., all the occupational classes in a society) form what is known as *a system of stratification.*[26] Taken together, all the systems of stratification in a society (e.g., the occupational system, the racial-ethnic system, the property system, etc.) form what is known as *the system of stratification* or *the distributive system* of that society.

As the latter term suggests, the basic function of these systems is to distribute the things of value that men produce in their life together in societies. These include not only the material products of the economy, such as food and clothing, but also intangible products, such as prestige and power. Some kind of distributive system is inevitable, since these things are usually in short supply (i.e., not enough is produced to satisfy the desires of all the members of society), and when people produce things through cooperative efforts, as they do in societies, there is no one obviously right way to distribute the product. For example, it is equally reasonable to argue that the products of the group's efforts be distributed on the basis of (1) the needs of individuals for these products, (2) the amount of effort individuals expend in their production, or (3) the degree of skill contributed by the producers, to mention but three of the possibilities. Even if a group settles on one of these principles, further disputes are likely. For example, if the members decide to apply the principle of effort, they still must decide how to measure effort. Should it be measured by the number of hours spent on the job or by the foot-pounds of energy expended? Or, if they select a different criterion, how does one compare a statesman's skills with those of a surgeon? In short, there is no one right way to handle this problem: arbitrary standards are inevitable. The only alternative is anarchy, given the natural tendency of individuals to put the satisfaction of their own needs ahead of the needs of most other people.

Not surprisingly, the subject of social stratification and inequality has given rise to one of the major controversies in modern sociology. The issue is whether distributive systems develop in response to the needs and requirements of society as a whole or in response to the power of elite groups within society. One school of sociologists stresses the inevitability of inequality, sometimes arguing that inequality is needed to motivate the abler members of society to seek the more important positions, sometimes arguing the social necessity of unequal authority. A second group argues that most inequality is simply

---

[26] Classes are sometimes called "strata," and a system of classes, or strata, is therefore called "a system of stratification." It may also be called a *class system.*

the result of force and fraud on the part of the more powerful and clever. A third group sees elements of truth in both views and tries to combine them in a synthetic perspective.[27] Though we can hardly resolve the controversy in this volume, we will offer materials that should help readers form their own views on the subject.

Conclusion   By way of conclusion, we can say that social structures are built on two basic principles: (1) the principle of the division of labor and (2) the principle of stratification. Because it is more efficient and more rewarding for men to divide up the tasks that are necessary for their survival and well-being, a system of functionally differentiated roles and groups gradually evolves in a society. But as this process of *functional* differentiation takes place, it is accompanied by a process of *status* differentiation. Thus, individuals, roles, and groups come to be differentiated in terms of status as well as in terms of the functions they perform; this, in turn, leads to the formation of classes. In some human societies, these possibilities have been realized in only the most limited way, but in others, social structures have become immensely complex.

Ideology

The last basic component of sociocultural systems is "ideology." This term refers to *a society's basic belief systems and their application to daily life.* The ideology of a society is made up of three important elements: (1) world views, (2) values, and (3) norms.

World views   Culture makes it possible for men to ask the question "Why?" "Why do some people enjoy greater success in life than others?" "Why did my child die?" "Why don't the rains come so our people won't starve?" By the asking of these questions, people express their culturally generated need for meanings.

To some extent, these questions are answered by what we call science, at least in modern industrial societies. "Your child died because it contracted a disease known as leukemia." "The rains did not come because of the presence of a high-pressure system in the area and a stationary front to the west." But even though such answers may be correct, they invite further questions. "Why did my child contract the disease?" Or, "Why was there this high-pressure system and this stationary front?" In other words, it is possible for us to ask questions in an infinite regress. At some point, however, we weary of explanations of explanations and ask the ultimate questions. "What is really real in this world?" "What are the forces that ultimately control human life?"

These are questions science cannot answer and never will. The

---

[27] For a brief introduction to the three "schools," see Lenski, *Power and Privilege,* chap. 1.

answers we give to these questions are answers based on faith.[28] This is not to say that reason plays no part in shaping them. Most people draw their inferences from observation and experience as carefully and as rationally as they can, but in the last analysis they are forced to take a leap of faith and say "I believe . . . "

One might suppose that the immense variability of human experience combined with this need for faith would result in an almost infinite variability in world views. Although it is surely true that world views vary greatly, there are forces that help promote agreement. From the standpoint of the individual, it is not reassuring to have a wholly unique view of the world and one's place in it. From the standpoint of society, too much divergence in this area can undermine the unity of the group.

In most societies of the past, a single world view tended to be dominant. Frequently there were variations on it, as in medieval societies where the educated classes had a somewhat different view from that of the illiterate peasant masses. In the modern world, however, a variety of circumstances have created a situation in which a much larger number of conflicting views compete for our loyalties. As a result, in most modern industrial societies world views are not the source of integration they were in the past. In the nineteenth and early twentieth centuries, many people thought that science might replace all the existing ideologies and provide a final, definitive world view. Today, however, as the nature of science and its limitations come to be better understood, this possibility has gone aglimmering. Today, we realize that though the findings, the method, and even the outlook of modern science are things that an educated person must take into account in his effort to define his own world view, science alone cannot create one and, in fact, explicitly avoids pronouncements on the *ultimate* nature of reality.

Values The beliefs that make up the ideology of a society include not only people's world views but also their "values." This term refers to *the generalized moral beliefs to which members of a group subscribe.* These include such things as the belief that lying, stealing, and murder are wrong and qualities such as generosity and bravery commendable.

Values tend to be tied to world views, with the world view usually providing a justification or rationale for the values, as well as for the actions these values encourage. Thus, Communists have long justified revolutionary violence on the grounds that feudalism and capitalism are doomed and that revolutions shorten the period of oppression and exploitation under the old order and speed the coming of a happy new era of justice and equality. Similarly, nineteenth-century Europeans justified the spread of the colonial

---

[28] See Peter Berger, *The Sacred Canopy: Elements of a Sociological Theory of Religion* (Garden City, N.Y.: Doubleday, 1961), chap. 1.

system in Asia and Africa on the ground that it was the white man's burden to be the carrier of civilization to these benighted lands.

As these examples suggest, one of the major functions of ideologies is to *legitimize* courses of action men want to follow. Ideologies have long been used to justify economic and political exploitation. This has been especially important in countries with marked social inequality. Pronounced differences in power and privilege have an explosive potential, and unless the poor and downtrodden are given some acceptable explanation for the practices that keep them poor and downtrodden, they are likely to revolt. Usually an explanation has been found to justify these practices, and the poor have suffered in silence.

Sometimes, however, rebels have been shrewd enough to see the need for a counter-ideology to fight the official one. Although the counter-ideology is not likely to persuade members of the class in power, it is essential for mobilizing the energies of the common people behind a revolutionary program. So long as the common people accept the old world view, they are psychologically immobilized. Marx saw this more clearly than most people, and his success in creating a new world view is largely responsible for the appeal and power of Marxist movements in many parts of the world today.

In the relationship between world views and values, it is sometimes difficult to determine which is the chicken and which is the egg. Logically, one would expect people to derive their values from their world views. But few of us are logicians, and those who are, are self-interested logicians. That is to say, most of us have special interests to defend, and, as a result, we find it convenient to make our world view serve our interests rather than the other way around. Not that this is necessarily a conscious process. Probably it is not in most cases, but the result is the same. Perhaps the best way to summarize what we know about this subject is to say that there seems to be a dialectic—a two-way exchange of influence—between world views and values, with each influencing the other.

In discussing values, it is important to distinguish between two sets of values that are often lumped together and treated as though they were the same. These are (1) pragmatic values and (2) ideal values.[29] Pragmatic values are at the core of all popular moral codes and are based on the recognition that members of the group need one another. Therefore, they condemn those kinds of actions which threaten to undermine the unity of the group (e.g., dishonesty, violence against fellow members, etc.) and encourage those actions which enable the group to satisfy its needs (e.g., hard work, honesty, etc.). Ideal values go much further. They set forth ideals for human conduct, but it is taken for granted that few, if any, will be able to live up to this standard (e.g., the Christian

---

[29] Lenski, *Power and Privilege*, p. 30.

Church has always taught that people should love their neighbors as themselves).

Since ideal values are so seldom realized, one might argue that they are of little social significance. But this is not true: their purpose is achieved if they stimulate us to go even a little way beyond the minimum level of performance called for in our group's pragmatic values. Ideal values are important in the crucial process of transforming us from the totally self-interested animals we are at birth to the partially group-oriented humans we must become.

Norms Values are always stated in general terms; they take no account of circumstances. Norms, by contrast, are the application of these general rules to specific circumstances. They are *behavioral prescriptions and proscriptions for the incumbents of specific roles in specific situations.*

Earlier, we defined roles as positions to which certain distinctive behavioral expectations and requirements are attached. "Norms" is the technical term for these expectations and requirements.

There are two basic types of norms. Those which are written down in some official code and systematically enforced by a governing authority are usually called "laws" or "regulations" or, in some cases, simply "rules." Contrasted with these more formally defined standards, every group and society also has many customary standards that, though unofficial and informal, are nonetheless regarded as important.

Some norms prescribe a single action in a certain situation and proscribe all others. Other norms define a range of alternative behavior that is acceptable: these alternatives may all be defined as equally acceptable, or some may be identified as preferred.

Violations of norms tend to generate guilt feelings on the part of the offender and punitive reactions on the part of others. These responses are due to the socialization process, which we shall examine more fully in Chapter 3. For now, the important point is that violations of norms are usually punished, while conformity tends to be rewarded. This system of norms and their related rewards and punishments is the core of every system of social control.

ENVIRONMENT

To round out our analysis of the structure and functioning of human societies, we must examine a final concept, one that is different from the others in that it is not a part of the society but external to it. Environment is *the surrounding complex of phenomena and forces that influence a society and are influenced by it.*

The relationship between a population and its environment is the most basic one in the whole world of nature. It is the basis of all ecological systems and the ultimate source of all evolutionary change. Since human populations are part of the biotic world, this relationship is equally important for them. Every society's survival basically depends on its ability to cope with its environment, to overcome the dangers and to utilize the resources.

In thinking about the environment, there is a tendency to focus exclusively on such things as mineral resources, climate, terrain, rivers and mountains, flora and fauna, and so on. These are obviously part of the environment of every human society, and terribly important to it. But there is more: other human societies. They, too, are part of the complex of phenomena and forces which surround a society and which influence it and are in turn influenced by it. Moreover, as human societies have grown larger and more powerful, this "social environment," as it might be called, has become increasingly significant as a source of societal problems—a threat often more serious than disease, wild animals, the elements, or any of man's other ancient environmental enemies. But the social environment has simultaneously become a major resource as well, thanks to the process of cultural diffusion—of which we shall say more in subsequent chapters. For now we will simply reiterate the essential point that no society can be analyzed without taking account of its environmental setting, a setting that includes other human societies as well as the biophysical environment.

APPENDIX: A FURTHER NOTE ON HUMAN NATURE

One aspect of the problem of human nature that has been much debated, and often quite unprofitably, is concerned with human values. Many scholars have taken the position that it is impossible to attribute any common set of values to people the world over—other than, perhaps, the very general self-seeking tendency noted previously. It is argued that some people seek physical comfort, some fame and honor, others aesthetic gratification, and so forth. Given these great differences, they argue, human nature can have nothing to do with the matter.

Recently, however, a psychologist, A. H. Maslow, developed a theory of human motivation that shows how such diverse goals and motivations might all spring from a common source. In a volume entitled *Motivation and Personality,* Maslow argues that people have a common inborn hierarchy of needs.[30] The most basic are physiological (the needs for food, water, sleep, protein, etc.). Next most basic are the safety needs. These are followed, in turn, by the "belongingness and love needs," the esteem needs, and the need for self-actualization. According to Maslow, the more basic needs are normally dominant until they are satisfied. The more fully they are satisfied, the stronger the higher needs become. In the case of individuals in whom the physiological and safety needs are fully met, the higher needs are usually dominant. In referring to one or another set of needs as dominant, Maslow does not claim that they alone are active. On the contrary, he suggests that several needs are likely to be operative at the same time, though all would not be equally compelling.

Though Maslow's theory can hardly be

---

[30] Maslow, *Motivation and Personality,* especially chap. 5. The brief summary of Maslow's theory given here does not do justice to his highly sophisticated and carefully qualified presentation. Hence, the reader is urged to read Maslow's argument firsthand.

called definitive, it is suggestive. Above all, it points the way to a resolution of the apparent paradox of diverse motivations and a common human nature.[31] It also may have special relevance for evolutionary theory and its application to contemporary social change. Thanks to the continuing industrial revolution, a number of societies are now, for the first time in history, in a position to satisfy most of the physio-logical and safety needs of the majority of their people. If Maslow is correct, this could result in a major shift in patterns of individual action, and this, in turn, could have far-reaching consequences for societies. This is a subject that deserves more attention than it has yet received from either sociologists or social psychologists.

---

[31] This is not to claim that all differences in motivation can be explained in this way. Some are undoubtedly the result of individual differences in heredity and of individual experiences of kinds unrelated to Maslow's theory.

CHAPTER THREE

Continuity, Innovation, and Extinction

In Chapter 2 we focused on the anatomy and physiology of human societies, that is, on the elements which comprise the structure of societies and on the function or functions each element performs. But if we are really to understand human societies, we must go beyond this—just as biologists have had to go beyond the study of anatomy and physiology to the study of organic evolution.

The theory of sociocultural evolution, like its counterpart in the biological sciences, is concerned with four basic processes:

1. *Continuity* (i.e., the persistence of phenomena over time)
2. *Innovation* (i.e., the emergence of new phenomena)
3. *Extinction* (i.e., the disappearance of certain older phenomena)
4. *Evolution* (i.e., basic trends over time)

In this chapter, we will consider the first three, thereby laying a foundation for our examination of sociocultural evolution in subsequent chapters. Since evolution is, in effect, the outcome of the combined operation of these three processes, we cannot hope to understand the basic trends of human history until we understand the processes of continuity, innovation, and extinction.

SOCIOCULTURAL CONTINUITY

Continuity, at first glance, appears to be irrelevant to evolutionary theory. In fact, it might even seem antithetical, since evolution means change and continuity can be thought of as the antithesis of change. When we think about it more carefully, however, we realize that evolution is change of a very special kind. It is change that implies continuity, because, in essence, it is *cumulative* change. In other words, it involves the addition of new elements to a continuing base of elements rather than the constant abandonment of existing elements and their replacement by new ones. Because of this, we cannot ignore continuity in any theory of sociocultural evolution.

Evidence of social and cultural continuity is all around us. The modern processes of paper making, printing, and bookbinding used in producing this book, for example, contain numerous elements that originated hundreds of years ago. The more basic elements, such as the alphabet and the very concept of books, are over three thousand years old. Other elements in our culture, such as the calendar, the concept of God, certain tools and techniques of cultivation, the basic techniques of metallurgy, and the concept of justice, to name but a few, are even older.

Forms of Sociocultural Continuity

Sociocultural continuity manifests itself in various ways, but two of the most important are customs and institutions. Customs are *learned patterns of behavior which are at least moderately widespread in a society and which endure for a significant period of time.* From the functional standpoint, customs may be regarded as traditional solutions to recurring problems. Certain problems arise repeatedly in every society. It would require an impossible expenditure of time and energy for every individual to work out his own solutions to them. Furthermore, most of the solutions would be less efficient than the standardized group solution that develops over a period of time. Sometimes, too, no particular solution is intrinsically superior; yet a standardized solution is necessary. A good example of this is the problem of which side of the road automobiles should drive on. It makes no difference whether they stay on the right or the left, but it is imperative that all drivers in a particular nation follow the same practice.

At this point, the question naturally arises as to how customs are related to norms. Norms, it will be recalled, are rules defining correct behavior in specific situations. Customs, by contrast, are the ways people *actually act* in those situations. Norms and customs are usually similar, but they are seldom identical, since certain violations of the norms tend to be customary. For example, driving somewhat in excess of the speed limit is the typical practice on certain highways in this country, even though this is clearly in violation of a legal norm.

Figure 3.1 Sometimes no particular solution to a society's problem is superior, yet a standardized solution is necessary. British laws require that vehicles travel on the left-hand side of roads and highways.

Similarly, the practice of sleeping on duty has long been customary on many police forces, especially during the midnight to 8 A.M. shift.

Rarely does a single custom exist in isolation. It is usually part of a larger structure of customary practices known as an *institution.* Thus, we often speak of the political, economic, religious, educational, or kinship institutions of a society, by which we mean the complex of customary practices in that area.

A British sociologist has referred to institutions as "frozen answers to fundamental questions."[1] Though this description exaggerates the static character of institutions, it vividly calls attention to the element of continuity inherent in every social institution. Change is present in social institutions, but it occurs within the context of a predominantly stable and continuing system of practices.

Causes of Sociocultural Continuity

Not surprisingly, a process as widespread and fundamental as sociocultural continuity is the result of a variety of factors. Some of these involve deliberate, conscious efforts to promote continuity and avoid change; others operate without conscious intent on anyone's part. Some depend on complex organizational arrangements; others operate very informally. To appreciate why sociocultural continuity has been so important in human societies, we must recognize the potency and diversity of the forces that promote it.

Some of the most powerful forces lie in *man's genetic heritage.* The very fact that this heritage itself changes so slowly ensures considerable continuity. One generation differs hardly at all from the next. In fact, there seem to have been few major genetic changes in our species in the last 35,000 years. Thus, man's body and what we have called his "human nature," together with all the problems that emanate from them, have remained pretty much the same for a long time.

Related to this, the individual's *inborn propensity for satisfying his needs as economically as possible* has also contributed to continuity. In most circumstances, economizing is best accomplished by sticking to customary practices. Change is not only risky; it usually requires new learning, and learning requires the expenditure of two of man's most precious commodities, time and energy. After providing for the necessities of life, most people have had little left of either. As a result, they usually have clung to traditional ways of doing things except in cases where the anticipated benefits of change clearly outweighed the anticipated costs or in trivial matters where nothing of value was at stake. Even the great revolutionaries of history have recognized the impossibility of *total* change and have never advocated it.

The process of aging is another important barrier to change. Older people usually have much stronger emotional ties with traditional practices than

---

[1] James K. Feibleman, *The Institutions of Society* (London: G. Allen, 1956), p. 52.

younger ones have. Moreover, learning new techniques and new ways of doing things becomes more difficult in later life. Yet, because power tends to be associated with age, this biological process acts as an important force for conservatism.

Another basic aspect of human nature that contributes to sociocultural continuity is *the prolonged helplessness of the human infant.* Unlike the offspring of most other species, the newly born human is incapable of satisfying even his most basic needs, and he remains in this condition, not for days or weeks, but for years. To survive into adulthood, he must master the traditional culture of his society, since it alone provides the resources he needs to cope with the problems of existence. Language is a good illustration of this. Until a child masters the linguistic symbols of his society, he is largely dependent on others; but once he masters them, he has an invaluable resource at his disposal. This applies to all the basic elements of his group's culture: *it pays the child to master them.*[2] Thus the desire of the older generation to preserve the traditional culture and transmit it to their offspring is more than matched by the desire of the younger generation to master it, particularly during the early formative years.

The process by which an individual learns the culture of his society is, as we have seen, the socialization process (page 29). The key to this process lies in the system of rewards and punishments that surrounds each of us from infancy on. Each person has, at birth, a potential for developing in a variety of different ways. More than that, in the early months and years of his life, he explores many of these possibilities. Some he finds are rewarding, while others result in unpleasant experiences. The normal individual responds by repeating those actions which have been rewarding and abandoning those which were not.

Figure 3.2 is a graphic representation of the situation in which most of us find ourselves. The larger circle represents the full range of possibilities open to us. The wedge represents the more limited range of behavior patterns approved by the culture of our society. When we experiment with actions that lie within the approved limits, we find that we are usually rewarded; when we go beyond these limits, we usually find the opposite. Sometimes, of course, we are punished when we act in accord with the norms and rewarded when we violate them. For example, a student who cheats on an examination and is not caught may receive a higher grade than one who is honest. Some instances of this are inevitable in almost any society, since those who do the sanctioning are not omniscient. In general, however, conformity with the norms is rewarded, deviance punished. As a result, by a process of conditioning that begins in infancy and continues throughout our lives, we

---

[2] Consider the early life of Helen Keller, prior to her discovery of the existence of symbols.

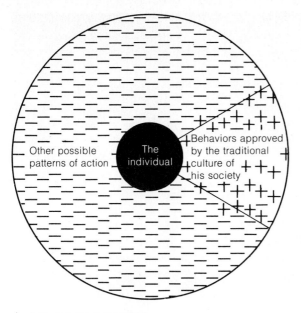

+ Actions that are rewarded

— Actions that are not rewarded

Figure 3.2 The sanction system surrounding the individual.

gradually become habituated to those patterns of action which are customary in our society and approved by it.

Figure 3.2 may be slightly misleading in one respect. It shows the limits of approved behavior for a single individual and may appear to suggest that the same boundaries apply for all members of that society. Actually, this is not the case. As we saw in Chapter 2, norms are rules of behavior governing the conduct of the incumbents of *specific roles*. What is correct for the incumbent of one role is not necessarily correct for the incumbent of another. For example, speech patterns suitable for sailors are not the same as those for clergymen—and vice versa. Similarly, there are marked differences in the norms of conduct for members of the middle and lower classes. The total range of behavior that is approved by a society for incumbents of all the various roles, then, is far greater than the range approved for any single role. Even so, the total range of approved behavior falls far short of what is possible.

To a considerable degree, every system of sanctions reflects *conscious and deliberate* efforts to promote continuity. The older generation naturally uses its resources to encourage adherence to the cultural standards it believes right and to discourage deviance from them. These standards are, after all, an important part of the precious residue of information gleaned by the group from generations of experience. If each generation had to start afresh and build its culture from its own experiences, mankind would never have escaped the Stone Age.

Figure 3.3 Some of the most effective socialization occurs in situations where no conscious effort is made to train or influence others.

The socialization process is not only a matter of deliberate efforts, however. Some of the most effective socialization occurs in situations where no conscious effort is being made to train or influence others. Many of the "rewards" and "punishments" experienced in everyday life are simply spontaneous by-products of normal social interaction. It is human nature to respond positively to actions we appreciate and value and negatively to those we do not. Therefore, because our values reflect our training and experience, we tend to respond positively to actions consistent with the traditional culture of our group and negatively to those which are not. Although there are exceptions to this, they are just that—exceptions.

We cannot fully appreciate the power of the socialization process, however, so long as we think of it as an external force to which we respond more or less reluctantly. It is, rather, an external force that so transforms our inner nature that it gradually becomes an internal force as well. As one writer puts it:

What happens in socialization is that the social world is internalized within the child. The same process, though perhaps weaker in quality, occurs every time the adult is initiated into a new social context or a new social group. Society,

> then, is not only something "out there," . . . but it is also "in here," part of our innermost being. Only an understanding of internalization makes sense of the incredible fact that most external controls work most of the time for most of the people in a society. Society not only controls our movements, but shapes our identity, our thought and our emotions. The structures of society become the structures of our own consciousness. Society does not stop at the surface of our skin. *Society penetrates us as much as it envelops us.*[3]

As a result, the socialized individual shares in the traditional culture of his society with a minimal sense of constraint. What is more, by his own actions, both deliberate and spontaneous, he reinforces the system of sanctions that surrounds others, thereby making his own contribution to sociocultural continuity.

Socialization continues into adulthood, for society is loath to abandon its efforts to shape its creatures until death or senility remove us from its reach. In modern industrial societies, adult socialization has grown in significance. This is due, in large measure, to the elimination of child labor. Cut off, as they are, from the basic economic institutions of society, many young people today must wait until their formal education has ended before they can really begin the serious business of learning to earn a livelihood.

The conservatism inherent in the socialization process is greatly reinforced by *most ideologies*. One of their chief functions is to preserve for future generations the basic insights of the past, which usually include the belief that the existing social order is a moral order, worthy of support. Established norms and values are thus justified by the society's overarching world view, and the whole ideological system acquires a sacred and conservative character. Ironically, this has been true even of revolutionary ideologies, such as Marxism. Once they win acceptance, they, too, acquire an aura of the sacred and become a force for continuity—and against change.

Still another factor contributing to sociocultural continuity is *the systemic character of sociocultural systems*. Most of the parts of these systems are linked to other parts in such a way that a change in one necessitates changes in others. For example, when, in the 1960s, the Swedes decided to drive on the right side of the road, this "simple" change necessitated hundreds of others and took months of planning. Cars and buses had to be redesigned, traffic signals moved, highway billboards relocated, and traffic laws rewritten. The changeover cost literally millions of dollars. Similar linkages are found throughout every sociocultural system. As a consequence, there are many changes that cannot be made without numerous additional ones; and though initially the benefits of the change may outweigh the costs, this may no longer be true when the costs of later changes are added.

---

[3] From *Invitation to Sociology* by Peter L. Berger. Copyright 1963 by the author. Reprinted by permission of Doubleday & Company, Inc. Emphasis added.

Benefits and Costs of Continuity

Until the modern era, most people accepted without question the principle that traditional ways of doing things are usually best. To say that a practice had been customary for centuries was necessarily to praise it. Today, however, we are less sure that traditional ways are best. Though many still prefer "the old ways," many others prefer change. Attitudes on the question of tradition versus change have become a divisive force in politics, economics, religion, art, scholarship, and many other fields. Conservatives emphasize the benefits of tradition, while liberals stress the advantages of change. Though we cannot hope to resolve such controversies, we can, perhaps, achieve a better understanding of the basic issue by examining both the benefits and the costs associated with continuity.

On the positive side, it is clear that sociocultural continuity yields a number of major benefits without which human life would be impossible. The development of customs greatly increases people's efficiency. If every problem had to be worked out again each time it was encountered, mankind would not survive for long. Similarly, if children did not inherit ready-made solutions to most of life's problems, they could not survive.

Beyond these individual benefits, there are social ones. None of us can live alone; we all depend on society. But a social system can function only if the actions of its members are mutually predictable, and sociocultural continuity is a requisite of predictability. The costs of unpredictable behavior patterns are dramatically illustrated by the many tragic misunderstandings that developed between the early European explorers and the peoples of both Africa and the New World.

Finally, as mentioned earlier, evolutionary progress is built on the foundation of cumulative change, and cumulative change presupposes the continuation of advantageous elements from the past. To express it somewhat differently, a sociocultural system incorporates the best solutions that the members of a society have found for their recurring problems. To ignore these solutions simply for the sake of change would be to abandon the group's chief resource in its struggle for survival.

Yet having said all this, we still must recognize that sociocultural continuity, or lack of change, can be costly. In the realm of technology, innovation usually leads to greater efficiency in the use of man's time and energy, a higher standard of living, and the opening of a wider range of options in many areas of life. Much the same is true in the realm of social organization.

Sociocultural continuity is likely to prove especially costly in a changing world. Either a society changes in response to changes in its environment, or the adequacy of its adaptation declines. This is inevitable in a world where societies compete for land and other essential resources, as technologically primitive peoples have learned in recent centuries. *In a changing world, there can be no final, perfect, or ultimate mode of adaptation to the environment.*

SOCIOCULTURAL INNOVATION

Forms of Innovation

Sociocultural innovation occurs in four basic forms: discoveries, inventions, diffusion, and alterations. Discoveries and inventions are probably the most familiar, though sometimes the distinction between them is blurred. In sociological usage, the term "discovery" is reserved for an innovation that provides the members of a society with new information, while "invention" refers to an innovation that is essentially a useful new combination of already existing information.[4] Thus, Columbus was a discoverer, while Gottlieb Daimler, the creator of the first automobile, was an inventor. Daimler combined in a novel way a number of technological elements that were already part of the cultural heritage of Western nations (i.e., the gasoline engine, running gears, drive shaft, carriage body, etc.). The "only" thing new was his combination of elements.

Diffusion is simply the transmission of existing information from one society to another, or from one subdivision of a society to another subdivision. Like invention and discovery, it is generally useful for the receiving society; unlike them, it adds nothing to the total store of human information. Nevertheless, the ease with which diffusion occurs is one of the chief reasons why sociocultural evolution moves so much faster than organic evolution.

Alterations, the final form of innovation, are by far the least important, though probably the most common. Unlike the others, they have no identifiable adaptive value. They frequently involve nothing more than a change in the *form* of certain symbols, as in linguistic changes. Linguists have shown, for example, that by the process of alteration all the different words for mother in the various Indo-European languages evolved, over thousands of years, from the same word. Similar changes occur in legends, songs, and other aspects of culture, especially when a society has no system of writing and must rely on the memory of its members. Sometimes alterations are simply the result of deliberate efforts to change things for the sake of change. Slang, for example, involves the purposeful distortion of words to create a distinctive vocabulary. Changing styles in art sometimes seem to reflect a similar process.

Causes of Innovation

Many factors contribute to innovation within a society, but for purposes of analysis, they may be divided into two categories: (1) environmental factors and (2) internal factors.

By now it should be clear that the relationship between a society and its environment is extremely important. Not only is the environment a so-

---

[4] For one of the earliest statements of this distinction, see F. Stuart Chapin, *Cultural Change* (New York: Century, 1928), p. 345.

ciety's source of sustenance, but also its various characteristics—including other societies—act as a set of conditions to which the society must adapt. Changes in the environment, therefore, generate pressures for compensatory changes in the society.

Several times in history, societies have had to make major adjustments in response to changes in their biophysical environments. The end of the Pleistocene Ice Age, for example, necessitated drastic changes in the sociocultural systems of Europe, which had been based on the highly specialized hunting of reindeer on open plains.[5] With the warming of the climate, forests began to spring up across Europe, and the reindeer retreated toward the Arctic regions where they are found today. As new species of plants and animals gradually replaced Ice Age species, societies had either to innovate or to perish.

The environment to which a society must adapt also includes the other societies with which it has any contact. A major change in one usually has consequences for the rest, frequently triggering a chain reaction of adjustments and innovations. In the last 5,000 to 10,000 years, the social environment has been much less stable than the physical and biotic and, as a result, has been a much more frequent source of change.

If environmental change were the only source of innovation, the rate would have been much lower than it has been. Innovations, however, are also the result of forces rooted in man himself and in his societal mode of life.

To begin with, as we have seen, people do not always learn perfectly everything their elders try to teach them. Errors occur in the process of transmitting the cultural heritage from one generation to the next, giving rise to alterations of various kinds. In addition, people are apparently motivated by their very nature deliberately to try new patterns of action. Sometimes they experiment with alternatives because they have become bored by routine and feel the need for new experiences. Sometimes the motivation is curiosity, a trait found among many of the higher animals but intensified by culture. Or the motivation may simply be material self-interest. Given man's desire to maximize his rewards, experimentation and innovation are inevitable. Besides all this, societal life produces problems that stimulate innovation. With population growth, for example, a simple technology and social structure may become inadequate; and change in one part of the sociocultural system often generates pressure for change elsewhere.

Man has been exploring his environment and experimenting with new methods of doing things from the earliest times. In the ensuing processes of discovery and invention, purposive behavior and accident—or chance—have often been curiously intermingled. For example, the great scientist Louis Pasteur discovered the principle and technique of immunization only after he accidentally injected a stale bacterial culture of chicken cholera into some an-

---

[5] See, for example, Grahame Clark, *The Stone Age Hunters* (London: Thames and Hudson, 1967), chaps. 3 and 5.

imals. When, unexpectedly, they survived, it occurred to him that a weakened culture might immunize against the disease.[6] Similarly, a key problem in the development of photographic techniques was solved when Louis Daguerre put a bromide-coated silver plate into a cupboard where, unknown to him, an open vessel of mercury was standing. When he returned the following day, he found that the latent image had begun to develop and surmised that fumes from the mercury were responsible.

Even though chance has played an important part in the process of innovation, *knowledge, intelligence, and purpose* have also been essential. An appreciation of the value of new information presupposes both intelligence and knowledge, and often purpose as well. It was more than accident that led Pasteur to discover the process of immunization and Daguerre the process of developing pictures. Both men had already acquired the knowledge that enabled them to appreciate the import of their accidental discoveries. Furthermore, both were actively seeking new information. Thus, in these cases as in most others involving chance, the outcome was due to a combination of chance, knowledge, intelligence, and purpose.

Given man's evolutionary history, this is exactly what we would expect. Man stands in an evolutionary line that has relied on learning as a basic means of adaptation, and the chief function of that learning is to enhance the value of experience. This experience comes to him both by chance and by his purposive action.

Figure 3.4 "If this doesn't result in one or two first-class inventions, nothing will."

[6] For a discussion of a number of interesting examples, including those here, see A. L. Kroeber, *Anthropology* (New York: Harcourt, Brace, 1948), pp. 353–355. For more recent examples, see Howard A. Rush, "Right Time and Place: Many Medical Discoveries Found to Result from Series of Accidents," *The New York Times*, June 8, 1969.

In the earlier stages of human history, chance was probably much more important in the innovative process than it is today. Accidental alterations were far likelier before the invention of writing and other methods of record keeping increased the accuracy with which information could be transmitted. Though we have no record of how important discoveries of the past occurred (e.g., fire-making, animal domestication, plant cultivation, etc.), it seems probable that chance played a significant part in these as well.

The rise of science, with its systematic methods of research and organized store of information, has further reduced the role of chance in the last century. Many modern inventions (e.g., submarines and rocket ships) were predicted years in advance of the construction of the first workable model. Similarly, most of the "newer" elements in the periodic table in chemistry were predicted long before their actual discovery. This decline in the importance of chance and the corresponding increase in the importance of purposeful action are natural by-products of the steady growth in the store of man's useful information.

The Rate of Innovation

Though innovation occurs in every human society, its *rate* is highly variable. In some societies, during some periods, the rate has been so low as to be virtually imperceptible; at other times, or in other societies, it has been extremely high. To understand the major trends in evolutionary history, we must first understand what is responsible for these variations.

Of all the factors involved in the rate of innovation, probably none has been more important than *the magnitude of the existing store of information in the group*.[7] The reason is simple. Invention, as we have seen, is one of the basic processes of innovation, and inventions are essentially *recombinations of existing elements of the culture*. It follows, therefore, that a society's potential for invention is a simple mathematical function of the number of elements available for combination. This is easily illustrated. Table 3.1 shows the number of combinations that are possible for various numbers of units or elements. Though two units can be combined in only one way, three units can be combined in four ways, and four units in eleven ways. In other words, *the addition of each new unit more than doubles the number of possible combinations*. Thus a mere fivefold increase in the number of units from two to ten leads to a thousandfold increase in the number of possible combinations, and when the number of units reaches twenty, over a million combinations are possible!

Of course, many of the elements of a sociocultural system cannot be combined in any useful way. For example, it is difficult to imagine a useful combination of the hammer and the saw. The number of possible combinations,

---

[7] For an early discussion of this point, see William F. Ogburn, *Social Change* (New York: Viking, 1922), chap. 6.

Table 3.1 Number of combinations possible for various numbers of units

No. of Units	Total Number of Combinations									Total
	2 at a Time	3 at a Time	4 at a Time	5 at a Time	6 at a Time	7 at a Time	8 at a Time	9 at a Time	10 at a Time	
2	1	0	0	0	0	0	0	0	0	1
3	3	1	0	0	0	0	0	0	0	4
4	6	4	1	0	0	0	0	0	0	11
5	10	10	5	1	0	0	0	0	0	26
6	15	20	15	6	1	0	0	0	0	57
7	21	35	35	21	7	1	0	0	0	120
8	28	56	70	56	28	8	1	0	0	247
9	36	84	126	126	84	36	9	1	0	502
10	45	120	210	252	210	120	45	10	1	1,013

therefore, is much greater than the number of *fruitful* ones. Moreover, inventions, combinations of existing information, add nothing to a society's potential; only discoveries do this. Nevertheless, despite these qualifications, the amount of available information is certainly a major factor in a society's rate of innovation.

A second cause of difference in the rate of innovation is *the size of societal populations.*[8] The more people looking for a solution to a problem, the quicker it will be found, other things being equal. Since societal populations vary so greatly (by ratios as high as 30 million to 1), this is another factor of considerable importance.

A third factor influencing the rate of innovation, and one of the most important in the modern world, is *the extent of intersocietal contact.* The greater the contact one society has with others, the greater its opportunities to appropriate their discoveries and inventions. In short, sociocultural contact enables a society to take advantage of the brainpower and cultural heritage of other societies.

The importance of this was beautifully illustrated by Ralph Linton, a leading anthropologist of the last generation. Analyzing American culture, he wrote:

> Our solid American citizen awakens in a bed built on a pattern which originated in the Near East but which was modified in Northern Europe before it was transmitted to America. He throws back covers made from cotton, domesticated in India, or linen, domesticated in the Near East, or wool from sheep, also domesticated in the Near East, or silk, the use of which was discovered in China. All of these materials have been spun and woven by processes invented in the Near East. He slips into his moccasins, invented by the Indians of the Eastern woodlands, and goes to the bathroom, whose fixtures are a mixture of European and American inventions, both of recent date. He takes off his pajamas, a garment

---

[8] Ogburn mentioned this factor briefly in his study but did not stress it. See ibid., 1950 ed., p. 110.

invented in India, and washes with soap invented by the ancient Gauls. He then shaves, a masochistic rite which seems to have been derived from either Sumer or ancient Egypt.

Returning to the bedroom, he removes his clothes from a chair of southern European type and proceeds to dress. He puts on garments whose form originally derived from the skin clothing of the nomads of the Asiatic steppes, puts on shoes made from skins tanned by a process invented in ancient Egypt and cut to a pattern derived from the classical civilizations of the Mediterranean, and ties around his neck a strip of bright-colored cloth which is a vestigial survival of the shoulder shawls worn by the seventeenth century Croatians. Before going out for breakfast he glances through the window, made of glass invented in Egypt, and if it is raining puts on overshoes made of rubber discovered by the Central American Indians and takes an umbrella, invented in southeastern Asia. Upon his head he puts a hat made of felt, a material invented in the Asiatic steppes.

On his way to breakfast he stops to buy a paper, paying for it with coins, an ancient Lydian invention. At the restaurant a whole new series of borrowed elements confronts him. His plate is made of a form of pottery invented in China. His knife is of steel, an alloy first made in Southern India, his fork a medieval Italian invention, and his spoon a derivative of a Roman original. He begins breakfast with an orange, from the eastern Mediterranean, a canteloupe from Persia, or perhaps a piece of African watermelon. With this he has coffee, an Abyssinian plant, with cream and sugar. Both the domestication of cows and the idea of milking them originated in the Near East, while sugar was first made in India. After his fruit and first coffee he goes on to waffles, cakes made by a Scandinavian technique from wheat domesticated in Asia Minor. Over these he pours syrup, invented by the Indians of the Eastern woodlands. As a side dish he may have the egg of a species of bird domesticated in Indo-China, or thin strips of the flesh of an animal domesticated in Eastern Asia which have been salted and smoked by a process developed in northern Europe.

When our friend has finished eating he settles back to smoke, an American habit, consuming a plant domesticated in Brazil in either a pipe, derived from the Indians of Virginia, or a cigarette, derived from Mexico. If he is hardy enough he may even attempt a cigar, transmitted to us from the Antilles by way of Spain. While smoking he reads the news of the day, imprinted in characters invented by the ancient Semites upon a material invented in Germany. As he absorbs the accounts of foreign troubles he will, if he is a good conservative citizen, thank a Hebrew deity in an Indo-European language that he is 100 per cent American.[9]

A fourth factor affecting the rate of innovation is *the stability of the environment to which the society must adapt.* The greater the rate of environmental change, the greater the pressure on the society to modify either its technology

---

[9] From: *The Study of Man* by Ralph Linton. Copyright, 1936, by D. Appleton-Century Company, Inc. Reprinted by permission of Appleton-Century-Crofts.

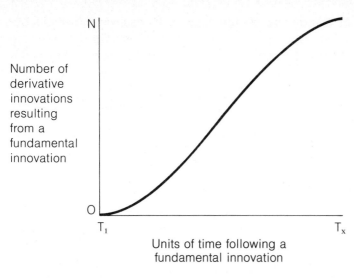

N

Number of
derivative
innovations
resulting
from a
fundamental
innovation

O

T_1

T_x

Units of time following a
fundamental innovation

Figure 3.5 S-curve pattern of derivative innovations resulting from a fundamental innovation.

or its social structure. As we noted before, the *social* environment usually changes much more rapidly than the biophysical. Especially important are events that upset the balance of power among neighboring societies, such as large-scale migrations, the building of empires, and similar developments.

Fifth, the rate of innovation is greatly influenced by *"fundamental" discoveries and inventions.* Not all discoveries and inventions are of equal importance; a few open the way for literally thousands of other innovations, while the majority have no such effect.[10] The steam engine is a good example of a fundamental invention of the recent past. Examples from earlier periods include the discovery of the principles of plant cultivation, of animal domestication, and of metallurgy, and the invention of the plow.

Sometimes a fundamental innovation will cause the rate of innovation to rise because it involves a principle that can be applied, with minimum effort and imagination, to hundreds, even thousands, of problems. This was true of both the steam engine and metallurgy. Sometimes, however, an invention or discovery earns the label "fundamental" because it so drastically alters the conditions of human life that hundreds or thousands of other changes become either possible or necessary. This was certainly the case with the discovery of the principles of plant cultivation, which, as we shall see in a later chapter, led to a host of major sociocultural changes.

Before leaving the subject of fundamental innovations, we should note that they have an impact that follows the pattern of the so-called S-curve, or logistic curve, shown in Figure 3.5. In other words, their immediate effect is a period during which derivative innovations occur at an accelerating rate. In time,

[10] Ogburn, 1950 ed., p. 107.

however, this rate begins to decline, as the number of possible derivations begins to be exhausted. How soon this happens depends on the nature of the fundamental innovation: some have a more limited number of possible derivatives than others. In every case, however, the long-term trend involves some approximation of the S-curve.

A sixth factor influencing the rate of sociocultural innovation is *the society's attitude toward innovation*. In some societies, innovation has been positively valued, at least in certain areas of life. Contemporary American society is a case in point: innovation or creativity is highly valued in art, science, technology, philosophy, entertainment, and recently even in theology. Sometimes it seems that an innovation can even be inferior to what it replaces and still be applauded. In most societies, however, traditional patterns have been highly valued, especially in ideology and social structure, and the idea of innovation for innovation's sake has been entirely alien.

Though the problem has not been studied as systematically as it should be, a society's attitude toward innovation is apparently greatly influenced by its prior experience with change. A society that has undergone an extended period of change and benefited from it will almost certainly favor innovation more than a society that has not had this experience. Societies' attitudes toward innovation also vary according to religious or other ideological influences. Some ideologies generate a very conservative and anti-innovational outlook; Confucianism is a classic example of such a faith. Judaism, Christianity, and Communism, by contrast, have been much more receptive to sociocultural innovation and change.

The "Multiplier Effect" in Innovation

Up to this point we have considered separately each of the factors influencing the rate of innovation. Actually, however, *most of the factors stimulating innovation are interdependent*. The nature of this interdependence is shown graphically in Figure 3.6. As indicated by the double-headed arrow linking size of population and size of the store of useful information, each of these factors affects the other. The greater the store of useful information, the larger the population that can be supported in a given geographical area and the larger the area that can be controlled by a single society. Conversely, the larger the population working on problems, the more rapidly the store of useful information tends to grow.

A similar relation exists between the size of the store of information and the degree of intersocietal contact. A greater store of useful information means more time free from the demands of providing daily sustenance to devote to intersocietal contacts, and it may also mean better means of transportation and communication to facilitate such contacts. Conversely, the more contact a society has with other societies, the greater its own store of information will become.

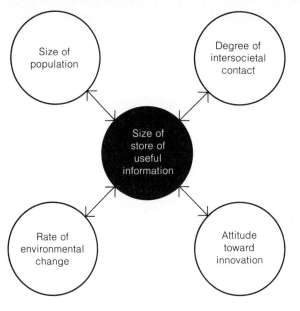

Figure 3.6 **Relations between factors responsible for variations in the rate of innovation.**

A society's store of information and changes in its environment are also related. An increase in the former will usually result in changes in either the biophysical or the social environment. Such changes, in turn, create the need for further change in the society and in its store of information, or else the level of the society's adaptation to the environment will decline.

Finally, the more useful information a society possesses, the more favorable its attitude toward innovation (because of rewarding experiences in the past); and, conversely, a favorable attitude toward change is likely to be favorable to growth in the store of information. In short, *the size of the store of information is linked to each of these other factors in a reciprocal relation.*

Because of these interrelations, a single innovation often gives rise to a whole series of others. Something analogous to the economist's multiplier effect seems to operate.[11] An increase in the store of useful information can easily contribute to increases in population, in the degree of intersocietal contact, and in the rate of environmental change, and to an improvement in attitudes toward innovation. These changes, in turn, are all likely to contribute to a further increase in the store of useful information.[12]

---

[11] For a discussion of the multiplier effect in economics, see Paul Samuelson, *Economics,* 6th ed. (New York: McGraw-Hill, 1964), pp. 231ff.

[12] Normally the multiplier involved in the innovation process is considerably less than 1.0. This means that the derivative effects of the initial innovation become smaller and smaller in magnitude until eventually they disappear. For example, if we imagine an initial innovation with an adaptive value of 100 and a multiplier effect of 0.5, the first derivative effect would have a value of 50, the second of 25, the third of 12.5, and so on, until the effects become imperceptible.

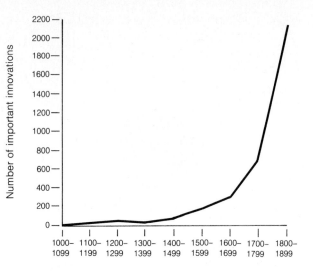

Figure 3.7 Number of important inventions and dis-coveries, by century, from 1000 A.D. to 1900 A.D.

The Long-term Rise in the Rate of Innovation

One of the most important facts of human history is the tremendous increase in the rate of innovation since early prehistoric times. Though one might suppose that this is largely a recent development, such is not the case. On the contrary, the trend has been going on for tens of thousands of years. Figure 3.7 shows the pattern for the past nine hundred years, and, as we shall see in Chapter 6, archaeological evidence traces the trend to man's earliest history.[13]

This is not to say there has been a constantly accelerating rate in every society or even that there has been an accelerating rate for the world as a whole in every century. At several points in history the rate of innovation remained fairly stable or even declined for a period. Nevertheless, the rate invariably turned upward again and became greater than ever before.

The reasons for this should be evident by now. As we have seen, technological information is cumulative, and each new bit of useful information increases the probability of getting more. Besides, technological advance makes possible larger populations, and larger populations mean more people looking for solutions to problems. It also leads to increased contacts between societies and to the more rapid diffusion of knowledge. Finally, the benefits resulting from all these developments gradually undermine historic prejudices against change and contribute to the emergence of new change-oriented ideologies.

Where will this trend end? No one can really say at this time. We can say only that sooner or later acceleration must cease. At some point, any further increase in the rate of innovation will almost certainly prove psychologically,

---

[13] See Table 6.2, p. 132.

and perhaps physically and economically, intolerable. Sometimes it seems we are already approaching that point.[14] When we think about the situation more carefully, however, we realize that considerable acceleration is still possible simply because so many innovations in today's highly specialized societies require little or no adjustment on the part of most people. With the extreme division of labor that has developed during the last century, an individual is seriously affected by only a small proportion of the many inventions and discoveries being made. In short, evolution appears to increase a society's ability to tolerate higher rates of innovation.

SOCIOCULTURAL EXTINCTION

Sociocultural extinction is the process whereby various social and cultural phenomena disappear from a society. This can happen abruptly and dramatically, as when the czarist government was overthrown in 1917, terminating countless social and cultural patterns. Or the process may be drawn out over an extended period, as in the gradual replacement of the horse and carriage by the automobile.

Sociocultural extinction often occurs as the result of processes at work

Figure 3.8 A case study of intrasocietal selection: horse-drawn carriages compete with early automobiles.

---

[14] We shall talk about this further in Chapter 15.

within a society, as in the examples just cited. In this case we speak of intrasocietal selection. When extinction results from a struggle *between* societies, it is intersocietal selection. Because they work in different ways and, to some extent, have different outcomes, each needs to be considered separately.

Intrasocietal Selection: The Selection of Elements within Societies

Because of the process of innovation, the members of human societies are often confronted with alternative solutions to problems. The choice a group makes in such a situation often leads to the extinction of one or more of the alternatives. Many factors influence people when they make these choices—the information available to them, their judgments concerning the probable benefits and costs of the various alternatives, and their values.

In keeping with the economizing principle stated earlier, people try to follow the course of action that promises the greatest rewards for the least expenditure of resources. This does not mean that they are strictly rational in their choices: many decisions are made on the basis of unexamined assumptions; in other cases, emotions play a significant role. But even when these factors are minimal, it can be extremely difficult to determine which of several possible alternatives will prove the most rewarding. This is especially true in matters of ideology. Technology poses less of a problem, with the result that the process of selection in that area moves more swiftly. To a lesser degree, this is also true of social structure, especially groups created for a single purpose, such as to make a profit or to defend a nation. Here, as with technology, alternatives are subjected to recurring tests, and their relative efficacy can be judged by a single standard (where multiple standards are involved, as in groups with diverse functions, it is much more difficult for men to agree on the relative efficacy of alternatives). Thus, with the passage of time, the sequence of choices made by the members of a society often produces a progression of structural forms, just as choices among technological alternatives usually produce a progression of technological forms.

One of the great ironies of evolution is the fact that the process of intrasocietal selection does not necessarily increase a society's chances of survival.[15] It may even reduce them. The explanation of this paradox is that the principles governing the selective process on the intrasocietal level are different from those which operate on the intersocietal level. Within societies, choices are made on the basis of the maximization principle, as applied by individuals and groups such as families, businesses, and labor unions. These decisions are based on what each judges to be its own best interests, and

---

[15] See Walter Goldschmidt, *Man's Way: A Preface to the Understanding of Human Society* (New York: Holt, 1959), p. 128. For the biological parallel, see Konrad Lorenz, *On Aggression,* translated by M. K. Wilson (New York: Bantam, 1967), pp. 36–38.

these often conflict with the best interests of the society as a whole, at least when judged from the standpoint of its chances of survival. For example, most American families prefer to spend their resources on things that contribute to their own immediate comfort and pleasure rather than on things that strengthen the nation economically, militarily, or morally.[16]

Human Societies as Imperfect Systems

This brings us to a characteristic of human societies that is frequently overlooked: though human societies may quite properly be called systems, they are very *imperfect* systems. A human society lacks the degree of coordination among its parts, and the degree of coordination between the parts and the whole, found in most of the things to which we apply the term "system."

Too often this term is used categorically: we tend to say that either something is a system or it is not. Like many other concepts, however, it becomes more meaningful when it is used as a variable. For purposes of definition we should say that a system exists *to the degree that* the actions of the parts are coordinated with one another and with the actions of the entity as a whole. When "system" is defined in this way, it is clear that human societies are less perfect systems than most of the other things to which this term has been applied. For example, there is much less internal conflict within insect societies than within human societies. Though insect populations are divided into different castes, they exhibit nothing comparable to the struggles between groups within human societies. Similarly, the coordination between the actions of the parts and the whole is much greater in insect societies, and in organisms and mechanical systems, than it is in human societies. In fact, there are few phenomena to which we apply the label "system" that show systemic properties less clearly than do human societies.

This suggests that we must use the term with considerable caution if we are not to distort our image of social reality. As we observed in Chapter 1, the cultural tools we create to serve us (and these tools include terms) can easily become our masters and end up shaping our perception of the world we are trying so hard to understand, preventing us from seeing it as it really is.

Intersocietal Selection: The Selection of Societies

While the selective process goes on within societies, eliminating first one, then another, of the elements of sociocultural systems, a similar process is taking place in which societies themselves are the units whose survival is in question.

---

[16] See John Kenneth Galbraith's discussion of this problem in *The Affluent Society* (Boston: Houghton Mifflin, 1958), especially chap. 18.

No adequate understanding of evolutionary history is possible if we ignore this second mode of selection.

The two processes differ from one another in a number of ways, but the most important difference is in the basis of selection. In intersocietal selection, the basic determinant has usually been *military power*. To survive, a society has had to be strong enough to protect its territory and its resources against the attacks of aggressive neighboring societies. Those too weak to defend themselves have usually been destroyed.

If this seems an unduly harsh view, one need only examine the historical record. Thousands of societies that once flourished no longer exist. If we look for the reason, we find that the great majority of them were simply unable to defend themselves. Defeated in war, they were absorbed, destroyed, or so crippled that they could not survive as autonomous units. The hundreds of Indian tribes that once flourished in North and South America and the many independent city-states that once dotted the Mediterranean world and the Middle East are good examples.

Figure 3.9   A doomed society: Navajo Indians of the American Southwest.

One of the widespread misconceptions of the modern era is that peace is the normal state of relations between societies and that hostility and war are abnormal conditions. Much as we might wish this were true, the historical record indicates otherwise. A study of eleven European countries, covering periods of 275 to 1,025 years, found that the incidence of war ranged from a low of 28 per cent of the years in the case of Germany to a high of 67 per cent in the case of Spain.[17] The mean was 47 per cent, indicating that on the average these eleven countries were engaged in some kind of military action almost every other year. Though we lack such systematic data for more primitive societies, the evidence we have suggests that warfare and fighting are common among many of them too.[18]

There are a number of reasons why wars and other struggles have been so common. Throughout most of history, the basic cause seems to have been the same that underlies competition in the rest of the biotic world, namely, *the limited supply of resources*.[19] A *finite* supply of resources, no matter how great, will never suffice for a population with an *infinite* capacity for growth. Unless its growth is checked somehow, every population, human or animal, eventually exhausts its supply of resources. In that situation, it will encroach on the territories and resources of neighboring populations. But since these resources are essential to the latter, they cannot allow this to happen. Conflict thus becomes inevitable, and in time the weaker groups are destroyed. In many ways, evolutionary history has been like a deadly game of musical chairs in which a succession of contestants has been eliminated because of their inability to defend their territorial bases.

In the case of man, the problem has been complicated by his possession of culture. To begin with, the problem of scarcity is more acute because culture multiplies human needs and desires enormously. The wants of animals are limited, but the more men have, the more they usually want. Thorstein Veblen, a pioneer American social scientist, saw this clearly. In his famous work, *The Theory of the Leisure Class,* he developed the thesis that once a society is able to produce more than the necessities of life, its members strive to acquire nonessential goods and services because of their prestige value.[20]

---

[17] Pitirim Sorokin, *Social and Cultural Dynamics,* ed. (New York: Bedminster Press, 1962), vol. III, chap. 10 and p. 352.

[18] See, for example, L. T. Hobhouse, G. C. Wheeler, and M. Ginsberg, *The Material Culture and Social Institutions of the Simpler Peoples* (London: Routledge, 1965, first published 1915), p. 232, or Colin K. Loftin, "Warfare and Societal Complexity: A Cross-Cultural Study of Organized Fighting in Preindustrial Societies" (unpublished Ph.D. dissertation, University of North Carolina, Chapel Hill, 1971).

[19] This is not to deny other causes of conflict between societies. Sometimes, however, what appear to be other causes partly or wholly disappear when we examine them, just as a close examination of the Crusades indicates that religious motivations were far from dominant for most of the leaders.

[20] Thorstein Veblen, *The Theory of the Leisure Class* (New York: Macmillan, 1899), now available in various paperback editions.

Since prestige is always a relative matter (i.e., it is a measure of one's standing in relation to others), it is impossible to satisfy the demand for goods and services that it generates, and scarcity is therefore inevitable no matter how much technology is improved or production increased. Many wars have been fought to provide, not the necessities of life for the masses, but glory and luxuries for their leaders.

Although military power has been the basic determinant of societal survival, other factors are involved, if only because they influence military power. For example, the greater a society's supply of manpower, the stronger it tends to be militarily. Similarly, the more advanced a society is technologically, the greater its military potential. A society's size and level of technological development, therefore, are major determinants of its chances of survival.[21]

Nonmilitary forms of power, too, sometimes affect societal selection. Recent studies in India, for example, show that Hindu society has been gradually destroying, through cultural absorption, scores of primitive societies along its borders.[22] In most instances, members of these tribes, or their leaders, are envious of the advantages afforded by membership in Hindu society. This leads them to adopt Hindu ways and to abandon the traditional culture of their own group. Even when only part of a tribe does this, it can be enough to undermine the autonomy of the group and bring about its eventual destruction. This pattern is likely to occur, however, only when a small, primitive society comes into contact with a large, advanced one.

Nonviolent extinction can occur in still other ways. A number of American Indian tribes, for example, were destroyed by smallpox epidemics. Other groups have disappeared because of internal struggles that resulted in schisms. Currently, another nonviolent form of societal extinction seems to be developing: the elimination of small nations that are unable to compete economically with the mass markets of larger nations and the resulting low unit costs of production. The formation of the European Economic Community could well be the prototype of a new pattern of societal merger and extinction.

Some Final Thoughts

Before we conclude this discussion of sociocultural extinction, several points need to be clarified. First, sociocultural selection is an immensely complex process: it reflects the influence of multiple—sometimes even contradic-

---

[21] Other factors, such as the morale of soldiers and the skill of their leaders, sometimes help account for the success or failure of a particular society at a particular time, but they are of relatively little importance in explaining the basic pattern of evolutionary history. They may explain, for example, why one Indian tribe defeated another Indian tribe, but they are irrelevant to the ultimate victory of the Europeans over all the thousands of Indian tribes in the New World. That was a matter of superior technology and superior numbers.

[22] See, for example, F. G. Bailey, *Tribe, Caste, and Nation* (Manchester, England: Manchester University Press, 1960).

tory—selective criteria, and it operates on every level of social organization from the family to the global "community" of societies. At the same time, however, the fact that there are basic patterns in the evolutionary process indicates that some selective forces are more powerful than others. This is obviously the case with respect to those which have a substantial effect on the survival chances of entire societies.

Second, any comparison of sociocultural selection with its counterpart in the biotic world—what Darwin called *natural* selection—is bound to point up the significance of man's conscious, rational faculty. Yet while we should never minimize this factor, neither should we exaggerate it. Blind, irrational forces have played a critical role in sociocultural selection more often than many of us recognize. The outcome of wars is not determined by people who sit back and compare the societies involved and decide, on rational grounds, that some deserve to survive more than others. Nor are competitive struggles among business firms resolved this way. In these arenas, survival is simply a function of military or economic power, and the process is not so very different from the one involved in struggles in the rest of the world of nature.

Finally, it should be noted that the destruction of a sociocultural system does not necessarily mean death for its members. Such populations are often absorbed into the ranks of the conquering society. This is one of the important differences between sociocultural evolution and organic evolution: the destruction of the genetic heritage of a species, as in the case of the passenger pigeon, means the destruction of the population that transmitted the heritage, but the destruction of the sociocultural heritage of a society, as in the case of many American Indian groups, can be accomplished simply by scattering the members and destroying the social bonds on which their cultural system depended.

CHAPTER FOUR

Sociocultural Evolution

Someone has said that the study of history is nothing but the study of one damned thing after another. And sometimes it does seem that way—that human history is just a tangled web of events, without any meaningful patterns or trends. But if we look more carefully and from a broad enough time perspective, we discover that there *are* significant patterns. The basic aim of evolutionary theory is to identify these patterns and explain them.

PATTERNS IN HISTORY

In its most general sense, the word "evolution" refers to a sequence of events that exhibits a directional trend of some kind. Human history reveals a number of such trends, and these provide the starting point for evolutionary analysis.

Although the origin of our species is still far from certain, the best guess is that our ancestral line first established itself 2 million years or more ago, probably in Africa. In any case, the numbers were minuscule, and the entire population was concentrated in a single, limited area. Since then, except for short-lived, localized declines, as in medieval Europe during the Plague, there has been a steady increase in numbers. Simultaneously, people have spread out over more and more of the earth's surface, eventually occupying every continent except Antarctica.

This growth and spread of the human population has been accompanied by technological advances that can be clearly traced in both the archaeological and the historical records. Wood and stone, for example, the chief materials used in tools and weapons through most of human history, were replaced or supplemented successively by bronze, iron, steel, and aluminum. For energy, man originally had to depend entirely on his own bodily strength. In time, this was supplemented by the energy of domesticated animals and subsequently by a variety of still more powerful energy sources.

The advances made in transportation and communication have also been extremely important. Throughout most of history, until he domesticated the horse and other animals, man depended exclusively on his own two legs to get around. More recently, steam, gasoline, and rocket engines have provided a degree of mobility undreamed of in the past. Comparable advances in communications have extended the reach of man's voice and the power of his vision.

Paralleling these trends, the historical record shows a fairly steady advance in the production of goods and services, culminating in the tremendous output of the modern era. The quantity and diversity available today would be incomprehensible to people of the past.

Individual societies have steadily grown in numerical and geographical size and in structural complexity. The current populations of China, India, the Soviet Union, and the United States far exceed anything known until recently. Structurally, such societies involve a diversity of occupations and a complexity in the division of labor never approached before, while stratification systems have contributed yet another complicating element.

Figure 4.1 Our shrinking planet: advances in transportation, which have helped mankind overcome the barriers of space and distance, constitute one of the basic patterns in history.

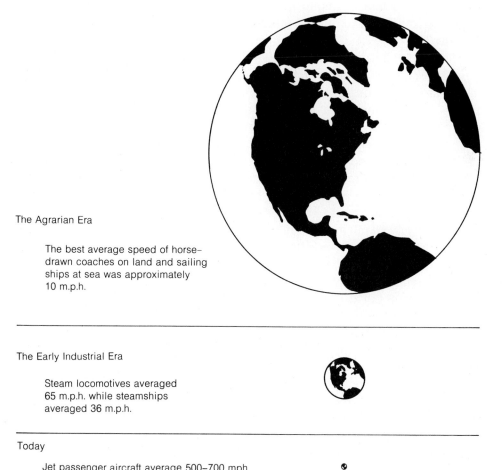

The Agrarian Era

The best average speed of horse-drawn coaches on land and sailing ships at sea was approximately 10 m.p.h.

The Early Industrial Era

Steam locomotives averaged 65 m.p.h. while steamships averaged 36 m.p.h.

Today

Jet passenger aircraft average 500–700 mph

This growth in the size and complexity of societies has been matched by a corresponding growth in the size and complexity of communities. Through most of the prehistoric period, settlements seldom had as many as a hundred members. Most groups had to move every few weeks or months to obtain an adequate food supply. The establishment of the permanent village was the first step in an evolutionary sequence that has brought us by stages to the modern megalopolis.

From the cultural standpoint, the trend has been toward increasing diversification. During the early part of human history, this resulted primarily from the expansion of the population into new environments, necessitating new modes of adaptation. The cultural patterns that evolved in societies in arctic regions were naturally different from those in temperate or tropical regions, the cultures in desert areas different from those in more fertile locations. In the last 5,000 to 10,000 years, however, cultural diversity has also been a reflection of increasing structural complexity, as stratification and other forms of in- trasocietal differentiation have created substantial cultural diversity *within* societies.

Another striking pattern in human history has been the acceleration in the *rate* of change. For a long, long time, change occurred at a glacial pace. Then, gradually, it began to accelerate and has continued to do so until the present—with the result that we now find ourselves in the midst of a sweeping social and cultural revolution of global proportions.

Finally, we can see that man's impact on the biophysical environment has steadily increased over the course of history. At first, it was limited to the very minor effects of man's activities as a hunter of animals and a gatherer of plants. With his discovery of the techniques of plant cultivation and animal domestication, it increased substantially. Since the Industrial Revolution, this impact has grown until man's very existence is threatened.

One could easily add to this list, but it should already be clear that human history is more than a set of unrelated events. There are, at the very least, a number of highly significant trends. But more than that, these trends give evidence of being interrelated.

A little reflection indicates that the common factor is *technological ad- vance.* This basic trend has been prerequisite for all the others we iden- tified[1]—as it has been for every major social revolution in history. Without tech- nological advance the human population today would be a tiny fraction of its actual size. Human societies would consist exclusively of small bands of primi- tive hunters and gatherers, living not very differently from the more advanced primates of our day. The rate of change would be imperceptible, man's impact

---

[1] One could argue that some part of a few of the trends would have been possible without technological advance, as in the case of the growth in numbers and the spread of the human population. The far more important point, however, is that most of this growth and spread would *not* have been possible except for technological advance, and most of the trends would not have occurred even on a minor scale.

on the environment negligible, differences between societies minor, and internal differentiation evident only along the lines dictated by age and by sex.

SOCIOCULTURAL EVOLUTION DEFINED

Having established the significance of technological advance, we are now ready to define sociocultural evolution. Stated briefly, it is *technological advance and its consequences*. These consequences are the trends we have already indicated, along with others that will become evident in later chapters.[2]

Our use of the word "advance" in the definition might appear to suggest that "evolution" is synonymous with "progress." Actually, most nineteenth-century evolutionists believed exactly that: for them, evolution was the story of man's noble ascent from the apes, of his moral advance and creation of a better world. But for contemporary evolutionists, sociocultural evolution has a much more restricted meaning, one with no implicit moral judgments. It refers only to technological advance and to the things that can be attributed to that advance. Since these include man's increasing capacity to destroy both himself and the biophysical environment on which he depends, it should be abundantly clear that when we use the word "progress," we mean it only in the basic sense of "a progression of events"—as when one speaks of the progress of a disease.

Another thing should be made clear: this definition does not imply that every aspect of societal history is part of the evolutionary process. On the contrary, it assumes that some sociocultural patterns function independently of technological advance. For example, there is no reason to suppose that most of the doctrinal differences between Christians and Muslims were caused by technology. By the same token, evolutionary theory does not pretend to account for the majority of sociocultural traits that distinguish societies at the same level of technological development—except, perhaps, for those traits which can be linked to earlier evolutionary differences that have been preserved through the process of continuity.[3]

WHY TECHNOLOGY?

To understand sociocultural evolution, it is not enough to recognize technology's unique role: we must also know the reason for it. Simply put, technology

---

[2] Though there is a unilinear directional trend involved in technological advance, this is not necessarily the case with all its consequences. For example, one can easily imagine a time when the human population will begin to level off or even decline in size. Far from being outside the scope of sociocultural evolution, such a trend would be an integral part of it, since it would be the direct result of technological advance—birth control techniques, for example, or an atomic war.

[3] Many of the differences between societies at the same level of development are explicable in *ecological* terms, however, and we shall often have occasion to take ecological factors into account.

is so important because it is equivalent to an extension or modification of man's basic organic equipment—his eyes, ears, arms, legs, brain, nervous system, and the rest of his "tools" and genetic heritage. Microscopes, telescopes, and television extend the range of his vision just as automobiles, airplanes, and boats extend the range of his movement. These things enable man to behave, at times, as if he had a new and radically different physical endowment—fantastic vision, unheard of powers of locomotion, and all the rest. Just as a genetic change in the basic organic equipment of an animal species produces a change in its way of life, so change in these cultural extensions of man's genetic equipment leads to change in his way of life. One might add: the more revolutionary the change in the equipment, whether organic or technological, the more revolutionary the change in life patterns that is likely to result.

Technological innovations that increase the flow of *energy* into societal systems are especially important.[4] A human population cannot survive without a steady, daily input of energy; and every social and cultural complexity over and above the members' bare survival requires an additional input. An increase in the energy flowing into a system will result in a corresponding increase in goods and services, a larger population, or both. And these, in turn, will stimulate further developments in the group's social structure, its ideology, the variable aspects of its population, and its language.

In short, then, a society's solutions to its technological problems function as a set of conditions that determines the *range* of solutions the society can apply to its other problems. Thus, a society that depends on a primitive hunting and gathering technology has a range of solutions that precludes large communities with thousands of residents, religious organizations led by elaborate hierarchies of priests, complex legal systems, factories, labor unions, universities, or any of dozens of other structural systems that the members of an industrial society take for granted. Neither will such a society develop complex, abstract ideologies or world views like those of Christianity, communism, and humanism, or accumulate a body of knowledge of the kind represented by chemistry, astronomy, psychology, and the other sciences. Rather, its population will be very small, its structure very simple, and its world view very limited.

Not only does technology set these outside limits on a society's development, it goes on to influence the society's choice of alternatives within those limits. For example, as we shall see in a later chapter, either a monarchical or a republican form of government is possible for an agrarian society. But at this particular level of technological development, the monarchical pattern is much more likely. Technology exerts this kind of influence even in the arts. As an illustration of this, E. Power Biggs, the noted organist and student of organ

---

[4] For classic statements of the importance of energy, see Fred Cottrell, *Energy and Society* (New York: McGraw-Hill, 1955), and Leslie White, *The Science of Culture* (New York: Grove Press, 1949), pp. 363–393.

Figure 4.2 A society's solutions to its technological problems function as a set of conditions that determine the range of solutions it can apply to its other problems: the Bushmen of Southwest Africa.

music, has shown how a composer's distinctive qualities reflect the kind of instrument available to him.[5] For example, Handel's concertos were written for the small eighteenth-century English organs, noted for their bright, gay tones, while Bach's famous Toccata in D Minor was apparently written to display the massive power and range of the organ of St. John's Church in Lueneburg. As a result, Bach's work is not nearly as impressive when played on the small English organs of that day, nor are Handel's concertos as pleasing on a north German instrument. And Spanish organ music, long considered inferior to northern European because of the poor impression it made on northern organs, is judged quite differently when played on the Spanish organs for which it was written.

The only element in societal systems that has remained at all impervious to the influence of technology is the genetic aspect of population. Since modern man replaced Neanderthal man approximately 35,000 years ago, genetic changes in our species have been negligible—that is, they have not been of the kind or magnitude that would necessitate a significant change in the structure or functioning of human societies.[6] Yet well over 99 per cent of technological change has occurred in just the last few thousand years!

---

[5] E. Power Biggs, "Dr. Schweitzer's Intuition Confirmed," *Saturday Review,* Aug. 31, 1968, pp. 41–43.

[6] See, for example, Theodosius Dobzhansky, *Mankind Evolving* (New York: Bantam, 1970), chaps. 11 and 12.

Having emphasized technology's impact on the other parts of societal systems, we must recognize that influences also flow in the opposite direction. However, except for those which originate in man's genetic nature (i.e., the *constant* aspect of population), these influences generally are in the form of feedback. In other words, they are responses to previous influences by technology. For example, advances in a society's subsistence technology increase its food production, which usually leads to an increase in numbers (one of the variable aspects of population). This growth in population, as we noted in the last chapter, is then likely to cause an increase in inventions and discoveries. But this impact of population on technology is really feedback from the earlier effects of technology.

In general, the effect of such feedback has simply been either to speed up or to retard the *rate* of technological advance. There has been much less effect on its content or direction, which have proved very difficult to control. When men have tried it, the results have often been quite different from what they intended. For example, the airplane was invented with only peaceful purposes in mind, but it was transformed into a devastating engine of war. Conversely, radar, which was developed to meet a military need, has been adapted to many peaceful purposes.

Most of what we have said can be summarized in a fairly simple diagram, Figure 4.3, which starts with the interaction of the human population (endowed only with its genetic attributes) and the biophysical environment. In response to the problems arising from this interaction, man has slowly built his technological repertoire of tools, techniques, and information, as extensions of,

Figure 4.3 Basic model of general evolution for the past 35,000 years.

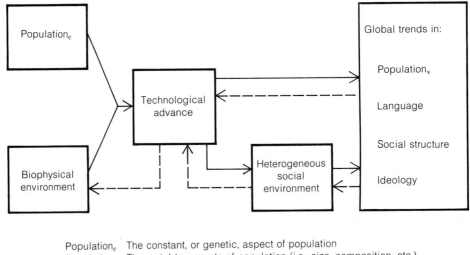

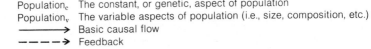

Population$_c$ The constant, or genetic, aspect of population
Population$_v$ The variable aspects of population (i.e., size, composition, etc.)
————→   Basic causal flow
— — — →   Feedback

and improvements on, his inherited organic equipment, techniques, and information (i.e., information contained in his genes). Every technological advance has been, for him, the functional equivalent of a genetic advance, some of them crucial, some less important.

This evolving system of technology, with its increasing power and effectiveness, has been largely responsible for all the other basic evolutionary patterns—the growth and spread of the human population, the increased production of goods and services, the increased cultural diversity, the growth in size and the increased structural complexity of societies and communities, and the accelerating rate of sociocultural change. In part, this influence has been direct, as indicated by the arrow from technological advance to the global trends in population$_v$, language, social structure, and ideology. But it also acts indirectly. Because societies do not advance technologically at the same rate, the social environment is gradually altered. What started out as a highly homogeneous environment from the standpoint of military and economic power is gradually altered into a highly heterogeneous one. In this changed environment, the weaker societies are marked for extinction, and with them their less developed sociocultural systems. The global trends in population$_v$, language, social structure, and ideology are thus substantially reinforced by the process of intersocietal selection.

Within our model we have indicated feedback at the appropriate points. If the time span of our model were extended to include more than the last 35,000 years, we would have to add a feedback arrow from technology to population$_c$. For man's use of tools and his development of hunting techniques in the Lower and Middle Paleolithic apparently played an important role in his organic evolution, contributing to his increased reliance on learning and communication as basic techniques of adaptation.[7] And today we seem to be on the threshold of a new kind of technological impact on our genetic heritage—deliberate genetic manipulation.

The Evolution of Evolution?

As long as people were unaware of the crucial role technological advance played in human life, they made no effort to bring the trend under rational control and make it more their servant and less their master. In recent years, however, as the rate of technological advance has risen to unprecedented levels, it has become impossible to ignore its impact. As more and more people recognize its effects—especially the delayed effects that manifest themselves only years or decades later—the demand for regulation of technological

---

[7] See, for example, William Laughlin, "Hunting: An Integrating Biobehavior System and Its Evolutionary Importance," in Richard Lee and Irven DeVore (eds.), *Man the Hunter* (Chicago: Aldine, 1968), pp. 304–320, or John E. Pfeiffer, *The Emergence of Man* (New York: Harper & Row, 1969), especially chap. 7.

innovation becomes increasingly insistent. Thus, we may be approaching a new stage in the evolutionary process—a stage in which technological advance finally provides man with enough information, enough resources, and enough pressure for him to bring the entire process under his control. Natural selection would then be replaced by conscious, rational selection. Were this to happen, it would be a development as revolutionary as the dawn of consciousness in animal life in the remote prehistoric past, as revolutionary as the beginnings of culture in man's own past. Each of those ancient developments was a giant step forward in the evolutionary process, and success in the effort to control the engine of "progress" could likewise initiate an important new phase in evolutionary history.

TECHNOSTASIS AND REGRESSION

Evolutionary theory does not assume that technological advance has been inevitable everywhere and all the time. Clearly it has not. Technostasis[8] and even technological regression have occurred frequently, and evolutionary theory must take account of this.

The significance of technostasis and regression depends to a considerable degree on whether one is considering *general* or *specific* evolution.[9] General evolution is the evolution of human societies as a whole the world over; specific evolution is the evolution of an individual society. Not surprisingly, technostasis and regression are much more relevant for specific evolution, since they have been infrequent phenomena on the global level but fairly common at the level of the individual society.

Many of the best examples of technostasis are provided by the various hunting and gathering societies that survived into the modern era. Though the cultures of these peoples have certainly changed in a number of respects, their basic technology appears to be much as it was ten thousand years ago or more.[10] Archaeological research indicates that technostasis was also characteristic of most hunting and gathering societies throughout most of the prehistoric era. By modern standards, the rate of technological advance was unimaginably slow.[11]

Technostasis has also been common among agrarian societies. The rate of progress in these societies was so slow that our country's Founding Fathers and their European contemporaries would have found themselves far

---

[8] "Technostasis" refers to the condition of a society when it is neither advancing nor regressing technologically.

[9] See Marshall Sahlins, "Evolution: Specific and General," in Marshall Sahlins and Elman Service (eds.), *Evolution and Culture* (Ann Arbor: University of Michigan Press, 1960).

[10] See, for example, Frank Hole and Robert Heizer, *An Introduction to Prehistoric Archeology* (New York: Holt, 1965), who write that "in many areas of the New World there was no discernible 'development' over the whole time of occupation. That is, economy, being in fine adjustment with the physical and cultural environment, remained stable. The changes that could be seen were stylistic . . . " (p. 242).

[11] See Chapter 6.

Figure 4.4 The collapse of the Roman Empire was the basis of one of the more striking examples of sociocultural regression: ruins of Roman theatre in modern Libya.

more at home, from the technological standpoint, in Roman society at the time of Christ than in present-day America.

Sociocultural regression is a far less common pattern, but it does occur. There are a number of documented cases in which valuable technological information was lost to a small primitive society because this information had been kept as the closely guarded secret of a single family or group that died off without sharing it with others. For example, one society lost the technique of canoe making this way, another the technique of making stone adzes.[12]

A more serious pattern of regression is associated with the breakdown of political institutions in more advanced societies. A classic example is pro-

---

[12] A. L. Kroeber, *Anthropology* (New York: Harcourt, Brace, 1948), p. 375.

vided by the events that followed the collapse of the Roman Empire. The fall of the Roman Empire was not the usual case in which a society is conquered by one on the same, or a higher, level of development. Rather, the Roman state was destroyed by technologically less advanced societies.[13] As a result, it was replaced by a number of much smaller, less advanced, and less efficient states. The well-articulated economy that had emerged under Roman aegis was disrupted, trade and commerce declined greatly, and the whole economy moved back toward a pattern of local self-sufficiency. As a consequence, urban populations were drastically reduced, and many industries disappeared or were severely restricted. For example, by the beginning of the sixth century the once numerous copper mines of Western Europe were virtually all shut down, not to be reopened until the tenth century; brass, an alloy of copper and zinc, seems not to have been manufactured again until the fifteenth century.[14] From the end of the sixth to the end of the tenth century, such ores as were mined (chiefly iron) were taken at much shallower depths, by much more primitive methods, and in much smaller quantities than in earlier periods.[15] Regression was also evident in most other fields of production.

Causes of Technostasis and Regression

These cases of technostasis and regression pose an interesting problem. Their deviance from the basic evolutionary pattern requires an explanation, but one that is consistent with our explanation of technological advance and its consequences.

In our discussion of technostasis and regression, we identified three distinctive forms of technostasis and two of regression. Since there is no reason to suppose they all result from the same cause, we must consider each in turn:

1. Technostasis in most hunting and gathering societies in the prehistoric era
2. Technostasis in hunting and gathering societies that survived into the modern era
3. Technostasis in most agrarian societies
4. Limited regression in some very small and isolated societies
5. General regression in a few large, developed horticultural and agrarian societies such as Rome and its successor states

Our analysis of sociocultural innovation and extinction in Chapter 3 provides us with the basic explanation for the widespread pattern of techno-

---

[13] The success of the barbarians was in no small measure the result of the internal conflicts that racked the Roman Empire.

[14] John Nef, *The Conquest of the Material World* (Chicago: University of Chicago Press, 1964), p. 8.

[15] Ibid., p. 7.

stasis in hunting and gathering societies of the prehistoric era. Most of these societies were poorly situated from the standpoint of advancing technologically. Above all, they lacked a large store of accumulated information on which to build. In addition, their small populations and their relative isolation put them at a disadvantage. Finally, throughout much of the prehistoric era the ready availability of new lands prevented population pressures from building up, thus slowing the deadly, but progressive, process of intersocietal selection.

With respect to technostasis in contemporary hunting and gathering societies, the explanation is partly the same as for hunting and gathering societies of the prehistoric era. The same factors that kept those societies at the primitive level for countless thousands of years also prevented advance in the surviving remnant during the last 8,000 to 10,000 years. From an evolutionary perspective, this extra several thousand years is not a very long period of time.

One may ask, however, why these few surviving hunting and gathering groups did not benefit from cultural diffusion, as so many others did, and evolve into some more advanced type of society. The answer seems to be that most of them were too remote from the centers of technical advance to be affected. A recent survey of ninety-two hunting and gathering societies reveals that 85 per cent of them were located in either the New World or Australia, areas cut off from the mainstream of technological development until the last several centuries.[16] Most of the rest were in such remote, isolated areas of the Old World as the Kalahari Desert, Arctic Asia, and the jungles of Malaysia.

In the case of limited regression (i.e., the loss of certain specific elements of technology) in small and isolated societies, the explanation is simple when the lost traits were secrets held by a single family. In other instances, the loss can be explained by the migration of a society to a new territory where some essential raw material was unavailable. For example, a group of Eskimo moved into an area so far north that there was no driftwood. By the time European explorers discovered them some generations later, the group no longer knew how to build seaworthy kayaks.[17]

The two remaining categories (3 and 5) involve agrarian societies. These pose a somewhat more difficult problem, which we will examine in detail in Chapter 8. For the present, however, we may note that in these societies both technostasis and regression are linked with certain basic developments in social structure. In the case of technostasis, the cause apparently lies in the emergence in agrarian societies of a highly exploitative social order in which few of the rewards for work or innovation went to the worker or innovator. Rather, they were monopolized by the members of a small, powerful, and wealthy elite

---

[16] These figures are adapted from Allan Coult and Robert Habenstein, *Cross Tabulations of Murdock's World Ethnographic Sample* (Columbia, Mo.: University of Missouri Press, 1965), p. 9. The societies referred to are those in which hunting and gathering were the dominant or codominant means of subsistence.

[17] Kroeber, p. 376.

that knew little about technology and cared less.[18] Under these conditions, people's natural inclinations to maximize their rewards were diverted into other channels. Potential peasant innovators knew that they could seldom hope to benefit from inventions or discoveries they might make. And the elite were so unfamiliar with the mundane world of technology that they were incapable of making any significant contribution.

Finally, the occasional instance of general regression, exemplified by Western Europe after the collapse of the Roman Empire, points again to social structure as a major contributing factor. The immediate cause of the decline was the breakdown of government. Because the government was unable to protect them, merchants could no longer move safely from town to town, and trade became increasingly unprofitable and dangerous. With the drastic curtailment of trade, the supply of many specialized products declined or disappeared, and skilled artisans were forced to turn to other activities (especially farming and soldiering) to earn a livelihood. With the reduction in numbers, or total elimination, of merchants, artisans, and government officials, the economic base of most urban communities was so badly undermined that they declined in size or even disappeared. The result was a reversion to a much more primitive form of agrarian society.

A somewhat similar pattern occurred in the Indus River Valley 2,000 years earlier. Beginning shortly after 3000 B.C. and continuing for more than 1,000 years, an impressive civilization flourished in this area.[19] Between 2000 and 1500 B.C., however, the cities in which this civilization was centered were destroyed or abandoned, and a period of technological and social regression set in. Not until 1,200 years later was writing again used in India.

These occasional developments in agrarian societies (i.e., general technostasis or regression) underline the importance of the process of feedback. Though the flow of influence from technology to social structure may be more important in the long run, the feedback from social structure to technology may prove crucial in the short run.

ALTERNATIVE EXPLANATIONS OF SOCIOCULTURAL EVOLUTION

Over the years, a number of alternative explanations of sociocultural evolution have been proposed. Though none has found lasting acceptance in scholarly circles, several of them have enough adherents among the public at large to merit our attention. Three in particular are in this category: (1) racial explana-

---

[18] For a classic statement of this, see V. Gordon Childe, *Man Makes Himself* (New York: Mentor, 1953), chap. 9. See also Thorstein Veblen, *The Theory of the Leisure Class* (New York: Modern Library, 1934, first published 1899), for an outstanding analysis of the logic underlying the actions of such elites.

[19] For a good description of this civilization, see Stuart Piggott, *Prehistoric India* (Harmondsworth: Penguin Books, 1950), chaps. 5 and 6.

tions, (2) geographical determinist explanations, and (3) "great man" explanations.

Racial explanations   In the nineteenth century, racial theories were widely accepted by scholars as well as laymen. In recent decades, scholarly support has almost disappeared and lay support has declined. Nevertheless, racial theories are still popular enough to require consideration.

Two basic observations gave rise to them. First, as a result of greater contact between the races in recent centuries, Europeans became increasingly conscious of their own technological and military superiority. Second, in the United States and certain other nations where immigration had produced racially heterogeneous populations, people of European extraction enjoyed higher status than those of African or Asian descent. Recognition of these patterns naturally led many people to the conclusion that Europeans are genetically superior.

This conclusion was reinforced for a time by the publication of the early results of intelligence testing conducted by the American Army during World War I. Tests of draftees showed that, on the average, whites scored substantially higher than blacks.[20] Further analysis of these tests revealed, however, that blacks from a number of Northern states had higher average scores than whites from a number of Southern states, indicating that the scores were determined, at least in part, by sociocultural influences.[21] Subsequent research has confirmed this. In studies made of black children in New York and Philadelphia, for example, the average IQ scores increased the longer the children were in these communities and the briefer their exposure had been to segregated Southern schools.[22] Other studies have shown that the IQ scores of blacks, like those of whites, vary substantially according to the class position of the family in which the child is raised.[23] These and other findings have made it clear that IQ tests do not measure what they were originally designed to measure, namely, the innate ability, or genetic potential for learning, of the individual. Rather, they measure innate ability in conjunction with socially differentiated opportunities for learning.[24] Since the latter cannot be fully controlled in experimental studies,

[20] See R. M. Yerkes (ed.), *Psychological Examining in the U.S. Army,* Memoirs of the National Academy of Sciences, Washington, D.C. 15 (1921), or Carl Brigham, *A Study of American Intelligence* (Princeton, N.J.: Princeton, 1923).

[21] See William C. Bagley, "The Army Tests and the Pro-Nordic Propaganda," *Educational Review,* 67 (1924), pp. 179–187, or Otto Klineberg, *Negro Intelligence and Selective Migration* (New York: Columbia, 1935), table 2, p. 2.

[22] Klineberg, graph 6, p. 27. See also Everett S. Lee, "Negro Intelligence and Selective Migration: A Philadelphia Test of the Klineberg Hypothesis," *American Sociological Review,* 16 (1951), pp. 227–233.

[23] See, for example, M. Deutsch and B. Brown, "Social Influences in Negro-White Intelligence Differences," *Journal of Social Issues,* 20 (1964), pp. 24–35.

[24] Recent research has begun to show how complex, and also how subtle, the influence of the social environment can be. For example, recent studies show that dietary deficiencies, both prenatal and those occurring after birth, can cause irremediable damage to a child's learning mechanism.

it is impossible to draw valid conclusions concerning racially based differences in learning potential.

On the societal level, the evidence regarding racial abilities is no less complex, especially if we take earlier centuries into account. Prior to the modern era, there was little if any evidence of the technological superiority of the European peoples. During the Dark Ages following the fall of Rome, when Western Europe reverted to a very primitive agrarian level, its societies were technologically and structurally much inferior to Chinese society, and even as recently as the twelfth century the superiority of Western European societies over certain West African societies was not great. One distinguished anthropologist of the last generation wrote that "in their arts and crafts these societies were little, if at all, inferior to medieval Europeans, while in the thoroughness of their political organization and the skill with which social institutions were utilized to lend stability to the political structure, they far exceeded anything in Europe prior to the sixteenth century."[25] Though this statement is an exaggeration, it is closer to the truth than most Europeans or Americans realize. In any case, when we enlarge our perspective to include the evidence of centuries other than our own, the basis for the racial theory is seriously weakened. In view of what we know at this time, it appears that racial differences have had little, if any, effect on the course of sociocultural progress. The sweeping claims made by racial theorists are simply not supported by the evidence.

Figure 4.5 The distribution of human health and energy on the basis of climate, according to Ellsworth Huntington.

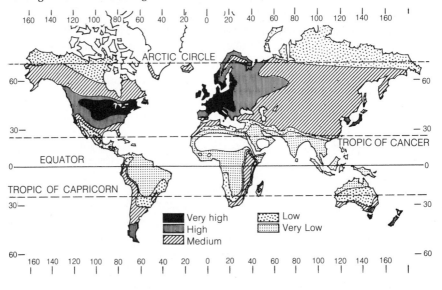

---

[25] Ralph Linton, *The Tree of Culture* (New York: Vintage Books, Knopf, 1959), p. 170.

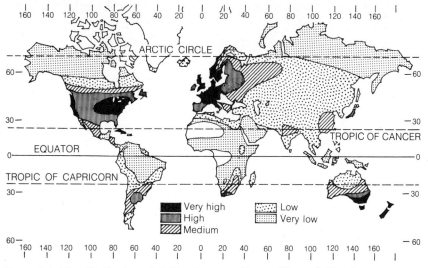

Figure 4.6 The distribution of civilization, according to Ellsworth Huntington.

Geographical determinist explanations Geographical determinist explanations were also much in vogue in the nineteenth century, but these, too, have now been largely abandoned, at least by serious scholars. One of the last important advocates of geographical determinism was Ellsworth Huntington, an American geographer of a generation ago. Huntington tried to prove that climatic factors were the chief determinants of sociocultural progress.[26] To do this, he compared indexes of progress with indexes of climate. This ultimately led to the preparation of two maps that showed a striking correlation between climatic conditions and the level of societal development in the twentieth century (see Figures 4.5 and 4.6).

 Unfortunately for Huntington, critics quickly found major flaws in his theory. They asked, among other questions, why the northeastern quarter of the United States, with one of the most favorable climates in the world, was inhabited throughout most of history by relatively primitive peoples, and why Greece, once one of the centers of civilization, should now be ranked among the underdeveloped nations, when there had been no substantial climatic change. Huntington's inability to provide satisfactory answers to such questions led to the theory's demise.

 Nevertheless, social scientists do recognize the importance of geographical factors in evolutionary history, as we have seen. For though every society's natural environment contains possibilities for development, the potentials are not the same. Climatic differences, for example, though not as important as Huntington made them out to be, are certainly significant. Some environ-

---

[26] See especially Ellsworth Huntington, *Mainsprings of Civilization* (New York: Wiley, 1945).

ments severely limit indigenous development. Since desert and arctic areas, for example, cannot support plant cultivation, normal evolutionary progression beyond the hunting and gathering stage is impossible.

Topography has played an important role by shaping patterns of intersocietal communication. Such features as oceans, deserts, and mountain ranges have prevented or seriously impeded the flow of information between societies, while other features, such as navigable rivers and open plains, have facilitated it. Considering how crucial the flow of information is in the evolutionary process, enormous differences in sociocultural development can be explained by this factor.

Finally, variations in the distribution of critical natural resources have been important in societal evolution. The presence of mineral resources, for example, or differences in their accessibility, undoubtedly influenced the course of development for many societies.

In summary, geographical factors have been much more important than racial ones. Far from contradicting the evolutionary explanation, *they are an integral part of it.* Problems arise only when enthusiasts like Huntington try to establish a deterministic explanation that ignores or minimizes the role of other crucial factors.

"Great man" explanations For a long time, history was largely the chronicle of the achievements and disasters wrought by a handful of famous men. To people schooled in this tradition, nothing was more natural than to suppose that the progress achieved by certain societies was primarily due to a few men of genius and that without them these societies would never have risen above the rest.

Social scientists, as well as the newer breed of historians, reject this view. Basically this rejection is the result of a better understanding of the nature of intelligence and the innovative process. One of the most damaging pieces of evidence against what has been called "the great man theory of history" was the discovery that many of the most important innovations of modern times were made almost simultaneously by two or more individuals working completely independently of one another. Following is a list of just a few of these simultaneous inventions and discoveries.

Sunspots: Fabricius, Galileo, Harriott, Scheiner, 1611
Logarithms: Napier, 1614; Bürgi, 1620
Calculus: Newton, 1671; Leibnitz, 1676
Nitrogen: Rutherford, 1772; Scheele, 1773
Oxygen: Priestley, Scheele, 1774
Water as H_2O: Cavendish, Watt, 1781; Lavoisier, 1783
Telegraph: Henry, Morse, Steinheil, Wheatstone and Cooke, 1837
Photography: Daguerre and Niepce, Talbot, 1839
Neptune: Adams, Leverrier, 1845

> Natural selection: Darwin, Wallace, 1858
> Telephone: Bell, Gray, 1876
> Phonograph: Cros, Edison, 1877
> Rediscovery of Mendel's laws: De Vries, Correns, Tschermak, 1900
> South Pole: Amundsen, December 1911; Scott, January 1912[27]

Half a century ago, 148 simultaneous innovations had been identified; since then, others have been added to the list. In a number of instances, as many as four or more persons produced the same innovation with no knowledge of the others' work. Though not denying the ability of the individuals involved, this finding suggests that few of those who have contributed most to the advance of knowledge were indispensable. In recent years, simultaneous inventions and discoveries have become so common that they are a serious matter for scientists. With so many working on the same problem and so little reward for running second, scientists often go to great lengths both to be first and to establish their claims to being first.[28]

The modern understanding of inventions as combinations of existing elements of culture not only explains the frequency of simultaneous inventions but also makes understandable the great da Vinci's inability to design a successful flying machine in the fifteenth century when lesser men succeeded four centuries later. Even Leonardo's genius was no substitute for the advances in technology that took place in the intervening period and were available to the Wright brothers and others. Sociocultural evolution obviously depends, not on the actions of a handful of great men, but rather on the accumulation of information by society as a whole.

---

[27] Adapted from William F. Ogburn and Dorothy S. Thomas, "Are Inventions Inevitable? A Note on Social Evolution," *Political Science Quarterly*, 37 (1922), pp. 93–98, and Kroeber, p. 342.

[28] See Warren Hagstrom, *The Scientific Community* (New York: Basic Books, 1965), or James D. Watson, *The Double Helix* (New York: Atheneum, 1968).

CHAPTER FIVE

Types and Varieties of Societies

Every branch of science is built on a foundation of comparisons. To understand anything in the world of nature—a plant, a star, a society, a rock formation—we are forced to compare it with other things, noting how it resembles them and how it differs.

Over the years, this process of comparison has gradually led to the discovery of many orderly patterns. This, in turn, has laid the foundation for a variety of classificatory systems—the Linnaean taxonomy and its successors in biology, the periodic table in chemistry, and the typology of market systems in economics, to name but three.[1]

Classification systems are essential in every area of study, because they enable us to order and organize our kaleidoscopic welter of experience. Without them, it would be impossible to develop general propositions about the world of nature—propositions that help us anticipate, and sometimes control, the forces of nature and the behavior of living things.

CLASSIFYING HUMAN SOCIETIES

Modern evolutionary theory had its beginnings in the work of seventeenth- and eighteenth-century European scholars who responded to the discovery of less advanced societies in the New World, Africa, and Asia by rethinking the age-old questions about man's origins and early development. This led, quite naturally, to comparisons of societies and efforts to differentiate between them and classify them.

As early as the eighteenth century, a number of scholars recognized the crucial importance of subsistence technology and based their schemes of classification on it.[2] These writers frequently differentiated between societies according to whether they depended on hunting, herding, or farming, and some of them claimed that these were successive stages through which every society necessarily passes in the evolutionary process.

Other early writers developed classificatory systems based on ideology. An early Italian writer, for example, claimed there were three kinds of

---

[1] The most basic classificatory systems of all are the vocabularies of languages.

[2] See Marvin Harris, *The Rise of Anthropological Theory* (New York: Thomas Y. Crowell, 1968), chap. 2, and Robert Nisbet, *Social Change and History* (New York: Oxford, 1969), chap. 4.

societies, the divine, the heroic, and the human, which reflected three stages in the evolution of man's intellect. Auguste Comte, the pioneer French sociologist, offered a similar typology. He divided human history into three stages, theological, philosophical, and scientific. This kind of typology, however, never found wide acceptance.

A more useful kind of typology originated with a nineteenth-century Danish museum curator, Christian Jurgensen Thomsen. Wrestling with the problem of how to organize his growing collection of prehistoric artifacts, he hit on the idea of grouping them by the types of materials from which they were made—stone, bronze, or iron. Recognizing that these were not just alternative materials that had been used contemporaneously, but rather that each had been the dominant material for tools and weapons in successive periods, Thomsen formulated the idea of an evolutionary sequence of Stone Age, Bronze Age, and Iron Age. Archaeologists later subdivided the first into Old, Middle, and New Stone Ages (traditionally referred to as the Paleolithic, Mesolithic, and Neolithic).

The system of classification used in this volume draws on the first and third of these early traditions and the work of a host of later scholars who refined and sharpened them.[3] Figure 5.1 provides a graphic summary of this system, which classifies societies by their basic mode of subsistence. The vertical dimension indicates the degree of overall technological advance: the higher the societal type, the greater its store of useful information and the more efficient and effective its tools and techniques. Simple hunting and gathering societies are the least advanced in this respect, industrial societies the most. As the diagram indicates, human societies may reach comparable technological levels by following different evolutionary paths, that is, by developing different but equally advanced subsistence technologies. Because of this, the categories cannot all be neatly ranked, one ahead of the other. Maritime and agrarian societies, for example, are roughly equal in terms of technological progress even though they employ very different subsistence technologies.

For a typology to be useful in theory and research, it must be as simple and unambiguous as the data permit. For this reason, the criteria used to classify societies have been held to a minimum. In most instances, a single criterion is used to differentiate between two adjacent categories (i.e., categories with a common boundary in Figure 5.1). For the same reason, the criteria are features whose presence in a society can be easily ascertained, the use of plows for example.

---

[3] Our special debt to the late V. Gordon Childe and to Walter Goldschmidt is indicated in the first edition of *Human Societies,* pp. 120–123. For an earlier and somewhat less satisfactory version of this system of classification, see Gerhard Lenski, *Power and Privilege: A Theory of Social Stratification* (New York: McGraw-Hill, 1966), pp. 91–93.

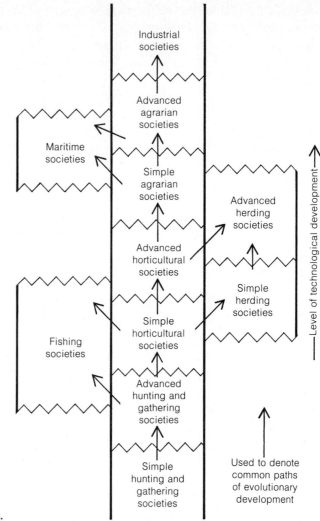

Figure 5.1 Basic types of human societies.

A society is classified as "hunting and gathering" when this is its primary mode of subsistence. This classification does not mean that the group never gets any of its material necessities by other means; most of the hunting and gathering societies studied in the last century have, in fact, relied on fishing or part-time horticulture to some degree. But when hunting and gathering is the *primary* mode of subsistence, we classify the society accordingly.

Simple hunting and gathering societies are those prehistoric societies of the Lower and Middle Paleolithic, the period prior to the last 35,000 years. These groups had only the most rudimentary technology. Their best weapon, for example, seems to have been nothing but a wooden spear.

The category of *advanced* hunting and gathering societies is reserved for the more advanced groups of the Upper Paleolithic, the Mesolithic, and more recent eras down to the present. The key developments setting these groups apart are the spear-thrower and the bow and arrow, weapons that appreciably increase the food-getting capability of a group.

The four categories of horticultural and agrarian societies constitute an evolutionary sequence of societies that depend primarily on plant cultivation. We could lump them all together, but in doing so we would lose many valuable insights into the nature of the evolutionary process. The best way to describe the relationship among these four types is to list *the minimal criteria* for each. As Table 5.1 indicates, if plant cultivation is the primary means of subsistence but the society has neither metallurgy nor the plow, the society is *simple horticultural.* If the society adds metal tools and weapons, it is *advanced horticultural.* If, in addition, it uses the plow, it is a *simple agrarian* society. Finally, if it has all these attributes and also manufactures *iron* tools and weapons, it is *advanced agrarian.*[4]

Fishing, herding, and maritime societies differ from the rest in that they are *environmentally specialized types.* They are distinguished from other societies at comparable levels of development, not so much in terms of their total technological repertoire, but rather in terms of the parts of it they *use.* They naturally rely disproportionately on those elements in their technology which are especially suited to the distinctive features of their unusual environments. Thus a fishing society relies primarily on the part of its technology that is most useful to a people located on a body of water. A herding society relies disproportionately on those elements of its technology which enable it to subsist on open grasslands with limited rainfall. Maritime societies, like fishing societies, utilized their proximity to water, though in a different way: being technologically more advanced, they adapted their technology to the use of waterways for trade and commerce at a time when the movement of bulky goods was much cheaper by water than by land.

Table 5.1 Minimal criteria for classification of horticultural and agrarian societies

Type of Society	Plant Cultivation*	Metallurgy*	Plow*	Iron*
Simple horticultural	+	−	−	−
Advanced horticultural	+	+	−	−
Simple agrarian	+	+	+	−
Advanced agrarian	+	+	+	+

*The symbol + means that the trait is present in the type of society indicated; the symbol − means it is not.

[4] In Africa south of the Sahara, most societies have long manufactured iron tools and weapons but have had a horticultural base. This has been because of the diffusion of the techniques of iron-making without a corresponding diffusion of the plow and agriculture. For purposes of analysis, these societies are classified as advanced horticultural, since they fail to meet the minimal criterion for agrarian societies (i.e., the presence of the plow).

With respect to level of technological development, herding societies are more varied than either of the other specialized types. For this reason, the category is divided into simple and advanced types. The basic distinction is that the latter employ horses or camels for transportation in work and warfare, while the former lack this important resource.

Industrial societies are the most recent to appear. The key development marking their emergence was the harnessing of new energy sources. Previously, the major sources were human and animal power, water, wind, and wood. Beginning in the eighteenth century, first coal, then petroleum, natural gas, hydroelectric power, and, most recently, atomic power have revolutionized subsistence activities. When these sources are dominant and industry replaces agriculture as the chief source of a society's income, the society is classified as "industrial."

The jagged lines along the upper and lower boundaries of the various societal types in Figure 5.1 indicate that a few of the most advanced groups within one type may be a bit more advanced overall than the least advanced societies in the next higher type. This apparent contradiction exists because of our decision to base the system of classification on the fewest possible criteria. As a result, a society that lacks a key differentiating element (e.g., the plow) may possess enough other technological elements to make it somewhat more advanced *overall* than a few of the least advanced societies that have the key element. Despite occasional incongruities of this kind, the benefits of this method of classification far outweigh the drawbacks.[5]

Finally, a word about *hybrid* societies. These are omitted from Figure 5.1 because they would clutter the diagram and make it difficult to read. Hybrid societies are those with two or more basic modes of subsistence. In some cases these societies are on the boundary between adjacent societal types. For example, a society might rely as much on fishing as on hunting and gathering. In another society, at a certain time in its history, a basic innovation like the plow may have spread to the point where roughly half the population uses it, while the other half still relies on an older tool or technique, such as the hoe. Neither society can be put in a single category, and we have to classify them as hybrids.

In other instances, the pattern of hybridization is more complex. This is particularly true when highly advanced societies come into contact with substantially less developed groups and crucial elements of technology diffuse from the former to the latter. Most contemporary African societies south of the Sahara are good examples of this: they can only be described as industrializing horticultural societies (see Chapter 14).

---

[5] The chief advantages are that (1) the information needed to classify a society is most likely to be available when few criteria are used and (2) with fewer criteria, fewer categories are required and fewer societies will be unclassifiable because of contradictory characteristics (i.e., some characteristics pointing to one classification, others to another).

Figure 5.2 **Hybrid societies use elements of technology from two or more basic societal types. India, an industrializing agrarian society, combines elements of the older agrarian way of life and the newer industrial one.**

SOCIETAL TYPES THROUGH HISTORY

As we have seen, people lived in simple hunting and gathering societies throughout most of human history. Advanced hunting and gathering societies, with their more advanced technology, began to appear 20,000 years ago.[6] For the next 8,000 years, or until about 10,000 B.C., these two were the only kinds of human societies on earth. Though there were many differences between individual groups as a result of environmental influences, people everywhere depended on hunting and gathering for their basic subsistence.

It is still not known just when this period of relative technological uniformity ended, but it seems to have been sometime during the Mesolithic era (10,000–7000 B.C.). The first new kind to emerge was probably the fishing society. The practice of fishing can be traced back into the Upper Paleolithic, but the primitive equipment used at that time pretty well rules out the possibility that any group was yet relying primarily on fishing for subsistence.[7] With the

---

[6] John E. Pfeiffer, *The Emergence of Man* (New York: Harper & Row, 1969) pp. 210–212.

[7] See Jacquetta Hawkes, *Prehistory* (New York: Mentor, 1965), chap. 6, for a good summary of archaeological finds relating to fishing. See also Grahame Clark and Stuart Piggott, *Prehistoric Societies* (New York: Knopf, 1965), chap. 7.

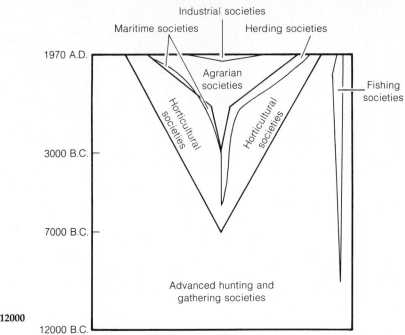

Figure 5.3   Societal types from 12000 B.C. to the present.

invention of true fishhooks, nets, traps, boats, and paddles in the Mesolithic, however, the stage was set for some favorably situated group to make the shift from hunting and gathering to fishing and gathering.

Simple horticultural societies probably came next, first appearing in the Middle East around 7000 B.C.[8] Though people began to use copper within the next 1,500 years,[9] it was not until nearly 4000 B.C. that metal tools and weapons became common enough to permit us to call any of these societies *advanced horticultural.*[10]

The plow seems to have been invented late in the fourth millennium, and this innovation, too, occurred in the Middle East.[11] By 3000 B.C. it was so widely adopted by societies in Mesopotamia and Egypt that we are justified in calling them simple agrarian.

Iron was discovered early in the second millennium B.C. but, like copper, did not become the dominant material in tools and weapons for a long

---

[8] Robert Braidwood, "The Earliest Village Communities of Southwestern Asia Reconsidered," and Karl Butzer, "Agricultural Origins in the Near East as a Geographical Problem," in Stuart Struever (ed.)*Prehistoric Agriculture* (Garden City, N.Y.: Natural History Press, 1971), pp. 222 and 249.

[9] James Mellaart, *Earliest Civilizations in the Near East* (London: Thames and Hudson, 1965), p. 105.

[10] See, for example, Leslie Aitchison, *A History of Metals* (London: MacDonald and Evans, 1960), vol. 1, p. 41.

[11] E. Cecil Curwen and Gudmund Hatt, *Plough and Pasture: The Early History of Farming* (New York: Collier Books, 1961), p. 64.

time.[12] Thus, the first *advanced* agrarian societies did not appear until the early years of the first millennium B.C.

The origin of herding societies remains something of a mystery. Evidence of animal domestication dates from about 9000 B.C., but the findings from the earliest site suggest a mixed economy.[13] Although we cannot say when people first relied on herding as their chief means of subsistence, it was probably some time after horticultural societies appeared.

Maritime societies date from the end of the third millennium B.C. The Minoans on the island of Crete were apparently the first to rely on overseas commerce as their primary economic activity.[14] Unlike other major societal types, maritime societies have not had a *continuous* history. After flourishing in the Mediterranean world for 2,000 years, they were wiped out by the growth of Roman power. During the Middle Ages, they enjoyed a revival for a number of centuries, only to disappear once more.

The last major societal type is the industrial. Although the basic inventions that mark the beginning of the modern technological revolution occurred in the eighteenth century, it was not until the nineteenth that Britain, pioneer in industrialization, reached the point where it could be classified as a truly industrial society. Since then numerous others have followed Britain's lead.

HISTORICAL ERAS

As Figure 5.3 makes clear, the composition of the universe of human societies has been constantly changing during the last 10,000 years. There was a time when every human society was at the hunting and gathering level of development; today, we have everything from hunting and gathering to industrial societies.

To understand the problems confronting a given society, it is not always enough to know what type of society it is. It may be equally important to know when it existed, since this tells us a great deal about its chances for survival. For example, the situation of hunting and gathering societies today is far more precarious than the situation of comparable societies 10,000 years ago. In the modern world such a group usually finds itself in the unenviable position of interacting with far more advanced, and hence far more powerful, societies. No matter where it is located, agents of industrialism are likely to be penetrating, using their vast resources to transform the conditions of life for the more primitive group. This may be done with the best of intentions—as in the case of medical, educational, or religious missions—but that makes little difference.

---

[12] Aitchison, pp. 102 and 111–113.

[13] Mellaart, p. 20.

[14] William H. McNeill, *The Rise of the West: A History of the Human Community* (New York: Mentor, 1965), p. 150.

Whatever the intentions, the net effect is to destroy or transform the sociocultural systems of technologically primitive peoples.

For analytical purposes, therefore, it is often useful to identify the historical era. Combining the era with what we know about the society itself, we can discuss problems and patterns much more intelligently.

Reduced to essentials, there have been four major eras in human history.

Hunting and gathering (to c. 7000 B.C.)
Horticultural (from c. 7000 B.C. to c. 3000 B.C.)
Agrarian (from c. 3000 B.C. to c. A.D. 1800)
Industrial (since c. A.D. 1800)

Until about 7000 B.C., hunting and gathering societies were the most advanced technologically.[15] They were then replaced by horticultural societies, which remained dominant until around 3000 B.C. At this point, agrarian societies emerged as the dominant form of societal organization, a position they held until the early part of the last century, when industrial societies displaced them. With each new era, the position of less advanced societies became increasingly precarious. Because of the process of intersocietal selection, their chances of survival went steadily down.

CORRELATES OF SOCIETAL TYPE AND CONSEQUENCES OF TECHNOLOGICAL ADVANCE

Beginning in Chapter 6, we will examine the major societal types one by one. First, however, we will look at some basic comparative data that illustrate the kinds of differences we can expect to find between them. We will have occasion to refer back to some of these data—especially those on population size—at a number of points in future chapters.

The richest source of systematic information on human societies is the Ethnographic Atlas published in most issues of *Ethnology*. This journal, founded by George Peter Murdock, provides a wealth of systematically coded data on hundreds of societies in all parts of the world. The data range from a people's subsistence technology to the kinds of games they play.

Though the journal has not classified societies by type, most of the data needed to do so are in the codes; when they are not, the original ethnographic reports usually provide them. We thus can apply our typology to this rich source of data, providing a systematic survey of evolutionary patterns.[16]

---

[15] Although fishing societies made their appearance prior to 7000 B.C. and were a somewhat more advanced form of societal organization, we do not speak of a "fishing era" for the simple reason that fishing can never be the dominant mode of subsistence except in very limited areas.

[16] Pioneering efforts in this direction include the work of Leonard T. Hobhouse, G. C. Wheeler, and M. Ginsberg, *The Material Culture and Social Institutions of the Simpler Peoples* (London: Chapman & Hall, 1915). Unfortu-

The tables that follow are based on information on the first 915 societies recorded in the Ethnographic Atlas. These societies were distributed as follows among the basic societal types:[17]

Hunting and gathering	151
Simple horticultural	76
Advanced horticultural	267
Agrarian (both simple and advanced)	96
Fishing	44
Herding (both simple and advanced)	60
Hybrids, maritime, industrial, and unclassifiable	221

In our analysis, we will omit hybrid societies in order to concentrate on the more basic types, and maritime and industrial societies because they are so few in number and the sources of data are questionable.[18]

Population Size

One of the most important consequences of technological advance is growth of population. There are two ways this may occur. First, when higher densities can be sustained in a given area, larger communities become possible. Second, when more communities can be united within a single political system, overall societal size increases.

Table 5.2 shows both of these patterns. In hunting and gathering societies, communities are extremely small, averaging only about forty people each. Since these local groups are nearly always autonomous—that is, independent societies in their own right—the average hunting and gathering society actually contains only about forty people. In simple horticultural societies, communities average nearly a hundred, but there, too, local groups are usually autonomous, so that community and society are the same size. At the level of advanced horticultural societies, however, there are important changes. Not only are communities larger, but multicommunity societies are the rule. Thus, though the average advanced horticultural *community* is only three times larger than the simple horticultural, the average advanced horticultural *society* is

---

nately, because of the eclipse of evolutionary theory after World War I, this outstanding piece of work did not have the impact it might otherwise have had. In recent years there have been a number of efforts to analyze systematically coded bodies of data using various samples of societies, but these have seldom employed an adequate societal typology. Much of this work is summarized in Raoul Naroll, "What Have We Learned from Cross-Cultural Surveys?," *American Anthropologist*, 72 (1970), pp. 1227–1288.

[17] See the appendix on pp. 503–507 of the first edition of *Human Societies* for details on the classification of societies.

[18] Specifically, the codes on industrial societies were often based on the study of a single community that could in no sense be regarded as representative of the society.

Table 5.2 Median size of communities and societies, by societal type

Type of Society	Median Size of Communities	Median Size of Societies	No. of Societies*
Hunting and gathering†	40	40	93–62
Simple horticultural	95	95	48–45
Advanced horticultural	280	5,800	107–84
Agrarian	‡	Over 100,000	58–48
Fishing	60	60	20–22
Herding	55	2,000	17–22

* Data are seldom available on a given subject for all 915 societies. This column indicates the number of societies for which data were available and on which the statistics are based. The first of the two figures indicates the number of cases on which the median size of communities is based, the second, the number for the median size of societies.

† In this table and subsequent tables, all the hunting and gathering societies referred to are *advanced* ones.

‡ Murdock's method of coding community size does not permit one to give a precise figure for the median size of communities in agrarian societies, since 57 per cent fall in a category labeled "one or more indigenous cities with more than 50,000 inhabitants." In other words, the content of the code shifts from a measure of central tendency to a measure of the upper limit of the range. It should also be noted that averages are much less meaningful in agrarian societies than in simpler societies owing to the greater range in size.

roughly sixty times larger than its simple horticultural counterpart. The trend continues in agrarian societies, where urban communities are common and the average society covers an even wider area. Since 60 per cent of the agrarian societies for which we have data fall into Murdock's top category of "100,000 or more," it is not possible to give an exact figure for them. But it is obvious that they are substantially larger than their nearest rivals among the less advanced types.[19]

Table 5.2 is also pertinent to our earlier discussion of the relative technological levels of fishing, herding, and horticultural societies. Fishing societies fall between hunting and gathering and simple horticultural societies in size. In community size, so do herding groups, but for societal size, which is more important, they stand between simple and advanced horticultural. It may seem strange that although herding communities are no larger than fishing communities, herding *societies* are more than thirty times larger than fishing societies. The explanation seems to be that fishing communities generally occupy unusually favorable environmental niches with respect to food, enabling them to build up local population densities higher than are normal for communities at their level of technological development, while herding peoples' environments are just the opposite. At the societal level, however, the technological superiority of herding societies permits them to expand geographically and develop

[19] This particular code was not reported in the Ethnographic Atlas in *Ethnology* but in an earlier paper of Murdock's entitled "World Ethnographic Sample," *American Anthropologist*, 59 (1957), pp. 644–687. This paper provided data on a sample of 565 societies and offered a more limited range of information. The computations reported in the tables in this chapter are our own.

politically to an extent impossible for the less advanced fishing groups. Moreover, political expansion is easier in the steppe and prairie environments of herders than in the coastal and river territories of fishing peoples, where there are a multitude of natural barriers.

These data call attention to an important qualification concerning the relationship between technological and structural development in a society. The latter tends to be a function of the former, but only to the extent that environmental conditions are held constant. To put it another way, *the level of structural development in a society is a function both of its level of technological development and of the abundance of resources in its environment.*

Permanence of Settlements

Technological advance also leads to more permanent settlements. Hunting and gathering peoples are generally nomadic; more advanced groups (except for herding peoples) are more settled. This is because hunting and gathering usually so depletes the supply of plants and animals in a small area that it becomes impossible to feed even a few dozen people on a permanent basis. Murdock's data show this clearly. Of 147 hunting and gathering societies, 90 per cent were nomadic,[20] in contrast to only 4 per cent of 377 horticultural and agrarian societies.

Division of Labor

Another result of technological advance is an increased division of labor. Table 5.3 shows how often certain tasks are performed by specialists in each of the

Table 5.3   Frequency of craft specialization,* by societal type (in percentages)

Type of Society	Metal Working	Weaving	Leather Working	Pottery	Boat Building	House Building	Average
Hunting and gathering	†	0	0	0	0	0	0
Simple horticultural	†	0	3	2	4	2	2
Advanced horticultural	100	6	24	24	9	4	28
Agrarian	100	32	42	29	5	18	38
Industrial‡	100	100	100	100	100	100	100
Fishing	†	0	0	0	9	4	2
Herding	95	11	22	†	†	0	21

* The term "craft specialization" as used here includes Murdock's category of industrial specialization.

† The activity in question is seldom found in this type of society.

‡ The figures for industrial societies are not from Murdock's data but are added simply for comparative purposes.

---

[20] Fourteen per cent of the hunting and gathering societies were classified as fully migratory, 61 per cent as seminomadic, and 15 per cent as semisedentary.

major types of societies. Such specialization is virtually unknown in hunting and gathering and simple horticultural societies. In advanced horticultural societies, it occurs with some frequency, becoming more prominent still in agrarian societies. Fishing societies closely resemble simple horticultural societies, while herding societies again are between the simple and advanced horticultural types.

Religious Beliefs

Religion is one area where we might suppose technology and societal type would have little effect. Yet, as Table 5.4 indicates, the basic beliefs typical of the simpler societies are quite different from those in the more advanced. Very few hunting and gathering, simple horticultural, or fishing societies share the underlying Jewish and Christian belief in a God who not only created the universe but remains actively interested in it and in the moral aspects of human life. Few of these societies, in fact, have even conceived of a Supreme Creator, and those that do usually assume him to be indifferent to man. In advanced horticultural societies, the pattern changes notably, and a majority of societies believe in an otiose (i.e., inactive) creator god. Belief in a Supreme Creator who is actively interested in his creation and supports moral conduct is a common pattern only in agrarian and herding societies.[21]

Social Inequality

Another aspect of life that might appear to be relatively immune to variations in subsistence technology is social inequality. Yet here, too, the evidence indicates that different types of societies have quite different patterns.

Table 5.4   Beliefs concerning God, by societal type (in percentages)

Type of Society	Beliefs*				Total	No. of Societies
	A	B	C	D		
Hunting and gathering	60	29	8	2	99	85
Simple horticultural	60	35	2	2	99	43
Advanced horticultural	21	51	12	16	100	131
Agrarian	23	6	5	67	101	66
Fishing	69	14	7	10	100	29
Herding	4	10	6	80	100	50

* A—no conception of Supreme Creator; B—belief in a Supreme Creator who is inactive or not concerned with human affairs; C—belief in a Supreme Creator who is active in human affairs but does not offer positive support to human morality; D—belief in a Supreme Creator who is active and supports human morality.

[21] This way of classifying religious beliefs is based on a method developed by G. E. Swanson in *The Birth of the Gods: The Origin of Primitive Beliefs* (Ann Arbor: University of Michigan Press, 1960), chap. 3.

Table 5.5 Presence of slavery in societies, by societal type (in percentages)

Type of Society	Percentage Having Slavery	No. of Societies
Hunting and gathering	10	142
Simple horticultural	14	66
Advanced horticultural	83	243
Agrarian	54	84
Fishing	51	43
Herding	84	50

As Table 5.5 indicates, slavery is extremely rare in both hunting and gathering and simple horticultural societies. In fishing and agrarian societies, however, it is found about half the time, while in advanced horticultural and herding societies it occurs in five out of six societies. The fact that agrarian societies are less likely to practice slavery than advanced horticultural and herding societies is interesting, because it indicates that evolutionary patterns sometimes assume a curvilinear form (i.e., they involve a reversal in direction). We will find other instances of this later on.

Table 5.6 supplements Table 5.5, showing that the decline in slavery associated with the rise of agrarian societies did not mean a reduction in social inequality as a whole. On the contrary, class systems are actually more common in agrarian societies than in any other. The trend shown in Table 5.5 certainly indicates a change in the *nature* of stratification, but not a general movement toward greater social equality.

Table 5.6 Presence of class systems, by societal type (in percentages)

Type of Society	Percentage Having a Class System*	No. of Societies
Hunting and gathering	2	143
Simple horticultural	17	69
Advanced horticultural	54	224
Agrarian	71	89
Fishing	32	41
Herding	51	49

* This includes those societies which Murdock codes as having "complex class systems," "dual stratification," and "elite stratification."

Other Correlates

We could easily add more tables of correlates, but these should suffice to show how substantial and varied the consequences of technological advance have been. This will become even more evident when we examine the major societal types individually.

TECHNOLOGICAL DETERMINISM?

Today, as in the past, efforts to understand the role of technology in human affairs have been hindered by the tendency of some scholars to take extreme positions on the subject. Over the years, one group has argued the case for a technological determinism that explains almost every sociocultural pattern.[22] To combat this exaggerated view and to uphold the importance of ideological factors, others have minimized or denied the importance of technology.[23] The unreasonableness of *both* positions has apparently escaped many social scientists, with the result that sociology and anthropology have been extremely slow in coming to a realistic assessment of technology's role in the evolutionary process.

Much of the confusion results from the failure to think in *probabilistic* and *variable* terms. Few, if any, significant social patterns are determined by a single factor. Where human societies are concerned, one rarely can say that A, and A alone, causes B. Usually B is due to the combined effect of a number of factors, and, although A may be the most important, it alone is not likely to be strong enough to determine the outcome. The most we can say, as a rule, is that if A is operative, B will be present *with some degree of probability.*

The problem is further complicated because so many of the B's we deal with are in variable form. For example, when we talk about a society's population, we are not interested in whether it exists, but in its relative size. The same is true of most of the phenomena we are concerned with—the *degree* of occupational specialization, the *frequency* of warfare, the *extent* of the authority vested in leaders, and so forth. To think in categorical, either-or terms about such things is misleading.

Clearly, then, the controversy over technological determinism has been a false issue. Technological factors are obviously incapable of explaining *all* social phenomena. On the other hand, the evidence indicates that they explain a great deal. How much they explain varies from subject to subject. We can see this in Table 5.7, which is a measure of the explanatory power of the sixfold societal typology used in analyzing Murdock's data.

---

[22] Leslie White, an anthropologist at the University of Michigan, has been the leading proponent of this point of view for many years. See, for example, his stimulating but extreme essay, "Energy and the Evolution of Culture," in *The Science of Culture* (New York: Grove Press, 1949), pp. 363–393.

[23] Talcott Parsons is one of many who have consistently minimized the role of technology in the process of social change. Though not as extreme as some in his views, he has been very influential. See *Societies: Evolutionary and Comparative Perspectives* (Englewood Cliffs, N.J.: Prentice-Hall, 1966), especially pp. 113–114, for a recent statement of his views.

To understand this table, turn back to Table 5.5 and note that the largest percentage spread occurs when hunting and gathering societies are compared with herding societies: slavery is found in 10 per cent of the former and 84 per cent of the latter, a difference of 74 percentage points. In Table 5.7 we see on the seventh line the variable "slavery practiced," with the value of 74

Table 5.7 Maximum range of percentage differences among six basic societal types* for selected variables

Variable	Maximum Range
Specialization in metal working	100
Leather working: wholly or largely a female activity	96†
Boat building practiced	91
Nomadic communities	87
Median size of communities 100 or more	80
Belief in God as active and moral force	78
Slavery practiced	74
Leather working practiced	71
Two or more levels of government above the local community	71
Pottery made	71
Class stratification	69
Games of strategy	68
Patrilocal residence	68
Urban communities of 5,000 or more	67
Bride price or bride service required	56
Weaving practiced	56
House construction: predominantly male activity	51
Patrilineal clans	51
Games of chance	50
Premarital virginity enforced for women	49
Weaving: predominantly male activity	46†
Specialization in leather working	42
Extended family system	33
Gathering: predominantly female activity	31
Specialization in pottery making	29
Specialization in fishing	29
Fishing: predominantly male activity	22†
Matrilineal clans	18
Specialization in house construction	18
Dowry system	15
Games of physical skill	13
Specialization in boat building	9
Boat building: predominantly male activity	8†
Specialization in hunting	7
Polyandry	1
Hunting: predominantly male activity	0†

* The societal types are those shown in Table 5.6 (page 107).

† Percentage difference based on those societies in which the specified activity is carried on and for which data on sexual specialization are available.

percentage points—the maximum range found in Table 5.5. Similarly, in Table 5.6, the maximum spread is 69 points (between hunting and gathering and agrarian societies), and this is the value shown on line 11 of Table 5.7 opposite the heading "class stratification."

The data shown in Table 5.7 are all based on tables similar to Tables 5.3 through 5.6, but they cover many additional topics. Industrial societies were not included in the calculations, since Murdock's data on them are inadequate. The basic point demonstrated by Table 5.7 is that *the differences between societal types cover the entire range of possibilities from 0 to 100 per cent*. At the lower level, variations in technology are obviously irrelevant or of little importance. In nearly every case this is because the activity in question is almost universally present or almost universally absent. Hunting, for example, is predominantly a male activity in *every* society in Murdock's sample, while, at the other extreme, polyandry (i.e., several men married to one woman) is practiced in less than 1 per cent of the societies. In such cases, there is little or no variance to be explained by technology—or by any other variable.

By contrast, where the values are large in Table 5.7, there is considerable variance to be explained, and technological differences appear to be of major importance. In still other instances, the variance may be considerable, but subsistence technology is of little help in explaining it. To ignore or minimize these differences would both misrepresent and oversimplify the complexities of the real world.

In summary, modern evolutionary theory does *not* take a deterministic view of technology's role: it views subsistence technology as but one force in a field of forces that, together, determine the total pattern of societal characteristics. Its position can be stated briefly in two propositions:

1. Technological advance is the chief determinant of that constellation of global trends—in population, language, social structure, and ideology—which defines the basic outlines of human history.

2. Subsistence technology is the most powerful single variable influencing the social and cultural characteristics of societies, individually and collectively—not with respect to the determination of each and every characteristic, but rather with respect to the total set of characteristics.

These propositions lead to the conclusion that the first step in analyzing any society must be to determine its basic mode of subsistence. This assures that we take into account, at the start of our analysis, the most crucial factor operating in societal evolution.

Our basic task for the rest of this volume will be to apply these propositions in a broadly comparative study of human societies. We will examine each of the major societal types that have emerged in the course of history, seeing how technological innovations have influenced developments in population, language, social structure, and ideology, and how developments in these areas have fed back to technology and influenced its development. We will, for obvious reasons, give special attention to the industrial and industrializing societies of our own day. Our ultimate goal is increased understanding of the basic forces responsible for sociocultural evolution, in the hope that this will help us understand, and even control to some extent, the process of change that is such a striking, and at times threatening, feature of the contemporary world.

PREINDUSTRIAL SOCIETIES

CHAPTER SIX

Hunting and Gathering Societies

Hunting and gathering societies are unique, for they alone span the whole of human history: from the emergence of the first men down to the present, there have always been societies obtaining their livelihood in this way. But as we have said before, the effects of industrialization make it unlikely that any will survive into the twenty-first century. Because these peoples add so much to our understanding of the development of human societies, we can at least be grateful that they survived long enough for trained observers to live among them and record their ways of life.

The surviving hunting and gathering societies have been for decades the focus of a major controversy among social scientists. Some scholars have seen these groups as the living counterparts of prehistoric hunting and gathering societies. Others have denied the legitimacy of any such comparison, arguing that these modern groups are products of an evolutionary process as extended as that of any modern industrial society.

Though the latter view prevailed for a time, there are signs of a reversal. Many archaeologists now refer to the hunting and gathering peoples of prehistoric and modern times as "analogous peoples" and acknowledge the benefits to their discipline of inferences drawn from ethnographic studies (i.e., studies of contemporary primitive societies).[1] A leading British archaeologist summed up the current view when he wrote that the archaeologist learns from the ethnographer

> how particular peoples adapt themselves to their environments, and shape their resources to the ways of life demanded by their own cultures: he thus gains a knowledge of alternative methods of solving problems and often of alternative ways of explaining artifacts resembling those he recovers from antiquity. Study of ethnography will not as a rule . . . give him straight answers to his queries. What it will do is to provide him with hypotheses in the light of which he can resume his attack on the raw materials of his study. In fact, the great value of

---

[1] For an example of the use of the term "analogous peoples," see Grahame Clark and Stuart Piggott, *Prehistoric Societies* (New York: Knopf, 1965), p. 133. On the value of inferences from ethnography, see Frank Hole and Robert Heizer, *An Introduction to Prehistoric Archeology* (New York: Holt, 1965), especially pp. 211–214 and chap. 16, or Grahame Clark, *Archaeology and Society: Reconstructing the Historic Past,* 3d ed. (London: Methuen, 1957), pp. 172–174. In several instances, contemporary hunters and gatherers have provided explanations for previously unexplained archaeological findings. See, for example, John E. Pfeiffer, *The Emergence of Man* (New York: Harper & Row, 1969), pp. 322–324.

ethnography to the prehistorian is that it will often suggest to him what to look for. . . . By constant reference to the culture of living or recently living societies, the prehistorian should be able to enrich and fortify his interpretation of the past, as well as bring into the open problems calling for further research.[2]

In our analysis we will follow the conservative procedure of presenting the findings of archaeology and ethnography separately. Only after we have done this will we explore the question of whether they provide consistent or contradictory images of hunting and gathering societies.

THE ARCHAEOLOGICAL EVIDENCE

Human Origins

It is easy to speak of "the dawn of human history" but not so easy to assign a date to it. Mankind, in the sense of Homo sapiens sapiens, or genetically modern man, is the product of a long and extended process of genetic evolution that only gradually differentiated our species from others of the primate order. For this reason it is highly arbitrary to say that human history began at any particular point. The only realistic approach is to identify certain critical developments in the process and try to establish their approximate dates.

For many years it was thought that using and making simple tools was the first significant step in the differentiation of our species from the rest of the primate order, but recent studies of chimpanzees living in their natural habitat show that they, too, use and even make simple tools.[3] If this reflects a genetic heritage that we share with chimpanzees, as now seems likely, we must look to some later development for the first distinctive step in man's evolutionary history. Scholars today believe that this came when tool-using and tool-making evolved into something more than incidental activities, which is all they are for chimpanzee societies. At some point, making and using tools—to dig up roots, crack open nuts or bones, and to do a variety of other things—became so frequent and so important in hominid[4] life that it was essential to survival. One contemporary anthropologist suggests that this point was reached about the time our ancestors began to make more or less standardized tools out of stone.[5] If so, this first important development took place about 2 or 3 million years ago.

---

[2] Clark, pp. 172–173. Quoted by permission of Methuen & Co., Ltd.

[3] Jane van Goodall, who lived alongside them and observed their behavior over extended periods, reports that they often use sticks and twigs as tools, especially for getting at termites, which they eat. When no suitable stick or twig is available, they break or bend one to a shape they can use. See "Chimpanzees of the Gombe Stream Reserve," in Irven DeVore (ed.), *Primate Behavior* (New York: Holt, 1965), pp. 441–443 and 473.

[4] This is a generic term that includes both modern man and his manlike prehistoric ancestors.

[5] Jane Lancaster, "On the Evolution of Tool-using Behavior," *American Anthropologist*, 70 (1968), pp. 56–66.

Second, and even more crucial, was the use of symbols and language. Unfortunately, the first symbols were almost certainly verbal, which could leave no record. To infer speech solely on the basis of rudimentary stone tools found with early hominids, as some have done, is unwarranted.[6] We really cannot safely infer the use of symbols prior to the time our ancestors began burying their dead, which was approximately 100,000 years ago.[7] This was also about the time that hominid brain capacity stopped increasing, which some scholars take as an indication that hominids were beginning to rely on cultural adaptation as a mechanism of survival.

The final step in man's evolution occurred when sociocultural adaptation replaced genetic adaptation as the *dominant* mode of response to the environment. One can argue that man, in the fullest sense of the term, did not even exist until this critical point was reached. Though precise dating is impossible, this development almost certainly occurred only in the last 30,000 to 40,000 years, or since the last major genetic change led to Neanderthal man's (*Homo sapiens neanderthalensis*) replacement by modern man (*Homo sapiens sapiens*). Prior to this, cultural change had been painfully slow[8]—even slower than genetic change in the hominid line. After this, *major* genetic change stopped (i.e., *Homo sapiens sapiens* was never superseded genetically), and major cultural change became increasingly frequent.

The Archaeological Time Frame

Archaeologists divide hominid history prior to the horticultural revolution into four major periods: Lower Paleolithic, Middle Paleolithic, Upper Paleolithic, and Mesolithic. These are all part of the Stone Age, when stone was the chief material used in cutting, scraping, and piercing tools and weapons. Paleolithic means "old stone age," and Mesolithic, "middle stone age." The Neolithic, or "new stone age," came after the horticultural revolution and will be dealt with in the next chapter.

The Lower Paleolithic was by far the longest period. Beginning at least 2 million years ago and lasting until about 100,000 years ago, when Neanderthal man appeared, it covers 95 per cent or more of hominid history. The approximate dates for the other periods are shown in Figure 6.1. The fact that each period was substantially shorter than the one before it is of considerable importance, as we will soon see.

During the early years of archaeological research, when investigations

---

[6] See, for example, Carleton S. Coon, *The Origin of Races* (New York: Knopf, 1962), p. 259.

[7] Alternatively, the first use of symbols may have been associated with the increase in big game hunting half a million years earlier, since such hunting usually requires close cooperation and cooperation usually requires some mode of communication.

[8] See Table 6.1, p. 131.

Dates	Dominant Hominid Type	Archaeological Period	Sociocultural Era
2,000,000 B. P. c. 650,000 B. P.	*Australopithecus*	Lower Paleolithic	Hunting and gathering
c. 100,000 B. P.	*Homo erectus*		
c. 35,000 B. P.	*Homo sapiens neanderthalensis*	Middle Paleolithic	
c. 8000 B.C.		Upper Paleolithic	
c. 7000 B.C.	*Homo sapiens sapiens*	Mesolithic	
c. 4000 B.C.		Neolithic	Horticultural
c. 3000 B.C. c. 800 B.C.		Bronze Age	Agrarian
A.D. 1800		Iron Age	Industrial

* The time dimension, it must be noted, is *not* drawn to scale; all dates prior to 35,000 B. P. are only rough estimates. The abbreviation B. P. stands for "before present."

Figure 6.1 Three time frames.*

were still limited to Europe, it was generally supposed that the dates for the various eras were the same everywhere. Today, as a result of research in other continents, we know better. For example, though the Lower Paleolithic ended in Europe about 100,000 years ago, it continued in eastern and central Africa for another 50,000 years.[9] Similarly, the Mesolithic survived for varying periods of time, ending in parts of the Middle East about 7000 B.C., in Britain and other parts of northern Europe about 3000 B.C. The dates in Figure 6.1, therefore, oversimplify the picture to some extent.

Simple Hunting and Gathering Societies of the Lower Paleolithic

As we have already noted, the hominids of the Lower Paleolithic were not men in the usual sense of the term. If by "man" we mean a creature whose mode of adaptation is primarily cultural and if we equate culture with the ability to use symbols, it is highly unlikely that the hominids of most of that era were true men. Students of the prehistoric past have concluded that the Lower Paleolithic's "almost unimaginable slowness of change demonstrates a lack of inventiveness that could only survive among societies without fully articulate speech."[10]

---

[9] Sonia Cole, *The Prehistory of East Africa* (New York: Mentor, 1965), pp. 44 and 164.

[10] Jacquetta Hawkes, *Prehistory*, UNESCO History of Mankind, vol. 1, part 1, (New York: Mentor, 1965), p. 172. See also Grahame Clark, *The Stone Age Hunters* (London: Thames and Hudson, 1967), p. 25; Clark and Piggott, p. 45; and Cole, pp. 120 and 123, who refers to the "astonishing slowness in cultural development" in this era.

Biological evidence points in the same direction. The cranial capacity of modern man ranges from 1,000 to 2,000 cubic centimeters, with an average of about 1,450 cubic centimeters.[11] By contrast, the cranial capacity of the australopithecines, the prehuman hominids that lived during most of the Lower Paleolithic, was only 375 to 680 cubic centimeters.[12] This is hardly distinguishable from the 350 to 750 cubic centimeter range of the modern gorilla. Though cranial capacity is not related to mental ability in modern man except in rare pathological cases, the gap between modern man and australopithecines, together with the similarity between the latter and modern primates, reinforces the conclusion indicated by the "unimaginably" slow rate of technological progress.

During the latter part of the Lower Paleolithic, perhaps around 650,000 B.P. (before the present), the australopithecines apparently evolved into Homo erectus, a hominid genetically closer to modern man. His cranial capacity of 775 to 1,225 cubic centimeters was substantially larger than his predecessors' and overlaps the lower range of modern man. More important, with the appearance of Homo erectus we see technological innovations beginning to set man apart from the rest of the animal world.

Our picture of life in the Lower Paleolithic is still extremely sketchy. What knowledge we have is based primarily on three kinds of evidence: (1) hominid skeletal remains, (2) skeletal remains of animals apparently eaten by

Figure 6.2 Ranges of cranial capacity of modern gorilla, Australopithecus, Homo erectus, and modern man.

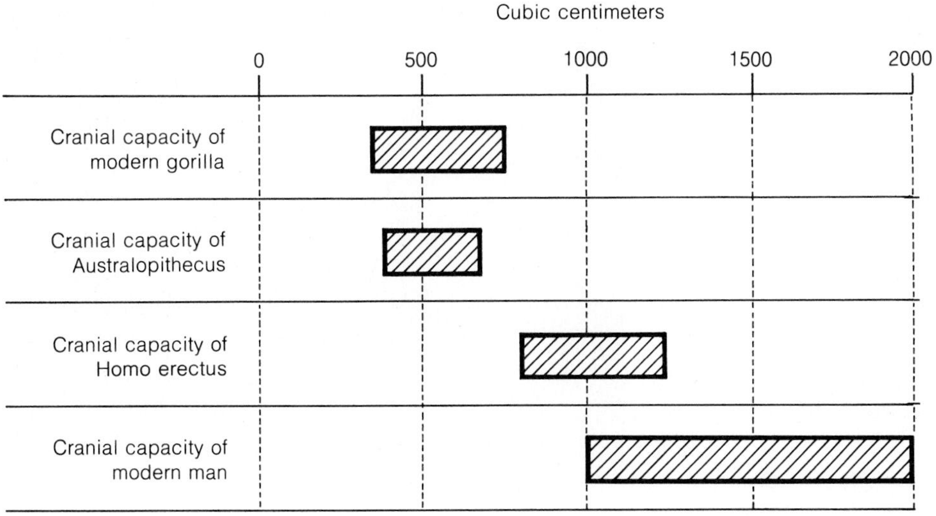

---

[11] C. Loring Brace, *The Stages of Human Evolution* (Englewood Cliffs, N.J.: Prentice-Hall, 1967), pp. 63–64.

[12] John Napier, *The Roots of Mankind* (Washington: Smithsonian Press, 1970), p. 194. We also use Napier's figure for the gorilla range; but his figure for the modern human average is contradicted by most other authorities.

these hominids, and (3) thousands of simple stone tools apparently used to skin animals, to cut off chunks of meat, and perhaps to sharpen wooden tools and weapons. In addition, there are a few fragments of wooden objects, as well as traces of organic material that cast a bit more light on our ancestors' diet.[13]

From at least the time of Homo erectus, man's ancestors differed from other primates by virtue of their substantial dependence on meat. Initially, they may have scavenged the remains left by carnivores, but long before the Lower Paleolithic ended, they were skilled hunters. A cave near Peking, containing the bones of Homo erectus, was filled with thousands of animal bones, and the fact that most of them had been split open indicates that these hominids had eaten the animals, opening the bones to get at the marrow. Most of the animals were large ones, indicating more than minor hunting skills.

Recent research suggests that reliance on hunting was crucial in the eventual development of symbols and culture. As one writer puts it:

> The amount of information which must be exchanged between plant eaters is small compared with that needed in group-hunting [by] large animals, wolves for example. Equally to the point is the lack of challenge or psychological stimulation involved in plant eating. Plants do not run away nor do they turn and attack. They can be approached at any time from any direction, and they do not need to be trapped, speared, clubbed, or pursued on foot until they are exhausted.[14]

Figure 6.3   Artist's reconstruction of the life of Homo erectus. This drawing from the British Museum is based on archaeological evidence from the cave near Peking.

---

[13] For a photograph of some of these rare wooden fragments, see François Bordes, *The Old Stone Age*, translated by J. E. Anderson (New York: McGraw-Hill, 1968), fig. 18.

[14] William S. Laughlin, "Hunting: An Integrating Biobehavior System and Its Evolutionary Importance," in Richard Lee and Irven DeVore (eds.),, *Man The Hunter* (Chicago: Aldine, 1968), p. 318. Quoted by permission.

Figure 6.4 Approximate areas of hominid habitation in the Lower Paleolithic.

The hunting of large animals by Homo erectus probably stimulated his processes of thought and his efforts to communicate to an extent that collecting plants, and even scavenging, could not.

The occupants of the Peking cave also used fire. Whether they could generate it is not known: most scholars believe that they merely preserved fires started by lightning or other natural causes. Fire was undoubtedly used for warmth and, from a fairly early date, for cooking as well. Remains of Homo erectus found in England reveal another important use—to harden the point of a wooden spear, which was apparently the most advanced weapon until the Upper Paleolithic. It is speculated that hominid hunters may also have employed fire to kill animals too large for them to handle any other way, driving them off cliffs or into swamps.

During most of the Lower Paleolithic, man's ancestors lived in caves or in crude shelters of branches and leaves like those still used by some modern hunting and gathering peoples (see Figures 6.12 and 6.13). By the latter part of the Lower Paleolithic (c. 300,000 B.P.), some were building more substantial dwellings. Recent excavations on the French Riviera have identified the remains of a number of oval structures 20 to 50 feet long and 12 to 18 feet wide, complete with hearths with low stone walls to protect them from the wind. The superstructure was apparently intertwined branches, with an opening in the top for smoke.[15]

Finally, archaeological evidence indicates that at least some Lower Paleolithic groups practiced cannibalism. In the cave at Peking, several of the

---

[15] Pfeiffer, pp. 123–126.

skulls were broken in a way that strongly indicates the brains were removed, presumably for food.

Beyond this, there is little we can say about life in the Lower Paleolithic except as inferences based on our observations of modern hunting and gathering societies. Since this takes us into the realm of ethnography, we will first complete our survey of the archaeological evidence.

Simple Hunting and Gathering Societies of the Middle Paleolithic

With the beginning of the Middle Paleolithic approximately 100,000 years ago, the human character of the tool-makers is no longer a matter of debate. This is the era dominated by Neanderthal man. Biologically, Neanderthal man was much more like modern man (i.e., Homo sapiens sapiens) than either australopithecus or Homo erectus were. With respect to the important matter of cranial capacity, he closely resembled Homo sapiens sapiens.

Culturally, the resemblance was not nearly so strong. But one thing, at least, indicates that Neanderthal man used symbols: he buried his dead and placed artifacts in the grave with them, strongly suggesting a belief in life after death. These artifacts included food, flowers, implements, and red ocher, which some scholars suspect was believed to have the life-giving properties of blood. At least one grave held animal bones and cinders, suggesting either burnt offerings or the remains of a funeral feast.[16] This evidence of abstract ideas is strongly indicative of speech and the use of symbols.

In other respects, however, the culture of Neanderthal man was closer to the Lower Paleolithic than to later periods. Apart from the burial of the dead, there seem to have been only three noteworthy developments. The first of these was the adoption of clothing. Though there is no direct evidence that Neanderthal man wore clothing, many archaeologists believe it would have been essential in the cold climates he was exposed to during much of his history.[17] The abundance of flint scrapers found at Neanderthal sites reinforces this hypothesis, since they could have been used to dress animal skins.

The second noteworthy innovation of Neanderthal man was his discovery of the usefulness of handles on tools. A handle usually multiplies the efficiency of a tool several times. In a striking tool, it increases the force of the blow by increasing the radius of the swing; in a cutting tool, it increases the force by bringing the more powerful muscles of the hand and arm to bear.[18] As far as we know, Neanderthal man never actually added handles to his tools, but he did discover the advantage of using the long bone of an animal as a

---

[16] For a good brief summary of Neanderthal burial remains, see Pfeiffer, pp. 167ff.

[17] See, for example, Clark and Piggott, p. 59.

[18] S. A. Semenov, *Prehistoric Technology*, trans. M. W. Thompson (New York: Barnes & Noble, 1964), p. 173.

kind of ready-made handle, with the end of the bone serving as the head of the tool.[19]

The third important change during this period was an apparent increase in violence, in the sense of man against man. Several skeletons have been found with clear indications of man-inflicted wounds (e.g., a flint projectile in a rib cage and a pelvis with a spear hole in it).[20]

Advanced Hunting and Gathering Societies of the Upper Paleolithic

With the appearance of modern man (Homo sapiens sapiens) approximately 35,000 years ago, the rate of technological innovation increased greatly. Important new tools and weapons appeared in such numbers (see Figure 6.5) that we are forced to recognize the emergence of a new type of society, one appreciably higher on the scale of technological progress than any of its known predecessors in the Lower and Middle Paleolithic. We will refer to such societies as *advanced* hunting and gathering societies to distinguish them from the earlier, more primitive groups. Since the innovations occurred over a 25,000-year period, the transition from simple to advanced hunting and gather-

Figure 6.5 Assorted Paleolithic tools. The large chopper or hand ax in the center dates from the Lower Paleolithic. Since no other types of tools or weapons from this era have been found, it is assumed that these were all-purpose implements. By contrast, people in the Upper Paleolithic used a much wider variety of tools and weapons, of which a few examples are shown on either side of the older chopper.

[19] Ibid.

[20] Pfeiffer, p. 172.

ing societies was gradual, and the latter term is far more applicable to societies late in the era than to those at the beginning.

Some of the most important innovations were in the manufacture of weapons. Though the spear had been used since Lower Paleolithic times, there were no significant improvements until the Upper Paleolithic, when several appeared. One of the first was the spear-thrower. Using the principle of the lever, it doubled the distance a spear could be hurled.[21] At the other end of the spear, the men of the Upper Paleolithic used sharpened bone points, and later they added barbs.[22]

The most important innovation in weapons, however, was the bow and arrow. Utilizing the principle of the concentration of energy, Upper Paleolithic man created a weapon of great usefulness and versatility. Its effective wounding range is roughly four times that of the spear and twice that of the spear thrown with the aid of a spear-thrower.[23] Furthermore, an arrow travels two and a half to three times faster than a spear. This is important not only because of the time advantage it affords the hunter but also because the force of the blow is a function of the speed of the missile.[24] Finally, in contrast with the spear, the bow and arrow permits the hunter to sight the missile at eye level, which greatly increases the accuracy of his aim.

Though less dramatic, the development of other tools was no less important. As one writer puts it, "In the Upper Paleolithic Age man began to make

Figure 6.6 Two comparisons of the spear and the bow and arrow.

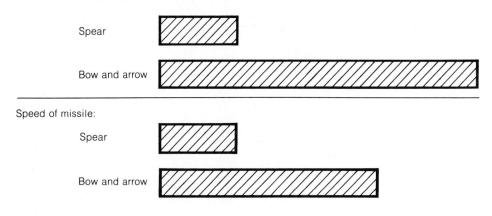

Effective wounding range:

Spear

Bow and arrow

Speed of missile:

Spear

Bow and arrow

---

[21] Semenov, pp. 202–203.

[22] E. Adamson Hoebel, *Anthropology,* 3d ed. (New York: McGraw-Hill, 1966), pp. 176–177, and Hawkes, pp. 212–213.

[23] This and the following statements concerning the bow and arrow are based on Semenov, pp. 202–204.

[24] These advantages are partly offset by the greater weight of the spear, which means that it might remain best for hunting animals with thick hides.

Figure 6.7 Reconstruction of an Upper Paleolithic settlement in Czechoslovakia.

the tool fit the task with an altogether new precision."[25] Innovations included such diverse tools as pins or awls, needles with eyes, spoons, graving tools, axes, stone saws, antler hammers, shovels or scoops, pestles and grinding slabs (for grinding minerals to obtain coloring materials), and mattocks.

In colder regions, Upper Paleolithic man usually lived in caves. This was not always possible, however, as in the case of the mammoth hunters who ranged from Czechoslovakia to Siberia and whose way of life forced them to remain in caveless country even during the winter. Figure 6.7 shows a modern reconstruction of one of their settlements. In addition to these tentlike structures, Upper Paleolithic people also built true earth houses.[26]

The discovery of these settlements is important, among other reasons because they provide us with information on the size of human communities in this era. In general, they were quite small, many with as few as six to thirty persons. One, spread out along a 2-mile stretch of river in France, may have housed as many as 400 to 600 persons, but this was exceptional and probably reflected their unusual fishing opportunities.[27]

Another significant innovation was the lamp, the oldest of them found in caves in Western Europe. These first lamps were simply shallow stone saucers, though some had a broad tongue extending from the rim to form a handle. Modern Eskimo use similar lamps today, with seal or walrus blubber for fuel and moss for a wick. Europeans of the Upper Paleolithic may have done the same, using other fats.[28]

The best-known innovation of Upper Paleolithic man is his art. The drawings on the walls of caves in Western Europe (see Figure 6.8) are world famous, but they are only one of the art forms developed in that era. There was

---

[25] Hawkes, p. 212.

[26] J. G. D. Clark, *Prehistoric Europe: The Economic Basis* (London: Methuen, 1952), pp. 132–133, and Pfeiffer, p. 214.

[27] Hawkes, pp. 184–188, and Pfeiffer, p. 212.

[28] Hawkes, pp. 229–230.

Figure 6.8 The stag hunt, an Upper Paleolithic
painting from the wall of a cave in Spain.

Figure 6.9 The Venus of Willen-
dorf, an Upper Paleolithic sculpture.

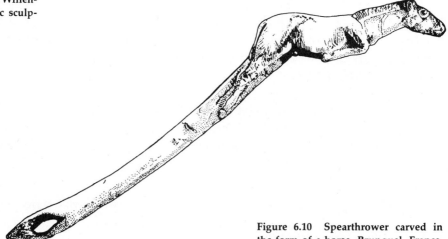

Figure 6.10 Spearthrower carved in
the form of a horse, Brunquel, France.

sculpture of various kinds (Figure 6.9), as well as bone and ivory carvings, often on the handles of weapons and tools (Figure 6.10).[29]

It would be hard to exaggerate the importance of these artistic remains, for they provide us with many insights into Upper Paleolithic life. Drawings of men dressed to resemble animals strongly suggest magical or religious practice, especially a belief in sympathetic magic. This belief—that anything done to an image, or a part, of a person or animal will affect that person or animal—is further evidenced by the fact that a great number of the drawings have spears or darts drawn or scratched into animals' flanks.[30]

Sympathetic magic was apparently also used to produce fertility, in both humans and animals. At least this is the most likely explanation for the numerous female figures with exaggerated evidences of pregnancy (see Figure 6.9). Most scholars think it is no coincidence that the artist ignored the facial features and devoted all his attention to the symbols of fertility.

Many examples of Upper Paleolithic art indicate the development of ceremonies or rituals. These are suggested by the drawings of men dancing and by engravings of processions of men standing before animals, with their heads bowed and their weapons resting on their shoulders in a nonthreatening position. It has been suggested that these men are following the practice of some modern hunters and are asking the forgiveness of the animals they plan to kill.[31] In short, Upper Paleolithic art reveals the growth of human consciousness and man's efforts to understand and control his environment, and attests to the gulf developing between him and the rest of the animal world.

Upper Paleolithic art also provides the first hints of the beginnings of occupational specialization. Several of the drawings may be early records of shamans or medicine men, though they may simply depict ordinary hunters engaged in stalking animals (see Figure 6.11). A stronger indication of specialization comes from a settlement site in Czechoslovakia. One of its three huts was still only partially excavated at last report, and little can be said about it, while the second appears to have been a communal longhouse occupied by five family groups. But the third was a small circular hut that was evidently used for making clay statuettes of animals and women, indicating the workshop of a shaman.[32]

A final development in the Upper Paleolithic was man's migration to

---

[29] On Upper Paleolithic art, see Peter Ucko and Andreé Rosenfeld, *Palaeolithic Cave Art* (New York: McGraw-Hill, 1967), or Grahame Clark, *The Stone Age Hunters,* chap. 4.

[30] Clark and Piggott, pp. 93–95.

[31] Hawkes, pp. 293–294, including fig. 35b.

[32] See Bohuslav Klema, "The First Ground-plan of an Upper Paleolithic Loess Settlement in Middle Europe and Its Meaning," in Robert Braidwood and Gordon Willey (eds.), *Courses toward Urban Life: Archeological Considerations of Some Cultural Alternatives* (Chicago: Aldine, 1962), pp. 199ff.

Figure 6.11 Cave drawings like "the sorcerer" strongly suggest magical or religious practice, especially a belief in sympathetic magic.

three new continents, North and South America and Australia.[33] Movement to the New World became possible because the sea level was lower during the last Ice Age, when vast quantities of water were held in glaciers. This created a land bridge in the Bering Strait, providing direct access from Siberia to North America.[34] There may have been a similar link with Australia, though present evidence indicates that Upper Paleolithic man had to travel a part of the way by

[33] For a summary of recent results of carbon dating in Australia, see Frederick McCarthy, "The Aboriginal Past: Archaeological and Material Equipment," in Ronald Berndt and Catherine Berndt (eds.), *Aboriginal Man in Australia: Essays in Honour of Emeritus Professor A. P. Elkin* (Sydney: Angus and Robertson, 1965), pp. 83–84. On the Americas, see R. F. Spencer, J. D. Jennings, et al., *The Native Americans* (New York: Harper & Row, 1965), chap. 1.

[34] Despite its latitude, much of this area was free from glaciers at this time. See Clark and Piggott, chap. 5, for a discussion of this movement and the relevant evidence. New findings are still coming in on this subject, however, and all conclusions, especially about the timing of the migration, are tentative.

water.[35] If so, we must assume another major technical achievement, the invention of boats. So far, the oldest boats date from the Mesolithic, but future research may provide evidence of earlier ones.

Advanced Hunting and Gathering Societies of the Mesolithic

With the Mesolithic, we come to the end of the era in which hunting and gathering were man's most efficient means of subsistence. Later, this simple way of life would be increasingly threatened, struggling to survive in the face of growing challenges from groups with more advanced and more efficient technologies. In the Mesolithic, however, if hunting and gathering societies had any competition, it was only from fishing societies, and these were confined to limited areas.

As we noted earlier, it is impossible to say just when the first fishing societies appeared, but archaeological evidence suggests that it was during the Mesolithic. The oldest remains of boats and boat equipment date from this period, as do the first true fishhooks, fish nets, and fish traps.[36] The widespread distribution of these artifacts indicates that fishing was practiced not just by true fishing societies but by many societies that continued to rely on hunting and gathering as their primary means of subsistence.

In Europe, many of the innovations in the Mesolithic reflect man's response to relatively rapid climatic changes.[37] As the glaciers retreated and temperatures moderated, forests began to grow where there had been open plains, and vast herds of reindeer gave way to game that traveled in small herds or individually. Human populations had to respond with equally drastic changes in their patterns of life, and increased reliance on fishing was only one of these adjustments.

Another important response to the changed environment was the gradual development of wood-working tools and skills. Axes with handles became common, and the adze was introduced. As we noted, the oldest known boat, a crudely dug out log found in Holland, was from this period—approximately 6400 B.C. A wooden paddle from an English site is about a thousand years older.

At this time the Middle East, unlike Europe, was largely open grassland. Here people first turned to the cereal grasses as a major source of food. During most of this period they seem to have simply harvested wild grains as they ripened. But before the end of the Mesolithic they discovered that the same

[35] See N. W. G. Macintosh, "The Physical Aspect of Man in Australia," in Berndt and Berndt, especially pp. 36–41.

[36] Hawkes, pp. 156–158, 213, and 226–228.

[37] See Grahame Clark, *The Stone Age Hunters*, pp. 92–108.

grains that were eaten could be planted to provide a new crop.[38] Numerous stone sickles unearthed at Mesolithic sites attest to this: they still show the distinctive sheen produced by the abrasive effects of thousands of stems of grass on the cutting surfaces of the blades. These sites also yielded pestles and mortars, apparently used for grinding grain, as well as clay-lined pits for storing it. A second major innovation in subsistence technology was the domestication of sheep.[39] These two developments formed the foundation for the first major social revolution in human history.

Even during the Mesolithic, however, these advances already had an impact. These Middle Eastern communities could now support larger populations and a more settled way of life. One cemetery, for example, contained eighty-seven individuals, another forty-five, and some of the graves reveal an elaborateness of construction not previously encountered.[40]

Despite its brevity, the Mesolithic era produced a variety of other innovations, including the domestication of the dog, the invention of the sledge and the ice pick (the latter used to open holes for winter fishing), and the development of basketry and leather working and the tools used for them. In addition, numerous improvements were made in traditional tools and weapons. Recent research shows that by various devices, such as changing the angle of the blade, men learned to strengthen stone tools and reduce their tendency to break under pressure.[41] As a result, the stone tools of the Mesolithic were considerably better than those of the Upper Paleolithic.

By the end of the Mesolithic, human societies had achieved an amazing diversity. They had adapted to tropic conditions, to arctic conditions, and to everything in between. People were living in forests, in open grasslands, and even in deserts. Though some groups still relied entirely on hunting and gathering, an increasing number were getting a part of their food from fishing, horticulture, or herding. In short, the Upper Paleolithic and the Mesolithic were periods of increasing change and variability.

The Changing Rate of Change in the Paleolithic and Mesolithic

The quickening pace of change in the Upper Paleolithic calls to mind our earlier hypothesis that the long-term evolutionary trend involves an acceleration of

---

[38] There is no direct evidence that this discovery was made during the Mesolithic, but we define horticultural societies as those which obtain more than half of their food supply from the cultivation of plants, and obviously this did not happen overnight. The discovery of plant cultivation must have occurred many years, and perhaps some centuries, before the first true horticultural societies appeared.

[39] Hawkes, p. 255, and James Mellaart, *Earliest Civilizations of the Near East* (London: Thames and Hudson, 1965), chap. 2.

[40] Clark and Piggott, p. 151, or Mellaart, pp. 26–27.

[41] Semenov, p. 203.

the rate of innovation. Before turning to the ethnographic evidence on modern hunting and gathering societies, we will take a close look at this matter to see whether archaeological data support or contradict it.

To help us explore this problem as systematically as possible, Table 6.1 lists all the known innovations of importance from Lower Paleolithic through Mesolithic times.[42] If this table errs, it is probably in its omission of later ones. For example, Mesolithic man's important change in the blade angle of stone tools is not included. If all such innovations were recorded, the list for the Upper Paleolithic and Mesolithic would be considerably longer.

Table 6.1 Technological and other innovations during the Lower, Middle, and Upper Paleolithic and Mesolithic eras

Era	Innovations*	
Lower Paleolithic	Stone chopping, cutting, and scraping tools† Wooden spear Fire-hardened spear point	Use of fire [Cannibalism]
Middle Paleolithic	Use of bone for tools Skin clothing (probable) Built-in handle for tools (i.e., long bone)	[Ceremonial burial] [Religion (probable)]
Upper Paleolithic	Spear-thrower Man-made dwellings Harpoon head Pins or awls Antler hammers Mattocks Stone saws Spoons Separate handles [Painting] [Magic (probable)]	Bow and arrow Lamps Fish gorgets Needles with eye Shovels or scoops Stone ax with hafted handle Graving tools Pestles and grinding slabs Boats (very possible) [Sculpture] [Ornaments]
Mesolithic	Boats (?) Fish nets Adze Plant cultivation Basketry Grinding equipment Sledge Comb	Fishhooks Fish traps Sickles Domestication of sheep Leather-working tools Paving Ice pick Domestication of the dog

* Items in brackets are nontechnological and are not counted in Table 6.2.

† These are multipurpose tools usually referred to by archaeologists as "chopping tools" or "hand axes." For purposes of Table 6.2 they will be considered a single innovation, since refinements of tools are not otherwise listed or counted.

[42] This table is based largely on Clark and Piggott, Semenov, and Hawkes.

Table 6.2   Rate of change during the Lower, Middle, and Upper Paleolithic and Mesolithic eras

Era	(A) Duration (in 1,000-Year Intervals)	(B) Number of Major Technological Innovations	(B/A) Rate of Innovation
Lower Paleolithic	1,900*	4	0.002
Lower Paleolithic	550†	3	0.005
Middle Paleolithic	65	3	0.046
Upper Paleolithic	25	17.5†	0.700
Mesolithic	3§	16.5‡	5.500
Mesolithic	1.2¶	16.5‡	13.750

* This estimate assumes that the Lower Paleolithic began 2 million years ago.

† This estimate assumes that the Lower Paleolithic began 650,000 years ago.

‡ Because of the great uncertainty concerning the era in which boats were invented, they are counted as half a unit in both the Upper Paleolithic and the Mesolithic.

§ This estimate assumes that the Mesolithic lasted approximately 3,000 years on the average.

¶ This estimate assumes that the Mesolithic lasted only 1,200 years in the area of minimum duration (i.e., the Middle East).

To complete the analysis, Table 6.2 shows the duration of each period, the number of major technological innovations in it (excluding the nontechnical items bracketed in Table 6.1), and, based on this information, the *rate* of innovation. Because of the difficulty of measuring the duration of the Lower Paleolithic and Mesolithic eras, alternative calculations are provided. For the Lower Paleolithic, one estimate includes the hominids of 2 million years ago, while a second takes the emergence of Homo erectus as its starting point. For the Mesolithic, one estimate is based on the period's average length of about 3,000 years in Europe and Asia, the other on its brief duration (1,200 years) in the crucial Middle Eastern area. Though these alternatives yield different values for the rate of change, they have no significant effect on the basic pattern: the calculations show a *sharply rising rate* of innovation. In fact, the lower estimate for the Mesolithic is a thousand times the higher estimate for the Lower Paleolithic! The magnitude of the difference is so great that it is difficult to imagine any new findings or more precise listing of major innovations could possibly alter the picture.[43]

THE ETHNOGRAPHIC EVIDENCE

Fortunately for the student of human societies, hunting and gathering societies did not disappear with the emergence of new kinds of societies. In remote

---

[43] For a similar conclusion, based on a less systematic survey, see Hawkes, pp. 172–173.

areas, especially in the New World and Australia, they continued to flourish. Though the settlement of these areas by Europeans and the spreading influence of industrialization are finally destroying them, we have detailed descriptions of many of these groups. Thus their loss is not as great a tragedy as it would have been had it occurred several hundred years earlier, when the civilized world possessed almost no firsthand knowledge of them.[44]

A hundred years ago, there were still large numbers of hunting and gathering societies in both the New World and Australia, and smaller numbers in Southwest Africa, parts of the rain forest in central Africa, certain remote areas in Southeast Asia and neighboring islands, and in Arctic Asia. As recently as 1788 there were probably 5,000 hunting and gathering societies in Australia alone[45] and almost certainly as many more in North America.

In our review, we will concentrate on those societies whose way of life has been least affected by contact with agrarian and industrial societies. Our primary concern will be with the more remote and isolated groups and with groups that were studied before social contacts and cultural diffusion transformed or destroyed their traditional social patterns.

Even with these limitations, our sample of societies is by no means homogeneous. This can be seen quite clearly in the 151 hunting and gathering societies in Murdock's sample. At one extreme, 13 per cent of these societies relied entirely on hunting and gathering for their subsistence; at the other extreme, 11 per cent relied on these techniques for only about half of their subsistence. Most of the groups (80 per cent) depended on fishing to some extent, with a few (15 per cent) obtaining nearly half of their subsistence from this source. A minority (23 per cent) derived part of their subsistence from horticulture, and a few (less than 5 per cent) got nearly half this way. In short, some were pure hunting and gathering societies, but most of them incorporated limited elements of a fishing or horticultural technology or both. In this respect they resembled those hunting and gathering societies of the Upper Paleolithic and Mesolithic which supplemented their food supply by fishing and those in the late Mesolithic which had begun the practice of horticulture.

Population Density and Size

Despite these variations, modern hunting and gathering societies[46] have a lot in common. To begin with, none is capable of supporting a large or dense popula-

---

[44] For good reviews of recent work on hunters and gatherers, see Lee and DeVore, op. cit., Carleton S. Coon, *The Hunting Peoples* (Boston: Little, Brown, 1971), and Elman Service, *The Hunters* (Englewood Cliffs, N.J.: Prentice-Hall, 1966).

[45] This figure is based on Elkin's estimate that there were approximately 300,000 aborigines in Australia at the time of the first white settlement. This estimate was divided by 60, a very generous estimate for the average size of these societies. See A. P. Elkin, *The Australian Aborigines,* 3d ed. (Sydney: Angus and Robertson, 1954), p. 10.

[46] When referring to "modern" hunting and gathering societies, we mean both those now in existence and those which survived into the modern era (i.e., the last several hundred years). In writing about these societies, the present tense is usually used for convenience.

tion. Even in the most favorable environment, such as north central and northern California prior to white settlement, the population density for small localities rarely reaches 10 persons per square mile and, over larger areas, seldom exceeds 3 per square mile. In less favorable environments, such as Australia, much of which is desert, population density drops well below 1 person per square mile.[47]

All communities, then, are small. The largest have only a few hundred people, and these occur only in very favorable environments or in groups that rely on horticulture or fishing to a considerable degree. The Ethnographic Atlas provides information on the size of local communities in 93 of the 151 hunting and gathering societies. Nearly two-thirds have fewer than 50 persons per community, and only two have more than 200.[48]

These two "exceptions" are quite interesting, incidentally, because far from disproving the importance of subsistence technology, they underline it. In both instances, the societies obtain nearly half their food from horticultural activities and fishing.[49] In other words, they almost qualify as more advanced societal types.

The importance of this can be seen when we divide the hunting and gathering category into two subcategories: (1) those societies which obtain 85 per cent or more of their food supply from hunting and gathering and (2) those which obtain only 50 to 85 per cent in this way. As Table 6.3 shows, the purer hunting and gathering communities are smaller, on the average, than those which depend on either fishing or horticulture to any great degree.

Societies, too, are small at this level of technological development. In more than 90 per cent of the groups in the Ethnographic Atlas, the local band or

Table 6.3 Size of hunting and gathering societies classified by percentage of food supply obtained from hunting and gathering

Percentage of Food Supply Obtained from Hunting and Gathering	Percentage of Societies with Average Community Size Less Than 50	Estimated Median Size	Number of Societies
86–100 per cent*	88	29	32
50–85 per cent*	54	48	61

* These figures are not precise measurements, but rather rough estimates made by Murdock and his associates, based on qualitative statements in ethnographic reports.

[47] See Martin Baumhoff, *Ecological Determinants of Aboriginal California Populations,* University of California Publications in American Archaeology and Ethnology, 49 (Berkeley, 1963), especially pp. 227 and 231. See also Elkin, op. cit., and his estimate of an aboriginal population of 300,000 prior to white settlement. Since Australia contains nearly 3 million square miles, this means an average density of only 1 person per 10 square miles. In Alaska, there was only 1 per 25 square miles at the time of its purchase by the United States (Hawkes, p. 183).

[48] Another recent study found an average of 25 members in 53 groups in Africa, India, and Australia. See Joseph Birdsell, "Some Predictions for the Pleistocene Based on Equilibrium Systems among Recent Hunter-Gatherers," in Lee and DeVore, p. 235.

[49] The first of these groups was the Miami Indians; the second, the Carrier Indians.

community is politically autonomous and hence constitutes a separate society. Of the fourteen exceptions, all but one are societies in which horticulture or fishing provides an important secondary source of subsistence.[50]

Nomadism

Modern hunting and gathering societies also tend to be nomadic. Some groups are reported to remain in an area for periods as short as a week.[51] On the other hand, a few communities (approximately 10 per cent in Murdock's sample) occupy permanent settlements. Again, all of these either rely on fishing or horticulture as important secondary sources of subsistence or are located in unusually favorable environments.[52]

The nomadic character of most hunting and gathering communities is an inevitable result of their subsistence technology. One anthropologist described the basic problem when he said of a group of African Pygmies that "after about a month, as a rule, the fruits of the forest have been gathered all around the vicinity of the camp, and the game has been scared away to a greater distance than is comfortable for daily hunting."[53] He went on to say that since "the economy relies on day-to-day quest, the simplest thing is for the camp to move." Except for variations in the frequency of moves, this description fits most hunting and gathering peoples.

Despite their nomadism, hunters and gatherers usually restrict their movements to well-defined territories. When the food supply in one area is depleted, they move to another, frequently settling in or near some former camp site. There may even be a regular circuit of sites that the group uses year after year. Moves are frequently stimulated by seasonal changes that reduce the supply of food in one section of a territory while increasing it in another—as with areas at different altitudes or with different ground covers.

---

[50] The one exception was the Chamacoco, a South American Indian group that lived in an area of almost constant warfare and slave raiding following Spanish settlement. This is probably the explanation for this group's "abnormal" organization, since warfare sometimes causes groups at this level of development to establish temporary alliances with neighboring communities, and continuous warfare might well lead to a more permanent relationship. For other instances of temporary alliances during wars, see I. Schapera, *The Khoisan Peoples of South Africa* (London: Routledge, 1930), p. 156, or Antonio Serrano, "The Charrua," in Julian Steward (ed.), *Handbook of South American Indians,* Smithsonian Institution, Bureau of American Ethnology, Bulletin 143 (Washington, D.C., 1946), vol. 1, p. 194.

[51] See, for example, John Garvan, *The Negritos of the Philippines* (Vienna: Ferdinand Berger, 1964), p. 27, or Edwin Loeb, *Sumatra: Its History and People* (Vienna: Institut für Volkerkunde, 1935), p. 283, on the Kubu.

[52] Only one of the 15 nonnomadic hunting and gathering societies in Murdock's sample depended on hunting and gathering for as much as three-quarters of its subsistence, whereas more than half of the 136 nomadic hunting and gathering societies were in this category. The one exception among the nonnomadic societies (the Nomlaki) was located in the Sacramento Valley of northern California, a territory as favorable for a hunting and gathering people as any in the world (see Baumhoff, pp. 205–231).

[53] Colin Turnbull, "The Mbuti Pygmies of the Congo," in James Gibbs (ed.), *Peoples of Africa* (New York: Holt, 1965), pp. 286–287.

Groups are generally deterred from entering new territories because of their unfamiliarity with them and their resources, and sometimes by fear of hostile neighbors. More than that, there is often a rather general fear of the unknown in these groups, which serves to accentuate the sacred or semisacred character their own territories have acquired through song and legend.[54] Thus, when a hunting and gathering band moves into new territory, it usually moves from necessity, not choice.

Economic Conditions

Given the combination of a primitive technology and a nomadic way of life, it is impossible for most hunting and gathering peoples to accumulate many possessions (see Figures 6.12 and 6.13). In describing the Negritos of the Philip-

Figure 6.12 Home and possessions of Paiute hunter in southern Utah in the 1870s.

---

[54] See, for example, Elkin, pp. 37–39.

Figure 6.13 Home and possessions of a Bushman family, Southwest Africa. See also Figure 4.2.

Figure 6.14 The quest for food is an important activity in every hunting and gathering society: Bushman boys gathering nuts.

pines, one observer reports that "the possessions of a whole settlement would not be a good load for a sturdy carrier."[55] A student of the Siriono of Bolivia reports that "apart from the hammocks they sleep in and the weapons and tools they hunt and gather with, they rarely carry anything with them."[56] As he explains, "being seminomadic, they do not burden themselves with material objects that might hamper mobility." The few other things they use can quickly be made from materials that are readily available throughout the area. The situation is virtually the same among the Bushmen of southwestern Africa. "It is not advantageous to multiply and accumulate in this society. Any man can make what he needs when he wants to. Most of the materials he uses are abundant and free for anyone to take. Furthermore, in their nomadic lives, without beasts of burden, the fact that the people themselves must carry everything puts a sharp limit on the quantity of objects they want to possess."[57] The few hunting and gathering groups that have been able to establish permanent settlements may accumulate more possessions, but even they are greatly limited by their primitive technology.[58]

The quest for food is an important activity in every hunting and gathering society. Since most of these societies have no way to store food for extended periods, the food quest is fairly continuous. Moreover, unlike our situation, every member of the group must participate and make his own contribution.

Until recently, most studies of hunting and gathering societies emphasized the uncertainty of the food supply and the difficulty of obtaining it.[59] Newer studies, however, often paint a brighter picture. Reports from the Pygmies of the Congo, the aborigines of Australia, the Tasadays of the Philippines, and even the Bushmen of the Kalahari Desert in southwestern Africa indicate that an ample supply of food can be secured without undue expenditure of time or energy.[60] This has led some anthropologists to swing to the other ex-

---

[55] Garvan, p. 29.

[56] Allan Holmberg, *Nomads of the Long Bow: The Siriono of Eastern Bolivia,* Smithsonian Institution, Institute of Social Anthropology, 10 (Washington, D.C., 1950), p. 11. See also Loeb, p. 300, who writes of the Orang Benua of Sumatra that "they carried all their possessions in a bamboo a foot long. These possessions consisted of blow-gun darts, a piece of poisoned wood on which they rubbed them, wood for making a fire [tinder?] and perhaps a small knife."

[57] Lorna Marshall, "The !Kung Bushmen of the Kalahari Desert," in Gibbs, pp. 257–258. Quoted by permission of Holt, Rinehart and Winston, Inc. See also Charles Hose and William McDougall, *The Pagan Tribes of Borneo* (London: Macmillan, 1912), pp. 190–191, on the Punan.

[58] See, for example, Walter Goldschmidt, *Nomlaki Ethnography,* University of California Publications in American Archaeology and Ethnology, 42 (Berkeley, 1951), pp. 333–335 and 417–428.

[59] See, for example, Loeb, p. 294, or Holmberg, pp. 30 and 91.

[60] Turnbull, pp. 287 and 297; Frederick McCarthy and Margaret McArthur, "The Food Quest and the Time Factor in Aboriginal Economic Life," in Charles Mountford (ed.), *Records of the American-Australian Expedition to Arnhem Land* (Melbourne: Melbourne University Press, 1960), pp. 190–191; Kenneth MacLeish, "The Tasadays: Stone Age Cavemen of Mandanao," *National Geographic,* 142 (August 1972), pp. 243–245; Richard B. Lee, "What Hunters Do for a Living, or How to Make Out on Scarce Resources," in Lee and DeVore, pp. 36–37.

treme and refer to hunters and gatherers as "the most leisured people in the world" and to their way of life as "the original affluent society."[61]

Neither extreme does justice to the diversity and changeability of the situations reported by the numerous observers who have lived among these peoples. Conditions vary considerably from group to group, and within a group they may vary from season to season. For example, the Indians of northern California usually had an abundance of food, but occasionally they encountered a shortage so severe that some of them starved.[62]

A very few societies, such as the recently discovered Tasadays, do not practice hunting. For the rest, hunting usually provides less food, in terms of bulk, than gathering. Yet hunting is valued more highly in virtually every one of these groups. There are several reasons for this. To begin with, meat is generally preferred to vegetables.[63] Whether this reflects a genetically based need, we do not know; certainly all individuals do not share this preference. In some groups, preference for meat may simply reflect its scarcity. Hunting also may be valued so highly because it provides excitement and challenge and an opportunity for the individual to excel. Added to all this is the fact that meat, unlike vegetables, is commonly shared beyond the immediate family, so success in hunting may be rewarded by widespread respect and deference. One leading anthropologist even suggests that sharing meat "is basic to the continued association of families in any human group that hunts."[64]

Because of the primitive nature of the technology, the division of labor in hunting and gathering societies is largely limited to distinctions based on age and sex. In these societies, as in all others to date, there are basic differences between men's and women's work. Hunting and military activity fall to the male, as do most political, religious, ceremonial, and artistic activities. The collection and preparation of vegetables and the care of children are women's responsibilities.[65] Some activities, such as constructing a shelter, may be defined as either men's or women's work, depending on the society.[66] Still other activities may be considered appropriate for members of both sexes. Table 6.4 shows the division of labor between the sexes in one society. Though some of

[61] See Service, p. 13, and Marshall Sahlins, "Notes on the Original Affluent Society," in Lee and DeVore, pp. 85–89.

[62] Goldschmidt, p. 417. See also Asen Balicki, "The Netsilik Eskimos: Adaptive Responses," and the comments of Lorna Marshall and Colin Turnbull, in Lee and DeVore, pp. 78–82, 94, and 341, for challenges to the recent effort to portray life in hunting and gathering societies as idyllic and trouble-free.

[63] See, for example, Lee, p. 40.

[64] Coon, *The Hunting Peoples*, p. 176.

[65] In the sample of hunting and gathering societies in the Ethnographic Atlas, hunting was entirely a male activity in 97 per cent of the cases and predominantly a male activity in the rest. On the other hand, gathering was wholly or largely a female activity in 91 per cent of the societies and predominantly a male activity in only 2 per cent (in the remainder the activity was shared by both sexes).

[66] Of the hunting and gathering societies in the Ethnographic Atlas, 57 per cent defined this as a male responsibility, 25 per cent as a female, and 18 per cent regarded it as appropriate to both sexes.

Figure 6.15 Bushman hunter, Southwest Africa.

the details are peculiar to this group, the overall pattern is fairly typical. Division of labor along age lines is also inevitable, since both the very young and the aged are limited in their capabilities.

In hunting and gathering societies there are no full-time occupational specialties, though some part-time specialization is usual. For example, most groups have at least a headman and a shaman or medicine man. When their services are required, they function in these specialized capacities, but, as one writer says of the headmen of the Bergdama and the Bushmen, "when not engaged on public business they follow the same occupations as all other people."[67] He adds that this is most of the time. Other specialists, much less common, may include part-time workers in certain arts and crafts and occasionally an assistant to the headman. Such individuals are most likely to be found in settled communities that depend less on hunting and gathering or in those with especially favorable environments.[68]

---

[67] I. Schapera, *Government and Politics in Tribal Societies* (London: Watts, 1956), p. 93. See also Holmberg's description of the Siriono headman or chief quoted on p. 176, and Hose and McDougall, op. cit., p. 190, on the Punan shaman.

[68] See, for example, Goldschmidt, pp. 331–332, and Elkin, pp. 254ff.

Within hunting and gathering groups, the family (either nuclear or extended[69]) is normally the only significant form of economic organization. Sometimes, when the practice of sharing is widespread and hunting and gathering are carried on as communal activities, even the family group ceases to be economically important.

With respect to subsistence, each local band is virtually self-sufficient. Some trade does occur, but except where contacts have been established with more advanced societies, the bartered items tend to be nonessentials, primarily objects with a status or aesthetic value. Trade between two hunting and gathering communities usually involves things that are scarce or nonexistent in one group's territory but fairly abundant in the other's (e.g., certain kinds of shells, stones, feathers, etc.).

Trade with advanced societies is more likely to involve essential items. For example, many groups obtain metal tools and weapons this way.[70] In the

Table 6.4   Division of labor between the sexes in Siriono society

Activity	Normally Male	Normally Female	Both Sexes
Hunting	x		
Fishing	x		
Extracting honey	x		
Weapon making	x		
Tool-making	x		
House building	x		
Preparing utensils	x		
Cooking		x	
Caring for children		x	
Twining string		x	
Twining hammocks		x	
Carrying water		x	
Collecting firewood		x	
Pot making		x	
Weaving		x	
Preparing feather ornaments		x	
Stringing necklaces		x	
Collecting			x
Dressing game			x
Burden carrying			x

Source: Adapted from Allan Holmberg *Nomads of the Long Bow: The Siriono of Eastern Bolivia*, Smithsonian Institute of Social Anthropology, 10 (Washington, D.C., 1950), table 2, p. 41.

---

[69] See p. 143 below for a discussion of the extended family.

[70] See, for example, Turnbull, pp. 287–288; Ivor Evans, *The Negritos of Malaya* (London: Cambridge, 1937), pp. 57 and 112–113; Garvan, p. 66; or Hose and McDougall, p. 191. Turnbull warns, however, that many scholars exaggerate the dependence of the Pygmies on the neighboring horticultural villagers. He maintains that they turn to the villagers only for luxuries and diversion. See *Wayward Servants: The Two Worlds of the African Pygmies* (Garden City, N.Y.: Natural History Press, 1965), pp. 33–37.

past, these imports were seldom important enough to alter seriously the basic character of these societies.[71] In recent years, however, as contacts with industrialized and industrializing societies have increased, the volume and importance of the imports have transformed most hunting and gathering groups into hybrid types.

Kinship and Marriage

Ties of kinship are vitally important in most hunting and gathering groups. It is hard for members of modern industrial societies to appreciate the tremendous significance of these ties among simpler peoples, since so much of our own social interaction is organized in terms of *non*kinship roles (as in relations between lawyer and client, teacher and student, or clerk and customer). But the fact is that people are deeply affected by the roles they occupy; roles even help shape self-images.

By contrast, social interaction in hunting and gathering societies is usually organized around kinship roles, and self-images are formed by involvement in them. One student of the Australian aborigines reports that "in a typical Australian tribe it is found that a man can define his relations to every person with whom he has any social dealings whatever, whether of his own or of another tribe, by means of the terms of relationship."[72] Another writer goes so far as to say of these people that "every one with whom a person comes in contact is regarded as related to him, and the kind of relationship *must be* ascertained so that the two persons concerned will know what their mutual behavior should be."[73] He adds that kinship ties are the anatomy and physiology of aboriginal society and "must be understood if the behavior of the aborigines as social beings is to be understood." Though there are exceptions to this, *kinship is usually the central organizing principle in hunting and gathering societies.*[74]

Viewed in evolutionary perspective, the family has often been described as the matrix, or womb, from which all the other more complex and more specialized forms of social structure have evolved. Although this may be an exaggeration, it points to a basic truth: in hunting and gathering societies, kin groups perform many of the functions that are performed by schools, business firms, governmental agencies, and other specialized organizations in larger, more advanced, and more differentiated societies.

Kin groups in hunting and gathering societies are of two types, nuclear and extended families. A nuclear family includes a man, his wife or wives, and

---

[71] The introduction of the horse and the gun among the Plains Indians of this country was an important exception to the usual pattern.

[72] A. R. Radcliffe-Brown, "The Social Organization of Australian Tribes," *Oceania*, 1 (1930), pp. 44–45.

[73] Elkin, p. 56 (Doubleday Anchor ed.); emphasis added.

[74] Service, *The Hunters*, pp. 32ff. For some exceptions, see Turnbull, *Wayward Servants*, pp. 109–112.

their unmarried children. Polygyny is widespread; only 12 per cent of the hunting and gathering groups in Murdock's Ethnographic Atlas are classified as monogamous. It does not follow, of course, that 88 per cent of *families* are polygynous: this would be impossible given the roughly equal numbers of men and women. Usually only one or two of the most influential men have more than one wife, and they seldom have more than two or three. This limited polygyny is possible because girls usually marry earlier than boys, and some men are forced to remain bachelors. Multiple wives appear to be an economic asset in these societies and, to some extent, a status symbol as well.

Divorce is permitted in virtually all hunting and gathering societies and is fairly common in some.[75] In others, however, it is made relatively difficult.[76] The most we can say is that there is great variability in this matter.

The nuclear family is usually part of a larger, more inclusive, and more important kin group known as the extended family.[77] The extended family typically includes a group of brothers and their families or a father and his married sons with their families; in any event, it is usually organized around kinship ties among *males.* This practice probably reflects the peculiar requirements of hunting.[78] Successful hunting often calls for extremely close cooperation—cooperation that presupposes years of close association in the activity and enables every individual to anticipate the moves of every other. Gathering has no such requirement. Since plants are stationary, no cooperation is required; if women go foodgathering in groups, it is largely for companionship. Furthermore, since animals, unlike plants, move about, hunters must have an intimate knowledge of the local environment. This kind of familiarity is acquired from early childhood on, and it is not readily transferable from one locale to another. Finally, the practice of keeping married sons within the family probably reflects, to some extent, simple male dominance and male preference.

The extended family is also important economically, for the ties of kinship among its members encourage the practice of sharing. When the daily acquisition of food is as uncertain as it is in many hunting and gathering societies, a nuclear family could easily starve if it had to depend exclusively on its own efforts. A family might be surfeited with food for a time and then suddenly have nothing. Or all the adult members of the family could be ill or injured at the same time. In either case the family would be dependent on the generosity of others. Although sharing can, and does, take place between unrelated persons, kinship ties reinforce the tendency. In this connection, it is

---

[75] See, for example, Elkin, p. 50; Evans, p. 254.

[76] See, for example, Garvan, p. 82.

[77] Service, p. 42.

[78] Coon, *The Hunting Peoples,* p. 192; Laughlin, "Hunting," pp. 318–320; Julian Steward, "Causal Factors and Processes in the Evolution of Pre-farming Societies," in Lee and DeVore, pp. 332–333; and Elman Service, *Primitive Social Organization: An Evolutionary Perspective* (New York: Random House, 1962), chap. 3, especially p. 61.

noteworthy that many hunting and gathering peoples create what we would call fictional ties of kinship when there is no "real" relationship by blood or marriage. These ties are just as meaningful to them as "true" kinship ties and serve to tighten bonds within the group.

By marrying outside the local group (a practice known as exogamy), a society gradually establishes a web of kinship ties with neighboring groups. According to one anthropologist, "One of the important functions of exogamy is that of opening territories so that peaceful movements can take place among them, and particularly so that any large temporary variations in food resources can be taken advantage of by related groups."[79] Akin to this is the custom of wife lending, practiced by hunting and gathering peoples as diverse as the Eskimo and the Australian aborigines.[80] As in the case of exogamy, the purpose seems to be to strengthen, restore, or create bonds between the men involved. Thus, if two individuals or two groups have had a quarrel, they may settle it by lending one another their wives. The practice is predicated on the assumption that women are prized possessions that one does not share with everyone. It would be a mistake to suppose, however, that women are merely property in these societies; they often have considerable influence in the life of the group and are far removed from the position of chattels.

Political Patterns

Politically, modern hunting and gathering societies are extremely primitive. As we have seen, most local communities are autonomous and independent entities even though they have an average population of less than fifty, including babes in arms. The primitive nature of their political systems is also evidenced by the limited development of specialized political roles and the very limited authority vested in them. The most common pattern is for a single headman to provide minimal leadership for the group.[81] The late Allan Holmberg, an anthropologist who lived among the Siriono of eastern Bolivia, wrote a description of their headmen that is close to being a portrait of the "typical" headman in a hunting and gathering society.

> Presiding over every band of Siriono is a headman, who is at least nominally the highest official of the group. Although his authority theoretically extends throughout the band, in actual practice its exercise depends almost entirely upon his personal qualities as a leader. In any case, there is no obligation to obey the orders of a headman, no punishment for nonfulfillment. Indeed, little

[79] Service, *Primitive Social Organization,* p. 49.

[80] See, for example, Elkin, pp. 134–137.

[81] Occasionally there might be a second official. See, for example, Kaj Birket-Smith, *The Eskimos,* rev. ed. (London: Methuen, 1959), p. 145; Goldschmidt, pp. 324–325; and Frank Speck, *Penobscot Man* (Philadelphia: University of Pennsylvania Press, 1940), pp. 239–240.

attention is paid to what is said by a headman unless he is a member of one's immediate family. To maintain his prestige a headman must fulfill, in a superior fashion, those obligations required of everyone else.

The prerogatives of a headman are few. . . . The principal privilege . . . if it could be called such, is that it is his right to occupy, with his immediate family, the center of the [communal] house. Like any other man he must make his bows and arrows, his tools; he must hunt, fish, collect, and plant gardens. He makes suggestions as to migrations, hunting trips, etc., but these are not always followed by his [people]. As a mark of status, however, a headman always possesses more than one wife.

While headmen complain a great deal that other members of the band do not satisfy their obligations to them, little heed is paid to their requests. . . .

In general, however, headmen fare better than other members of the band. Their requests more frequently bear fruit than those of others because headmen are the best hunters and are thus in a better position than most to reciprocate for any favors done them.[82]

There are similar reports on most other hunting and gathering societies.[83] In a number of instances it is said that the headman "held his place only so long as he gave satisfaction."

Occasionally the headman enjoys a bit more power and privilege. For example, among the Arunta of Australia the headman "has, *ex officio,* a position which, if he be a man of personal ability, but only in that case, enables him to wield considerable power. . . ."[84] Among the Bergdama of southwestern Africa, the headman "is treated with universal respect, being specified as a 'great man' by adults and 'grandfather' by children; he usually has the most wives (sometimes three or more); he has the pick of all wild animal skins for clothing himself and his family, and only his wives wear necklaces or girdles of ostrich eggshell beads; and he receives portions of all game killed in the chase, and tribute from men finding honey."[85]

At the opposite extreme are a number of groups that do not even have a headman. This is true of 12 per cent of the hunting and gathering societies in the Ethnographic Atlas sample. In such cases, decisions that affect the entire

---

[82] Holmberg, pp. 59–60. Quoted by permission of the Smithsonian Institution Press. Following an older usage, Holmberg refers to the leaders of Siriono bands as "chiefs." In current usage, such persons are usually referred to as "headmen," and the term "chief" is reserved for the leaders of tribes or other multicommunity societies. For this reason, the term "headman" has been substituted.

[83] See, for example, John Cooper, "The Ona," in Steward, *Handbook,* vol. 1, p. 117; A. R. Radcliffe-Brown, *The Andaman Islanders* (Glencoe, Ill.: Free Press, 1948), p. 47; Hose and McDougall, p. 182, on the Punan of Borneo; Speck, p. 239, on the Penobscot of Maine; Schapera, *The Khoisan Peoples,* p. 151, and Roland Dixon, "The Northern Maidu," in Carleton S. Coon (ed.), *A Reader in General Anthropology* (New York: Holt, 1948), p. 272.

[84] Baldwin Spencer and F. J. Gillen, *The Arunta: A Study of a Stone Age People* (London: Macmillan, 1927), vol. 1, p. 10.

[85] Schapera, *Government and Politics,* p. 117. Quoted by permission of C. A. Watts & Co., Ltd. See also A. H. Gayton, *Yokuts-Mono Chiefs and Shamans,* University of California Publications in American Archaeology and Ethnology, 24 (Berkeley, 1930), pp. 374–376.

group are arrived at through informal discussions among the more respected and influential members, typically the heads of families.[86]

The limited development of political institutions in hunting and gathering societies stands in sharp contrast to the situation in more advanced societies (see Table 6.5). It stems from the primitive nature of the groups' subsistence technology and their resultant small size and relative isolation, which make it possible for them to handle their political problems very informally: consensus is achieved much more readily in a small, homogeneous group of a few dozen people (of whom only the adults, and often only the adult males, have a voice) than in a larger, more heterogeneous community of hundreds or thousands. A headman is valuable to a small group only if he contributes special knowledge, insight, or skills. This is why we so often read in ethnographic reports that the headman of a hunting and gathering band "held his place only so long as he gave satisfaction" and that his influence "depends almost entirely upon his personal qualities as a leader."

Even if the leader of a hunting and gathering band were ambitious and eager to increase his power, the technology of his society would prevent him from getting far. Unlike leaders in more advanced societies, he would find it impossible to build and maintain an organization of dependent retainers to do his bidding, or to obtain a monopoly of the more powerful weapons. Except for the physically handicapped, every man is able to provide for his own material needs. The materials for making weapons lie ready at hand, and every man is trained to make and use them. If worse comes to worst, a man can usually leave the band he is in and join another.[87] Thus, there are no opportunities for building political empires, even on a small scale.[88]

Given the rudimentary nature of political institutions in hunting and gathering societies, one might suppose that there are few restrictions on an

Table 6.5 Degree of power of political leaders, by societal type

Societal type	Degree of power (in percentages)			No. of Societies
	Substantial	Moderate	Slight	
Hunting and gathering	9	18	73	11
Horticultural	50	33	17	24
Herding	88	13	0	8

Source: Derived from data in Leo Simmons, *The Role of the Aged in Primitive Society* (New Haven, Conn.: Yale, 1945).

[86] See, for example, Colin Turnbull, *Wayward Servants*, chaps. 11 and 12, or *The Forest People* (New York: Simon & Schuster, 1961), on the Mbuti Pygmies. As he indicates, the office of headman is sometimes found among these people, but it has been more or less forced on them by the Bantu villagers and is of little significance except in their contacts with these villagers.

[87] See, for example, Schapera, *Government and Politics*, p. 193, or Turnbull, *Wayward Servants*, pp. 100–109.

[88] The limiting effects of a hunting and gathering technology will become clearer in subsequent chapters, as we observe the growth of political systems in horticultural and agrarian societies.

individual. In one sense this is true; there are few imposed by political authorities — no courts, no police, no prisons. The individual is hardly free, however, to do as he wishes. To begin with, his freedom is limited by the nature of his society's technology. Compared with members of more advanced societies, hunters and gatherers are very restricted in where they can go and what they can do.

But there are also social restraints. No human society can afford to be indifferent to the actions of its members, and even in the absence of formal political authority, the group controls human conduct. Though there are minor variations from one hunting and gathering society to another, we see the same basic pattern of social control in groups as far apart as the Kaska Indians of the Canadian Northwest, the Andaman Islanders of Southeast Asia, the Bushmen of Southwest Africa, and the Punan of Borneo.[89] In each of these groups there are three basic types of social restraints. First, there is blood revenge, whereby the injured person, aided, perhaps, by his kinsmen, punishes the offender himself. As one student of the Bushmen put it, "when disputes arise between the members of the band . . . there is no appeal to any supreme authority, [since] . . . there is no such authority. . . . The only remedy is self-help."[90] Usually this mode of social control is invoked only when the victim of the offense is a single individual or a family. When an entire band suffers because of the actions of a member, the method of control is group pressure. For example, if a man refuses to do his fair share in providing food, he is punished by losing the respect of others.[91] In the case of more serious offenses, the penalty may be ostracism or even banishment. The third method of control applies primarily to violations of ritual proscriptions. In such cases, the group believes that spontaneous supernatural sanctions operate, and fear of them is usually an effective deterrent. For example, the Andaman Islanders believe that killing a cicada causes bad weather, and the Bushmen believe that girls who do not observe the restrictions imposed on them at puberty change into frogs.[92] All three methods are very informal and thus are feasible only in a small group with intimate and continuous contact among its members.

Equality and Inequality

The rudimentary nature of the political system and the primitive nature of the technological system contribute to yet another distinctive characteristic of

---

[89] See John Honigmann, *The Kaska Indians: An Ethnographic Reconstruction,* Yale University Publications in Anthropology, 51 (1954), pp. 90–92 and 96–97; Radcliffe-Brown, *The Andaman Islanders,* pp. 48–52; Schapera, *The Khoisan Peoples,* pp. 151–155; and Hose and McDougall, p. 182.

[90] Schapera, *The Khoisan Peoples,* p. 152.

[91] Radcliffe-Brown, *The Andaman Islanders,* p. 50.

[92] Ibid., p. 51, and Schapera, *The Khoisan Peoples,* p. 152.

modern hunting and gathering societies: minimal inequality in power and privilege. Differences between individuals are so slight, in fact, that a number of observers have spoken of a kind of "primitive communism." To some extent this is justified. As we have seen, political authority with the power to coerce is virtually nonexistent. Differences in *influence* exist, but only to the degree permitted by those who are influenced and only as a result of their respect for another individual's skills or wisdom. Should he lose this respect, he also loses his influence.

The chief exceptions to the near equality in wealth and economic privilege occur among the handful of nonnomadic groups, where some modest inequalities are reported.[93] In most societies, differences in wealth are very minor. Many factors are responsible for this. For one thing, the nomadic way of life prevents any substantial accumulation of possessions. Moreover, the ready availability of most essential resources (e.g., wood for bows, flint for stone tools, etc.) precludes the need to amass things, while technological limitations greatly restrict the variety of things that can be produced. The absence of any coercive political authority is also a factor. Finally, there is the widespread practice of reciprocity, or sharing, in most of these groups.

As a general rule, the concept of private property has only limited development among hunting and gathering peoples. Things that an individual uses constantly, such as his tools and weapons, are always recognized as his, but fields and forests are the common property of the band (see Table 6.6). The territorial rights of bands, however, are often taken quite seriously, and outsiders are frequently obliged to ask permission to enter another group's territory to seek food.[94] Animals and plants are normally considered the common property of the band until they are killed or gathered, when they become the property of the individual. Even then, his use of them is hedged about by the rule of sharing.[95]

Table 6.6 Frequency of private ownership of land, by societal type

Societal type	Frequency of Private Ownership of Land (in percentages)				No. of Societies
	General	Frequent	Rare	Absent	
Hunting and gathering	0	0	11	89	9
Horticultural	36	23	23	18	22

Source: Derived from data in Leo Simmons, *The Role of the Aged in Primitive Society* (New Haven, Conn.: Yale, 1945).

[93] See, for example, Goldschmidt, pp. 330–341.

[94] See, for example, Evans, p. 21; Marshall, "!Kung Bushmen," p. 248; or Radcliffe-Brown, p. 29. For an exception, see Birket-Smith, pp. 145–146. For intermediate cases, see Honigmann, pp. 84, 88, and 96; Elkin, p. 45; and H. Ling Roth, *The Aborigines of Tasmania* (London: Kegan Paul, Trench, Trubner, 1890), p. 71.

[95] Sometimes certain trees become the private property of an individual who stakes a special claim to them, but this is uncommon and the number of trees involved is generally small. See, for example, Radcliffe-Brown, *The Andaman Islanders*, p. 41, or Goldschmidt, p. 333.

A successful hunter does not normally keep his kill for himself alone or even, in most cases, for his family.[96] The reason for this is the same as that which underlies the popularity of insurance in industrial societies: *it is an effective method of spreading risks.* As we have seen, poor hunting conditions, ill health, or just a streak of bad luck can render any individual or family incapable of providing for itself, and sharing food greatly enhances the entire group's chances of survival. Most of the societies that failed to develop this practice have probably been eliminated.

Despite the near equality of power and wealth, there is inequality in prestige in most hunting and gathering societies. The interesting thing about this, from the viewpoint of a member of an industrial society, is the extent to which prestige depends on the *personal* qualities of an individual rather than on such impersonal criteria as the offices or roles he occupies or the possessions he controls. This is, of course, a natural consequence of the limited development of specialized offices and roles and the limited opportunities for the accumulation of possessions and wealth. But it sharply differentiates these societies from our own.

Writing of the Andaman Islanders, A. R. Radcliffe-Brown reports that they accord honor and respect to three kinds of people: (1) older people, (2) people endowed with supernatural powers, and (3) people with certain personal qualities, notably "skill in hunting and warfare, generosity and kindness, and freedom from bad temper."[97] Though he does not say so explicitly, men are apparently more likely than women to become honored members of the group. For the most part, these same criteria are employed by other hunting and gathering peoples, with skill in oratory often honored as well.[98]

Because personal criteria are so important, the systems of stratification in these groups have an openness about them not found in more advanced societies. Almost no organizational or institutional barriers block the rise of talented individuals. For example, even where the office of headman is inherited, as it is in approximately half the societies,[99] others can surpass him in achieving honor, and he himself may fail to win even a modicum of it. The study of the Siriono Indians, quoted earlier, reports the case of such a headman, an individual who was a very poor hunter and whose status, as a result, was low. The importance attached to age also contributes to the openness of the system. Almost any individual who survives long enough is likely to attain a fair degree of honor and respect.

---

[96] See, for example, McCarthy and McArthur, "Aboriginal Economic Life," pp. 179–180; Schapera, *The Khoisan Peoples,* pp. 100–101; Radcliffe-Brown, *The Andaman Islanders,* p. 43; Hose and McDougall, p. 187; or Speck, p. 47.

[97] Radcliffe-Brown, *The Andaman Islanders,* pp. 44–48.

[98] See, for example, Goldschmidt, pp. 324–326.

[99] Among the sample of hunting and gathering societies in the Ethnographic Atlas, 54 per cent had provision for the hereditary transmission of the office, usually to a son of the previous headman.

Tribal Ties

As we have noted a number of times, local hunting and gathering bands are usually autonomous. Rarely are two or more communities brought under a single leader, and when it happens, it usually involves groups no longer completely dependent on hunting and gathering.

Despite the absence of formal organizations beyond the local level, there are frequently *informal* structures. The most inclusive of these, and the most nearly universal as well, is the tribe—a group of people who speak a distinctive language or dialect, possess a common culture that distinguishes them from other peoples, and know themselves, or are known, by a definite name.[100] Unlike a society, a tribe is not necessarily organized politically. On the contrary, few are, at least among hunting and gathering peoples.

Though there is no direct evidence, most tribes appear to have been formed by the process of societal fission. When the population of a hunting and gathering band grows too large for the resources of the immediate area, it splits into two groups. Division may also occur because of conflict within a band.[101] In either case, although a new group is formed, its members continue to share the language and culture of the parent group. Normally the new group locates somewhere near the old one, if for no other reason than because their technology and accumulated experience become less relevant the further they move and the more the environment differs from the one they have been used to. As this process of fission occurs, a cluster of autonomous bands with the same language and a similar culture will emerge, forming a new tribe.

As this suggests, among hunters and gatherers the tribe is more important as a cultural unit than as a social unit. One writer, describing the Bushmen, reports that the tribe "has no social solidarity, and is of very little, if any, importance in regulating social life. There appears to be no tribal organization among the Bushmen, nothing in the nature of a central authority whose decisions are binding on all the members of the tribe, nor is collective action ever taken in the interests of the tribe as a whole. The tribe in fact is merely a loose aggregate of hunting bands which have a common language and name."[102] This description applies to most tribes of hunters and gatherers. Occasionally, as in Australia, an entire tribe comes together for some important event, but this is not typical.

From the structural standpoint, the chief significance of these tribal groupings lies in their evolutionary potential: with technological advance, they may become political units. Even among societies still on the hunting and gathering level, there is some evidence of movement in this direction. In a few of the

---

[100] This definition is based on Hoebel, *Anthropology*, p. 572, and Elkin, *The Australian Aborigines*, p. 25.

[101] Examples are provided by the Punan of Borneo (Hose and McDougall, p. 183) or the Mbuti Pygmies of Africa (Turnbull, *Wayward Servants*, pp. 100–109).

[102] Schapera, *The Khoisan Peoples*, p. 76. Quoted by permission of Routledge & Kegan Paul, Ltd.

more favorably situated sedentary groups, for example, several villages have been brought together under the leadership of a single individual.[103] This step was undoubtedly facilitated by the common cultural heritage of the groups involved.

Religion

Few facets of primitive life have received as much attention in the last hundred years as religion. Yet, paradoxically, there are few areas where our understanding is less satisfactory. One reason is that too many writers have twisted the facts to fit their preconceived theories.[104] As a result, we have many very plausible but mutually contradictory theories and a minimum of systematic analysis.

Another difficulty is the great diversity of beliefs and practices among hunting and gathering peoples. Primitive technological systems restrict men's freedom less in the realm of religious ideas than in most other areas.[105]

At a minimum, however, we can say that religion in some form has been found in every carefully studied hunting and gathering society of the modern era. In every group there is evidence that people have grappled with the problems of ultimate causation and meaning.[106] In myths and legends, they have developed explanations for most of the recurring features of life. Most of these peoples believe the world is populated with countless unseen spirits that influence the course of events in the world around them.[107] These spirits can be responsible for the success or failure of the hunt, for unexpected deaths or accidents, for illness, for births, or for unexpected good fortune. Many, perhaps most, of these spirits reside in material objects such as plants, animals, rocks, or other natural phenomena (a belief known as animism).

Although these beliefs may appear crude and unscientific, scholars who have studied them carefully have shown that sometimes they embody

---

[103] See, for example, Goldschmidt, p. 324.

[104] For a more detailed discussion of this point as it applies to the religion of the Australian aborigines, see W. E. H. Stanner, "Religion, Totemism and Symbolism," in Berndt and Berndt, pp. 207–237.

[105] In part, the diversity of religious beliefs and practices is the result of cultural diffusion from more advanced societies. Apparently the diffusion of religious ideas occurs more easily than other types of diffusion (e.g., the diffusion of complex structural systems). See, for example, Loeb's comments on the religious ideas of various hunting and gathering peoples on Sumatra (*Sumatra*, pp. 216–217, 286–289, etc.). See also Hose and McDougall, p. 186.

[106] See, for example, W. E. H. Stanner's comments on this as it applies to the Australian aborigines, in "The Dreaming," in William Lessa and Evon Vogt (eds.), *Reader in Comparative Religion*, 2d ed. (New York: Harper & Row, 1965), p. 162. See also Evans, chaps. 14–18 and 24; Garvan, chap. 14; Turnbull, *The Forest People;* and others.

[107] William D. Davis, *Societal Complexity and the Sources of Primitive Man's Conception of the Supernatural* (unpublished Ph. D. dissertation, University of North Carolina, Chapel Hill, 1971), chap. 5. Davis reports such beliefs in all but one of the eleven hunting and gathering societies he studied.

profound insights and moving sentiments.[108] In particular, these religions proclaim that the world is far more complex and mysterious than it appears on the surface—a belief shared not only by the major world religions but by modern science as well.

Religious differentiation within a hunting and gathering society is minimal, religious conflict negligible. There are none of the sectarian differences found in more advanced societies, except those introduced by missionary efforts or other contacts with advanced societies. This does not mean that the members of a society have identical beliefs and practices. Rather, whatever differences exist are considered either complementary in nature or unimportant.[109]

Figure 6.16 Bushman shaman in trance.

[108] See especially Stanner, "Religion, Totemism and Symbolism," pp. 215–216, or "The Dreaming," p. 159, and the Australian aboriginal concept of "the eternal dream time," which Stanner suggests may best be translated as "everywhen." See also Turnbull, *The Forest People,* especially chaps. 4 and 8.

[109] The religious distinctions between men and women among the Australian aborigines are a good example of complementary differences (see Elkin, chap. 7).

Figure 6.17 A Siberian shaman of the eighteenth century, as seen by a Dutch traveler. Note the antler headdress and compare with "the sorcerer," Figure 6.11.

The one really important religious distinction in most hunting and gathering societies is the role of shaman or medicine man. The shaman is an individual who is believed to have special powers as a result of his distinctive relationship with the spirit world. He uses these powers in various ways, but one of the most common is healing.[110] He may also use them to ensure the success of hunting expeditions, to protect the group against evil spirits and other threats, and generally to ensure the group's well-being. Shamans do not always use their special power for the benefit of others, however. They may employ it to punish people who have offended them.[111]

Because of their role, shamans usually command respect and often are more influential than the headmen.[112] Sometimes, as with the Northern Maidu in California, the headman "was chosen largely through the aid of the shaman, who was supposed to reveal to the old men the choice of the spirits."[113] The role of shaman tends to be profitable, since others are usually happy to offer gifts in exchange for help or to maintain goodwill. One early observer of the Indians of Lower California wrote that successful shamans were able "to obtain their food without the trouble of gathering it . . . for the silly people provided them with the best they could find, in order to keep them in good humor and to

---

[110] See Service, *The Hunters,* p. 70.

[111] For descriptions of shamans and their practices, see Evans, chaps. 19–20; Coon, *The Hunting Peoples,* chap. 16; Honigmann, pp. 104–108; Schapera, *The Khoisan Peoples,* pp. 195–201; Radcliffe-Brown, *The Andaman Islanders,* pp. 175–179; Elkin, chap. 11; or Gayton, pp. 392–398.

[112] See, for example, Dixon, p. 282.

[113] Ibid., p. 272.

enjoy their favor."[114] Though the shaman is normally a man, a woman may become one if she has had psychic experiences and if, like other shamans, she can prove her power through healing and other feats.

Socialization and Education

The socialization of the young in hunting and gathering societies is largely an informal process in which children learn both through their play and through observing and imitating their elders. Colin Turnbull, who lived among the Pygmies of the Congo, writes:

> For children, life is one long frolic interspersed with a healthy sprinkle of spankings and slappings. Sometimes these seem unduly severe, but it is all part of their training. And one day they find that the games they have been playing are not games any longer, but the real thing, for they have become adults. Their hunting is now real hunting; their tree climbing is in earnest search of inaccessible honey; their acrobatics on the swings are repeated almost daily, in other forms, in the pursuit of elusive game, or in avoiding the malicious forest buffalo. It happens so gradually that they hardly notice the change at first, for even when they are proud and famous hunters their life is still full of fun and laughter.[115]

At a relatively early age, boys are allowed to join the men on the hunt, participating in any activities they are capable of. Fathers commonly make miniature bows as soon as their sons can handle them and encourage the boys to practice. Girls assist their mothers in their camp-site duties and in gathering vegetables and fruits. Thus the children prepare for their future roles.

This informal socialization is often supplemented by a formal process of initiation that marks the transition from childhood to manhood or woman-hood.[116] Initiation rites vary considerably from one society to another, though girls' ceremonies are usually linked with their first menstruation. The rites for boys commonly involve painful experiences (e.g., circumcision, scarification, or knocking out a tooth), which prove their courage and thus their right to the privileges of manhood. As a rule, these rites are also the occasion for a youth's introduction to his group's most sacred lore. This combination of experiences helps to impress on the young the value and importance of such information.

Compared with horticultural and herding societies, hunting and gathering societies put more stress on training the child to be independent and self-

---

[114] Jacob Baegert, S. J., *Account of the Aboriginal Inhabitants of the California Peninsula*, in Coon, *A Reader in General Anthropology*, p. 79. See also Radcliffe-Brown, *The Andaman Islanders*, p. 177.

[115] Turnbull, *The Forest People*, p. 130. © 1961 by Colin M. Turnbull. By permission of Simon & Schuster, Inc.

[116] See, for example, Elkin, chap. 7; Marshall, "!Kung Bushmen," pp. 264–267; Turnbull, "The Mbuti Pygmies," pp. 306–307; or Coon, *The Hunting Peoples*, chap. 14.

Table 6.7 **Emphases in child rearing, by societal type**

Societal Type	Child-rearing Emphases (in percentages)					No. of Societies
	1*	2*	3*	4*	5*	
Hunting and gathering	36	36	14	14	0	22
Horticultural and herding	3	8	3	36	51	39

Source: Based on Herbert Barry III, Irving L. Child, and Margaret K. Bacon, "Relation of Child Training to Subsistence Economy," *American Anthropologist*, 61 (1959), table 2.

*(1) Self-reliance stressed much more than obedience
 (2) Self-reliance stressed somewhat more than obedience
 (3) Self-reliance and obedience stressed equally
 (4) Obedience stressed somewhat more than self-reliance
 (5) Obedience stressed much more than self-reliance

reliant, less on obedience (see Table 6.7). This is apparently an adaptation to a subsistence economy in which it is imperative to have "venturesome, independent adults who can take initiative in wresting food daily from nature." [117] By contrast, venturesomeness and independence are less necessary—and may even be undesirable—in technologically more advanced horticultural and herding societies.

The Arts and Leisure

Modern hunting and gathering peoples in widely scattered parts of the world have produced a variety of artistic works. Some are strikingly similar to the cave drawings and carvings of the prehistoric hunters and gatherers of the Upper Paleolithic. The motivation behind these efforts is not always clear, but in some cases it is plainly religious, in others, magical. [118] And sometimes it appears to be simply aesthetic.

Music, too, plays a part in the lives of at least some hunters and gatherers. Turnbull has written in detail of *molimo* festivals, in which songs and the music of a primitive wooden trumpet are central. [119] These festivals have great religious significance and express the people's devotion to, and trust in, the forest. As with the visual arts, music is sometimes purely for enjoyment. [120] Dancing is another valued feature of life in many of these societies, and, again, the motives for it are varied.

[117] Herbert Barry III, Irving L. Child, and Margaret K. Bacon, "Relation of Child Training to Subsistence Economy," *American Anthropologist*, 61 (1959), p. 263.

[118] Some of the best evidence of religious motivation comes from Australia (see Elkin, pp. 191–192 or 232–234). For an example of art employed as an instrument of sympathetic magic, see Evans, pp. 130ff.

[119] Turnbull, "The Mbuti Pygmies," pp. 308–312, *The Forest People,* chap. 4, and *Wayward Servants*, pp. 259–267.

[120] See, for example, Hose and McDougall, p. 192, and Speck, pp. 270ff.

Figure 6.18 Australian aborigine painting a design on a piece of bark. The design is based on tribal legend.

Storytelling is also important in the leisure hours. Turnbull tells us that the Pygmies "are blessed with a lively imagination," and he provides several delightful examples.[121] The stories told by hunters and gatherers range from accounts of the day's experiences on the hunt (often embellished to hold the listeners' attention) to the sacred myths and legends passed down over many generations. Legends commonly deal with the origins of both the world and the group, which are often considered identical. Stories about great heroes of the past and their exploits are popular and often provide justification for the group's customs. Sacred myths and legends, as we have seen, frequently enter into initiation rites, especially for boys, and they are sometimes accompanied by music and dance. This complex interweaving of art, religion, entertainment, and education provides a strong foundation for tradition and for sociocultural continuity.

In their free hours, adult hunters and gatherers, like adults everywhere, enjoy gossip, small talk, and other nonessential activities. Games are played in virtually every hunting and gathering society, but it is interesting to note that games of strategy have little or no place there, while games of chance are more

121 Turnbull, *The Forest People,* p. 135.

SONG OF THE ELEPHANT HUNTERS

The following song was sung by Pygmy hunters just before they set out on an elephant hunt. The headman was joined in the choruses by the entire group. The song was recorded by a visiting French missionary.

In the weeping forest, under the evening wind,
The night, all black, lies down to sleep, happy.
In the sky the stars escape trembling,
Fireflies flash and go out,
Up high, the moon is dark, its white light is out.
The spirits are wandering,
    Elephant hunter, take up your bow!
      Chorus: Elephant hunter, take up your
        bow!

In the timid forest the tree sleeps, the leaves
    are dead,
The monkeys have closed their eyes, hanging
    high from the branches,
The antelopes glide by with silent steps,
They nibble the cool grass, cocking their ears,
    alert,
They raise their heads and listen, a little fright-
    ened,
The cicada falls silent, cutting off his grating
    sound,
    Elephant hunter, take up your bow!
      Chorus: Elephant hunter, take up your
        bow!

In the forest that the great rain lashes,
Father elephant walks heavily, baou, baou,
Carefree and fearless, sure of his strength,
Father elephant whom nothing can vanquish,
Among the tall forest trees that he breaks, he
    stops and moves on,
He eats, trumpets, and searches for his mate,
Father elephant, we hear you from afar,
    Elephant hunter, take up your bow!
      Chorus: Elephant hunter, take up your
        bow!

In the forest where nothing moves through but
    you,
Hunter, lift up your heart, glide, run, leap, and
    walk,
The meat is in front of you, the huge piece of
    meat,
The meat that walks like a hill,
The meat that rejoices the heart,
The meat that will roast at your hearth,
The meat your teeth sink into,
The beautiful red meat and the blood that we
    drink steaming,
    Yoyo, Elephant hunter, take up your bow!
      Chorus: Yoyo, Elephant hunter, take up
        your bow!

From Carleton S. Coon, *The Hunting Peoples* (Boston: Little, Brown, 1971), pp. 114–115. Reprinted by permission of Little, Brown and Company and Jonathan Cape Ltd.

common than in any other type of society (see Table 6.8). If a society's games reflect the experiences its members have in their everyday lives, the prevalence of games of chance in hunting and gathering societies suggests that hunters and gatherers have less sense of control over the events in their daily lives than more advanced peoples.

Table 6.8   Types of games, by societal type

| Type of Society | Percentage of Societies Having Games of: | | | No. of Societies |
	Physical Skill	Chance	Strategy	
Hunting and gathering	96	83	0	117
Simple horticultural	83	33	7	30
Advanced horticultural	90	37	68	41
Agrarian	92	60	60	25
Fishing	93	63	3	30
Herding	89	44	56	9

Source: George Peter Murdock's Ethnographic Atlas sample of 915 societies.

Demographic Patterns: Birthrates and Death Rates

The basic determinants of population size are birthrates and death rates. These, together with the rates of in- and out-migration, are the only immediate determinants of population change in a society. All other factors (e.g., famines, wars, etc.) make their influence felt through one of these four.

It is usually difficult to determine these rates in hunting and gathering societies. Ethnographers have generally been more interested in such things as the details of childbirth rituals and the intricacies of marriage rules than in the birthrate or typical family size. Such evidence as we have, however, indicates that birth and death rates are usually quite high. In Greenland, from 1922 to 1930, the average annual birthrate among the Eskimo was 42.3 per thousand inhabitants, more than twice that of modern industrial societies.[122] In a Canadian Eskimo group that had minimal contact with the outside world, the average number of births per married woman was 5, and for women of forty-five or older the average was over 10. Among the Bushmen, it is reported, pregnancies "follow in rapid succession during the course of married life, and it often happens that another child, or even two, may be born while the first is still at the breast."[123] The Negritos of Malaya have apparently been somewhat less prolific, if we may judge from one small study: a group of thirty-two men aged forty and over had 151 children, an average of nearly 5 apiece, with the prospect of more to come.[124] Finally, among the Punan of Borneo "large families are the rule; a family with as many as eight or nine children is no rarity."[125]

One should not assume, however, that these societies are swarming

[122] Birket-Smith, p. 44; compare with Table 11.1, p. 321, which shows the rates for industrial societies.

[123] Schapera, The Khoisan Peoples, p. 116.

[124] Evans, p. 16.

[125] Hose and McDougall, p. 183.

with children. To begin with, the infant mortality rate is also high. Over 40 per cent of those 151 children born to the thirty-two Negrito fathers were already dead at the time of the study. The study of the Bushmen refers to the "high infant mortality caused by the natural hardships and strenuous conditions of Bushmen life,"[126] and the study of the Eskimo of Greenland speaks of "the very high mortality among infants."[127] Added to this, infanticide is practiced with some frequency in most hunting and gathering societies.[128] Among the Bushmen, at least, it is extremely common. Their children are not weaned until they are three or even four years old, and those born in the meantime are, as the Bushmen put it, "thrown away."[129] Because of the high birthrate, over half their children apparently die this way, and, after the toll from natural causes, relatively few children survive: the average woman rears only two or three children.

Accidents, illness, and food shortages also contribute to the high death rates, sometimes directly, sometimes by causing premature aging. An ethnographer who lived among the Siriono of South America, for example, estimates that the average life span of those who survived infancy was only thirty-five to forty years, by which time the stresses of their way of life had rendered most people decrepit.[130] At one time, it was believed that death rates were uniformly high for all hunting and gathering societies, but more recent evidence indicates that there are at least some exceptions.[131]

ARCHAEOLOGICAL AND ETHNOGRAPHIC EVIDENCE COMPARED

Having completed our review of both the archaeological and the ethnographic evidence on hunting and gathering societies, we are now in a better position to consider the relationship between prehistoric man and modern primitives, a problem that has divided students of human societies for years. Though indiscriminate comparisons of the two populations can be misleading, our evidence indicates that careful comparisons are not only valid but extremely valuable.[132]

---

[126] Schapesa, *The Khoisan Peoples*, p. 116.

[127] Birket-Smith, p. 46.

[128] One survey revealed that infanticide was practiced in twelve out of fifteen hunting and gathering societies, and thirteen of them also practiced abortion. See John Whiting, "Effects of Climate on Certain Cultural Practices," in Ward Goodenough (ed.), *Explorations in Cultural Anthropology: Essays in Honor of George Peter Murdock* (New York: McGraw-Hill, 1964). The tabulations are our own and are based on table 9, pp. 528–533.

[129] Schapera, *The Khoisan Peoples*, p. 116.

[130] Holmberg, *Nomads of the Long Bow*, p. 85. A more general survey concluded that "individuals who live as long as fifty years are rare" in hunting and gathering societies (cited by Service, *Primitive Social Organization*, p. 80).

[131] Lee, "What Hunters Do for a Living," p. 36, and Frederick Dunn, "Epidemiological Factors: Health and Disease in Hunter-Gatherers," in Lee and DeVore, pp. 221–228.

[132] For similar comparisons, see Grahame Clark, *The Stone Age Hunters*, op. cit., and Pfeiffer, op. cit.

To avoid confusion, however, we must recognize that modern hunters and gatherers can in no sense be equated with the hunters and gatherers of the *Lower* and *Middle* Paleolithic. Any comparability is strictly between these modern groups and the hunters and gatherers of the late Upper Paleolithic and the Mesolithic.

We can see why, now that we are familiar with both sets of evidence. The similarities between modern hunters and gatherers and those of the late Upper Paleolithic and the Mesolithic are many and basic; the differences are fewer and much less important.[133] Similarities occur in such crucial matters as technology and mode of subsistence, size of local groups, the existence of relative equality,[134] and minimal occupational specialization. Similarities in art suggest further similarities in religious belief and practice.

The differences are largely of three types. First, in many modern hunting and gathering societies there are certain elements that originated in more advanced societies (e.g., some metal tools and some religious ideas); this could not happen, of course, in the Upper Paleolithic and the Mesolithic. Second, modern groups, unlike the prehistoric ones, are often crowded into the least desirable territories.[135] Finally, in the modern era, hunters and gatherers have no opportunity for territorial expansion, which means that population growth is impossible and deaths and births must balance. Prehistoric hunters and gatherers, happily, were not always subject to this harsh restriction.

As we have seen, the archaeological record is much less complete than the ethnographic, being silent on many subjects about which the latter provides a wealth of information. Therefore, when the ethnographic record shows patterns that are consistent for all or most modern groups and when these patterns do not depend on conditions peculiar to the modern era, scholars now increasingly regard them as applicable to the advanced hunting and gathering societies of the late Upper Paleolithic and the Mesolithic. This is a result of our growing awareness of the *limiting* nature of a hunting and gathering technology and economy.[136] Given a primitive technology and economy, it is utterly impossible to have large settlements, highly developed governments,

---

[133] We are excluding here those modern hunting and gathering peoples who have been socially and culturally overwhelmed in recent years by contact with more advanced societies. This is becoming increasingly common, and we must therefore rely heavily on older (especially pre-World War II) studies of such peoples.

[134] This is indicated by the absence of differentiation in burial remains from the Upper Paleolithic and Mesolithic. By contrast, in more advanced societies of later eras one finds clear evidence of distinctions between rich and poor, the former having many rare and obviously costly objects buried with them.

[135] Though not always, by any means. Many of the areas they occupied in Australia and the New World were highly desirable. Furthermore, the value of territory to an advanced society is not necessarily the same as its value to hunters and gatherers. On the contrary, they often differ.

[136] See, for example, Clark and Piggott, *Prehistoric Societies* pp. 130ff., or Hole and Heizer, *Introduction to Prehistoric Archeology*, pp. 225–226.

literacy, schools, a high degree of occupational specialization, a market economy, a complex class system, and a host of other things.

What *is* possible is small communities, usually autonomous, usually nomadic, led by headmen who have almost no authority and govern by persuasion. These groups are likely to be composed of a number of nuclear families linked by ties of kinship into an extended family. These kinship ties will probably be very important to both the individual and the community. The division of labor is likely to be almost entirely along the lines of age and sex, with very limited occupational specialization a possibility. Possessions are certain to be few, near equality in wealth the rule. Finally, birth and death rates will both be high by the standards of modern industrial societies.

There may be limited variations on these themes. Societies in very favorable locations and those with a somewhat more advanced technology (e.g., those able to supplement their food supply by fishing or horticulture) will probably be a bit larger, somewhat less nomadic, a little more developed politically and specialized occupationally, and a bit wealthier and less egalitarian. These differences, however, will not be great.

At the same time, there are certain aspects of life where the hunting and gathering technology seems completely irrelevant. Observations of modern hunters and gatherers indicate that this is true of divorce. Every possibility, ranging from the complete absence of divorce to the most casual practice of it, has been noted.

Between the extremes, there are a number or areas where a hunting and gathering technology neither determines the pattern nor is irrelevant. Rather, it seems to predispose the group to adopt a particular alternative without completely precluding the others. Some marriage practices are a case in point: a minority of modern hunting and gathering societies (12 per cent of those in the Ethnographic Atlas sample) are monogamous, even though the great majority permit polygyny. Apparently, a hunting and gathering technology and the characteristics that accompany it are not strong enough to preclude either of these possibilities, but neither are they irrelevant. In statistical terms, one would say that the characteristics of hunting and gathering societies increase the probability of occasional polygyny and reduce the probability of strict monogamy.

Since there is no reason to think that relevant conditions were different in late Upper Paleolithic or Mesolithic times, it is reasonable to suppose that roughly comparable probabilities prevailed then. In short, except where there is no distinctive pattern for modern hunting and gathering societies (as in the case of divorce) or where relevant conditions have changed (as in the case of death rates, which are influenced by the availability of new territories), we can probably assume substantial similarity between the advanced hunting and gathering societies of the late prehistoric era and those of recent centuries.

CHAPTER SEVEN

Horticultural Societies

Ten thousand years ago some long-forgotten inhabitants of the Middle East began to raise part of their food instead of relying, as men had always done, on wild plants. Little did they dream how greatly this innovation would change the conditions of human life! Little did they dream that they were laying the foundation for the growth of cities, the rise of empires, and the emergence of civilization!

We will probably never know the exact circumstances that led to this important step, since writing was not yet invented and archaeological excavations are unlikely to tell us. Experts have made some educated guesses, however, and any one of them, or a combination, may be correct.[1] One explanation links the beginning of horticulture with environmental changes in the Middle East at the end of the last Ice Age. According to an early version of this hypothesis, these changes forced societies in the Fertile Crescent to develop new methods of subsistence. A later version suggests that melting glaciers forced coastal populations to move inland in such numbers that they triggered a deadly process of intersocietal selection. Other experts, however, see the shift to horticulture simply as the inevitable result of man's expansive tendencies in combination with his increased store of information about the biophysical environment—in other words, just one more step along man's evolutionary path, requiring no conditions other than the development of his store of information to the appropriate point.

This much we know for certain: for hundreds of years, many hunting and gathering societies of the Middle East had been harvesting the wild grasses from which our modern cereals were developed. For these people to shift from harvesting these grains in the wild to planting part of their last harvest to ensure an ample one next time was an innovation no more radical than hundreds of others, especially for groups already used to storing grain. If the change seems dramatic or revolutionary to us, it is because we, with the advantage of hindsight, know how far-reaching its consequences proved to be.

Regardless of what caused the shift to horticulture, everything we know

---

[1] Stuart Streuver (ed.), *Prehistoric Agriculture* (Garden City, N.Y.: Natural History Press, 1971), parts II and IV, or E. Cecil Curwen and Gudmund Hatt, *Plough and Pasture: The Early History of Farming* (New York: Collier Books, 1961), chap. 10.

about the division of labor in primitive societies suggests that it was the work of women.[2] Women are much more likely to have gathered and stored wild cereals, and in modern horticultural societies they are the ones who generally do the planting, cultivating, and harvesting. Men, by contrast, are much more likely to have domesticated animals, since hunting and herding have always been predominantly male activities.

SIMPLE HORTICULTURAL SOCIETIES IN PREHISTORIC ASIA AND EUROPE

Although we may never know precisely where and when the first horticultural society came into being, recent archaeological research has established the general area and approximate time, as we have indicated. It happened somewhere in the Middle East about 7000 B.C. Currently the chief contenders for the honor are Asia Minor, Palestine, and the hill country to the east of the Tigris River. In each of these areas, ancient settlements dating from that period have been found in which horticulture was apparently the primary means of subsistence.[3]

From this area of initial development, horticultural techniques spread both east and west until horticultural societies were eventually established at points as distant as Britain and China. By the time they became established in those areas, however, the horticultural societies of the Middle East were already evolving into agrarian societies.

During recent years our knowledge of these early horticultural societies has been advanced substantially by developments in the field of archaeology, including the excavation of new sites and the more extensive exploration of older ones. Biologists and geologists have contributed a great deal to our understanding of the environmental conditions of that era. And most important of all is the post–World War II development of a new technique for dating archaeological remains. With this technique, known as radiocarbon dating, prehistoric materials up to about 50,000 years of age can, for the first time, be dated with a fair degree of accuracy, and many formerly unanswerable questions can now be resolved.[4]

---

[2] V. Gordon Childe, *What Happened in History,* rev. ed. (Baltimore: Penguin, 1964), pp. 65–66.

[3] See, for example, Robert Braidwood and Bruce Howe, "Southwestern Asia Beyond the Lands of the Mediterranean Littoral," in Robert Braidwood and Gordon Willey (eds.), *Courses Toward Urban Life: Archeological Considerations of Some Cultural Alternatives* (Chicago: Aldine, 1962), pp. 137, 152–153, and 346, or James Mellaart, *Earliest Civilizations of the Near East* (London: Thames and Hudson, 1965), pp. 12, 32–38, 47–50, and 81.

[4] The technique is so named because it measures the amount of radioactive carbon remaining in dead material. For a good description of the technique, see Frank Hole and Robert Heizer, *An Introduction to Prehistoric Archeology* (New York: Holt, 1965), pp. 145–150.

Characteristics of the Societies

In traditional archaeological usage, the period in which simple horticultural societies were dominant in a region is known as the Neolithic, or New Stone Age. This name was chosen because in early excavations in Europe and the Middle East, some strata yielded distinctive stone axes, adzes, and hammers that had been smoothed by grinding or polishing. Prior to the discovery of radiocarbon dating, these tools were one of the best indicators of the relative age of the stratum and its place in evolutionary history.

As research progressed, however, and more and more sites were excavated, it became increasingly clear that these tools were neither the most distinctive feature of Neolithic societies nor their greatest technological achievement. Rather, their most important innovations were in the area of subsistence technology: for the first time in history, men were *producing* their food, and hunting and gathering were relegated to a secondary role.

In this connection, it is important to recognize that these early horticultural societies had a mixed economy. Horticulture was their basic means of subsistence, but it was supplemented by herding, hunting, or gathering in various combinations.[5] The presence of livestock in many of these early societies was especially important, as we will soon see.

Archaeologists have come to recognize that the term "Neolithic" focuses attention on the wrong thing, and a number of them now refer to the period in which these societies were dominant as "the era of effective food production."[6] We will call it simply "the horticultural era."

Most archaeologists now regard the emergence of horticultural societies as the first great social revolution in human history. From a long-term evolutionary standpoint, in which time is measured in centuries or millenniums, this view is certainly justified. It would be wrong to assume, however, that the rate of change seemed revolutionary to the participants. As far as we can judge today, the process was so gradual that the changes occurring during a lifetime were probably neither very numerous nor overwhelming.

One of the best indications of this slow rate of change is the evidence that people in the Middle East had already been relying on cereal grains during much of the Mesolithic. Techniques of harvesting, storing, grinding, and cooking grains were apparently well established long before the techniques of cultivation were developed. Furthermore, as we have noted, hunting, and to some extent gathering, continued to play an important part in the lives of the early horticulturalists. We may also assume that there was considerable continuity in other areas of life, especially kinship, religion, and politics. The survival

---

[5] Braidwood and Howe, p. 140; Curwen and Hatt, p. 33; Mellaart, chaps. 3ff.; V. Gordon Childe, "The New Stone Age," in Harry Shapiro (ed.), *Man, Culture, and Society* (New York: Oxford Galaxy, 1960), p. 103.

[6] See Braidwood and Willey, op. cit., or Robert Braidwood, "Domestication: The Food-producing Revolution," in *International Encyclopedia of the Social Sciences* (New York: Macmillan and Free Press, 1968), vol. 4, pp. 245–247.

of fertility cults, indicated by the widespread presence of female figurines in Neolithic remains, is one evidence of this.[7]

Our use of the term "revolutionary" in connection with the rise of horticultural societies, then, is based primarily on our awareness of the long-term implications of the change. To begin with, the shift to horticulture meant more permanent settlements. No longer did groups have to move about constantly in search of game and other food. On the contrary, the practice of horticulture forced them to stay in one place for extended periods. In the Middle East and in southeastern Europe, truly permanent settlements seem to have been established. Elsewhere, simple horticulturalists usually have had to move their settlements every few years, because their primitive methods of cultivation seriously deplete the soil.[8] Why this was not necessary in the Middle East and in southeastern Europe is still a mystery, since modern research indicates that only fertilization (by alluvial deposits or by man), irrigation, the use of the plow, or crop rotation permits land to be kept under continuous cultivation,[9] and so far there is no evidence of any of these practices. We do know, however, that these early horticulturalists kept livestock, and it is possible that the value of manure was discovered at an early date.[10] This practice may not have spread simply because of the greater availability of arable land elsewhere.

In any case, the shift from hunting and gathering to horticulture substantially increased the permanence of human settlements, enabling people to accumulate many more possessions than they ever had before. This is evident in the archaeological remains left by horticulturalists of the Neolithic era. Tools and weapons are much more numerous and varied than in Paleolithic and Mesolithic sites, and for the first time there are large, bulky objects such as stone cups and bowls and pottery.[11] Dwellings also became more substantial. Some buildings contained several rooms and a small courtyard (see Figure 7.1) and were made of materials like sun-dried clay blocks, capable of lasting for as long as two generations.[12] Even more noteworthy is the appearance of such things as religious shrines or ceremonial centers, village walls, and occasional paved or timbered (corduroy style) roadways or alleys; though none of these are typical of simple horticultural communities, neither are they rare.[13]

The change from hunting and gathering to horticulture also resulted in

---

[7] Jacquetta Hawkes, *Prehistory*, UNESCO History of Mankind, vol. 1, part 1, (New York: Mentor, 1965), pp. 442–452; Mellaart, p. 42; Childe, "The New Stone Age," p. 107.

[8] Childe, "The New Stone Age," pp. 100–101.

[9] See, for example, B. H. Farmer, "Agriculture: Comparative Technology," in *International Encyclopedia of the Social Sciences*, vol. 1, pp. 204–205, or Curwen and Hatt, p. 68 and chap. 16.

[10] Childe, *What Happened in History*, pp. 64–65.

[11] Mellaart, pp. 50–51, or Jean Perrot, "Palestine-Syria-Cilicia," in Braidwood and Willey, pp. 156–157.

[12] Hawkes, pp. 384–395; Childe, "The New Stone Age," pp. 104–105; or Perrot, pp. 154–155.

[13] Hawkes, pp. 395–401, and Mellaart, pp. 40–42.

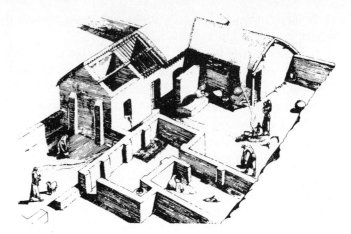

Figure 7.1   Reconstruction of a farmhouse of the early horticultural era, Hassuna, Iraq (c. 5500–5000 B.C.).

larger settlements and denser populations. Jarmo, one of the oldest horticultural villages yet discovered, contained twenty to twenty-five houses and an estimated population of 150,[14] nearly four times that of the average hunting and gathering band. Neolithic villages in Europe had from eight to fifty houses, suggesting populations ranging up to at least 200.[15] In several cases there were even more striking concentrations of population. One of the most famous is the town located on the site of Jerico nearly 6,000 years before the days of Joshua. Recent excavations there uncovered a community that apparently housed 2,000 to 3,000 inhabitants.[16] Still more recent excavations of Çatal Hüyük in Asia Minor revealed a community occupying an even larger area and, presumably, with a larger population.[17]

These two communities, though obviously exceptional, illustrate another development associated with the rise of horticultural societies—the rapid expansion and growing importance of trade and commerce.[18] Modern scholars feel that the "great" size of Jericho and Çatal Hüyük was not simply the result of the practice of horticulture. As one writer has put it, "It is . . . most unlikely that [horticulture] should have flourished more at Jericho, 200 metres below sea-level, than elsewhere in Palestine. Some other resource must have existed, and this was probably trade."[19] As he points out, Jericho commanded the resources

---

[14] Mellaart, p. 47

[15] Childe, "The New Stone Age," p. 105. Elsewhere Childe speaks of twenty-five to thirty-five households as "a not uncommon number" in central Europe and southern Russia. See *What Happened in History*, p. 66.

[16] Mellaart, p. 36, or Hawkes, p. 310.

[17] Mellaart, pp. 81–101.

[18] See, for example, Childe, "The New Stone Age," p. 106, or *What Happened in History*, pp. 67–68. See also Braidwood and Howe, p. 138.

[19] Mellaart, p. 36. See also p. 84 for his views on Catal Hüyük.

of the Dead Sea, notably salt, bitumen,[20] and sulfur, all useful materials in simple horticultural societies and not available everywhere. This view of Jericho as an early center of trade is supported by the discovery there of products such as obsidian from Asia Minor and cowrie shells from the Red Sea. In the case of Çatal Hüyük, obsidian (i.e., volcanic glass, a material much sought after for use in weapons and other things) seems to have been the key local resource responsible for its growth. Even in small villages far removed from such centers as Jericho and Çatal Hüyük, there is evidence of trade. For example, shells from the Mediterranean were found in the sites of Neolithic villages and in graves throughout the Danube Basin and far down the Oder, Elbe, and Rhine river valleys in northern Europe.[21]

The growth of trade and commerce suggests an increase in occupational specialization, at least in the chief commercial centers. Direct evidence of this has been found in a number of sites. For example, a community south of Jericho yielded a number of small workshops where such specialized craftsmen as a butcher, a bead maker, and a maker of bone tools worked.[22] This kind of specialization, however, was apparently limited to the emerging trade centers.[23]

Meanwhile, most communities remained largely self-sufficient, and most families still produced nearly everything they used.[24] Important innovations continued in the domestic arts, the most notable being the invention of pottery and weaving.[25] Pottery is so common in Neolithic sites that for a long time no site was considered truly Neolithic unless pottery was present. Recent research has shown, however, that pottery did not appear until some time after the emergence of the first horticultural societies.[26]

There is little evidence of warfare during the early Neolithic. Graves rarely contain weapons, and most communities had no walls or other defenses.[27] Some, it is true, had ditches and fences, but these were more suitable for protection against marauding animals than against human enemies. The walls surrounding Jericho, on the other hand, were obviously defenses against human foes.[28] Later in the Neolithic the picture changed drastically and warfare

---

[20] Bitumen was used to fix blades in handles, mend pottery, etc. (ibid., pp. 20–21).

[21] Childe, "The New Stone Age," p. 106.

[22] Mellaart, pp. 43–44.

[23] See Childe, *What Happened in History*, p. 67.

[24] Childe, "The New Stone Age," p. 106, and *What Happened in History*, p. 67.

[25] For a good review of these developments, see Hawkes, pp. 401–410 and 414–417, or V. Gordon Childe, *Man Makes Himself* (New York: Mentor, 1953), pp. 76–80.

[26] See, for example, Mellaart, chap. 8.

[27] Childe, "The New Stone Age," p. 107, or *What Happened in History*, p. 74.

[28] Hawkes, p. 358, or Mellaart, pp. 33–36.

became increasingly common. In this period battle-axes, daggers, and other arms appear in the grave of every adult male. The reason for this change is not clear, but some scholars think it was linked with the growth of population and the resulting scarcity of new land suitable for horticulture. It may also have been related to declining opportunities for hunting, a traditional male activity. Warfare, with its demands for bravery and skill in the use of arms, would be a natural substitute, and if women were doing most of the work of tending the gardens, as is the case in most contemporary horticultural societies, men would have had substantial time on their hands to spend in this activity. Moreover, the frictions created by growing pressure for land would provide a ready-made justification. Finally, some experts suspect that the increase in warfare was linked with the increase in wealth, especially in the form of cattle, which could be stolen so easily.[29]

Diffusion

From its origins in the Middle East, the new way of life spread east and west. Simple horticultural societies were eventually established throughout almost all of Europe and North Africa. In Asia, their spread was more irregular, and they never did develop in certain large areas where the land was unsuited to plant cultivation.[30]

From the evolutionary standpoint, this new way of life spread rather rapidly, but from the perspective of an individual lifetime, the pace was extremely slow. The distance from the Middle East to China is approximately 5,000 miles, and it took the new technology at least 3,000 years, possibly more, to cover it. The movement westward was even slower: 4,000 years were required to reach Britain, 3,000 miles away. In other words, the new way of life spread only a mile or two per year on the average.

Various factors contributed to the spread of horticulture, but one of the more important was the growth of population. Given the tendency for human populations to increase until checked by the limitation of resources, population pressures would naturally build up in the original area of horticultural practice, leading to the formation of new settlements on the outer fringes. This meant that horticulturalists either moved into previously unoccupied territory or took over the territory of hunters and gatherers. In the latter case, the advantage would clearly lie with the horticulturalists. By remaining in one area for a number of years, a group of horticulturalists would usually so reduce the supply of game that the territory would become unattractive to hunters and gatherers. And

---

[29] Childe, "The New Stone Age," p. 107.

[30] See, for example, H. D. Sankalia, *Prehistory and Protohistory in India and Pakistan* (Bombay: Bombay University Press, 1962), pp. 152–155, or Sir Mortimer Wheeler, *Early India and Pakistan* (London: Thames and Hudson, 1959), pp. 80ff.

should the latter be tempted to fight for their "rights," they would typically find themselves outnumbered by a ratio of more than 2 to 1, if the populations of contemporary groups are any indication.[31]

In the process of diffusion, there was a definite tendency for the whole cluster of horticultural traits to spread together, but there were exceptions. Weaving, for example, apparently never reached horticultural Britain, and large trading centers like Jericho and Çatal Hüyük were limited to the Middle East.[32] On the other hand, certain elements of the horticultural way of life were adopted by some groups that still relied primarily on hunting and gathering. In parts of northeastern Europe and northern Asia, for example, pottery and polished stone axes, both basic horticultural, or Neolithic, innovations, came to be widely used by hunting and fishing peoples.[33] Developments such as these demonstrate the need for those irregular boundaries between societal types shown in Figure 5.1 (page 96).

The spread of horticulture to China is especially interesting, because China provides us with one of the first points of contact between prehistory and history. Horticulture reached China late enough, and writing developed there early enough, that some memory of the early horticultural era was preserved in legends that were eventually written down. For a long time scholars believed that this material was entirely fictional, but modern archaeological research has substantiated enough of it that it is now regarded as an intermingling of fact and fiction.[34]

According to legend, China's earliest inhabitants were hunters, but the increase of population eventually forced a shift to horticulture. As one source recounts, "The ancient people ate meat of animals and birds. At the time of Shen-nung [an early legendary ruler and culture hero] there were so many people that the animals and birds became inadequate for people's wants and therefore Shen-nung taught the people to cultivate."[35] Other sources relate that Shen-nung introduced pottery and describe the era as a period of peace and self-sufficiency. "During the Age of Shen-nung people rested at ease and acted with vigor. They cared for their mothers, but not for their fathers. They lived among deer. They ate what they cultivated and wore what they wove. They did not think of harming one another." This preference for mothers is intriguing, because it is so contrary to the later Chinese tradition yet conforms to one of the

---

[31] For the ethnographic evidence, see Table 5.2, p. 104.

[32] On the absence of weaving in Britain, see Hawkes, p. 326.

[33] Ibid.

[34] See Kwang-chih Chang, *The Archaeology of Ancient China* (New Haven, Conn.: Yale, 1963), pp. 130–131. See also Curwen and Hatt, pp. 16–18, on truths contained in ancient traditions.

[35] The quotations in this paragraph are all from Chang, pp. 131–133, and are used by permission of the Yale University Press.

distinctive characteristics of contemporary horticultural societies (see page 189 below). Finally, there is a legend describing the Age of Shen-nung as the last era in which men were free from coercive political authority. "People were administered without a criminal law and prestige was built without the use of force. After Shen-nung, however, the strong began to rule over the weak and the many over the few."

Technological Advance

During the horticultural era, technological progress was almost continuous, especially in the Middle East. In addition to the invention of pottery making and weaving, metals were discovered and the basic principles of working them were developed. Thus the simple horticultural societies of the latter part of the era were appreciably more advanced than their predecessors three thousand years earlier. The societies that flourished throughout Mesopotamia around 4000 B.C. are a good example of this. These groups apparently shared a common culture, called the Ubaid culture after one of the sites where its remains are found.

Ubaid culture was notable in many ways. To begin with, large settlements were relatively common. This is indicated by the size of cemeteries (one of which contained more than 1,000 graves) as well as by the large temples that

Figure 7.2 Artist's reconstruction of the Ubaid temple at Tepe Gawa.

dominated these communities.[36] A variety of technical skills were highly developed. Some copper tools and weapons were used, at least in the northern area, while in the south, sickles and other tools were made from clay fired at high temperatures, a process that produced a remarkably efficient substitute for the stone unavailable in that area.[37] Trade became extensive throughout Mesopotamia (facilitated by simple sailboats plying the myriad waterways).[38] This undoubtedly contributed to the wide diffusion of Ubaid culture. As one writer says, "Never before had a single culture been able to influence such a vast area, if only superficially."[39] Compared with these societies, the first horticultural societies of the seventh millennium appear primitive indeed. The difference between them is a measure of the tremendous progress achieved by the simple horticulturalists of the Middle East during the first part of the horticultural era.

ADVANCED HORTICULTURAL SOCIETIES IN PREHISTORIC ASIA AND EUROPE

Each of the many inventions and discoveries of the horticultural era increased man's control over his environment to some degree. None, however, had such far-reaching effects as the use of metal in weapons and tools. This is why we use metallurgy as the basic criterion for differentiating between simple and advanced horticultural societies. To be more specific, we classify societies as advanced horticultural only when the use of metal weapons and/or tools was widespread. Societies in which they were rare, or in which metals were used only for artistic and ceremonial artifacts (as in some South and Central American Indian groups where gold was the only metal known), are better classified as simple horticultural, since the impact of metallurgy on societal life was so limited.

Middle Eastern Beginnings

To the nontechnically inclined, the shift from stone to metal may suggest a radical break with the past and the introduction of something completely new. Actually, however, the use of metals evolved from the use of stone by a series of surprisingly small steps.

Since the Upper Paleolithic, and perhaps even before, men had been keenly aware of the different kinds of stone. Certain types, because of their

---

[36] Mellaart, pp. 130–131, and V. Gordon Childe, *New Light on the Most Ancient East* (London: Routledge, 1952), pp. 118ff.

[37] Childe, *New Light,* p. 115, and Hawkes, p. 425.

[38] Childe, *New Light,* p. 115.

[39] Mellaart, p. 130.

hardness, were recognized as most suitable for tools and weapons. Men were also attentive to differences in rock color, which led them to select some for ornamental purposes, others as sources of pigments. This interest in unusual rocks undoubtedly attracted men to copper. In its native form, copper appears as purplish green or greenish black nuggets that, when scratched or rubbed, show the yellowish red kernel of pure copper.

At first, copper was simply hammered cold into small tools and ornaments such as awls, pins, and hooks. A few articles made by this method have been found in sites dating to the middle of the sixth millennium B.C.[40] Sometime shortly after 5000 B.C., men discovered the technique of annealing.[41] By alternately heating and hammering the metal, they made it less brittle and thus could use it for a wider variety of objects. The heat from a simple wood fire was sufficient for this process. Subsequently (late in the fifth millennium B.C.), men discovered techniques for extracting copper from various kinds of ores by means of smelting, as well as ways to melt "pure" copper and cast it in molds.[42]

These discoveries illustrate again the cumulative character of technological progress. Both smelting and melting copper require higher temperatures than a simple wood fire can produce. This requirement strongly suggests that these important discoveries came after the invention of pottery and the pottery kiln.[43] And these inventions, in turn, presupposed settled communities where heavy and bulky objects could be accumulated.

As far as we can judge, the use of copper tools and weapons increased rather slowly for 1,500 to 2,000 years.[44] Various factors were responsible for this. For one thing, until smelting techniques were discovered, the supply of copper was extremely limited. Even when copper was available, it often had to be carried some distance to potential users, and primitive methods of transportation made this costly. Second, because metal working (particularly smelting and casting) was probably mastered by only a few, these specialists may have treated their skills as a kind of magic, as smiths in modern horticultural societies often do, in order to protect their lucrative monopoly. Finally, since any man could make his own tools and weapons out of stone, most people were undoubtedly reluctant to switch to the costlier product.[45] Thus, though copper was discovered as early as the middle of the sixth millennium B.C., no truly advanced horticultural society (i.e., one in which metal tools and weapons were

---

[40] Ibid., p. 105.

[41] R. J. Forbes, *Studies in Ancient Technology* (Leiden, Netherlands: Brill, 1964), vol. 9, p. 30, or Leslie Aitchison, *A History of Metals* (London: MacDonald and Evans, 1960), vol. 1, p. 21.

[42] Aitchison, p. 40.

[43] Ibid., or Forbes, vol. 8, p. 26.

[44] Childe, *Man Makes Himself*, p. 99.

[45] V. Gordon Childe, *The Bronze Age* (London: Cambridge, 1930), p. 11.

widespread) seems to have developed before the end of the fifth millennium or the early part of the fourth (i.e., around 4000 B.C.).[46]

If this is true, then the period when advanced horticultural societies flourished in the Middle East was relatively brief: agrarian societies may have appeared as early as the *latter* part of the fourth millennium. The pattern was similar in most of Europe and in India. In fact, China is the only major area in the Old World where advanced horticultural societies flourished for an extended period.

Because of this and because of the limitations of the archaeological record, it is difficult to describe the advanced horticultural societies of most of prehistoric Europe and Asia as accurately as we would like. Other sources of information on societies of this type, notably the modern ethnographic record, are much more rewarding. Except in the case of China, the most we can say with assurance about these early societies is that during the time they flourished there was continued growth in the size and density of populations, continued progress in technology, further increases in occupational specialization and trade, greater urbanization of the population (i.e., more people freed from the task of raising their own food), marked development of religious and political institutions, and increasing social inequality. In short, societies became larger, more productive, and more differentiated.

The Chinese Experience

China was something of an exception to the usual evolutionary pattern at the advanced horticultural level, basically because this era lasted so much longer there than anywhere else in the ancient world. Modern research indicates that it extended from early in the second millennium B.C. to the middle of the first.[47] The plow, for reasons unclear, was slow to reach China, thus delaying China's attainment of agrarian status. The resultant prolongation of the advanced horticultural era there was undoubtedly a factor in China's achievement of an overall level of technological development that surpassed most other horticultural societies.

One indication of this superiority is the fact that the dominant metal in China during most of this era was not copper, as in the Middle East and Europe, but bronze. This is significant, because bronze, whose manufacture represents an important advance in metallurgy (involving, as it does, the principle of alloying), is a great deal harder than copper and thus opens up important new possibilities for a society. In the Middle East, the technique of making bronze

---

[46] See, for example, Childe, *New Light,* p. 116. There is still some uncertainty about this point.

[47] On the emergence of advanced horticultural societies and the early use of metals, see Te-k'un Cheng, *Archaeology in China: Shang China* (Cambridge, England: Heffer, 1960), chap. 10; Chang, chap. 6; William Watson, *China: Before the Han Dynasty* (New York: Praeger, 1961), chap. 2. On the emergence of agrarian societies, see Chang, pp. 197–198, or Cho-yun Hsu, *Ancient China in Transition* (Stanford, Calif.: Stanford, 1965), pp. 130–132.

was not really understood until the early part of the third millennium B.C., some time *after* the first agrarian societies had made their appearance.[48] These variations in the sequence of such major innovations as bronze and the plow warn us of the inadequacy of *unilinear* theories of evolution, which assume that all societies follow exactly the same evolutionary path. Some variation is the rule, not the exception.

When the advanced horticultural era in China (i.e., China of the Shang and most of the Chou dynasties) is compared with the simple horticultural period, the differences are striking. During the earlier era, northern China was covered with numerous small, largely self-sufficient, autonomous villages. In the later period, the villages were no longer autonomous, and a few of them had become towns of some size and substance.

The emergence of these towns was largely the result of the military success of village leaders, and this success, in turn, resulted from the possession of bronze weapons. As one scholar summarized this period, "In the course of a few centuries the villages of the plain fell under the domination of walled cities on whose rulers the possession of bronze weapons, chariots, and slaves conferred a measure of superiority to which no [simple horticultural] community could aspire, however populous and well fed."[49]

The importance of this development can hardly be exaggerated. For the first time in Chinese history, men found the conquest of their fellow men to be a profitable alternative to the conquest of nature. Much the same thing happened in other parts of the world during this stage in societal development. Thus, beginning in advanced horticultural societies and continuing in agrarian, we find as much, or more, energy expended in war as in the age-old struggle for subsistence. One might almost say that bronze was to man's conquest of his fellow man what plant cultivation was to his conquest of nature. Both made major breakthroughs possible.

From the military standpoint, China's advanced horticulturalists enjoyed a great advantage over the simple horticulturalists. Recently excavated burial remains show that these warriors wore elaborate armor, including helmets, carried shields, and were equipped with spears, dagger-axes, knives, hatchets, and reflex bows capable of a pull of 160 pounds.[50] In addition, they used horse-drawn chariots carrying teams of three men.

These peoples also enjoyed numerical superiority over less advanced groups in the land: every victory brought more people under their control,

---

[48] Some bronze seems to have been manufactured accidentally a few centuries earlier as a result of using copper derived from ores containing tin, but the deliberate and conscious alloying of metals did not begin until after 3000 B.C. See Forbes, vol. 9, pp. 151–152.

[49] Watson, p. 57.

[50] Cheng, pp. 206–207.

enabling them to enlarge their armies still further.[51] This could not have been accomplished by a hunting and gathering society, where primitive technology made it impossible for conquerors to incorporate a defeated people into their group. At that level of development, the economic surplus (i.e., production in excess of what is needed to keep producers producing) was too small and irregular. But with the introduction of horticulture, the situation changed dramatically. For the first time in history, the conquest, control, and exploitation of other groups became possible—*and profitable.* All that remained to transform this possibility into a reality was an advance in military technology that would give one society a definite advantage over its neighbors. That advance was bronze. It tipped the balance of military power decisively in favor of the advanced horticulturalists.

The earliest advanced horticultural society in China of which we have any archaeological knowledge was established by the Shang people in either the eighteenth or the sixteenth century B.C.[52] Though Shang society was ruled by a single dynasty for at least 500 years, its structure was basically feudalistic. In most regions, especially those remote from the capital, effective power was in the hands of feudal lords, who paid tribute to the king and supported him militarily but otherwise enjoyed great autonomy.[53] They were so independent, in fact, that they often waged war among themselves. The same was true in the Chou dynasty that followed.

During the Shang and Chou periods, marked social inequality was the rule. Societies were divided into two basic classes, a small warrior nobility and the great mass of common people.[54] The warrior nobility was the governing class and lived in the walled cities, which served as their fortresses, and it was they who enjoyed most of the benefits of the new technology and the new social system. The chief use of bronze was to manufacture weapons and artistic and ceremonial objects for the benefit of this class (see Figure 7.3). Almost none of this relatively scarce material was made available to the common people for farm tools.[55] Much the same situation existed in the Middle East and Europe for 2,000 years or more. As one writer put it, this was a world in which metals

---

[51] Shang kings, for example, mounted "many military expeditions with an army of between 3,000 and 5,000 men." Ibid., p. 210, and Hsu, p. 67.

[52] According to ancient Chinese legends, the Shang dynasty was preceded by a Hsia dynasty. For a time, both were thought to have been fictional, but archaeological research has proved the existence of the Shang dynasty, and most scholars now assume there was an earlier Hsia dynasty and that it could have ruled over an advanced horticultural society. See Chang, pp. 130–131, or Cheng, pp. xix–xxii.

[53] Cheng, pp. 200–206.

[54] Ibid., pp. 200–215 and 248. For a more detailed picture of the system of stratification in the Chou era, see Hsu, op. cit. In reading this book one must keep in mind that the Chan Kuo period, the "period of the warring states," is included, and by then, north central China seems to have reached the agrarian level of development.

[55] Watson, p. 141, and Chang, pp. 195ff.

Figure 7.3 Bronze ritual vessels from late eleventh or early tenth century B.C., found in tomb in Shensi province, China. Each vessel had its prescribed and specific use.

played a major role in the military and cultural spheres but not in the economic.[56]

Kinship ties were extremely important in the political systems of advanced horticultural China. Membership in the governing class was largely hereditary, and as far as possible leading officials assigned the major offices under their control to kinsmen.[57] The origins of these noble families are unknown, but it seems likely that such families were descended from the village headmen of the simple horticultural era and from the close associates of early conquerors.

The walled towns where the aristocracy lived, small by modern standards, were nonetheless an important innovation. One recently excavated town, probably an early capital of the Shang state, covered slightly over 1 square mile.[58] The size of the walled areas, however, does not tell the full story of these towns, especially in the earlier period, for many of the common people had their homes and workshops outside the protected area and cultivated nearby fields.

[56] Aitchison, p. 97.

[57] Hsu, pp. 3–7 and chap. 4.

[58] Chang, p. 150.

The walled area, while basically a fortress and place of residence for the governing class, was also a political and religious center. Religious activities were quite important and were closely tied to the political system—so closely, in fact, that one writer describes the Shang state as "a kind of theocracy."[59] Though this is an overstatement, ancient inscriptions prove that the ruler did perform major religious functions and was what we would describe today as head of both church and state.

The physical structure of those early urban centers was impressive and reflected the evolution of the state and its newly achieved ability to mobilize labor on a large scale. One scholar estimates, for example, that it required the labor of 10,000 men working eighteen years to build the wall around an early Shang capital. Such massive undertakings apparently utilized large numbers of captives taken in war, many of them subsequently used as human sacrifices.[60]

Not much is known about the daily life of the common people, but their chief functions were obviously to produce the economic surplus on which the governing class depended and to provide the manpower for the various projects and military campaigns. Not all labor was of the brute, physical type, however. Some men were occupational specialists who provided the new and unusual luxury goods that the governing class demanded for display and for ceremonial purposes; others produced military equipment.[61] Although many of these specialists were probably part-time farmers, the growth of occupational specialization was undoubtedly accompanied by a significant growth in trade.

Despite their increasingly exploitative character, the advanced horticultural societies of China made important progress in a number of areas. The more important innovations included writing, money, the use of the horse, probably irrigation, and possibly the manufacture of iron just before the first agrarian society. In addition, there were lesser innovations too numerous to mention, some of them Chinese inventions or discoveries, others the result of diffusion. In most cases, it is impossible to determine which are which.

HORTICULTURAL SOCIETIES IN PREHISTORIC AMERICA

Scholars have long debated whether knowledge of the principles of plant cultivation spread through the Old World from a single source or whether they were discovered independently more than once. Proof of multiple, independent discoveries would be very difficult to come by, and we may never know for certain. Currently the majority of scholars seem inclined to the view that the knowl-

---

[59] Watson, p. 106. See also Hsu, pp. 15ff., on the interrelations between religion and politics in Chou China.

[60] Chang, pp. 150 and 159.

[61] Ibid., p. 171.

edge originated in a single place and spread from there, but their arguments are hardly compelling.[62]

Fortunately, we do not need to solve that problem in order to prove that human progress beyond the hunting and gathering level did not depend on a single lucky accident or stroke of genius. The sociocultural isolation of the New World during most of the last 9,000 years provides the basis for this assertion. Recent archaeological research in Mexico shows that plant cultivation began there no later than 3700 B.C. and possibly as early as 7000 B.C.[63] Since horticulture did not reach eastern Asia until at least 4000 B.C., and probably much later, it is impossible to explain plant cultivation in the New World by diffusion from Asia. Diffusion from Europe or North Africa is even less likely. Moreover, the slow and gradual development of horticulture in the new World, together with the uniqueness of the plants involved, suggests an indigenous process rather than an established way of life imported from abroad.[64]

This independent development is important because it gives us an opportunity to test the hypothesis that technology limits the kinds of social structures a society can develop and predisposes it to adopt certain patterns. If subsistence technology is as important as ecological-evolutionary theory asserts, the basic structural patterns in the horticultural societies of the New World should not be too different from the patterns in Europe and Asia.

Simple Horticultural Societies

Though plant cultivation in the New World began no later than the first half of the fourth millennium B.C., there were no true horticultural societies (i.e., societies obtaining at least half of their subsistence by this method) until the middle or latter half of the second millennium.[65] These appeared first in Mexico and spread from there both north and south. By the time of European exploration and settlement, they covered a good part of the New World. The rate of diffusion was very similar to that in the Old World. For example, it took approximately 2,200 years for simple horticultural societies to spread from their point of origin near Mexico City to the head of the Ohio River near Pittsburgh, a distance of about 2,000 miles.[66]

---

[62] While the diffusion hypothesis seems likely in the case of the various cereal grains, it is less convincing in the case of the root crops, such as taro, yams, and manioc, which are grown chiefly in tropical and semitropical areas. The area in which root crops have been cultivated is so different from that of the cereals, and the techniques of cultivation so different, that it is difficult to believe that knowledge of cereal cultivation served as the basis for the cultivation of root crops. Unfortunately, this problem has been ignored in most discussions of the question.

[63] Gordon Willey, "Mesoamerica," in Braidwood and Willey, p. 88.

[64] Ibid., p. 100.

[65] Ibid., pp. 91ff., and Robert Braidwood and Gordon Willey, "Conclusions and Afterthoughts," in Braidwood and Willey, pp. 335 and 344ff.

[66] Braidwood and Willey, p. 347.

Figure 7.4   Aerial view of the ruins of the ancient town of Teotihuacan, near Mexico City.

Similarities between prehistoric simple horticultural societies in the two hemispheres are striking. In both areas the shift from hunting and gathering to horticulture was associated with an increase in population size and density, a more settled village life, increased wealth or possessions, more substantial dwellings and other buildings, the beginning of craft specialization, the appearance of markets, increased trade, the establishment of relatively permanent religious centers, and even such specifics as the manufacture of ground stone implements and pottery and the discovery of the principles of metallurgy.[67] There is also evidence in both areas that militarism increased after horticultural societies became well established.

At the same time, however, certain differences between the two hemispheres warn against an overly deterministic view. In parts of Mexico and Guatemala, a number of the simple horticultural societies of the prehistoric era

[67] For developments in the New World, see Willey, pp. 91–101; Donald Collier, "The Central Andes," in Braidwood and Willey, pp. 169–174; or Gerardo Reichel-Dolmatoff, *Colombia* (New York: Praeger, 1965), chap. 5.

evolved to a degree normally associated with more advanced societies. During the first millennium A.D., they developed numerous settlements that are remarkable not only for their size but also for their material and intellectual achievements. The best known of these were developed by the Maya of Yucatán.

From the standpoint of size, Mayan communities were much larger than simple horticultural settlements in the Old World. In some cases, populations reached 10,000 or more.[68] The most impressive material accomplishments were massive temple complexes, some of which have survived for more than a thousand years. The intellectual achievements are no less remarkable and include the invention of a primitive, ideographic system of writing, a numeral system that included the concept of zero centuries before this was invented in the Old World, and an amazingly accurate calendar.[69]

In any comparison of simple horticultural societies, the Maya are unique.[70] Despite their lack of metal, they achieved a level of societal development comparable in many respects to advanced horticultural societies. This raises a question with important implications for our understanding of societal development: how did they do it?

Part of the explanation lies in the nature of horticultural systems in general and of theirs in particular. A contemporary Mayan, using about the same techniques his ancestors used in pre-European times, can raise enough corn in 190 days to supply the basic needs of several families for a year.[71] Even making allowance for the labor required for other subsistence needs, and making adjustments for such technological advances as metal tools, it is clear that the native economy was able to free large numbers of people from the work of providing their own food—at least as long as the supply of good land lasted. These people could devote themselves to a variety of specialized activities, ranging from the construction of temple complexes to their maintenance and operation. There may have been a similar potential in the simple horticultural systems of the Old World, but, if so, it was not utilized until the advent of metal.

A second key to the puzzle apparently lies in the role of religion in Mayan societies. A striking feature of every major settlement is the centrality

---

[68] The size and nature of some of these centers is a subject of much debate. Some claim they housed as many as 200,000 residents; others argue that they were merely religious centers with relatively small residential populations that served the surrounding peoples. For the two views, see Sylvanus Morley, *The Ancient Maya* (Stanford, Calif.: Stanford, 1946), p. 315, and J. E. S. Thompson, "A Survey of the Northern Mayan Area," *American Antiquity,* 2 (1945), pp. 2–24. Even if the early Mayan centers were not residential, however, it appears that later Mexican settlements were.

[69] On the Maya, see Morley, chap. 12. On the more general distribution of these intellectual skills, see Willey, pp. 91ff., or Victor von Hagen, *The Ancient Sun Kingdoms of the Americas* (Cleveland: World Publishing, 1961), pp. 47–58.

[70] This statement and many of those which follow apply not only to the Maya but also to a number of other less well known groups nearby.

[71] Morley, pp. 154–158. For figures from other parts of the horticultural world, see R. F. Watters, "The Nature of Shifting Cultivation," *Pacific Viewpoint,* 1 (1960), p. 93.

Figure 7.5 Mayan temple at Tikal.

and dominance of the complex of temple buildings. The priests who directed the construction of these massive buildings obviously had great authority or influence. We will never know for certain how they acquired their power, but it is probably more than coincidence that this large-scale temple construction began about the same time as the development of the calendar, writing, and the numeral system.[72] Since these innovations all were made by the priestly class or soon became their monopoly and since this knowledge was essential in determining the timing of crucial events in the annual horticultural cycle (planting, harvesting, etc.), the common people may have spontaneously accorded the priests high status and readily followed their leadership.[73] The influence of the

[72] Morley, p. 209, and Willey, pp. 94–96.

[73] Morley, pp. 144–147.

priests was further enhanced by such practices as prophecy, divination, and healing, all of which increased the people's dependence on them, and by the fact that they worked in close alliance with the governing nobility.

Finally, these societies occupied an area rich in a fortunate combination of soft and hard rock. The hard rocks, basalt and diorite, were admirably suited to cutting the softer limestone and sandstone. Furthermore, the softer stones were kinds that tend to harden after exposure to the elements, which greatly enhanced their value.[74] Few other simple horticulturalists have been so favorably situated.

The Mayan case is yet another reminder that there are alternative paths in societal evolution, though some, of course, have been followed much more often than others. The usual pattern at the simple horticultural level has been the formation of many small, relatively undifferentiated, autonomous farming villages. Because of the productivity of the horticultural economy, however, the formation of occasional trading centers like early Jericho has been one alternative. Another has been the development of larger and more complex "theocratic" communities like those created by the Maya and their neighbors.

No one can say with certainty why one, rather than another, of these alternatives was adopted, but nontechnological factors were undoubtedly important, especially in the case of the temple builders of the New World. Before temple construction was begun, their technology was apparently unexceptional. Thus we must look elsewhere for an explanation.

As we have seen, the environment provided these people with exceptionally fine building materials, but obviously these were not the stimulus for temple building. This could have come only from the religious system. Apparently out of appreciation to the gods for their blessings, especially for their help in certain critical horticultural activities, the Maya voluntarily offered them a portion of both their harvest and their labor. Under the direction of the priests, these contributions provided the material base for the development of an elaborate temple cult. Thus the surplus was taken from its producers before it could be consumed in the usual way, that is, by a simple increase in the number of farmers eking out a bare subsistence. Instead, these societies embarked on a course that checked population growth and led to institutional and occupational specialization on an impressive scale, and to the growth of social inequality.

This pattern of development is remarkably similar to the one that evolved in some very advanced horticultural societies of the Middle East in the fourth millennium B.C. In those groups, too, religion played an essential role in the preservation of the surplus and the creation of a more differentiated social

---

[74] Ibid., chap. 14.

Figure 7.6 Human sacrifice, from carving on the Mayan Temple of the Jaguars, Chichen Itza, Mexico.

system. They, too, had an intellectual elite of priests who introduced writing and counting, devised calendars, and developed the science of astronomy. Here, too, these skills apparently enhanced the priests' status, giving them the necessary power to develop an elaborate temple cult. The similarities extend even to the construction of massive temples.[75] The chief difference between the early theocracies of the Middle East and those of Mexico is that the former did not emerge until *after* the discovery of the basic principles of metallurgy.

Before leaving the Maya, we must take at least brief note of the dark side of their religious heritage, the practice of human sacrifice (see Figure 7.6). By modern standards, this involved a chillingly barbaric ceremony. One writer describes the ceremony this way:

> The victim was presented in the nude, his body painted blue, his head decorated with a pointed headdress. The place of execution was either the precinct of the temple, or the summit of the pyramid where the altar was erected; the altar of sacrifice was a heavy stone with a convex surface. Four assistants or *chaces,* also painted blue, took hold of the four limbs of the victim and laid him on his back on the stone so that his thorax projected. The sacrificer or *nacom,* equipped with a flint dagger, opened the lower left part of the breast, put his hand into the incision, tore out the beating heart, placed it on a plate and gave it to the priest or *chilán.* The *chilán* quickly smeared with blood the image of the god in whose honor the ceremony had been celebrated. The *chaces* threw the still warm body to the bottom of the pyramid where the priests of lower rank stripped it of all its skin, except for the hands and feet. The *chilán* dressed himself in this bloody skin and danced in company with the spectators. When the victim had been a particularly valiant soldier, the scene was accompanied by ritual cannibalism. The hands and feet were reserved for the *chilán.*[76]

Practices of this kind have been relatively common in horticultural and simple agrarian societies in both the Old World and the New.

---

[75] For discussions of these developments, see, among others, Childe, *Man Makes Himself,* chap. 7, or Henri Frankfort, *The Birth of Civilization in the Near East* (Bloomington: Indiana University Press, 1959), pp. 58ff.

[76] From Paul Rivet, *Maya Cities,* translated by M. Kochin and L. Kochin (New York: Putnam, 1960), p. 78. Quoted by permission of G. P. Putnam's Sons.

Advanced Horticultural Societies

The earliest use of metal in the Western Hemisphere was in central Peru around 1000 B.C.[77] At first, as in the Old World, relatively pure pieces of metal were simply hammered into ornaments, except that gold, not copper, was the most common metal. Later, techniques for melting, alloying, casting, and smelting were developed. Not long after the time of Christ, copper began to be used in tools and weapons with considerable frequency, and the first advanced horticultural societies appeared during the first half of the first millennium.[78] From

Figure 7.7   Ruins of Incan fortress. Note the careful masonry; no mortar was used by the Incas.

---

[77] Victor von Hagen, *The Desert Kingdoms of Peru* (London: Weidenfeld and Nicholson, 1965), p. 82, or Collier, p. 169.

[78] Collier, p. 170, or Julian Steward and Louis Faron, *Native Peoples of South America* (New York: McGraw-Hill, 1959), p. 99.

Peru, metallurgy spread north, and it reached Mexico early in the second millennium A.D.[79]

In most respects, the *advanced* horticultural societies of Peru resembled the *simple* horticultural societies of Mexico (the use of metal tools and weapons never became widespread enough in Mexico to justify calling any of the Mexican societies advanced). Both had numerous semiurban settlements with populations sometimes in excess of 10,000. Both also had architectural structures of massive proportions. These were usually of a religious nature in both instances, though religion seems to have been somewhat less central to societal life in Peru. A wide variety of crafts were highly developed in both areas, and social inequality was pronounced. And in both cases there was a small privileged elite of nobles and priests, set apart from the masses of common people whose labors supported them and their activities.

There were also a number of differences. Most were minor, but two deserve attention. First, the intellectual achievements of the Peruvians were somewhat inferior to those of the Mexicans. In particular, they had no system of writing—though they did have a primitive system of record keeping based on an intricate technique of knotting ropes.

The second important difference was in the political realm. Small, independent city-states were the rule in Mexico until a relatively late date.[80] In Peru, on the other hand, empire building began simultaneously with the use of metals for weapons.[81] During the first millennium A.D., conquests were on a very modest scale; the largest Peruvian state controlled only 20,000 square miles.[82] But in the centuries that followed, empires steadily grew in size, culminating in the Incan empire. This was the largest empire created by any native people in the New World and one of the largest ever created by a horticultural people anywhere. In the short space of a century, a series of Incan rulers built an empire of 350,000 square miles and several million inhabitants.[83]

HORTICULTURAL SOCIETIES IN THE MODERN ERA

In recent centuries, horticultural societies have been found in four parts of the world—the islands of the Pacific, southern Asia, Africa below the Sahara, and the New World. Most of those in the Pacific and the New World were simple hor-

---

[79] See von Hagen, *Ancient Sun Kingdoms*, p. 62, or Forbes, *Studies in Ancient Technology*, vol. 8, p. 14. Some of the Indians in what is now the United States cold-hammered pure copper prior to contact with Europeans. It is not known whether this represents an independent discovery on their part or was the result of diffusion from Mexico. See Forbes, vol. 9, pp. 2–5.

[80] Morley, pp. 159–161.

[81] Collier, pp. 170–173; Steward and Faron, pp. 86–100.

[82] Von Hagen, *The Desert Kingdoms*, p. 31.

[83] Steward and Faron, pp. 115 and 121.

Figure 7.8 Sketch of a village of simple horticulturalists in North Carolina, by John White (c. A.D. 1585).

ticultural societies; those in Africa and Asia were generally advanced. Before European expansion and colonialism in the sixteenth century, horticultural societies occupied about as much of the earth's surface as any societal type. Since then, however, they have declined greatly, not only as a result of conquest and absorption by more advanced societies but also because of hybridization resulting from cultural diffusion. Except in hybrid form (i.e., as industrializing horticultural societies), it is doubtful that they will survive much longer.

Simple Horticultural Societies

Simple horticultural societies are found today in only three parts of the world: the remote interior of the Amazon River basin; certain islands of the Pacific, particularly New Guinea; and parts of the hill country of Southeast Asia. In recent centuries, they also occupied much of North and South America.

All these groups practice some version of "slash-and-burn" or "swidden" horticulture. This involves the periodic clearing of new land to replace gardens that have lost their fertility and have been abandoned. Clearing is typically done by girdling or cutting trees and undergrowth and, after they have dried, setting fire to them. The ashes fertilize the ground, and the garden is then planted amid the stumps and debris (see Figure 7.9). The basic tools are wooden hoes and digging sticks. Women normally have the primary responsibility for the routine tasks of gardening, men for the occasional and

Figure 7.9 Women planting taro in a simple horticultural society in New Guinea. Note the stumps which remain in the cultivated area: most horticulturalists do not clear fields as completely as agriculturalists, who use the plow.

more strenuous tasks, such as clearing the land. Usually within a few years weeds take over and the soil loses its fertility, so new gardens must be cleared. The old ones are allowed to revert to jungle or forest and remain unused for decades until nature restores the soil's fertility. Then, the villagers return to the area and repeat the cycle all over again.

In most matters where comparisons are possible, the simple horticultural societies of modern times are strikingly similar to the type most common in prehistoric times. In other words, they are usually small, largely self-sufficient, politically autonomous villages with populations ranging from a few dozen to a few hundred.[84] Compared with modern hunting and gathering societies, their settlements are much more permanent; most groups move only every few years, when the soil is exhausted.[85] As in prehistoric times, the groups' relative permanence results in a greater accumulation of goods and the construction of more substantial buildings.[86] These developments are associated with a more diversified production of goods and services and an increase in trade.[87] Finally, as in the simple horticultural societies of the later Neolithic, warfare is fairly common.[88]

As with hunting and gathering societies, the ethnographic record not only supports the view provided by archaeology but broadens and enriches it. For example, modern studies show that kinship ties are extremely important in simple horticultural societies. In many instances, especially in the less advanced societies, these ties provide the basic framework of the social system.[89] This is hardly surprising in view of the small size of these groups: the average individual is related in some way to many, perhaps most, of those with whom he comes into contact and must consider his kinship obligations in all his dealings with them. The virtual absence of competing social structures (e.g., craft guilds, political parties, etc.) further enhances the importance of kinship.

Kinship systems in these societies are sometimes very complex, with intricate systems of rules governing relations between numerous categories of

---

[84] A careful comparison of societies in the two eras suggests that modern simple horticulturalists may be a bit less advanced than their prehistoric predecessors. For example, more than a third of those in Murdock's sample did not make pottery and more than half did not engage in weaving, both common practices in simple horticultural societies of prehistoric times.

[85] Only 10 per cent of the hunting and gathering societies in the Ethnographic Atlas sample maintained fairly permanent settlements, and virtually all these relied on either fishing or horticulture as a secondary source of subsistence. By contrast, 87 per cent of the simple horticultural societies maintained such settlements.

[86] A number of simple horticultural groups have built structures 50 or more feet long. See Gunnar Landtman, *The Kiwai Papuans of British New Guinea* (London: Macmillan, 1927), p. 5, or Gerhard Lenski, *Power and Privilege* (New York: McGraw-Hill, 1966), p. 121.

[87] Lenski, pp. 124–125.

[88] Ibid., p. 122.

[89] See, for example, Steward and Faron's statement (op. cit., p. 300) with reference to villagers who occupied most of the northern half of South America that "kinship was the basis of society throughout most of this area." Many similar statements could be cited.

Figure 7.10 Leisure among the Yanamamö. The man is the boy's mother's brother, and the relationship between them is a warm and important one, as in many horticultural societies.

kin. Extended family groups are common and usually very important, since they perform a number of essential functions for their members.[90] Above all, they function as mutual aid associations, providing the individual with protection against his enemies and with economic support. Although both these functions are important, the former is critical, for the political system is too primitive at this level to provide police services. Extended families also perform important regulatory functions in the area of marriage, and they sometimes have important religious functions as well. Finally, the most powerful or respected extended family often assumes leadership functions for the entire community, with its head serving as headman for the village.

One interesting and significant feature of kinship systems in these societies is the emphasis many of them give to ties with the mother's relatives. In this respect, horticultural societies, both simple and advanced, are unique. This can be seen clearly in the Ethnographic Atlas sample, where the percent-

[90] See E. Adamson Hoebel, *Anthropology*, 3d ed. (New York: McGraw-Hill, 1966), pp. 374–376, for a good brief summary of these functions.

age of societies having matrilineal kin groups (i.e., descent traced through the maternal line) is as follows:[91]

Hunting and gathering societies   10%
Simple horticultural societies   26%
Advanced horticultural societies   27%
Agrarian societies   4%

Figure 7.11 Yanamamö woman harvesting plantain, a type of banana that is usually cooked before eating. Plantain and manioc (a starchy tuber) provide about 70 percent of the Yanamamö's caloric intake.

[91] For similar findings based on Murdock's earlier sample of 565 societies, see David Aberle, "Matrilineal Descent in Cross-cultural Perspective," in David Schneider and Kathleen Gough (eds.), *Matrilineal Kinship* (Berkeley: University of California Press, 1961), table 17.4, p. 677.

Another indication of the importance attached to kinship on the female side is the frequency with which married couples are expected to live with or near the wife's parents (i.e., the practice known as matrilocality). Using the Ethnographic Atlas sample again, the frequency in different societal types is:

Hunting and gathering societies	3%
Simple horticultural societies	15%
Advanced horticultural societies	5%
Agrarian societies	1%

These unusual patterns are apparently linked with the women's contribution to subsistence in horticultural societies: in many of these groups, the women do most of the work of cultivation (see Table 7.1). Where men engage in activities that also make a substantial contribution to the subsistence of the group—hunting or herding, for example—matrilineal and matrilocal patterns are not as likely to develop. But where the men do not make a significant contribution, these patterns are much more common (see Table 7.2).[92]

Though village autonomy is still the rule in simple horticultural societies, as in hunting and gathering, multicommunity societies are more common.[93] These societies usually consist of only a handful of villages, seldom more than ten.[94] Usually they have been formed by a process of confederation involving villages that belong to a single tribe.[95] In most instances, military considerations, either offensive or defensive, provide the motivation to confederate.

Table 7.1 **The division of labor between the sexes in horticultural and agrarian societies**

Type of society	Percentage distribution			Total	Number of societies
	Horticulture primarily a female responsibility	Both sexes share equally	Horticulture primarily a male responsibility		
Simple horticultural	37	49	14	100	51
Advanced horticultural	50	27	23	100	142
Agrarian	7	37	56	100	43

Source: George Peter Murdock's Ethnographic Atlas sample of 915 societies.

[92] Aberle reached a similar conclusion (op. cit., p. 725). He states that "in general, matriliny is associated with horticulture, in the absence of major activities carried on and coordinated by males. . . ."

[93] Multicommunity societies constitute only 2 per cent of all pure hunting and gathering societies (i.e., those in which fishing and horticulture are not important secondary sources of subsistence) but comprise 23 per cent of all simple horticultural societies.

[94] Lenski, pp. 119–120.

[95] For an early statement of this process, see Lewis Henry Morgan, *Ancient Society* (Cambridge, Mass.: Belknap Press, 1964, first published 1877), pp. 109ff.

Table 7.2   Matrilineality and matrilocality among simple horticultural societies, by percentage of subsistence obtained by hunting and herding

Percentage of subsistence obtained by hunting and herding*	Percentage of societies matrilineal	Percentage of societies matrilocal	Number of cases
26 per cent or more	13	6	16
16 to 25 per cent	25	17	28–29†
Less than 15 per cent	39	22	23

Source: George Peter Murdock's Ethnographic Atlas sample of 915 societies.

* These figures are estimates (see footnote, Table 6.3).

† Information was available on matrilineality for 28 societies, on matrilocality for 29.

Despite the formation of these larger, more inclusive societies, the power of political leaders remains quite limited in nearly all simple horticultural societies. Except in matters of war and relations with other societies, local villages enjoy virtual autonomy. Both the village headman and the tribal chief depend more on persuasion than on coercion to achieve their goals. In part this is a result of the limited development of the governmental system, which means a leader has few subordinates so dependent on him that they are obliged to carry out his instructions. In part it is due to the absence of weapons that a governing class could monopolize to control the rest of the population; bronze weapons, for example, because they are expensive and must be made by specialists, lend themselves to monopolization by a wealthy minority.

In some simple horticultural societies, shamans also serve as headmen or chiefs because of the awe or respect in which they are held.[96] In other societies, secular leaders assume important religious functions and become quasi-religious figures. As one writer notes, a "chief's influence is definitely enhanced when he combines religious with secular functions."[97] In short, in many simple horticultural societies of the modern era, just as in the prehistoric past, church and state are closely linked and sometimes almost become one.

The only other important basis of political power in these societies is membership in a large and prosperous kin group. As we noted previously, the senior member and leader of the largest, most powerful, or most respected

---

[96] This dual role seems to have been quite common in South America. See Steward and Faron, p. 301, on the Indians of eastern Brazil and the Amazon Basin, or Julian Steward, "The Tribes of the Montaña and Bolivian East Andes," in Julian Steward (ed.), *Handbook of South American Indians,* Smithsonian Institution, Bureau of American Ethnology, Bulletin 143 (Washington, D.C., 1946–1950), vol. III, p. 528. For a slightly different pattern in North America, see Irving Goldman, "The Zuni Indians of New Mexico," in Margaret Mead (ed.), *Cooperation and Competition among Primitive Peoples,* rev. ed. (Boston: Beacon Press, 1961), p. 313.

[97] Robert Lowie, "Social and Political Organization," in Steward, *Handbook,* vol. V, p. 345. For examples of this, see Steward, *Handbook,* vol. III, pp. 85, 355, 419, and 478. See also Steward and Faron, p. 244.

lineage group often becomes the village headman or the tribal chief.[98] At a minimum, he can usually count on the support of his kinsmen, a substantial political resource in a society with such limited political development.

Social inequality is generally rather limited, though societies differ in this. Although extremes of wealth and political power are absent, substantial differences in prestige are not uncommon. Political and religious leaders usually enjoy high status, but this depends far more on their achievements than on mere occupancy of the office. There are few sinecures in these societies. Other bases of status include military prowess (which is highly honored in nearly all societies), skill in oratory, age, lineage, and in some cases wealth in the form of wives, pigs, and ornaments.[99] Each society has its own peculiar combination of these criteria.

The more advanced the technology and economy in one of these groups, the greater social inequality tends to be. Societies that practice irrigation, own domesticated animals, or practice metallurgy for ornamental and ceremonial purposes are usually less egalitarian than groups that have not taken these steps. We can see this when we compare the villagers of eastern Brazil and the Amazon River basin with their more advanced neighbors to the north and west who, in pre-Spanish days, practiced irrigation and metallurgy (since they used gold, which is too soft for tools and weapons, they cannot be considered advanced horticulturalists). Hereditary class differences were absent in the former groups but quite common in the latter, where a hereditary governing class of chiefs and nobles was set apart from the larger class of commoners.[100]

Modern ethnographers have found warfare to be much more common among horticulturalists than among hunters and gatherers (see Table 7.3). This finding parallels the evidence from archaeology, where all the signs indicate

Table 7.3 Incidence of warfare, by societal type (in percentages)

Type of Society	Frequent	Intermediate	Rare or Absent	Number of Societies
Hunting and gathering	0	55	45	11
Simple horticultural	45	55	0	11
Advanced horticultural	93	0	7	14

Source: Derived from Leo Simmons, *The Role of the Aged in Primitive Society* (New Haven, Conn.: Yale, 1945). The calculations are our own.

---

[98] See, for example, Alfred Métraux, *Native Tribes of Eastern Bolivia and Western Matto Grosso,* Smithsonian Institution, Bureau of American Ethnology, Bulletin 134 (Washington, D.C., 1942), p. 39, on the Araona, or Leopold Pospisil, "Kaupauku Papuan Political Structure," in F. Ray (ed.), *Systems of Political Control and Bureaucracy in Human Societies, Proceedings of the 1958 Meetings of the American Ethnological Society* (Seattle, Wash.), p. 18.

[99] For a more detailed discussion of these bases of status, see Lenski, pp. 126–131.

[100] See Steward and Faron, pp. 302–303, on the former, and pp. 213–214, 243, 248–249, on the latter.

Figure 7.12 Yanamamö men, intoxicated on ebene, a hallucinogenic drug, prepare for a "friendly" duel with a neighboring village with which they are allied. Such duels often turn violent and culminate in war.

that warfare increased substantially during the horticultural era. Now, as in the past, combat may serve as a psychic substitute for the challenge and rewards of hunting, which loses much of its honorific status with the shift to horticulture. Moreover, skill in warfare is probably essential in areas where population pressures and more stable settlement patterns combine to create a deadly game of musical chairs, whose losers often face societal extinction.

As warfare grows in importance in a society, several new patterns develop. Above all, there is the cult of the warrior, which heaps honors on successful fighters. Record keeping and publicity are no less important to these warrior heroes than to modern athlete heroes, and, in the absence of statisticians and sports writers, they invent techniques of their own—especially trophy taking. Some of the more popular trophies are scalps, skulls, and shrunken heads, all of which are preserved and displayed like modern athletic trophies.[101]

Ceremonial cannibalism, a surprisingly widespread practice among simple horticultural societies, may have developed as a by-product of trophy

---

[101] Data provided by Leo Simmons, *The Role of the Aged in Primitive Society* (New Haven, Conn.: Yale, 1945), show that scalp taking or headhunting was a frequent practice in only one of five hunting and gathering societies but in thirteen of fourteen horticultural societies.

Figure 7.13   The Jivaro Indians of western South America collected heads as trophies of their prowess and developed a special technique for shrinking and preserving them. The skin was removed from the skull and hot sand repeatedly poured in to dry and shrink it, after which the lips were sewed together.

collecting. Utilitarian cannibalism, or eating other humans to satisfy serious hunger, is an ancient practice, traceable to distant prehistoric times, but ceremonial cannibalism seems to be a more recent invention. The basic idea underlying it is that one can appropriate for oneself the valued qualities of a conquered enemy by eating his body.[102] Ceremonial cannibalism is usually surrounded by a complex, and often prolonged, set of rituals, as the following account from South America indicates.

> The prisoners taken by a Tupinamba war party were received with manifestations of anger, scorn, and derision, but after the first hostile outburst, they were not hampered in their movements nor were they unkindly treated. Their captors, whose quarters they shared, treated them as relatives. The prisoners generally married village girls, very often the sisters or daughters of their masters, or, in certain cases, the widow of a dead warrior whose hammock and ornaments they used. They received fields for their maintenance, they were free to hunt and fish, and they were reminded of their servile condition by few restrictions and humiliations.
>
> The period of captivity lasted from a few months to several years. When, finally, the date for the execution had been set by the village council, invitations were sent to nearby villages to join in the celebration. The ritual for the slaughter of a captive was worked out to the most minute detail. The club and cord which figured prominently in the ceremony were carefully painted and decorated in accordance with strict rules. For three days before the event, the village women danced, sang, and tormented the victim with descriptions of his impending fate. On the eve of his execution a mock repetition of his capture took place, during which the prisoner was allowed to escape but was immediately retaken; the man who overpowered him in a wrestling match adopted a new name, as did the ceremonial executioner.
>
> The prisoner spent his last night dancing, pelting his tormentors, and singing songs which foretold their ruin and proclaimed his pride at dying as a warrior. In the morning he was dragged to the plaza by old women amidst shouts, songs, and music. The ceremonial rope was removed from his neck and tied around his waist, and it was held at both ends by two or more men. The victim was once more permitted to give vent to his feelings by throwing fruit or potsherds at his enemies. The executioner, who appeared painted and dressed in a long feather cloak, derided the victim, who boasted of his past deeds and predicted that his relatives would avenge him.
>
> The actual execution was a cruel game. The prisoner was allowed sufficient freedom of movement to dodge the blows aimed at him; sometimes a club was put in his hands so that he could parry the blows without being able to

---

[102] Lest this idea appear utterly fanciful, it should be noted that in recent years experimental psychologists have trained various kinds of animals to do specific things and then have ground up their brains and injected the resulting chemical extracts into untrained animals, with the effect that the untrained animals displayed the learned pattern of behavior, indicating a chemical transfer of learning. See Fred Warshofsky, *The Control of Life* (New York: Viking, 1969), pp. 165–167.

strike back. When at last he fell, his skull shattered, everyone shouted and whistled. Old women rushed in to drink the warm blood, children were invited to dip their hands in it, and mothers smeared their nipples so that even infants could have a taste. While the quartered body was being roasted on a babracot the old women, who were the most eager to taste human flesh, licked the grease running from the sticks. Certain delicate or sacred portions, such as the fingers and the grease around the liver, were given to distinguished guests.[103]

The high incidence of warfare in simple horticultural societies serves to keep the channels of vertical mobility open. Almost every boy becomes a warrior and thus has a chance to win high honors and great influence. At the same time, however, a comparison of hunting and gathering with simple horticultural societies reveals a strengthening of those elements in the social system which make it possible for favored members of one generation to transmit their advantages to their children. To begin with, the general structural development associated with horticultural societies contributes to that end. The occupants of key positions, such as headmen, are somewhat less dependent on their personal skills than are their counterparts in hunting and gathering groups. The institutional structure of many of these societies has evolved to the point where a leader no longer needs to prove that he is the best man in the group but only that he is competent to fill the position. In large part this is possible because a headman or chief frequently has assistants to help him, as well as other resources beyond his own personal abilities. Another factor with a similar effect is the greater amount of private property, such as pigs and valued ornaments, that can be passed from one generation to the next. Finally, there is the greater strength of extended family groups and the greater inequality among them. On balance, therefore, the accident of birth—being born into one family rather than another—counts for more in simple horticultural societies than in hunting and gathering societies.

Advanced Horticultural Societies

For several centuries, advanced horticultural societies have been limited to two parts of the world, sub-Saharan Africa and Southeast Asia. In sub-Saharan Africa they occupied almost all the land until recently; other types of societies—hunters and gatherers, herders, and fishers—were relatively few in number. In Southeast Asia, on the other hand, agrarian societies occupied most of the land.

These advanced horticulturalists of modern times differ in one important respect from their prehistoric predecessors: the dominant metal in their

---

[103] Alfred Metraux, "Warfare-Cannibalism-Trophies," in Steward, *Handbook,* vol. V, pp. 400–401. Quoted by permission of the Bureau of American Ethnology.

Figure 7.14 Partial view of a village of advanced horticulturalists, Dahomey.

societies has been iron, not copper or bronze. This fact is important, because iron ore is so much more plentiful than copper and tin that it can be used for ordinary tools as well as weapons. However, because it is so much more difficult to reduce the ore to metal, the manufacture of iron was the last to develop.

The history of Africa proves once again that the evolutionary process does not compel societies to follow exactly the same pattern of development. Bronze was never the dominant metal in most of Africa below the Sahara. During the period when bronze was dominant in the Middle East, cultural contacts between Egypt and the territories to the south were minimal. By the time there was sufficient contact to permit diffusion of specialized skills like metallurgy, iron had become dominant.[104]

Compared with hunting and gathering or simple horticultural societies, advanced horticultural societies are usually larger and more complex. Table 5.2 (page 104) summarizes the evidence from Murdock's sample. Communities in advanced horticultural societies are three times larger than those in simple horticultural societies and seven times larger than those in hunting and gathering societies. A comparison of societies is even more striking: on the average,

---

[104] Sonia Cole, *The Prehistory of East Africa* (New York: Mentor, 1965), p. 299.

advanced horticultural societies are 60 times the size of simple horticultural and 140 times the size of hunting and gathering societies.

As one would expect, advanced horticultural societies are also structurally more complex. Of those in Murdock's sample, some have as many as *four* layers of government above the local community; no simple horticultural society in the sample has more than *two* layers. These data also show that village autonomy is the rule in simple horticultural societies, the exception in advanced horticultural. In 79 per cent of the former, villages are autonomous; in 71 per cent of the latter, they are *not.*

Another evidence of structural complexity is the extent of occupational specialization. Table 5.3 (page 105) shows that craft specialization is much more common in advanced horticultural societies than in simple ones. In six basic areas, craft specialization occurred an average of only 2 per cent of the time in simple horticultural societies but 28 per cent of the time in advanced.

Murdock's data also show that social inequality increases markedly with the emergence of advanced horticultural societies. Class stratification was reported in only 17 per cent of the simple horticultural societies, as opposed to 54 per cent of the advanced (see Table 5.6, page 107). In addition, the class

Figure 7.15 Basket weaver at work beside his home, Guinea.

systems of the latter are generally more complex, involve greater degrees of inequality, and are more often hereditary.[105] The presence of slavery in 83 per cent of the advanced but only 14 per cent of the simple horticultural societies is a striking illustration of this (see Table 5.5, page 107).

One consequence of the more fully developed economy and stratification system in advanced horticultural societies is their increased emphasis on the economic aspect of marriage. In almost every one of these societies, marriagable daughters are viewed as a valuable economic property, and men who want to marry them must either pay for the privilege or render extended service to their prospective in-laws. Fortunately for young men with limited resources, extended kin groups tend to view marriage as a sensible investment and are often willing to loan suitors part of the bride price. This economic approach to marriage is much more common in advanced horticultural societies than in either hunting and gathering or simple horticultural societies (see Table 7.4).

The growth in social inequality is closely linked with the growth of government. A generation ago, Meyer Fortes, one of the pioneer students of African political systems, argued that most African societies fell into one of two basic categories: those "which have centralized authority, administrative machinery, and judicial institutions—in short, a government—and in which cleavages of wealth, privilege, and status correspond to the distribution of authority" and those which have none of these attributes.[106] Though recent studies suggest that this twofold division is something of an oversimplification, they confirm that African societies differ in the ways Fortes described and that there is a strong relationship between the development of the state and the growth of social inequality.[107]

Table 7.4 Association of economic transaction with marriage, by societal type

Type of Society	Percentage of Societies Requiring Economic Transaction with Marriage	Number of Societies
Hunting and gathering	49	148
Simple horticultural	61	74
Advanced horticultural	97	265

Source: George Peter Murdock's Ethnographic Atlas sample of 915 societies.

[105] Of the simple horticultural societies, 15 per cent had hereditary systems of stratification, compared to 47 per cent of the advanced horticultural societies. None of the simple societies had complex systems of stratification (i.e., three or more classes apart from slaves), compared with 7 per cent of the advanced.

[106] Meyer Fortes, in Meyer Fortes and E. E. Pritchard (eds.), African Political Systems (London: Oxford, 1940), p. 5.

[107] In one study of twenty-two African horticultural societies, a correlation of .67 (Kendall's tau) was found between level of political development and level of social inequality (see Lenski, p. 163). See also Basil Davidson with F. K. Buah, A History of West Africa: To the Nineteenth Century (Garden City, N.Y.: Doubleday Anchor, 1966), p. 174.

African societies afford a valuable opportunity to study the early stages of political development. A leading student of East African political systems suggests that a critical step in the process occurs when the head of some strong extended family group begins to take on, as retainers, men who are not related to him, thus breaking out of one of the traditional limitations on power and its expansion.[108] These retainers are usually individuals who have been expelled from their own kin groups for misconduct or whose groups have been destroyed in war or some natural disaster, and they offer their allegiance and service in exchange for protection and a livelihood.

Since there is a natural tendency for men in this position to turn to the strongest families, power begins to pyramid. This is reinforced by the wealth of such a group, which permits it to buy more wives to produce more sons and warriors, and by the development of myths that explain the group's success by attributing magical powers to its leader. The final link in this chain of state building is forged when less powerful families, and even whole communities, are brought under the control of the head of a strong family group—either by conquest or by the decision of the weaker groups to put themselves under the strong group's protection. When this happens, each of the subordinate groups is usually allowed to retain its land, and its leader his authority within the group, but the group is compelled to pay tribute. The leader of the dominant group then uses these revenues to support his kinsmen and retainers, thereby increasing their dependence on him and, it is hoped, their loyalty to him as well.

Sometimes the state-building process is stimulated by intrafamily and interfamily feuds that get out of hand. Where strong political authority is lacking, feuds are a serious matter. Individuals and families are forced to redress their own grievances, which often sets off a deadly cycle of action and reaction. More than one East African group has voluntarily put itself under the authority of a strong neighboring leader just to break such a cycle and reestablish peace among its members.

One might suppose that these processes, once set in motion, would continue until eventually all Africa was brought under a single authority. But powerful countervailing forces prevented this. Technological limitations, especially in transportation and communication, were most important. Advanced horticulturalists in Africa, as in the New World, had no knowledge of the wheel and used no draft animals until contact with Europeans. As a result, the further a ruler's power extended into outlying areas, the weaker it became. These areas were vulnerable to attack by foreign enemies, and, even more serious, they were vulnerable to revolt. From the territorial standpoint, Mali was probably the largest kingdom that ever developed in sub-Saharan Africa. In the early four-

---

[108] See Lucy Mair, *Primitive Government* (Baltimore: Penguin, 1962), especially chap. 4. The discussion that follows is based largely on her work.

teenth century, it controlled approximately 500,000 square miles in the western Sudan.[109] Most African kingdoms were much smaller.

By the standards of modern industrial societies, the governments of Africa's advanced horticultural societies were extremely unstable. Revolts were a common occurrence, not only in outlying provinces but even in the capitals. These were seldom, if ever, popular risings. Rather, they were instigated by powerful members of the nobility, often the king's own brothers, a pattern so common that the Zulus developed a proverb that "the king should not eat with his brothers lest they poison him."[110]

In virtually every politically advanced society of horticultural Africa

Figure 7.16 Woman spreading rice to dry in the sun, Liberia.

---

[109] Estimated from the map in Davidson, p. 56.

[110] I. Schapera, *Government and Politics in Tribal Societies* (London: Watts, 1956), p. 169. See also the Swazi proverb that "nobles are the chief's murderers."

Figure 7.17 Early bronze casting of Dahomean chief and his entourage of relatives and retainers. Note the fine workmanship. This is a native art form in West Africa, predating European contact.

there was a sharply defined cleavage between a hereditary nobility and the mass of common people. Historically, this distinction grew out of the state-building process.[111] Nobles were usually descendants either of past rulers and their chief lieutenants or of hereditary leaders of subordinated groups. They comprised a warrior aristocracy supported by the labors of the common people. Below the commoners there was often a class of slaves, many of them captives taken in war, and, as in other horticultural societies, they were frequently slaughtered as human sacrifices.

In the advanced horticultural societies of Africa, as in the New World and elsewhere, religion and politics were intimately related. In many instances the king was viewed as divine or as having access to divine powers.[112] This undoubtedly served to legitimate many tyrannical and exploitative practices. And it helps explain why no efforts were made to establish other kinds of political systems: given the ideological heritage of these societies, such a thing was inconceivable. This ideology did not protect a ruler against attacks from his

---

[111] See, for example, Davidson, chap. 14.

[112] See, for example, George Peter Murdock, *Africa: Its Peoples and Their Culture History* (New York: McGraw-Hill, 1959), p. 37.

kinsmen, however, because they shared his special religious status and were also qualified to assume the duties and privileges of the royal office—if they could seize it.

A comparison of the politically advanced societies of sub-Saharan Africa with those which remained autonomous villages shows that the former were more developed in other ways as well. They were far likelier to have full-time craft specialization, for example, and they were also more likely to have urban or semiurban settlements—a few with populations of 20,000 or more.[113]

Before concluding this discussion of advanced horticultural societies in the modern era, a brief comment on those in Southeast Asia is necessary. The striking feature of these societies is their relative backwardness, especially from the standpoint of political development. In most instances they remain on the level of village autonomy, and when multicommunity societies do develop, they invariably are small.[114] Urban or semiurban settlements are absent. The reason appears to be ecological. Centuries ago, after this region came under the domination of more powerful agrarian societies, horticultural societies usually survived only in hill country where transportation was difficult and the land unsuited for the plow and permanent cultivation. This combination of more powerful neighbors and the deficiencies of their own territories apparently prevented all but the most limited development and caused these groups to be looked down upon, and often exploited, by their agrarian neighbors. The Montagnards (or hill people) of Vietnam are a classic instance of this.[115]

Ecological factors of a different type had a similar effect in certain parts of Africa: political development was quite limited in the tropical rain forests. Apparently the lush vegetation and other hindrances to the movement of armies and goods made it impossible to build and maintain extensive kingdoms.[116]

HORTICULTURAL SOCIETIES IN EVOLUTIONARY PERSPECTIVE

Few events in human history can match in importance the discovery of the principles of plant cultivation. It is no exaggeration to say that the discovery of horticulture in the realm of technology was comparable to the invention of symbols in the realm of communication. Each was a decisive break with the animal world. Hunting and gathering, like the use of signals, are techniques

---

[113] See, for example, P. C. Lloyd, "The Yoruba of Nigeria," in James Gibbs (ed.), *Peoples of Africa* (New York: Holt, 1965), pp. 554–556.

[114] For an example of a multicommunity society, see P. R. T. Gurdon, *The Khasis* (London: Macmillan, 1914). This author reports that these people were divided into fifteen small states averaging 15,000 in population and controlling about 400 square miles apiece (pp. 1 and 66).

[115] The term "Montagnards" refers to a number of separate and independent groups of horticulturalists in the Vietnam highlands.

[116] Lenski, pp. 160–162. See also Davidson, pp. 76–77.

man inherited from his prehuman ancestors. Horticulture and symbols, by contrast, are uniquely human.

Of the many enormous changes that accompanied horticulture, three stand out: (1) the growth of the human population, (2) the greater permanence of their settlements, and (3) the potential for a stable economic surplus. More people meant more minds at work on the problems of human life, with all that implies for the rate of technological advance. More permanent settlements meant more opportunity for people to accumulate possessions, hence a greater incentive for them to exercise inventiveness and creativity in the productive realm. A stable economic surplus meant new organizational opportunities, particularly in the areas of occupational and institutional specialization. Collectively, these developments added up to a revolutionary change in the conditions of human life.

Not all horticultural peoples took full advantage of the new opportunities; some remained on the level of the relatively undifferentiated, autonomous village. This suggests that horticulture is a necessary condition, but not in itself a sufficient *cause,* for the emergence of more complex social systems. The formation of such systems requires some specialized institution that will appropriate part of what is produced before population growth consumes all of it. Religious institutions have often performed this function, motivating men to offer up their surplus to the gods, and to the priests who serve them. In other instances political institutions collect the surplus by means of taxes and tribute. In either case, part of the population is freed from the task of providing its own food supply and is able to engage in specialized activities of various kinds.

Before concluding this summary, a brief comment on the ethical consequences of the horticultural revolution is needed, lest anyone still suppose that the technological and structural progress of horticultural societies implies ethical progress. As numerous scholars have noted, it is one of the great ironies of evolution that progress in the technological and structural spheres is often linked with ethical *regress.* Horticultural societies provide several striking examples. Some of the most shocking, by the standards of our own society, are the increases in headhunting, scalp taking, cannibalism, human sacrifice, and slavery, all more common in the technologically progressive horticultural societies than in the more backward hunting and gathering groups.

Another development that many would regard as ethical regression is the decline in the practice of sharing and the growing acceptance of economic and other kinds of inequality. This is not as simple a matter as it seems on the surface, however. As we have seen, inequality is the inevitable accompaniment of an economic surplus in societies at this stage of development. And that surplus seems to be a prerequisite for the development of civilization—with all that implies—and for improvement of the standard of living. In other words, without an economic surplus, all the benefits of technological advance would be swallowed up by population growth, and the result would simply be more people living at the subsistence level. Our view of the ethics of this growth in inequality, therefore, depends largely on whether we take a short-term or a long-term view. If we judge it from the standpoint of the generations adversely affected, we will conclude that it was ethically regressive. But if we judge it from the standpoint of all subsequent generations, we might very well take the opposite view. We will want to return to this problem in the final chapter.

CHAPTER EIGHT

Agrarian Societies

To a modern city dweller, the plow may not sound much like the basis of a major social revolution. Yet history shows it was exactly that. Agrarian societies have far surpassed horticultural societies in size, complexity, and military power. Not surprisingly, they have also displaced them over vast areas.

The etymologies of the words "horticulture" and "agriculture" suggest some of the reasons for this. Horticulture comes from the Latin words *hortus,* or "garden," and *cultura,* "cultivation." Agriculture, by contrast, comes from *ager,* which means "field." Agriculture, therefore, means cultivation on a larger scale, with greater permanence,[1] with a more powerful and effective tool, and with greater yields.

To appreciate the importance of the plow, we need to keep in mind two basic problems that confront farmers everywhere: controlling weeds and maintaining the fertility of the soil.[2] With traditional horticultural tools and techniques, both of these problems grow more severe the longer a plot is cultivated. Weeds multiply faster than horticulturalists with their hoes can root them out. At the same time, the soil's nutrients seep into the ground, below the reach of plants and too deep to be brought back to the surface with hoes or other simple tools. Within a few years, the yield usually becomes so small that the cultivator is forced to abandon the plot and move elsewhere.[3]

The plow, if it did not eliminate these problems, at least reduced them to manageable proportions and made the permanent cultivation of fields a common practice for the first time in history. Because it turns the soil over to a greater depth than the hoe, the plow buries weeds, not only killing them but adding humus to the soil. Deeper cultivation also brings back to the surface the nutrients that have seeped below root level.

The invention of the plow paved the way for another crucial innovation, the harnessing of animal energy.[4] As long as the digging stick and hoe were

---

[1] Fields, unlike gardens, are normally cultivated continuously, for generations or even centuries.

[2] This paragraph and the one that follows are based on B. H. Farmer, "Agriculture: Comparative Technology," in *International Encyclopedia of the Social Sciences* (New York: Macmillan and Free Press, 1968), vol. 1, pp. 204–205.

[3] In a few instances, horticulturalists have been able to maintain continual cultivation because of irrigation (natural or artificial) or fertilization (ibid., p. 204).

[4] See Gudmund Hatt, "Farming of Non-European Peoples," in E. Cecil Curwen and Gudmund Hatt, *Plough and Pasture: The Early History of Farming* (New York: Collier Books, 1961), pp. 217–218.

the basic tools of cultivation, men and women had to supply the energy. But the plow could be pulled, and it did not take long for people to discover that oxen could do the job. The importance of this discovery can hardly be exaggerated, since it established a principle with broad applicability. As V. Gordon Childe has stated, "The ox was the first step to the steam engine and the [gasoline] motor."[5]

More immediately, however, the harnessing of animal energy relieved people of one of the most exhausting forms of labor required by the new mode of food production and led to greatly increased productivity. With a plow and a pair of oxen, a person could cultivate a far larger area than he could with a hoe.[6] In addition, the use of oxen led, in many societies, to stall feeding, and this in turn led to the use of manure, a practice that contributed further to soil fertility.[7] In short, the shift from the hoe to the plow not only meant fields kept permanently under cultivation and larger crops; it also meant the potential for a much larger economic surplus and new and more complex forms of social structure.[8]

SIMPLE AGRARIAN SOCIETIES

The earliest evidence of the plow comes from Mesopotamian cylinder seals and Egyptian paintings dating from a little before 3000 B.C.[9] Modern research indicates that the plow, like so many other innovations since the Paleolithic, presupposed certain earlier inventions and discoveries—underlining again the cumulative nature of technological change. The first plows of the Mesopotamians and the Egyptians were simply modified versions of the hoe, the basic farm implement of all advanced horticultural societies. In the earliest period, the plow was probably pulled by men, but before long, cattle and oxen began to be used.

As in the case of horticulture, the techniques of agriculture spread by

---

[5] V. Gordon Childe, *What Happened in History* (Baltimore: Penguin, 1964), p. 89.

[6] Gordon Childe, *Man Makes Himself* (New York: Mentor, 1951), p. 100.

[7] Farmer, p. 205.

[8] See Childe, *Man Makes Himself*, p. 100. In recent years, some have argued that horticulture is more efficient than agriculture in the tropics and that horticultural societies should not be considered less advanced that agricultural. Though there are some areas where horticulture is more efficient, these are rare (a 1957 study by the Food and Agriculture Organization of the United Nations showed that only 7 per cent of the world's population were using horticultural techniques, and often only because of ignorance of the alternative). Furthermore, horticultural societies clearly have not achieved the efficiency in other areas of technology or the complexity of social structure and ideology that agrarian societies have. Though we know of no single paper that provides a comprehensive, balanced analysis of this problem, we recommend R. F. Watters's excellent paper, "The Nature of Shifting Cultivation: A Review of Recent Research," *Pacific Veiwpoint,* 1 (1960), pp. 59–99, especially pp. 77–95.

[9] E. Cecil Curwen, "Prehistoric Farming of Europe and the Near East," in Curwen and Hatt, pp. 64–65; or C. W. Bishop, "The Origin and Early Diffusion of the Traction Plow," *Antiquity,* 10 (1936), p. 261.

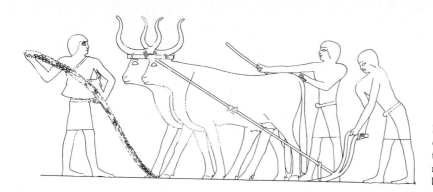

Figure 8.1 Early Egyptian ox-drawn plow (c. 2700 B.C.). Note the primitive method of harnessing the animals—a simple bar attached to their horns.

diffusion until agrarian societies were eventually established throughout most of Europe and much of North Africa and Asia. For reasons that remain obscure, use of the plow never spread to sub-Saharan Africa until the period of European colonialism. In the New World, too, it was unknown until introduced by Europeans.

The full impact of the new technology was not felt immediately in either Mesopotamia or Egypt. Nevertheless, the shift to agriculture was quickly followed by several important developments, notably the invention of writing, the rise of urban communities,[10] and the beginnings of empire building (which in Egypt led to the unification of the entire country under a single ruler for the first time in history). This was the period that historians refer to as "the dawn of civilization."

As we have seen, similar developments occurred (though at later dates) in horticultural societies in China and Mexico, proving that an agrarian economy was not a *necessary* precondition for literacy, urbanism, and large-scale imperialism. But the rarity of these phenomena in horticultural societies and their frequency in agrarian societies indicate that the shift to agriculture, by increasing productivity, greatly increased the probability of their occurrence.

The Role of Religion in the Formation of a Surplus

In early Mesopotamia and Egypt, religion was an extremely powerful force in the life of society. Mesopotamian theology held that "man was . . . created for one purpose only: to serve the gods by supplying them with food, drink, and

---

[10] Recently some scholars have argued that Egypt had no cities at this time. See, for example, John A. Wilson, "Civilization without Cities," in Carl Kraeling and Robert Adams (eds.), *City Invincible: A Symposium on Urbanization and Cultural Development in the Ancient Near East* (Chicago: University of Chicago Press, 1960), pp. 124–136, or William McNeill, *The Rise of the West: A History of the Human Community* (New York: Mentor, 1963), pp. 87–88. Although there were surely differences between Egyptian and Mesopotamian cities, it seems to be semantic gamesmanship to deny the existence of Egypt's cities. Several commentators on Wilson's paper made just this point (see Kraeling and Adams, pp. 136–162). Especially telling was the comment of one Mesopotamian specialist, who noted that when the Assyrians came to Egypt, they spoke of "hundreds of cities" (Kraeling and Adams, p. 140).

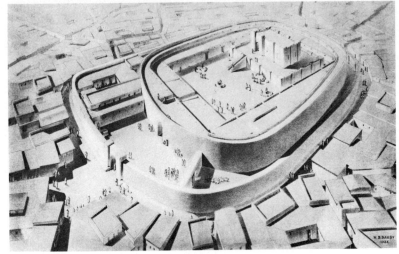

Figure 8.2 Early Mesopotamian temple and its environs: temple oval at Khafaja.

shelter so that they might have full leisure for their divine activities."[11] Each temple was believed to be, quite literally, the house of a particular god, and each community had its own special deity. Priests and other attendants constituted the god's court or household, and their chief task was to minister to his needs. Another responsibility was to mediate between the god and the community, trying to discover his will and appease his anger. In order for them to perform these tasks, temples and their staffs had to be supported by a steady flow of goods. Over the years, the temples were continually enlarged and became increasingly costly. In fact, they became, in many respects, substantial business enterprises, a development that apparently provided the stimulus for the invention of writing, which was originally a means of recording the temple's business activities.[12] Many scholars have described the early Mesopotamian city-states as theocracies, since the local deity was regarded as the real ruler and the king merely as his "tenant farmer."[13]

Egypt was also a theocracy, but of a different type. One scholar compared the Egyptian and Mesopotamian patterns this way:

Egypt's theocracy was of a totally different kind from that of [Mesopotamia]; instead of the earthly ruler being but the chosen representative and the "tenant farmer" of the sovereign deity, Pharaoh was himself a god, and his government was divine simply because it was Pharaoh's. The other gods did not and could

[11] Samuel Noah Kramer, *The Sumerians: Their History, Culture, and Character* (Chicago: University of Chicago Press, 1963), p. 123.

[12] Childe, *Man Makes Himself*, pp. 143–144.

[13] See, for example, Sir Leonard Woolley, *The Beginnings of Civilization*, UNESCO History of Mankind, vol. 1, part 2, (New York: Mentor, 1965), pp. 116, 119, 198, 449ff., etc.

not dispute his authority. To whatever deity of the Egyptian pantheon the local temple might be dedicated, yet Pharaoh's statues adorned it and, likely as not, the reliefs on the walls celebrated Pharaoh's exploits.[14]

To his subjects Pharaoh "was the incarnation, the living embodiment, of the god of any district he happened to be visiting; he was their actual God in living form, whom they could see, speak to, and adore."[15] Like the gods of the Mesopotamian city-states, he was theoretically the owner of the land and hence entitled to a portion of all that was produced, and, as in Mesopotamia, his revenues supported a small army of specialists (e.g., officials, craftsmen, soldiers, etc.).

In later years there was a secularizing trend, especially in Mesopotamia.[16] By then, however, societies had developed other institutional arrangements—notably political ones—to ensure the continued transfer of the economic surplus from the peasant producers to the governing class. Nevertheless, religion continued to play an important role as a legitimizing agency: it provided a rationale to justify the operation of the political system and its economic consequences.

The experience of Mesopotamia and Egypt thus supports our earlier impressions (based on Mexico and China) concerning the role of religion in the formation of an economic surplus. Technological advance creates the possibility of a surplus; religion can transform this possibility into a reality. Technological advance makes it *possible* for farmers to produce more than they need to stay alive and productive; religion can motivate them to *do* it and go on to convince them that they should turn the surplus over to others. Although this has sometimes been accomplished in other ways (e.g., the political system sometimes provides the motivation and rationale), it is significant that in at least four cases—Mesopotamia, Egypt, Mexico, and China—religion apparently played this critical role. This is an aspect of the evolutionary process which our own highly secularized generation is apt to overlook.

Scale of Organization

In the first few centuries after the shift to agriculture, there was striking growth in the size of a number of communities, especially in Mesopotamia.[17] These

---

[14] Sir Leonard Woolley, *Prehistory* (New York: Harper & Row, 1963), vol. 1, part 2, p. 127. Reprinted by permission.

[15] Margaret Murray, *The Splendour That Was Egypt* (London: Sidgwick & Jackson, 1949), p. 174.

[16] On Mesopotamia, see Woolley, p. 356, or A. Leo Oppenheim, *Ancient Mesopotamia: Portrait of a Dead Civilization* (Chicago: University of Chicago Press, 1964), pp. 84–85. On Egypt, see Ralph Turner, *The Great Cultural Traditions: The Foundations of Civilization* (New York: McGraw-Hill, 1941), vol. 1, p. 187, or George Steindorff and Keith Seele, *When Egypt Ruled the East,* rev. ed. (Chicago: Phoenix Books, 1963), p. 83.

[17] Robert Adams, "Factors Influencing the Rise of Civilization in the Alluvium: Illustrated by Mesopotamia," in Kraeling and Adams, p. 33.

became the first full-fledged cities in history. The largest of them were in-variably the capitals of the largest and most prosperous societies. Although it is impossible to obtain accurate figures on the size of the cities and towns of the third and second millenniums B.C. and scholars disagree on the interpretation of the evidence, some believe that one or more of these cities passed the 100,000 mark.[18]

Egypt was the largest of the simple agrarian societies of ancient times and politically the most stable. She enjoyed the unique distinction of surviving as a united and independent nation throughout most of the simple agrarian era. This achievement was due to her unique ecological situation: no other society had such excellent natural defenses and was so little threatened by powerful neighbors.

In the second half of the second millennium, Egypt embarked on a pro-gram of expansion that brought under her control all the territory from Syria to the Sudan. There were also other important empires in this era, especially those established by the Babylonians in the eighteenth century B.C. and the Hittites in the thirteenth century B.C. Babylonia succeeded briefly in uniting most of Meso-potamia, while the Hittites conquered much of what is now Turkey and Syria.

Organizational Development: Growth of the State

These conquests posed serious organizational problems for the rulers of early agrarian societies. Traditional modes of government organized around an ex-tended family proved completely inadequate for administering the affairs of societies whose populations now sometimes numbered in the millions. Though rulers continued to rely on relatives to help them perform the most essential

Figure 8.3 Egyptian soldiers attacking a fortress (c. 1940 B.C.).

---

[18] See, for example, Kramer, pp. 88–89; Woolley, p. 125; or Kingsley Davis, "The Origin and Growth of World Ur-banism," *American Journal of Sociology*, 60 (1955), p. 431. See also Oppenheim, p. 140, who, though declining to estimate size, reports Nineveh to have been larger than Ur (generally thought to have been over 100,000) and Uruk nearly as large.

Figure 8.4 This model of a royal granary was found in the tomb of Meket-Re (c. 2000 B.C.). Note the scribes and other officials recording the deliveries of grain.

tasks of government, they were forced to turn increasingly to others. One expedient was to incorporate a conquered group as a subdivision of the state, leaving its former ruler in charge, but in a subordinate capacity. Eventually, however, all of the more successful rulers found it necessary to create new kinds of organizational structures, not based on ties of kinship.

We can see these newer patterns developing in both military and civil affairs. The first armies, for example, were simply organizations of all the able-bodied men in the society.[19] During this period, wars were of short duration and were fought only after the harvest was in. In fact, the period following the harvest came to be known as the "season when kings go forth to war." This limitation was essential because, with the shift to agriculture, the male's responsibilities in farming had greatly increased.

As long as wars were brief and limited to skirmishes with neighboring peoples, this arrangement was adequate. But once rulers became interested in empire building, the traditional system proved impossible. As early as the middle of the third millennium in Mesopotamia, would-be empire builders established small, but highly trained, professional armies. For example, Sargon,

---

[19] Woolley, pp. 185ff., or Steindorff and Seele, pp. 89–90.

the famous Akkadian king, had a standing army of 5,400 men who "ate daily before him."[20] As far as possible, recruits were sons of old soldiers, and thus a military caste was gradually created. The Egyptians followed a similar policy except that they relied chiefly on foreign mercenaries. These new armies soon came to be *royal,* rather than national, armies. Their expenses were paid by the king out of his enormous revenues, and the profits resulting from their activities were his also. Not only were these armies useful in dealing with foreign enemies, they also served as a defense against internal threats.[21]

In civil affairs, too, the casual and informal practices of simpler societies proved inadequate. As states expanded and the problems of administration multiplied, new kinds of governmental positions were created, and a governmental bureaucracy began to take shape.[22] In addition to the many officials who comprised the royal court and were responsible for administering the king's complex household affairs, there were officials scattered throughout the countryside to administer the affairs of units ranging from small districts to provinces with hundreds of villages and towns. Each official had a staff of scribes and other lesser officials to assist him, and written records became increasingly important as administrative problems grew more complex.[23]

Throughout most of the history of the simple agrarian societies of antiquity, writing was a specialized art mastered by only a few individuals after long apprenticeships.[24] This is easily understood, considering the complex, prealphabetic systems of writing then in use. Even after a process of simplification that lasted over 2,000 years, cuneiform script still had between 600 and 1,000 distinct characters. Before a person could learn to read or write, he had to memorize this formidable array of symbols and learn the complex rules for combining them. The Egyptian hieroglyphic and hieratic scripts were equally complicated. Thus, those who could write formed a specialized occupational group in society—the scribes—and their services were much in demand. For the most part this occupation was filled by the sons of the rich and powerful, since only they could afford the necessary education.[25] Because of the political importance of their skill and the limited supply of qualified personnel, most scribes were at least marginal members of the governing class.

---

[20] Woolley, p. 188. Later armies were even larger.

[21] Turner, p. 312.

[22] McNeill, p. 68; Turner, pp. 310–311; Steindorff and Seele, chap. 9; Pierre Montet, *Everyday Life in Egypt: In the Days of Rameses the Great,* trans. A. R. Maxwell-Hyslop and Margaret Drower (London: E. Arnold, 1958), chap. 10; Oppenheim, pp. 70ff., 230ff., and 276–277.

[23] Oppenheim, p. 276. As one writer reports, "Sumerian bureaucracy has left us a staggering number of texts; we are unable to venture a guess as to how many tablets beyond the far more than 100,000 now in museums may be buried in southern Mesopotamia."

[24] Childe, *Man Makes Himself,* pp. 148–149, or Childe, *What Happened in History,* p. 144.

[25] See especially Kramer, p. 231, or Samuel Noah Kramer, *It Happened at Sumer* (Garden City, N.Y.: Doubleday, 1959), p. 3.

Figure 8.5 Two sides of a limestone tablet found at Kish, Mesopotamia, bearing some of the oldest known picture writing (c. 3500 B.C.). Included are the signs for head, hand, foot, threshing sledge, and some numerals.

One consequence of the growth of empires and the development of bureaucracy was the establishment of the first formal legal systems. Over the centuries every society had developed certain concepts of justice, as well as informal techniques for implementing them. The most common solution seems to have been to rely on blood revenge by the injured party and his relatives. Recognizing the anarchic tendencies inherent in this system, men began to seek settlement by arbitration, turning quite naturally to the most respected and most powerful members of the community. In this way, headmen and other political leaders gradually acquired judicial powers. Then, as empires grew, peoples of diverse cultures were brought within the framework of a single political system. In many instances, the official appointed to rule over an area was not a native and would therefore be unfamiliar with local conceptions of justice (which varied considerably from place to place). This generated pressure to clarify and standardize judicial practice, which eventually led to the promulgation of formal codes of law. The most famous of these was the Code of Hammurabi, the great Babylonian empire builder of the early second millennium.

The Development of Monetary Systems

Money as we think of it was absent in the first simple agrarian societies. There were, nevertheless, certain standardized media of exchange. Barley served this function in ancient Mesopotamia, wheat in Egypt. Wages, rents, taxes, and various other obligations could be paid off in specified quantities of these grains.[26]

As media of exchange, grains were less than ideal, since they were both perishable and bulky. So, from a fairly early date, various metals, particularly silver and copper, were used as alternatives.[27] Initially, they were circulated in the form of crude bars of irregular size and weight, and their use was restricted to major transactions, since metal was still relatively scarce. La-

---

[26] See Turner, p. 263, or Childe, *What Happened in History*, p. 118.

[27] Childe, *What Happened in History*, pp. 118–119.

ter, as metals were easier to obtain, smaller units were made to facilitate local trade, and their sizes and weights were gradually standardized. As the last stage in the process, governments assumed the responsibility for manufacturing metallic currencies, and full-fledged monetary systems appeared. This did not occur, however, until the very end of the simple agrarian era.

The growth of monetary systems had tremendous implications for societal development. Money has always acted as a lubricant, facilitating the movement, the exchange, and ultimately the production of goods and services of every kind. A money economy greatly enlarges the market for the things each individual produces, because his products can be sold even to people who produce nothing he wants. Thus the effective demand for goods and services is maximized.

One immediate consequence of the emergence of a money economy is the growth of opportunities for merchants, or middlemen, who purchase goods which they themselves do not want but which they know are wanted by people without access to the producers. Once a class of merchants has come into being, they serve not only to satisfy existing demands but to create new ones. By displaying new and uncommon articles, they generate needs and desires that did not exist before and thereby stimulate economic activity.

In the long run, a money economy subverts many of the values of simpler societies, especially the cooperative tendencies and traditionalism inherent in extended family systems. In their place it fosters a more individualistic, rationalistic, and competitive orientation and lays a foundation for many of the attitudes and values that underlie modern industrial societies.

These developments were very limited in the simple agrarian societies of the ancient Middle East. The newly emerging monetary economies barely penetrated the rural villages, where most of the people lived. Even in the cities and towns, the role of money was quite limited compared with what we are accustomed to. In short, the major impact of money still lay in the future.

Sociocultural Cleavages

In the simple agrarian societies of the ancient world, there were several very important lines of cleavage. First, there was the cleavage between the small governing class and the much larger class of people who, having no voice in political decisions, had to turn over all or most of their surplus to the governing class. Second, there was the division between the urban minority and the vast majority of peasant villagers. Finally, there was the cleavage between the small literate minority and the illiterate masses.

As Figure 8.6 indicates, these three lines of cleavage tended to converge. As a result, the small governing class lived in a very different world from that of the illiterate, rural, peasant majority—despite the fact they were members of the same society. One historian has pointed out that the invention of writing intensified the great social cleavage between the governing class

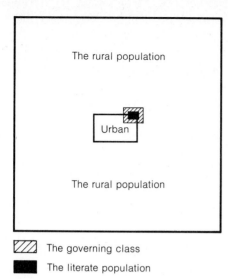

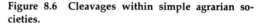

Figure 8.6 **Cleavages within simple agrarian societies.**

and the governed and led to the formation of two increasingly distinct subcultures.[28] The subculture of the common people was a mixture of primitive superstition and the kind of practical knowledge they needed in their daily lives. It was extremely parochial in outlook and knew little of the world beyond the village. The subculture of the governing class, by contrast, incorporated many of the refinements we would identify with "civilization." It included elements of philosophy, art, literature, history, science, and administrative techniques, and above all, a contempt for physical labor of any kind (except warfare) and for those who engage in it. In short, the governing classes not only possessed a different body of information, they had a different set of values.

In many respects the differences *within* simple agrarian societies were greater than those *between* them. An Egyptian peasant in the latter half of the second millennium B.C. could have adapted far more easily to the life of a Babylonian peasant than to the life of a member of the governing class of his own society. As this gulf widened, members of the governing class found it increasingly difficult to recognize the ignorant, downtrodden peasants as fellow human beings. The scribes of ancient Egypt were fond of saying that the lower classes were "without heart" (meaning that they lacked intelligence) and therefore had to be driven with a stick like cattle.[29]

Slowdown in the Rate of Technological Innovation

Another significant development in these societies was a marked slowdown in the rate of technological innovation and progress, beginning within a few cen-

---

[28] See Turner's excellent treatment of this topic, pp. 317–323.

[29] Adolf Erman, *Life in Ancient Egypt,* translated by H. M. Tirard (London: Macmillan, 1894), p. 128.

turies after the shift from horticulture to agriculture. Childe described the change this way:

> Before the [agrarian] revolution comparatively poor and illiterate communities had made an impressive series of contributions to man's progress. The two millennia immediately preceding 3,000 B.C. had witnessed discoveries in applied science that directly or indirectly affected the prosperity of millions of men and demonstrably furthered the biological welfare of our species by facilitating its multiplication. We have mentioned the following applications of science: artificial irrigation using canals and ditches; the plow; the harnessing of animal motive-power; the sailboat; wheeled vehicles; orchard husbandry; fermentation; the production and use of copper; bricks; the arch; glazing; the seal; and—in the earliest stages of the revolution—a solar calendar, writing, numerical notation, and bronze.
>
> The two thousand years after the revolution—say from 2,600 to 600 B.C.—produced few contributions of anything like comparable importance to human progress. Perhaps only four achievements deserve to be put in the same category as the fifteen just enumerated. They are: the "decimal notation" of Babylonia (about 2,000 B.C.); an economical method for smelting iron on an industrial scale (1,400 B.C.); a truly alphabetic script (1,300 B.C.); aqueducts for supplying water to cities (700 B.C.).[30]

Childe went on to note that two of these four innovations, the smelting of iron and the development of the alphabet, "cannot be credited to the societies that had initiated and reaped the fruits of the urban revolution" but rather were the products of somewhat less advanced neighboring societies.[31]

On first consideration, this slowing of the rate of technological advance seems an unlikely development. Larger populations, improved communications, and the greater store of knowledge available to potential innovators should have produced still higher rates of innovation. The fact that they did not poses an important problem.

As scholars such as Childe have seen, the explanation lies in the transformation of the social structure and ideology of the societies involved.[32] Specifically, the development of the state and the growth of social inequality that followed the shift from horticulture to agriculture created a situation in which those who were engaged in the daily tasks of production were gradually reduced to the barest subsistence level, and held there, by their more powerful superiors. Thus these peasant producers lost the normal incentive for creativity; any benefits that might result from an invention or discovery would simply be

---

[30] Childe, *Man Makes Himself*, p. 180, quoted by permission of C. A. Watts & Co., Ltd. See also McNeill, p. 53, or Childe, *What Happened in History*, pp. 183ff.

[31] *Man Makes Himself*, p. 181. Elsewhere, Childe adds a third innovation (or a fifth to the total list), the invention of glass in Egypt. See *What Happened in History*, p. 183.

[32] See Childe, *Man Makes Himself*, chap. 9, for a classic discussion of this subject. The analysis that follows is heavily indebted to Childe's provocative discussion but varies in some details and emphases.

appropriated by the governing class.[33] At the same time, the governing class, though motivated to create a more productive economy, no longer had the necessary knowledge of, and experience with, subsistence technology and thus were in no position to make creative innovations. In short, expertise and incentive were inadvertently divorced, with disastrous results for technological progress.

Under the circumstances, it is hardly surprising that the governing class turned increasingly to warfare and conquest as the most promising means of increasing their wealth. Warfare was something they understood; furthermore, in their system of values it was one of the few occupations considered appropriate for members of their class. The energies of this powerful and influential class were thus turned from the conquest of nature to the conquest of man.[34] And this, thanks to the new, more productive technology, could be a highly profitable enterprise. With the peasants producing much more than they needed to survive and remain productive, a steady flow of taxes, tithes, and rents was coming in to support the host of specialists that catered to the whims of the governing class, as well as the army of soldiers and officials that implemented their wishes.

These developments help explain the advances in social organization made during this period. Having cut themselves off from the sweaty world of work and directed their efforts instead to conquest, the governing class found a new challenge for their creative talents in the area of social organization. The exercise of power and the manipulation of others were activities in keeping with their dignity. Furthermore, they were rewarding: the better organized an army or government, the greater its chances of success in struggles with other groups.[35]

Some believe that the great influence of organized religion in these societies also contributed to the technological slowdown.[36] The religions of the simple agrarian societies of the ancient Middle East inculcated an inordinate respect for the powers of magic, which undoubtedly discouraged interest in technological innovation. It is not clear, however, that superstition and magic were more prevalent in these societies than in those which preceded them, so the argument is not completely persuasive.

ADVANCED AGRARIAN SOCIETIES

During the period in which simple agrarian societies dominated the Middle East, the most important technological advance was the discovery of the tech-

---

[33] It is possible that the problem was even more serious and that the mental capacities of many peasants were impaired by protein-deficient diets and limited learning opportunities in early childhood.

[34] See Childe, *What Happened in History*, p. 184.

[35] For a classic statement of this principle, see Gaetano Mosca, *The Ruling Class*, translated by Hannah Kahn (New York: McGraw-Hill, 1939), p. 53.

[36] See especially Childe, *Man Makes Himself*, chap. 9.

nique of smelting iron. Prior to this, bronze was the most important metal. But since the supply was always limited[37] and the demands of the governing class always took precedence over the needs of peasants, bronze was used primarily for military and ornamental purposes. It never really replaced stone and wood in ordinary tools, particularly agricultural tools, and so its impact on the economy was limited.

Men knew of iron at least as early as the first half of the third millennium B.C., but apparently only in its meteoric form, which is very scarce.[38] Sometime during the second millennium, the Hittites of Asia Minor discovered iron ore and invented a technique for smelting it. For centuries they kept this a closely guarded secret, which brought them both economic and military advantage. Then, about 1200 B.C., their nation was destroyed. This led to the rapid dispersal of both the Hittite people and the technique of iron smelting.

As one would expect, in view of the nature of the class structure of simple agrarian societies, the initial use of iron was limited largely to the governing class. Some of the earliest iron objects recovered from Egypt were a dagger, a bracelet, and a headrest found in the tomb of the pharaoh Tutankhamen. Prior to the military collapse of the Hittites, iron was five times more expensive than gold, forty times more than silver. Only later, perhaps during the eighth century B.C., was it commonly used for ordinary tools. Thus, not until this period were there true advanced agrarian societies—though the Middle Eastern societies of the previous three of four centuries were certainly transitional types.

During this transitional period two further discoveries greatly enhanced the value of iron. First it was found that if the outer layers of the iron absorbed some carbon from the fire during the forging process, the metal was somewhat hardened. Later it was discovered that this carburized iron could be hardened still further by quenching the hot metal in water, thus producing steel. With these developments, iron became not only more common than bronze but also more useful for both military and economic purposes. As one writer has said, "After the discovery of quench-hardening, iron gradually passed into the position from which it has never subsequently been ousted; it became the supremely useful material for making all the tools and weapons that are intended for cutting, chopping, piercing or slashing."[39]

From its point of origin in the Middle East, iron-making spread until eventually it was practiced in nearly all of the Old World, even in many horticultural societies. By the time of Christ, advanced agrarian societies were firmly established in the Middle East, throughout most of the Mediterranean world,

---

[37] This was because of the scarcity of tin, an essential component.

[38] For a good summary of the early history of iron, see Leslie Aitchison, *A History of Metals* (London: MacDonald and Evans, 1960), vol. 1, pp. 97–110. The discussion that follows is based largely on Aitchison.

[39] Ibid., p. 113.

and in much of India and China. Within the next thousand years, the advanced agrarian pattern spread over most of Europe and much of Southeast Asia and expanded further in India and China. Still later it was transplanted to the European colonies in the New World. Advanced agrarian societies still survive in hybrid form in much of Asia, the Middle East, and Latin America, where they constitute the majority of the problem-ridden, underdeveloped nations of our day. We will examine these partially industrialized agrarian societies in Chapter 14.

Technology

Compared with simpler societies, advanced agrarian societies enjoyed a very productive technology. Unfortunately, however, the same conditions that slowed the rate of technological advance in simple agrarian societies continued to operate. As a result, their progress was not nearly what one would expect on the basis of their size, the degree of communication among them, and, above all, their store of accumulated knowledge.[40]

Nevertheless, over the centuries quite a number of important innovations were made. A partial list would include the catapult, the crossbow, gunpowder, horseshoes, a workable harness for horses, stirrups, the wood-turning lathe, the auger, the screw, the wheelbarrow, the rotary fan for ventilation, the clock, the spinning wheel, porcelain, printing, iron casting, the magnet, water-powered mills, windmills, and, in the period just preceding the emergence of the first industrial societies, the workable steam engine, the fly shuttle, the spinning jenny, the spinning machine, and a number of other power-driven tools. As a result of these and other innovations, the most advanced agrarian societies of the eighteenth century A.D. were considerably superior, from the technological standpoint, to their predecessors of 2,500 years earlier.

This rise in the level of technological efficiency was not uniform throughout the agrarian world, despite diffusion. Knowledge still spread slowly in most cases, and some areas were considerably ahead of others. During much of the advanced agrarian era, especially from A.D. 500 to A.D. 1500, the Middle East, China, and parts of India were technologically superior to Europe.[41] In part, this was simply a continuation of older patterns: the Middle East, in other words, was the center of innovation for more than 5,000 years following the horticultural revolution. Even more important, however, were the effects of the collapse of the Roman Empire. For centuries afterward, Europe was divided into scores of petty kingdoms and principalities that had only enough

---

[40] See, for example, Charles Singer's comparison of the level of technology in the ancient empires of Egypt and Mesopotamia prior to 1000 B.C. and later in Greece and Rome, in "Epilogue: East and West in Retrospect," in Charles Singer (ed.), *A History of Technology* (Oxford: Clarendon Press, 1956), vol. II, pp. 754–755.

[41] Ibid., pp. 754–772.

resources to maintain the smallest urban settlements and the most limited number of occupational specialists. Therefore, Europeans were inactive on many of the most promising and challenging technological frontiers of the time. Though they made relative gains during the later Middle Ages—thanks largely to the diffusion of knowledge from the East—they did not really catch up until the sixteenth century and did not take the lead until even later.

Scale of Organization

In any comparison with simple agrarian societies, the greater organizational development of the advanced is very evident on both the societal and the communal levels. On the societal level, there is roughly a tenfold differential between the largest society in each of the two categories. The largest simple agrarian society was probably Egypt in the latter half of the second millennium, at which time it controlled roughly 800,000 square miles.[42] By contrast, the Russian empire in the mid-nineteenth century covered nearly 8 million square miles; even as early as the reign of Peter the Great (1689–1725), it covered nearly 6 million square miles.[43] Several other advanced agrarian societies built empires that far surpassed that of the ancient Egyptians. These include the Spanish empire in the eighteenth century (5 million square miles), the Chinese empire at various times since the first century B.C. (up to 4 million square miles),

Figure 8.7 Medieval town of Montepeyroux, France, now almost deserted.

[42] See, for example, Turner's map, p. 232.

[43] Jerome Blum, *Lord and Peasant in Russia from the Ninth to the Nineteenth Century* (Princeton, N.J.: Princeton, 1961), p. 278. One might object that much of the Russian empire was sparsely settled, but the same was true of the Egyptian empire.

Table 8.1 Estimated populations of medieval European cities

City	Date	Population
Venice	1363	78,000
Paris	1192	59,000
Florence	1381	55,000
Rome	1198	35,000
London	1377	35,000
Barcelona	1359	27,000
Naples	1278	22,000
Hamburg	1250	22,000
Brussels	1496	19,000
Antwerp	1437	14,000
Frankfort	1410	10,000
Amsterdam	1470	7,500
Zurich	1357	7,400
Berlin	1450	6,000
Geneva	1404	4,200
Vienna	1391	3,800
Dresden	1396	3,700
Leipzig	1474	2,100

Source: J. C. Russell, *Late Ancient and Medieval Population* (Philadelphia: The American Philosophical Society, 1958), pp. 60–62.

the Umayyad empire in the eighth century (3 million square miles), and the Roman Empire in the second century (2 million square miles).[44]

Populations, too, were much larger. The most populous simple agrarian society, Egypt, probably had fewer than 15 million members.[45] By contrast, the largest advanced agrarian society, mid-nineteenth-century China, had approximately 400 million.[46] Though that was exceptional, India reached 175 million in the middle of the nineteenth century, and the Roman and the Russian empires each had at least 70 million people.[47]

---

[44] See, for example, the reference maps in T. W. Wallbank et al., *Civilization*, 5th ed. (Chicago: Scott, Foresman, 1965), vol. I, pp. 658–671.

[45] This estimate was based on the known boundaries of these societies and on the fact that the Roman Empire, which was much larger and contained a much smaller percentage of uninhabitable land, had a maximum population of only about 70 million. See *The Cambridge Ancient History* (London: Cambridge, 1939), vol. XII, pp. 267–268. It is also noteworthy that in Roman times Egypt had a population of only 6 to 7 million. Even if allowance is made for the greater size of the Egyptian empire in the days of Egypt's independence, it is difficult to imagine a total population much in excess of 15 million. See Charles Issawi, *Egypt in Revolution: An Economic Analysis* (New York: Oxford, 1963), p. 20.

[46] Chung-li Chang, *The Chinese Gentry: Studies on Their Role in Nineteenth-Century Chinese Society* (Seattle: University of Washington Press, 1955), p. 102.

[47] On India, see Kingsley Davis, *The Population of India and Pakistan* (Princeton, N.J.: Princeton, 1951), pp. 24–25; on Rome, see *The Cambridge Ancient History*, pp. 267–268; on Russia, see Blum, p. 278.

Similar differences are found at the communal level. The populations of the largest cities in simple agrarian societies were probably not much over 100,000, if that. By contrast, the upper limit for cities in advanced agrarian societies may have been as high as 1 million—although, as with all population figures from earlier times, there is considerable uncertainty.[48] Only the capitals of great empires ever attained such a size, and they maintained it but briefly. Cities of 100,000 were more numerous than in simple agrarian societies, though still quite rare.[49]

Differentiation of Parts

Growth in the scale of organization was accompanied by an increasing differentiation of the parts. For the first time, there was significant economic specialization by regions and by communities, and it was accompanied by increased occupational specialization.

The Roman Empire provides a good illustration of both regional and communal specialization. North Africa and Spain were noted as suppliers of dried figs and olive oil; Gaul, Dalmatia, Asia Minor, and Syria for their wine; Spain and Egypt for salted meats; Egypt, North Africa, Sicily, and the Black Sea region for grain; and the latter for salted fish as well.[50] The tendency toward specialization at the community level is illustrated by a passage from a manual for wealthy farmers, written in the second century B.C., which advised:

> Tunics, togas, blankets, smocks and shoes should be bought at Rome; caps, iron tools, scythes, spades, mattocks, axes, harness, ornaments and small chains at Cales and Minturnae; spades at Venafrum, carts and sledges at Suessa and in Lucania, jars and pots at Alba and at Rome; tiles at Venafrum, oil mills at Pompeii and at Rufrius's yard at Nola; nails and bars at Rome; pails, oil urns, water pitchers, wine urns, other copper vessels at Capua and at Nola; Campanian baskets, pulley-ropes and all sorts of cordage at Capua, Roman baskets at Suessa and Casium.[51]

---

[48] See, for example, Gideon Sjoberg, *The Preindustrial City: Past and Present* (New York: Free Press, 1960), pp. 80ff.; Jerome Carcopino, *Daily Life in Ancient Rome: The People and the City at the Height of the Empire* (New Haven, Conn.: Yale, 1940), pp. 16–21; George Sansom, *A History of Japan* (Stanford, Calif.: Stanford, 1963), vol. III, p. 114; and Irene Taeuber, *The Population of Japan* (Princeton, N.J.: Princeton, 1958), p. 27. For a much more cautious view, see Amos H. Hawley, *Urban Society: An Ecological Approach* (New York: Ronald, 1971), pp. 32–35.

[49] Davis reports that there were still "less than 50" that large in 1800 ("The Origin and Growth of World Urbanism," p. 434). At this time no society could be classified as an industrial society, though the new industrial techniques were certainly beginning to have some effect.

[50] Turner, p. 911.

[51] F. R. Cowell, *Cicero and the Roman Republic* (London: Penguin, 1956), p. 79. Quoted by permission of Penguin Books.

Figure 8.8 Occupational specialization in an advanced agrarian society: silversmith in his shop, Manama, Babrun Island, Persian Gulf.

Similar patterns are reported in other agrarian societies.[52] Even at the village level a measure of specialization was not uncommon. In the agricultural off season, peasants often turned to handicrafts to make ends meet, and certain villages gradually developed a reputation for a particular commodity.

In the larger urban centers, occupational specialization reached a level that surpassed anything achieved in simpler societies. For example, a tax roll for Paris from the year 1313 lists 157 different trades.[53] The clothing industry alone contained such specialized occupations as wool comber, wool spinner, silk spinner (two kinds), headdress maker (seven kinds, including specialists in felt, fur, wool and cotton, flowers, peacock feathers, gold embroidery and pearls, and silk), and girdle maker. Though such specialization could be found only in the largest cities, smaller cities often had forty or fifty different kinds of

---

[52] See, for example, Blum, pp. 126 and 394–395, on Russia, or Ralph Linton, *The Tree of Culture* (New York: Vintage Books, Random House, 1959), p. 231, on China.

[53] S. B. Clough and C. W. Cole, *Economic History of Europe* (Boston: Heath, 1941), p. 25.

Figure 8.9 Occupational specialization in an advanced agrarian society: baker rolling dough, Saudi Arabia.

craftsmen, and even small towns had ten or twenty.[54] In addition to craft specialists, urban centers contained specialists in government, commerce, religion, education, the armed forces, and domestic service. The list should also include specialists engaged in illegal occupations, since these were a normal component of cities and towns in advanced agrarian societies.

The Polity

In nearly all these societies, the state was the basic integrative force. It was inevitable in any society created by conquest and maintained for the benefit of a tiny governing class that coercive power would be required to hold the natural antagonisms of its subjects in check. In exercising this power, a state welded together formerly disparate groups, unifying them politically and often, over a period of time, culturally as well.

At the head of nearly every advanced agrarian state was a single individual, the king or emperor. Monarchy was the rule, republican government an infrequent exception limited almost entirely to the least powerful and least

---

[54] Ibid. See also Blum, pp. 16 and 126.

[55] Gerhard Lenski, *Power and Privilege: A Theory of Social Stratification* (New York: McGraw-Hill, 1966), pp. 197–198.

developed societies and to those on the margins of the agrarian world.[55] The prevalence of monarchical government seems to have been the result of the militaristic and exploitative character of societies at this level. Governments were constantly threatening, or being threatened by, their neighbors. And all the while they were in danger from internal enemies: dissatisfied and ambitious members of the governing class, eager to seize control for themselves, and restless, hostile members of the numerically dominant lower classes. Under such conditions, republican government was nearly impossible.[56]

Because of a tendency to romanticize the past, many people today are unaware of the frequency of both internal and external conflict in the great agrarian empires. In Rome, for example, thirty-one of the seventy-nine emperors were murdered, six were driven to suicide, four were forcibly deposed, and several more met unknown fates at the hands of internal enemies.[57] Though Rome's record was worse than most, internal struggles occurred in all advanced agrarian societies.[58]

Peasant risings were also indicators of internal stress. One expert states that "there were peasant rebellions almost every year in China," and an authority on Russia reports that in the short period from 1801 to 1861, there were no less than 1,467 peasant risings in various parts of that country.[59] Most of these disturbances remained local only because authorities acted swiftly and ruthlessly. Had they not, many would have spread as widely as the famous English revolt of 1381 or the German Peasants' War of 1524–1525.[60]

External threats were no less frequent or serious, and warfare was a chronic condition. A survey of the incidence of war in eleven European countries in the preindustrial period found that, on the average, these countries were involved in war nearly every second year.[61] Such conditions obviously required strong centralized authority. Societies without it were eliminated in the selective process, unless they happened to occupy a particularly remote and inaccessible territory.

Most members of the governing class considered political power a prize

---

[56] For the effect of war on the forms of government, see Herbert Spencer, *The Principles of Sociology* (New York: Appleton, 1897), vol. II, part 5, chap. 17; Pitirim Sorokin, *Social and Cultural Dynamics* (New York: Bedminister Press, 1962), vol. III, pp. 196–198; or Stanislaw Andrzejewski, *Military Organization and Society* (London: Routledge, 1954), pp. 92–95.

[57] These figures were calculated from A. E. R. Boak, *A History of Rome to 565 A.D.,* 3d ed. (New York: Macmillan, 1943), and Harold Mattingly, *Roman Imperial Civilization* (Garden City, N.Y.: Doubleday Anchor, 1959), using Mattingly's list of emperors, pp. 351–355.

[58] For figures on several other societies, see Lenski, p. 235.

[59] Wolfram Eberhard, *Conquerors and Rulers: Social Forces in Medieval China* (Leiden, Netherlands: Brill, 1952), p. 52, and Blum, p. 558.

[60] For an interesting popular account of the former, see Philip Lindsay and Reg Groves, *The Peasants' Revolt, 1381* (London: Hutchinson, n.d.).

[61] Sorokin, vol, III, chap. 10, especially p. 352.

to be sought for the rewards it offered rather than an opportunity for public service, and the office of king or emperor was the *supreme* prize. This is the only interpretation one can put on the perennial struggle for power within agrarian states or the use made of it after it was won. Efforts to raise the living standards of the common people were rare, efforts at self-aggrandizement typical.[62] In many of these societies, government offices were bought and sold like pieces of property that purchasers used to obtain the greatest possible profit. Office holders typically demanded payment before they would act on any request, and justice was typically sold to the highest bidder. No wonder the common people of China developed the saying "To enter a court of justice is to enter a tiger's mouth."[63]

These practices reflected what is known as the proprietary theory of the state, according to which the state is a piece of property that its owners may use, within rather broad and ill-defined limits, for their personal advantage.[64] Guided by this theory, agrarian rulers and governing classes saw nothing immoral in the use of what we (not they) would call "public office" for private gain. To them, it was simply the legitimate use of what they commonly regarded as their "patrimony." It is said of the Ptolemies of Egypt, for example, that they showed the first emperors of Rome "how a country might be run on the lines of a profitable estate."[65] In the case of medieval Europe, we read:

> The proprietary conception of rulership created an inextricable confusion of public and private affairs. Rights of government were a form of private ownership. "Crown lands" and "the king's estate" were synonymous. There was no differentiation between the king in his private and public capacities. A kingdom, like any estate endowed with elements of governmental authority, was the private concern of its owner. Since "state" and "estate" were identical, "the State" was indistinguishable from the prince and his personal "patrimony."[66]

The proprietary theory of the state can be traced back to horticultural societies and, in a sense, even to hunting and gathering groups. In those simpler societies, the private and public aspects of political leadership were hopelessly confused. When a surplus first began to be produced, at least part of it was turned over to the leader, who held it as trustee for the group. As long as the surplus was small and in the form of perishable commodities, there was

[62] See, among others, Lenski, pp. 210–242 and 266–284, for more detailed documentation.

[63] Robert K. Douglas, *Society in China* (London: Innes, 1894), p. 104.

[64] See Max Weber, *The Theory of Social and Economic Organization,* trans. A. M. Henderson and Talcott Parsons (New York: Free Press, 1947), pp. 341–348, and Max Weber, *Wirtschaft und Gesellschaft,* 2d ed. (Tübingen: Mohr, 1925), vol. II, pp. 679–723.

[65] Mattingly, p. 137. See also Turner, vol. II, p. 620, or Michael Rostovtzeff, *The Social and Economic History of the Roman Empire,* rev. ed. (Oxford: Clarendon Press, 1957), p. 54.

[66] Hans Rosenberg, *Bureaucracy, Aristocracy, and Autocracy: The Prussian Experience 1660–1815* (Cambridge, Mass.: Harvard, 1958), pp. 5–6. Quoted by permission of Harvard University Press.

Figure 8.10 One use of the economic surplus in an agrarian society: the Taj Mahal, a tomb erected by Mogul emperor Shah Jahan in memory of his favorite wife.

little the leader could do with it except redistribute it, thereby winning status for his generosity. Eventually, however, as we saw in Chapter 7, it grew large enough to permit him to create a staff of dependent retainers who could be used to enforce his wishes. At this point, the proprietary theory of the state was born. Later rulers merely applied it on an ever-expanding scale, as productivity and the economic surplus steadily increased.

Recent research provides a good picture of the extremes to which rulers and governing classes have carried the proprietary principle. In late nineteenth-century China, for example, the average income for families not in the governing class was approximately 20 to 25 taels per year. By contrast, the governing class averaged 450 taels per year, with some receiving as much as

200,000.[67] The emperor's income, of course, was considerably larger than even this. To cite another example, the English nobility at the end of the twelfth century and early in the thirteenth had an average income roughly 200 times that of ordinary field hands, and the king's equaled that of 24,000 field hands.[68] Putting together the evidence from many sources, it appears that the combined income of the ruler and the governing class in most advanced agrarian societies equaled not less than half of the total national income, even though they numbered 2 per cent or less of the population.[69]

Despite their many similarities, the political systems of advanced agrarian societies did vary in a number of ways, the most important being the degree of political centralization. In some societies the central government was very strong; in others its powers were severely limited. In the main, these differences reflected the current state of the perennial struggle between the ruler and the other members of the governing class. A king or emperor naturally wanted the greatest possible control over his subordinates, and the latter just as naturally wanted to minimize it. When the ruler was dominant, the political system was despotic, autocratic, or absolutist; when the governing class was relatively free from monarchical control, the system tended to be feudalistic or oligarchic.

Since land (including the peasants who worked it) and political office were the most valuable resources in agrarian societies, struggles between rulers and the governing class usually revolved around their control. In a few instances, extremely powerful rulers like the Ottoman emperor Suleiman and the Mogul emperor Akbar managed to gain almost complete control over these resources. During their reigns, both land and offices were held at the ruler's pleasure and were subject to instant confiscation should the services of the holder be judged unsatisfactory.[70] A Dutch traveler of the early seventeenth century left a vivid picture of the situation in the Mogul empire at that time.

> Immediately on the death of a lord who has enjoyed the King's [favor], be he great or small, without any exception—sometimes even before the breath is out of the body—the King's officers are ready on the spot and make an inventory of the entire estate, recording everything down to the value of a single piece, even

---

[67] Chung-li Chang, *The Income of the Chinese Gentry* (Seattle: University of Washington Press, 1962), Summary Remarks, supplement 2, and chap. 1.

[68] On the king's income, see Sir James H. Ramsay, *A History of the Revenues of the Kings of England: 1066–1399* (Oxford: Clarendon Press, 1925), vol. I, pp. 227 and 261. For the income of the nobility, see Sidney Painter, *Studies in the History of the English Feudal Barony* (Baltimore: Johns Hopkins, 1943), pp. 170–171. For the income of field hands, see H. S. Bennett, *Life on the English Manor: A Study of Peasant Conditions, 1150–1400* (London: Cambridge, 1960), p. 121.

[69] Lenski, pp. 219 and 228.

[70] See, for example, Albert Lybyer, *The Government of the Ottoman Empire in the Time of Suleiman the Magnificent* (Cambridge, Mass.: Harvard, 1913), or W. H. Moreland, *The Agrarian System of Moslem India* (Allahabad, India: Central Book Depot, n.d.).

to the dresses and jewels of the ladies, provided they have not concealed them. The King takes back the whole estate absolutely for himself, except in a case where the deceased has done good service in his lifetime, when the women and children are given enough to live on, but no more.[71]

In Turkey under Suleiman, the chief officers of state were recruited from the ranks of specially trained slaves over whom the sultan held life-and-

Figure 8.11 Working equipment for a member of the governing class in sixteenth-century Germany.

Figure 8.12 Armor of a Japanese nobleman of the sixteenth century.

[71] F. Pelsaert, *Jahangir's India,* Translated by W. H. Moreland and P. Geyl and quoted by B. B. Misra, *The Indian Middle Classes* (London: Oxford, 1961), p. 47. Quoted by permission of W. Heffer and Sons, Ltd.

death power.[72] At the other extreme, during much of the medieval period, Europe's feudal lords were virtually autonomous. Though their lands were typically royal grants given in exchange for pledges of service, rulers usually lacked the power to enforce these pledges.[73]

Although examples of both extremes can be found, the usual pattern was something in between. Typically, the powers of the ruler and the governing class were fairly evenly balanced. Various factors influenced the balance and determined the precise location of a society on what might be called the autocracy-oligarchy scale. In general, the larger a state and the poorer its transportation and communication, the easier it was for members of the governing class to infringe on royal prerogatives.[74] A great deal also depended on the personal qualities of the ruler. Ruthless, energetic, and intelligent men were usually able to improve their positions, while those who lacked these qualities were apt to see them weakened. A ruler who was successful in foreign wars was especially likely to dominate his governing class, since conquests provided him with new resources to distribute and these always strengthened the bonds of "loyalty." The case of William the Conqueror is a classic example.

Patterns of inheritance and succession also greatly influenced the balance of power. A system of primogeniture in the governing class tended to prevent the breakup of large estates, keeping this crucial base of power intact.[75] Rules governing succession to the throne were equally important. Where there was a principle of automatic succession, as in most European countries, children and other weak individuals could become rulers, providing the governing class with an excellent opportunity to increase its powers.[76] By contrast, where there was an open contest, there were few weak rulers. To become ruler of the Mogul empire, for example, a prince had to kill his own brothers. This system produced a succession of strong emperors who held the rights of the governing class to the barest minimum.[77]

Finally, the balance of power depended on the unity of the governing class. When it presented a united front, it could exert far more pressure than

---

[72] Lybyer, pp. 47–58 and 115–117.

[73] See, for example, James Westfall Thompson's statement that "the medieval state was a loose agglomeration of territories with rights of property and sovereignty everywhere shading into one another," in *Economic and Social History of the Middle Ages* (New York: Appleton-Century-Crofts, 1928), p. 699. See also Marc Bloch, *Feudal Society*, trans. L. A. Manyon (Chicago: University of Chicago Press, 1962), especially chaps. 14–24; Blum, chap. 2; or Sidney Painter, *The Rise of the Feudal Monarchies* (Ithaca, N.Y.: Cornell, 1951), *The English Feudal Barony*.

[74] For a more detailed discussion of the factors influencing this balance, see Lenski, pp. 234–240.

[75] See, for example, Karl Wittfogel, *Oriental Despotism: A Comparative Study of Total Power* (New Haven, Conn.: Yale, 1957), pp. 79ff.; Alan Simpson, *The Wealth of the Gentry, 1540–1660* (London: Cambridge, 1961), pp. 107–108; Blum, pp. 82 and 378; Misra, pp. 44 and 50; and Jean Hippolyte Mariéjol, *The Spain of Ferdinand and Isabella*, translated by Benjamin Keen (New Brunswick, N.J.: Rutgers, 1961), pp. 276–277.

[76] See, for example, Painter, *The Rise of the Feudal Monarchies*, pp. 127–129.

[77] Moreland, pp. 92–100.

when it was torn by internal conflicts. Skillful rulers recognized this and typically sought to exploit differences in rank, wealth, ethnicity, region, and religion for their own advantage.[78]

The Economy: An Overview

Because politics and economics were always tightly intertwined in advanced agrarian societies, those who dominated the political system also dominated the economic system. The leading office holders in government were usually the chief landholders as well, and in these societies land was the most important economic resource. As one economic historian expressed it, "In pre-market societies [among which he includes agrarian], wealth tends to follow power; not until the market society [does] power tend to follow wealth."[79]

As this statement suggests, the economies of agrarian societies operated on a very different basis from those of modern industrial societies. In resolving the central economic questions—how resources should be used, what should be produced and in what quantities, and how the products should be distributed—the basic market forces of supply and demand were much less important than the arbitrary decisions of the political elite. In other words, these were *command* economies rather than market economies.[80]

The economy of an advanced agrarian society consisted of two distinct parts: its rural-based agricultural sector and its urban-based commercial and industrial sector. These were not of equal importance, however: a leading student of ancient history recently estimated that the Roman state derived approximately twenty times more tax revenue from agriculture than from trade and industry. He went on to say that "this apportionment of the burden of taxation probably corresponded roughly to the economic structure of the empire. All the evidence goes to show that its wealth was derived almost entirely from agriculture, and to a very small extent from industry and trade."[81] The same could be said of every other agrarian society. It does not follow, however, that the urban economy was of little interest to the governing class. On the contrary, it was of tremendous interest, because it provided them with the luxuries they valued so highly. The urban economy, however, depended on the rural economy and on its ability to produce a surplus that could support the urban population.

---

[78] For examples of the application of the policy of "divide and rule," see Mariéjol, pp. 264ff., or Rosenberg, pp. 152ff.

[79] Robert Heilbroner, *The Making of Economic Society* (Englewood Cliffs, N.J.: Prentice-Hall, 1962), p. 27. See also H. R. Trevor-Roper, "The Gentry 1540–1640," *The Economic History Review Supplements*, no. 1 (n.d.), or Bloch, who wrote of "that age when true wealth consisted in being the master" (p. 192).

[80] Heilbroner, pp. 9–44.

[81] A. H. M. Jones, *The Later Roman Empire 284–602: A Social, Economic and Administrative Survey* (Oxford: Blackwell, 1964), vol. I, p. 465.

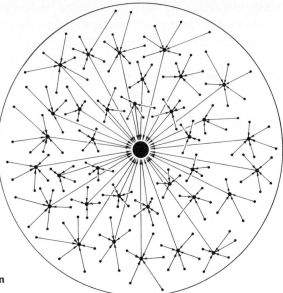

**Figure 8.13 Graphic representation of the flow of goods in
advanced agrarian societies.**

In many respects the economy of the typical agrarian society reminds
one of a tree with roots spreading in every direction, constantly drawing in new
resources. Graphically, the pattern was that shown in Figure 8.13. At the center
of the society was the national capital, controlled by the king or emperor and
the leading members of the governing class. Surrounding it were various
provincial or regional capitals controlled by royal governors and other
members of the governing class. Each of these, in turn, was surrounded by
smaller county seats and market towns, controlled by the lower-ranking
members of the governing class. Finally, each of these towns was surrounded
by scores of small villages. In the larger empires, there was often another layer
interposed between the county seats and the regional capitals.

In this system, there was a steady flow of goods from the smaller units
to the larger, or from the villages to the county seats and from there to the
regional and national capitals. Basically this flow was through taxation, but it
was supplemented by rents, interest on debts, tithes, and profits, all of which
helped transfer the economic surplus from the peasant villagers to the urban-
based governing class and their allies and dependents.

Some scholars have argued that this was actually a symbiotic relationship in which the villagers freely exchanged the goods they produced for
goods and services produced in the urban centers. Although there was an element of this, the historical record shows that basically it was a one-sided, coercive relationship in which the peasants were forced to give far more than they
received. The peasants recognized this, even if some modern scholars do not,

and they greatly resented it, as indicated by the frequency of their protests and hopeless revolts.[82]

With what they retained of their surplus after paying taxes, rents, interest, and other obligations, peasants could go to the urban centers and trade for commodities that were not available in their villages (e.g., certain metal tools, salt, etc.). Towns and cities were also religious centers in many cases, and the peasants often used these facilities. Finally, the peasants benefited to some degree from the maintenance of law and order provided by urban-based governments, even though the law was used disproportionately to protect the rights of the governing class and keep the peasants in their place. The maintenance of order is especially important in an agrarian society, where so much depends

Figure 8.14 The city as a religious center: Hindu temple in Nepal.

[82] See page 227 above on peasant revolts. See also G. G. Coulton, *The Medieval Village* (London: Cambridge, 1926), chaps. 11 and 24–25.

on the success of each harvest and each harvest depends on months of effort. Disruption at any point in the agricultural cycle can be disastrous for everyone.

The Rural Economy

In most advanced agrarian societies, the ruler and the governing class (including the religious leaders) owned a grossly disproportionate share of the land. Though there are no precise figures for earlier times, the traditional pattern can still be seen in many parts of Latin America, the Middle East, and Southeast Asia. Even now, a minority of 1 to 3 per cent of the population owns from one-third to two-thirds of the arable land in these countries, as shown in Table 8.2.

Not only did the governing class usually own most of the land, but it often owned most of the peasants who worked it. Systems of slavery and

Table 8.2 **Landholdings of the governing class in selected nations in the mid-twentieth century**

Nation	Percentage of Population	Percentage of Arable Land Owned
Chile	1.4	63
Northeast Brazil	2	48
Portugal	0.3	39
Southern Spain	1.8	50+
Egypt	0.4	34
	3	56
Jordan	3.5	37
Lebanon	0.2	50
	1.4	65
Iraq	3	67
North-central India	1.5	39
	3.3	54
South Vietnam	2.5	50

Sources: Chile—Frederico Gil, *The Political System of Chile* (Boston: Houghton Mifflin, 1966), p. 148; Northeast Brazil—Josue de Castro, *Death in the Northeast* (New York: Random House, 1966), p. 154; Portugal—Herminio Martins, "Portugal," in Margaret Archer and Salvador Giner (eds.), *Contemporary Europe* (New York: St. Martin's, 1972), p. 66; Spain—Salvador Giner, "Spain," in Archer and Giner, p. 134; the Middle Eastern nations—Morroe Berger, *The Arab World Today* (Garden City, N.Y.: Doubleday Anchor, 1964), pp. 196–199; North-central India—Baljit Singh and Shridhar Misra, *Land Reforms in Uttar Pradesh* (Honolulu: East-West Center Press, 1964), p. 28; South Vietnam—*The Washington Post,* October 17, 1965, p. A 8.

Figure 8.15 Peasant using the traditional wooden plow, Iran.

serfdom have been common in agrarian societies, with large landholdings and large numbers of slaves or serfs normally going hand in hand. Thus it was only natural that a nineteenth-century Russian nobleman who owned 2 million acres of land also owned nearly 300,000 serfs.[83] Rulers, understandably, had the largest holdings. Prior to the emancipation of the serfs in Russia, the czar owned 27.4 million of them.[84]

But even when the peasant owned his own land and was legally free, he usually found it difficult to make ends meet. A bad crop one year, and he had to borrow money at usurious rates, sometimes as high as 120 per cent a year.[85] In any event, there were always taxes, and these usually fell more heavily on the peasant landowner than on his wealthier neighbor, either because of special exemptions granted the latter or simply because of his greater ability to evade such obligations.[86] If a peasant did not own his land, he had to pay rent,

---

[83] Blum, pp. 369–370.

[84] Ibid., pp. 356–357.

[85] Sjoberg, *The Preindustrial City*, p. 215.

[86] See, for example, Chang, *Income of the Chinese Gentry*, pp. 37–51.

**Figure 8.16   Peasants trans-
planting rice, Indonesia.**

which was always set high. In addition, he was often subject to compulsory labor service, tithes, fines, and obligatory "gifts" to the governing class.[87]

Because the number and variety of obligations were so great, it is difficult to determine just how large the total was, but in most societies it appears to have been not less than half the total value of the goods the peasants produced.[88] The basic philosophy of the governing class seems to have been to tax the peasants to the limit of their ability to pay.[89] This philosophy is illustrated by a story told of a leading Japanese official of the seventeenth century who, returning to one of his estates after an absence of ten years and finding the villagers in well-built houses instead of the hovels he remembered, exclaimed, "These people are too comfortable. They must be more heavily taxed."[90]

Living conditions for most peasants were very primitive, and it is doubtful that they were as well off as hunters and gatherers. For example, the diet of the average peasant in medieval England consisted of little more than

---

[87] For a survey of these obligations, see Lenski, pp. 267–270.

[88] Ibid., p. 228.

[89] See, for example, Blum, p. 232, or Moreland, p. 207.

[90] Sansom, *A History of Japan,* vol. III, p. 29.

the following: a hunk of bread and a mug of ale in the morning; a lump of cheese and bread with perhaps an onion or two to flavor it and more ale at noon; a thick soup or pottage with bread and cheese in the evening.[91] Meat was rare and the ale usually thin. Household furniture consisted of a few stools, a table, and a chest to hold the best clothes and any other treasured possessions.[92] Beds were uncommon; most peasants simply slept on earthen floors covered with straw. Other household possessions were apparently limited to cooking utensils.

In some cases, the lot of the peasant was worse than this. Conditions frequently became so oppressive that it was impossible to eke out a livelihood and the peasants were forced to abandon their farms.[93] In China, conditions were so wretched that female infanticide was widely practiced. One nineteenth-century scholar indicated that in some districts as many as a quarter of the female infants were killed at birth.[94] Sometimes signs were posted in these areas: "Girls may not be drowned here." Though obviously an extreme case, the conditions that fostered it were by no means limited to China.

To compound the misery created by their economic situation, peasants were often subjected to cruel treatment. Families were sometimes split up if it served their master's economic interests.[95] Peasants often found it difficult to defend their wives and daughters from the amorous attentions of the governing class, and in some areas the lord of the manor maintained the notorious *jus primae noctis*.[96] Finally, peasants were subject at all times to the whims and tempers of their superiors, who might invoke severe punishments even for minor offenses. Petty thievery was often punished by death, frequently by cruel and frightful means.[97]

To the governing class, all this seemed only natural, since most of them, like their predecessors in simple agrarian societies, viewed peasants as essentially subhuman. In legal documents in medieval England, a peasant's children were not his *familia,* but his *sequela,* meaning "brood" or "litter."[98] Estate records in Europe, Asia, and America often listed the peasants with the

[91] Bennett, p. 236.

[92] Ibid., pp. 232–236.

[93] See, for example, Moreland, p. 147, on India, or Blum, pp. 163, 266–268, 309–310, and 552ff., on Russia.

[94] Douglas, p. 354.

[95] Blum, pp. 424 and 428, on Russia, and Gunnar Myrdal, *An American Dilemma* (New York: McGraw-Hill, 1964), p. 931, on the American South.

[96] Literally, the right of the first night (i.e., the right to deflower a bride on her wedding night). See Coulton, pp. 80 and 464–469; Blum, pp. 426–427; G. M. Carstairs, "A Village in Rajasthan," in M. N. Srinivas (ed.), *India's Villages* (Calcutta: West Bengal Government Press, 1955), pp. 37–38.

[97] Bennett, p. 196; Coulton, pp. 190–191, 248–250, and 437–440.

[98] G. G. Coulton, *Medieval Panorama* (New York: Meridian Books, 1955), p. 77, or Thompson, p. 708.

livestock.[99] Even so civilized a Roman as Cato the Elder argued that slaves, like livestock, should be disposed of when no longer productive.[100]

As shocking as these views seem today, they were not completely illogical. So divergent were the ways of life of the governing class and the peasantry, and so limited their contacts (normally a class of officials and retainers stood between them[101]), it is perhaps more surprising that some members of the privileged class recognized their common humanity than that the majority did not.

Despite the heavy burdens laid on them, not all peasants were reduced to the subsistence level. By various devices, many contrived to hide part of their harvest and otherwise evade their obligations.[102] A small minority even managed, by rendering special services to the governing class or by other means,

Figure 8.17 Peasant village, Colombia.

[99] William Stubbs, *The Constitutional History of England* (Oxford: Clarendon Press, 1891), vol. I, p. 454, n., Wolfram Eberhard, *A History of China*, 2d ed. (Berkeley: University of California Press, 1960), p. 32; and Yosoburo Takekoshi, *The Economic Aspects of the History of the Civilization of Japan* (New York: Macmillan, 1930), vol. I, pp. 60–63.

[100] See Boak, *A History of Rome*, p. 127, or Cowell, *Cicero and the Roman Republic*, p. 64. For an example of the application of Cato's principle in medieval Europe, see Bennett, p. 283.

[101] See, for example, Bloch, p. 337, or George Homans, *English Villagers of the 13th Century* (Cambridge, Mass.: Harvard, 1942), p. 229.

[102] See, for example, Morton Fried, *The Fabric of Chinese Society: Study of the Social Life of a Chinese County Seat* (New York: Praeger, 1953), pp. 104–105; Moreland, pp. 168 and 207; and Bennett, pp. 100–101, 112–113, and 131ff.

Figure 8.18 Country home of a member of the governing class, Colombia. The owner of this hacienda seldom stays in it, preferring his other home in the city of Cali.

to rise a bit above their fellows, operating larger farms and generally living a bit more comfortably.[103]

For the majority, however, the one real hope for a substantial improvement in their lot lay, ironically, in the devastation wrought by plagues, famines, and wars. Only when death reduced their numbers to the point where good workers were in short supply was the governing class forced to bid competitively for the peasants' services, raising their income above the subsistence level.[104] Normally, however, high birthrates kept this from happening or, when it did, soon brought about a return to the former situation.

The Urban Economy

When we think of the great civilizations of the past, most of us conjure up images of Rome, Constantinople, Alexandria, Jerusalem, Damascus, Baghdad, Babylon, and the other great cities that loom so large in the historical record. Thus it is with a sense of shock that we discover that rarely if ever did all the urban communities, large and small together, of one of these societies hold more than 10 per cent of its population, and often much less.[105]

---

[103] See, for example, the franklins in thirteenth-century England (Homans, pp. 248–250).

[104] May McKisack, *The Fourteenth Century* (Oxford: Clarendon Press, 1959), pp. 331–340; Lindsay and Groves pp. 30, 34, and 63; Charles Langlois, "History," in Arthur Tilley (ed.), *Medieval France* (London: Cambridge, 1922), pp. 150–151; and Paul Murray Kendall, *The Yorkist Age* (Garden City, N.Y.: Doubleday, 1962), pp. 171ff.

[105] Sjoberg, p. 83; Lynn White, *Medieval Technology and Social Change* (Oxford: Clarendon Press, 1962), p. 39; Henri Pirenne, *Economic and Social History of Medieval Europe* (New York: Harvest Books, n.d., first published 1933), p. 58; J. C. Russell, *British Medieval Population* (Albuquerque: University of New Mexico Press, 1948), p. 305; Blum, pp. 268 and 281.

How can this be? The explanation is that we have been victims of an illusion. Because history was recorded by literate men—men who nearly always lived in cities and towns and regarded the life of the rural villages as unworthy of their attention—the record is primarily of city life, particularly the life of the governing class.

The most striking feature of the cities and towns of these societies was the great diversity of people who lived in them. Urban residents ranged from the most illustrious members of the governing class to beggars and other destitute people who barely managed to stay alive. Unlike the majority of cities and towns in modern industrial societies, these were not primarily industrial centers. Though considerable industrial activity was carried on in them, their political and commercial functions, and frequently their religious ones, were more important.

Since the cities and towns were the centers of government, most members of the governing class preferred to live in them.[106] As a result, urban populations included not only the necessary complement of civil and military officials, but the extensive households of the governing class as well. Servants were far more numerous in these societies than in ours, both because of the absence of labor-saving devices and because the governing class viewed manual work of any kind as degrading. Furthermore, one of their chief forms of status competition was to see who could maintain the most luxurious households. The household staff of the head of one small kingdom, Edward IV of England, numbered 400.[107] A more important ruler, such as the Roman emperor at the height of the empire, had thousands. As one historian put it, one "is dumbfounded by the extraordinary degree of specialization [and] the insensate luxury."[108] One group of servants was responsible only for the emperor's palace clothes, another for his city clothes, another for those he wore to the theater, yet another for his military uniforms. Other servants attended strictly to eating vessels, a different group to those used for drinking, another to silver vessels, and still others to gold vessels and those set with jewels. For entertainment, the emperor had his own choristers, an orchestra, dancing women, clowns, and dwarfs. Lesser members of the governing class obviously could not maintain household staffs as elaborate as this, but many had staffs of hundreds, and some had a thousand or more.[109] All this was made possible by the labors of the peasantry.

Part of the peasants' surplus also went to support two important groups that were allied with the governing class yet separate from it. The first of these

---

[106] They were also attracted to them because they were the social and cultural centers of their societies. See Sjoberg, pp. 108–116. This pattern also prevailed in the American South. See Samuel G. Stoney, *Plantations of the Carolina Low Country* (Charleston: Carolina Art Association, 1938), p. 36.

[107] Kendall, p. 157.

[108] Carcopino, *Daily Life in Ancient Rome,* p. 70.

[109] Ibid., and Kendall, pp. 202 and 206.

was the clergy, of whom more will be said shortly. The second was the merchant class. Merchants were a peculiar group in the structure of agrarian societies. Although some of them were extremely wealthy, they were rarely accepted as equals by members of the governing class—even by those less wealthy than they. For merchants worked to obtain their wealth, and this, by the values of the governing class, was unpardonable.[110] Nevertheless, the latter avidly sought the goods that the merchants sold and coveted their wealth, acquiring it whenever they could by taxes, marriage, or outright confiscation.[111] The attitude of the merchants toward the governing class was equally am-

Figure 8.19 Like modern advertisers, merchants often created a demand for their goods, especially luxuries: market scene, Morocco.

[110] See, for example, Sjoberg, pp. 183ff. For an interesting illustration of the persistence of this pattern into the latter part of the nineteenth century in England, see W. Somerset Maugham, *Cakes and Ale* (New York: Pocket Books, 1944), p. 29.

[111] On acquisition by marriage, see Elinor Barber, *The Bourgeoisie in 18th Century France* (Princeton, N.J.: Princeton, 1955), p. 89, or Sansom, vol. III, pp. 128–129. On confiscation, see Misra, pp. 25–27; Takekoshi, vol. II, pp. 251ff.; Kendall, p. 181; or Ramsay, vol. I, p. 58.

bivalent: they both feared and envied them, but, given the chance, they emulated their way of life and sought to be accepted by them.

Like modern advertising men, the merchants of agrarian societies often created the demand for their goods, thereby spurring productivity. And like modern advertisers, they were primarily interested in creating a demand for luxuries. One reason for this was the high cost of moving goods. With the primitive transportation available, only lightweight luxury items, such as silks, spices, and fine swords, could be moved very far without the costs becoming prohibitive. A report on China shortly after World War II indicates the enormous differential between traditional and modern methods of transportation there. To ship 1 ton of goods 1 mile, the costs were as follows (measured in United States cents):[112]

Steamboat	2.4	Animal-drawn cart	13.0	Pack donkey	24.0
Rail	2.7	Pack mule	17.0	Pack horse	30.0
Junk	12.0	Wheelbarrow	20.0	Carrying by pole	48.0

Figure 8.20 The cost of moving goods was extremely high in agrarian societies because of the primitive methods of transportation: market scene, Saudi Arabia.

[112] John Lossing Buck, *Secretariat Paper No. 1. Tenth Conference of the Institute of Pacific Relations* (Stratford on Avon, 1947), reprinted in Irwin T. Sanders et al., *Societies Around the World* (New York: Dryden Press, 1953), p. 65.

Figure 8.21 Craft specialization was highly developed in agrarian societies: Indian potter at work.

Figures from Europe are strikingly similar: in 1900, for example, it cost ten times more to move goods by horse-drawn wagon than by rail.[113] In short, modern methods of transportation have slashed this expense by 80 to 95 per cent.

The prosperity of the merchant class was due in no small measure to the labors of another, humbler class with which they were closely affiliated—the artisans, who numbered approximately 3 to 5 per cent of the total population.[114] Except for the peasantry, this class was the most productive element in the economy. Most artisans lived in the urban centers and, like the rest of the urban population, were dependent on the surplus produced by the peasants. Craft specialization was rather highly developed in the larger urban centers, as we have seen.

The shops where artisans worked were small by modern standards and

---

[113] Clough and Cole, *Economic History of Europe*, p. 445.

[114] See, for example, John Nef, *The Conquest of the Material World* (Chicago: University of Chicago Press, 1964), p. 69.

bore little resemblance to a modern factory. In Rome in the first century B.C., a shop employing fifty men was considered very large.[115] A pewter business employing eighteen men was the largest mentioned in any of London's medieval craft records, and even this modest size was not attained until the middle of the fifteenth century.[116] Typically, the shop was also the residence of both the merchant and his workmen, and work was carried on either in the living quarters or in an adjoining room.[117]

The economic situation of the artisans, like that of the merchants, was variable. In Peking at the time of World War I, wages ranged from $2.50 a month for members of the Incense and Cosmetic Workers Guild to $36 a month for members of the Gold Foil Beaters Guild.[118] In general, those in highly skilled trades and some of the self-employed fared moderately well by agrarian standards. Apprentices and journeymen in less skilled trades, however, worked long hours for bare subsistence wages. In Peking, for example, a seven-day workweek and ten-hour workday were typical, and many artisans remained too poor to marry.

Merchants and artisans in the same trade were commonly organized into guilds. These organizations were an attempt to create, in an urban setting within agrarian societies, a functional approximation of the extended-family group of horticultural societies. Many guilds spoke of their members as brothers, for example, and functioned as mutual aid associations, restricting entry into the field, forbidding price cutting, and otherwise trying to protect the interests of their members.[119] But because a guild included merchant employers as well as artisan employees, the former were dominant, controlling key offices and adopting policies that benefited them more than the artisans.[120]

Beneath the artisans in the social structure of the cities were a variety of other kinds of people, including unskilled laborers who supplied much of the animal energy required by the system. The working conditions of these men were usually terrible, and injuries were common. As a result, their work life was short. For example, early in the present century, the average Peking rickshaw man was able to work only five years, after which he was good for little except begging.[121] The class of unskilled laborers shaded off into still more deprived

---

[115] Cowell, p. 80. See also William Woodruff, *Impact of Western Man: A Study of Europe's Role in the World Economy* (New York: St. Martin's, 1966), p. 254.

[116] Sylvia Thrupp, *The Merchant Class of Medieval London* (Ann Arbor: Ann Arbor Paperbacks, University of Michigan Press, 1962), p. 9.

[117] See, for example, Nef, p. 78.

[118] Sidney Gamble, *Peking: A Social Survey* (New York: Doran, 1921), pp. 183–185.

[119] Thrupp, pp. 19, 30, etc.

[120] Ibid., pp. 23 and 29–31; James Westfall Thompson, *Economic and Social History of Europe in the Later Middle Ages, 1300–1530* (New York: Century, 1931), p. 398.

[121] Gamble, p. 283.

THE SHAME OF A TOWN THAT SOLD ITS DAUGHTERS

This was the caption of a story that *The Washington Post* ran on an inside page April 27, 1972. It reports the recent recurrence of a practice that was once moderately widespread in agrarian societies. The subtitle of the article was "When the rice crop failed in northern Thailand."

Dork Kham Tai, Thailand—Like the golden acacia, after which it is named, this northern Thailand country town has lost its blossoms and gone to seed.

Its golden flowers were its daughters. By count of its own district's embarrassed and chagrined officials, 100 girls aged 14 to 20 years, mostly belonging to poor rice-farmer families, were sold to madams and pimps last year for service in Bangkok's red-light district known as Sukhothai.

A drought had struck the rice crop, and many families in this lean countryside were desperate for food, as well as for seed

and fertilizer for next season's crop. Their teenage daughters were the most salable commodity, for northern Thailand women have a reputation for prettiness and for docility.

The selling price ranged, depending upon youth and beauty, from 1,000 to 5,000 baht, about $50 to $250. The servitude in the world's oldest profession ends only after they have worked off their bond, plus sizeable "interest and upkeep."

This story was reported by Jack Foisie.
© *Los Angeles Times*. Reprinted by permission.

---

groups—the unemployed, the beggars, and the criminals. The high birthrates of agrarian societies resulted in an oversupply of unskilled labor, and such people drifted to the cities, hoping to find some kind of employment. As long as they were young and healthy, they could usually get work as day laborers. But after they were injured or lost their youth and strength, they were quickly replaced by fresh labor and left to fend for themselves, usually as beggars or thieves. No agrarian society found a solution to this problem. But then, the leading classes were not expecially interested in finding one. The system served their needs quite well just the way it was.

Many of the sisters of the men who made up the urban lower classes found their livelihood as prostitutes. Moralists have often condemned these women as though they elected this career in preference to a more honorable one. The record indicates, however, that most of them had little choice: their only alternative was a life of unrelieved drudgery and poverty as servants or unskilled laborers, and many could not even hope for that.[122] The men they might have married were too poor to afford wives, and the system of prostitution was often, in effect, a substitute for marriage forced on many men and women

---

[122] In Asia many were sold into prostitution by their parents. See Gamble, p. 253. Many more, in every part of the world, were ignorant country girls seeking work in the city who were trapped by hired procurers, while still others were driven to prostitution by unemployment and lack of funds. See M. Dorothy George, *London Life in the XVIIIth Century* (London: Kegan Paul, Trench, Trubner, 1925), pp. 112–113.

by society. To be sure, the poor were not the only ones to avail themselves of the services of prostitutes, nor were all girls in the "profession" because of poverty. But economic factors were clearly the chief cause of its high incidence.

The number of profitable working years for prostitutes was hardly longer than that for the rickshaw boys, porters, and others who sold their animal energies for a meager livelihood. As a result, the cities and towns in agrarian societies often swarmed with beggars. Estimates by contemporary observers and officials suggest that beggars comprised from a tenth to as high as a third of the total population of urban communities.[123] The proportion was not so high for the society as a whole, of course, since many of the rural poor migrated to the cities and towns in the hope of finding greater opportunities.

Demographic Patterns

As we have noted, the population potential of advanced agrarian societies far surpassed that of simpler societies, rising slowly over the centuries in response to technological advances in food production. Thus China's population gradually increased from about 50 million in the middle of the second century A.D. to around 240 million in the late eighteenth century and then, more rapidly, to 400 million by the middle of the nineteenth.[124] Japan's grew from about 10 million in the thirteenth century to 35 million in 1875, and Britain's from 1 million in the eleventh century to 6 million in the early eighteenth.[125]

Birthrates have always been high in advanced agrarian societies, averaging about 40 births per year per thousand population, more than double that of modern industrial societies.[126] In general, there seems to have been little interest in limiting the size of families, since large families, particularly ones with many sons, were valued for both economic and religious reasons. From the economic standpoint, children were viewed by peasants as an important asset, a valuable source of cheap labor.[127] As members of a modern industrial society, we are often ignorant of the amount of work required on a peasant farm.

---

[123] See, for example, Frederick Nussbaum, *A History of the Economic Institutions of Modern Europe* (New York: Crofts, 1933), or Frank Aydelotte, *Elizabethan Rogues and Vagabonds* (Oxford: Clarendon Press, 1913), p. 4.

[124] Eberhard, *History of China*, pp. 108 and 274, and Chang, *The Chinese Gentry*, p. 102.

[125] Taeuber, *The Population of Japan*, pp. 20 and 41; Russell, p. 235, and D. V. Glass and D. E. C. Eversley, *Population in History* (Chicago: Aldine, 1965), p. 240, on England.

[126] Warren Thompson and David Lewis, *Population Problems*, 5th ed. (New York: McGraw-Hill, 1965), p. 386; O. Andrew Collver, *Birth Rates in Latin America: New Estimates of Historical Trends and Fluctuations* (Berkeley, Calif: Institute of International Studies, 1965), pp. 26–30; Glass and Eversley, pp. 467, 532, 555, and 614. One of the lowest rates for an agrarian society prior to the twentieth century was for eighteenth-century Sweden, and it was nearly 36 per thousand (Glass and Eversley, p. 532).

[127] See, for example, Horace Miner, *St. Denis: A French-Canadian Parish* (Chicago: Phoenix Books, The University of Chicago Press, 1963), p. 65; Berger, p. 116; Coulton, *The Medieval Village*, p. 322; Manning Nash, *The Golden Road to Modernity: Village Life in Contemporary Burma* (New York: Wiley, 1965), pp. 265–266.

Religion added another incentive for large families, either by encouraging cults of ancestor worship in which perpetuation of the family line was essential or simply by declaring large families to be the will of God.[128] The chief deterrent to large families was probably the reaction of women to the strains and risks of repeated pregnancies; but because they were subordinant to their husbands, who favored large families, their views counted for little.[129]

Despite their high birthrates, advanced agrarian societies grew slowly. Sometimes they failed to grow at all or even declined in size. The reason, of course, was that death rates were almost as high as birthrates and sometimes higher. Wars, disease, accidents, and starvation all took their toll. Infant mortality was especially high before the development of modern sanitation and medicine. Recent studies show that the average child born in Rome 2,000 years ago could not expect to live more than twenty years.[130] Even as recently as the seventeenth century, the children of British queens and duchesses had a life expectancy of only thirty years, with nearly a third dead before their fifth birthday. Youngsters of the elite who survived the dangerous infant years still had a total life expectancy of only a little more than forty years.[131] For the common people, conditions were even worse. With death rates averaging nearly 40 per thousand per year, life expectancy could not have been much over twenty-five years.

The larger cities were notoriously unhealthy places, especially for the common people. The citizens of Rome, for example, had a shorter life expectancy than those, in the provinces.[132] England in the early eighteenth century presented a similar situation. During the first half of that century, there were an estimated 500,000 more deaths than births in London.[133] Some of the reasons for this become clear when we read descriptions of sanitary conditions in medieval cities. As one historian depicts them:

> The streets of medieval towns were generally little more than narrow alleys, the overhanging upper stories of the houses nearly meeting, and thus effectually excluding all but a minimum of light and air. . . . In most continental towns and some English ones, a high city wall further impeded the free circulation of air. . . . Rich citizens might possess a courtyard in which garbage was collected and occasionally removed to the suburbs, but the usual practice was to throw everything into the streets including the garbage of slaughter houses and

---

[128] See, for example, John Noss, *Man's Religions,* rev. ed. (New York: Macmillan 1956), pp. 227, 304ff., and 420–421; Miner, pp. 65–66.

[129] Miner, p. 170.

[130] Harrison Brown, *The Challenge of Man's Future* (New York: Viking Compass, 1956), p. 75.

[131] H. Hollingsworth, "A Demographic Study of the British Ducal Families," in Glass and Eversley, tables 2 and 5, pp. 358 and 360.

[132] Brown, p. 75.

[133] Warren Thompson, *Population Problems,* 3d ed. (New York: McGraw-Hill, 1942), p. 73.

Figure 8.22 The streets of medieval towns were generally little more than alleys effectively excluding all but a minimum of light and air: street scene, France.

other offensive trades. . . . Filth of every imaginable description accumulated indefinitely in the unpaved streets and in all available space and was trodden into the ground. The water supply would be obtained either from wells or springs, polluted by the gradual percolation through the soil of the accumulated filth, or else from an equally polluted river. In some towns, notably London, small streams running down a central gutter served at once as sewers and as water supply. . . . In seventeenth century London, which before the Fire largely remained a medieval city, the poorer class house had only a covering of weatherboards, a little black pitch forming the only waterproofing, and these houses were generally built back to back. Thousands of Londoners dwelt in cellars or horribly overcrowded tenements. A small house in Dowgate accommodated 11 married couples and 15 single persons. . . . Another source of unhealthiness were the church vaults and graveyards, so filled with corpses that the level of the latter was generally raised above that of the surrounding ground. In years of pestilence, recourse had to be made to plague pits in order to dispose of the harvest of death.[134]

This account calls attention to one of the striking demographic characteristics of advanced agrarian societies: the disasters that periodically overtook

---

[134] M. C. Buer, *Health, Wealth, and Population in the Early Days of the Industrial Revolution, 1760–1815* (London: Routledge, 1926), pp. 77–78. Quoted by permission of Routledge & Kegan Paul Ltd.

Figure 8.23 Street scene, Peru: note the overhanging upper story.

Figure 8.24 Sanitation standards were minimal in most agrarian societies: open air butcher shop, Saudi Arabia.

them and produced sharp peaks in the death rates.[135] The most devastating of all, the Black Plague that hit Europe in the middle of the fourteenth century, is said to have killed a third of the population of France and England, half that of Italy, and to have left the island of Cyprus almost depopulated.[136] Crop failures and famines seldom affected such large areas, but they were much more frequent and could be just as deadly where they struck. One Finnish province lost a third of its population during the famine of 1696–1697, and many parts of France suffered comparable losses a few years earlier.[137] Even allowing for a considerable margin of error in the reports of such disasters, it is clear from other kinds of evidence—for example, the severe labor shortages and the abandonment of farms that followed plagues and famines—that the number of deaths was huge. Because of these disasters, the growth of advanced agrarian populations was anything but continuous.

Religion

During the era in which advanced agrarian societies were dominant, a number of important changes occurred in the religious sphere. The most important by far was the emergence and spread of three new religions, Buddhism, Christianity, and Islam. Each proclaimed a supranational or universal faith, and each succeeded in creating a community of believers that transcended societal boundaries. In all the older faiths, religious belief and affiliation were determined by the accidents of birth and residence. Where one lived determined the god or gods one worshiped, for the prevailing view was that there were many gods and that, like kings, each had his own people and territory.

The ancient Israelites were perhaps the first to reject this view and move toward a more universalistic outlook. Centuries before the birth of Christ, the prophets proclaimed that there was only one God and that he ruled over the entire world. For a time, Judaism was a missionary religion and won converts in many parts of the Roman world.[138] This phase ended, however, when the early Christian missionaries won most of these Gentile converts over to their faith. After this, the implementation of the universalistic vision became the mission of Christians and Muslims, who eventually converted, at least nominally, most of the population of Europe, North Africa, and the Middle East and some of the people of India, central Asia, China, and Southeast Asia.

Buddhism, the other great universal faith, began in India as a heretical offshoot of Hinduism and spread through most of Southeast Asia, China, Korea, and Japan, though it later died out in the land of its origin. Older ethnic faiths, such as Hinduism, Confucianism, and Shintoism, still survived in much of Asia,

---

[135] D. E. C. Eversley, "Population, Economy, and Society," in Glass and Eversley, p. 52.

[136] Warren Thompson, p. 58. See also Brown, p. 32.

[137] K. F. Helleiner, "The Vital Revolution Reconsidered," in Glass and Eversley, p. 79.

[138] See Kenneth Scott Latourette, *A History of Christianity* (New York: Harper, 1953), pp. 15–16.

Figure 8.25 Worshippers listening to sermon at Badhshahi (royal) Mosque, Lahore, Pakistan.

but even they now incorporated some elements of universalism in their thought.

The spread of the new universal faiths reflected the broader social and intellectual horizons opened up by improved transportation and the spreading web of trade relations. Empire building, too, helped weaken parochial or "tribal" views. As men's knowledge of other societies increased, and with it their awareness of the essential unity of mankind, the basic postulate of the older ethnic faiths was gradually undermined.

Another important development was the growing separation of religious and political institutions.[139] Compared with the situation in advanced horticultural and simple agrarian societies, the state had become much more secular. Kings and emperors were still said to rule "by the grace of God," the divine right of kings was generally accepted, and occasionally a ruler claimed to be a god; but few rulers functioned as high priests, and theocracies (i.e., states in which a priesthood rules in the name of a god) were almost unknown. This separation was part of the much more general trend toward institutional specialization that is so basic in the evolutionary process from the horticultural era on.

Despite the growing *organizational* separation of politics and religion,

---

[139] See Robert Bellah, "Religious Evolution," *American Sociological Review*, 29 (1964), pp. 367–368.

Figure 8.26 Religious procession in the village of Marin, Venezuela.

the two systems continued to work closely together, and political and religious leaders were normally allied. This was especially evident in struggles between the governing class and the common people. When rebellious voices challenged the right of the governing class to control the economic surplus produced by the peasants, the clergy usually defended the elite, asserting that their power had been given them by God and any challenge to it was a challenge to his authority.[140] By legitimizing the actions of the governing class in this way, the clergy reduced the need for costly coercive efforts.

In appreciation for this, and also because of their own religious beliefs, agrarian rulers were often extremely generous with religious groups, giving them large grants of land and special tax exemptions. In effect, a symbiotic relationship was established, with religious groups legitimizing the actions of the governing class in return for generous financial support. Modern research indicates that religious groups frequently owned as much as a quarter or a third of a nation's land.[141]

Despite such profitable alliances, most religions fostered some concern for distributive justice. This is especially evident in Judaism and Christianity.[142] One historian captured the contradictory nature of the medieval

---

[140] See, for example, Lenski, pp. 7–9. See also Kendall, pp. 232ff.

[141] Lenski, pp. 257–258.

[142] Ibid., pp. 262–266, for a more detailed treatment of this aspect of religion.

church in this discerning characterization: "Democratic, yet aristocratic; charitable, yet exploitative; generous, yet mercenary; humanitarian, yet cruel; indulgent, yet severely repressive of some things; progressive, yet reactionary; radical, yet conservative—all these are qualities of the Church in the Middle Ages." [143]

Magic and Fatalism

Before we leave the subject of ideology, two other aspects of the world view of agrarian societies deserve comment: (1) the widespread belief in the efficacy of magic and (2) the equally widespread attitude of fatalism. [144] Logically, these are contradictory. If magic really works, people do not need to be fatalistic, and if they are true fatalists, they should have no confidence in magic. But people are seldom completely logical in their view of life. In their more optimistic moments they often hope for things they know are impossible. Considering the tremendous pressures operating on the masses of common people in agrarian societies, and their limited sources of information, it is hardly surprising that so many of them held these mutually contradictory views. At least they offered a ray of hope.

The prevalence of these beliefs, however, was another factor that contributed to the slow rate of technological advance in agrarian societies. Neither belief was likely to motivate men to try to devise better tools and techniques. On the contrary, one encouraged them to look to magic for the solutions to their problems, and the other convinced them that success was, after all, simply a matter of fate.

Kinship

Kinship ties continued to be important for the individual in advanced agrarian societies. Their importance for society, however, was greatly diminished compared with hunting and gathering or horticultural societies. The explanation for this lies in the growth in the scale of organization. As long as communities and societies were small, the kinship system could serve as an integrative force for the entire population. Later, when the growth of population made this impossible, the largest and most powerful extended family in a society, supplemented perhaps by its dependent retainers, could still provide enough men to staff the political system. By the time the level of advanced agrarian societies was reached, however, even this became impossible. Civil and military offices were so numerous that not even the largest extended family could fill them all.

---

[143] James Thompson, *Economic and Social History of the Middle Ages*, p. 684.

[144] See, for example, Carlo Levi, *Christ Stopped at Eboli* (New York: Farrar, Straus, 1947), chaps. 11ff., for a good description of the role of magic in one agrarian community. On fatalism, see, for example, Edward Banfield, *The Moral Basis of a Backward Society* (New York: Free Press, 1967), pp. 36–37, 41, 107ff., etc.

Thus, the kinship system could no longer provide the structural basis for the political system.

Family ties still played a significant role in politics, however. Many civil and military offices in agrarian societies were a family's patrimony, handed down from father to son like any other family possession. The classic case of this was the royal office itself in most societies, but the pattern was much more widespread than that. When offices were not privately owned, they were often closed to anyone who was not a member of the nobility or whose family did not qualify by less formal criteria as one of "the right families." Even when these criteria were not invoked in the allocation of offices, family ties were still important. Family funds might be needed to purchase an office, for example; and those who had it in their power to assign an office were naturally influenced by their own families' interests. Although similar practices still occur in modern industrial societies, they are usually a violation of the law and lack public approval. But in advanced agrarian societies, these practices were usually an accepted part of life, and there was little criticism, and still less punishment, of those who engaged in them.

In the economic realm, the family was usually the basic unit of organization. This was equally true in urban and in rural areas. Businesses were almost always family enterprises; the corporate form of enterprise, owned jointly by unrelated persons, was virtually unheard of, even in the largest cities. And in rural areas the basic work unit was the family.

It is not unfair to say that in these societies the family was largely an economic and political organization. While this can be demonstrated in many ways, some of the best examples are associated with marriage. For instance, because of its economic implications, marriage was considered much too important to be decided by young people, and marriages were usually arranged by the parents, often with the aid of marriage brokers.[145] Sometimes the young couple did not even meet until the ceremony itself. In selecting spouses for their children, parents were primarily concerned with the economic and status implications of the match and only secondarily with other matters. Marriage arrangements often involved an outright economic transaction, either the payment of a bride price (i.e., payment for the bride) or a dowry.[146] Among members of the governing class, marriages were usually arranged with an eye to their political implications: by skillful management of its children's marriages, a family could do a great deal to improve its political position.

As one would suppose, marriages contracted in this way did not always produce psychological or sexual compatibility between the spouses, but then, this was not necessarily expected. For those pleasures, wealthier men often

---

[145] Sjoberg, *The Preindustrial City*, pp. 146ff.

[146] Ibid., p. 155.

turned to mistresses and concubines. Despite this, marriage ties were usually quite durable because of their strong economic or political bonds.

Within the family, male dominance was the rule. Obedience was generally held to be the highest ideal for women and children.[147] This was but part of the general authoritarian pattern that characterized so much of the life of agrarian societies.

Leisure and the Arts

Though life for the great majority of people in agrarian societies entailed long hours of tiring work and was exceedingly grim in other ways, most people had some time for leisure and recreation.[148] It is impossible to recount all their uses of such time, as this was one area where innovative tendencies were not unduly restricted. Weddings and religious festivals were important occasions for people to get together for a good time, with singing and dancing their basic entertainment and alcoholic beverages adding to the merriment in most societies.

Figure 8.27 "Peasant Wedding," by Pieter Breughel the Elder (1520?–1569).

---

[147] Ibid., pp. 163ff.; Henry Orenstein, *Gaon: Conflict and Cohesion in an Indian Village* (Princeton, N.J.: Princeton, 1965), pp. 53–57; Kendall, *The Yorkist Age*, chaps. 11 and 12; L. F. Salzman, *English Life in the Middle Ages* (London: Oxford, 1927), pp. 254–256.

[148] For descriptions of the uses of leisure in agrarian societies, see Margaret Wade Labarge, *A Baronial Household of the Thirteenth Century* (New York: Barnes & Noble, 1966), chap. 10; Bennett, *Life on the English Manor*, chap. 10; or Coulton, *Medieval Panorama*, chaps. 8 and 44.

People also amused themselves with games and contests, courtship and love-making, gossiping and storytelling, and a host of other activities.

Class distinctions were evident in leisure activity as in any other, with falconry, jousting, and chess among the activities generally identified with the governing class. But some forms of entertainment, such as archery and dice, had a universal appeal. Gambling in particular was popular with every class.

The rise of professional entertainers was part of the general trend toward occupational specialization. Actors, minstrels, jesters, clowns, acrobats, jugglers, prostitutes, and geishas were a few of the more familiar. In general, the status of such people was extremely low, probably because of their economic insecurity and their excessive dependence on the favor of others. Yet an entertainer who had a powerful patron might find his work quite lucrative.

Recreation was frequently raucous and crude; it could also be brutal and violent. Cockfights and dogfights were very popular, public hangings often drew large, exuberant crowds, and wedding parties and other festivities frequently ended in drunken brawls. In fact, violence typically followed drinking. From what we know of life in agrarian societies, it would appear that alcohol simply removed a fragile overlay of inhibitions, revealing people's frustrations and bitterness.

But if the agrarian world at play was often unattractive, its artistic accomplishments were quite the opposite. In their sculpture, their painting, their architecture, these societies left monuments of lasting beauty. Thousands of cathedrals, churches, mosques, pagodas, temples, and palaces, and all the treasures within them, testify to an impressive development of the arts during that era. Achievements in literature were probably no less impressive, though language barriers make it difficult for us to appreciate them as fully.[149] Developments in music during most of the agrarian era seem to have been less spectacular than in the other arts. Toward the end of the era, however, the invention of new instruments and the genius of composers like Bach, Mozart, Beethoven, and Chopin combined to produce an outburst of magnificent music that has transcended societal boundaries in unprecedented fashion.

Most artists were subsidized by the governing class or the religious elite, drawing on the economic surplus extracted from the peasant masses. Thus, the artistic achievements of agrarian societies were a product of the harshly exploitative social system. Yet, if the peasants had been allowed to keep the surplus, the result would simply have been more poor people. Again, as with horticultural societies, this link between an exploitative class system and cultural achievements reminds us of the difficulty we face in passing ethical judgments on complex sociocultural systems.

---

[149] Robert Frost once said that "poetry is what gets lost in translation," and anyone who has ever tried seriously to translate a poem understands the enormity of the language problem.

Cleavages and Conflicts

The sociocultural cleavages dividing advanced agrarian societies were similar to those in simple agrarian societies. Most important of all was the division along class lines. In advanced agrarian societies, however, this could no longer be described simply as a cleavage between the governing class and the rest of the population. The class structure had become more complex. Some merchants were now wealthier than some members of the governing class, for example, and between these privileged classes and the mass of common people was a growing middle class of self-employed artisans, small merchants, minor officials, lesser members of the clergy, and well-to-do peasants. In conflicts with the poor, the wealthy merchants and the middle class usually aligned themselves with the governing class, but at other times they did their best to advance their own interests at the expense of the governing class.

The cleavage between city people and country folk was still there, intensified, if anything, by greater urbanization. Towns and cities could no longer be described as overgrown villages. They had developed their own distinctive way of life, one that seemed completely alien to the visiting peasant or the migrant from a rural area. And because of the concentration of the literate and privileged classes in the urban centers, the villages seemed to city dwellers to be social and cultural backwaters, their residents ignorant and uncouth. There was a great deal of barbed humor by city people at the expense of country "yokels," and by country people at the expense of city "slickers" who were not quite as smart as they thought they were when confronted with the problems of rural life.

The cleavage between literate and illiterate continued, the chief difference being that in advanced agrarian societies most of the privileged class were literate. Writing was no longer a craft specialty. In most societies, this spread of literacy was greatly facilitated by the invention of the alphabet, though the Chinese experience shows that the alphabet was not essential.

Religion was the basis of an important new cleavage in many advanced agrarian societies. Although religious conflicts existed in simple agrarian societies, they were largely power struggles within the governing class, and most people had little interest in their outcome. With the rise of the new universal faiths, however, the common people were often drawn into these struggles. In many areas, especially in the Middle East and India, this led to the formation of largely endogamous (that is, inbred), culturally differentiated, and hostile religious groups. Each group sought control of the machinery of government in order to protect and further its own special interests. Members of religious minorities were often discriminated against politically, economically, and legally.

On the whole, the divisions within advanced agrarian societies were more serious than those within simple agrarian societies. In particular, they were much more likely to lead to violence. Earlier, we noted the frequency of peasant risings. Though most of these were local incidents involving small numbers of people, some spread and became large-scale insurrections. In either case, they were something new in history. Nor was it only the peasants who revolted against the governing class. The artisans followed suit on a number of occasions, as did the merchants.[150] And these groups, unlike the peasants, sometimes emerged victorious. In Europe, the merchants were so successful in their challenges to the governing class that eventually *they* became the governing class in many cities and towns. From the evolutionary perspective, this proved to be a very important development indeed.

Sociocultural Variations

In surveying societies at the same level of development, it is natural to empha- size those characteristics which are found in all of them, or are at least wide- spread, and to slight the differences, thus giving an impression of greater uni- formity than really exists. Obviously there have been variations in every area of life in advanced agrarian societies, and we have noted many of them in pass- ing or hinted at them in qualifying phrases, saying that a particular pattern was found in "most" or "many" of these societies.

Technologically, for example, the first advanced agrarian societies were much more like their simple agrarian predecessors than like the ad- vanced agrarian societies of Europe on the eve of the Industrial Revolution. Fur- thermore, the size of societies in this category ranged all the way from tiny prin- cipalities to great empires. Most were monarchies, but a few were republics. Similar variations occurred in almost every area of life.

Clearly, then, variation is to be expected among societies at the ad- vanced agrarian level—indeed, at *every* level of societal development. There is, however, one important difference: in the simpler societal types (i.e., hunting and gathering, fishing, and simple horticultural), intratype variation results primarily from differences in the biophysical environment. We see this clearly when we compare the Eskimo with the Australian aborigines, or the Bushmen of the Kalahari Desert with the Pygmies of the rain forest. In advanced agrarian societies, on the other hand, differences in biophysical environment have been responsible for relatively little intratype variation. This is exactly what evolu- tionary theory would lead us to expect, since the further a society advances on the evolutionary scale, the greater its ability to overcome the limitations im- posed by the biotic and physical world.

Differences in the *social* environment of advanced agrarian societies, however, have sometimes been responsible for rather important intratype varia-

[150] See, for example, H. van Werveke, "The Rise of the Towns," in *The Cambridge Economic History of Europe* (London: Cambridge, 1963), vol. 3, pp. 34–37; L. Halphen, "Industry and Commerce," in Tilley, pp. 190–192; or Pirenne, *Economic and Social History of Medieval Europe,* pp. 187–206.

tion. This is especially evident when we compare frontier societies with other advanced agrarian societies. A frontier society is one that is in the process of expanding into the territories of technologically simpler societies. The most familiar example for Americans is the European settlement of the New World; other instances include the British settlement of Australia and New Zealand, the Dutch or Boer settlement of South Africa, Russia's settlement of Siberia, and the earlier German thrust into Slavic territories.

Frontiers are especially interesting because they provide a unique opportunity for departures from the sociocultural patterns so deeply entrenched in agrarian societies. Those who respond to the challenges of the frontier, to its dangers and its opportunities, are primarily men with little to lose, with little stake in the established order. But they also possess a willingness to take great physical risks and a proclivity for independence and innovation. As a result, new ways of life commonly develop in frontier areas, innovations are accepted much more readily, and older rigidities give way.[151]

One of the most significant changes that occurs is the breakdown of the traditional class system. Except where the native population is enslaved or enserfed—as in much of Latin America—or where slaves are imported—as occurred in the Caribbean and the southern United States—a highly egalitarian system of small farms is likely to develop. This is what happened in Canada, the United States outside the southern region, Australia, New Zealand, Siberia, and the former German-Slavic frontier. In such areas, there is always a serious shortage of manpower; men are suddenly much more valuable than they were in the older, settled areas with their typical surplus of labor. On the frontier, there are neither enough farmers to cultivate the newly opened land nor enough fighters to defend it. It is not surprising, then, that frontier life produces a striking independence of spirit and a stubborn resistance to authority. Having risked their lives to establish themselves in a new territory, frontiersmen are not prepared to hand over their surplus to anyone. Thus, frontier conditions often break down the sharp inequalities and exploitative patterns characteristic of agrarian societies.

Unhappily, however, this condition is usually temporary. As the resistance of the native population comes to an end and the land begins to fill up with the original settlers' descendants, as roads are built and governmental authority is established, there is a waning of the spirit of independence and individualism, opportunities for resistance decline, and the traditional system begins to assert itself. To be sure, this does not happen overnight. On the contrary, it is likely to take a century or more. But in the end, the typical agrarian pattern prevails.

Only one thing has ever prevented this from happening—the onset of industrialization. In a number of instances during the last century and a half, the

---

[151] See, for example, Frederick Jackson Turner, *The Frontier in American History* (New York: Holt, 1920), or James G. Leyburn, *Frontier Folkways* (New Haven, Conn.: Yale, 1936).

Industrial Revolution generated a new demand for labor before the demands of the frontier had been satisfied and thus aborted a return to the old system. This happened in the United States in the nineteenth century and subsequently in Canada, Australia, and New Zealand. All these societies were thus spared the agony of slowly sliding back into the classic agrarian pattern in which a massive, impoverished peasantry is dominated and exploited by a small, hereditary aristocracy.

In the United States, this process actually got fairly well under way in much of the South because of its system of slavery. But the Confederacy's defeat in the Civil War and the South's eventual industrialization gradually halted the process. In other parts of the country, the process had not really developed very far before the forces of industrialization intervened.

Looking back, it seems clear that the frontier experience was excellent preparation for the Industrial Revolution. Most important, perhaps, it established a tradition of innovation and a receptivity to change that were lacking in other agrarian societies. Also, by creating a more egalitarian class system, the frontier prepared the way for the more open and fluid class systems of modern industrial societies. These facts undoubtedly help explain the relative ease with which the overseas English-speaking democracies have made the transition to the industrial era and also why they have been in the forefront with respect to productivity, standard of living, and political stability. It is interesting to speculate, however, how different the situation in these societies might be had they been settled a thousand years sooner and a more typical agrarian social system taken root.

CHAPTER NINE

Specialized Societal Types

Up to this point in our survey of human societies, we have concentrated on those types which are in the mainstream of evolutionary history, those which developed their technologies around the resources of fields and forests. The types of societies to which we now turn have adapted to more specialized, less typical environments—two to aquatic conditions, the third to semidesert grasslands and other marginal environments. Though these specialized societies have contributed to sociocultural evolution in numerous ways, their overall contribution has been more limited than that of the mainstream societies. This is because of their smaller numbers and size and the specialized nature of the problems with which they have dealt in their subsistence activities. Because of their more limited contribution, we will not examine them in the same detail as the others.

FISHING SOCIETIES

Actually, it is something of a misnomer to call any group a "fishing" society, for none ever depended exclusively on fishing for its food supply.[1] Except in the Arctic, nearly all fishing peoples obtain fruits and vegetables by foraging or cultivation. Many of them also supplement their diet by hunting or, occasionally, by raising livestock. To call a society a fishing society, then, simply indicates that fishing and foraging are its most important subsistence activities.

In recent centuries, fishing societies have been found in many parts of the world, but they have been most common in the northwestern part of North America—Oregon, Washington, British Columbia, Alaska, and the arctic regions of Canada. They have occurred less frequently in northern Asia and among the islands of the Pacific (most of the Pacific peoples have been simple horticulturalists) and in scattered parts of Africa, South America, and elsewhere.

Historically, fishing societies are probably the second oldest type, emerging in the Mesolithic era, or about a thousand years before the first horti-

---

[1] According to Murdock's Ethnographic Atlas, the Manus of New Guinea come as close to full dependence on fishing as any people in the world. See *Ethnology*, vol. 6, no. 2 (April 1967), pp. 170–230. Yet, as Margaret Mead indicates in her report, these people also depend heavily for their subsistence on garden products that they obtain through trade from neighboring peoples and to a lesser degree on pigs that they raise and obtain through trade. See Margaret Mead, *Growing Up in New Guinea* (New York: Mentor, 1953, first published 1930), especially pp. 173–174.

Figure 9.1   African fishing village, Dahomey.

cultural societies. The actual practice of fishing is, of course, even older and more widespread and has provided a supplementary source of subsistence in most societies since at least Upper Paleolithic times.

In some ways fishing societies might be regarded simply as specialized hunting and gathering societies, adapted to aquatic environments rather than terrestrial. One might argue that the chief difference is simply that fish, rather than land animals, are the object of the chase and that the technology of the group is modified accordingly. But this ignores a crucial fact: fishing economies usually have a potential for supporting larger, more sedentary populations than hunting and gathering economies. There are two reasons for this. First, because fish have much higher reproductive rates than most land animals, especially the larger animals on which hunters depend, primitive fishing people are less likely to deplete the food resources of their territory. As a result, it is easier for them to establish permanent settlements, with all this implies for the accumulation of wealth and the growth of social inequality.

A second basic difference is that fishermen usually work only a small fraction of the food-producing territory. When primitive people fish a large body of water, such as an ocean, a sea, or a large lake, their simple boats prevent them from going very far. As a result, even if they catch all the fish in the territory they work, the supply is quickly replenished by the great surplus spawned in adjacent areas. Nothing like this can happen on land, at least not after hunting and gathering bands occupy all the habitable territory in an area. This second difference reinforces the effects of the first.

Thus, even though fishing societies are technologically as primitive as hunting and gathering societies, we would expect them to be somewhat larger, more sedentary, and in other ways a bit more advanced.[2] This is, in fact, precisely what we find. With respect to size, they are half again as large: Murdock's sample shows that the average size of fishing communities is approximately 60, the average size of hunting and gathering groups only 40.[3] With respect to sedentariness, only 10 per cent of the hunting and gathering societies live in permanent settlements, compared to 49 per cent of the fishing societies.

Their political systems also indicate the greater potential inherent in a fishing economy. Less than 10 per cent of hunters and gatherers are organized into multicommunity societies, in contrast to nearly a quarter of the fishing societies. Social inequality, too, is more pronounced and more common: slavery is reported in slightly over half of the fishing societies. A system of hereditary nobility is also much more common in fishing societies than in hunting and gathering societies (32 per cent versus 2 per cent). Finally, as another indication of their economic development and greater wealth, fishing peoples are much more likely to link marriage with some economic transaction. This happens in 77 per cent of these groups but in only 48 per cent of the hunting and gathering societies.

In terms of structural development, fishing societies have about as much in common with simple horticultural societies as with advanced hunting and gathering societies.[4] Depending on the criterion, they sometimes lean more toward one, sometimes the other. For example, in community size they more closely approximate advanced hunting and gathering societies;[5] in permanence of settlements they are midway between the other two;[6] and in frequency of multicommunity societies they are almost indistinguishable from simple horticultural.[7]

From an evolutionary standpoint, the line of development represented by fishing societies has been something of a blind alley. Unlike the mainstream types, no fishing group ever evolved into a more advanced soci-

---

[2] For an earlier discussion of this point, see Gordon Hewes's excellent paper, "The Rubric 'Fishing and Fisheries,'" *American Anthropologist,* 50 (1948), pp. 241–242.

[3] See Table 5.2, p. 104 above.

[4] For a good illustration of this, see Philip Drucker's excellent description of the Indians of the Pacific Northwest, in *Cultures of the North Pacific Coast* (San Francisco: Chandler, 1965).

[5] The averages are hunting and gathering, 40; fishing, 60; simple horticultural, 95.

[6] The percentages for permanent settlements are hunting and gathering, 10; fishing, 49; simple horticultural, 87.

[7] The percentages are hunting and gathering, 10; fishing, 23; simple horticultural, 21.

Figure 9.2   The Shui-jen, or water people of south China, are descended from fishing peoples of an earlier time. They still depend on fishing for their livelihood and remain separate from the mainland population.

ety.[8] The reasons for this are quite simple. To begin with, the areas suited to a predominantly fishing economy are not only very limited; they are scattered and strung out along thin coastal strips, so that it would be virtually impossible to consolidate several groups into one larger political entity.[9] Instead, when neighboring horticultural societies become powerful enough, fishing societies are usually conquered and absorbed. Then, even though fishing con-

---

[8] Unless, perhaps, some evolved into maritime societies. To date, however, there is no real evidence that this ever happened. Maritime societies seem to have evolved out of advanced horticultural or agrarian societies.

[9] See Hewes, pp. 240–241.

tinues in the area, it is only a minor part of the economy of the larger society, and the leaders of the fishing groups are reduced to the status of minor officials, too weak to hold onto the local surplus for local use. As a result, fishing communities in agrarian societies have often been socially and culturally less advanced (except in subsistence technology) than fishing communities in more primitive fishing societies. Typically, their situation is no better than that of peasant villages, and for the same reason—their surplus is confiscated by the more powerful elements in the society.[10]

Though fishing societies did not give rise to more advanced societal types, they were not evolutionary blind alleys in the same sense as animals like the dinosaurs, whose entire line was wiped out and who therefore made no lasting genetic contribution. The technological advances made by fishing societies, far from being lost, have become part of the cultural heritage of almost every modern society.

HERDING SOCIETIES

Herding societies, like fishing societies, represent an adaptation to specialized environmental conditions. Other than that, the two have little in common. Their environments are very different, and their technologies, although overlapping somewhat, are basically on different levels.

Technologically, herding groups cover the same range of development as horticultural and simple agrarian societies. Animals were first domesticated about the same time plants were first cultivated, and the two practices typically went hand in hand in the horticultural and agrarian societies of the Old World.[11] In some areas, however, crops could not be cultivated because of insufficient rainfall, too short a growing season (in northern latitudes), or mountainous terrain. This was true of much of central Asia, the Arabian peninsula, and North Africa, and parts of Europe and sub-Saharan Africa. Because it was often possible to raise livestock in these areas, however, a new and different type of society gradually come into being.[12]

A pastoral economy usually necessitates a nomadic or seminomadic way of life.[13] In fact, "nomad" comes from an early Greek word meaning a "herder of cattle."[14] In the sample of herding societies in the Ethnographic

---

[10] For an interesting account of one such group, see Wilmond Menard, "The Sea Gypsies of China," *Natural History,* 64 (January 1965), pp. 13–21.

[11] This was not true in most of the New World, where there were almost no domesticated animals.

[12] Usually these societies have also had some secondary means of subsistence, frequently horticulture or agriculture on a small scale.

[13] See, for example, Lawrence Krader, "Pastoralism," in *International Encyclopedia of the Social Sciences* (New York: Macmillan and Free Press, 1968), vol. II, pp. 456–457, or Carleton Coon, "The Nomads," in Sydney Fisher (ed.), *Social Forces in the Middle East* (Ithaca, N.Y.: Cornell, 1955), pp. 23–42.

[14] John L. Myres, "Nomadism," *Journal of the Royal Anthropological Institute,* 71 (1941), p. 20.

Figure 9.3 Bedouin family camped in ruins of a deserted town, Saudi Arabia.

Atlas, more than 90 per cent are wholly or partially nomadic. In this respect they closely resemble hunters and gatherers.

Herders are also like hunters and gatherers in the size of their communities. On the average, they are a bit smaller than fishing communities and much smaller than simple horticultural, as the following population figures show.

Hunting and gathering societies	40
Herding societies	55
Fishing societies	60
Simple horticultural societies	95

The explanation for this is primarily environmental. Given the limited resources of their territories, large and dense settlements are impossible.[15]

Despite the small size of their communities, herding *societies* are usually fairly large. Whereas the typical hunting and gathering, fishing, or simple horticultural society contains but a single community, the average herding society contains several dozen.[16] Thus the median population of herding societies far surpasses those of the other three types.

Hunting and gathering societies	40
Fishing societies	60
Simple horticultural societies	95
Herding societies	2,000

The size of herding societies results from the combined influence of environment and technology. Open grasslands, where the majority of herders live,

---

[15] Krader reports that the average density of population in Mongolia was less than 1 per square mile, and among the Tuareg of Africa it was even lower (op. cit., pp. 458–459).

[16] The percentages of single-community societies were 90, 78, 77, and 13, respectively, in Murdock's Ethnographic Atlas sample.

present few natural barriers to movement. Furthermore, since early in the second millennium B.C., many of the herding peoples have mastered the art of horseback (or camel) riding, which greatly facilitates political integration.

The basic resource in these societies is livestock, and the size of the herd is the measure of the man. Large herds signify not only wealth but power, for only a strong man or the head of a strong family can defend such vulnerable property against rivals and enemies. Thus, in most of these societies, and especially in the more advanced (i.e., those with horses or camels and herds of larger animals such as cattle), marked social inequality is the rule. Hereditary slavery, for example, is far more common in herding societies than in any other type.[17] Other kinds of inequality are also very common, especially inequality of wealth.[18]

With respect to kinship, herding societies are noteworthy on at least two counts. First, they are more likely than any other type of society to require the payment of a bride price or bride service.[19] Second, they are the most likely to require newly married couples to live with the husband's kinsmen.[20]

These strong patriarchal tendencies have several sources. To begin with, they reflect the mobile and often militant character of pastoral life. Raiding and warfare are frequent activities, and, as we have noted before, these activities stimulate the growth of political authority. Moreover, the basic economic activity in these societies is man's work. In this respect they stand in sharp contrast to horticultural societies, where women so often play the dominant role in subsistence activities. It is hardly coincidence that horticultural societies are noted for their frequent female-oriented kinship patterns, herding societies for the opposite.

Herding societies are extremely interesting from the religious standpoint. Their concept of God corresponds to the Jewish and Christian concept more closely than any other group's. In forty of the fifty herding groups for which the Ethnographic Atlas has data, there is a belief in a Supreme Deity who created the world and remains actively concerned with its affairs, especially with man's moral conduct. This combination of beliefs is rare in other societies, except agrarian, where it occurs in two-thirds of the cases.[21] But even there, as Table 9.1 makes clear, its occurrence varies directly with the importance of herding activities to the particular group.

For those familiar with religious history, this relationship is not surprising. The Hebrews, who played such an important role in the rise and spread

---

[17] Found in 62 per cent of these societies as against 3 to 37 per cent of the rest.

[18] As shown in Table 5.6, p. 107, class stratification, by Murdock's definition, is present in 51 per cent of these societies.

[19] This requirement is found in 93 per cent of these societies, compared to 37 to 86 per cent of other types.

[20] This requirement occurs in 97 per cent of herding societies, compared to only 49 to 79 per cent of other types.

[21] Among the rest, it is most common in advanced horticultural societies, but even there it occurs in only 16 per cent of the cases; in the other types, the frequency ranges from 2 to 10 per cent.

Table 9.1 Religious beliefs of agrarian societies, by percentage of subsistence derived from herding

Percentage of Subsistence from Herding	Percentage Believing in Active, Moral Creator God	Number of Societies
36–45	92	13
26–35	82	28
16–25	40	20
6–15	20	5

Source: George Peter Murdock's Ethnographic Atlas sample of 915 societies.

of monotheism, were originally a herding people. And Islam, one of the most uncompromisingly monotheistic faiths, enjoyed most of its early successes among the herding peoples of the Arabian peninsula.

Why this relationship developed is far from clear, but the fact is undeniable. One can find repeated evidence of the affinity between the pastoral way of life and these religious concepts in biblical texts that describe God as a shepherd and his people as sheep. The shepherd's relationship with his flock has apparently suggested answers to the perennial questions concerning man's nature and destiny and the power that ultimately controls them. These answers have not been obvious to all herding peoples, however; a number of pastoral groups in Asia and Africa have come up with very different ones. The most we can say is that pastoral life increases the probability that men will arrive at these kinds of answers.

One of the most important technical advances made by herding peoples was utilizing the energy of horses, and later camels, for transportation. This practice originated in the eighteenth century B.C., when certain herding groups in the Middle East began to harness horses to chariots.[22] This gave them an important military advantage over their less mobile agrarian neighbors and enabled them to win control of much of the Middle East—at least until their techniques spread to the more numerous agrarian peoples. Herders later learned to *ride* their horses, which led to a new wave of conquests, beginning in the ninth century B.C.[23] During the next 2,500 years, a succession of advanced herding groups attacked agrarian societies from China to Europe and frequently conquered them. The empires and dynasties they established include some of the most famous in history—the great Mongol empire, for example, founded by Genghis Khan early in the thirteenth century A.D. and expanded by his suc-

[22] See William McNeill, *The Rise of the West: A History of the Human Community* (New York: Mentor, 1965), pp. 126ff., or Ralph Turner, *The Great Cultural Traditions* (New York: McGraw-Hill, 1941), p. 259.

[23] For a good discussion of this important subject, see McNeill, pp. 256ff.

cessors. At the peak of its power, the Mongol empire stretched from Eastern Europe to the shores of the Pacific and launched attacks against places as far apart as Austria and Japan. Other famous empires and dynasties founded by herding peoples include the Mogul empire, established in India by one branch of the Mongols, the Manchu dynasty in China, the Ottoman empire in the Middle East, and the early Islamic states established by Muhammad and his followers.

Despite their frequent military victories, herding peoples were never able to destroy the agrarian social order. In the end, it was always they, not the agrarian peoples, who changed their mode of life. There were a number of reasons for this, but it was primarily because the herders were motivated chiefly by greed. They saw agrarian societies as rich prizes and coveted the luxuries that their governing classes enjoyed. After a few early conquerors tried to turn fields into pastures, they realized they were, in effect, killing the goose that lays the golden eggs, and abandoned the effort. Thus, despite many impressive victories, the limits of the herding world were never enlarged.

Although herding continued to be an important secondary source of subsistence in the agrarian world, it was the primary source only in areas not suited to cultivation. In recent centuries, even these areas have, in most cases, been brought under the control of agrarian or industrial societies, and herding societies, like other preindustrial types, are vanishing.

MARITIME SOCIETIES

Maritime societies have been the rarest of all the basic societal types. Not one survives today. Yet they once played an important role in the civilized world.

Technologically, maritime societies had a lot in common with agrarian societies. What set them apart was the way they used their technology to take advantage of the opportunities afforded by their environmental situation. Located on large bodies of water in an era when it was cheaper to move goods by water than by land, these peoples found trade and commerce far more profitable than either fishing or the cultivation of their limited land resources and gradually created societies in which overseas trade was the chief economic activity.

The first maritime society in history was probably developed by the Minoans on the island of Crete, late in the third millennium B.C. We are told that the wealth and power of the Minoan rulers "depended more upon foreign trade and religious prerogative than upon the land rents and forced services."[24] The island location of Minoan society was important not only because it afforded access to the sea but also because it provided protection against more powerful agrarian societies. Maritime societies always required the absence of pow-

---

[24] Ibid., p. 111.

Figure 9.4 Maritime societies usually developed on islands or peninsulas: aerial view of Tyre, an important maritime society of the ancient world. When Tyre was a leading Phoenician city, there was no land bridge connecting it to the mainland.

erful neighboring societies, and for this reason they usually developed on islands or peninsulas that were difficult to attack by land (see Figure 9.4). Their only military advantage was in naval warfare.

During the next 1,500 years a number of other maritime societies were established in the Mediterranean world. These included the Mycenaeans, or pre-Hellenic Greeks of the second millennium B.C., the Phoenicians, the Carthaginians, the Athenians, and the Corinthians.[25] The spread of the maritime pattern was largely, perhaps wholly, the result of diffusion and the migration of maritime peoples.

Eventually, all these groups were conquered by societies of other types and either destroyed or absorbed as subunits. This was not the end of overseas trade and commerce, of course, since these remained important activities in advanced agrarian societies. It was, however, a temporary end to societies in which they were the dominant economic activities. Then, more than a thousand years later, there was a revival of maritime societies during the Middle Ages. Venice and Genoa are the best known, but there were others (e.g., Danzig, Luebeck) in northern Europe. The last important maritime society was Holland, which in the seventeenth and eighteenth centuries apparently derived the major part of its income from overseas trade.[26]

---

[25] In the case of Athens, for example, it is estimated that by the fourth century B.C. only 20 per cent of the cereals consumed were grown in Attica and the rest were imported. See V. Gordon Childe, *What Happened in History* (Baltimore: Penguin, 1964), p. 207.

[26] England moved far in this direction in the seventeenth, eighteenth, nineteenth, and early twentieth centuries but probably never quite reached the point where her dependence on overseas commerce exceeded her dependence on, first, agriculture and, later, industry. Nevertheless, because of the great growth of overseas commerce, she took on a number of the characteristics of maritime societies.

In many ways maritime societies resembled advanced agrarian societies, particularly in their urban centers. But there were also a number of important differences. To begin with, most maritime societies were much smaller, usually containing only a single city and its immediate rural hinterland. Athens was probably typical in this respect; at its height it covered only about 1,000 square miles.[27] Only two maritime societies ever developed empires worthy of the name, and, significantly, both of these (the Carthaginian and Dutch) were *overseas* empires.[28] In each case the empire was created more as an adjunct of commercial activity than as a militaristic venture.

This curious feature is linked with other, more basic peculiarities of maritime societies. In a largely agrarian world in which monarchy was the normal—almost universal—form of government, maritime societies were usually republics. Athens is the most familiar example, but there were numerous others. Although monarchies were not unheard of, they were most common in the earlier periods, suggesting that they were a carryover from an earlier, premaritime tradition.

The explanation for the republican tendency in maritime societies seems to be that commerce, rather than warfare and the exploitation of peasant masses, was the chief interest of the governing class. Being less involved in military activities than the typical agrarian state, these nations had less need for a strong, centralized, hierarchical government. An oligarchy of wealthy merchants could do the job, since their primary responsibilities would be to regulate commercial competition and to provide naval forces to defend their access to foreign ports. The fact that navies were the chief military arm of maritime states was also important, for navies, unlike armies, are usually busy in places far from the seat of government. This affords a considerable measure of protection for civilian leaders, for it greatly reduces the risk of military coups.

Another peculiarity of maritime societies was their unusual system of values and incentives. As we saw in the last chapter, the governing class in agrarian societies typically viewed work of any kind as degrading. Since this was the class that all others emulated, their view of economic activity rubbed off on the rest. This was especially evident in the case of merchants, who, when they became wealthy, usually gave up their commercial activities. As we noted, this antiwork ethic undoubtedly contributed to the slowdown in the rate of technological innovation and progress. In maritime societies, by contrast, the merchants were the dominant class, and a very different view of economic activity prevailed. Though much more research is needed on the subject, there is reason to believe that the rate of technological advance was greater in maritime

---

[27] Alvin Gouldner, *Enter Plato: Classical Greece and the Origins of Social Theory* (New York: Basic Books, 1965), p. 6.

[28] On the less familiar Carthaginian empire, see Donald Harden, *The Phoenicians* (New York: Praeger, 1963), chaps. 5 and 6.

Figure 9.5 Venetian room showing the wealth which commercial activities brought to merchants and officials of maritime societies.

societies than in agrarian and that maritime societies made disproportionate technological and economic contributions to the emergence of modern industrial societies. Moreover, the rate of technological advance in *agrarian* societies was apparently correlated with the sociopolitical strength of its merchant class. In other words, the greater their social status and political influence, the greater the society's rate of technological and economic innovation.[29]

PRELIMINARY RECAPITULATION

Having completed our survey of the various types of preindustrial societies, we are ready to consider the three types of societies that are most important today—industrial, industrializing agrarian, and industrializing horticultural. Before we turn to them, however, it may be well to pause and look back over the

---

[29] Compare, for example, the status of merchants and the rate of innovation for Europe, during the sixteenth, seventeenth, and eighteenth centuries, with the situation in India. Both were higher in Europe. Although this could have been coincidence, the evidence suggests a causal link.

long evolutionary span and see how some of the more crucial developments in human history relate to our basic theoretical framework.

Beginnings

Man as we know him is the product of a tremendously long evolutionary process. The first significant step occurred far back in the Paleolithic, when the tools our ancestors had been making for so long became essential to their survival. The second step in the sequence was the use of symbols and language, beginning, perhaps, at the start of the Middle Paleolithic, about 100,000 years ago. Finally, in the Upper Paleolithic, no more than 35,000 to 40,000 years in the past, the last major step was taken: sociocultural evolution replaced organic evolution as the dominant mode of human adaptation.

Man and his hominid ancestors have apparently always lived in societies. Although the basic elements of societal life are therefore attributable to our genetic heritage, this is not the whole story: the more complex societal patterns that have developed rest on cultural foundations. Were the key elements of the cultural heritage of modern industrial societies somehow lost, they could not survive; there would be a rapid regression to a far more primitive level of organization. Though this is not likely to happen, it is possible, for cultural information is seldom shared by all members of a society. Thus, a large number of people might survive a disaster and yet not possess, among them, enough technological information to maintain more than a rudimentary social system.

Throughout most of the prehistoric period, technological progress was painfully slow. There were fewer advances during all the hundreds of thousands of years of the Lower Paleolithic than in the last century alone. This was due to the very small number of people, the paucity of information they had to work with, and the poor communication between societies. Later, as population and information increased, the rate of technological advance gradually accelerated. Even so, progress was infinitely slower than it is today.

Diversification and Progress

Until about ten thousand years ago, every human group was a hunting and gathering society. They were hardly carbon copies of one another, however. Because of man's gradual spread over the earth, societies were forced to adapt to many kinds of environments, ranging from arctic to tropical. There probably were also many differences in marriage patterns, religious practices, and other aspects of life, but the archaeological record is silent on this. Since there is considerable variation in these areas among modern hunters and gatherers, however, there is no reason to suppose it was any different then.

The emergence of the first fishing societies during the Mesolithic was an important new step. Man had at last devised techniques and tools that

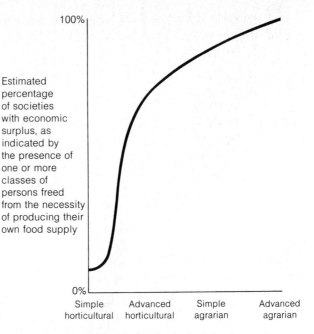

100%

Estimated
percentage
of societies
with economic
surplus, as
indicated by
the presence of
one or more
classes of
persons freed
from the necessity
of producing their
own food supply

0%

| Simple | Advanced | Simple | Advanced |
| horticultural | horticultural | agrarian | agrarian |

Level of technological development

Figure 9.6 Estimated percentage of societies that have an economic surplus, by level of technological development.

enabled him to take advantage of the resources of a radically different kind of environment, one that could support population growth, more permanent settlements, and multicommunity societies. These, in turn, made possible the production of new kinds of goods and services, the accumulation of property, and the elaboration of ritual and ceremony—in short, a significant enrichment of human life.

Not long afterward, an even more revolutionary development occurred when men discovered the basic techniques of plant cultivation and animal domestication. For the first time, relatively permanent settlements could be maintained in almost any environment. Previously this had been possible only in coastal areas where fishing was carried on and in a few unusual areas like northern California. The larger populations and greater permanence of settlement that fishing groups enjoyed were now possible for other societies, and to an even greater degree. But from the evolutionary standpoint, the most important development was the formation of an economic surplus, since this opened up so many structural and ideological possibilities.

Forming a surplus was not, however, an automatic by-product of horticulture; many horticultural societies, and even a few agrarian ones, did not take this step (see Figure 9.6). Horticulture, though *necessary* for the formation of a surplus, was not enough: a farmer had to be motivated to produce more than his family required. In a considerable number of societies, religion provided this incentive.

Once an economic surplus was established, some people could forget about subsistence activities and devote all their time and energy to other things. Although some specialization occurs without it, an economic surplus has been essential for any significant increase in a society's division of labor.

The surplus also led to increased status and class differentiation. Those who were powerful enough to control the surplus became the governing class in a society and were supported by the mass of common people, whose duty was to produce all they could.

As the productive capacity of a society increased, there gradually emerged an intermediate class of specialists who catered to the governing class and helped them produce, and dispose of, the surplus. Servants, retainers, officials, merchants, craftsmen, soldiers, and clergy formed most of the new class. As a rule, they lived near the governing class, often in the same households, and these clusters of people became the nuclei of the gradually emerging urban communities.

With the creation of stable surpluses, warfare became increasingly profitable. No longer were powerful and aggressive groups limited to hit-and-run raids and plundering expeditions. Now they could establish permanent control over weaker groups and take their surplus, in the form of tribute or taxes, on a regular basis. In short, conquest and empire building became feasible for the first time in history, opening up a road to wealth that soon proved far more attractive to rulers and governing classes than the more pedestrian route of technological innovation.

These developments made the progress of intersocietal selection even more important than it had been before. Since military advantage lay with the larger, technologically more advanced, and organizationally more efficient societies, these generally survived at the expense of their opposites. Similarly, militaristic and exploitative societies had an advantage over more peaceful and humane ones.

Meanwhile, despite many developments that should have stimulated technological advance, the rate of innovation actually began to *slow* after the rise of the first agrarian societies. This appears to have been the first major break in the long process of acceleration that began far back in the Paleolithic. The new ideologies and the exploitative social structures generated by the agrarian revolution were primarily responsible for this retardation.

As societies grew in size and complexity, ties of kinship became increasingly unsatisfactory as the basis for social organization and had to be supplemented and replaced by more formal ties. From the standpoint of societal cohesion, political ties between a ruler and his subjects were the most significant addition. These were supplemented by an expanding network of commercial ties generated by economic institutions, and by ideological and communal ties created by religious institutions. These newer integrative forces, however, could no more prevent the development of intrasocietal antagonisms and conflict than kinship bonds could. If anything, antagonisms were more serious, since they now involved groups and classes of men, rather than individuals, and the issues were so much more complex.

This points up a basic irony of sociocultural evolution: in the process of solving one problem, men usually create others. Sociocultural evolution is thus not only a problem-solving process but a problem-producing one. Sometimes, in fact, it almost seems to be a process whereby men trade old problems for new ones.

Why, then, have men tried so hard to achieve progress if its fruits are not sweeter? To begin with, we must remember that much of this progress has not been a matter of choice. Many hunting and gathering groups would probably have preferred to continue their traditional way of life, but their lands were confiscated by societies with a more advanced technology. Other groups have had the same experience. The process of intersocietal selection, then, has not been a voluntary one.

But this is not the whole answer. Many individuals and many societies have voluntarily, even eagerly, adopted more efficient tools and techniques and new ways of doing things, because they believed the gains would outweigh the costs. And they were right—up to a point. Technological advance usually has meant more food, better health, longer life, less exhausting labor, and greater leisure for most people in the generation that initially adopted the advance—and often for their children and grandchildren as well. But those who took this step had no way of knowing that their technological advance would lead to such an increase in population that all the gains would be wiped out in just a few generations, leaving their descendants little or no better off than people were before the innovation. And, even if they had known, they would not have chosen differently.

Until recently, the members of advanced societies (especially agrarian) had known only one way to halt this frustrating chain of events: a system of social organization that ruthlessly appropriated everything the common people could spare and gave it to the governing class.[30] No dramatic increase in population was likely to ensue under this system; death rates and birthrates remained about equal. In this way, some of the benefits of technological advance were preserved, if only for a tiny minority of the population. For the masses, however, conditions seldom improved.

Once this system was firmly established in a society, it was virtually impossible to turn back to a less sophisticated technology. For one thing, because the population was larger and denser than it had been before, such a reversal would have meant starvation for large numbers of the common people. Nor would the governing class have allowed it; from their viewpoint, tech-

---

[30] Population growth might also have been controlled by abortion, infanticide, monasticism, prostitution, and the like; but these techniques never were adopted widely enough to solve the problem.

nological advance was a fine thing. The elites in agrarian societies have almost always been better off than their counterparts in less advanced groups. Most agrarian societies thus found themselves virtually "locked into" the technological status quo. They could not afford to turn back, and they could move forward only very slowly.

This, then, was the situation that prevailed on the eve of the Industrial Revolution.

Part III

INDUSTRIAL AND INDUSTRIALIZING SOCIETIES

CHAPTER TEN

The Industrial Revolution

During the past nine thousand years, human societies have undergone several revolutionary transformations. The only one that is fully documented, however, is the Industrial Revolution. Thus it affords a unique opportunity to study a socio-cultural revolution and its underlying causes. We will begin by clarifying what we mean by "Industrial Revolution" and then briefly review its history.

THE CONCEPT OF THE INDUSTRIAL REVOLUTION

Toward the end of the nineteenth century, economic historians began using the term "Industrial Revolution" to refer to the series of dramatic technological and economic innovations that occurred in England during the period from about 1760 to 1830.[1] In their view, the mechanization of the textile industry, technical advance and expansion in the iron industry, the harnessing of steam power, the establishment of the factory system, and other, related developments of that period revolutionized the English economy. What had still been essentially an agrarian system (or agrarian-maritime) in the middle of the eighteenth century became an industrial system by the middle of the nineteenth.

In more recent years, many scholars have questioned the time limits assigned the Industrial Revolution by earlier writers, claiming it is a mistake to put a terminal date on a revolution which, they maintain, is still continuing.[2] Others argue that the starting date is too late, that the acceleration in industrial activity began not in the middle of the eighteenth century but in the middle of the sixteenth.[3]

Both of these criticisms have some merit. The rate of technological advance did, in fact, begin to accelerate at least two hundred years before 1760. But it does not follow that we are justified in treating those earlier developments as part of the Industrial Revolution. If it is to be meaningful, this term must be reserved for *developments that led directly to a substantial increase in the eco-*

---

[1] See especially the lectures of Arnold Toynbee (uncle of the contemporary historian), delivered at Oxford in 1880–1881 and recently republished under the title *The Industrial Revolution* (Boston: Beacon Press, 1956). Though not the first to use the term, Toynbee did much to give it currency in scholarly circles.

[2] See, for example, Robert Heilbroner, *The Making of Economic Society* (Englewood Cliffs, N.J.: Prentice-Hall, 1962), pp. 101–102.

[3] See, for example, John Nef, *The Conquest of the Material World* (Chicago: Univessity of Chicago Press, 1964), especially part 2.

nomic importance of industrial activity. Refinements and improvements of older techniques do not qualify unless they significantly increased the proportion of the population dependent on industrial activity or the percentage of the gross national product obtained from this source.[4] Using these criteria, we cannot put the start of the Industrial Revolution much, if any, before the middle of the eighteenth century.[5] The earlier events, however, obviously contributed to the later ones.

The other criticism of the dates is sounder: the Industrial Revolution definitely was not over by 1830. Only its first phase ended at that time. Subsequently, there have been at least three other phases, and each has contributed substantially to the importance of industrial activity in the societies involved, as well as to the general transformation of the societies themselves.

We cannot assign precise dates to these phases, since they are all rather arbitrary divisions in what is essentially a continuous process of development. However, the use of even approximate dates can help us to see more clearly the progression of events. In the initial phase, which began in mid-eighteenth century England, the revolution was centered in the textile, iron, and coal industries, and the invention of the first true steam engine was probably the most important innovation. The second phase got its start in the middle decades of the nineteenth century and was characterized by rapid growth in the railroad industry, the mass production of steel, the replacement of sailing ships by steamships, and application of the new technology to agriculture. Around the turn of the century, the Industrial Revolution entered a third phase, whose areas of rapid growth were the automobile, electrical, telephone, and petroleum industries. World War II marked the beginning of the fourth phase, distinguished by remarkable development in aviation, aluminum, electronics, and plastics. Today, we are entering a fifth phase, in which the utilization of nuclear power, rocket engines, computers, and automation are some of the most important features.

Our review will deal with the Industrial Revolution as it has developed in the world as a whole, not as it has developed in individual societies. The phases are not stages that a society must invariably pass through to become industrialized. On the contrary, latecomers are likely to skip over certain phases, or at least parts of them, and to combine elements from different

---

[4] If such refinements and improvements were included, it would be hard to avoid dating the start of the Industrial Revolution in the Mesolithic, since technological progress of some kind, however slow, has been virtually continuous since then. One cannot use the criteria stated in the text above to date the *end* of the Industrial Revolution, since many societies have already reached the point where there is virtually no room for increase in the proportion of the population dependent on industrial activity or in the percentage of the GNP obtained from this source, yet the revolution in the techniques and tools of production is obviously continuing. The only standard we can use to mark the end of the Industrial Revolution would be a drastic slowing in the rate of growth of technological innovation.

[5] See especially Phyllis Deane and W. A. Cole, *British Economic Growth 1688–1959: Trends and Structure* (London: Cambridge, 1962), chap. 2.

phases. For example, an underdeveloped nation today will often develop its railways, highways, and airways simultaneously.

First Phase

The first phase of the Industrial Revolution, as we just noted, began in the middle of the eighteenth century and lasted about a hundred years. Geographically, it was centered in England, where there was a great burst of technological innovation. Many of the best-known innovations occurred in the textile industry and were of two kinds—machines that increased the efficiency of human labor and machines that harnessed new sources of power. The flying shuttle is a good example of the first—and a good example, too, of the way one invention stimulated others. Because it enabled one weaver to do the work formerly done by two, spinners could no longer keep up with the demand for yarn. This disruption of the traditional balance between spinning and weaving triggered a succession of additional inventions. First, the traditional spinning wheel was replaced by the spinning jenny, which enabled a worker to spin 4 threads simultaneously and, after a number of modifications, 120 threads! But although the spinning jenny was a tremendous improvement from the standpoint of speed, its yarn was so coarse and loose that flax had to be mixed in with the cotton to produce a satisfactory fiber. This was remedied with the water frame, a machine that could satisfactorily spin pure cotton, and later with the spinning mule, whose cotton threads were stronger and finer. All these advances in spinning reversed the earlier situation: now weaving was the bottleneck in the industry—until a new series of innovations in weaving machines helped restore the balance.

Figure 10.1 Replica of James Hargreaves' spinning jenny.

By the end of the eighteenth century, the new looms were so large and heavy that they were almost impossible to operate. To work the treadle of one machine even at a slow speed, for example, required two powerful men—and they had to be spelled after a short time.[6] This led to a search for alternative sources of power. One possibility was waterpower, which had already been used for a variety of purposes for many centuries. But England was poorly supplied with suitable streams and rivers, and the wheels and troughs used in water systems were extremely inefficient.[7] Eventually, James Watt developed the first true steam engine,[8] a source of power that could be employed anywhere, and by the end of the century it had been adapted for use in the textile industry.

The net effect of these innovations was such a rapid expansion of the British textile industry that between 1770 and 1845 its contribution to the national income increased more than fivefold.[9] Though unspectacular by recent standards, this was a striking rate of growth by traditional agrarian standards. Remember, too, that the actual increase in production was even larger, since per unit costs of production dropped considerably during this period.

Another industry that expanded greatly during the first phase of the Industrial Revolution was iron manufacturing. Despite an increasing demand for iron, technical difficulties held its manufacture back until late in the eighteenth century. One problem was England's growing shortage of wood, which was needed to make charcoal for smelting and refining. This problem was partially solved early in the century, when someone found that coke could be substituted for charcoal, at least in the smelting process. But a serious bottleneck remained. Because it is hard and brittle, pig iron, before it can be used for most purposes, must be converted into wrought, or malleable, iron. Again, the process required charcoal, and it was very slow—until development of the double process of puddling and rolling. These innovations opened the way for rapid expansion: in 1788, England produced only 68,000 tons of iron; by 1845, twenty-four times that.[10]

Between them, the iron industry and the steam engine substantially increased the demand for coal. The steam engine also helped alleviate the ancient problem of flooding in coal mines, providing power to pump out the water that constantly seeped into shafts and tunnels. The growth of the coal industry, though not quite so dramatic as that of the iron industry, was still impressive: in

---

[6] Paul Mantoux, *The Industrial Revolution in the Eighteenth Century,* rev. ed. (London: Cape, 1961), pp. 243–244.

[7] Ibid., p. 312.

[8] Earlier in the century, Thomas Savery and Thomas Newcomen invented the atmospheric engine, which laid the foundation for Watt's work. Its only practical use, however, was to pump water out of mines.

[9] Deane and Cole, p. 212.

[10] For 1788, see Clive Day, *Economic Development in Europe* (New York: Macmillan, 1942), p. 134; for 1840, see Deane and Cole, p. 225.

1760, Britain produced barely 5 million tons; by 1845, the figure had risen over ninefold.[11]

No discussion of developments in this period would be complete without mention of the machine-tool industry. Although it never achieved the size or financial importance of the textile, iron, and coal industries, it was crucial for technological progress, because it produced the increasingly complex industrial machinery. This industry, which began undramatically with the invention of the first practical lathe, was soon producing machines capable of precision work to the thousandth of an inch.[12] For many years, a single tool was used for drilling, boring, grinding, and milling; but, gradually, specialized tools were designed for the various operations.

Another basic advance in the eighteenth century was the production of machines with interchangeable parts. This greatly facilitated industrial growth, since damage to one part of a complex machine no longer meant that the entire machine had to be discarded or a new part specially manufactured. Spare parts could now be kept on hand and replacements made on the spot by mechanics with limited skills and equipment.

During this initial phase of the Industrial Revolution, shortly after 1800, Britain became the first nation in which industry replaced agriculture as the most important form of economic activity.[13] The United States would not reach this point for another seventy years.[14]

Second Phase

The second phase of the Industrial Revolution began in the middle decades of the nineteenth century. Expansion continued at a rapid pace in the textile, iron, and coal industries, but now there were breakthroughs in a number of others as well. By the end of the century industrialization had occurred in most segments of the British economy. Meanwhile, the Industrial Revolution began to play a significant role in some of the other countries of northwestern Europe and in the United States.

One of the most important developments during this phase was the application of the steam engine to transportation, something inventors had been trying to accomplish for decades. Finally, about 1850, most of England was linked together by a network of railroads.[15] The results were tremendous:

---

[11] Deane and Cole, pp. 55 and 216.

[12] W. S. Woytinsky and E. S. Woytinsky, *World Population and Production: Trends and Outlook* (New York: Twentieth Century Fund, 1953), p. 1147.

[13] Ibid., tables 30 and 37.

[14] U.S. Bureau of the Census, *Historical Statistics of the United States, Colonial Times to 1957*, p.139.

[15] J. H. Clapham, *An Economic History of Modern Britain*, 2d ed. (London: Cambridge, 1930), vol. I, pp. 391–392.

Figure 10.2 Model of the DeWitt Clinton, built in New York City in 1831. On its first run between Albany and Schenectady, it covered 12 miles in less than an hour.

the lower cost of moving goods by rail contributed to a reduction in the price of many heavy, bulk commodities, and this, in turn, led to greater demand. In addition, railroads helped break down local monopolies and oligopolies (i.e., markets with only a few sellers), which added to the competition and further lowered prices. Thus, England gradually became a single giant market for an increasing number of commodities, a development destined to have far-reaching consequences.

Even before the steam engine was adapted to land transportation, it had been used on water. For many years, however, it was limited to coastal and river shipping, both because inefficient engines made it impossible to bunker enough wood or coal for long voyages and because paddle wheels worked poorly in high seas. Then, in only a few decades, efficient compound engines solved the problem of bunkering fuel; iron and steel began to replace wood, making possible longer and larger ships with greater carrying capacity (the upper limit in length for wooden vessels was only about 300 feet); and the screw propeller replaced the cumbersome and easily damaged paddle wheel.[16] After this, steamships increased so rapidly that by 1893 world steam tonnage exceeded sailing tonnage.

In the iron industry, meanwhile, a way was finally found to produce steel cheaply and in large quantities, making it available for many new purposes.[17] Between 1845 and the early 1880s, Britain's production of iron and steel

---

[16] S. B. Clough and C. W. Cole, *Economic History of Europe* (Boston: Heath, 1941), pp. 594–595.

[17] Ibid., pp. 535–537.

increased more than fivefold.[18] This meant that in less than a century and a half, the increase was 500-fold! And the quality of the product was vastly superior.

The tremendous growth in railroads and use of steamships and the expansion of the iron industry all combined to increase the demand for coal. Though there were no spectacular breakthroughs in mining techniques, improved engines and other products of the steel industry pushed production up fivefold.[19]

A number of new industries emerged in addition to the railroads, none as important at the time, but some destined to surpass them later on. The rubber industry developed after Charles Goodyear's discovery of the technique of vulcanization, which prevented rubber goods from becoming sticky in hot weather, stiff and brittle in cold. About the same time, Samuel Morse and several others invented the telegraph, and this quickly became the basis of another new industry. A method for making dyes from coal tar helped establish the chemical industry. Then, in the 1860s, the electric dynamo was invented, and the door was opened for the use of electricity in industry. A second crucial development in this field, the invention of the transformer, overcame one of the greatest impediments to the use of electricity: the loss of energy during long-distance transmission. The petroleum industry also got its start in these years chiefly by providing a substitute for whale oil in lighting homes.

The Industrial Revolution began to make an impact even on agriculture, through improved equipment (e.g., sturdier steel plows), new kinds of machines (e.g., threshing machines, mowers, reapers, steam plows, etc.), and synthetic fertilizers from the growing chemical industry. The result was a substantial increase in productivity. In Germany, for example, production per acre rose 50 per cent in only twenty-five years.

All during this period, industrialization was spreading rapidly across Europe, especially the western part, and to North America. Before the century closed, Britain had lost her position of economic and technological leadership. The iron and steel industry illustrates the trend: although Britain nearly doubled her production of pig iron between 1865 and 1900, her share of the world market dropped from 54 to 23 per cent.[20] Her chief rivals were the United States and Germany, whose production of pig iron increased more than sixteenfold and eightfold respectively. The American share of the market jumped dramatically from 9 to 35 per cent, while the German share rose from 10 to 19 per cent.

As these figures indicate, though industrialization was spreading, it was still largely limited to a few countries. The United States, Britain, Germany, and

---

[18] Deane and Cole, p. 225.

[19] Ibid., p. 216.

[20] Clough and Cole, p. 538.

France, for example, produced 84 per cent of the world's iron in 1900. A similar picture emerges when we look at national shares of all manufacturing activity. In 1888, the percentages are estimated to have been as follows:[21]

United States	32%
Britain	18%
Germany	13%
France	11%
All other countries	26%

Incidentally, the fact that "all other countries" contributed more to *all* types of manufacturing than they did to iron production alone (even though the figures for all types of manufacturing were from an earlier date) reflects the more rapid spread of the new technology in light industries, such as textiles, than in heavy industries. This resulted both because light industries required less capital and because their pace of development had already slowed considerably, reducing the need for highly skilled and innovative personnel.

The last factor points up a final characteristic of this phase of the Industrial Revolution: the growing dependence on science and engineering. Before 1850 most of the major advances were made by simple craftsmen, or by gentlemen amateurs. After that, key inventions came primarily from people with formal technical or scientific training. This was especially true in the chemical industry, but it was evident in others as well.

Third Phase

Around the turn of the century, the Industrial Revolution entered a phase that lasted until the beginning of World War II. One of its most dramatic and significant developments was the expansion of the automobile industry. Just as remarkable as this industry's rate of growth were the repercussions it had on other industries: in 1937, for example, the American automobile industry consumed 20 per cent of the nation's steel, 54 per cent of its malleable iron, 73 per cent of its plate glass, 80 per cent of its rubber, and 90 per cent of its gasoline.[22] The key inventions, of which the gasoline engine was the most important, were all made some years before the industry actually began production at the end of the century. In 1900 no more than 20,000 automobiles were produced in the entire world, with France the largest producer.[23] By 1913 world production had risen to 600,000, with the United States turning out more than 80 per cent;

---

[21] Calculated from Woytinsky and Woytinsky, p. 1003.

[22] Ibid., p. 1164.

[23] This figure is an estimate based on Clough and Cole's report of French production in 1902 (p. 773) and Woytinsky and Woytinsky's report of American production in 1900 and 1902 (p. 1168).

Figure 10.3 Early assembly line: dropping the Ford engine into the Model T chassis, Highland Park, Michigan.

by 1929 world production passed the 6 million mark, with America's share 85 per cent.[24]

The electrical industry was another that grew fantastically during the third phase. Between 1900 and 1940 the capacity of all the generating plants in the world increased 200-fold.[25] Again the United States led the way, producing 40 to 45 per cent of the world's electrical power.

The proportional growth of the petroleum industry was less dramatic, because it had already enjoyed substantial growth before 1900. Even so, production in 1940 was thirteen times larger than it was in 1900.[26]

The telephone industry, too, grew rapidly in this period. Between 1900

---

[24] Woytinsky and Woytinsky, pp. 1165–1166, including fig. 328.

[25] Ibid., p. 966.

[26] The 1900 figure is estimated from information provided by Woytinsky and Woytinsky, pp. 897–900; the 1940 figure is from fig. 257, p. 897.

Table 10.1 Percentage distribution of world industrial output (excluding handicrafts), by nation, in 1888 and 1937

Nation	1888	1937
United States	32	34
United Kingdom	18	10
Germany	13	10.5
France	11	5
Russia	8	10
Japan	No data	4
All others	18	26.5

Source: Calculated from W. S. Woytinsky and E. S. Woytinsky, *World Population and Production: Trends and Outlook* (New York: Twentieth Century Fund, 1953), pp. 1003–1004.

and 1940, the number of telephones in the United States increased from 1.4 million to 20.8 million, and by the latter date, the industry had investments valued at $5 billion.[27]

During this phase, as during the second, the Industrial Revolution was felt not only in new sectors of the economy but in new parts of the world as well, which meant some change in the relative ranking of nations. While the United States continued in the lead, Britain, Germany, and France all lost ground relatively (see Table 10.1) despite substantial growth in absolute terms. The chief gains were registered by nations that were just beginning to industrialize. The gains by Russia and Japan were especially noteworthy.

Fourth Phase

No previous war had ever been as dependent on industrial activity as World War II, and every major nation made tremendous efforts to increase its output of military supplies. One of the most important long-term consequences of this was the great stimulus it gave the aviation industry. In the United States, the production of aircraft rose from 3,600 in 1938 to more than 96,000 in 1944.[28] Though this rate could not be sustained once the war ended and military needs were reduced, the air transport industry expanded rapidly. Between 1940 and 1970, the number of passenger-miles flown by scheduled airlines rose from 1.2 billion to 130 billion, and the number of ton-miles flown in hauling freight and mail rose from 14 million to over 4 billion.[29] Despite somewhat slower growth,

---

[27] J. Frederic Dewhurst and Associates, *America's Needs and Resources* (New York: Twentieth Century Fund, 1955), p. 317, and U.S. Bureau of the Census, *Statistical Abstract of the United States, 1963*, p. 516.

[28] Woytinsky and Woytinsky, p. 1171.

[29] *Statistical Abstract, 1963*, p. 586, and *Statistical Abstract, 1971*, p. 556.

European airlines flew more than 45 billion passenger-miles in 1969.[30] The year 1958 marked a significant shift in transportation patterns: for the first time, planes covered more passenger-miles in America than trains, and they also replaced steamships as the chief carriers of transatlantic travelers.

Just as automobiles spurred the petroleum industry, so aviation spurred aluminum. Though it was first manufactured in the nineteenth century, its production was quite limited until Germany and Italy started building their air forces in the 1930s. In three decades (from 1938 to 1969), world production increased more than twenty times, and it is still increasing as new uses continue to be found.[31] As in most of the rapidly expanding industries of the third and fourth phases, American production was a major share, about half of the world's aluminum output since World War II.

Electronics is another industry with roots in an earlier period that came into its own in the fourth phase. Its products fall into two chief categories: component materials, such as transistors, diodes, electron tubes, resistors, and capacitors; and end products, such as computers, testing and measuring equipment, industrial control equipment, microwave communications systems,

Figure 10.4 Final assembly area for B-52 bombers, Boeing plant, Wichita, Kansas.

[30] Calculated from United Nations, *Statistical Yearbook, 1970,* p. 458.

[31] The 1938 figure is calculated from J. Frederic Dewhurst and Associates, *Europe's Needs and Resources: Trends and Prospects in Eighteen Countries* (New York: Twentieth Century Fund, 1961), p. 627; the 1969 figure is from *Statistical Abstract, 1971.* p C59.

television and radio equipment, phonographs, tape recorders, and high-fidelity systems. The military needs of World War II stimulated rapid development in electronics and led to a number of spectacular technological breakthroughs. Radar, the most important, gave impetus to the invention of transmitters and detectors capable of using wavelengths far shorter than those used in radio. The war also accelerated the development of "miniaturization," as well as servomotors—small power units that respond instantly to signals—and it contributed to the perfection of feedback systems, in which machines not only act but react. These innovations laid the foundation for automated equipment and computers. Unfortunately, it is almost impossible to obtain statistics on the tremendous growth of this industry, because its productivity is still recorded under a number of separate, traditional headings in government records.

The plastics industry is another that came into its own during this phase. Its origins go back to 1861, when nitrocellulose was plasticized with camphor to produce artificial ivory and used as a substitute for horn in spectacle frames. Thanks to many subsequent developments, plastics have become the most versatile of modern materials: they can now be manufactured to almost any set of specifications. Not surprisingly, the industry has mushroomed: as recently as the late 1930s, world output was under 200,000 tons; by 1969, it was nearly 28 million and growing, with American production half of the total.[32]

During the fourth phase, several of the rapid-growth industries of the third phase maintained their high rate of growth. Between 1940 and 1969, world output of electricity increased ninefold, world production of motor vehicles and petroleum sevenfold.[33] Again, the United States was a major producer, its 1969 contribution ranging from 22 per cent of the world total in petroleum to 34 per cent in motor vehicles.

From the standpoint of the geographical distribution of industrial activity, the most striking feature in the fourth phase was the rise of the Soviet Union (compare Tables 10.1 and 10.2). England, France, and Germany continued to decline in relative terms. The United States, however, held the lead it gained in the second half of the nineteenth century.

Tables 10.1 and 10.2 show the total industrial outputs of nations, but they do not indicate their relative degree of industrialization. For that we need a per capita measure of industrial activity. As Table 10.3 shows, this changes the picture considerably. The lead of the United States and the Soviet Union is markedly reduced and the relative position of the smaller nations improved. Little Denmark, for example, passes the Soviet Union.

---

[32] The figure for the late 1930s is based on Woytinsky and Woytinsky's statement about output in the United States and other countries in that period (p. 1201); the 1969 figure is from United Nations, *Statistical Yearbook, 1970,* p. 287, but translated into short tons.

[33] Production figures for 1940 may be found in Woytinsky and Woytinsky, pp. 897, 966, and 1167; the 1969 figures are from United Nations, *Statistical Yearbook, 1970,* pp. 212, 320, and 369.

Table 10.2   World industrial output, by nation, 1969, as indicated by consumption of electrical energy*

Nation	Percentage Share of World Industrial Output
United States	34
Union of Soviet Socialist Republics	16
Germany (East, West, and Berlin)	7†
China	6
Japan	5
United Kingdom	4
Canada	3
France	3
All others	22

Source: Derived from United Nations, *Statistical Yearbook, 1970*, table 138.

* For a comparison of consumption of electrical energy with an alternative measure of industrial output (i.e., value added by industrial activity), see *Human Societies*, 1st ed. table 11.2, p. 325.

† The energy consumption of West Berlin was estimated in the absence of data.

Table 10.3   Per capita energy consumption, by nation, 1969

Nation	Energy*	Nation	Energy	Nation	Energy
United States	10,774	South Africa	2,746	Syria	477
Canada	8,794	Romania	2,628	Algeria	470
Czechoslovakia	6,120	New Zealand	2,623	Turkey	461
Sweden	5,768	Italy	2,431	Egypt	221
Belgium	5,429	Israel	2,154	Bolivia	218
Australia	5,200	Argentina	1,544	Thailand	197
Denmark	5,142	Spain	1,354	India	193
United Kingdom	5,139	Yugoslavia	1,243	Ghana	155
West Germany	4,850	Chile	1,210	Kenya	148
Netherlands	4,661	Greece	1,150	Indonesia	98
Norway	4,430	Mexico	1,044	Pakistan	93
Soviet Union	4,199	Lebanon	689	Tanzania	58
Poland	4,052	South Korea	641	Burma	58
Finland	3,576	Peru	623	Haiti	31
France	3,518	Albania	608	Afghanistan	26
Ireland	2,953	Portugal	603	Ethiopia	23
Hungary	2,888	China	505	Nepal	11
Japan	2,828	Brazil	481	Upper Volta	10

Source: United Nations, *Statistical Yearbook, 1970*, table 138.

* Measured in kilograms of coal equivalent consumed per person per year.

As Table 10.3 makes clear, there is tremendous variation in the degree of industrialization. For purposes of classification, we will regard as industrial societies those *nations that consume at least 2,000 kilograms of coal equivalent per person per year*. Obviously, however, this is an arbitrary cutoff point on what is essentially a *continuum of development*.

Fifth Phase

Recent developments leave no doubt that the Industrial Revolution is entering a fifth phase, characterized by a rapid increase in the use of nuclear power, rocket engines, computers, and automation. For some time, the trends have been in motion: in 1955, the world's first nuclear installation began operating in the Soviet Union, with a capacity of 5,000 kilowatts; fourteen years later, installations in fifteen nations were producing more than 64 billion kilowatt-hours.[34]

CONSEQUENCES OF THE INDUSTRIAL REVOLUTION

From an early date it was clear that the Industrial Revolution meant far more than a change in techniques of production, that it had enormous implications for every aspect of life. Though our chief concern is with the long-run consequences of the revolution, we cannot ignore its immediate effects on the lives of those who first experienced the transition from the agrarian way of life to the industrial.

Immediate Consequences

The first indication of serious change came with the invention of the new spinning and weaving machines in the late eighteenth century. Because of their great size and weight, they could no longer be operated in people's homes, as had been the case, but required specially constructed buildings and an inanimate source of power, such as a steam engine or waterfall. In short, the new technology forced the creation of the factory system.

Factories required a dependable supply of labor. A few of the early factories were built in open countryside, but their owners quickly found they could not hire enough workers unless they built adjoining tenements, which in effect created new urban settlements. Most factories were built in or near existing towns, and the cry that went out from them for workers coincided with the declining need for labor on the farms.

Although the ensuing migration into urban areas was not a new phenomenon, its magnitude was, and most communities were unable to cope with the sudden influx. The migrants themselves were badly prepared for their new

---

[34] United Nations, *Statistical Yearbook, 1965*, p. 353, and *Statistical Yearbook, 1970*, p. 377.

way of life. Sanitary practices that had been tolerable in sparsely settled rural areas, for example, became a threat to health, even to life, in crowded urban communities whose sanitary practices had never been more than adequate at best.

Equally critical problems resulted from the abrupt disruption of social relationships. Severed ties of kinship and friendship could not be replaced overnight, while local customs and institutions that had provided rural villagers at least a measure of protection and support were lost for good. It was an uprooted, extremely vulnerable people who streamed to the towns and were thrown into situations utterly foreign to them and into a way of life that often cul-

Figure 10.5 Early English industrial town, Staffordshire.

minated in injury, illness, or unemployment. A multitude of social ills—poverty, alcoholism, crime, vice, mental and physical illness, personal demoralization—were endemic.

Town magistrates and other local officials had neither the means nor the will to cope with rampant problems in housing, health, education, and crime. Cities and towns became more crowded, open space disappeared, and people accustomed to fields and woodlands found themselves trapped in a deteriorating situation of filthy, crowded streets and tenements, polluted air, and long workdays, rarely relieved by experiences of either hope or beauty.[35]

The misery of the new urban dwellers was compounded by the harshness of the factory system, which often operated along quasi-penal lines.[36] Regardless of how hard life had been before, country folk had at least had some control over their own hour-to-hour movements; but now, work was, if anything, longer, more arduous, more confining. Women and children, though they had always worked extremely hard in their homes and fields, now worked in factories with dangerous, noisy machinery or in dark and dangerous mines.

Figure 10.6 Superintendent and spinner in North Carolina textile mill, 1909. One quarter of the employees in this mill were as young as this girl, or younger.

---

[35] J. L. Hammond and Barbara Hammond, *The Town Labourer: 1760–1830* (London: Guild Books, 1949, first published 1917), vol. I, chap. 3.

[36] Ibid., chaps. 2 and 6–9, or J. T. Ward (ed.), *The Factory System* (New York: Barnes & Noble, 1970), vols. I and II.

CHILDREN AND THE FACTORY SYSTEM

The following testimony was given to a Parliamentary committee investigating working conditions in 1832 by Peter Smart. Similar testimony was provided by numerous others.

Q. Where do you reside?

A. At Dundee.

Q. Have you worked in a mill from your youth?

A. Yes, since I was 5 years of age.

Q. Had you a father and mother in the country at the time?

A. My mother stopped in Perth, about eleven miles from the mill, and my father was in the army.

Q. Were you hired for any length of time when you went?

A. Yes, my mother got 15 shillings for six years, I having my meat and clothes.

Q. What were your hours of labor, as you recollect, in the mill?

A. We began at 4 o'clock in the morning and worked till 10 or 11 at night; as long as we could stand on our feet.

Q. Were you kept on the premises constantly?

A. Constantly.

Q. Locked up?

A. Yes, locked up.

Q. Night and day?

A. Night and day; I never went home while I was at the mill.

Q. Do the children ever attempt to run away?

A. Very often.

Q. Were they pursued and brought back again?

A. Yes, the overseer pursued them and brought them back.

Q. Did you ever attempt to run away?

A. Yes, I ran away twice.

Q. And you were brought back?

A. Yes; and I was sent up to the master's loft, and thrashed with a whip for running away.

Q. Do you know whether the children were, in point of fact, compelled to stop during the whole time for which they were engaged?

A. Yes, they were.

Q. By law?

A. I cannot say by law; but they were compelled by the master; I never saw any law used there but the law of their own hands.

Source: *Parliamentary Papers, 1831–32,* vol. XV.

Minor infractions of complex rules, such as whistling on the job or leaving a lamp lit a few minutes too long after sunrise, led to fines, more serious infractions to floggings. One observer of the period wrote poignantly of hearing children, whose families could not, of course, afford clocks, running through the streets in the dark, long before time for the mills to open, so fearful were they of being late.[37]

The immediate effects of industrialization have been traumatic for vast numbers of people in virtually every society that has made the transition from

---

[37] Hammond and Hammond, vol. I, pp. 32–33.

agrarianism. The details vary, but the suffering was no less acute in the Soviet Union than in England. Whether life for the new urban working class was better or worse than it had been for the peasants and the urban lower classes of the old agrarian societies is still a matter of debate.[38] But one point is not debatable: the transition to an industrial economy has almost always exacted a cruel price in terms of human suffering and demoralization for countless millions of people.

Long-run Consequences

In subsequent chapters, we will examine in detail the new societies and the distinctive life patterns that have resulted from two centuries of industrialization. For the moment, however, we will note just a few of the most important and most striking consequences outside the realm of technology. Collectively, these changes in population, social structure, ideology, and language add up to a revolution without parallel in human history, from the standpoint of scope as well as speed[39]

1. World population has multiplied five times just since 1750, a rate of growth at least seven times higher than the rate during the agrarian era.
2. The rural-urban balance in advanced industrial societies has been completely reversed: agrarian societies were 90 per cent rural; advanced industrial are 90 per cent urban.
3. The largest communities of the industrial era are already ten times the size of the largest of the agrarian era.
4. Women in industrial societies have only a third to a half as many children as women in preindustrial societies.
5. Life expectancy at birth has almost tripled in advanced industrial societies.
6. The per capita production and consumption of goods and services in advanced industrial societies is at least ten times greater than in traditional agrarian societies.
7. The division of labor is vastly more complex.
8. Hereditary monarchical government has almost disappeared in industrial societies, and democratic systems of government have generally replaced it.
9. The functions of government have been greatly enlarged.

---

[38] Compare and contrast the work of Hammond and Hammond, op. cit., or Eric Hobsbawm, "The British Standard of Living, 1790–1850," *Economic History Review*, 2d ser., 10 (1957), pp. 46–61, with Thomas Ashton, "The Standard of Life of the Workers in England, 1790–1830," *Journal of Economic History*, 9 (1949), supplement, pp. 19–38, reprinted in Friedrich Hayek (ed.), *Capitalism and the Historians* (Chicago: University of Chicago Press, 1954).

[39] Documentation for these assertions will be found in Chapters 11–14.

10. Free public educational systems have been established in all industrial societies, and illiteracy has been virtually eliminated.
11. New ideologies have spread widely (notably socialism and humanism), while older ones inherited from the agrarian era either have been substantially modified or have declined.
12. Worldwide communication and transportation networks have been created that have, for all practical purposes, rendered the entire earth smaller than England of the agrarian era.
13. A global culture has begun to emerge, as evidenced in styles of dress, music, language, technology, and organizational patterns.
14. The family has almost ceased to be a significant unit of production in the economy.
15. The role of women in the economy and in society at large has changed substantially.
16. The role of youth is also changing, and youth groups and youth cultures have become a significant factor in the life of industrial societies.

And all this in only 200 years!

CAUSES OF THE INDUSTRIAL REVOLUTION

For more than a century, scholars have debated the causes of the modern economic and social revolution, particularly the question of why it occurred just where and when it did. The basic disagreement has been over the importance of technological and economic factors relative to ideological factors. Although this controversy continues, there is growing agreement that no single factor can fully account for the emergence of modern industrial societies and that they resulted from an unusual combination of events. Had not all or most of these events occurred when they did, and in conjunction with one another, agrarian societies might still be the dominant societal type today, and remain so for many centuries to come.

Historical Perspective

Before we begin to look for the causes of the Industrial Revolution, we should recall how the structure of agrarian societies impeded technological progress: a tiny governing class that controlled the economic surplus and used it for their own advantage, and thus had every reason to be interested in more efficient methods of production, could not, because of their disdain for manual labor, make technological contributions. Furthermore, they regarded war and the conquest of other societies as a surer and more honorable way to wealth. Meanwhile, the common people, technically knowledgeable, lacked incentive: if a peasant built a better mousetrap, he could be sure the benefits would go to someone else. In short, technological expertise and economic incentive were divorced. And to make matters worse, religion usually encouraged an inordinate respect for tradition and an unprofitable confidence in magic.

These conditions prevailed not only in the simple agrarian societies of the ancient Middle East but in virtually every agrarian society throughout history. Forces that might otherwise have generated technological advance were largely canceled out by the system of social organization. Not that there were *no* advances in agrarian societies; but the rate of advance was much slower than one would expect from the size of their populations, the extent of contact between societies, and the amount of information available.

Another point to keep in mind in considering the causes of the Industrial Revolution is the fact that this was the first important technological and economic revolution to originate in northwestern Europe. All the other crucial technological breakthroughs of the last ten thousand years had occurred in or near the Middle East—plant cultivation, animal domestication, the metallurgical discoveries, the invention of the plow, and the invention of the sailing ship. During most of this time, northwestern Europe was a remote and underdeveloped cultural backwater. What progress it made was chiefly the result of diffusion from more advanced centers.

The first indication that northwestern Europe might become something more than a second-rate outpost of civilization came in the thirteenth, fourteenth, and fifteenth centuries, when it began catching up, partly through its own inventions and discoveries. For the most part, however, Europe remained dependent on diffusion until the beginning of the sixteenth century.[40]

It is easy to forget these facts in an age when we take for granted the technological superiority of northwestern Europe and its overseas settlements. But if we are to understand the Industrial Revolution, it is essential that we keep in mind just how recent the current pattern really is. For this will lead us to ask, What happened at that particular point in history to shift the locus of technological innovation to an area that had always been one of the more backward regions of Eurasia?

Conquest of the New World

When we put it that way, our attention is inevitably drawn to two unique events: (1) the discovery and conquest of the New World and (2) the Protestant Reformation. By almost any criterion, these were the two most significant developments in Western Europe in the fifteenth and sixteenth centuries.

Every schoolboy knows that Columbus "discovered" the New World in 1492. What he sometimes forgets is how quickly the task of exploration and

---

[40] See, for example, Charles Singer, "Epilogue: East and West in Retrospect," in Charles Singer (ed.), *A History of Technology* (Oxford: Clarendon Press, 1956), vol. II, pp. 755ff.

conquest was accomplished. By 1533 the two leading empires of the New World, the Aztec and Incan, had already been subjugated. These victories, and others that followed, brought immense new resources under the control of West Europeans.

The impact on Europe was tremendous. Colonial governments quickly began shipping back vast quantities of gold and silver, with the result that the Continent's supply tripled between 1500 and 1650.[41] One important consequence of this increase was to hasten the spread of a cash economy and the demise of the old barter system. Though money had been used for more than 2,000 years, the supply of precious metals had been so limited that many payments were still made in kind rather than in cash—especially in rural areas, but by no means only there.

This situation seriously hindered both economic and technological advance, because an economy that operates on the basis of barter is not flexible and the flow of resources from areas of oversupply to areas of short supply tends to be sluggish. Furthermore, it is difficult to calculate economic advantage in a barter system. The more widely money is used, however, the easier it is for people to calculate their costs and income and determine which of the alternatives open to them is likely to yield the greatest profit. This is extremely important in breaking down barriers to technological innovation. In a society where technological progress has been halting and uncertain for centuries and where there is no efficient accounting system, people with money to invest will generally conclude that traditional forms of investment are best. Also, where money is scarce, people tend to state obligations (wages, rents, debts, and so on) in relatively inflexible and traditional terms, which makes the economy less responsive to changing conditions and new opportunities. But all this began to change in Western Europe during the sixteenth and seventeenth centuries because of the inflow of precious metals from the New World.

The gold and silver had a second important effect: it produced inflation. This was a natural consequence of the greatly increased supply of money together with the much more limited increase in the supply of goods. Prices doubled, tripled, even quadrupled within a century. As is always the case under such conditions, some people prospered and others were hurt. In general, those with fixed incomes, notably the landed aristocracy and wage-earners, were hurt. But entrepreneurs of all sorts tended to benefit. This meant a marked improvement in the position of the merchants relative to the governing class. More of the economic resources of European societies began to wind up in the hands of men who were interested in, and knew something about, both economics and technology. More than that, these were men oriented to rational profit making (a far from typical orientation in agrarian societies) and therefore motivated to provide financial support for technological innovations that would increase the

---

[41] Clough and Cole, *Economic History of Europe,* pp. 127–128.

efficiency of men or machines. The rise in prices in the sixteenth century was "at once a stimulant to feverish enterprise and an acid dissolving all customary relationships."[42]

The benefits to Europe that resulted from the discovery and conquest of the New World were not limited to the sixteenth and seventeenth centuries. Though the flow of gold and silver began to decline within a century, other commodities started flowing back, and the colonies in the New World provided new and growing markets for European products. In the period from 1698 to 1775, Britain's trade with its colonies increased more than fivefold.[43] All of this strengthened the position of European merchants and provided new sources of capital that they could divert into industrial development as the opportunity arose.

The Protestant Reformation

Only twenty-five years after Columbus discovered the New World, Martin Luther took the first decisive steps in what came to be known as the Protestant Reformation. For more than half a century, scholars have debated the nature of the relationship between this epoch-making religious revolution and subsequent developments in economics and technology. On one point, however, there is no room for argument: Christian nations in general, and Protestant nations in particular, are unique in the modern world by virtue of their high level of economic development (see Table 10.4). Added to this is the fact that the Industrial Revolution got its start in a predominantly Protestant nation, which remained the leader in industrialization until another predominantly Protestant nation took over.

The modern controversy over the relationship between Protestantism and economic development stems largely from the work of Max Weber. Reacting against what he regarded as the overly economic, Marxian interpretation of history, Weber sought to show that the most important economic development of modern times, the rise of capitalism, owed a great deal to the new religious outlook promoted by the reformers, the Calvinists and the Puritans in particular.[44] Although the reformers did not intend to produce an economic revolution, Weber believed that this had been an unintended by-product of their labors and that various aspects of the new Protestant teachings had con-

---

[42] R. H. Tawney, *Religion and the Rise of Capitalism* (New York: Mentor, 1947), p. 117.

[43] Ibid., p. 257.

[44] For the basic statements of Weber's views, see *The Protestant Ethic and the Spirit of Capitalism,* translated by Talcott Parsons (New York: Scribner, 1958); *The Sociology of Religion,* translated by Ephraim Fischoff (Boston: Beacon Press, 1963); and *From Max Weber: Essays in Sociology,* translated by H. H. Gerth and C. W. Mills (New York: Oxford, 1946), pp. 302–322. For a good summary of his views, see Reinhard Bendix, *Max Weber: An Intellectual Portrait* (Garden City, N.Y.: Doubleday, 1960), chaps. 3–8.

tributed to it. In the first place, the reformers laid great stress on the importance of work as a form of service to God. Luther, for example, insisted that all honest forms of work are Christian callings just as truly as the ministry or priesthood. This challenged both the medieval Catholic view of work as basically a penalty for sin and the traditional aristocratic view of work as degrading and beneath the dignity of a gentleman. At the same time, it supported the merchants and craftsmen in their efforts to legitimize their way of life. Second, the new Protestant faiths undermined traditionalism and trust in magic and encouraged the growth of rationalism. Though the reformers dealt with these things only in the area of religion—and even there only imperfectly—they stimulated a trend that ultimately had broad ramifications. Some branches of Protestantism, for example, encouraged their adherents to plan their lives in rational terms rather than simply live from day to day, as the name Methodist implies. Third and finally, many of the newer Protestant faiths emphasized the value of denying the pleasures of this world and living frugally, a practice that led those who were economically successful to accumulate capital. To the extent that they followed these teachings, Weber argued, men developed a new outlook on life: they worked harder, acted more rationally, and lived more thriftily. In short, men's personalities were remolded by the Reformation in ways that helped undermine the traditional agrarian economy and stimulate economic and technological in-

Table 10.4 Median energy consumption for groups of nations classified by dominant tradition religion, 1969

Dominant Traditional Religion	Median Energy Consumption[a]	No. of Nations
Protestant[b]	5,141	10
Eastern Orthodox[c]	3,060	4
Roman Catholic[d]	914	31
Muslim[e]	208	24
Eastern religions (Buddhism, Hinduism, etc.)[f]	193	13
Preliterate tribal faiths[g]	70	25

Sources: United Nations, *Statistical Yearbook, 1970,* table 138, and Bruce Russett et al., *World Handbook of Political and Social Indicators* (New Haven, Conn.: Yale, 1964), tables 73–75.

[a] Kilograms of coal equivalent consumed per person per year in median nation in each category.

[b] United States, United Kingdom, Australia, New Zealand, Scandinavia (including Iceland), and East Germany.

[c] U.S.S.R., Bulgaria, Romania, and Greece.

[d] Most of Latin America, southern and eastern Europe (except Yugoslavia and Albania), Ireland, Belgium, France.

[e] Middle East (except Israel and Lebanon), Indonesia, Pakistan, Afghanistan, Iran, North Africa, Sudan, Chad, Niger, Mali, Mauritania, Senegal, Guinea, and Somalia.

[f] Southern and eastern Asia (except Indonesia and Malaysia).

[g] Sub-Saharan Africa (except South Africa, Rhodesia and Muslim nations indicated in note e).

Note: Nations of mixed background (e.g., West Germany, Canada, Ethiopia, Yugoslavia) and very small nations (e.g., Mauritius, Malta, Kuwait) were omitted.

novation. In later years, Weber modified his views to the extent of recognizing that the roots of what he called the "Protestant Ethic" (i.e., the new view of work) lay in *pre*-Reformation Christianity and ancient Judaism. Thus he would not have been surprised by the differences shown in Table 10.4 between the Eastern Orthodox and Roman Catholic countries on the one hand and the Muslim and Oriental faiths on the other.

Weber's work has been attacked from many quarters.[45] The most serious criticism has stressed his neglect of the effects of economics on religion. Weber recognized this relationship but in some of his best-known writings purposely chose to ignore it.

Probably none of Weber's critics has been more influential and perceptive than the English economic historian R. H. Tawney, who pointed out that Calvinism and Puritanism were influenced from the very beginning by the fact that their leaders were townsmen and city dwellers and by the heavy representation of merchants and craftsmen in their membership. He wrote:

> As was to be expected in the exponents of a faith which had its headquarters at Geneva, and later its most influential adherents in great business centers, like Antwerp with its industrial hinterland, London, and Amsterdam, its leaders addressed their teachings, not of course exclusively, but none the less primarily, to the classes engaged in trade and industry, who formed the most modern and progressive elements in the life of the age. In doing so they naturally started from a frank recognition of the necessity of capital, credit and banking, large-scale commerce and finance, and the other practical facts of business life. They thus broke with the tradition which, regarding a preoccupation with economic interests "beyond what is necessary for subsistence" as reprehensible, had stigmatized the middleman as a parasite and the usurer as a thief. They set the profits of trade and finance, which to the medieval writer, as to Luther, only with difficulty escaped censure as *turpe lucrum,* on the same level of respectability as the earnings of the laborer and the rents of the landlord. "What reason is there," wrote Calvin to a correspondent, "why the income from business should not be larger than that from landowning? Whence do the merchant's profits come, except from his own diligence and industry?"[46]

Calvinism and Puritanism did not, of course, condone all forms of business activity. But they did accord business in general a measure of legitimacy and respectability denied it by nearly all earlier ideologies. Wherever Calvinist thought became dominant, profit seeking was viewed not as a necessary evil or as a means of upward mobility but as a legitimate and useful activity in its own right.

---

[45] For an introduction to the critics, see Robert W. Green (ed.), *Protestantism and Capitalism: The Weber Thesis and Its Critics* (Boston: Heath, 1959). This volume gives brief excerpts from a number of the leading critics and provides a useful bibliography on pp. 115–116.

[46] Tawney, pp. 92–93. Quoted by permission of Harcourt, Brace & World, Inc.

Tawney also pointed out that Calvinism gradually changed after its founder's death, neglecting some of his teachings while emphasizing those which were more congenial with the needs and aspirations of the commercial class, by then an important part of the membership of the group. For example, the corporate elements in Calvinism were weakened and the individualistic elements strengthened. Thus the group abandoned the practice of excommunication, which had been an important means of discipline in the earlier years, and left discipline more and more to the conscience of the individual—enlightened, presumably, by Calvinist teaching. This in turn led to a gradual withdrawal of the church from the realm of economics and the elimination of even those restraints on economic activity which Calvin had retained. In Tawney's view, the social teachings of the Puritans and other later Calvinists were a complex mixture "derived partly from the obvious interests of the commercial classes, partly from [their] conception of the nature of God."[47]

On many points, Tawney agreed with Weber. He shared his view of the importance of Luther's doctrine of the calling—the doctrine that all who do honest work have Christian vocations and therefore serve God. He, too, appreciated the importance of the Calvinist and Puritan condemnation of self-indulgence. In short, like Weber, he believed that the Protestant Reformation established a new system of values and created a new type of personality, both more conducive than their older counterparts to economic and technological progress. Tawney put it this way:

> [Calvinist] teaching, whatever its theological merits or defects, was admirably designed to liberate economic energies, and to weld into a disciplined social force the rising bourgeoisie, conscious of the contrast between its own standards and those of a laxer world, proud of its vocation as the standard-bearer of the economic virtues. . . . Calvinism stood, in short, not only for a new doctrine of theology and ecclesiastical government, but for a new scale of moral values and a new ideal of social conduct.[48]

The Agricultural Revolution

A third development that contributed to the Industrial Revolution was the agricultural revolution in eighteenth-century England. This earlier revolution has been largely forgotten because of the more dramatic events that followed on its heels. Nevertheless, at the time, it was recognized as very important, and it clearly contributed to the rise of industry.

The agricultural revolution, like the industrial, was stimulated by the economic disturbances generated by the discovery of the New World. The rise

---

[47] Ibid., p. 192.

[48] Ibid., p. 98. Quoted by permission of Harcourt, Brace & World, Inc.

in prices caused severe losses among the landowning class, who realized something would have to be done if they were ever to regain their prosperity. Fortunately, the more rational and experimental outlook stimulated by the growth of the money economy and the rise of Protestantism had begun to permeate even the rural landowning class, everywhere noted for its conservatism and traditionalism, and during the eighteenth century, a number of them began seriously looking for ways to increase the yields of their estates. This led to several important innovations. Early in the century, a brother-in-law of the prime minister discovered a system of crop rotation that enabled farmers to stop leaving a quarter of their land fallow each year. By rotating barley, clover, wheat, and turnips, land could be kept in continuous production without depleting its resources. As the word spread, farm yields increased considerably. Later in the century, another wealthy landowner discovered the principle of selective breeding, simultaneously making a small fortune for himself from his stud farm and improving the size and quality of British livestock. Several innovative landowners developed machines to help mechanize farming and increase the efficiency of farm labor. One of them also authored a textbook designed to rationalize farming practices, claiming his methods had increased the annual profits on his 20-acre farm from £131 to £334 in just ten years. Though his claims were questioned, the book was extremely popular and helped to increase the efficiency of English farming.

Another important development in the eighteenth and early nineteenth centuries was the passage of the infamous enclosure acts, which gave wealthy landowners control of several million acres of common pastureland, woodland, and scattered strip holdings of small yeoman farmers. This worked a terrible hardship on the common people. As Oliver Goldsmith described in his poem "The Deserted Village," many poor farmers were forced to abandon what was left of their small holdings and migrate to the developing industrial centers. These ruthless seizures were clearly stimulated by the shift to a money economy and the spread of capitalism. Their ultimate effect was to destroy the traditional, inefficient system of agriculture and replace it with a large-scale, capitalistic, and rationalistic system of enterprise. From this time on, English farming began to take on the character of a modern business.

From the standpoint of the Industrial Revolution, all these developments were very important. In the first place, the agricultural innovations resulted in the production of more food with less manpower, thus releasing a considerable portion of the population from the need to farm. Though this removed the basic limitation on the growth of urban populations, the increased agricultural efficiency could not, *by itself,* have ensured urban growth, since the additional food might have been consumed by a growing rural population. The enclosure acts, as harsh and immoral as they were, prevented this by forcing the excess rural population to migrate to the new industrial towns, thus providing the manpower needed by the expanding industries. Without these changes in England's agriculture, it is doubtful that the Industrial Revolution would have developed nearly as rapidly as it did, and it might have stalled completely at some early point because of insufficient manpower, insufficient agricultural resources, or both.

The Benefits of Cumulation

The Industrial Revolution also owed a great deal to the simple cumulation of technological knowledge that had occurred over the centuries of the agrarian era. Although the rise of agrarian societies was associated with a marked slowing of the rate of technological advance, this was not the same thing as a complete halt in the innovative process. Some new inventions and discoveries were made, and the store of useful information did increase, if slowly.

Because sociocultural innovation is cumulative and because the number and types of inventions are a function of the already existing store of technical knowledge, the odds that there would be some kind of a major technological breakthrough were bound to be greater in the eighteenth century than in the fifteenth and greater in the fifteenth than in the first century A.D. or the tenth century B.C. This does not mean that the Industrial Revolution was *inevitable* by the eighteenth century, or even by the twentieth. On the contrary, if the developments we have enumerated had not occurred, agrarian societies might still be the most advanced in the world.

Concluding Note

As our analysis indicates, the causes of the Industrial Revolution were probably more complex than the causes of earlier technological revolutions. Unlike its predecessors, this one required the disruption, or at least the weakening, of a well-established social structure and the rejection of a deeply rooted ideology.

The discovery of the New World and the Protestant Reformation seem to have been the chief catalytic agents that triggered the essential changes. They undermined the structural and ideological foundations of the agrarian way of life and thereby freed creative forces that had been severely curbed for a long time. Then, with a relatively broad base of accumulated information to build on, it was only a matter of time until men would make the inventions and discoveries that were at the heart of the Industrial Revolution. And, as subsequent events proved, it did not take long at all!

CAUSES OF THE CONTINUING INDUSTRIAL REVOLUTION

As Weber noted more than half a century ago, any explanation of the economic and social revolution of modern times must address itself to two problems. After we have dealt with its origin, we still must explain its continuation.

Although the origin has easily been the more controversial of the two, we cannot simply take the continuing revolution for granted, as though it were inevitable or its causes self-evident. On the contrary, because we live in the era of that continuing revolution, we have a special interest in the forces changing our societies and our lives.

The Institutionalization of Innovation

Modern industrial societies have not been content to remove impediments to technological advance; they have consciously tried to stimulate it. One of the most important steps has been the democratization of educational systems and the extension of educational opportunities to citizens of every class. Another has been the redefinition of the nature of educational institutions: whereas their sole function used to be the transmission of the cultural heritage of the past, in the last century institutions of higher education have increasingly become research centers as well.

More recently, business groups and government agencies have discovered the importance of research and have set up research units within their own organizations. Expenditures for scientific research and development in this country rose from $166 *million* in 1930 to nearly $28 *billion* in 1972.[49] For the

Figure 10.7 Ultrahigh speed liquid zonal centrifuge at Atomic Energy Commission's Oak Ridge Laboratory. This machine was developed to permit high efficiency separation of the components of human and animal cells.

---

[49] U.S. Department of Commerce, *Long-term Economic Growth: 1860–1965* (1966), p. 198, and *Statistical Abstract, 1972*, table 842.

first time in history, human societies are systematically searching for solutions to their problems.

Modern research becomes more fruitful every year, thanks to increasingly sophisticated methods of observation and measurement, which run the gamut from the electron microscope to public-opinion polling. These techniques permit far more precise comparisons between the performances of proposed innovations and those older tools and techniques which they are designed to replace, while newer methods of cost accounting provide more accurate comparisons of relative costs and profits.[50] These comparisons naturally speed the acceptance of useful innovations and thus contribute to the continuing revolution in modern technology.

The Changing Nature of Warfare

Although there are many reasons for the growing emphasis on research, the most important (as gauged by financial support) is the changing nature of warfare. Prior to the Industrial Revolution, military technology changed slowly. Among nations on the same level of development, victory was usually determined by the sizes of the armies and the organizational and tactical skills of their commanders.

Today, all this is changed. Military technology becomes obsolete in a few years. The sizes of armies and the skills of their commanders are becoming—perhaps already are—less important than the productive capacity of a nation's economy and the technological skill of its engineers and scientists. If they want to maintain their relative military status, the leading nations must invest increasing amounts in military research, including biological, chemical, and space research, as well as the more traditional kinds. It is hard to see how this costly acceleration of military research can be halted without either the formation of a single world state to end military rivalries or a nuclear war that would so cripple these societies that they could not continue research activities of *any* kind.

Population Control

Another enormously important factor in the continuing revolution is man's newly achieved ability to control the birthrate. By now it should be clear that population growth can easily offset any gains in productivity that result from technological advance. Unless this is prevented, most people are doomed to live at,

---

[50] Critics have noted, however, that these modern methods of accounting fail to take account of human values that are not monetized. For example, they make no allowance for the high value many people place on the preservation of rare or beautiful species of birds and animals threatened by commercially profitable activities. Some efforts are being made to change this, but the problem is a difficult one.

or near, the subsistence level — and life at that level is not conducive to innovation and progress.

In past centuries, various techniques of population control were tried, but none was really successful. With the Industrial Revolution, the need became even more acute, as advances in medicine and sanitation drastically cut the death rate. Infant mortality was greatly reduced, with the result that many more people survived into the reproductive years.

Fortunately, the Industrial Revolution also brought advances in chemistry and related fields that led to better methods of birth control. As a result, the birthrate in modern industrial societies has been substantially reduced, and the growth in productivity has, for the first time in history, far outrun the growth in population. This in turn has made it possible — again, for the first time — for all segments of the population to share in the benefits of technological advance: the historic necessity of keeping millions of people at the subsistence level has been eliminated. The slower rate of growth also makes it feasible to educate more of the population. All these factors combine to produce more people who are physically and intellectually equipped, and psychologically motivated, to contribute to the ongoing process of change.

Increased Information and Improved Communications Facilities

The continuing technological revolution is also simply an inevitable consequence of the increased store of information and the improved facilities for transmitting it within and between societies. Since inventions are recombinations of existing elements of information, the larger the store of such elements, the greater the potential for further innovation. Thus, advances made back in the early stages of the Industrial Revolution laid the foundation for advances occurring now, as well as for those yet to come.

Today, millions of books and technical publications disseminate information widely and quickly, and the growing use of computers promises to accelerate the process even more. Telephones and modern transportation are also crucial, facilitating contacts between people working on related problems.

The New Ideology

Not surprisingly, the changes of recent centuries have resulted in a radical shift in human values. In the past, people generally looked on innovation and change as undesirable, even dangerous, and departures from tradition were usually considered wrong until proved otherwise. This attitude has been almost reversed in industrial societies. In the arts, for example, innovation is often praised simply for its own sake, without regard to aesthetic criteria. Many people are so ready to applaud the artist who does something — anything — no one has done before, that prizes have been awarded to entries submitted as hoaxes. In education, too, a higher value is now placed on innovation. Rote learning is scorned by many educators, and "creativity" has come to be the quality most sought in students, particularly in leading colleges and universities. Even in business and religion, there is a tendency to value the new above the old, regardless of its merits by other standards.

Whatever else its consequences, this shift in values makes it easier for technological innovators to gain a hearing for their ideas. Ideology, which once slowed the rate of innovation, has now become a stimulant.

Future Prospects

Since the middle of the eighteenth century, the Western world has been caught up in a technological revolution that has radically transformed the conditions of human life. Any thoughtful person, after surveying this period of history, is bound to wonder, "What next?"

Before we tackle this question, however, we should take a careful look at contemporary industrial and industrializing societies, since they are the products of the revolution thus far. They will be our chief concern in the next four chapters. After we have examined them, we will be in a better position to consider that most difficult question of all—the question of the future.

CHAPTER ELEVEN

Industrial Societies: Part 1

In the century and a half since England became the first industrial society, she has been joined by more than a score of other nations, including most of those in Europe, all the English-speaking democracies overseas, Japan, South Africa, and Israel. Some of these nations have barely crossed the threshold separating agrarian from industrial societies (see page 296), while others have moved well beyond this point. We will be chiefly concerned with the latter, since they provide us with our clearest picture of what industrial societies are like when the agrarian elements are most nearly eliminated.

If we were to carry this logic to its extreme, we would focus exclusively on American society, since it is currently the most advanced of all the industrialized nations. But this would be a mistake, since no society is the prototype of all the others. Although industrial societies have a lot in common, they are not carbon copies of one another any more than agrarian societies are. Their differences are every bit as important as their similarities, because they provide us with some idea of the range of alternatives that are possible for industrializing nations. For this reason alone, we could not limit our analysis to a single society.

THE TECHNOLOGICAL BASE

During the early stages of the Industrial Revolution, many elements of the agrarian way of life continued relatively unchanged. Today, however, in societies that are well into the fourth or fifth phase, the old order has largely vanished. Nowhere, of course, is this more true than in the realm of technology.

One of the best indications of the dramatic nature of the change is the shift away from the sources of energy that agrarian societies relied on for so long. Traditionally, people and animals were the chief sources of the energy required by "work"—meaning activities such as pushing, pulling, lifting, cutting, and digging, which have been, or theoretically could be, performed by the muscle power of man, but *not* activities such as providing heat, light, or refrigeration.[1] To some extent muscle power was supplemented by water harnessed by waterwheels and wind harnessed by sailing ships and windmills. As recently as

---

[1] This definition of "work" is based on J. Frederic Dewhurst and Associates, *America's Needs and Resources* (New York: Twentieth Century Fund, 1955), pp. 905–906.

Figure 11.1 Diesel engine works, Denmark.

1850, these traditional sources supplied over 87 per cent of the energy used in work in the United States. Today they account for less than 1 per cent.[2] In their stead, we rely on coal, petroleum, natural gas, hydroelectric power, and nuclear power. Except for coal, these sources were still untapped in 1850, and even coal was not used in performing work until the invention of the steam engine.

Not only have energy *sources* changed, but the quantities produced have multiplied enormously. In 1850, all the prime movers in the United States (i.e., steam engines in factories, sailing vessels, work animals, etc.) had a capacity of 8.5 million horsepower; by 1970, this had risen to 20 *billion,* more than a 200-fold increase in per capita terms.[3]

---

[2] For 1850, see ibid., p. 1116; by the early 1960s the figure had apparently dropped below 1 per cent, according to reports on the increase in the newer energy sources. See, for example, U.S. Bureau of the Census, *Statistical Abstract of the United States, 1963,* table 716, and compare with Dewhurst and Associates, Tables 25.3 and 25.4.

[3] U.S. Bureau of the Census, *Historical Statistics of the United States: Colonial Times to 1957,* ser. S 1–14, (1960), and U.S. Bureau of the Census, *Statistical Abstract of the United States, 1971,* p. 781.

This remarkable jump in the production and consumption of energy was closely linked with increases in the production and consumption of a wide variety of raw materials. Consider iron and steel, for example: American production rose from 20,000 tons in 1820 to 225 million tons in 1970,[4] Britain's from 7,000 tons in 1750 to 48 million tons in 1970.[5] In each case, the increase was more than 6,000-fold.

Equally dramatic growth is evident in the production and consumption of many other raw materials. In one recent year, the United States produced 4.6 tons of sand and gravel for every man, woman, and child in the population, 4.3 tons of stone, 2.8 tons of coal, 2.4 tons of crude petroleum, 0.4 tons of iron ore, 775 pounds of cement, 580 pounds of clay, 440 pounds of salt, 370 pounds of phosphate rock, 200 pounds of lime, 100 pounds of gypsum, 100 pounds of uranium ore, and 65 pounds of sulfur, to cite but a few items.[6] Altogether, mineral production equals 16 tons per person per year!

Statistics like these simply document the fact that advanced industrial societies have established a radically new relationship with the biophysical environment. Man's ability to mobilize energy and information has increased so rapidly that he is suddenly able to level mountains, redirect rivers, erase forests, and remove mineral deposits from deep below the earth and the sea. He can even moderate the effects of climate with modern systems of heating, cooling, and irrigation.

As environmentalists continually remind us, this enormous power to manipulate the biophysical environment has been anything but a simple success story and may yet turn into a major disaster. Certainly we are all painfully aware of rivers converted into sewers, giant lakes unable to support marine life, even oceans beginning to show signs of trouble, and we are conscious that in areas around the globe our life-sustaining atmosphere is becoming life-threatening, many forms of plant and animal life have been, and are being, irrevocably destroyed, and such critical resources as fossil fuels are being depleted at a rate that threatens the security of future generations. In short, modern technology, in the process of solving many of man's historic problems, has emerged as an alarming source of new ones.

Since this unprecedented use of the earth's resources is at the very heart of the technological revolution, it follows that a society's rate of energy consumption (see Table 10.3, page 295) is a good indicator of its technological development. It is, in fact, the best measure available for recent years, but,

---

[4] The 1820 figure is from W. S. Woytinsky and E. S. Woytinsky, *World Population and Production: Trends and Outlook* (New York: Twentieth Century Fund, 1953), p. 1101; the 1970 figure is from *Statistical Abstract, 1971,* tables 1070 and 1171.

[5] The 1750 figure is from the Woytinsky and Woytinsky, p. 1100; the 1970 figure is from United Nations, *Statistical Yearbook, 1971,* tables 121 and 122, and is converted to short tons.

[6] Production figures are from *Statistical Abstract, 1971,* table 1040. Per capita calculations are our own.

unfortunately, the necessary data are not available for most societies prior to World War II. Happily, we have an alternative: a society's *per capita income* has been shown to be highly correlated with its energy consumption. Using this measure, we can observe the magnitude of the change that occurs when a society moves from the agrarian to the advanced industrial level.

Per capita income in the United States underwent a dramatic increase—from approximately $400 per person per year in 1871 to approximately $3,900 in 1970 (the 1871 figure and all figures for earlier decades used in this section have been adjusted to take account of inflation in the intervening years).[7] As striking as this nearly tenfold increase is, it actually understates the

Figure 11.2   The Krupp steel works at Rheinhausen operates twenty-four hours a day, producing two million tons of steel a year.

[7] The 1871 figure is estimated from data provided in *Historical Statistics of the United States*, ser. F 1–5 and 6–9. It was assumed that the ratio of national income to gross national product was the same in 1869–1873 as in 1897–1901. The 1970 figure is from *Statistical Abstract, 1971*, p. 308. Price adjustments were based on data on p. 330 and in *Historical Statistics of the United States*.

magnitude of the difference between a typical advanced agrarian society of the past and American society today, since by 1871 this country was already well on the road toward industrialization. In fact, as we noted in the last chapter, the value of its industrial production surpassed its agricultural production as early as the 1880s. Therefore, to get an accurate idea of the productive level of traditional agrarian societies, we must turn either to European nations during much earlier stages of industrialization or to the underdeveloped nations of more recent years.

In the first category, both Britain and Sweden can provide us with good data. In Britain, per capita income in 1801 seems to have been somewhere near $165 per year, in Sweden in 1861, approximately $180.[8]

Data from societies still predominantly agrarian in the twentieth century are remarkably similar. In 1938, the earliest year for which reliable estimates are available for most of them, per capita income was estimated to have been as follows:[9]

Greece	$209
Colombia	195
Egypt	171
Peru	167
Turkey	163
Mexico	158
Brazil	136
India	92
China	46

Like Britain in 1801 and Sweden in 1861, however, these societies had already experienced some degree of industrialization, which suggests that if this influence could be stripped away, the figure for the typical agrarian society prior to the Industrial Revolution would not be much in excess of $100 per person per year. Even if we double this to allow for the likelihood that production was underreported in rural areas, the current American figure represents almost a twentyfold increase.

But even this figure fails to do justice to the magnitude of the economic transformation. Modern industrial societies not only can provide a higher income per capita, they also support much larger populations within a given territory. In England, for example, the population has multiplied more than seven-

---

[8] These figures are our own calculations. The British figure is based on data presented by Phyllis Deane and W. A. Cole, *British Economic Growth, 1688–1959* (London: Cambridge, 1962), tables 72 and 90, the Swedish on data presented by Woytinsky and Woytinsky, p. 387, with adjustments for the changing values of the dollar, pound, and krone.

[9] These figures are based on those in Woytinsky and Woytinsky, pp. 389–390, and are multiplied by 2.71 to take account of the effects of inflation between 1938 and 1970.

fold since 1750.[10] To get a better estimate of the effect of the Industrial Revolution on the productive capacity of societies, then, we have to multiply this increase in per capita income by the increase in population. When we do this, we find that the most advanced modern industrial technology has a productive capacity approximately 100 times greater than that of traditional agrarian societies of the recent past. Small wonder that this has triggered a major social revolution.

DEMOGRAPHIC PATTERNS

Growth in Numbers

On the eve of the Industrial Revolution, during the early years of the eighteenth century, the population of the entire world was about 600 million.[11] Today, less than three centuries later, it is approaching 4 billion.[12] To many people, there is nothing startling about a sixfold increase in a 250- to 300-year period. But to demographers, such a rate of change is revolutionary. Throughout most of the agrarian era, world population apparently grew about 0.1 per cent per year;[13] today, it is averaging 2 per cent, twenty times the traditional rate.[14] At the lower rate, the population doubled every 700 years; at the present rate, it doubles every 35 years.

Although the long-term population growth has been greatest in industrial societies, the hybrid societies of Asia, Africa, and Latin America are growing more rapidly now that modern sanitation and medical technology have eliminated many of their historic scourges. Unfortunately, other aspects of the new technology, notably techniques of contraception and of production, have not spread so readily, with the result that many of these nations now face a demographic catastrophe (see Chapter 14).

In Europe, the birthplace of the Industrial Revolution, population has increased "only" about fivefold since 1700. This is partly due to the heavy migration of Europeans to the New World and Oceania. If we take the whole area of European settlement into account, the increase is nearly ninefold (from about 135 million to 1,235 million). And were it not for the newer methods of

---

[10] Judith Ryder and Harold Silver, *Modern English Society* (London: Methuen, 1970), p. 310. The United States has grown even more rapidly, but that is less relevant to the present problem, since the American population never came close to reaching its agrarian potential.

[11] This estimate is based on A. M. Carr-Saunders, *World Population* (Fair Lawn, N.J.: Oxford University Press, 1936), p. 42, and Walter F. Willcox, *Studies in American Demography* (Ithaca, N.Y.: Cornell, 1940), p. 45.

[12] See United Nations, *Demographic Yearbook, 1970.*

[13] Warren Thompson and David Lewis, *Population Problems,* 5th ed. (New York: McGraw-Hill, 1965), pp. 383–385.

[14] United Nations, *Demographic Yearbook, 1970,* table 1.

birth control, the combined populations of Europe, the Americas, and Oceania alone would almost certainly be 3 billion, possibly more. The rate of growth of industrial societies is clearly no measure of their *potential for sustaining numbers.* If Europeans were willing to live at the subsistence level, as millions do in Asia, Europe alone might support a population of several billion.

Fertility and Mortality

To understand the modern demographic revolution, we have to look beyond the figures on total population to those on fertility and mortality. They reveal the striking fact that the great increase in population during recent centuries was achieved without any increase in the birthrate. In fact, it occurred in spite of a substantial *decline* in many parts of the world.

Throughout most of history, human societies maintained a demographic equilibrium, with their birthrates and death rates roughly balancing each other. Over the long run, the birthrate was usually a little higher than the death rate, with the result that there was a slow increase in population.[15] This modest growth was made possible by technological advance. In the short run, of course, the death rate often exceeded the birthrate because of wars, famines, and plagues. Most societies apparently established an equilibrium at about 40 births and 40 deaths per 1,000 population per year.

Then, during the eighteenth century, the death rates of some societies began to drop as a result of their increased productivity, improved transpor-

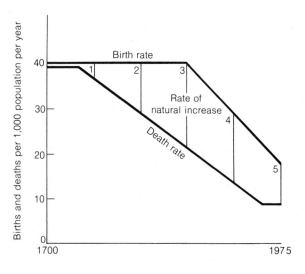

Figure 11.3   Trends in fertility, mortality, and natural increase in industrialized societies. The vertical lines measure the natural increase at five different points in time.

---

[15] Occasionally, however, there were long-run declines. For example, Egypt is estimated to have had a population of 6 to 7 million in Roman times but only 2.5 million in 1798. See Charles Issawi, *Egypt in Revolution: An Economic Analysis* (New York: Oxford University Press, 1963), p. 20.

tation (which eliminated localized famines resulting from crop failures, formerly an important cause of death), and advances in sanitation and medicine. The trend continued until, today, the death rate in the more advanced industrial societies is under 10 per 1,000 per year.

The decline in the birthrate was much slower. In most of the new industrial societies, there was no permanent decrease until the end of the nineteenth century. This combination of a traditional birthrate and a steadily declining death rate naturally resulted in a sharply rising rate of natural increase, as shown by the growing length of the first three vertical lines in Figure 11.3.

So far, not a single industrial society has achieved a demographic equilibrium (i.e., zero population growth), but sooner or later, every one of them must. Their only choice will be the level at which it occurs. It could be at the old level of 40 births and 40 deaths per 1,000 per year; but this would mean a very short life expectancy for most people. It could, alternatively, occur in the neighborhood of 12 to 14 per 1,000 per year, which would mean a life expectancy of 70 to 80 years for the average person. An equilibrium could hardly be established at 10 or less per year in the near future, for that presupposes an average life expectancy of 100 years or more in a population in equilibrium, and medical science has made only limited progress in raising the life expectancy of older people.[16] It is quite possible, however, that there will continue to be some population growth in most industrial societies for several more genera-

Table 11.1 Crude birthrates for selected industrial societies, 1970

Nation	Crude Birthrate*	Nation	Crude Birthrate*
West Germany	13.3	France	16.7
Sweden	13.6	Poland	16.7
Finland	13.7	Italy	16.8
East Germany	13.9	United States (1971)	17.2
Denmark	14.4	Canada (1969)	17.5
Belgium	14.7	U.S.S.R.	17.5
Hungary	14.7	Netherlands	18.4
Austria	15.1	Japan	18.9
Czechoslovakia	15.8	Australia	20.5
Switzerland	15.9	Romania	21.1
Norway	16.2	Ireland	21.8
United Kingdom	16.2	New Zealand	22.1
Bulgaria	16.3	South Africa (whites only)	24.0
		Israel	27.0

Sources: United Nations, *Demographic Yearbook, 1970*, table 13, and U.S. Bureau of the Census, *Current Population Reports*, Ser. P-25, no. 481 (April 1972), p. 1.

* The term "crude birthrate" refers to the number of live births per 1,000 population per year.

[16] Death rates of 10 or less can occur in societies that are growing fairly rapidly even if the average life expectancy is 70 years or less. But in a stable population, death rates this low can occur only if the average life expectancy is 100 years or more.

tions, with the death rate remaining around 10 and the birthrate somewhat higher, perhaps 15.

Almost no one wants to return to the traditional situation in which nature held sway and man had virtually no control over this vital aspect of his life. In most industrial societies the birthrate is already below 20 (see Table 11.1). The only exceptions are nations recently settled by Europeans and still under-populated, such as New Zealand and Australia, marginal industrial societies, such as Ireland and Romania, or nations in which the dominant population feels threatened by a lack of numbers, as in Israel and South Africa.

SOCIAL STRUCTURE: INTRODUCTION AND OVERVIEW

Scale of Organization

Despite their great technological achievements, or actually because of them, industrial societies have not set any spectacular records for size. From the demographic standpoint, China, an industrializing agrarian society, remains the largest society ever formed by man. Its present population, which is believed to be approaching 800 million, puts it far ahead of the largest industrial society, the Soviet Union, with approximately 240 million. India, another hybrid society, also far surpasses the Soviet Union. Its present population is around 550 million.

Industrial societies are not especially impressive from the geographical standpoint either. As we noted in Chapter 8, czarist Russia built an empire covering nearly 8 million square miles. Under Communist leadership, the boundaries have been enlarged to embrace 8.6 million square miles, hardly a remarkable increase.

But comparisons such as these are misleading. Industrial societies have a capacity for expansion, both demographic and geographic, that far exceeds the potential of agrarian societies. Inventions like the airplane and the radio have made the entire planet smaller today than England was just a few centuries ago. One can now communicate with people on the other side of the world in a matter of minutes, and meet them in a matter of hours. From the technical standpoint, it would be easier to govern the entire world today than it was to govern most small kingdoms in the not far distant past. Within the next century or two, therefore, a substantial expansion in average societal size is likely, and a single global society well within the realm of possibility.

So far, however, industrial societies have been extremely zealous in guarding their national sovereignty. Moreover, the new military technology has made war an increasingly costly and risky road to expansion. Nations now stand to gain much more by peaceful economic development than by wars of conquest. In this respect, industrialization has reversed a relationship that existed throughout most of the agrarian era.

If societal expansion does come, then, it will probably result from pressures generated by economic competition. In the modern world, the low cost of moving goods has forced firms in every country to compete with their foreign counterparts. In this situation, firms based in the small countries are usually at a serious disadvantage: having a smaller volume of sales to begin with, they cannot spread their fixed costs over as many units, and as a result they wind up with higher prices. (In the automobile industry, for example, the design costs for a new model are fixed costs: they will be the same regardless of whether millions are produced or only a few hundred thousand. By contrast, the costs of the materials that go into the cars are variable costs: the more cars made, the greater the expenditures for these items.) Since the price of most commodities is a function of both fixed and variable costs, the producer with the largest volume of sales enjoys an advantage over his competitors, especially in an industry where fixed costs are a significant part of the total (see Table 11.2). In this situation, the largest producer usually increases his share of the market at the expense of the other firms, because he can consistently underprice them or offer a better product at a lower price. In the end, he will probably drive them into bankruptcy unless they have some offsetting advantage, such as greater organizational efficiency, tariff protection, or the like.

In response to this problem, a number of small countries have formed customs unions, which eliminate tariffs on goods shipped between member nations. This was tried first by Belgium, the Netherlands, and Luxembourg (the Benelux Union); later, by most of the nations of Western Europe (the European Economic Community). Although these new arrangements have helped West European firms compete with American firms in world markets, they have not been achieved without some loss of national sovereignty, and undertakings of this sort may prove to be the first step toward political unification.

The most striking development with respect to the scale of organization in the industrial era has been the formation of global political entities—first the League of Nations, now the United Nations. Though their powers have been minimal, the very fact of their existence is indicative of the changes wrought by

Table 11.2 Relationship of sales volume to per unit costs of production

Firm	No. of units sold	Variable costs*	Fixed costs†	Total costs	Cost per unit‡
A	10,000	$10,000	$5,000	$15,000	$1.50
B	8,000	8,000	5,000	13,000	1.63
C	5,000	5,000	5,000	10,000	2.00

* Variable costs need not be exactly proportional to sales, but they have been shown this way to simplify the illustration.

† Normally, fixed costs would not be exactly the same for the several firms, but they have been shown this way to simplify the illustration.

‡ Cost per unit equals total cost divided by sales volume.

the Industrial Revolution. A few centuries ago, organizations like these could not have functioned. Today, despite the limitations imposed on the United Nations, there is a real possibility that it may yet evolve into a more inclusive kind of political system than the world has ever seen.

Industrialization also means growth in the size of organizations at the community level. In agrarian societies, the largest communities never had much over a million inhabitants. Prior to the Industrial Revolution, this figure was attained only a few times, and then only by the capitals of empires that controlled the resources of vast territories. Today, approximately 130 cities have populations of 1 million or more, and only a minority are national capitals.[17] Moreover, 11 cities have more than 5 million; and Greater New York and Tokyo have already passed the 10 million mark and are still growing. By the end of the century, some students of urbanism expect to see the cities on the east coast of the United States linked up in a giant megalopolis stretching from Boston to Washington. Although this is by no means a certainty, most of the technology needed to maintain such a community is already available. If these expectations are not realized, it will probably be because people *choose* not to live that way—not because they are unable to.

Differentiation of Parts

From the structural standpoint, industrial societies are by far the most complex that have ever existed. No other type of society has contained such a variety of differentiated subunits. This is true both of the roles individuals fill and of the groups of which these roles are a part.

Nowhere is this complexity more evident than with respect to occupational roles: the U.S. Department of Labor has identified more than 20,000 different kinds of jobs in this country.[18] The meat-packing industry nicely illustrates the extremes to which occupational specialization has been carried. Here are a few of the more specialized jobs in that industry, each a full-time, forty-hour-a-week job:

aitchbone breaker	jowl trimmer
belly opener	leg skinner
bladder trimmer	lung splitter
brain picker	rump sawyer
gland man	side splitter
gut puller	skull grinder
gut sorter	snout puller
head splitter	toe puller

---

[17] *The World Almanac, 1972*, pp. 154 and 584–585.

[18] See *Dictionary of Occupational Titles* (Washington, D.C.: Government Printing Office, 1965), vol. I, p. xv.

Figure 11.4 **Extreme occupational specialization is characteristic of industrial societies: IBM assembly line.**

("What does your daddy do?" "Oh, he's a snout puller over at the packing house.")

In recent years, automated machinery has replaced human labor in many highly specialized blue-collar jobs, but this has been more than offset by the growing number of equally specialized white-collar jobs. In the medical profession, for example, the general practitioner is rapidly being replaced by a growing variety of specialists.[19] The same thing is happening in the academic world: the general historian is being replaced by the specialist in eighteenth-century German history or nineteenth-century French history. This pattern is repeated in most other professional and managerial occupations.

Specialization is also evident in the tremendous variety of associations found in every industrial society. Here is a small sample of nationwide groups in the United States today:

> Aaron Burr Association
> Acoustical Society of America
> Actors Equity Association
> Administrative Management Society
> Adult Education Association of the U.S.A.
> Advertising Federation of America

---

[19] The percentage of physicians in general practice in the United States dropped from 48 to 15 per cent between 1950 and 1970. See U.S. Bureau of the Census, *Statistical Abstract of the United States, 1968,* table 86, and *Statistical Abstract, 1972,* table 95

Aerospace Industries Association of America
Aerospace Medical Association
Agricultural History Society
Air Force Association
Air Force Sergeants Association
Air Lines Pilots Association
Air Pollution Control Association
Aircraft Owners and Pilots Association
Alcoholics Anonymous
Altrusa International
Aluminum Association
American Amputation Foundation
American Anthropological Association
American Federation of Labor and Congress of Industrial Organizations
American Latvian Association
American Legion Auxiliary
American Medical Association

A recent issue of *The World Almanac* listed over a thousand such groups, even though it omitted most religious groups, labor unions, and political parties.[20]

Community specialization is also common in industrial societies with the production of automobiles, textiles, tobacco, recreation, educational services, or governmental services, to name a few, often concentrated in a single city or group of cities. We find specialization even at the national level. In a world dominated by advanced industrial societies, some countries concentrate on oil, others on rubber, coffee, sugar, or manufactured goods. Were the world not still divided into autonomous nation-states that are concerned with maintaining balanced economies, this tendency would be even more pronounced, for greater national specialization is technically feasible and, from an international standpoint, would certainly be more profitable.

Increased Social Interaction: Advances in Transportation and Communication

The amount of social interaction in a modern industrial society would stagger the imagination of the members of simpler societies. To a large extent, this unprecedented level of interpersonal contact is the natural result of increasing urbanization: communities are larger, people live closer together, and increased contact is inevitable. Industrialization also has an effect: home is now the workplace of only a small minority of men; children spend half their days in crowded schools; and women are increasingly drawn outside the home by paid employment, as well as a variety of other responsibilities and opportunities.

---

[20] *The World Almanac, 1970*, pp. 691–705.

The revolutionary advances in communication and transportation have played a major role in breaking down former barriers to social contact. Political leaders often travel over 100,000 miles in a single year (Democratic presidential candidate George McGovern traveled 200,000 miles during the 1972 campaign). Ordinary citizens, too, travel more than ever before: Americans have recently been averaging *at least* 7,000 to 10,000 miles every year.[21] In addition to the contacts resulting from all this movement, hundreds of millions more are made daily by telephone and mail. On a typical day in the United States, there are currently 500 million telephone conversations and more than 200 million communications by mail.[22]

The mass media have opened up yet another avenue of interaction. Moreover, they reach even people whose other contacts are limited by lack of transportation, poor health, or geographical isolation. Although the flow of communication is in only one direction, and the image at best only two-dimensional, the impact is tremendous. This was strikingly illustrated at the time of President Kennedy's assassination: millions of people all over the world watched the television coverage of ensuing events, many of them weeping openly and later reporting that they had experienced a depth of involvement and a sense of loss comparable to what they felt after a death in their own family.

One consequence of the growth of social interaction has been the steady erosion of *localism* and *local subcultures*. Local dialects and customs, so marked in agrarian societies, and local loyalties are being replaced by national norms and national loyalties. From the standpoint of cultural diversity, this is a great loss, as evidenced by the tiresome similarity of most American cities and towns.

A more serious consequence of the rise of the mass media has been the increased opportunity for tiny elites to manipulate people's thinking. This problem is especially critical with television and movies, for not only are they the most vivid and dramatic of the media, they also appeal disproportionately to that part of the population with the fewest alternative sources of information. What is more, the impact of the audiovisual media is such that it is easy for the uncritical, unsophisticated viewer to come away believing he has been an eyewitness to events, when, in fact, he was exposed to a severely limited, or even badly distorted, representation. During peace demonstrations in the 1960s, for example, camera crews often zeroed in on the most unkempt and unattractive participants, with the result that many viewers were sure they knew precisely the type of person who was questioning America's involvement in Vietnam.

Where television and the press are operated as commercial enterprises, there is a natural tendency for them to focus on the bizarre, the dramatic, and the startling, since this ensures larger audiences and larger audi-

---

[21] This estimate is based on reports of automobile and air transportation. These show that *intercity* traffic alone averaged nearly 5,000 miles per person per year. See *Statistical Abstract, 1972*, table 874.

[22] *Statistical Abstract, 1971* tables 751 and 759.

ences ensure higher profits. Thus, exciting but trivial events usually receive far more coverage than much more important events conducted in a lower key. In politics, for example, personalities are likely to be featured, issues played down.

When the mass media are operated by governments, deliberate attempts to manipulate public thinking are even more frequent. One-party states in particular are notorious for introducing distortions, though French experience demonstrates that the problem can also arise in multiparty states. Though the desire to change other people's thinking and persuade them to new ideas is neither new nor inherently bad, there is real reason for concern when a few individuals can so directly and so subtly influence the minds of so many.

THE ECONOMY

Urbanization of Production

In agrarian societies, productive activities were centered in the rural villages, agriculture was the dominant industry, and farmers were a substantial majority of the labor force. In addition to farming, the rural population often engaged in a variety of crafts during the off-season, welcoming the chance to supplement their meager incomes. Urban populations were small, and many urban residents, leisured members of the governing class, were not gainfully employed, while those who were, often produced nonessential or luxury goods and services for the upper classes.

The Industrial Revolution changed all this. As we saw in the last chapter, the new machines that were invented required factories and large concentrations of people living nearby. While the new industries generated a growing demand for workers in the cities and towns, advances in agriculture reduced the need for farm workers. And so, before the end of the eighteenth century, there began that massive migration which only now shows signs of having run its course.

Today, in the more advanced industrial societies, the historic distribution of population has been reversed. Whereas less than 10 per cent of the people in agrarian societies lived in urban areas, 90 per cent or more of the people in advanced industrial societies do so. Yet even that dramatic comparison understates the difference, for the city dwellers of modern industrial societies are much more urban than the city dwellers and townspeople of the agrarian era. Their communities, of course, are much larger on the average (e.g., more than one-third of the American population now lives in communities of 1 million or more and more than two-thirds in communities of 50,000 or more).[23] But it is

---

[23] *Statistical Abstract, 1971,* table 16, and *The World Almanac, 1972,* p. 154. The figures cited refer to Standard Metropolitan Areas.

Figure 11.5 The city dwellers of modern industrial societies are much more urban than the city dwellers and townspeople of the agrarian era: view southwest from the top of the RCA Building, New York City.

more than that: they are much further removed culturally from the historic rural way of life. For example, during harvests city dwellers of the agrarian era often suspended their activities to go work in the fields.[24] In industrial societies today, that would be inconceivable.

Rural life, too, has been transformed far beyond anything the simple statistical reversal could indicate. One sign of this is the fact that since 1970 American farmers have earned more from *non*farm activities than from selling

[24] S. B. Clough and C. W. Cole, *Economic History of Europe* (Boston: Heath, 1941), p. 48, or G. G. Coulton, *Medieval Panorama* (New York: Meridian Books, 1955, first published 1938), pp. 282ff.

Figure 11.6 The traditional family farm is a dead or dying institution in most industrial societies: harvesting wheat in North Dakota.

crops, livestock, and other products.[25] Only about one farmer in three reports that he derives more than half of his income from farm activities. Similar trends are being reported in other countries.[26]

The traditional family farm is a dead or dying institution in most industrial societies. In the Soviet Union and in most East European societies, it was eliminated fairly quickly by government edict and replaced with large agricultural cooperatives and state farms. In most other industrial societies, the process has been more gradual and market forces have been primarily responsible for the demise of this institution. In both cases, however, the underlying cause has been the technological revolution, which has made large, highly mechanized farms much more efficient and productive than small, traditional ones. Today, in the United States, for example, a single diesel tractor may cost as much as $40,000, while the total investment in land and buildings required for a profitable farm is well over $100,000 in most areas.[27] Unable to raise this kind of capital (and the need for new capital is continuous, since not only must

[25] AP wire-service story in *Raleigh News and Observer*, Aug. 7, 1972, p. 27.

[26] See, for example, Daniel Chirot, "Sociology in Romania: Review of Recent Works," *Social Forces*, 51 (1972), pp. 100–101.

[27] Edward Higbee, *Farms and Farmers in an Urban Age* (New York: Twentieth Century Fund, 1963), pp. 10 and 54 and tables 1 and 13, His figures have been adjusted upward to allow for the inflation of the last decade.

equipment be replaced but the acreage needed to break even keeps rising), most farm families have been forced to sell out. Their places are increasingly taken by agrobusinesses—highly capitalized and mechanized, even automated, corporate enterprises run by salaried managers and employing wage labor.

Changing Patterns of Employment

The decline in the farm population is only part of the massive shift in employment patterns that accompanies industrialization. In traditional preindustrial societies, as we have seen, the vast majority of people are employed in what are known as *primary industries,* those which produce raw materials (such as farming) or extract them (such as mining). Then, in the early stages of industrialization, there is a rather rapid shift of manpower to *secondary industries,* which process the raw materials and turn out finished products, and to *tertiary industries,* which perform services (such as retail trade, education, government). As industrialization progresses, the secondary industries grow less rapidly and may even decline somewhat in relative numbers, while the service industries continue their rapid growth.

We can observe this pattern within the labor force of a single industrializing nation, or we can view it comparatively, using data from societies at different stages of industrialization. Table 11.3 compares five nations that range from Thailand, just beginning the process, to the United States, the most advanced, and illustrates how the percentage of the labor force in primary industries steadily declines. The percentage in secondary industries, namely manufacturing and construction, rises sharply up to the point of industrialization represented by Spain, then stabilizes or even declines slightly. By contrast, the percentage in service industries shows a steady and continuing increase.

Table 11.3   Distribution of labor force among industrial categories for five nations (in percentages)

Society	Primary Industries*	Secondary Industries†	Tertiary Industries‡	Total
United States	4.9	31.6	63.5	100.0
Japan	19.5	33.1	47.4	100.0
Spain	30.1	35.6	34.3	100.0
Mexico	55.4	17.3	27.3	100.0
Thailand	82.2	3.9	13.9	100.0

Source: International Labour Office, *Yearbook of Labour Statistics, 1971,* table 2a.

* Agriculture, fishing, forestry, mining, quarrying, hunting.

† Manufacturing, construction.

‡ All other industrial classifications.

The Rise of Market Economies

In *The Making of Economic Society,* Robert Heilbroner writes:

> Looking not only over the diversity of contemporary societies, but back over the sweep of all history, [the economist] sees that man has succeeded in solving the production and distribution problems in but three ways. That is, within the enormous diversity of actual social institutions which guide and shape the economic process, the economist divines but three overarching *types* of systems which separately or in combination enable humankind to solve its economic challenge. These three great systemic types can be called economies run by Tradition, economies run by Command, and economies run by the Market.[28]

In a traditional economy, the basic questions of production and distribution—what shall be produced? in what quantities? and for whose benefit?—are answered by simply continuing to do things as they were done previously. In a command economy, the opinions and values of those who control the government provide the answers. In a market economy, the basic economic decisions are made through a complex interaction of the forces of supply and demand, reflecting the opinions and values of all the individuals and organizations in the society, *but in proportion to their wealth.*

The economies of most societies are actually a complex blend of all three of these elements, but the majority of modern industrial societies are unique by virtue of the strength and importance of the market element. Prior to the Industrial Revolution there was no society with what could properly be called a *market economy*—that is, an economy in which the basic problems of production and distribution were settled primarily by the free play of market forces.[29]

Several conditions must exist before there can be a true market economy.[30] To begin with, the economy must be monetized: money must become a pervasive element in the daily life of every member of society, and most of the goods and services people value must be available for a price. Further, land, labor, and capital must be mobile; traditional restraints on their use or transfer have to be eliminated. People must be free to sell ancestral lands if that is profitable; workers must be free to leave their jobs and take new ones if they can get higher wages; and businessmen must be free to use their capital

---

[28] Robert Heilbroner, *The Making of Economic Society* (Englewood Cliffs, N.J.: Prentice-Hall, 1962), p. 9. Quoted by permission of Prentice-Hall.

[29] See, for example, Karl Polanyi's statement that "previously to our own time no economy has ever existed that, even in principle, was controlled by markets. . . . Though the institution of the market was fairly common since the later Stone Age, its role was no more than incidental to economic life." From *The Great Transformation: The Political and Economic Origins of our Time* (Boston: Beacon Press, 1957), p. 43. Maritime societies may have been an exception to this assertion, but unfortunately we lack the data to test the possibility.

[30] Heilbroner, pp. 42–44 and 64–65.

however they wish. Restraints on economic activity based on family sentiments, religious taboos, social customs, or organizational restrictions (guild restrictions on output, for example, or legal restrictions on the migration of serfs and slaves) must be minimal. In short, individual economic advantage, as measured in monetary terms, must become the decisive determinant of economic action.

As we have seen, the discovery of the New World gave a powerful impetus to the first requirement: the great flow of bullion from the Spanish colonies increased the supply of precious metals in Western Europe severalfold. At the same time, the Protestant Reformation and the ideological changes that followed it, such as eighteenth-century deism and the Enlightenment, weakened traditional social bonds that had immobilized both men and property. These same factors also sparked the Industrial Revolution. Once that was under way and the economy had begun to change, the effect tended to be cumulative. Each change stimulated further change; the more resources that came under the control of Western Europe's entrepreneurial class, for example, the better they were able to promote further change.

By the end of the nineteenth century, it looked as if every industrial society would soon have a largely market economy. Industrial societies were coming increasingly under the control of political parties dominated by businessmen committed to the philosophy of laissez faire capitalism or free enterprise. Following the teachings of Adam Smith, the pioneer economist, this new governing class argued that the most productive economy, and the most beneficial, was one that was entirely free of governmental restrictions. The only role government should play in society's economic life, according to these men, was the role of policeman to ensure the fulfillment of contracts. They were firm believers in the principle that "that government governs best which governs least."

Shift toward a Mixed Market-Command Economy

It was not long, however, before it became evident that the new market economy was not the unmitigated blessing its enthusiasts made it out to be. In the pursuit of profits, businessmen adopted practices that were obviously harmful to others. In an attempt to cut labor costs, many employers fired adult workers and replaced them with children, simultaneously creating adult unemployment and endangering the health and safety of children. In other instances, efforts to reduce costs resulted in dangerous working conditions and the production of shoddy, even unsafe, merchandise.

Protests soon began to be raised, sometimes by social reformers like Robert Owen, sometimes by poets and novelists like Thomas Hood and Upton Sinclair. Even before the middle of the last century, the British Parliament began enacting legislation to protect society against the extremes of free enterprise. The Factory Acts of 1833 and 1844, the Mines Act of 1842, and the Ten

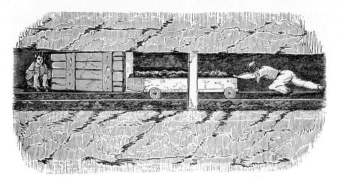

Figure 11.7 The Mines Act of 1842 prohibited the employment of boys under the age of ten in mines.

Hour Law of 1847 prohibited the employment of children under the age of nine in textile factories restricted children under thirteen to six and a half hours' work per day in factories, forbade the employment of women or of boys under ten in the mines, limited women and young people aged thirteen to eighteen to ten working hours per day, and provided for inspectors to enforce these laws.[31] By 1901, the minimum age for child labor in England was raised to twelve, and in 1908 limitations were finally imposed on the working hours of men. Other legislation forced employers to provide for the safety of their employees in dangerous industries and established the first minimum wage. In Germany under Bismarck, new laws provided for sick leave and for workmen's compensation in the case of injuries sustained on the job. The crowning achievement of German legislation in this period was the Old Age and Security Law of 1889.

Before the end of the century, another major defect in the market system became evident: its tendency to lose its competitive character and evolve in the direction of monopolistic enterprise. This danger was especially apparent in industries where fixed costs were a significant part of total costs (see page 323). A large company, because it could spread its fixed costs over a larger volume of sales than its competitors could, was thus in a position either to undersell them or to match their price but offer a superior product. Either way, the larger company would gradually win its rivals' customers, further increasing its advantage. Were market forces allowed to operate without any restriction, smaller competitors would eventually be driven out of business.

In some instances, monopolies seemed preferable to competition. In the telephone industry, for example, rival firms operating within the same territory would complicate communications and increase costs. In a number of other industries—public utilities—a monopoly or, at most, limited competition seemed preferable to free enterprise and an unregulated market system. Such monopolies could not be permitted, however, to set their own prices and conditions of service: governmental controls were imperative. Thus, beginning in the nineteenth century, local, state, and national governments established regulative agencies. In the United States, the first such agency at the national level

---

[31] Clough and Cole, pp. 693–698.

was the Interstate Commerce Commission, established in 1887 to regulate the operation of the railroads.

In most industries, however, monopolies were considered undesirable in the United States. Congress passed the Sherman Antitrust Act in 1890 to prevent their formation. Although it has not been very vigorously enforced, this Act has served as a deterrent. A number of industries might now be dominated by a single company had not the managers of the leading firms been fearful of the legal consequences. For example, economists have testified before Congress that economies of scale have long made it possible for General Motors to substantially undersell all its competitors. But rather than face anti-trust action, its managers have chosen to price their cars competitively, offering, perhaps, a bit more for the money and taking advantage of the situation primarily through higher profits.

The situation in which a market is dominated by a very few sellers—known as oligopoly—is a common occurrence both in this country and abroad. Table 11.4 gives some indication of the current situation here. As a rough rule of thumb, economists consider an industry oligopolistic when as few as four companies control 50 per cent or more of production.[32] This standard

Table 11.4 Percentage of production accounted for by the four largest companies in selected industries in the United States, 1967

Industry	Percentage	Industry	Percentage
Motor vehicles	92	Radio and TV receivers	49
Steam engines	88	Steel mills	48
Cereal preparation	88	Metal office furniture	38
Chewing gum	86	Petroleum refining	33
Typewriters	81	Textile machinery	31
Cigarettes	81	Flour products	30
Woven carpets	76	Weaving mills	30
Metal cans	73	Meat packing	26
Home refrigerators	73	Mattresses and bedsprings	26
Tires	70	Pharmaceuticals	24
Soap and detergents	70	Frozen fruits and vegetables	24
Aircraft	69	Fluid milk	22
Explosives	67	Paints	22
Thread mills	62	Dolls	19
Synthetic rubber	61	Newspapers	16
Cookies and crackers	59	Soft drinks	13
Phonograph records	58	Wooden home furniture	12
Distilled liquor	54	Women's dresses	7
Roasted coffee	53	Fur goods	5

Source: U.S. Bureau of the Census, *Census of Manufacturers, 1967* (Washington: 1971), vol. 1, chap. 9, table 5.

[32] G. Warren Nutter, "Industrial Concentration," in *International Encyclopedia of the Social Sciences* (New York: Macmillan and Free Press, 1968), vol. 7, p. 221. Senator Philip Hart of Michigan introduced a new antitrust bill in the U.S. Senate in 1972 that used the "four companies–50 per cent of sales" criterion as one of three indicators of "monopoly power." See *The Washington Post*, July 23, 1972, p. A-8.

can be deceptive, however, because degree of national concentration means different things in different industries, depending chiefly on whether the market is local, regional, or national. The newspaper industry, for example, might appear highly competitive, because according to government statistics the four largest companies produce only 16 per cent of the papers. But a moment's reflection reminds us that most newspapers produce for a local market, and in most of our communities, over 90 percent of them in fact, the paper or papers are owned by a single person or firm.[33] Thus Table 11.4 understates the extent of oligopoly in this country.

Where oligopoly prevails, the law of supply and demand often stops functioning, primarily because collusion between firms is so easy. Collusion can take a variety of forms. A fairly common practice in the construction industry is the rigging of bids, whereby firms get together and decide among themselves which one will take which job and then bid accordingly, with the "low" bid set as high as they dare. Price leading, a perfectly legal practice, appears to be standard procedure in several major industries: one firm, usually the largest, sets its prices at a level that ensures profits for all and maximum profits for the larger firms. In this situation, competition is largely restricted to such secondary matters as design and advertising.

Another development that has weakened the role of market forces has been the increase in what is commonly known as vertical integration, the process by which a company gets control of companies in other industries that either supply it with materials or buy its products.[34] A furniture manufacturer, for example, might buy up a number of lumber companies and sawmills to provide his raw materials and then buy into retail establishments that handle the furniture he turns out. In this way, he eliminates a lot of the uncertainties of the market situation. Another device with a similar purpose is to establish interlocking directorates, which bring the top officials or directors of a company on which one depends for some essential commodity or service onto the controlling board of one's own company. This device is widely used to bring officers of financial institutions on the boards of firms that require ready access to large amounts of capital.[35]

Finally, the market system has been weakened by the changing nature of warfare. World War II demonstrated beyond any doubt that success in all-out modern war requires the mobilization of all of a nation's economic resources.[36] Obviously this effort cannot begin with the outbreak of hostilities: it must be

---

[33] Ben Bagdikian, "Why Newspapers Keep Dying," *The Washington Post*, July 23, 1972, p. B-5.

[34] John Kenneth Galbraith, *The New Industrial State* (New York: Signet Books, 1968), pp. 38–39.

[35] Peter C. Dooley, "The Interlocking Directorates," *American Economic Review*, 59 (1969), pp. 314–323.

[36] See, for example, Donald M. Nelson, *Arsenal of Democracy* (New York: Harcourt, Brace, 1946), or Albert Speer, *Inside the Third Reich* (New York: Avon, 1970), parts II and III.

planned and implemented far in advance. In societies that wish to maintain a strong military position, this inevitably leads to the development of a military-industrial complex from which most of the elements of free enterprise are eliminated. For one thing, there is only one buyer for the product, the government. Often there is only one producer as well, and seldom more than a handful, for a particular weapons system. The situation is prejudicial to an open market in yet another way: the military is disinclined to shop around for bargains ("more bang for the buck"), both because this increases security risks and because truly competitive bidding might cause companies to cut corners and turn out defective products. So long as the military has the taxing power of the government behind it, it has little motivation to economize. Finally, when major weapons systems are involved, there are usually few companies in a society that have both the equipment and the engineering skills required. Thus, there is a natural tendency for market forces to be replaced by the principles of command in the vast and important area of military procurement, even in a society whose leaders constantly affirm their commitment to the principles of free enterprise.

We could summarize most of the foregoing by saying that the last two hundred years have revealed three basic flaws in the market mechanism. First, not only does it fail to protect the weaker and more vulnerable members of society, such as the industrial worker and the consumer, but it compels the strong to act ruthlessly if they wish to remain strong. Second, the market system has what might be called a built-in self-destruct element, which causes most free competitive markets to evolve into monopolistic markets unless checked by governmental intervention. (Marx saw this more than a century ago when he argued that capitalism contains the seeds of its own destruction.) Finally, the market system cannot respond adequately to the *corporate* needs of society, as contrasted with the needs and desires of individuals.

This final weakness is particularly evident during societal crises, such as wars, depressions, or the current environmental crisis. As long as individuals and organizations are free to act according to what they perceive as their own best interests, the more short-sighted tend to win out. Corporations that respond to the environmental problem by installing expensive antipollution devices, for example, will find themselves at a disadvantage in competition with firms that do not.

For a variety of reasons, then, even those societies whose members are ideologically most committed to free enterprise have been backing away from the market system. Public rhetoric to the contrary, the economies of these societies can now be described only as a highly complex mixture of market and command economies. And if we can judge from recent trends (see, for example, Table 11.5), the command component of these economies will probably continue to gain at the expense of the market component. There seems little danger, however, that the market component will disappear altogether: the

Table 11.5   Trends in corporate economic concentration, United States and Sweden

	Percentage Share of Total Value Added	
United States	1947	1967
50 largest companies	17	25
200 largest companies	30	42
	Percentage of Industrial Employment	
Sweden	1942	1964
50 largest companies	16	21
200 largest companies	25	32

Sources: U.S. Bureau of the Census, *Census of Manufacturing, 1967* (1971), vol. 1, chap. 9, table 1; Swedish Finance Department, State Public Investigations (SOU), *Ägande och inflytande inom det privata näringslivet: Koncentrationsultredningen, V* [Ownership and influence in the private sector of the economy] (Stockholm, 1968.,) p. 7.

experience of the socialist societies of Eastern Europe suggest that this would not be a rewarding alternative.

Economic Trends in Eastern Europe

In societies controlled by Fascist or Communist regimes, market forces have usually been relegated to a very secondary position.[37] This is only what we would expect, given the strong ideological and programmatic commitments of these parties. Guided by a vision of a "better" society, their leaders have sought to mobilize all their nations' resources to achieve their goals. Since they could never persuade everyone to accept their program voluntarily, they have had to rely on the techniques of command, which has meant, in effect, a planned economy. The succession of Five-Year Plans adopted by the Soviet Union is a classic example of this.

In recent years Communist leaders have become increasingly aware of the limitations inherent in this type of economic system. First in Yugoslavia, then in the Soviet Union, and later throughout all Eastern Europe, elements of the market system were reintroduced into areas of the economy from which they had been excluded for years.[38] The reason for this reversal seems to have been the inefficiencies of centralized planning. To be really effective, economic planning must take account not only of all the thousands of commodities produced but also of all the interrelations among them, since the production of one commodity is always contingent on the availability of many others. One Soviet economist is reported to have argued that a sound plan for the Soviet machine

---

[37] For a good discussion of the economy in Nazi Germany, see Franz Neumann, *Behemoth: The Structure and Practice of National Socialism* (New York: Oxford, 1942), part II.

[38] See, for example, Alec Nove, *The Soviet Economy*, rev. ed. (New York: Praeger, 1966), especially chap. 9; Harry G. Shaffer, *The Communist World: Marxist and Non-Marxist Views* (New York: Appleton Century Crofts, 1967), pp. 226ff.; or Erik de Mauny, *Russian Prospect* (New York: Atheneum, 1970), chap. 4.

industry alone would require provision for more than 15 billion interrelations.[39] Because it is impossible to coordinate successfully such a fantastic number of relationships, shortages have repeatedly developed in some commodities, surpluses in others.

The great virtue of the market system is its automatic mechanism for balancing supply and demand. When the demand for a product goes up, so does the price, giving producers an incentive to turn out more of it. Conversely, a slump in the demand for something lowers prices and reduces incentives. All this is accomplished without costly centralized planning.

Until recently, the market system was so identified with capitalism that it was unthinkable for Soviet leaders. In the last decade, however, Soviet economists have shown that the market mechanism is not necessarily linked with private enterprise and that its reintroduction into socialist economies would not stimulate a revival of capitalism. With this point clarified and with the more pragmatic orientation of the new generation of Soviet leaders, the way was cleared for experimentation. This experimentation has been successful enough that nearly all the socialist nations in Eastern Europe are now employing market mechanisms to some degree.

The introduction of market mechanisms into socialist economies suggests that in the future there may well be less variation in this important aspect of industrial societies than there has been in the past.[40] Both socialist and nonsocialist societies are moving toward a more balanced type of economy, in which both market and command will play important roles. Market forces will be used to achieve greater efficiency, while command will be used to protect the corporate interests of society and to limit the degree of social inequality. This is not to say, of course, that differences between economic systems will be eliminated (East European socialist governments seem determined to prevent the reestablishment of privately owned enterprises, for one thing), but they will probably be reduced.[41]

New Types of Economic Organizations

The economies of agrarian and maritime societies were usually organized around three types of units—family enterprises, guilds, and state enterprises. Of these, only state enterprises play a major role in modern industrial societies. Guilds have banished entirely and family enterprises have declined to the point

---

[39] Joseph Alsop, "Matter of Fact," *The Washington Post*, Jan. 13, 1964.

[40] Many Soviet scholars feel that American social scientists try to blur the differences. For a good statement of their view, see Alex Simirenko (ed.), *Soviet Sociology: Historical Antecedents and Current Appraisals* (*Chicago: Quadrangle, 1966*), *pp. 327–339.*

[41] See, for example, Jean Marchal and Bernard Ducros (eds.), *The Distribution of National Incomes: Proceedings of a Conference held by the International Economic Association* (London: Macmillan, 1968), pp. xiii–xiv and 274.

where they play at best a secondary role and in some nations not even that. In their stead, a number of new kinds of organizations have emerged, among them corporations, cooperatives, labor unions, and professional and industrial associations. These, together with state enterprises, constitute the major economic units in industrial societies.

Corporations The modern business corporation easily ranks as one of the most important inventions of modern times, and, like many major innovations, it evolved gradually. Its origins go back to the middle of the sixteenth century, when English and Dutch merchants, trading with remote areas, banded together in what came to be known as joint stock companies.[42] This form of organization had several advantages over family enterprises and partnerships. Above all, it permitted people to pool capital, thus spreading their risks. This was extremely important in ventures where risks were great and large investments essential. In addition, a joint stock company, unlike a family enterprise or a partnership, was not disrupted by the death of one of the owners. Either his heirs inherited his stock, or, if they wanted to get the money out of the enterprise, they could sell the stock to someone else. This was not possible in a partnership, since the law required (as it still does) that if one of the partners died or wished to withdraw, the partnership had to be dissolved and the assets distributed.

During the next several centuries, the joint stock company, or corporation, gradually spread to new fields of enterprise. More important, a series of changes made this form of organization safer and more attractive to investors. For one thing, the development of preferred stock (i.e., shares that had first claim on profits and assets in the case of bankruptcy) provided a safer form of investment, and the organization of stock markets facilitated the exchange of stock. Most important of all, however, was the adoption of the principle of limited liability. Prior to the nineteenth century, stockholders in most corporations, like owners of family businesses and members of partnerships, had unlimited liability in case of bankruptcy. This meant that they stood to lose not only their investment in the company but all their other possessions as well if these were needed to satisfy the claims of creditors. This naturally made investors extremely cautious; unless they had firsthand knowledge of a business and those running it, they were taking a great risk. The passage of laws limiting the liability of stockholders to the investment itself greatly stimulated the flow of capital into this new form of enterprise.

In today's industrial societies, nearly all the largest and most powerful private enterprises are organized as corporations. In the United States in 1969, for example, 83 per cent of all business was done by corporations, and among

---

[42] See, for example, Clough and Cole, *Economic History of Europe,* pp. 148ff. See also Edward S. Mason, "Corporation," in *International Encyclopedia of the Social Sciences,* vol. 3, pp. 396–403.

larger concerns (i.e., those with annual receipts of $500,000 or more), they accounted for 96 per cent of the total.[43] The very largest concerns, those with annual profits in the hundreds of millions or billions of dollars, are all corporations. At the present time, privately owned corporate assets constitute more than 70 per cent of this nation's wealth.[44] A single firm, American Telephone and Telegraph, has assets totaling $50 billion, and General Motors has had receipts averaging over $20 billion annually since 1965. AT & T has more than 3 million shareholders, GM more than 1.3 million.[45]

As corporations have grown, their character has changed substantially. Most important, control of the largest ones has been slipping from the owners to the top managers.[46] As one observer recently put it, "Almost everyone now agrees . . . that, typically, control is in the hands of management; and that management normally selects its own replacements."[47] The chief cause of this shift is the fragmentation of stock ownership, an almost inevitable by-product of enormous corporate growth. In AT & T for example, no single person owns as much as 1 per cent of the stock, and most own only a minute fraction of 1 per cent. Furthermore, the stockholders are scattered around the world. Mobilizing a majority of the voting stock to wrest control from the managers would be extremely difficult.

The growing power of managers in industry is part of a larger trend in modern societies. In government, education, religion, labor, and other areas as well, organizations have become so large, and administrative problems so complex, that those who constitutionally hold ultimate power (e.g., the voters, stockholders, trustees, or members) cannot possibly exercise more than the most limited control over the administrators and managers.[48] Under the circumstances, most of the responsibility for day-to-day decisions gravitates into the hands of the latter.

---

[43] Calculated from *Statistical Abstract, 1972,* table 747.

[44] Calculations based on data for 1968 in ibid., tables 553 and 762.

[45] *Moody's Public Utility Manual, 1971,* pp. 1080 and 1086, and *Moody's Industrial Manual, 1971,* pp. 2625 and 2627.

[46] See A. A. Berle, Jr., and Gardner Means, *The Modern Corporation and Private Property* (New York: Macmillan, 1932), especially book 1, or Robert A. Gordon, *Business Leadership in the Large Corporation* (Berkeley: University of California Press, 1961), on American corporations. For the trend in Europe, see P. Sargant Florence, *Ownership, Control, and Success of Large Companies: An Analysis of English Industrial Structure and Policy, 1936–1951* (London: Street and Maxwell, 1961), or David Granick, *The European Executive* (Garden City, N.Y.: Doubleday Anchor, 1964).

[47] E. S. Mason (ed.), *The Corporation and Modern Society* (Cambridge, Mass.: Harvard, 1959), p. 4.

[48] For a classic statement of the problem, see Robert Michels, *Political Parties: A Sociological Study of the Oligarchical Tendencies of Modern Democracy,* translated by Eden Paul and Cedar Paul New York: Dover, 1959, first published in 1915). Michels's study is of special interest because he focused on the Socialist parties of Western Europe, which had an intense commitment to democratic principles; yet, as he demonstrates, even they could not avoid the development of an administrative oligarchy in their own organizations.

Labor unions   One of the most striking differences between agrarian and industrial societies is the development of organizations designed to advance the interests of the common people. The two most obvious examples are working-class political parties and labor unions.

The origins of modern labor unions can be traced back to the latter part of the eighteenth century, when small groups of workingmen, in both England and the United States, banded together to negotiate with their employers on wages, hours, and working conditions. During the nineteenth century the movement had many ups and downs, but over the long run the gains outweighed the losses. Laws forbidding union organization and strikes were gradually repealed and more stable organizations established, until, by 1900, there were 2 million union members in Britain and nearly a million each in the United States and Germany.

Today, labor unions claim approximately 20 million members in the United States; and union-backed political parties hold office, or have held or shared office, in Britain, Scandinavia, the Low Countries, France, Italy, Austria, the United States, and Australia. In English-speaking nations, unions have been the dominant force in the workingmen's movement, and labor parties have grown out of them; on the Continent, the reverse has been true.

As corporations have grown in size, so have unions: the United Auto Workers, for example, currently has about 1.5 million members. Size is essential in bargaining with corporate giants like General Motors, whose profits in one recent year were more than $2 billion.

With their growth in size and power, and with their increasing respectability, labor unions have lost a lot of their former idealistic and reformist fervor. Under the leadership of often elderly administrators and bureaucrats, they tend to play a rather cautious and conservative role, both economically and politically. Many of them now see their chief task as simply maximizing the wages of their own members, thus assuring them a larger share of the benefits of an affluent society.

The function of labor unions in one-party societies has been quite different from what it is in democratic nations.[49] In both communist and fascist nations, unions have been used by the dominant party as an instrument of social control. In theory, the unions are instruments of the workers, in practice, largely instruments of the Party and the governing elites. Recently there have been some indications that unions may play a more independent role in the future, but so far this is more promise than reality.

---

[49] See, for example, Emily Clark Brown, *Soviet Trade Unions and Labor Relations* (Cambridge, Mass.: Harvard, 1966), or Roy Medvedev, *Let History Judge: The Origins and Consequences of Stalinism*, translated by Colleen Taylor and edited by David Joravsky and Georges Haupt (New York: Knopf, 1971), p. 534.

Professional associations   Another new form of economic organization is the professional association. With increasing frequency, professional people (e.g., doctors, lawyers, teachers, chemists, accountants, architects, etc.) have organized into associations ostensibly designed to ensure high standards of performance in their fields but, in practice, functioning largely to advance their economic and other interests. The most publicized, and most controversial, of these organizations in the United States has been the American Medical Association. As a result of its aggressive efforts, the medical profession has become the most lucrative single occupation in the country. In one-party nations, these associations, like unions, are primarily instruments of the Party, though the fact that professionals need long training, and are thus hard to replace, has sometimes made their organizations more difficult for the Party to control and manipulate.

Cooperatives   A fourth important organizational innovation is the cooperative. Its development is related to that of socialism and trade unionism. It, too, grew out of the efforts of workingmen to improve their situation.

In its earliest stages, leaders of the cooperative movement tried to establish cooperative communities, like the one Robert Owen founded in New Harmony, Indiana, in the 1820s. Very soon, however, the energies of the movement were channeled into consumers' and producers' cooperatives. Consumers' cooperatives were retail stores owned by groups of consumers, with the profits either shared by the members or turned back into the movement to help establish other cooperative ventures. Producers' cooperatives were associations of craftsmen or farmers who banded together, formed their own busi-

Figure 11.8   Cooperative housing development, Sweden.

Figure 11.9 Collective farm workers in the Ukraine.

nesses in competition with privately owned enterprises, and shared the profits among themselves.

In many industrial societies, including the United States, the cooperative movement has had only limited success, with cooperatives accounting for no more than a small percentage of the total volume of business in any industry except agriculture. This is not the situation everywhere, however. In Scandinavia in particular, cooperatives are an important element in the economy: at least a third of the wage-earners in these countries belong to a cooperative, with the ratio highest in Denmark.[50] Farmers' cooperatives have been an important element in the Danish economy since the latter half of the nineteenth century, with nine-tenths of the farm population organized into one large cooperative by 1939. In recent years, Sweden's cooperatives have controlled much of her agricultural production and urban housing, a third of her retail trade, and a tenth of her wholesale trade and nonfarm production. In general, cooperatives have been most successful in agriculture, housing, and retail and wholesale trade—industries whose capital requirements are not so great as in, say, manu-

---

[50] J. Frederic Dewhurst et al., *Europe's Needs and Resources: Trends and Prospects in Eighteen Countries* (New York: Twentieth Century Fund, 1961), p. 754. See also Marquis W. Childs, *Sweden: The Middle Way*, rev. ed. (New Haven, Conn.: Yale, 1947).

facturing, and in which small enterprises are not at such a serious competitive disadvantage.

Cooperatives have also found a place in the economies of East European nations. In the Soviet Union they have functioned primarily as a transitional arrangement during the shift from private to state enterprise, especially in agriculture, where collective farms, a form of cooperative, have played a major role for a long time.[51] Even as recently as 1965, cooperatives still produced 42 per cent of the nation's farm products.[52]

Over the years, state enterprises have grown so, at the expense of cooperatives, that one could almost predict the eventual elimination of cooperatives in East Europe. But this may be premature, in view of the efforts of these nations to decentralize their economies and move toward a mixed market-command system. Cooperatives could become a valuable kind of organization under these circumstances. We should add that the experiments of the Yugoslavs, economically as well as politically often the pioneers of Eastern Europe, point in this direction. By allowing workers a voice in plant policy and a share in plant profits, they have adopted the principle, if not the name, of the cooperative mode of organization.

Continuing Forms of Organization

Along with these newer kinds of economic organization, certain older ones have managed to survive and, sometimes, to flourish. These include the family-owned enterprise, which survives in most industrial societies, even in some of the East European nations. In Poland and Yugoslavia, for example, there are still privately owned farms and small businesses, though they are hedged about with many restrictions, particularly on their size. In nonsocialist societies, family businesses operate in a wide variety of fields, though they are being crowded out by newer forms of organization, especially the corporation. Farming was the last major industry to remain predominantly under family control, but even there, as we have seen, corporations and cooperatives are taking over.[53]

An older form of organization that has fared far better is the state-operated enterprise, which for thousands of years flourished in agrarian societies and even in some advanced horticultural societies. In modern industrial societies, the role of state enterprises varies considerably. In some, notably the

---

[51] Nove, pp. 41–45. See, also, Robert C. Stuart, *The Collective Farm in Soviet Agriculture* (Lexington, Mass.: Lexington Books, 1972).

[52] Philip Raup, "Some Consequences of Data Deficiencies in Soviet Agriculture," in Vladimir Treml and John Hardt (eds.), *Soviet Economic Statistics* (Durham, N. C.: Duke, 1972), p. 265.

[53] For an excellent description and analysis of trends in American agriculture, see Higbee, *Farms and Farmers.* For a similar volume on Europe, see P. Lamartine Yates, *Food, Land and Manpower in Western Europe* (London: Macmillan, 1960).

East European nations, they are dominant. For example, state enterprises in the U.S.S.R. account for 98 or 99 per cent of nonagricultural production, and nearly half of agricultural.[54] Their role is much smaller in the United States; yet even here they operate the postal system, many electric and water companies, some bus companies, some hospitals and other health facilities, many insurance programs, most educational institutions, some housing facilities, quite a few recreational facilities, many transportation facilities (e.g., highways, ports, passenger trains, etc.), and many banking services.

West European nations stand somewhere between the United States and the East European nations with respect to the scope of state enterprises. Railroads there, for example, are 90 to 100 per cent government-owned.[55] Of the scheduled airlines in Western Europe, only Swissair is less than half government-owned, and radio and television broadcasting are entirely government enterprises in every country but the United Kingdom and Luxembourg. The state also plays a major role in Europe's electric, gas, insurance, banking, mining, iron, and steel industries and, in some countries, in the automobile, chemical, and machine-tool industries as well.

---

[54] Nove, pp. 28–29.

[55] This and the following statements are based on Dewhurst et al., *Europe's Needs and Resources,* pp. 436–440.

CHAPTER TWELVE

Industrial Societies: Part 2

THE POLITY

The Democratic Trend

Sensitive as we are today to the undemocratic elements in the political systems of modern industrial societies, it often comes as a shock to learn that one of the more striking changes associated with the rise of industrial societies has been the growth of political democracy. Yet this is clearly the case. The agrarian societies from which most modern democratic nations evolved were, as we have seen, largely monarchical, and popular participation in political decision making was negligible. Maritime societies, although often republican, were oligarchic at best. In brief, popular involvement in political decision making in most industrial societies today, imperfect though it is, represents a substantial change from the situation in the agrarian era.

Not all industrial societies have been democratic, of course. Dictatorial regimes flourished in a number of these societies in the past, and they still exist, though somewhat modified, in Eastern Europe today.[1] Also, the government of South Africa, though moderately democratic where its white minority is concerned, denies virtually all political rights to the nonwhite majority. In addition, Britain, the Scandinavian countries, the Low Countries, and Japan retain certain monarchical trappings. But even these countries, in most instances, reflect the democratic drift that is linked with the industrialization process. In the case of the constitutional monarchies, the real power lies in the hands of democratically elected officials; kings and emperors are little more than ceremonial heads of state. As for dictatorships, some of them have been eliminated (e.g., Germany and Italy), while others have been liberalized so that a somewhat larger proportion of the population has at least a little influence in the political process (e.g., Hungary, Poland, and even, to some degree, the Soviet Union).[2] Though the level of democratic participation achieved in these nations

---

[1] Dictatorships also exist in Greece, Brazil, Spain, and a number of other countries that cannot yet be considered industrial societies.

[2] For example, in the 1967 parliamentary elections, Hungarians were permitted to choose between rival candidates for the first time since the Communist seizure of power. According to press reports, there were lively contests in many cases. Similar steps had been taken previously in Poland, and in the Soviet Union some popular participation is now permitted at the nomination stage. See John Reshetar, *The Soviet Polity* (New York: Dodd, Mead, 1971), pp. 218–225. It should also be noted that in 1971 or 1972, East Germany allowed members of its parliament to vote according to their consciences on the issue of abortion, with the result that there was a divided vote for the first time.

falls far short of what exists in most other industrial societies, the *trend* is important. In recent years, significant reversals have occurred in only two industrial societies, South Africa and Czechoslovakia, and even in these cases the prospects of an eventual resumption of the earlier trend are fairly good. Furthermore, in the case of Czechoslovakia, the reversal resulted from foreign intervention, while South Africa is a marginal industrial society with a very unusual ethnic-racial structure. Such a reversal has not occurred in a truly advanced industrial society as a result of internal developments except in Germany in the 1930s, a country struggling with a most unusual combination of problems.

In discussions of political systems, democracy is often treated in categorical, rather than variable, terms. Too often we simply say that nations are, or are not, democracies, ignoring variations in the degree of citizen participation in the political process. This is a serious mistake, for no large society has ever enjoyed pure democracy. This would mean, in effect, equal participation of every citizen in every decision—a practice that would result in utter chaos and the abandonment of every other useful activity. Even the most democratic nations achieve no more than representative democracy, a system in which most of the adult population are permitted, at infrequent intervals, to cast ballots for a limited number of candidates for public office and, between elections, to voice their support or criticism of the actions of the elected officials. Without denying the democratic elements present in such a system, it is clear that everyone does *not* have an equal voice in political decisions. Professional politicians and party functionaries always have disproportionate influence, and so, as a rule, do the wealthy who finance election campaigns and otherwise subsidize and influence elected officials.[3]

Once we recognize the impossibility of pure democracy in large organizations, it is easier to distinguish the varying degrees of democracy attained by different societies, or by a particular society at different times. The United

Table 12.1   Voters as a percentage of the British population aged twenty-one and over

1831	5.0
After First Reform Act, 1832	7.1
After Second Reform Act, 1867	16.4
After Third Reform Act, 1884	28.5
After 1918	74.0
After Equal Franchise Act, 1928	96.9

Source: Judith Ryder and Harold Silver, *Modern English Society: History and Structure, 1850–1970* (London: Methuen, 1970), p. 74.

---

[3] See, for example, Henry Ehrmann, *Organized Business in France* (Princeton, N.J.: Princeton, 1957), pp. 224ff.; V. O. Key, Jr., *Politics, Parties, and Pressure Groups,* 3d ed. (New York: Thomas Y. Crowell, 1952), especially chap. 18; or Drew Pearson and Jack Anderson, *The Case Against Congress* (New York: Simon & Schuster, 1968), especially parts II and IV.

States, for example, enjoys a much greater degree of democracy today than it did at the beginning of the nineteenth century. The elimination of property restrictions on the franchise, the direct election of senators, women's suffrage, the voting provisions in recent civil rights legislation, the "one man, one vote" decisions of the Supreme Court, the vote for eighteen-year-olds, and the McGovern Commission reforms in the Democratic Party—all these have increased either the percentage of Americans allowed to participate in the electoral process or the effectiveness of their participation. Similar trends can be observed in the recent history of other highly democratic nations, such as Britain and Sweden (see Table 12.1).[4]

Causes of the Democratic Trend

The democratic trend resulted primarily from the Industrial Revolution and the forces that gave rise to it. We have already seen how the discovery of the New World weakened the power of the traditional governing class in Western Europe and strengthened the position of the merchant class. This class had long been noted for its republican tendencies, both in maritime societies and in the urban centers of agrarian societies. Then, during the seventeenth and eighteenth centuries, the merchants made their bid for a major share of the political power in Britain, France, and the United States. They could not have done this legitimately, however, if they had not been supported by an ideology that replaced the ancient belief in the divine right of rulers and justified the transfer of political power to them and their allies. This ideology, which had been developing over many years, maintained that the powers of government are derived from the consent of the governed. The new philosophy was invaluable in the political struggles of that era, for it convinced the merchants and their allies that what they were doing was right and just. Without that impetus, they might have failed completely.

Among the various factors that contributed to the rise and spread of the new democratic ideology, Protestantism looms large. Whatever else the Reformation accomplished, it proved that established authority *could* be challenged and overthrown. But beyond that, the Protestant doctrine of the priesthood of all believers had political implications of a revolutionary nature; and though Luther and Calvin did not recognize that fact, others soon did. Both the bitter German Peasants' Revolt of 1524–1525 and the Leveler movement a century later in England were stimulated by it. That doctrine also led to the adoption of democratic or semidemocratic polities by many of the more radical Protestant groups, such as the Anabaptists, Mennonites, Baptists, Quakers, Puritans, and

---

[4] In Sweden, for example, property restrictions on the franchise were not finally eliminated until after World War I. See Dankwort Rustow, *The Politics of Compromise: A Study of Parties and Cabinet Government in Sweden* (Princeton, N.J.: Princeton, 1955), pp. 84–85.

Figure 12.1 Luther's doctrine of the priesthood of all believers had political implications of a revolutionary nature; though Luther did not recognize this, others soon did.

Presbyterians. It is no coincidence that democratization began in ecclesiastical governments some generations before it began in civil governments and that when it did begin in civil government, its early successes were chiefly in countries where ecclesiastical democratization had already made considerable headway. The first major and enduring victory of the democratic movement was in the United States, a country which since colonial days had been a refuge for the more radical and more democratic Protestant groups.

The discovery of the New World also contributed to the rise of the new democratic ideology. From an early date Europeans were fascinated by stories of the American Indians, and many believed their way of life revealed the condition of man in a state of nature. A myth, or mystique, quickly developed about "the noble savage," who, free from the fetters of autocratic government, achieved true nobility of character.[5] The monarchical form of government was increasingly depicted by intellectuals as a corrupting and unnatural institution. Building on this view of primitive man, political theorists like John Locke and Jean Jacques Rousseau propounded the "social contract" theory of government, which maintained that government is the creation of the people and therefore answerable to them. These ideas, together with the democratic outlook stimulated by Protestantism, successfully mobilized popular sentiment against monarchical governments and hastened their decline.

As important as these influences were, it is doubtful that the democratic movement would have succeeded without the technological contribution of the Industrial Revolution. To begin with, industrialization eliminated the traditional need for large numbers of unskilled and uneducated workers living at or near the subsistence level. As new sources of energy were tapped and new machines invented, societies had to produce more skilled and educated workers. Such people, however, are much less likely to be politically apathetic and servile. On the contrary, they tend to be self-assertive, jealous of their rights, and politically demanding.[6] Such characteristics are essential in a democracy, for they counterbalance and hold in check the powerful oligarchical tendencies present in any large and complex organization.

Industrialization also made possible the remarkable development of the mass media. To a great extent, this has been a response to the spread of literacy and to the increased demand for information generated by the rising level of education. Through newspapers, magazines, radio, and television, the average citizen of a modern industrial society is vastly more aware of political events than his counterpart in agrarian societies. Although much of the information he receives is extremely superficial and distorted, it nevertheless generates interest and concern. Thus the media not only satisfy a need, they also stimulate it.[7]

Finally, industrialization, by stimulating the growth of urban communities, further strengthened democratic tendencies. Isolated rural communities have long been noted for their lack of political sophistication and for their patriarchal and paternalistic political patterns. Urban populations, by contrast, have

---

[5] See, for example, *The Conquest of Granada,* by the seventeenth-century poet John Dryden, in which he wrote:

> I am as free as Nature first made man,
> Ere the base laws of servitude began,
> When wild in woods the noble savage ran. (Part I, act 1, sc. 1)

[6] Many recent studies have documented the relationship between high rates of literacy and education on the one hand and democratic government on the other. See, for example, Daniel Lerner, *The Passing of Traditional Society: Modernizing the Middle East* (New York: Free Press, 1958), especially pp. 63–64 and 86–89, or S. M. Lipset, *Political Man* (Garden City, N.Y.: Doubleday, 1960), pp. 53–58.

[7] On the relationship between democracy and the development of the mass media, see Lerner, op. cit., and Lipset, pp. 51–52.

always been better informed and more willing to challenge established authority. Thus, merely by increasing the size of urban populations, industrialization
contributed to the democratic trend.

Political Parties

The growth of democracy and the rise of industrial societies have produced a
totally new kind of political organization, the mass political party, which serves
to mobilize public opinion in support of political programs and candidates.
Wherever there are more candidates than offices, there is a process of selec-

**Figure 12.2 The rise of industrial societies has produced a totally new kind of political organiza-
tion, the mass political party: the British Labour Party assembled in convention.**

tion, and the candidates supported by organizations are usually the ones who survive.

At the present time, party organizations differ in several respects. Some, including the Republican and Democratic parties in the United States, are largely pragmatic, brokerage-type parties. This means they have no strong ideological commitments and no well-defined political programs. Their chief goal is to gain control of public offices in order to trade favors with special-interest groups, giving preferential legislative treatment in exchange for electoral and financial support. This cannot be said publicly, of course, and so party rhetoric takes the form of glittering generalities about service to the nation. In this type of party, discipline is weak or nonexistent, since each elected official is a free agent, permitted to work out his own "deals." Some degree of party unity is maintained, however, because, once an interest group establishes close ties with the officials of a certain party, it usually prefers to continue working with them. This unity is reinforced by the tendency of the more ideologically inclined to separate into opposing camps, liberals gravitating toward one party, conservatives toward the other. Sometimes the more ideologically inclined win control of the party machinery, as the Goldwaterites did in 1964 and the McGovernites did in 1972, but these periods are usually short-lived.

In contrast to the brokerage-type parties, most of those formed in the latter part of the nineteenth century and the first half of the twentieth had strong ideological commitments. Such parties, including both the Fascist parties of the right and the Socialist and Communist parties of the left, usually had well-developed programs for what they regarded as the rehabilitation of society and, in most instances, were willing to be defeated again and again rather than compromise with principles they held sacred.

Since World War II, however, many of these parties have become less ideological and more pragmatic. The Communists of Yugoslavia are a good example of the newer trend. This reversal seems to be rooted in the high rate of technological and social change characteristic of industrial societies. Political programs devised in the last century, or even in the early decades of this one, have become obsolete in many respects, especially in their more specific prescriptions. Modern Socialists and Communists, therefore, increasingly find themselves obliged to innovate, both politically and economically. Most West European Socialist parties, for example, have abandoned, or substantially modified, their former objective of nationalizing all basic industries, while East European Communist parties have introduced the profit mechanism into their economies and elections between competing candidates into their polities.[8]

In addition to pragmatic, brokerage-type parties and ideological

---

[8] See, for example, Kurt Shell, *The Transformation of Austrian Socialism* (New York: University Publishers, 1962), especially chaps. 6 and 7; Rustow, chap. 8; or Albert Parry, *The New Class Divided: Science and Technology vs. Communism* (New York: Macmillan, 1966), chap. 7. See also n. 2 above. For evidence of a counter-trend in Sweden, see Leif Lewin, *Planhushallnings debatten* (Stockholm: Almqvst S. Wicksell, 1967).

parties, two other types deserve mention. The first is based on subgroup loyalties, sometimes ethnic, more often religious. The Catholic parties of Western Europe are the best example. The other major type is the nationalistic party, of which the German National Socialist, or Nazi, Party is a classic example. Nationalist parties are quite common today in underdeveloped countries, especially in those recently freed from colonial rule; but they are very rare in industrial societies. It is not hard to see why this is so: a nationalist party cannot prosper unless there is some overriding national concern. Germany developed such a concern as a result of the Versailles Treaty following World War I, and the National Socialists capitalized on it. This pattern was not repeated after World War II despite Germany's second loss, perhaps because of the disclosure of the many Nazi atrocities. Widespread feelings of national guilt, together with the postwar economic boom, effectively blunted any sense of grievance.

Though nationalistic parties are rare in industrial societies today, nationalistic elements occur, in varying degrees, within other parties. This is especially true of the more conservative parties, most of which have a long tradition of nationalistic concerns.[9] This tendency will undoubtedly continue as long as international tensions and conflicts remain.

Political Conflict and Stability

Every social system generates internal conflict, and industrial societies are no exception. Nevertheless, they are remarkable for their success in channeling it into nonviolent forms. Compared with agrarian societies in particular, they are far less prone to revolution and serious political upheavals. This is especially true of those societies which are past the transitional or early phase of industrialization. In fact, a recent study of sixty-two nations found a strong, positive correlation of .965 between level of political stability and level of socioeconomic development.[10]

There are a number of reasons for this. First, the greater productivity of these societies and the more equitable distribution of goods and services[11] give the majority of the population a vested interest in political stability. Revolution and anarchy are costly for most members of advanced industrial societies.

---

[9] This is the result of the dominant role of the upper classes in these parties. Members of upper classes find it easy to identify their own private interests with the national interest, since they benefit disproportionately from national prosperity.

[10] Ivo Feierabend and Rosalind Feierabend, "Aggressive Behaviors within Polities, 1948–1962: A Cross-National Study," *Journal of Conflict Resolution*, 10 (1966), table 3. The measure used in Yule's Q. Results of this study suggest that rates of political instability are greatest in societies making the transition from agrarian to industrial, though results were not statistically significant. See the term "correlation" in the Glossary for an explanation of the meaning of the coefficient .965.

[11] See Gerhard Lenski, *Power and Privilege: A Theory of Social Stratification* (New York: McGraw-Hill, 1966), pp. 308–313, or Phillips Cutright, "Inequality: A Cross-National Analysis," *American Sociological Review*, 32 (1967), pp. 562–578.

Second, the democratic ideology strengthens the allegiance of most segments of the population to the government and weakens support for revolutionary movements. Especially noteworthy in this connection is the loyalty shown the government by the military and the absence of military coups in the more advanced industrial societies.[12] Finally, the very complexity of the structure of industrial societies seems to generate a readiness to compromise controversial issues. This is partly because there are so many people in intermediate positions between the contending groups (e.g., people with modest property holdings standing between those with great wealth and those with little or none). These people are likely to benefit more from peaceful compromise and to shy away from extreme or violent solutions. Contrary to Marxian predictions, this has been true of the great majority of blue-collar workers. Moreover, since the complexity of industrial societies means that each individual simultaneously fills a number of roles and often belongs to a variety of groups, people who are opponents in one controversy are likely to be allies in the next. For example, middle- and working-class Catholics who are divided over labor-management controversies may very well find themselves allies on church-state issues. This, too, has a moderating effect.

Although political conflicts are restrained in industrial societies, they are still there in a variety of forms and involve a wide range of issues. The most common type of conflict is between the "haves" and the "have-nots," and, in most democratic, multiparty nations, this conflict is the most important single factor defining the basic framework for partisan politics. Typically, some parties openly appeal to the working class and other disadvantaged elements in the population, promising improved conditions if they are elected. Opposing parties rely for support on the more privileged elements in the population, though they usually avoid stressing this in their campaign rhetoric. Nevertheless, the relationship is recognized by most people.

Britain provides a good example of the typical relationship between economic class and party preference. As Table 12.2 shows, support for the Labour Party has been more than twice as strong in the working class as in the

Table 12.2 Party preferences of the British population by economic class (in percentages; average of four samples)

Class	Labour	Liberals and Conservatives	Total
Upper and middle classes	27	73	100
Working class	61	39	100

Sources: Adapted from Robert Alford, *Party and Society* (Chicago: Rand McNally, 1963), p. 136, and Richard Rose, "Class and Party Divisions: Britain as a Test Case," *Sociology*, 2 (1968), pp. 129–162.

[12] Though military coups have been common in many parts of the world in recent decades, it is impossible to find a pure case in a truly advanced industrial society.

Table 12.3 Relationship between economic class and party preference in nine industrial societies*

Society	Percentage Point Difference
Norway	58
Finland	49
Italy (males only)	37
Australia, average of 7 surveys	35
Britain, average of 4 surveys	34
West Germany	31
France, average of 2 surveys	22
United States, average of 9 surveys	17
Canada, average of 10 surveys	7

Sources: Robert Alford, *Party and Society* (Chicago: Rand McNally, 1963), p. 136; Richard Rose, "Class and Party Divisions: Britain as a Test Case," *Sociology*, 2 (1968), pp. 129–162; Erik Allardt and Yrjö Littunen (eds.), *Cleavages, Ideologies and Party Systems: Contributions to Comparative Political Sociology in Transactions of the Westermarck Society* (Helsinki: The Academic Bookstore, 1964), vol. X, pp. 102 and 212; S. M. Lipset, *Political Man* (Garden City, N.Y.: Doubleday, 1960), pp. 225 and 227; Morris Janowitz, "Social Stratification and Mobility in West Germany," *American Journal of Sociology*, 64 (1958), p. 22; *Gallup Political Index*, report no. 17 (October 1966), p. 15 and inside back cover; Roy Pierce, *French Politics and Political Institutions* (New York: Harper & Row, 1968), table 10.

* As measured by percentage difference between upper- and middle-class support of liberal or leftist parties and working-class support.

middle and upper classes. The strength of this relationship between party preference and economic class is quite variable in industrial societies, and Britain's position is intermediate. Class differences are most pronounced in the Scandinavian countries, least pronounced in the North American, as Table 12.3 shows. The limited relation between class and party preference in the latter is due in part to the absence of working-class parties with strong ideological commitments. All the major parties in the United States and Canada are pragmatic, brokerage types, which tend to play down class-related issues rather than emphasize them.

Another factor that influences the relation between economic class and party preference is the presence of important ethnic and religious divisions within the population. It is probably no coincidence that the three countries in Table 12.3 with the strongest relation between class and party preference are also the three most homogeneous from an ethnic and religious standpoint. By contrast, Canada has for years been torn by struggles between an English-speaking Protestant majority and a very large French Catholic minority. In both Canada and the United States, religion and ethnicity are at least as powerful as economic class in determining party preference. In a number of countries, religious groups even sponsor their own political parties. The most powerful of

Figure 12.3 French-Canadian separatists demonstrating in Montreal. Canada has been torn for years by struggles between its large French-speaking minority and its English-speaking majority.

these are the predominantly Catholic parties in Italy, Germany, Austria, Belgium, and the Netherlands. In the Netherlands, three of the four major parties are organized along religious lines: one Catholic, one conservative Calvinist, and one liberal Calvinist.

Modern industrial societies differ dramatically from traditional agrarian societies by virtue of their willingness to permit ethnic and religious minorities and the economically disadvantaged to participate in the political process. In agrarian societies, such groups had little or no political power. In industrial societies, by contrast, these groups have sometimes won control of the machinery of government, or at least a share in it, as the Socialists have done in Scandinavia and Britain, the French Catholics in Canada, and the Catholics in the Netherlands.

The Growth of Government

Apart from the rise of democracy, the most important political change associated with industrialization is the great growth of government. The range of the activities and the diversity of the functions performed by government are much greater in modern industrial societies than in any other type of society. In a traditional agrarian society, the government's chief functions were the preservation of law and order, defense, taxation, and the support of religion. In modern industrial societies the last has sometimes been dropped, but dozens of new ones have been added.

Table 12.4   Annual per capita expenditures by governments in five industrial societies and five industrializing agrarian societies

Society	Per Capita Expenditures
Industrial societies	
United States	$920
Sweden	785
Australia	320
Italy	200
Japan	130
Industrializing agrarian societies	
Greece	110
Yugoslavia	50
United Arab Republic	45
Brazil	25
Ceylon	20

Sources: Calculated from United Nations, *Statistical Yearbook, 1970,* tables 180 and 186, and United Nations, *Demographic Yearbook, 1971,* table 4.

Table 12.4 compares per capita expenditures by the governments of a few industrial and industrializing agrarian societies. As this table indicates, the ranges are quite different. Per capita expenditures average seven times greater in industrial nations. If data were available for orthodox Communist-bloc nations, most of which fall into the first group, and if the influence of industrialization could be eliminated from the developing nations, the difference would be even larger.

This difference results primarily from the greater productivity of industrial societies: they produce more, and therefore they can afford to do more. But not only are their per capita expenditures larger; a much higher proportion of their gross national product goes for government activities. In one recent year, government expenditures in twenty-two industrial societies averaged 24.1 per cent of their gross national products. By contrast, government expenditures in seventeen industrializing agrarian societies averaged only 15.2 per cent, or about three-fifths as much.[13]

The broader scope of government is closely linked with its increasing democratization. As the masses of common people gain a voice in government, they demand services seldom, if ever, provided in agrarian societies. They want educational opportunities, job training, assistance when they are old or sick or unemployed, protection against dishonest businessmen, recreational facilities,

---

[13] These figures are arithmetic means; medians equaled 24.5 and 15.0 per cent respectively. These figures were calculated using United Nations, *Yearbook of National Account Statistics, 1964,* part C. The figures reported are for all levels of government from local to national.

and many other things. The provision of such services further strengthens democratic tendencies, since an educated, economically secure population usually participates more intelligently and effectively in the democratic process and is less likely to be attracted to nondemocratic programs than an illiterate and economically insecure population.[14]

Another factor contributing to the growth of government in an industrial society is the greater interdependence of its population. We have seen how occupational specialization has progressed to the point where virtually everyone is engaged in specialized work. Everyone, therefore, is dependent on the labors of others and on the maintenance of the complex system of exchange by which goods and services reach the ultimate consumer. In a society like this, a disruption at any point in the economy will have adverse consequences for almost everyone.

Similarly, in a society geared to a high degree of interaction among its members, dependable systems of transportation and communication are essential. And in its urban centers, where people live cheek by jowl, well-organized fire, police, and health services are imperative. Private individuals and organizations are unable to assume these responsibilities: only government can commandeer the resources and exercise the authority needed to deal with such fundamental problems.

The Growth and Transformation of Government Bureaucracies

One of the best measures of the growth of a government's activity is the size of its bureaucracy. In the United States, for example, the number of employees of the federal government has gone steadily up for the last century and a half.[15]

1816	5,000
1861	37,000
1901	239,000
1941	1,438,000
1971	2,852,000

This increase far outdistanced the growth of the population as a whole. While the latter increased 20-fold, the number of federal employees shot up nearly 600-fold. Contrary to what a lot of people think, it is not only the federal bureaucracy that has been growing: between 1940 (the earliest year for which national

---

[14] See, for example, Lipset, chaps. 2 and 4.

[15] U.S. Bureau of the Census, *Statistical Abstract of the United States, 1971,* table 601, and U.S. Bureau of the Census, *Historical Statistics of the United States: Colonial Times to 1957,* ser. Y 241–250 (1960). Similar trends are reported in other countries. In France, for example, civil servants increased from 3.7 per cent of the labor force in 1866 to 16.7 per cent in 1962. See Jacques Lecaillon, "Changes in the Distribution of Income in the French Economy," in Jean Marchal and Bernard Ducros (eds.), *The Distribution of National Income* (London: Macmillan, 1968), pp. 45 and 47.

totals are available) and 1970, the number of employees in state and local government increased 200 per cent, while the general population grew only about 55 per cent.[16]

The great growth in the powers of governments and the size of their bureaucracies has made top administrative officials (i.e., civil servants) powerful figures in every industrial society. Although this might be interpreted as simply a perpetuation of the old agrarian pattern with its dominance by a hereditary governing class, it is not. Government offices are no longer regarded as private property to be bought and sold and transferred to one's children. Rather, they are usually assigned on the basis of competitions in which technical competence, training, and experience are the chief criteria. Furthermore, in the exercise of office, officials are expected to act on the basis of the public interest rather than private advantage. Although this ideal is obviously not fully achieved, there is still a marked contrast between the practices of officials in most modern industrial societies and the practices of those in traditional agrarian societies. The United States has discovered this, to its regret, in trying to deal with the officials of many of the governments of Southeast Asia, the Middle East, and Latin America.

In large measure, the explanation for this change lies in the new democratic ideology, which asserts that the powers of government are derived from the people and should therefore be instruments of the people. This is in sharp contrast to the traditional proprietary ideology of agrarian societies, which defined the state as the property of the ruler. When modern officials use public office for private advantage, they are subject to severe censure and, in some cases, even to guilt feelings. Such restraints were largely absent in agrarian societies.

Despite the less venal behavior of public officials in industrial societies, the great power they exercise is a matter of concern. In the first place, where brokerage-type parties are dominant, plenty of leaders are perfectly willing to accept bribes and "honest graft," as they call it, if they think they can get away with it. But even when leaders are basically decent and responsible, a problem still exists, for their conception of what constitutes a wise and responsible use of power is not necessarily shared by others. Like everyone else, they have biases. The fact that most high officials are recruited from the more prosperous segments of society creates one kind of bias.[17] The fact that they are exposed, with increasing frequency, to specialized professional training creates another (e.g., a common criticism of American city managers is their preoc-

---

[16] U.S. Bureau of the Census, *Statistical Abstract of the United States, 1972*, table 674, and *Historical Statistics of the United States*, ser. Y 205–222.

[17] On the social origins of federal officials, see W. L. Warner et al., *The American Federal Executive* (New Haven, Conn.; Yale, 1963), table 33B.

cupation with technical efficiency, which they often promote at the expense of democratic values).[18]

So far the critics of official power have not come up with any feasible alternative. The sheer size and complexity of government in a modern industrial society makes mass participation in the decision-making process impossible. A substantial delegation of power, therefore, is inevitable, and those to whom the power is delegated will generally do what they deem appropriate. In short, there are decided limitations to the applicability of democratic principles in any large-scale organization.

Warfare

Sometimes, in our more pessimistic moments, we feel that war is a universal, inevitable feature of human life. Yet when we examine the record carefully, we find that under some conditions, war has been rather infrequent or absent altogether. Historically, wars have been most common when (1) population pressures forced societies to compete for limited space, (2) technological advance was slow and conquest was a more promising route to riches than economic development, and (3) a small governing class controlled the political life of societies.

Because these conditions were maximized during the long agrarian era that preceded the Industrial Revolution, it is easy to suppose that the patterns of that era—which constitutes most of recorded history—reflect a basic element in man's nature. A broader view of history, however, shows that the incidence of warfare has varied and, like most social patterns, has responded to changing social conditions. This suggests that we would be foolish to assume its inevitability.

In several respects, the developments associated with the Industrial Revolution give us reason to hope that war may be less common in the future than it was in the past, or at least less than during the agrarian era. Although world population is still growing very rapidly, there are effective and acceptable techniques for controlling it. These techniques have already reduced the rate of population growth in industrial nations to a point well below the growth rate of the gross national product. Though this will be a great deal more difficult to accomplish in the rest of the world, for reasons we will explore in Chapter 14, it can be done—provided wealthier nations are willing to help. Population control in the underdeveloped nations would simultaneously improve the standard of living for all their people and eliminate one of the traditional causes of war.

Another development, the democratic revolution, has destroyed the political monopoly of the governing class in a large number of societies.

---

[18] See, for example, Edward Banfield and James Wilson, *City Politics* (Cambridge, Mass.: Harvard and M.I.T., 1963), chap. 13 and conclusion.

Although wars of aggression may sometimes be profitable for a small governing class, they seldom are, or ever were, for the majority of citizens. The natural, deep-seated resistance to war makes it difficult for leaders of a democracy to commit their nation to this course. Usually it can be done only if people feel their national survival is threatened, or through a determined propaganda effort. Such an effort will naturally be easier for the elite if the war is fought exclusively in enemy territory and affects the civilian population only minimally. This explains in large part why democratic, industrial nations have become involved in conflicts with underdeveloped nations as often as they have in recent decades.

Finally, modern technology has produced weapons so destructive that they could, in a few hours of all-out war between the major powers, erase all mankind's gains of the last several hundred years—and possibly mankind as well. This fact has strongly reinforced the general reluctance to accept war as the solution to difficulties, particularly when more than one major power is involved.

These developments do not ensure the end of war, of course. But they do increase the probability of peaceful coexistence and competition between the major powers. When wars do occur, they are much more likely to involve nonindustrial societies, although one or more industrial nations may be brought in, as happened in Korea and Vietnam. But war between the major powers will be avoided if at all possible. If it does occur, it is not likely to come about, as in

Figure 12.4 Center of the city of Hiroshima, one year after the bomb.

agrarian societies of the past, simply because the ruler of a nation sees an opportunity for economic and political self-aggrandizement. Rather, it would probably result from an escalation of emotions on both sides that finally destroyed inhibitions rooted in reason. Happily, this possibility has become less likely as the danger has come to be recognized.

SOCIAL STRATIFICATION

Prior to the Industrial Revolution, every major technological advance led to an increase in social inequality. This was true of the horticultural revolution, and it was true of the agrarian. During the early stages of the Industrial Revolution, it seemed that the age-old pattern would be repeated once again and that industrial societies would emerge as the least egalitarian societies in all of human history.

More recently, however, as a number of societies have reached a more advanced stage of industrialization, this trend toward increasing inequality, which began ten thousand years ago, has begun to falter, even to show signs of a reversal. This has not meant a return to the highly egalitarian patterns of hunting and gathering societies. Far from it. But it has meant a somewhat more equitable distribution of power, privilege, and prestige than was characteristic of either early industrial or advanced agrarian societies.

As we saw in Chapter 2, the basic function of any society's system of stratification is to distribute the things of value that people produce in their life together in society. These include not only material goods but also power and prestige. An individual's access to all of them depends to a great degree upon his own, or his family's, status with respect to such key resources as occupation, education, wealth, ethnicity, political status, age, and sex. We cannot hope to understand the distributive process in advanced industrial societies without taking into account all these separate, but interrelated, systems of stratification.

It is important to note at the outset that the distributive process in an industrial society is affected, to a significant degree, by the ideological commitments of its politically dominant group. In East European societies, the dominant class consists of people who occupy key positions in the Communist Party and are committed to a socialist ideology. In most other industrial societies, the dominant class is made up of people who manage giant private corporations or own great fortunes and who are committed to a capitalist ideology. Socialist societies put far more emphasis on economic equality than nonsocialist societies have, while the latter have been more concerned with political equality. But as important as the differences are, they should not be allowed to obscure basic underlying similarities: in every industrial society, for example, people with advanced education are highly rewarded, as are those in key managerial and political offices. Similarly, power tends to be concentrated in older male hands, and minority ethnic groups tend to be discriminated against.

Occupational Stratification

For the vast majority of people the most obvious determinant of their access to society's rewards is their position in the occupational system of stratification. In the United States today, there are a number of persons who hold positions that pay a million dollars or more a year in salary, bonuses, and fringe benefits. Meanwhile, others are unable to find employment of any kind. Between these extremes, the great majority have jobs that provide anything from bare subsistence to substantial affluence.

In the socialist societies of Eastern Europe, occupational inequality is generally not as great as in nonsocialist societies, but it is still substantial. At the lower extreme, workers on poor collective farms and many pensioners and unemployables in the cities barely eke out an existence, while at the upper extreme, high Party and government officials, scientists, writers, and entertainers enjoy great affluence, including multiple homes, servants, vacations in exclusive resorts, and so forth.[19] A Soviet writer recently reported that in the last years of Stalin's reign, the incomes of some high-ranking officials, though not the very highest, were a hundred times the average worker's, several hundred times the most poorly paid worker's.[20] Since then, however, there has been a deliberate effort to reduce this differential.

The basic structure of the occupational system of stratification is remarkably similar in socialist and nonsocialist societies. In both, managerial and professional occupations are the most highly rewarded, skilled technicians and skilled manual workers come next, then the lower echelons of nonmanual workers (such as clerks) and semiskilled manual workers. And—again in both societies—unskilled manual laborers, small farmers, and farm laborers have the lowest incomes and the least power and prestige. The chief difference between the two systems is the position of self-employed businessmen. In nonsocialist societies their status depends on the amount of capital they control, but generally they rank high (usually on a par with managers and professionals). In socialist societies their position is extremely ambiguous: they often enjoy large incomes, but they also run the risk of imprisonment and are viewed by much of the public as engaged in morally questionable activities.[21] Their extreme status inconsistency resembles that of racketeers and others involved in illegal or immoral activities in nonsocialist societies.

---

[19] On the lower classes in Soviet society, see Andrei Amalrik, *Involuntary Journey to Siberia*, translated by Manya Harari and Max Hayward (New York: Harcourt Brace Jovanovich, 1970), chaps. 5ff. On the more favored classes, see Roy Medvedev, *Let History Judge: The Origins and Consequences of Stalinism*, translated by Colleen Taylor and edited by David Joravsky and Georges Haupt (New York: Knopf, 1971), pp. 540–541, or Jan Szczepański, *Polish Society* (New York: Random House, 1970), pp. 94–95.

[20] Medvedev, p. 540.

[21] See Szczepanski, pp. 95 and 137–138.

Figure 12.5 One of the basic divisions in the occupational structure of modern industrial societies is that which separates manual from nonmanual workers.

One of the most basic divisions in the occupational hierarchy is that separating manual from nonmanual workers. This is, of course, the basis for the popular distinction between the working and middle classes: people in families headed by manual workers usually think of themselves, and are thought of by others, as members of the working class, while people who belong to families headed by nonmanual, or white-collar, workers are thought of as middle class. Nonmanual jobs tend to be more rewarding not only in terms of income, but working conditions, job security, chances for upward mobility, and prestige as well.

Neither of these classes is a homogeneous entity: each has significant internal divisions. In nonsocialist countries there is an upper-middle class composed of proprietors, managers, officials, and professionals, and a lower-middle class consisting of people like clerks, salespeople, and secretaries. The division in socialist societies is similar, except for businessmen, as we noted, but what we will call the upper-middle class is usually referred to there as the

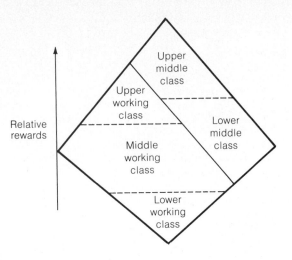

Figure 12.6 **Many skilled manual workers are more highly rewarded than many clerks and other non-manual workers today, even in nonsocialist societies. In socialist societies this tendency is even more marked.**

intelligentsia (a reflection of the educational prerequisites for entry into the class).[22]

In both types of societies, the working class has at least three fairly distinct skill levels. Its elite are highly skilled workers who have usually served long apprenticeships to master their trades. Included are such people as tool-and-die makers, electricians, and plumbers. Beneath them is a stratum of semi-skilled workers of the kind found on assembly lines, and on the bottom are those with minimal skills, such as laborers, domestic servants, and most other service workers.

But the occupational system of stratification is more complex than this breakdown reveals. For example, Figure 12.6 illustrates that many skilled members of the upper segment of the working class are more highly rewarded than many clerks and other members of the lower-middle class. For socialist societies, the line dividing the middle and working classes would be tilted a bit more toward the vertical to reflect the more favored position of the upper working class; for nonsocialist societies it might be tipped a bit more toward the horizontal. Fifty or seventy-five years ago, that line would have been even closer to the horizontal for all industrial societies. Since then, however, the middle and upper segments of the working class, through the efforts of labor unions and working-class parties, have considerably improved their relative position, while the largely unorganized lower-middle class has lost ground.

An even more significant change in the occupational system of stratification has been the great proportional increase of higher-status occupations. As Table 12.5 shows, in the United States, white-collar workers, who comprised

Table 12.5   Frequency distribution of adult population among occupational classes, United States, 1900 and 1972 (in percentages)

Occupational Class	Both Sexes		Males Only	
	1900	1972	1900	1972
Upper white-collar	10	24	10	27
Lower white-collar	7	24	7	13
Upper blue-collar	11	13	13	21
Middle blue-collar	13	16	10	19
Lower blue-collar*	21	19	18	15
Farmer and farm laborer	38	4	42	5
	100	100	100	100

Sources: Figures based on data in U.S. Bureau of the Census, *Historical Statistics of the United States: Colonial Times to 1957*, ser. D72–122 (1960), and U.S. Bureau of the Census, *Statistical Abstract of the United States, 1972*, table 366.

* Includes service workers

only 17 per cent of the labor force at the turn of the century, are now 48 per cent. Even if one considers the occupations of men only (on the assumption that their jobs are the chief determinant of family status), the trend is still impressive: from 17 to 40 per cent. These gains have been accompanied by a reduction in the least rewarding occupational categories, unskilled manual work and farming. Industrialization and technological advance have thus effected a drastic restructuring of the occupational hierarchy, eliminating many low-status occupations, which are physically so demanding, and replacing them with higher-status positions with greater rewards attached to them.

It is no longer valid, as it was in agrarian societies, to depict the occupational hierarchy as a pyramid, with the masses of people concentrated at or near the bottom. In advanced industrial societies, the structure more nearly approximates a diamond, with the largest concentrations in the middle levels. A table on income distribution would show the diamond pattern more clearly than Table 12.5, since the rewards of members of the upper-middle class vary considerably.

Property Stratification

The most basic difference between the stratification systems of socialist and nonsocialist societies involves the locus of power. In the socialist nations of Eastern Europe, power is concentrated in the hands of those who dominate the *political* system of stratification, the leaders and key officials of the Communist Party. In nonsocialist societies, power tends to be concentrated, though not nearly to the same degree, in the hands of those who dominate the *property* system of stratification, the wealthy, propertied elite.

Virtually everyone in nonsocialist nations owns some property: even the

Table 12.6   Distribution of wealth and distribution of investment assets, by wealth categories, United States, 1962

Net-worth Category	Percentage of Population	Percentage of Wealth Owned	Percentage of Investment Assets Owned
Under $1,000	25	0.04	0.05
$1,000–$4,999	17	2	0.3
$5,000–$9,999	14	5	0.9
$10,000–$24,999	24	19	7
$25,000–$49,999	11	19	10
$50,000–$99,999	5	16	17
$100,000–$499,999	2	20	35
$500,000 or more	0.3*	19	29
Total	98.3†	100	99.3†

Source: Based on data in *Federal Reserve Bulletin* (March 1964), pp. 285–293.

* This is our estimate; officially listed as "less than 0.5 per cent."

† These columns do not add up to 100 per cent because of rounding procedures.

poorest usually have a few possessions. But most of the wealth belongs to a strikingly small minority. Data on this subject are hard to come by: the most recent for the United States were gathered for the Federal Reserve Board in the 1960s and show that a mere 7 per cent of the population owned over half of the wealth (see Table 12.6). More striking still, barely 2 per cent owned a majority of the nation's investment assets.

Yet even this fails to tell the whole story. As we saw in the last chapter, the ownership and the control of investment assets are not the same thing where modern corporate enterprises are involved. Ownership of a small quantity of stock in a giant corporation means absolutely nothing so far as influence over corporate policy is concerned; control of company policy rests in the hands of top management and owners of substantial blocks of stock. Since these managers are invariably in that tiny group which owns most of the nation's investment assets, the 2 per cent that owns "only" 50 per cent actually controls about 90 per cent. Only such economically inconsequential enterprises as family farms and businesses escape their control.

If the power of this elite were confined to the economy, it would be impressive; when it spills over into the polity, as it frequently does, it is awesome. This situation arises because of the tremendous costs of modern election campaigns. *Time* magazine referred to the 1972 election in this country as "The $400,000,000 Election."[23] The more powerful the office, the greater the costs: the two major presidential candidates alone spent a total of about $80 million. As a consequence, most candidates for important public offices become heav-

---

[23] See the cover and feature story in the Oct. 23, 1972, issue.

ily indebted to the small number of wealthy individuals and organizations able to finance their candidacies. In exchange for hefty campaign contributions, politicians offer special tax breaks, lucrative government contracts, and other financial benefits that cost the public billions of dollars a year.

Sometimes these "repayments" are political actions that benefit only a single individual or group (as when the Nixon administration dropped an anti-trust case against International Telephone and Telegraph in exchange for a substantial campaign contribution). Even more significant, however, are actions that are designed to advance the interests of the propertied elite as a whole at the expense of everyone else in the society. There is an abundance of tax legislation, for example, that favors income earned from investments over income earned by work. A classic illustration is provided by the notorious mineral depletion allowances that excuse the owners of oil wells and coal mines from paying taxes on much of their income because these valuable resources are gradually being used up and someday their wells and mines will be worthless. As more than one critic has observed, no such consideration is shown the working people, whose chief resources—their bodies—are also being depleted.

As a result of special legislation designed for the benefit of the propertied class, it is now possible for people with annual incomes of $1 million and more to incur *no federal income tax obligation at all.* In 1969 there were 745 people with incomes of $100,000 or more who escaped all federal income tax obligations, despite the fact that their combined incomes totaled more than $338 million; included among them were 52 individuals with incomes averaging well over $3 million apiece.[24] Two years earlier it was reported that one individual with an income of nearly $20 million escaped scot-free and that another multimillionaire had incurred no tax obligation at all for more than a dozen years in a row.[25] All of this while people with less than $5,000 a year were being taxed an average of 9 per cent of their incomes.

The dominance of the propertied elite is not reflected only in tax benefits, of course. In countless ways, subtle and not so subtle, their influence pervades the life of society. Government policy on education, health care, environmental pollution, and even relations with other nations is affected by the fact that so many of those who make the decisions are obligated to the propertied class. Thus, they cannot decide issues of war and peace simply on the ground of justice or national security; they must also take into account the implications for giant corporations whose profits depend on a continuing demand for costly weapons systems. In finding solutions to the health needs of the nation, they must consider the massive campaign contributions of the American Medical Association and the drug industry, aware that any program which threatens the

---

[24] U.S. Department of the Treasury, *Statistics of Income, 1969: Individual Income Tax Returns,* table 1.9.

[25] *Newsweek,* Feb. 24, 1969, p. 65.

Table 12.7   Distribution of wealth in the United States and in Sweden compared

	Percentage of Wealth Held	
Wealth Category	United States	Sweden
Top 2 per cent	39	20
Top 10 per cent	61	39
Top 25 per cent	80	56
Top 50 per cent	96	75
Bottom 50 per cent	4	25

Sources: *Federal Reserve Bulletin* (March 1964), pp. 285–293, and Swedish Finance Department, State Public Investigations (SOU), *Ägande och inflytande inom det privata naringslivet: Koncentrationsutredningen, V* [Ownership and influence in the private sector of the economy] (Stockholm, 1968), 7, table 6/4b. Minor corrections were required in United States data to make them comparable to the Swedish data.

financial interests of those groups is dangerous for a politician to support. The United States is not unique in all of this; the situation in France, Italy, Japan, Canada, West Germany, and other nonsocialist nations is similar in many respects.[26]

Yet despite its immense power in most nonsocialist societies, in none of them does the propertied elite have anything approaching total control. The democratic political system ensures at least some measure of influence for the more numerous, but less wealthy, segments of the population, provided they organize effectively. Groups as dissimilar as Common Cause and Welfare Rights Mothers and techniques as disparate as running candidates for office and organizing protest rallies can be used by members of democratic societies to fight the propertied elite and protect their own interests.

The most potent opposition to the power of the propertied class, however, has come from working-class parties. In some countries, such as Sweden, Norway, and Denmark, these parties have held office much of the time since the 1930s. In other countries, such as the United States, there is no real working-class party, and both major parties are substantially under the control of the propertied elite. But even in a country like Sweden, where the Social Democrats have been in office continuously since the mid-1930s, the working class has had only modest success in its efforts to effect a redistribution of income and reduce the economic and political power of the propertied elite (see Table 12.7).[27]

---

[26] On Canada, see John Porter, *The Vertical Mosaic: An Analysis of Social Class and Power in Canada* (Toronto: University of Toronto Press, 1965), part II, especially chaps. 7–9 and 12–13; on France see Ehrmann, *Organized Business in France,* chap. 5.

[27] Swedish Finance Department, State Public Investigations (SOU), *Ägande och inflytande inom det privata näringslivet: Koncentrationsutredningen, V* [Ownership and influence in the private sector of the economy] (Stockholm, 1968), or Jörgen Ullenhag, *Den Solidariska Lönepolitiken i Sverige* (Stockholm: Scandinavian University Books, 1971).

Political Stratification

According to democratic theory as taught in public schools and extolled by politicians, the members of society are all made politically equal by giving each of them a single vote. But most people soon learn that this is not the way democracy works, either in nonsocialist or in socialist societies (all East European societies profess to be democratic and regularly hold elections).[28] In George Orwell's felicitous phrase, all men may be equal, but some are more equal than others. There is, in other words, a political hierarchy, just as there are hierarchies of wealth and occupation, and an individual's status in this hierarchy affects his access to rewards. This is especially true in one-party societies.

The political system of stratification so important in the socialist societies of Eastern Europe has a structure both simpler and more sharply defined than that of nonsocialist societies. The top stratum in the political hierarchy, and the dominant class in these societies, consists of full-time Party workers, or functionaries, and their families. In the Soviet Union they are known as the *apparatchiki,* (literally, "members of the apparatus or machine"; in effect, organization men). Milovan Djilas, communism's famous heretic, denounced

Figure 12.7 Leonid Brezhnev, chief of the apparatchiki in the Soviet Union following Nikita Krushchev.

---

[28] Several East European nations even have more than one political party, but as a leading Polish sociologist explains, political decision making is all carried out within the Communist Party's Politburo (Szczepański, p. 54).

this group, calling it "the new class" to direct attention to its striking similarity to the power-wielding, privilege-seeking, exploitative classes of other societies.[29]

Numerically, the *apparatchiki* and their immediate families are only a fraction of 1 per cent of the population;[30] but their near monopoly of political and economic power gives them a strength far out of proportion to their numbers. When the class first came to power, idealists and political zealots dominated it; but once its position was secure, careerists began to infiltrate, and the class became increasingly concerned with its own special interests, as Djilas noted.

Beneath the Party functionaries is the much larger class of ordinary Party members. In the Soviet Union, it includes about 9 per cent of the adult population. A minority of these members are volunteer activists who provide leadership in the lower echelons of Party affairs; the majority play a much more limited role, like most church members in this country.

Still lower in the political class system of a one-party state are those people who, though outside the Party, are not regarded as hostile to it: people who would like to join the Party but lack relevant qualifications, others who are covertly hostile to the Party and stay outside as a matter of principle, and still others who are politically apathetic. This class normally includes the vast majority of the population.

Finally, at the bottom of the system are people who are regarded as enemies of the Party. The size of this class varies considerably from time to time and from country to country, and the circumstances of its members vary from mere police surveillance to imprisonment, torture, and execution.[31]

The effects of one's status in this hierarchy are substantial, although they have sometimes been surprisingly inconsistent. For instance, shortly after World War II, when 2,000 former Soviet citizens were asked their opinion of thirteen occupations within the Soviet Union, the position of Party secretary ranked first in terms of material benefits—ahead of doctor, scientist, engineer, officer in the armed forces, or factory worker—but only eighth with respect to safety from

---

[29] Milovan Djilas, *The New Class: An Analysis of the Communist System* (New York: Praeger, 1959), especially pp. 37–39. For a more recent treatment of the subject by a Soviet author and Party member, see Medvedev, op. cit. Although Medvedev focuses on the Stalin era, and refrains from using the term "new class," the situation he describes is strikingly similar to Djilas's description, and it is clear that he regards the problem as a continuing one.

[30] Estimates of the number of *apparatchiki* range from 100,000 to 250,000. See Merle Fainsod, *How Russia Is Ruled*, 2d ed. (Cambridge, Mass.: Harvard, 1963), pp. 206–207; Jerry Hough, "The Party *Apparatchiki*," in H. Gordon Skilling and Franklyn Griffiths (eds.), *Interest Groups in Soviet Politics* (Princeton, N.J.: Princeton, 1971), p. 49; and Reshetar, *The Soviet Polity*, p. 170. With spouses and children, the group might total 750,000 at most, or 0.33 per cent of the population.

[31] See, for example, Amalrik, op. cit.; Medvedev, op. cit.; Zhores Medvedev and Roy Medvedev, *A Question of Madness* (New York: Knopf, 1971); or Alexander Solzhenitsyn's novels, *One Day in The Life of Ivan Denisovich*, *The First Circle*, and *The Cancer Ward*.

arrest.[32] Since Stalin's death, the role of *apparatchik* has become much safer, so this inconsistency no longer exists.

The ordinary Party member, too, enjoys advantages. The most important of these today is probably access to good jobs. As one writer puts it, "Although there are a few exceptions, managers generally can not move up even to the plant-director level without first becoming Communist Party members."[33] The situation is the same in the professions, though not quite to the same degree.[34] One consequence of this has been a disproportionate representation of managers and professionals in Party ranks, an ironic development in a party committed to the dictatorship of the proletariat. In fairness, however, we should note that the post-Stalinist leadership has tried to correct the imbalance, and the proportion of white-collar workers in the Party has been reduced a bit, from 51 to 45 per cent since 1956.[35]

Democratic multiparty societies also have political class systems, but they lack the extremes of reward and punishment and they are not as important in the life of the nation. In their general structure, they resemble the political class system of one-party states. At the top is a class of people for whom politics is a vocation. Although most of these professionals depend on politics for their livelihood, some, like the Kennedys, are people of wealth who are involved for other reasons. In a number of countries, including the United States, party activity can be extremely lucrative. For example, in 1964 President Johnson's family had a fortune valued at $9 to $14 million, "amassed almost entirely while Mr. Johnson was in public office; mainly [after] he entered the Senate and began his rise to national power in 1948."[36] Similarly, Richard Nixon has become a millionaire since entering politics.[37] Theirs are not isolated cases, at least not among politicians in brokerage-type parties. Typically, these men seem to feel they are entitled to use their public offices for private gain and regard the income as a kind of "broker's fee" paid by the special interests they serve.[38] Though the ethics of such practices are dubious, to say the least, most

---

[32] Peter Rossi and Alex Inkeles, "Multidimensional Ratings of Occupations," *Sociometry*, 20 (1957), p. 247. The role of *apparatchik* was most dangerous in the 1930s, when 110 of the 139 members of the Party's Central Committee were arrested in a five-year period from 1934 to 1939, with most eventually being executed. Lower echelons of Party functionaries were equally vulnerable. See Medvedev, chap. 6.

[33] David Granick, *The Red Executive* (Garden City, N.Y.: Doubleday Anchor, 1961), pp. 22–23.

[34] Nicolas DeWitt, *Education and Professional Employment in the USSR* (Washington, D.C.: National Science Foundation, 1961), pp. 536–537.

[35] See Reshetar, table on p. 171.

[36] *The New York Times,* June 10, 1964, p. 25.

[37] Reported by the Committee for the Reelection of the President during the 1972 campaign.

[38] See, for example, Sen. Russell Long's comments on the hearings on the unethical conduct of Sen. Thomas Dodd. He stated that at least half of the senators who were on the committee investigating Dodd could not stand a similar investigation. For an earlier study of the use of political power for private gain, see Harold Zink, *City Bosses in the United States* (Durham, N.C.: Duke, 1930), pp. 37–38.

political leaders stay carefully within the law (as interpreted by fellow members of the political class).

In ideologically oriented democratic parties, such as the Social Democrats in Scandinavia or the Labour Party in Britain, leaders are much less likely to use their positions for private financial advantage. Their rewards are chiefly power, fame, and the satisfaction of implementing their beliefs.

A second important class in most multiparty nations is composed of wealthy individuals and business leaders who take an active interest in politics but do not make it their vocation. These men, the so-called fat cats, provide political organizations with one of their most essential ingredients—money. Some of them seem to want only the excitement of political participation and other psychic benefits, but most are interested in more substantial rewards (e.g., oil depletion allowances, special tax advantages, lucrative government contracts, etc.).

Beneath the professional politicians and wealthy contributors is a class of volunteer workers. This is a very mixed group and includes people motivated by political ideals, by private ambition (such as the hope of joining the ranks of the professionals), or by a combination of both. This class is always small, seldom more than a few per cent of the population, and it has a high rate of turnover.[39]

The lowest rung in the political system in multiparty states is occupied by the great majority of citizens whose political activity is limited to voting and a vague identification with one or another of the parties. As voting records show, many people do not take even this much interest in the political process: 40 per cent of the adult population does not even bother to vote in presidential elections in the United States.[40]

In the political class system, as in some of the others, an individual tends to benefit in proportion to his investment of time and money. For this reason, a disproportionate share of the benefits accrue to the professional politicians and their wealthy allies. Fortunately, their opportunities for self-aggrandizement are at least somewhat limited by the widespread right of suffrage, which serves as a check on their self-seeking tendencies: they know that if they push their private advantage too far, they can be voted out of office.

Educational Stratification

The roots of educational stratification go far back in history. Even in hunting and gathering societies, shamans enjoyed greater power and prestige because of their special knowledge. After the invention of writing and the formation of

---

[39] See, for example, Maurice Duverger, *Political Parties,* trans. by Barbara North and Robert North (London: Methuen, 1959), p. 114, or Angus Campbell et al., *The American Voter* (New York: Wiley, 1960), pp. 90–93.

[40] *Statistical Abstract, 1972,* table 597.

schools early in the agrarian era, educational stratification became increasingly important. As we saw in Chapter 8, only a minority learned to read and write, because the costs of education were prohibitive for peasants. The literate were primarily children of the middle and upper classes, and this skill ensured that they would remain at that level. For the top positions in society, however, education was seldom of crucial importance; at most, literacy was required, sometimes not even that. Because these positions were usually filled by inheritance, the best-educated men tended to occupy the middle levels of the governmental and religious establishments and used their skill in the service of the elite.

Some elements of the older system have carried over into modern industrial societies. Above all, an individual's educational opportunities and attainments are still linked with the class position of his parents, and children of the powerful and wealthy stand a better chance of obtaining a university education, especially at the best institutions, than the children of the poor. (This is true in both socialist and nonsocialist societies.) But it is easy to exaggerate the similarity between the old system and the present one. Both the new technology and the new democratic ideology have created a need for a populace that is, at least, literate. Literacy is imperative for participation in a modern bureaucratized economy, and it is equally important for the effective operation of a democratic political system. Fortunately, as technology and ideology have created this need, they have provided the means and the motivation for meeting it: technology has become so productive that child labor is no longer needed, and the new ideology has made education a basic right of every child.

As a result, there is no longer the traditional cleavage between a literate minority and an illiterate majority.[41] Illiteracy has, in fact, almost disappeared in advanced industrial societies. At the same time, other educational distinctions have become important, particularly those based on amount of education. In the United States, an individual is often categorized according to whether he has less than a high school education, a high school diploma, a college diploma, or an advanced degree. As a result of the bureaucratization of government and industry, the great majority of jobs in the United States, and increasingly in other industrial societies as well, have educational prerequisites, and the individual who lacks them is automatically ineligible. This affects not only his chances of being hired but also his chances for promotion.[42] In this respect, modern bureaucratic personnel practices have created a civilian counterpart of the military caste system, with its sharp cleavage between officers and enlisted men. Just as the ceiling for the promotion of

---

[41] In the United States, however, there are a large number of persons who, though technically literate (i.e., they can sign their names and read or write a few simple words), cannot read and write well enough to use these skills in their work. Such persons are often referred to as "functional illiterates."

[42] See, for example, Alexander Matejko, "From Peasant into Worker in Poland," *International Review of Sociology,* 3 (1971), pp. 27–75.

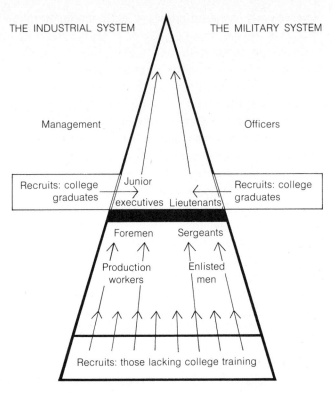

Figure 12.8 Recruitment and promotional patterns in modern industry compared with those in the military.

privates is normally the rank of sergeant, so the ceiling for production workers tends to be the rank of foreman or possibly plant superintendent. Higher ranks are reserved for people with more education, and they are recruited outside the organization. Figure 12.8 illustrates this pattern.

A good measure of the importance of education today is found in recent census data on the relationship between education and income. In 1970 these were the median annual incomes of American males in the peak earning years (i.e., forty-five to fifty-four):[43]

0–7 years of education	$ 6,274
8 years of education	7,839
1–3 years of high school	8,842
4 years of high school	10,328
1–3 years of college	12,034
4 years of college	15,237
5 years or more of college	18,311

The educational elite today appear to have much more influence on public policy than their counterparts in the past. This is not to say that they have

---

[43] U.S. Bureau of the Census, *Current Population Reports,* ser. P-60, no. 80 (October 1971), table 49.

become politically dominant or that advanced academic degrees are necessary for top political office. However, college or university training has become almost a prerequisite for top office, while political leaders are increasingly forced to rely on the educational elite for help in making major decisions.[44] The role of physical scientists and engineers in planning military and space programs, and of social scientists in economic and social policies, is taken for granted today. This pattern is by no means limited to the United States. In the Soviet Union, for example, the startling reintroduction of market mechanisms was due in no small measure to the efforts of economists, and physical and medical scientists have had comparable influence in other areas of public policy.[45] Although the political elite are interested only in the information these experts can provide, it is hard to get it in pure form; almost invariably, the personal values of the experts intrude, but often so subtly as to be unrecognized even by the experts themselves. As a result, today's educational elite have a much larger voice in high-level decision making than their predecessors in agrarian societies ever had.

Racial, Ethnic, and Religious Stratification

Most industrial societies have racial, ethnic, or religious cleavages. Canada, for example, has a serious cleavage between its French- and English-speaking groups, Belgium between Flemings and Walloons, Germany between Protestants and Catholics, and the United States between whites and blacks—to name but a few of the more important ones. As long as groups like these have no effect on how goods and services and other benefits of a society are distributed, they are not really a part of the system of social stratification. But when membership in such a group has an appreciable influence on one's access to those things, the group becomes a part of the system. In that case, the group becomes, in effect, a class: it is an aggregation of people who stand in a similar position with respect to some resource that influences their access to power, privilege, or prestige. It is obviously a special kind of class, however. For one thing, the resource involved is the individual's *membership in a group,* rather than his personal wealth, occupation, etc. For another thing, classes like these have a greater degree of group or class consciousness than most others, more, say, than people with a high school diploma, more even than manual workers as a whole. Finally, it is often more difficult to move into or out of such a class. Because of these differences, some sociologists call this type of class a *status group;* and in instances where movement into or out of the group is virtually impossible the label *caste* is often used.

---

[44] See, for example, R. Barry Farrell, *Political Leadership in Eastern Europe* (Chicago: Aldine, 1970), table 5/1.

[45] For a popular account of the role of the educational elite in Soviet society and its intrusion into politics, see Parry, *The New Class Divided,* and Skilling and Griffiths, chap. 7.

The most striking example of this type of stratification in the United States involves the two major racial groups. Since early in this country's history, blacks have been a subordinated group. Before the Civil War this was underlined by the legal position of the majority of blacks, who were slaves and the property of members of the white group. Even before the Emancipation Proclamation, some blacks achieved considerable success in the occupational, educational, and property systems of stratification, but despite this they continued to suffer from handicaps imposed on them because of their identification with the black group. Their access to clubs, churches, housing, and services of almost every kind was much more limited than that of whites with comparable status in other systems of stratification.

Today, many of these limitations have been removed. Recent civil rights legislation ensures blacks equal treatment in stores, hotels, restaurants, and other business establishments, at least in most sections of the country. But racial discrimination continues in housing, club membership, and some other areas. Even more important, the general cultural and economic deprivation of recent centuries has left many blacks unable to take full advantage of the new opportunities. So much basic learning occurs while a child is small that large numbers of black children with poorly educated, low-income parents are already badly handicapped when they begin school. These youngsters generally make slow progress and leave school poorly equipped to compete in the occupational system. It is hardly surprising, therefore, that the median income of black men has not been much more than half that of white men in recent years ($4,157 versus $7,011 in 1970).[46]

Although the white population is sometimes thought of as a unit, it is, of course, divided along both ethnic and religious lines. From the ethnic standpoint, people of British extraction enjoy the highest status, then those of other northwestern European ancestry, followed by those of southern and eastern European ancestry.[47] Among religious groups, Protestants rank first, followed by Catholics, then by Jews. These rankings reflect the historic dominance of the Protestants of British ancestry who first settled this country. Until about 1830, most of the white population were Anglo-Saxon and Protestant, and these people occupied the dominant positions in all the major institutions. Since most of the later immigrants were poor, had little education, and were unable to speak English, they tended to fill the more menial positions. The more they had in common with the older stock, the more readily they were accepted in marriage and in the better jobs, clubs, and neighborhoods. Northwestern European Protestants were thus accepted more readily than southern and east-

---

[46] *Current Population Reports,* ser. P-60, no. 80, table 48.

[47] Members of minority groups usually adopt the dominant group's prestige evaluations for groups other than their own. Sometimes they even adopt its evaluation of their own group. See, for example, Emory Bogardus, *Social Distance* (Yellow Springs, Ohio: Antioch Press, 1959), pp. 26–29.

Figure 12.9 Much basic learning occurs while a child is small: learning opportunities in Harlem.

ern European Catholics and Jews. Although most ethnic differences within the white population are disappearing, religious differences have proved much more resistant. Some scholars, in fact, see the religious cleavage as a relatively "permanent" feature of American life.[48]

Ever since the Civil War, the Democratic Party has been the political instrument for most of the groups that have felt discriminated against by the nation's political, economic, and social elite (i.e., wealthy Northern Protestant families of British origin). This is the reason the Democratic Party has traditionally attracted such diverse groups as Southern whites, blacks, Catholics, Jews, and the working class. The Republican Party, by comparison, has tended to be the political instrument for the historically dominant groups and has sought to protect their advantages.

In Canada, the most serious cleavage is along religious and ethnic lines, dividing French-speaking Catholics from English-speaking Protestants. Although the French Catholics settled the country first, they were conquered by the British, who dominated the political system from the eighteenth century on. The problem was further aggravated because the English-speaking Protestants

---

[48] For one of the first statements of this point of view, see Ruby Jo Reeves Kennedy, "Single or Triple Melting Pot? Intermarriage Trends in New Haven, 1870–1940," *American Journal of Sociology*, 49 (1944), pp. 331–339. For more recent statements, see Will Herberg, *Protestant-Catholic-Jew* (Garden City, N.Y.: Doubleday, 1956), and Milton Gordon, *Assimilation in American Life: The Role of Race, Religion, and National Origins* (Fair Lawn, N.J.: Oxford University Press, 1964).

industrialized while the French Catholics clung to the agrarian way of life. As a consequence, the English Protestants also dominated the economy, even in Quebec, the home province of the French Catholics.[49] In recent years the French have succeeded in eliminating many discriminatory practices through political action, but a minority of them still favor secession.[50]

Despite the current importance of racial, ethnic, and religious stratification in a number of industrial societies, there is reason to believe their importance will decline in the years ahead. With the spread of the democratic-egalitarian ideology, the more powerful and privileged classes have been forced to make concessions. On the whole, they have preferred to give ground in the racial-ethnic-religious area, rather than in the political and economic, because they stand to lose less that way. For example, when blacks are given equal opportunities in the job world, it is not the jobs of the managerial and professional classes that are threatened but the jobs of white workingmen. Similarly, when social facilities are integrated, the clubs of the wealthy are the last to be affected. As an old Latin proverb put it, "It is easy to be generous with other people's property," and as embattled elites have discovered in the modern world, it is easier to give away other people's privileges. People with wealth and occupational status do not need to depend on racial, ethnic, or religious status; therefore, when there are pressures for change toward a more democratic and egalitarian social order, this is the area in which they are most willing to make concessions. Here they are likely to be supported by the educational elite, since they, too, find this form of change relatively painless. And those intellectuals who are themselves members of minority racial, ethnic, and religious groups have everything to gain and nothing to lose.

Age and Sex Stratification

Age and sex have been bases of social differentiation in every society throughout history. The social roles of men and women have differed, as have the roles of children, adults, and the aged. In almost every case, these role differences have been linked to status differences in power, privilege, and prestige.

The ultimate basis of these distinctions lies in human biology.[51] Children are both physically and intellectually less developed than adults. Having had fewer chances to acquire experience and information, they are at a competitive disadvantage. For women, the primary handicap has been quite

---

[49] See, for example, Everett C. Hughes, *French Canada in Transition* (Chicago: University of Chicago Press, 1943), especially chap. 7. See also Porter, *The Vertical Mosaic*, chap. 3.

[50] One survey showed that an eighth of all French Canadians favored it, and a quarter of the college-educated, who are the leaders and molders of public opinion. See *Maclean's*, 76 (Nov. 2, 1963), p. 14.

[51] This is not to deny the important influence sociocultural systems have on age and sex status systems.

different. Throughout most of human history, the limitations imposed by frequent pregnancy, lactation, and the care of small children prevented women from competing with men in political and military activities, traditionally the basic determinants of power and prestige. Except through the institution of the family, women had little access to the goods and services produced by societies.

There are elements of both continuity and change in the systems of age and sex stratification in industrial societies. Middle-aged and older people continue to be dominant in the political, property, and occupational systems. In recent years, for example, the median age of United States senators has been fifty-six, and, with the Senate's system of seniority, committee chairmen have been even older.[52] One national study of business leaders indicated a median age of fifty-four; another, limited to the managerial elite, showed a median of sixty-one.[53] A study of American military leaders found their average age was fifty-four; and a study of the very wealthy showed that the average age of men with estates valued at $5 million or more was sixty-nine.[54] The situation is similar in other advanced industrial societies, including the Soviet Union.[55] On the other hand, younger people are now challenging the authority of their elders to a degree that was unthinkable in agrarian societies.

As far as sex stratification is concerned, although men continue to be dominant both politically and occupationally, women have made substantial gains in at least the property and educational systems. Laws that restricted their right to own property have been eliminated in most industrial societies, and in the United States women now own much of the wealth.[56] Similarly, former barriers to higher education have been largely eliminated. Even in the political arena, women have made substantial gains. As recently as 1900, women were permitted to vote only in New Zealand and four states in this country.[57] Today they enjoy this right in every advanced industrial society.

In the occupational world, the historical distinction between men's work and women's work has begun to blur. This has been made possible by the great reduction in the birthrate and the changing nature of work activities. In some societies women now enter the labor force in almost the same numbers

---

[52] Calculated from Donald Matthews, *U.S. Senators and Their World* (Chapel Hill: University of North Carolina Press, 1960), fig. 1.

[53] W. Lloyd Warner and James Abegglen, *Occupational Mobility in American Business and Industry, 1928–1952* (Minneapolis: University of Minnesota Press, 1955), p. 30, and Mabel Newcomer, *The Big Business Executive* (New York: Columbia, 1955), p. 112.

[54] Calculated from Morris Janowitz, *The Professional Soldier* (New York: Free Press, 1960), p. 63, and Robert Lampman, *The Share of Top Wealth-Holders in National Wealth: 1922–1956* (Princeton, N.J.: Princeton, 1962), tables 48 and 49.

[55] Hough, table 1.

[56] Lampman, p. 96. This study shows that among the rich, women now own about 40 per cent of the wealth.

[57] William J. Goode, *World Revolution and Family Patterns* (New York: Free Press, 1963), p. 55.

as men. In one recent year, women constituted 48 per cent of the labor force in the Soviet Union.[58] This figure was inflated somewhat as a result of the heavy death toll among Soviet men in World War II; but even if there had been equal numbers of both sexes in the population, women would still have made up 43 per cent of the labor force. In the United States, too, the percentage of gainfully employed women has steadily risen. In 1890 only 19 per cent of women fourteen or older worked outside the home. Today this figure is nearly 40 per cent, with women constituting 37 per cent of the labor force.[59]

Despite these increases, women are still far from achieving occupational equality and are concentrated in the less remunerative occupations. In

Figure 12.10 Locomotive engineer, U.S.S.R.

[58] International Labour Office, *Yearbook of Labour Statistics, 1971*, p. 43.

[59] Calculations based on *Statistical Abstract, 1972*, tables 34 and 341.

1970, only 8 per cent of Americans earning $10,000 or more per year were women.[60] A similar situation prevails in other industrial societies.[61] To some extent this is because women are handicapped during the early, and often critical, years of employment, when childbearing and child rearing interrupt their careers. But it is frequently a matter of choice: many women prefer marriage and homemaking. These factors have traditionally led most employers to favor men for the more responsible and demanding positions. This, in turn, reinforces the disinclination of many women to compete in the job market.

Consequences of Social Stratification

The unequal distribution of power, privilege, and prestige divides the members of industrial societies as surely as it did the members of agrarian societies. Those who have similar resources and backgrounds tend to associate with one another and to stand apart from the rest. This inevitably leads to the formation of class-based subcultures and class-based communities.

The differences that divide the classes are partly economic. The poor obviously cannot afford many of the things that are an integral part of the middle-class way of life, and the middle classes cannot afford many of the things that are essential to the upper-class way of life. But it is not only material differences that are divisive. Differences in values and world views, in experience and information, in social norms (especially the etiquette of daily life), and even in speech, are equally important.

It would be impossible to describe here all the differences that sociologists have found between the classes in modern industrial societies. The subject fills volumes.[62] Suffice it to say that hardly any aspect of life is untouched. Even one's chances for survival are influenced by one's class membership: white babies born in the United States today can expect to live seven years longer than nonwhite babies.[63] Class also affects many basic personality traits, since its influences begin to operate immediately after birth. To a large degree, a person's needs and desires, his goals and ambitions, and even his self-image are molded by the system of stratification. And not least of all, class affects his chance of success in school and in the world of work. Sometimes these influences are extremely subtle: children of the poor, for example, frequently suffer

---

[60] Calculated from U.S. Bureau of the Census, *Current Population Reports,* ser. P-60, no. 78 (May 1971), table 5.

[61] Though much has been made of the fact that women constitute three-quarters of the doctors in the Soviet Union, this occupation is not especially lucrative there, and the leading physicians continue to be men. The same seems to be true in most other fields. See, for example, Lotta Lennon, "Women in the USSR," *Problems of Communism,* 20 (July–August 1971).

[62] For a good summary of much of this, see Harold M. Hodges, *Social Stratification: Class in America* (Cambridge, Mass.: Schenkman, 1964), especially chaps. 6–11.

[63] *Statistical Abstract, 1971,* table 69.

Figure 12.11 Shaw's play "Pygmalion" and "My Fair Lady," the musical comedy based on it, revolve around class differences in speech and etiquette and their role as barriers to upward mobility.

permanent mental impairment because their mothers' diet during pregnancy, or their own early diet, was deficient in protein.

Despite our physical proximity to people of other classes, most of us never have the opportunity to see their lives "from the inside." At best, we are spectators who watch from a distance—and often misunderstand what we see. (This is what black militants are saying when they insist that whites are unable to "think black.") Talented novelists and other writers have often helped to bridge this gap by sharing insights or their own experiences, while sociologists and anthropologists now add to our understanding of what it means to live in other classes.[64] But it is important to remember that vicarious experiences are no substitute for direct, personal, life-long experience.

From the standpoint of society, one of the most important consequences of stratification is the dissension it generates between individuals and between classes. Where there is opportunity for upward mobility, competition is inevitable: this is a natural consequence of the maximizing tendency in human nature. Where status is primarily ascribed, however, class conflict often ensues. People born into classes to which many of the good things of life are denied are likely to join with others in the same situation and try to force society to make more rewards available to them, while those in the favored classes usually resist these efforts. We see this continually in struggles between

[64] See, for example, A. B. Hollingshead, *Elmtown's Youth* (New York: Wiley, 1949); St. Clair Drake and Horace Cayton, *Black Metropolis* (New York: Harcourt, Brace & World, 1945); Elliot Liebow, *Tally's Corner* (Boston: Little, Brown, 1967).

workers and employers, in racial conflicts, and in student efforts to get more power in the affairs of universities and colleges and in the larger society.

The stakes in struggles like these can be extremely high. In industrial societies, the outcome, more often than not, has favored the *less* advantaged class, resulting in a fairly steady, if slow, reduction in social, economic, and political inequality. Even if this is not always evident in short-run comparisons, it becomes clear as soon as we compare the more advanced industrial societies of the modern world with agrarian societies of the past (see *Social Inequality: Two Trends,* below).

Vertical Mobility

Compared with agrarian societies, industrial societies afford far more opportunities for individuals to better themselves. In the agrarian era, high birthrates ensured an oversupply of labor in almost every generation. At every social level, a certain percentage of the children were forced to work in an occupation less rewarding than their fathers' or to join the ranks of the beggars, outlaws, prostitutes, and vagabonds. Though some did improve their situations, the downwardly mobile were much more numerous.

In industrial societies, conditions are strikingly different. While birthrates have been falling, technology has been increasing the proportion of high-status occupations (see Table 12.5). As a result, the situation has been reversed: there is now more upward than downward mobility. A recent survey by the U.S. Bureau of the Census compared the occupations of men today with those of their fathers and found that two and a half times as many had risen from blue-collar occupations to white-collar as had dropped from white-collar to blue-collar.[65] Even if we divide the urban occupational hierarchy into three or four levels, the ratio of upward to downward mobility is about the same. This ratio is higher than in most other countries (owing, apparently, to the more rapid expansion of higher-status occupations here), but nearly every industrial society has eliminated the excess of downward mobility.[66]

This has undoubtedly been a factor in reducing the threat of the working-class revolution predicted by Marx and Engels. If, in every generation, a quarter or more of the sons of workingmen are able to rise into the ranks of the middle class, resentment against the system is almost certain to be less than if only a few per cent move up the ladder, as Marx and Engels expected. Furthermore, since those who rise are generally some of the most talented and ambi-

---

[65] Calculated from U.S. Bureau of the Census, *Current Population Reports,* ser. P-23, no. 11 (May 1964), table 1

[66] A few surveys indicate an excess of downward mobility, but there is reason to believe that these results sometimes are owing to the failure to ensure that respondents report the father's occupation when he was *their age.* This is important, because mobility also occurs within careers, and here, too, upward mobility is more common than downward.

tious members of their generation, a lot of potential leadership for protest movements is permanently lost to the working class.

It is probably no coincidence that a great deal of the leadership and support for protest movements in advanced industrial societies has come from members of racial, ethnic, or religious minorities. Upward mobility for such people is difficult, sometimes impossible. Unable to escape the limitations society imposes on them, many are apt to turn their energies to social protest, especially programs designed to eliminate the differential between their own group and more favored ones.

Social Inequality: Two Trends

When we began our examination of systems of stratification, we noted the trend toward increasing social inequality that started with the horticultural revolution 10,000 years ago and continued down to the early stages of the Industrial Revolution. We also noted that with further industrialization this trend was halted, even reversed. Before concluding our review of stratification, we need to take a closer look at this important development and at one other critical trend as well.

In advanced agrarian societies of the past, systems of inequality were often built right into the legal codes. There was no pretense that people were equal: some were legally recognized as privileged nobility, some as commoners, others as slaves or serfs, and legal rights and privileges varied accordingly. Democracy as we understand it was completely unknown in these societies; political decisions were the God-given prerogative of a tiny elite. The rest of the population had no influence: only the possibility of revolt or revolution, if conditions became too oppressive, set limits on the freedom of the elite. Economically, the ruler and the governing class usually received not less than half of the national income, sometimes as much as two-thirds.[67]

In advanced industrial societies, the legal bases of inequality have been virtually eliminated. In Britain and a few others, titles of nobility remain, but the special rights that were once attached to them have been largely stripped away. It is true, of course, that people still receive unequal treatment in courts of law, in both socialist and nonsocialist societies,[68] but the situation has improved greatly since the time when the poor were often hanged for the theft of an egg or a loaf of bread.

Except in the one-party states of Eastern Europe, opportunities for participation in the political decision-making process have been increased substantially. The right of franchise has gradually been enlarged until virtually the entire population is able to vote (see Table 12.1). Though the value of such

---

[67] Lenski, *Power and Privilege*, p. 228.

[68] On the United States, see Edwin Sutherland, *White Collar Crime* (New York: Holt, 1949); on the Soviet Union, see Amalrik, *Involuntary Journey to Siberia,* or Medvedev and Medvedev, *A Question of Madness.*

Figure 12.12 Public housing project for low-income families, Denmark. Compare this with American public housing projects.

limited participation may seem questionable at times, the record of the Scandinavian democracies shows what is possible; and even in countries like the United States and Canada, much of the legislation reflects the influence of less advantaged segments of the population. Although no society has anything approaching pure democracy, a much larger percentage of the population in industrial societies has some voice in political decision making.

If socialist societies lag in terms of political equality, they appear to be ahead in terms of economic equality. Substantial differences in income still exist, but they are, as we have seen, less than in nonsocialist societies, far less than in traditional agrarian. Even in nonsocialist societies, the upper 2 per cent of the population does not appear to receive more than 25 per cent of the national income, and usually less than that.[69] Though far more than their proportionate share, it represents a significant reduction in inequality.

The factors responsible for the recent egalitarian trend are primarily the same ones that led to the democratic trend (see page 347), which is simply part of the larger movement away from the extreme social inequality that developed in agrarian and early industrial societies.[70] But one other point should be

---

[69] Lenski, pp. 308–313.

[70] Ibid., pp. 313–318, for a more thorough discussion of this subject.

emphasized—the speed and magnitude of the increase in productivity in industrial societies. When national income is rising rapidly and promises to continue to rise as long as political and economic stability are maintained, the dominant classes find it in their interest to make some concessions to the lower classes to prevent costly strikes, riots, and revolutions. Even though they give ground in *relative* terms, they come out far ahead in *absolute* terms in an expanding economy. For example, an elite would enjoy a substantially greater income if it settled for "just" 25 per cent of the national income in a $900 billion economy than if it stubbornly fought to preserve a 50 per cent share and, in the process, provoked so much internal strife that the economy stalled at the $100 billion level. In short, the new technology has provided the elites of industrial societies with an option undreamed of in agrarian societies; and judging by the results, it has proved highly attractive.

But as the new technology has helped to reduce the level of inequality *within* industrial societies, it has had the opposite effect for the world as a whole. The gap between rich and poor nations has been widening ever since the start of the industrial era. One leading expert estimates that in the 100 years between 1860 and 1960, the wealthiest quarter of the world's nations increased their share of the world's income from 58 to 72 per cent, while the share of the bottom quarter fell from 12.5 to 3.2 per cent.[71] With the new technology gradually eroding the barriers between societies, this trend is bound to grow in relevance for everyone. We will return to this subject in Chapter 14, where we will examine the complex problems of societies that are struggling to industrialize in the shadow of far wealthier and more powerful societies.

---

[71] L. J. Zimmerman, *Poor Lands, Rich Lands: The Widening Gap* (New York: Random House, 1965), table 2.8, p. 38.

CHAPTER THIRTEEN

Industrial Societies: Part 3

KNOWLEDGE AND BELIEFS

Knowledge

During the last five centuries, the bounds of human knowledge have expanded tremendously. The voyages of exploration that began in the fifteenth century gave man his first accurate concept of the earth. The astronomers of the sixteenth and seventeenth centuries laid the foundation for a realistic view of our solar system. More recently, physicists, chemists, biologists, geologists, and astronomers have given us a vision of a universe of infinite complexity, whose age must be measured in billions of years and whose size can be expressed only in billions of light-years. Finally, in the last hundred years, the social sciences have begun the task of demythologizing the social order, challenging ancient theories about the nature of man and society and subjecting virtually every aspect of human life to systematic scrutiny.

Until the nineteenth century, the search for new knowledge was carried on largely outside the universities, because they perceived their function to be the transmission of the wisdom of the past—especially the cultural traditions of the governing class. Their curricula included classical literature, philosophy, theology, history, mathematics, and a smattering of traditional science (i.e., Ptolemaic astronomy, Aristotelian biology, etc.).

By the middle of the nineteenth century, the physical and biological sciences had advanced to the point where the universities found it difficult, even embarrassing, to ignore them, and departments and faculties of chemistry, physics, astronomy, geology, and biology were gradually established. Later, the social sciences were introduced into the curriculum, though the process is still far from complete, especially in European universities. The new sciences were frequently opposed by the older disciplines, which rejected the view that knowledge is acquired chiefly by experimentation and controlled observation rather than by meditation, inspiration, or the study of ancient authorities.

As the various sciences became established in the universities, the concept of the university's purpose gradually changed. Whereas teaching had once been the central responsibility (just as it still is in elementary and secondary schools), the search for new knowledge became equally important. In fact, in the leading universities it now takes precedence. This is due not only to the interests and ambitions of scientists, but even more to the demands of political and economic leaders who have discovered that science is often the best source of the information essential to their various enterprises. Thus, they pour increasing sums of money into scientific activity in the universities and frequently set up research centers within government and industry to work on applied problems.

Man's elaborate search for information about his environment has produced such fantastic results that there has literally been a revolution in his view of the world. Although much of the new information is understood only by a small scientific elite, particularly in the more technical fields, public education and the mass media have carried at least a general understanding of the crucial findings to most members of industrial societies.

Because the practical application of this vast store of information has proved so rewarding, people have virtually abandoned their reliance on magic. Even the least educated members of industrial societies are disinclined to take it seriously in most areas of their lives. There has also been a substantial decline in fatalism: people today are usually inclined to believe that something can be done about their problems, particularly the technical ones.

Religion

The spread of scientific knowledge has shaken and unsettled many traditional beliefs, as well as the institutional systems based upon them. Nowhere is this more evident than in the area of religion. The thought forms of all the great historic faiths—Judaism, Christianity, Islam, Hinduism, and Buddhism—bear the imprint of the agrarian era during which they evolved, and this poses serious problems for contemporary man; for many beliefs about the physical world and the social order that were "self-evident" to people in agrarian societies appear alien and primitive to those in industrial societies. This has generated an acute theological crisis for all the major faiths. Their intellectual leaders must continually translate the valid elements of their traditions into modern terms. And this is not always easy: somehow they must steer a course between irrelevant orthodoxy and heretical innovation.[1] The turmoil within the Roman Catholic Church since Vatican Council II is but one in a series of intellectual crises experienced by religious groups in recent centuries.

Beginning as early as the eighteenth century, new religious movements were established with the aim of reconciling world views with the new knowledge and thought forms. In eighteenth-century England and America there was Deism, a forerunner of later Unitarianism. In France at the time of the Revolution, the new authorities created the Cult of Reason and the Cult of the Supreme Being, while the common people established the Cult of the Martyrs of Liberty. In the nineteenth century, such efforts became even more frequent.

---

[1] See, for example, the writing of recent theologians and theological popularizers, such as Rudolf Bultmann, Paul Tillich, Dietrich Bonhoeffer, John Robinson, and Harvey Cox.

The most successful of the new movements, however, proved to be Communism. Karl Marx, its founder, propounded a faith that became highly popular among the working people and peasants in societies struggling to make the difficult transition from the agrarian way of life to the industrial. His followers eventually succeeded in seizing control of societies that contain a third of the world's population, and they have turned the educational systems and mass media of these societies into instruments of propaganda for the faith.

From a functional standpoint, Marxism is remarkably similar to the great historic faiths. Like them, it provides answers to the ultimate questions of human existence and guidance for the individual perplexed by the problems of life. Friedrich Engels, Marx's lifelong collaborator, commented on this when he wrote:

> The history of early Christianity has notable points of resemblance with the modern working class movement. Like the latter, Christianity was originally a movement of oppressed people: it first appeared as the religion of slaves and emancipated slaves, of poor people deprived of all rights, of peoples subjugated or dispersed by Rome. Both Christianity and the workers' socialism preach forthcoming salvation from bondage and misery; Christianity places this salvation in a life beyond, after death, in heaven; socialism places it in this world, in a transformation of society. Both are persecuted and baited, their adherents are despised and made the objects of exclusive laws, the former as enemies of the human race, the latter as enemies of the state, enemies of religion, the family, social order. And in spite of all persecution, nay, even spurred on by it, they forge victoriously, irresistibly ahead. Three hundred years after its appearance Christianity was the recognized state religion in the Roman world empire, and in barely sixty years socialism has won itself a position which makes its victory absolutely certain.[2]

This was written in 1894, twenty-three years before the Russian Revolution. More recently, the Soviet poet Evgeny Evtushenko, in his autobiography written for Western readers, referred to Communism as "my religion." And Svetlana Alliluyeva, Stalin's daughter, spoke of her conversion to belief in God as marking the end of her belief in Communism, indicating the functional equivalence of the two competing world views in her life.[3] Finally, countless non-Communist scholars have observed the striking functional similarities between Communism and the great historic faiths. Maurice Duverger, the French political scientist, is typical of these. He writes:

> The party not only provides [the militant Communist] with organization for all his material activities, more important still it gives him a general organization of

[2] From Lewis Feuer (ed.), *Marx and Engels: Basic Writings on Politics and Philosophy* (Garden City, N.Y.: Doubleday, 1959), pp. 168–169. Copyright in 1959 by Lewis S. Feuer. Reprinted by permission of Doubleday & Company, Inc.

[3] See Evgeny Evtushenko, *A Precocious Autobiography* (New York: Dutton, 1963), p. 42, and Svetlana Alliluyeva, *Twenty Letters to a Friend,* translated by P. J. McMillan (New York: Harper & Row, 1967).

ideas, a systematic explanation of the universe. Marxism is not only a political doctrine, but a complete philosophy, a way of thinking, a spiritual cosmogony. All isolated facts in all spheres find their place in it and the reason for all their existence. It explains equally well the structure and evolution of the state, the changes in living creatures, the appearance of man on the earth, religious feelings, sexual behavior, and the development of the arts and sciences. And the explanation can be brought within the reach of the masses as well as being understood by the learned and by educated people. This philosophy can easily be made into a catechism without too serious a deformation. In this way the human spirit's need for fundamental unity can be satisfied.[4]

Because of its basic functional similarity to religions such as Christianity, Judaism, and Islam, many scholars refer to Communism as a secular, or nontheistic, religion. This designation is largely a matter of taste and depends on whether the term "religion" is restricted to a belief in God or a supernatural realm, or applied to any basic system of beliefs about the force or forces that ultimately shape the nature and destiny of man and the world. (The more inclusive definition, incidentally, would apply not only to Communism and other modern nontheistic faiths but also to classical Buddhism and the parts of Hinduism that also fall outside the more restricted definition.)

In addition to Marxism, a host of other secular religions have sprung up in the last 100 years. Some, like Marxism and the historic faiths, have been formally organized (for example, Nazism, Ethical Culture, or the cult formed by Ayn Rand). But many have remained highly amorphous, as in the case of the various brands of Humanism preached by John Dewey, Bernard Shaw, Sigmund Freud, and Bertrand Russell. Instead of forming congregations or organizations of believers—a necessity in the agrarian era—these leaders have relied on books, magazines, and other mass media to spread their gospels. They have also had a great deal of support in universities, where many faculty members have been their missionaries.

These techniques have proved quite successful. Although it is difficult to estimate the number of followers of these newer faiths, they are at least a substantial minority in every industrial society, and a majority in some. They include large numbers of people who still call themselves Christians or Jews, but whose beliefs and practices bear little relation to the historic tenets of these faiths.

The rise of these new secular religions directs attention to one of the most striking changes in the realm of ideology: the shift in man's conception of the force or forces that ultimately shape his destiny and the world's. In the agrarian era, these forces were largely (though not entirely) conceived of in *per-*

---

[4] Maurice Duverger, *Political Parties: Their Organization and Activity in the Modern State,* translated by Barbara North and Robert North (London: Methuen, 1959), pp. 118–119. Quoted by permission of Methuen & Company, Ltd.

Figure 13.1 Three recent religious leaders: Karl Marx, founder of Marxism; Paul Tillich, Protestant theologian; Bertrand Russell, Humanist spokesman.

sonal terms. God (or the gods) was the ultimate power and, like man, was thought of as a reasoning Being with emotions. Even those religious leaders who rejected crude anthropomorphic conceptions of God still emphasized the spiritual qualities he has in common with man. Today, by contrast, many more people are inclined to think of the ultimate power or powers in impersonal terms. This is true not only in the secular religions but in the historic faiths as well. It can be seen, for example, in the writings of Christian theologians like Paul Tillich, who described God as "the ground of all being."[5]

The nature of the ultimate power in the universe, to which religious symbols refer, has certainly not changed. What *has* changed is man's informa-

---

[5] For a good popular account of the newer developments by an advocate of the impersonal view, see Bishop John A. T. Robinson, *Honest to God* (Philadelphia: Westminster Press, 1963).

tion and experience—and it is from these sources that he draws his conclusions about the nature of ultimate reality. Because his senses are so limited, man has no choice but to rely on analogies and inferences in his efforts to comprehend something as complex as "ultimate power."

During the agrarian era, man's experience of power in both society and nature pointed to a world controlled by spiritual or personal forces. In society, the actions of governments clearly reflected the whims and eccentricities of their rulers: as the Founding Fathers of this country observed, those were governments of men, not of laws. In the natural world, the situation seemed very similar: nature was often unpredictable and, like government, seemed to be responding to the whims and wishes of an arbitrary ruler rather than to laws.

Today, man's observation and experience suggest a different conclusion. The world of nature revealed by modern physics, chemistry, and astronomy often appears to be a world of machinelike regularity and predictability. Although it is true that elements of irregularity and unpredictability do occasionally appear (e.g., the Heisenberg principle in physics or mutations in genetics), most people simply accept them as part of a pattern not yet fully understood, or even dismiss them as unimportant exceptions to the rule. In the social world, too, power is much more impersonal. The forces of the market system, which can financially ruin a man without anyone having willed it, are a classic example. In the political realm, the growth of bureaucracies and their increasing impersonality have transformed the character of government. Modern bureaucracies are usually no respecters of persons; as Franz Kafka and other writers have pointed out, they follow rules and procedures with an often mindless impersonality.

Because men do draw inferences about ultimate power from their experience and observation of power in societies and in nature, it would be surprising if many had not moved toward a more impersonal conception since the Industrial Revolution.[6] We cannot say, of course, which view is more valid: this is a question science is incapable of answering.[7] Today, as in the past, our most basic beliefs ultimately rest on the foundation of faith.

KINSHIP

Declining Functions of Kin Groups

Kin groups have been the matrix from which every other form of social organization evolved. In the simplest societies, almost every aspect of life was cen-

---

[6] Many, of course, continue to look elsewhere for clues to the nature of ultimate power and find them in such things as meaningful personal relationships or even in drug experiences. Some would even argue that the very coldness and impersonality of so much of modern life and the modern world view generate this kind of reaction in more sensitive spirits.

[7] See, for example, Peter Berger, *The Sacred Canopy* (Garden City, N.Y.: Doubleday, 1967), p. 100; or William J. Goode, *Religion among the Primitives* (New York: Free Press, 1964), p. 23.

tered within the family. Kin groups were all-purpose organizations that provided for their members' political, economic, educational, religious, and psychic needs.

This could not last. As societies grew in size and complexity, relationships had to be established between individuals who were not related to one another. And people who were related had to become involved in relationships that violated the norms of the kinship system—for example, an individual of inferior rank in his extended family might find himself in a position where he exercised political authority over kinsmen of higher rank.

Although the functions of kin groups began to change thousands of years ago, no other type of society ever altered their role so drastically as modern industrial societies. In agrarian societies, the family was still the basic unit of production, and the state was normally the property of the royal family. Education, too, was still predominantly a family responsibility; most boys learned the male role by assisting their fathers, and girls the female role by assisting their mothers. Even when a boy was apprenticed to a master craftsman, he lived in the craftsman's household in a kind of pseudofamilial relation.

By contrast, in advanced industrial societies, ties of kinship are greatly reduced. The extended family is often so scattered that meaningful relations among its members are nearly impossible.[8] The nuclear family is no longer the basic unit of production, as it was in agrarian societies. In politics, family ownership of the state has been eliminated; and nepotism, though it still occurs occasionally, is no longer accepted as normal or legitimate. Finally, the schools have assumed many of the family's responsibilities of training and supervising children.

Today the family's basic function is to order the private and personal aspects of the lives of its members. This means continued responsibility for some of its historical functions—reproduction, child rearing, and the channeling of sexual behavior—as well as new or enlarged responsibilities with respect to personality development, affective relationships, and the consumption of goods and services.

One of the clearest indications of the change is in the area of courtship and marriage. In most horticultural, herding, agrarian, and maritime societies, marriage was thought of largely in economic terms (and in the governing class, in political terms as well). This was reflected in the practice of arranged marriages, in which the parents took the major responsibility for deciding whom their son or daughter would marry, and in the requirement of a bride price or a dowry. For companionship, men looked to other men, women to other women. For love and sexual satisfaction, the more prosperous men often kept mistresses or concubines, whom, unlike their wives, they were able to choose.

By contrast, people in industrial societies view marriage largely in

---

[8] The extended family is not dead by any means, especially in the working class. Its importance, however, has definitely declined since the Industrial Revolution.

Figure 13.2 Chaperoning, arranged marriages, dowry, and bride price have almost ended since the Industrial Revolution. Members of industrial societies view marriage more in romantic than in economic terms.

romantic terms. As our movies, magazines, and music testify, it is the union of a man and a woman who are attracted to one another physically and psychologically and who expect to find continuing pleasure in one another's company. Parents may offer advice, but as likely as not it will be ignored. Bride price and dowry are irrelevant, and mistresses have lost their former respectability. On the other hand, if the marriage fails to live up to expectations, there are far fewer economic, moral, or legal impediments to its dissolution.

The fact that the divorce rate is not higher than it is, however, suggests that it is easy to underrate the real functional importance of the nuclear family. In societies where people move so frequently and are involved in such a variety of organizations, they have plenty of opportunity to develop superficial relationships. Yet their mobility makes it harder for them to achieve sustained, intimate relations of the kind that involves all aspects of an individual's personality—including the memory of shared experiences. If sustained primary-group ties are essential for the development of emotionally mature and stable personalities, as social psychologists believe, then this function of the family is actually growing in importance.

Changing Composition of the Nuclear Family

The Industrial Revolution has changed not only the family's functions, but its composition as well. Above all, there has been a drastic reduction in the number of children, as Table 13.1 indicates. British marriages contracted around 1860 produced a median of six children. Only two generations later, the median had dropped to two. Families with eight or more children declined from 33 per cent of the total to only 2 per cent.

Though the decline was more rapid in Britain then in most industrial societies, the general pattern has been similar. In the United States, for example, the average number of children ever born to women who had just reached the end of the childbearing years (aged forty-five to forty-nine) dropped as follows:[9]

1880	5.4
1910	4.7
1940	3.0
1970	2.9

For British women married around 1925, the comparable figure was about 2.3.

In industrial societies today, families with more than four children are unusual; the majority have one to three. The United States has been something of an exception, but even here the pattern is changing. After World War II, its

Table 13.1 Distribution of British families of various sizes for marriages contracted around 1860 and 1925

Number of children born	Percentage of families with specified number of children	
	Marriages around 1860	Marriages around 1925
None	9	17
One	5	25
Two	6	25
Three	8	14
Four	9	8
Five	10	5
Six	10	3
Seven	10	2
Eight	9	1
Nine	8	0.6
Ten	6	0.4
Over ten	10	0.3
Total	100	101

Source: Royal Commission on Population, *Report* (London: H. M. Stationery Office, 1949), p. 26.

[9] Warren Thompson and David Lewis, *Population Problems*, 5th ed. (New York: McGraw-Hill, 1965), Table 9.6, and U.S. Bureau of the Census, *Statistical Abstract of the United States, 1972,* table 69. These figures are only for women who have been married.

birthrate shot up to 26.6 per 1,000 population, and as recently as 1964 was still above 20.0. Beginning in 1958, however, it began to decline rather rapidly and by the first quarter of 1972 had dropped all the way to 15.8.[10] So, while there are currently more large families here than in most other industrial societies, this distinction will not continue much longer.

Comparisons like the one in Table 13.1 are misleading if we assume that they reflect differences in the number of children actually living within a family at the same time. For one thing, in the earlier period the death rate among children was much higher than it is today. Table 13.2 shows how the rate for Swedish children has declined since the eighteenth century (these figures are used because Sweden has some of the oldest reliable statistics in this area). In the middle of the eighteenth century, 43 per cent of Swedish children died before they reached the age of five.[11] Of those who survived, 14 per cent died before they were twenty. In other words, half of the children were dead before their twentieth birthday. By contrast, in the middle of the twentieth century, 97 per cent of the Swedish children lived at least that long. Obviously, with so many deaths in the first years of life, the number of children *living* in an agrarian family was considerably lower than the number of children *born* into it.

Another factor that reduced the number of children living with their parents at any given time was the long duration of the childbearing period. Women who had eight, ten, or more children often bore them over a twenty-year period or longer. By the time the youngest child was five or ten, many of his older brothers and sisters had probably left home or died. Thus, although nuclear families were certainly larger in agrarian societies, the number of family members actually living together at one time was not as different as the birthrates suggest.

A second noteworthy change in the composition of the family is the elimination of the last vestiges of polygyny. Industrial societies are the only major type in which polygyny has never been socially approved. Among pre-

Table 13.2 Average annual death rates, by age, Sweden, 1751–1959 (rate per 1,000 population)

Age	1751–1780	1881–1910	1955–1959
0–4	86.6	36.3	4.2
5–9	13.8	5.9	0.5
10–14	7.2	3.6	0.4
15–19	7.0	4.6	0.7

Source: From *Statistical Abstract of Sweden,* as cited in Warren Thompson and David Lewis, *Population Problems,* 5th ed. (New York: McGraw-Hill, 1965), p. 374.

[10] Press release of U.S. Bureau of the Census, June 3, 1972.

[11] The figure of 43 per cent is arrived at by taking the average annual death rate of 86.6 per 1,000 shown in Table 13.2 and multiplying by 5 (for the first five years of life) and dividing by 1,000 (the base against which the annual death rate was calculated).

literate societies, only 13 per cent insist on monogamy;[12] in agrarian societies, monogamy is more common, though still far from universal (until recently, polygyny was practiced throughout the whole of the Muslim world extending from the East Indies to Morocco). The shift in industrial societies reflects the changing character of the family, especially the growing importance of affective ties between husband and wife and the declining importance of economic functions.

Finally, the modern family includes fewer relatives outside the nuclear group; households today seldom accommodate aged grandparents, unmarried aunts and uncles, or even grown children. This is no longer necessary in most families because modern urban communities provide so many alternative facilities—apartments, nursing homes, restaurants, laundries, and so on. Moreover, as these facilities have developed, changes have occurred in societal values: most members of industrial societies are extremely jealous of their privacy and apparently regard it more highly than they do the advantages that go with more inclusive households.

Changing Role of Women

One of the major consequences of the decline in the birthrate has been the emancipation of women from many of the restrictions previously imposed on them by their sex. Before the discovery of modern methods of contraception, most married women were destined to spend the prime years of their lives bearing children, nursing them, caring for them when they were sick and dying, rearing them if they survived, doing domestic chores, tending a garden, and often helping in the fields. It is hardly surprising, therefore, that women seldom played significant roles outside the home or made outstanding contributions to the arts. (Read Virginia Woolf's fascinating little fable about the fate of the talented Judith Shakespeare.)[13]

When technological advance opened up the possibility of limiting family size by preventing conception, women from the upper and upper-middle classes were the first to take advantage of it. They were prepared to do so not only by their wealth and education but by a class tradition that emphasized leisure as a mark of status.[14] Women from these same classes also provided much of the leadership for the early women's movements, whose initial goals were to obtain some of the rights traditionally reserved for men (e.g., the vote) and to protect working women, then mostly from the lower classes, from some of

---

[12] This is our own calculation based on 603 hunting and gathering, horticultural, fishing, and herding societies in Murdock's sample of 915 societies (see p. 102 above). We have omitted 104 hybrid societies, most of which are preliterate. If these were included, the figure would rise to 15 per cent.

[13] Virginia Woolf, *A Room of One's Own* (New York: Harbinger, n.d., first published 1929), pp. 48–50.

[14] Thorstein Veblen, *The Theory of the Leisure Class* (New York: Macmillan, 1899), chap. 3.

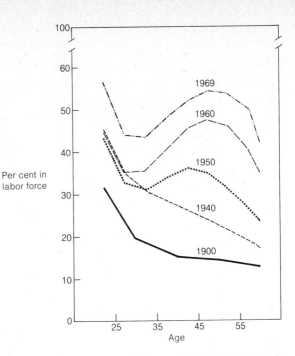

Figure 13.3 Female labor force participation in the United States, by age: 1900 to 1969.

Source: V. K. Oppenheimer, "Demographic Influence on Female Employment and the Status of Women," *American Journal of Sociology*, 78 (Jan. 1973), p. 948.

the more onerous features of employment outside the home (e.g., the twelve-hour day, night work, etc.).

Though this first phase of the movement did not achieve full equality for women, its accomplishments were substantial. In addition to winning women the right to vote, to hold office, to own property in their own names, to enter universities, and to enter most professions and occupations, the movement established the legitimacy of employment for women of the middle and upper classes. Previously, there had never been any opportunities outside the home for these women, other than serving as governess to a wealthy family, working in a family-owned business, or entering a nunnery. Thus, in opening such occupations as nurse, teacher, secretary, and social worker, the movement effected a major revolution. After these early successes, however, the movement virtually died out.

The newer women's rights movement, which got under way in the 1960s, picks up where the earlier one left off. It seeks to eliminate the remaining forms of economic inequality between the sexes—unequal pay, unequal access to jobs, and unequal opportunities for promotion. But it goes further: despite substantial differences in the specific goals and methods of its leaders, the basic message of the movement is that women must break out of the restrictive molds in which society casts them.

In various ways, leaders of the movement maintain that women, like men, should be allowed to develop, to perform, and to relate to those around them, not as females but as human beings, except in situations where one's sex is truly relevant. Thus their great hostility to the mentality (so widespread in the media and advertising industries) that portrays women largely as sex objects. They also point out that the range of aptitudes, emotional qualities, and potential is so similar for men and women that in most instances it is false to make distinctions on that basis. Thus their demands for equal pay, or for women on the Supreme Court. Furthermore, they resent the view that women should necessarily be content with a wife-mother role, while men take it for granted that their husband-father role will be supplemented by a meaningful role outside the family. Thus their emphasis on government-subsidized day-care centers to remove the largest remaining impediment to women's access to society's opportunities and challenges. The ideas emanating from the new women's movement promise to have far-reaching effects. While the first female jockeys and Senate pages were making news, for example, a number of young men were breaking the sex barrier in nursing.

The smaller families and modern conveniences that have made some married women so eager and able to work outside the home have simultaneously made the role of full-time homemaker look more attractive to others of their sex. Many women prefer to use their greatly increased freedom in political work, volunteer service, creative activities, talent development, or simply in socializing or otherwise indulging themselves. Meanwhile, of course, many women who are forced to hold down boring or unpleasant jobs for financial reasons would welcome the opportunity to stay home.

It is obvious that women's role in society has changed dramatically since the agrarian era and that there will be a great deal more change in the future. The basic accomplishment of the women's rights movement has been the enormous extension of the range of choice for women. Ideology has played a part in this, chiefly by making women more aware of the new possibilities open to them and motivating them to work to take advantage of them. But the dominant role has clearly been played by technological advance. Without modern techniques of contraception, and without modern machine technology, most women would still be confined to the nursery and the kitchen.

Divorce

During the last century, the divorce rate in the United States has risen substantially. In 1890 it was 0.5 per 1,000 population per year. By 1971 it had risen more than sevenfold to 3.7.[15] Many people have concluded from this that a high divorce rate is an inevitable result of industrialization.

Recently, however, careful cross-national comparisons have cast doubt

---

[15] *Statistical Abstract, 1972,* table 86.

Table 13.3   Number of divorces per 1,000 population for a sample of industrial and industrializing agrarian societies

Nation	Rate
Industrial societies	
United States (1971)	3.7
U.S.S.R. (1970)	2.6
Hungary (1970)	2.3
Austria (1969)	1.4
England (1970)	1.2
Canada (1968)	0.6
Italy (1970)	0.0
Industrializing agrarian societies	
Morocco (1955)	2.9
United Arab Republic (1968)	1.9
Cuba (1967)	1.3
Tunisia (1968)	0.8
Iraq (1967)	0.4
Ceylon (1967)	0.2
Spain (1970)	0.0

Sources: United Nations, *Demographic Yearbook, 1970,* table 23, and U.S. Bureau of the Census, *Statistical Abstract of the United States, 1972,* table 86.

on that view.[16] Statistics assembled by the United Nations show great variation among societies at similar stages of industrialization and remarkable similarities among societies with very different economies (see Table 13.3). This makes it difficult to claim that industrialization is the major cause of high divorce rates. Rather, it appears that in this area, technology is not as important as the beliefs and values of the people who control the nation's political system. For example, under Stalin, divorce laws became extremely strict in the Soviet Union, and the divorce rate was very low. Following his death, his successors relaxed the laws and the rate rose rapidly.[17] A similar change recently occurred in Italy following liberalization of the divorce law.

In general, Muslim, Socialist, and Protestant societies have been more permissive in this respect, and Buddhist and Catholic societies more strict. But there are exceptions to this. For example, as Table 13.3 shows, Muslim Iraq, as a result of recent restrictive legislation, now has a divorce rate only one-third that of Catholic Austria.

Industrialization is not totally irrelevant to divorce patterns, however. Fewer children, nursery facilities, and more job opportunities for women have

---

[16] See especially William J. Goode, *World Revolution and Family Patterns* (New York: Free Press, 1963).

[17] See, for example, Vladimir Gsovski, "Family and Inheritance in Soviet Law," in Alex Inkeles and Kent Geiger (eds.), *Soviet Society* (Boston: Houghton Mifflin, 1961), pp. 533–535. Between 1956 and 1962, the rate nearly doubled. See United Nations, *Demographic Yearbook, 1963,* p. 655.

made it much easier for women to establish and maintain their own households. Thus divorce in an industrial society does not usually force a woman to return to her father's household or to become dependent on a brother or uncle, as it would in an agrarian society.

Widowhood and Remarriage

In agrarian societies, at least half of all families were broken during the child-bearing and child-rearing years by the death of one or both parents. In mid-eighteenth-century Sweden, for example, the probability was about 0.51 (i.e., 51 chances per 100 marriages), in late eighteenth-century France around 0.61, and early in this century, about 0.71 in India.[18]

In most countries this pattern resulted in frequent remarriages. Individuals who survived to old age had often had several spouses. Marriages between widows and widowers were common and led to merged families with complicated combinations of half brothers and half sisters. Fairy tales about cruel step-

Figure 13.4 Prior to industrialization, a very high proportion of families were broken during the child-bearing, child-rearing years by the death of one or both parents.

[18] Calculated from Thompson and Lewis, p. 374; J. Bourgeois-Pichat, "The General Development of the Population of France since the Eighteenth Century," in D. V. Glass and D. E. C. Eversley (eds.), *Population in History* (Chicago: Aldine, 1965), p. 498; and W. S. Woytinsky and E. S. Woytinsky, *World Population and Production: Trends and Outlook* (New York: Twentieth Century Fund, 1953), p. 181.

mothers and stepfathers bear witness of the unhappy situations that often resulted.

In modern industrial societies, widowhood before middle age is relatively infrequent. In the United States the probability that one spouse will die between the ages of twenty and forty-five is only 0.11.[19] This means that the likelihood of a nuclear family's disruption before the children are grown was actually considerably greater in agrarian societies despite the rise in the divorce rate in many industrial nations.

Loosening of Ties

Another basic change in family life is the loosening of ties among the members. The agrarian family, as we have seen, was usually a work group. This was almost invariably the case among peasants, who were a substantial majority of the population, but it was typical of artisans, too. The place of work and the place of residence were normally the same, and all the members of the family, including children, shared in the work.

In industrial societies the pendulum has swung to the opposite pole. Very few men work at home, and most work too far away to return even for the midday meal. Married women, also, work outside the home or are away for other activities, while the schools draw children out of the family for a major part of their waking hours. As a result, family members spend much less time together than they did in agrarian societies. A child in the lower grades may be with his teacher more than with his mother. Similarly, a teen-ager may spend more time with his friends than with his parents, and a businessman may see more of his secretary than of his wife. This situation is bound to have an effect on family ties.

A classic illustration of the problem is the familiar dinner table dialogue in which the parents ask the children, "What happened at school today?" or the wife asks her husband, "What happened at work?" The standard answer is, "Oh, nothing." This does not really mean that nothing happened but rather that nothing happened that could be easily explained or that would be meaningful to people unfamiliar with the setting. The frequency with which this response is given is a good measure of the loosening of family ties.

This is not necessarily bad, however, even from the standpoint of its effect on family solidarity. Family ties were frequently *too close* in the past and as likely to generate hate and resentment as love and goodwill. (There is a good illustration of this point in the next chapter, page 452.) In a modern industrial society, family unity rests more on a foundation of common interests and mutual attraction than it did when social and economic necessity offered people so

---

[19] Calculated from *Statistical Abstract, 1971*, p. 54.

few alternatives. Despite its negative aspects, then, the new situation seems about as conducive to harmonious relations within the family as the old.

YOUTH COMMUNITIES AND THEIR SUBCULTURES

One of the most striking developments in industrial societies, especially in the United States, has been the emergence of communities of young people with highly distinctive subcultures.[20] These have no counterpart in agrarian societies, where virtually everyone in his teens or twenties is already integrated into the world of work. In those societies, children are usually given simple chores when they are very small, and their responsibilities gradually increase until, by their mid-teens, they can pretty well handle adult responsibilities.

In industrial societies, however, the new technology reduced the need for labor to such an extent that young people came to be viewed as a threat in the job market. Labor unions fought to make "child" labor illegal, and their efforts were reinforced by the enactment of compulsory school attendance laws. As a result, the historical involvement of young people in the economy has been drastically curtailed, and with it their opportunities for participation in the adult world.

But if the new technology has created a problem, it has also provided a solution of sorts: the tremendous affluence of modern industrial societies has made it possible to build schools and universities in unprecedented numbers. This solution has had an obvious appeal: the kind of education that was once the special privilege of the upper classes becomes available to the majority of youth. In addition, such an educational system can supply the skilled labor force required by the new technology. Schools and universities have thus grown at a fantastic rate. Table 13.4 shows the trend in the United States during the last 100 years. By 1971, 95 per cent of Americans aged fourteen through

Table 13.4   Growth of the student population in the United States, 1871–1971

Date	Enrollment in public schools, grades 9–12	Enrollment in colleges and universities	Total	Percentage of American population enrolled
1871	80,000	50,000	130,000	0.3
1900	520,000	240,000	760,000	1.0
1930	4,400,000	1,100,000	5,500,000	4.4
1971	14,060,000	8,090,000	22,150,000	10.1

Sources: U.S. Bureau of the Census, *Historical Statistics of the United States: Colonial Times to 1957* (1960), pp. 207, 210, and 211, and U.S. Bureau of the Census, "School Enrollment in the United States, 1971," *Current Population Reports*, ser. P-20, no. 234 (March 1972), tables 2 and 3.

---

[20] See, for example, Jack Douglas, *Youth in Turmoil: America's Changing Youth Cultures and Student Protest Movements* (Chevy Chase, Md.: National Institute of Mental Health, 1970).

Figure 13.5 Hare Krishna festival, San Francisco.

seventeen and 32 per cent aged twenty and twenty-one were students. Even among people from thirty to thirty-four, 5 per cent were still in school.[21]

As these figures suggest, educational institutions have expanded far beyond what is necessary to prepare people for a place in the economy.[22] In effect, high schools and universities have been forced to perform a glorified "baby"-sitting function for an increasing number of students—students who attend, not because they have any real interest in either the liberal or the vocational aspects of education, but because no other viable options are open to them.

Dropping out of school does little to improve the situation for most young people. Those who quit during secondary school usually have trouble getting decent jobs, and even college dropouts find good jobs scarce. As a result, many drift into street gangs, communes, and similar groups whose membership is recruited almost entirely from this age level. These groups typically operate in the vicinity of high schools and colleges, and their membership often includes some who are still enrolled.

The number and variety of youth groups in advanced industrial so-

[21] U.S. Bureau of the Census, "School Enrollment in the United States, 1971," *Current Population Reports,* ser. P-20, no. 234, (March 1972).

[22] See, for example, Randall Collins, "Functional and Conflict Theories of Educational Stratification," *American Sociological Review,* 36 (1971), pp. 1002–1019.

cieties today are staggering. In this country, there are currently groups as diverse as the Jesus freaks, Hare Krishna cultists, environmentalists, back-to-the-land communalists, urban communalists, remnants of SDS, other white political activists of every stripe, a wide variety of black separatists and militants, women's libbers, homosexual groups, counter-culture types, drug groups of various kinds, ghetto gangs, and motorcycle gangs. What kinds there will be by 1980 is anyone's guess, since things change so fast in this area.

Despite this obvious diversity, certain common themes recur repeatedly in youth groups—and this applies not only to the current crop but to their predecessors as well.[23] To begin with, these groups are characterized by their attraction to the new and different and by the succession of fads and fashions they adopt. Although their basic values remain fairly constant from year to year (e.g., resistance to adult authority, the desire for fun and excitement, etc.), the way they are expressed constantly changes, as styles in music, speech, and clothing illustrate. To some extent these changes are the result of clever manipulation and exploitation by businessmen, both young and old. But they are also a device that these communities use to maintain the boundary between themselves and the adult community. The more rapidly fads and fashions change, the harder it is for adults to keep up with them. This forces adults to keep their distance and prevents them from moving in and dominating the youth scene. It also provides a criterion by which otherwise dominant adults can be judged inferior. (This is a common pattern in lower-status groups: religious sects made up of poor people, for example, have often made asceticism a virtue and hence a basis for condemning the rich.)

Another characteristic of youth communities is their rejection of adult values and adult authority. Sometimes it almost seems that their values are simply inversions of adult values. And related to this is a third important characteristic: intolerance of nonconformity. This is so despite their own tendency to flout the standards of the adult community. Deviation from the group's standards is often punished severely, frequently by ridicule and ostracism. This harsh treatment is apparently necessary because many young people feel great ambivalence; they are torn between a basic respect for the values of the adult community and the desire to be accepted by their peers. Without discipline, there would probably be so many defections from the group and its standards that it could not survive. As long as the majority of its members can be held in line, however, the legitimacy of the subculture and its right to a measure of autonomy can be maintained. In many respects the situation is similar to that of workingmen when unions were first being formed. The majority of workingmen, too, were ambivalent, and it took rigorous discipline to establish the right of the group to a measure of autonomy.

Unfortunately, the analogy breaks down at one point: workingmen did

---

[23] Not all of the following description is meant to apply to every group.

not usually become owners and managers of industry, but young people do eventually become adults. As a result, the growing separation between adults and youth can cause serious problems, for many of the decisions that are crucial to a person in his adult years are made while he is still part of the youth community and subject to its values. Given the conflict between the values of the two communities, many early decisions later prove unsound.

A classic example of this is the heavy investment some boys make in athletics at the expense of their studies. In their peer group, where athletic success is often rewarded far more highly than academic success, this makes good sense. With rare exceptions, however, high school and college athletes find the demand for their skills in the adult world very disappointing. One in a hundred may have a brief career as a professional athlete, and only a minority of these find it really rewarding. Unfortunately, early decisions are often irreversible: not many men can return to high school in their middle twenties and make up what they neglected years before. A similar situation exists with respect to marriage. Decisions with lifelong consequences are often made while the individual is still a member of the youth community. But the qualities that make a person a desirable date frequently prove irrelevant to his or her desirability as a marriage partner.

Youth communities and their distinctive subcultures have a number of far-reaching consequences for industrial societies. In the long run, however, the most important is likely to be their effect on the processes of social change. Opposition to the values of the older generation predisposes each new generation to favor the new and the experimental. In this way, it becomes an important force for social and cultural change. Some observers of the contemporary scene have claimed to see the new youth culture as a powerful new moral force as well. But this seems dubious if one keeps in mind the whole range of innovations with which the youth culture is associated (e.g., heroin). It is safer to conclude that moral progress is no more inevitable today than it ever was. The new technology simply opens up new possibilities—for both good and evil.

LEISURE AND THE ARTS

No preindustrial society ever offered such varied opportunities for filling leisure hours as modern industrial societies provide. With electronic aids, one can vicariously explore the moon, follow sports events in distant places, or enjoy "command" performances by the world's greatest artists, dead as well as living, all in the privacy of one's own living room. If one is inclined to physical activity, the affluent society offers everything from miniature golf to skydiving.

Industrial societies are also unique with respect to the commercialization of their recreation, the vicarious nature of so much of their leisure-time activities, and their dependence on man-made aids in the search for pleasure. Both entertainment and the manufacture of equipment for leisure activities are major industries. Ironically, even when members of industrial societies "return to nature," they often take along every conceivable substitute for the conveniences of urban life they can cram into their trailers and campers.

One of the happier features of leisure in modern societies is its relative democracy. Many of the gross inequalities of agrarian societies have been drastically reduced. The shorter workweek of the average citizen furnishes the time, and mass production and general affluence the means, for him to participate in a wide variety of sports, hobbies, and other activities. Unattractive as it is in many respects, the very commercialization of entertainment has expanded opportunities for new kinds of careers, thus enabling far more people to develop their abilities more fully.

Although the influence of the new technology is most obvious in things

Table 13.5   Uses of leisure time by the Soviet urban population, by educational level, 1963

| | Percentage engaging in specified activity | | | |
| | | By level of education | | |
Frequency and type of activity	Total population	Primary	Secondary	Higher
At least several times a week:				
Reading newspaper	89	83	95	95
Listening to radio	79	80	80	75
Strolling, hiking	45	30	51	39
Playing with children	41	42	45	41
At least several times a month:				
Reading a book	75	67	82	83
Attending a movie	73	66	79	72
Visiting, having guests	64	66	69	54
Watching television*	45	37	49	55
Evening of dancing	21	20	25	11
Visiting bars, cafes	14	14	15	13
At least several times a year:				
Attending theater	42	28	50	56
Attending outdoor concerts	37	28	43	37
Attending sports events	32	26	36	32
Travel and outings	31	21	38	37
Hobbies	26	22	26	31
Visiting museums and galleries	24	15	26	31
Sports participation	22	14	26	21
Attending symphonies	18	10	16	35
Creative art work	14	10	18	20

Source: Adapted from A. B. Grushin, "Kak vy provodite svobodnoe vremia" [How do you spend your free time?], *Komsomolskaia Pravda*, Feb. 24–26, 1966. The percentages shown are based on a national urban sample of the Soviet population interviewed in 1963 and numbering 2,730.
* The low rate of television watching reflects limited opportunities at the time of the study. Nearly 80 per cent of those living in cities of 500,000 or more reported watching television at least several times per month, compared to less than 18 per cent in cities of under 10,000.

Figure 13.6   The modern symphony orchestra is a triumph of technology as well as of art: the New York Philharmonic at Philharmonic Hall, Lincoln Center.

like water skiing and photography, its impact on the fine arts has also been substantial. The modern symphony orchestra is a triumph of modern technology, and trends in painting reflect the influence of materials and processes not available to artists of an earlier era. But perhaps the most important consequence of the new technology in this area is an indirect one: traditional standards have given way to neophilia, the belief that "newer is better." This could not occur except in societies inured to, and favorably disposed toward, change in other areas.

Once again, the new technology reveals its potential for both good and ill. The nearly explosive increase in world travel, for example, could contribute so much to understanding among the peoples of the world, yet frequently it simply fans prejudice and animosity. Similarly, the mass media have almost unlimited potential both for creating and for alleviating society's problems. And although playing together can be highly effective in bridging the generation gap, such activities as golf and TV viewing have been divisive in more than a few families.

INTRATYPE VARIATION: TRENDS AND PROSPECTS

In recent decades there has been a great deal of variation among industrial societies. The differences have been especially pronounced between the one-party nations of Eastern Europe with their command economies, on the one hand, and democratic-capitalistic nations on the other. Twenty-five years ago it seemed that these were fundamentally different kinds of industrial societies, both stable and durable, both with excellent chances of surviving for the indefinite future.

But the picture has changed. Signs of convergence have been increasingly evident for a number of years. Since Stalin's death in 1953, and even more since the Twentieth Party Congress in 1956, there has been a definite, though slow and halting, movement away from the extremes of totalitarianism and political repression in the U.S.S.R. Compared with the Stalin years, the present system seems almost liberal, even though political dissent is still likely to lead to prison sentences, Siberian exile, or commitment to a mental institution.[24] In the economic area, there has been a clearly discernible shift away from the more extreme forms of the command economy. For a number of years, market forces have been permitted to operate in certain areas of the economy, and the role of centralized planning has been somewhat curtailed. These trends, as we have noted, are not limited to the Soviet Union, but extend throughout most of Eastern Europe.[25]

The capitalist democracies, meanwhile, have taken steps to increase governmental intervention in their economies and to restrict the free play of market forces. Even as conservative a President as Richard Nixon found it expedient to introduce wage and price controls of a sort, as did the British Prime Minister, Edward Heath, a Conservative. These are only two developments in a trend toward a mixed command-market economy that began decades ago. Politically, there is little evidence of any sustained or general trend away from democratic standards, though some profess to see this in such actions as the arrest of the Berrigan brothers or the trial of Daniel Ellsberg. This kind of thing is not new, however, as the arrest and imprisonment of Socialist leader and war critic Eugene Debs during World War I reminds us. Moreover, repressive developments like these have probably been more than offset by such liberalizing developments as the Civil Rights Act of 1965 (which gave the vote to large numbers of Southern blacks) or the McGovern Commission reform of the Democratic Party (which substantially increased the numbers of women, minorities, and young people among party officials and delegates).

Signs of convergence are not restricted to the political and economic areas. A declining birthrate, the movement of women into the labor force, the

---

[24] See, for example, the experiences of Andrei Sinyavsky, Yuri Daniel, General Pyotr Grigorenko, Andrei Amalrik, Yuri Galanskov, or Zhores Medvedev. On the other hand, authorities have failed to move against such dissidents as Roy Medvedev, Alexander Solzhenitsyn, and Andrei Sakharov.

[25] Czechoslovakia is clearly a special case, though it should be noted that its difficulties since 1968 were the result of an effort by Czech and Slovak Communists to push political and economic liberalization much more rapidly than the more cautious Soviet leaders would tolerate. Thus, there has been no lack of liberalizing forces within Czech society.

growth of urban populations, the growing importance of education, the growth of tertiary industries, the generation gap, the emergence of a distinctive youth culture—all these and many more are common trends in industrial societies.

These societies are not, of course, moving toward a single, uniform pattern. Differences will certainly remain; but they will probably be less marked than those which separated Hitler's Germany or Stalin's Russia from the Western democracies. The explanation for the convergence seems to be that some social systems are more costly and less satisfactory than others. If they are considered essential for ideological reasons, they can be maintained for some time by a dictatorial regime willing to pay the price. But it must be a regime run by a dedicated elite firmly committed to ideological principles. And such elites seldom remain in control for long. Though they can sometimes lead a successful revolution, once its success is assured they begin to be crowded out by pragmatic, self-seeking careerists who are far more interested in promoting their private interests than in implementing a set of abstract ideals.

As far as we can judge from the experience of industrial societies to date, extremely centralized polities and economies cost more to maintain than less centralized ones. Therefore, they are less common than democratic polities and economies that mix the elements of market and command. However, as some nations have proved, the costs are not impossible if a powerful minority of zealots is determined to make the rest of society pay the price.

PROGRESS AND PROBLEMS

In many ways modern industrial societies can be regarded as the crowning achievement in man's long struggle to build a better life. Never before has he had such a store of accumulated information or been able to harness such powerful forces in his own behalf. Never has a group of societies been as secure from the threat of starvation.

Yet for all his achievements, man is not free from problems—not even from the threat of extinction. The problems he faces today, however, differ from his earlier ones in one respect at least: they are increasingly problems of man's own making, by-products of the material progress of which he is so proud. Today more than ever, we can appreciate the reversal of an old saying: invention has, indeed, become the mother of necessity—and with a vengeance.

Examples of this are everywhere. The drug thalidomide is typical: it nicely solved the problem of sleeplessness for many people, but when taken by women early in pregnancy (often before the fact of pregnancy was known), it frequently resulted in badly deformed babies. Though an extreme case, it is not atypical. The drug industry alone could furnish thousands of other examples.

We are only now beginning to discover how many elements of the new technology have these harmful "side effects." Cigarettes produce lung cancer, factories and automobiles pollute the air, sewage systems make cesspools of beautiful rivers and lakes, insecticides destroy valuable wildlife, and supersonic jets shatter nerves and windows alike.

But it is not only the new technology that creates problems. New, highly bureaucratized systems of social organization, with their impersonal—sometimes mindless—operations, are the source of plenty of others. People whose needs do not fall neatly into one of the prepackaged routines that these organizations are "programmed" to handle can wind up horribly frustrated. And even those who manage to avoid this are likely to be alienated by the organization's impersonality.

Yet for all the shortcomings of modern industrial societies, it is doubtful that many people would elect the traditional agrarian way of life, with its widespread poverty, hunger, injustice, ignorance, exploitation, and disease. When people talk about the superiority of the great civilizations of the past, they reveal either an ignorance of the past or an unusual set of values. Taken as a whole, the agrarian way of life is decidedly inferior to the industrial, and the best evidence of this is the eagerness with which most members of agrarian societies industrialize or migrate to industrial societies when they have the chance and the reluctance of members of industrial societies to migrate to agrarian societies.

The inescapable conclusion, therefore, is that industrial societies, for all their defects, represent a significant advance over agrarian societies—and not only in technological terms. While some individuals may not share this judgment, the vast majority clearly do.

CHAPTER FOURTEEN

Industrializing Societies

Despite the rapid spread of industrialization during the last two centuries, less than a third of the world's population live in societies that can be called "industrial" as we have defined the term. The great majority, however, do live in societies that have been substantially influenced by the Industrial Revolution—either by the diffusion of modern industrial technology or by its products obtained through trade. These influences have produced a large number of societies that are best described as *industrializing agrarian* and *industrializing horticultural* societies—the ones we commonly refer to as the underdeveloped, or developing, nations.

These nations are in a transitional phase, moving from the older agrarian or horticultural way of life to the modern industrial. Social scientists usually refer to this as the *modernization* process, a process that involves *all* aspects of the life of society, not just the technological. Unfortunately, the transitional period is proving to be longer and more difficult than most scholars had expected. For both theoretical and practical reasons, then, these societies merit careful study.

In most analyses, industrializing agrarian and industrializing horticultural societies are lumped together indiscriminately. This is a serious mistake, since the two types differ in a number of important respects. In this chapter, therefore, we will deal with them separately.

First, however, a word concerning the place of other preindustrial types in the contemporary world. As we noted earlier, quite a number of hunting and gathering, fishing, and simple horticultural societies did survive into the modern era in remote and isolated areas. But recent advances in transportation have opened up most of these areas and removed this once effective source of protection. As a result, most of these groups have either been destroyed or herded onto reservations where they live as wards of their conquerors, usually under conditions that make their traditional way of life impossible. Even the few groups that still preserve a high degree of autonomy (e.g., the Bushmen in southwestern Africa) have usually adopted some tools and other elements from more advanced societies and thus are no longer pure types. This does not make them *industrializing* societies, of course; that implies something utterly beyond their adaptive capacities. Groups with such a primitive subsistence base could not possibly evolve into anything so advanced in the little time that is still available to them. They are, at best, unusual hybrids with a very limited future.

Maritime societies disappeared years ago, most of them absorbed by expanding agrarian societies. Herding societies have been more resistant, but in recent years they, too, have been largely absorbed into expanding industrial, industrializing agrarian, or industrializing horticultural societies. Though tribes of herdsmen remain distinct subgroups in many societies (Saudi Arabia, Iraq, Morocco, Kenya, etc.), because they are minority groups they do not set the tone for the society as a whole. There are a few societies in which herding peoples are dominant or nearly so—for example, Mongolia, Somalia, and Upper Volta—and others where herding is of major importance—including Jordan, Saudi Arabia, Mauritania, and Afghanistan, but research on these societies has been very limited, and they are not, as a group, very important on the world scene. Therefore we will not attempt to examine their special characteristics and problems here.

INDUSTRIALIZING AGRARIAN SOCIETIES

By one criterion, at least, industrializing agrarian societies are the most important type in the world today: more people live in them than in any other type of society. But this is not the only reason for their importance. These societies have, for decades, been struggling with problems that constantly threaten to overwhelm them. Despite a measure of industrialization, the majority of their citizens are as poor as the common people ever were in traditional agrarian societies. At the same time, improved education and the mass media have raised their hopes and expectations and given them a sharp awareness of a better kind of life. This contradiction has created a revolutionary situation that threatens to involve the entire world.

Sometimes it is suggested that the basic problem of the underdeveloped countries is simply their technological and economic backwardness. Actually, however, their problems are much more complex than that and involve all their major social institutions—polity, economy, family, religion, and education—as well as the attitudes and values of their people.

Technology and Productivity

Technologically, an industrializing agrarian society is a bewildering mixture of the ancient and the modern. Peasant farmers using techniques and tools very much like those their forefathers used 2,000 years ago work in sight of such marvels of modern technology as the Aswan Dam in Egypt or the Tata Iron and Steel Works in India.

Unfortunately from the developmental standpoint, the old technology is much more common, especially in the agricultural sector of these economies. In one recent year, an average of 55 per cent of the labor force of forty-six industrializing agrarian nations was engaged in agriculture, and yet pro-

Figure 14.1 The old and the new: Indian farmer plowing with his bullocks under high-power electric transmission lines.

duced only 26 per cent of the gross domestic product.[1] This differential would have been even greater if many of these countries did not have income from relatively modern plantations (tea, rubber, etc.) operated by foreigners from industrial societies.

There are marked differences in the level of technological and economic development among industrializing agrarian societies. With per capita energy consumption as a measure, levels range from only 11 kilograms of coal equivalent per year in Nepal to 1,544 in Argentina. The average for all industrializing agrarian societies is actually closer to Nepal's: in 1969 the median for forty-seven of them was only 328.

In general, the level of technological development is higher in the Middle East, North Africa, and Latin America than in southern and eastern Asia. Median figures for per capita energy consumption in these areas in 1969 were as follows:[2]

Middle East and North Africa	474 (N = 12)
Latin America	221 (N = 19)
Southern and eastern Asia	156 (N = 16)

---

[1] These figures are medians. The calculations are based on United Nations, *Yearbook of National Accounts Statistics, 1969*, table 3, and Food and Agriculture Organization of the United Nations, *Production Yearbook, 1970*, table 5. Here, as elsewhere in this chapter, we have ignored the new microstates such as Kuwait, Gabon, and Mauritania.

[2] These calculations are based on United Nations, *Statistical Yearbook, 1970*, table 138. N is the number of nations on which the energy consumption figure is based.

These figures do not include the industrial societies in those areas (e.g., Japan and Israel).

Many discussions of the underdeveloped countries give the impression that they are technically and economically stagnant or, at the very least, developing less rapidly than industrial societies. But data assembled by the United Nations show that this is not the case. Since 1938, the productivity of the industrializing societies has increased at almost exactly the same rate as that of industrial societies.[3] Unfortunately, however, they have far surpassed industrial societies in population growth (see below), and this, combined with the low base point from which they started, has served to keep their increases in *per capita* income small. Thus, during the decade from 1958 to 1968, the gain was only $3 per person in Indonesia, $8 in India, $11 in Ceylon, $30 in Thailand, $43 in Egypt, and $103 in Brazil, compared with $693 in Japan, $780 in West Germany, and $1,212 in the United States.[4] Because of the extreme social inequality that characterizes most of these societies, it is quite possible that even these meager gains did not reach the masses of people. Yet Americans continue to be puzzled by the appeal of communism in the Third World.

Demographic Patterns

With the introduction of modern medicine and sanitation, death rates have been cut drastically in almost every industrializing agrarian society. But except in

Table 14.1   Crude birthrates for selected industrializing agrarian societies, 1970 or most recent year for which data are available

Society	Crude birthrate*	Society	Crude birthrate*
Pakistan	50.9	Mexico	41.3
Saudi Arabia	50.0	Turkey	39.6
Indonesia	48.3	Brazil	37.8
Libya	45.9	Korea (North and South)	36.6
Philippines	44.7	China	33.1
Colombia	44.6	Lebanon	27.3
Cambodia	44.6	Chile	26.6
Haiti	43.9	Argentina	20.7
India	42.8	Spain	19.8
Peru	41.8	Greece	17.4

Sources: United Nations, *Demographic Yearbook, 1970,* table 13.

* Number of births per 1,000 population per year.

[3] For the period 1938–1961, see United Nations, Department of Social and Economic Affairs, *The Growth of World Industry, 1938–1961* (New York: 1965), table 4; for the years 1960–1969, see United Nations, *Statistical Yearbook, 1970,* table 4.

[4] These figures have all been corrected for inflation and thus are stated as changes in *real* income. The data on income change are from United Nations, *Statistical Yearbook, 1970,* table 184; the correction for inflation is based on data in U.S. Bureau of the Census, *Statistical Abstract of the United States, 1971,* table 526.

Table 14.2   Increases in gross domestic product and in per capita gross domestic product for three sets of societies, 1950–1969

Set of societies	Percentage increase in GDP,* 1950–1969	Percentage increase in per capita GDP,* 1950–1969
Industrial societies, except		
Communist bloc	141	93
Industrializing societies:		
East and Southeast Asian	134	53
Latin American and Caribbean	160	57

Source: Adapted from United Nations, *Statistical Yearbook, 1970,* table 4.

* Gross domestic product equals gross national product minus net income from abroad.

rare cases, birthrates have remained high, averaging over 40 per 1,000 population annually (see Table 14.1). Year in, year out, the populations of the underdeveloped nations continue to swell, consuming most of their hard-won gains in productivity.

Table 14.2 shows in detail the cost of uncontrolled population growth for the industrializing nations of southern and eastern Asia and Latin America. Had they been able to maintain a balance between births and deaths from 1938 to 1961, their per capita income would have grown at a faster rate than industrial societies experienced during that period. Instead, they fell further behind, even in Latin America, where the average annual increase in gross national product was greater than in industrial societies.

Uncontrolled population growth is a serious problem for industrializing societies not only because it means so many more mouths to feed but also because it complicates the entire process of societal development. For one thing, mass public education is prohibitively expensive in these nations, and yet without it the population is not equipped for most kinds of jobs in modern industry. This forces large numbers of people to find employment in traditional industries, especially farming. But even there they cannot be accommodated except by subdividing already small farms to the point where they are hopelessly inefficient and the introduction of modern machinery is impossible. In Egypt, for example, 70 per cent of the farm owners had less than half an acre in 1950.[5] As one writer observed, "Most of those who are working the land work not because the land requires their labor but because they require the work."[6] He went on to say that as early as 1939 it was estimated that 10 per cent of Egypt's farmers could have supplied all the necessary labor if Egypt's farms had been even half as mechanized as America's were. The story is much the same in other industrializing agrarian societies.

---

[5] Manfred Halpern, *The Politics of Social Change in the Middle East and North Africa* (Princeton, N.J.: Princeton, 1963), p. 80.

[6] Ibid.

Figure 14.2 Peasant family, Colombia.

Another complication results from the fact that the surplus population is too poor to buy anything but the most basic traditional commodities. Thus they do not generate a demand for the many kinds of industrial products that are an essential component of the economy of every industrial society. Finally, this surplus population compounds all the other problems by its own productive achievements: an abundance of children. The society is thus trapped in a vicious circle.

In view of all this, it is hardly surprising to learn that there is a correlation of −.49 between the birthrate and the average annual growth of per capita productivity.[7] This indicates a strong relationship between high birthrates and low rates of economic progress.

In recent years the leaders of a few of these industrializing societies have finally begun to grasp the seriousness of the population problem and its relation to economic growth. Efforts have been made to encourage married

[7] See Glossary for an explanation of correlation coefficients. The study cited was Bruce Russett et al., *World Handbook of Political and Social Indicators* (New Haven, Conn.: Yale, 1964), p. 277, and was based on data from fifty-five nations.

couples to adopt modern methods of contraception, but in most cases these have not been very successful. Considering the limited funds invested in these programs, one could hardly expect anything else. An increasing number of social scientists believe, however, that investments in birth control would accomplish far more in raising the standard of living than equal investments in industry—at least at this point in the developmental process.

The Economy

The economies of industrializing societies can be divided into two basic parts. The traditional component is very similar to the economy of the typical agrarian society of the last 2,000 years. The tools and techniques are much the same, and so, unhappily, is the level of productivity. In contrast, the modern—or at least modernizing—component uses tools, techniques, and patterns of economic organization that have, for the most part, been borrowed from industrial societies.

Obviously, this division results in tremendous internal variation within each developing nation. The people in some areas are living just about the way their forebears did for a thousand years or more, while other areas are already well on the way to industrialization. Table 14.3 shows the situation in Greece, but a similar situation exists in most societies of this type.

But the modernizing sector of these societies is not simply a scaled-down version of the economy of the average industrial society—a few small steel mills, a small automobile plant or two, some textile mills, wholesale and retail distributors, and so forth. Compared with more advanced economies, the modern sector in the average underdeveloped country is very one-sided or imbalanced and very highly specialized.

To understand why this is so, we have to recognize the tremendous difference between the circumstances under which these nations are industrializing and those under which Western Europe and the United States in-

Table 14.3   Some indicators of regional differences in Greece, 1961–1962

Indicators	Attica or Greater Athens	Thrace
Per capita consumption of electric energy in kilowatt-hours	833	34
Private cars per 10,000 inhabitants	168	8
Percentage of households with inside baths or showers	30	2
Percentage of households with drinking water installation	72	21
Number of inhabitants per doctor	305	3,293
Number of inhabitants per hospital bed	70	588

Source: Centre of Planning and Economic Research, *Draft of the Five Year Economic Development Plan for Greece* (Athens, 1965), p. 147, cited by Nikos Mouzelis and Michael Attalides, "Greece," in Margaret Archer and Salvador Giner (eds.), *Contemporary Europe* (New York: St. Martin's, 1972), p. 187.

Figure 14.3 Two views of an industrializing society: Croatian peasants plowing near Karlovac; new apartment buildings in Belgrade.

dustrialized. Today's developing nations have to make the transition in a world dominated politically and economically by *already* industrialized nations, nations that have well-established home markets with high volumes of sales, nations that have become the builders of industrial machinery for the rest of the world. Add to this the relatively low cost of moving goods today, and the industrializing countries are left without much of a competitive advantage *even in their home markets;* European, American, and Japanese firms can easily undersell Latin American and Asian manufacturers in a wide variety of fields, especially in the heavy industries.

As a result, many of the industrializing societies have been forced into a peculiar ecological niche: they have become the producers of the world's raw materials. Furthermore, because of pressures generated by world markets and by their own desire to maximize income, they often become dangerously specialized. For example, 100 per cent of Saudi Arabia's foreign exchange comes solely from the sale of petroleum products, 76 per cent of Chile's from copper, and 76 per cent of Cuba's from sugar (see Table 14.4). Of forty-one industrializing agrarian societies for which data are available, fifteen rely on a single commodity for over half of their foreign earnings, while another sixteen rely on only one for at least a quarter.[8]

Table 14.4   Leading exports of selected industrializing agrarian societies and percentage dependence on these exports for foreign exchange

Society	Commodity	Percentage Dependence
Saudi Arabia	petroleum	100
Iraq	petroleum	94
Chile	copper	76
Cuba	sugar	76
Malaysia	lumber	72
Colombia	coffee	63
Panama	bananas	60
United Arab Republic	textiles	60
Jamaica	bauxite and alumina	58
Bolivia	tin	53
Indonesia	petroleum	48
Cambodia	rubber	40
Brazil	coffee	35
Pakistan	textiles	31
Argentina	meat	27
India	textiles	27
Thailand	rice	20
Mexico	textiles	16
Spain	fruits and nuts	10

Source: Adapted from United Nations, *Yearbook of International Trade Statistics, 1969.*

---

[8] These calculations are based on United Nations, *Yearbook of International Trade Statistics, 1969.*

Any nation that depends so heavily on just one commodity is highly vulnerable to shifts in the world economy that affect its specialty. Technological innovations in particular—things like synthetic rubber and synthetic fibers—can permanently reduce, or even eliminate, demand for the product. This sensitivity to change naturally creates an unstable "boom or bust" atmosphere, hardly conducive to rational economic planning and development by businessmen or government. Instead, it encourages a speculative attitude whose goal is to make quick profits and then transfer capital to less risky ventures.

Despite their drawbacks, these specialized industries are an important source of income for developing nations and help them accumulate the capital that is so essential for industrialization. In addition, they increase the number of people with modern skills and a modern economic orientation. A society simply cannot industrialize and modernize without large numbers of such individuals.

It is still too early to say whether the benefits of specialized industries will, in the long run, outweigh the costs. A lot will depend on the attitude of the more advanced nations. If countries like the United States, Japan, the Soviet Union, and the members of the European Economic Community regard industrializing nations simply as pawns to be manipulated and exploited for economic and political advantage, the long-term benefits for the developing nations are likely to be small. On the other hand, if the leading nations act responsibly, they can set the less developed ones on a more hopeful course. This is one area in which modern statesmen have a truly important choice confronting them.

The Polity

One of the greatest hindrances to modernization and industrialization in these societies has been the kind of governing class they inherited from the past. This class had a good thing going for centuries, and its contemporary members have usually seen no need for change. The ideal society, for them, is the kind that flourished before intellectuals, students, and the common people ever heard of liberty, equality, democracy, socialism, and communism. From their perspective, change is something to be feared and fought—or occasionally, as in the case of aid programs sponsored by industrial societies, exploited for their own benefit.

In the last 100 years, however, a growing number of voices have been raised against the old order and its backward-looking, exploitative character. In some instances proponents of modernization have seized control of the government, with the idea of using the power of the state as a force for political, economic, and social change. These modernizers have been a heterogeneous lot. Some have been military men with a strong spirit of nationalism, like Ataturk and Nasser; some, civilians and democratic socialists, like Nehru. A number have been Communists, like Lenin, Tito, Mao Tse-tung, and Castro, while in at least one case—Iran—the monarch himself played this role.

Figure 14.4 Modernizers have been a heterogeneous lot. Some have been military men like Nasser, some Communists like Castro, while in at least one case—Iran—the monarch himself played this role.

Would-be modernizers usually have found, however, that it is not enough simply to win control of the government. To implement their plans, they must have the support of thousands of lower- and middle-level officials who are both efficient and honest. Unfortunately, such men are hard to find in societies that for centuries have neglected education and viewed government office as a means for self-aggrandizement. As a result, the efforts of the top leaders are often frustrated by the incompetence and corruption of lesser officials.[9]

One of the most basic questions confronting the leaders of industrializing societies today concerns what role the state should play in the industrializing and modernizing process. In recent decades there have been two radically different models for them to choose from, one provided by the Western democracies, especially Britain, France, and the United States, the other by the communist nations, the Soviet Union and China in particular. In practical terms, the choice has been between a society in which the state plays a limited role in the economy and other areas of life and there are free elections and parliamentary rule, and a society in which the state directs and controls the economy and other areas and a strong executive authority dominates the government without permitting free elections.

Until World War II, most would-be modernizers chose the Western democracies for their model. Parliamentary government and free elections looked as if they were the key to progress. The adoption of democratic forms by underdeveloped nations, however, seldom produced the expected results. Democratic governments were often toppled by military juntas representing the old order. Even the ones that survived such threats rarely experienced the economic progress they had anticipated.

In recent decades, the rapid advances made by the Soviet Union and the promises contained in Marxist theory made that model an attractive alternative. The key to progress in the communist model has been the systematic, and if necessary ruthless, mobilization of a society's resources by a regime with a definite plan for the future.

For some years now, many leaders in underdeveloped countries have found the choice difficult. On the one hand, they have been attracted by the liberal, humane, and pragmatic principles of the democratic model. On the other hand, they have been impressed by the ability of an authoritarian system to mobilize resources and by its promise of greater political stability and economic progress. Many leaders have come to doubt that a full-fledged democratic system can be both stable and economically progressive in a society characterized by widespread poverty and illiteracy among the common people,

---

[9] See, for example, A. H. Hanson, *The Process of Planning: A Study of India's Five-Year Plans, 1950–1964* (London: Oxford University Press, 1966), part II, especially chap. 8; Peter Franck, "Economic Planners," in Sydney Fisher (ed.), *Social Forces in the Middle East* (Ithaca, N. Y.: Cornell, 1955), pp. 137–161; Louis Walinsky, *Economic Development in Burma, 1951–1960* (New York: Twentieth Century Fund, 1962), part V, especially chap. 29; or Lennox A. Mills, *Southeast Asia* (Minneapolis: University of Minnesota Press, 1964), chap. 11.

exploitative traditions among the old upper class, and a critical shortage of technical skill and capital.

As a result, many leaders have recently begun experimenting with various hybrid forms, incorporating elements from both of the new models while often retaining some elements of their societies' traditional systems. Egypt's Nasser stated the goals and methods of these hybrid types as well as anyone. The six objectives of the Egyptian revolution, according to him, were "elimination of imperialism and its helpers, elimination of feudalism, elimination of monopoly and its domination of the government, the establishment of universal social justice, the formation of a strong, patriotic, national army, and the creation of sound democratic life."[10] In his view, however, democracy could not be put first, for the effort to establish it would undermine the whole revolutionary effort. In an address to the nation in 1954, he said, "There will be democracy and freedom, but we must first be free from exploitation, despotism, and slavery. I cannot understand how there can be freedom if I am not free to find my bread and make a living, and free to find employment."

In recent years, a growing number of Western social scientists have reluctantly concluded that truly democratic regimes are less well equipped to survive the terrible political stresses in these societies and at the same time provide the rate of economic growth essential for their future.[11] This is not to say that democracy is impossible in these countries: Ceylon, Chile, Costa Rica, and India prove otherwise.[12] These are the exceptions, however, not the rule. Of fifty-seven industrializing agrarian societies in 1972, not more than nine could be considered full-fledged democracies.[13] Several others were moving in that direction and might be called semidemocratic. A number of others contained democratic elements, but these were generally subordinated to authoritarian elements, both traditional and modern.

The most serious deficiency of democratic regimes in industrializing nations is their apparent inability to keep up with the nondemocratic and mixed types in the vital area of economic growth. Table 14.5 shows the record of the past twenty years, and as the figures in the right-hand column indicate, the gap

---

[10] Halpern, p. 244.

[11] See, for example, David Apter, *The Politics of Modernization* (Chicago: University of Chicago Press, 1965), or S. M. Lipset, *The First New Nation* (New York: Basic Books, 1963), p. 11. For other references on the subject, see the footnotes to the article by Charles Moskos and Wendell Bell, "Emerging Nations and Ideologies of American Social Scientists," *The American Sociologist,* 2 (1967), pp. 67–71. Moskos and Bell challenge the view cited above, but although their article serves as a valuable criticism of deterministic tendencies in some of their opponents (i.e., tendencies to deny that the liberal democratic model can *ever* be made to work in industrializing societies), their basic argument is not convincing.

[12] Moskos and Bell, op. cit., mention a number of other industrializing countries they regard as democratic, but many of these are either industrial or industrializing horticultural societies or inappropriate for other reasons (e.g., Greece has since fallen to a military junta).

[13] Here, as elsewhere, we have not counted the microstates.

Table 14.5 Average annual growth rates of per capita real gross domestic product in democratic and nondemocratic industrializing agrarian societies compared, 1950–1969 (in percentages)*

Time period	Democratic societies	Nondemocratic societies	Difference
1950–1959	1.4[a]	2.4	1.0
1960–1964	0.9[b]	2.3	1.4
1963–1969	1.4[c]	3.8	2.4

Sources: United Nations, *Statistical Yearbook, 1965,* tables 183 and 184, and United Nations, *Statistical Yearbook, 1970,* table 178.

* The average here is the median; real gross domestic product equals gross national product minus net income from abroad, measured in constant dollars (i.e., effects of inflation controlled).
[a] The democratic nations in this period were Brazil, Ceylon, Chile, India, Pakistan, the Philippines, and Uruguay.
[b] The democratic nations in this period were Brazil, Ceylon, Chile, Greece, India, Jamaica, the Philippines, and Uruguay.
[c] The democratic nations in this period were Ceylon, Chile, Colombia, India, Jamaica, the Philippines, and Uruguay.

between democratic and nondemocratic societies has been widening. The difference between a 1.4 per cent annual growth rate and a 3.8 per cent growth rate may look unimpressive, but it means the difference between doubling a nation's per capita income in *fifty* years as opposed to only *twenty*. For people who no longer accept poverty as inevitable, that extra thirty years may make democratic government a luxury they are not willing to pay for.

One cannot be dogmatic about what industrializing nations will do, since nations, like individuals, are free to choose uneconomical alternatives—that is, alternatives that reflect their ideological commitments. In general, however, the poorer an individual or a nation, the likelier it is to prefer the alternative that is economically most attractive. This suggests that democracy's prospects in the underdeveloped countries of the world are not very favorable for the next decade or two.

Social Stratification

Systems of stratification in industrializing agrarian societies are as varied as the polities and economies with which they are linked. Some are still predominantly agrarian in character (see Chapter 8), with only minor admixtures of modern elements. Others are much more modern, but even they differ in degree of modernization and in how far the polity leans toward the liberal democratic or the authoritarian model.

The composition of the upper class clearly reflects these variations. The stronger the traditional element in the polity and the less developed the economy, the more likely that the upper class will be an aristocracy of long-established, wealthy, landowning families that consider the control of government, army, church, and other basic social institutions their natural right. Regardless

Figure 14.5 Upper-class housing, Colombia.

of whether the government is constitutionally a monarchy, a republic, or a democracy, in fact it is an oligarchy.

The middle class is usually very small, mostly merchants, lesser officials, lesser members of the religious establishment, and a small number of prosperous peasants. With industrialization, however, it includes increasing numbers of business and professional men with modern skills, members of the civil service with modern educational qualifications, and teachers trained in the newer disciplines.

Then, as political modernization and industrialization progress, the leading members of these new occupations begin to penetrate the upper class. Some of the most successful businessmen rival, or even surpass, the old aristocracy in terms of wealth, while politically active individuals challenge the old elite's control of the government. This does not mean that the aristocracy accepts these new groups as social equals; on the contrary, it rejects them for as long as possible. The result is that there are, for a time, two largely separate and parallel systems of stratification. The traditional system is strongest in the rural areas, the newer one in the cities. With increasing modernization, however, the newer elements gradually become dominant politically, economically, and even socially, though the process is usually not completed until some time after the society has become fully industrialized.

In societies that adopt the authoritarian pattern, or lean in that direction, the old upper class is usually destroyed more quickly. Sometimes this is accomplished by imprisonment and execution, sometimes by confiscation of property and denial of access to political office. In these societies, just as in industrial societies under Communist control, the new political elite is the dominant class. But it is an ironic footnote to history that a disproportionate number of this new elite come from the upper and middle classes of the old regime.

As all of this suggests, industrialization and political modernization drastically alter the value of social resources. Land-ownership and membership in old aristocratic families become less valuable in the system of stratification, while modern education and membership in the modernizing party or movement become much more so. In societies that are modeled after the liberal democracies and permit large-scale private enterprise, ownership of factories, banks, and other large businesses is also a very valuable resource.

The value of modern education, especially training in engineering and science, is substantial in both authoritarian states and democracies. This has had one interesting, though almost certainly temporary, consequence: it places the younger generation in a relatively advantageous position. This advantage is often reinforced by the effects of political revolutions. Because they are usually the work of younger men who distrust the older generation and prefer to surround themselves with their age peers, revolutions tend to be followed by a period in which youth is an asset and younger men are promoted much faster than they would be otherwise.

Figure 14.6 Lower-class housing, Rio de Janeiro.

The major variations in the composition of the lower classes in these societies are the result of differences in level of economic development. The less development, the larger the peasant class and the smaller the urban working class, especially those in factories and other modern industries. Conversely, the more development, the fewer peasants and the more urban workers. At one extreme, 80 to 95 per cent of the labor force in Nepal, Laos, Afghanistan, Haiti, and Vietnam are still engaged in agriculture, and only a small percentage in industry. At the opposite extreme, countries like Argentina, Chile, Portugal, and Spain have less than half of their workers in agriculture and 20 to 30 per cent in manufacturing.[14]

Life is grim for large numbers of the lower classes in most industrializing agrarian societies. High birthrates, moderate and declining death rates, and inadequate educational systems combine to ensure a constant oversupply of unskilled labor, and the situation is naturally aggravated by the economy's shift from men to machines. The excess population typically migrates from rural areas to the cities, where there are at least some employment opportunities for the young and able-bodied. But, as in agrarian societies of the past, aging, accidents, and illness soon deprive them of their economic value, especially when there is a steady stream of fresh labor moving into the cities.

The only industrializing agrarian societies that seem to have solved this problem are communist nations, such as the People's Republic of China and Cuba. There, according to almost all reports, beggary, prostitution, and widespread unemployment and underemployment have been eliminated by drastic authoritarian measures. In effect, the leaders of these nations have traded the political liberties and many of the economic privileges of the small middle class and the elite for the economic benefit of the much more numerous lower class.

Cleavages and Conflict

Few societies in history have had such serious internal divisions as the majority of those now undergoing industrialization. Most of them are torn not only by the ancient cleavages that have always existed in agrarian and horticultural societies, but by some which are peculiar to societies industrializing at this particular time.

Most basic of the older cleavages in industrializing agrarian societies is that between the few who control the nation's resources and the vast majority who supply the labor and get little more than the barest necessities in return. The traditional cleavages between urban and rural populations and between the literate minority and the illiterate majority are also present, though they may

---

[14] International Labour Office, *Yearbook of Labour Statistics, 1971*, table 2A, and Food and Agriculture Organization of the United Nations, *Production Yearbook, 1970*, table 5.

OH! CALCUTTA!

Modern Calcutta is a city of outrageous paradoxes: a hell hole of filth and disease, whose poor curse it and their bad luck in living there; a city of matchless fascination for its richest citizens, who would not live anywhere else, and for prosperous foreign visitors.

Satahu Sahni, one of its poorer citizens, pulls a rickshaw for a living. He works from 6 A.M. to midnight, earning 52 cents a day. He lives in a one-room hut with his wife and two children. They spend about 40 cents a day for food alone, which provides tea and cookies for breakfast, a wheat cake for lunch, and rice and dried peas for supper. Satahu says of his work, "This job shouldn't be done by any human being, but I couldn't find any other thing to do."

Up and down hills, through broiling molten tar, across rough cobblestones, hauling heavy carts often loaded with more than one passenger as well as freight, Satahu and his fellow rickshaw men run day after day. Summer temperatures that are often above 100, and high humidity, cause a few each day to simply slip from between the shafts of their carts and drop dead. "It's really quite awful actually," said a British-educated Calcuttan, who has his own air-conditioned Mercedes and never rides in a rickshaw. "Not only do the poor runners die, but many passengers are injured when the rickshaws tip over backwards. Quite awful." But Satahu is fortunate compared to the hundreds of thousands of jobless persons and beggars in Calcutta who have no home at all and are forced to sleep on the open sidewalks at night and beg for a little food each day.

Adapted from a copyrighted story of the
Associated Press, April 19, 1970, by permission.

be less pronounced now that advances in transportation and communication have reduced the isolation, and hence the ignorance, of the rural and the illiterate.

As we have already seen, the struggle to industrialize and modernize creates its own cleavages and conflicts. There is a split within the more favored classes, for example, between those educated along traditional lines and those with modern scientific and technical training. These groups have difficulty understanding one another and are mutually prejudiced. Another new cleavage separates the landowning aristocracy and the new elite of industrial entrepreneurs, who frequently surpass the older group in wealth. But there are others as well.

As the patrimonial, monarchical system found in most agrarian societies breaks down, many new groups become politically active and many new issues become politically relevant. This is true even in societies where democratic principles are observed more in the breach than in practice. For example, the political unrest and other changes associated with industrialization often exacerbate historic tensions between religious and ethnic groups. One can see this in such widely scattered countries as Vietnam, Indonesia, India, Lebanon, Iraq, and Guyana, to name but a few whose interethnic or interreligious conflicts have been especially serious. The breakdown of the older political system and efforts to establish a modern regime can also produce serious tensions between civilian political leaders and the military. Struggles between these groups have caused crises in many Latin American, Middle Eastern, and Asian nations. In more democratic countries, mass political parties have introduced yet another cleavage. Although support for the various parties does tend to follow other lines of cleavage, it is seldom a perfect reflection of them. Therefore, it creates further divisions within an already badly divided population.[15]

Finally, the rapid rate of change characteristic of industrializing societies invariably creates a cleavage between the generations. Though there are no valid measures, this gap appears to be more serious than the generation gap in societies that have already industrialized. This conclusion is suggested both by the frequency and bitterness of the conflicts between students and political authorities in these nations and by the frequency of revolutionary activity by "young Turks" (the Kemalists in Turkey after World War I, Nasser's associates in Egypt, the Fidelistas in Cuba, Ben Bella in Algeria, the early Apristas in Peru, etc.). We would expect such a split, of course, in societies changing so rapidly. The experiences of the different generations, and thus the information and values on which they base their actions, are so dissimilar that conflict is almost inevitable. Universities are often the centers of discontent, because they bring together large numbers of people who have maximum exposure to new ideas but very little power to implement them. The result, not surprisingly, is often explosive.

Education and Economic Development

The importance of education for economic growth is abundantly clear: the most prosperous nations are those that have invested heavily in education. In the United States, Japan, and the Soviet Union—three of the most striking examples of economic growth—"high levels of national expenditure on education preceded industrialization."[16] In czarist Russia as early as the end of the last century, 44 per cent of the men between thirty and thirty-nine were literate, and in

[15] See, for example, Myron Weiner, *Party Building in a New Nation: The Indian National Congress* (Chicago: University of Chicago Press, 1967).

[16] Neil Smelser and S. M. Lipset (eds.), *Social Structure and Mobility in Economic Development* (Chicago: Aldine, 1966), pp. 29ff. Statistics cited in this paragraph are from the same source.

urban areas the figure was as high as 69 per cent. In Japan, half the male population was literate a generation before that; and in the United States, 90 per cent of white adults were literate as early as 1840.

Other studies of the relation between education and economic progress reinforce this conclusion. A recent survey of sixty-eight nations found a correlation of .42 between the rate of annual growth of per capita production and the percentage of children aged five to nineteen attending school and a correlation of .49 between growth and the literacy rate.[17]

Developments in a number of industrializing countries, however, suggest that it is not enough for them simply to provide more education regardless of content. Many of these nations have seriously overemphasized the humanities and classical forms of higher education at the expense of the sciences and engineering. In both Eastern and Western Europe, from one-third to one-half of university students study science or engineering, compared to only 23 per cent in Asia and 16 per cent in Latin America.[18]

These figures are important not only because industrializing societies so urgently need technical and engineering skills but also because they have so much trouble absorbing the nontechnical professionals they turn out. In India, for example, where, recently, 58 per cent of the students were enrolled in the humanities, fine arts, and law,[19] many graduates simply cannot find jobs that utilize their skills. Unwilling to accept lesser employment (a reflection of the traditional value system of agrarian elites and would-be elites), they become a kind of intellectual proletariat with deep-seated hostilities toward the existing social order. Because such people are easily attracted to revolutionary movements, there is increased political instability, and this in turn hampers economic progress. In short, far from aiding economic growth, an oversupply of nontechnically trained students in a society can actually hinder it.

One might ask why the leaders of these societies allow this kind of educational imbalance to develop. There are several reasons. First, in allowing the humanities to dominate their educational systems, they are following the example of the oldest and most prestigious educational institutions in the world—Oxford, Cambridge, and the famous Continental universities—as well as their own native traditions. Second, it costs much more to provide technical education, and these nations have very limited resources. Finally, it has not been very long since the nature of this problem first became evident. Perhaps in the light of experience these nations will begin to revise their educational programs.

---

[17] See the Glossary for an explanation of correlation coefficients. The study cited is Russett et al., *Political and Social Indicators,* p. 277.

[18] Smelser and Lipset, p. 37, and Jan Szczepanski, *Polish Society* (New York: Random House, 1970), table 15, p. 115.

[19] Smelser and Lipset, p. 37.

Belief Systems and Ideologies

Most leaders of modernizing movements are convinced that social and economic progress require more than increased capital and improved techniques of production. New creeds and new gods are needed to arouse and mobilize the common people, who, after centuries of frustration, are so often apathetic and take a fatalistic view of life. Ironically, even such a dogmatic and supposedly orthodox Marxist as Mao Tse-tung has come to place the spiritual struggle for men's minds and souls on a par with, or even ahead of, the struggle to transform the economy.

Today, in all but the most backward parts of the industrializing agrarian world, there is an intellectual ferment and clash of ideas between the advocates of traditional belief systems and the proponents of newer ones. The situation is often extremely complicated, because both traditionalists and modernizers are themselves divided on many points, while still others favor various blends of the old and the new.

A lot of the intellectual and ideological resistance to modernization has come from advocates of the traditional faiths. In southern and eastern Asia, this means Buddhism, Hinduism, and sometimes Islam; in the Middle East, Islam; in the Balkans, Eastern Orthodoxy; in Latin America, Spain, and Portugal, Roman Catholicism. In all these areas, religious leaders have often been the leaders of conservative and traditionalist movements as well. This is hardly surprising, considering the historical role of these groups in agrarian societies and the nature of their beliefs. In general, they believe that the quest for truth is essentially complete: what men need to know has already been revealed—in the Vedas, or in the Koran, or to the Sangha, or to the Church. True wisdom, in their opinion, lies in turning to religious authorities for guidance and following their directions. In describing the traditionalist approach to education in the Middle East

Figure 14.7 Two faiths.

today, one writer has said, "Education, as far as it is under the control of the ulema [the spiritual leaders of the Muslim community], is still bound up with authoritarianism, rote learning, and a rigid devotion to ancient authorities—providing only already known solutions to already formulated problems."[20] Traditionalist education in Latin America and southern and eastern Asia is very similar. This approach sees little need for change, unless it is to root out whatever modernizing influences have crept in.

In the late nineteenth and early twentieth centuries, many Western intellectuals thought these older faiths would simply die out as their adherents came to recognize the "obvious" superiority of Western creeds such as Protestantism, Humanism, and Socialism. All three of these newer faiths were then winning converts, especially among the better educated, and it looked as if it were only a matter of time until the older faiths would vanish altogether.

Since World War I, however, and even more since World War II, the situation has changed drastically in many areas. With the development of nationalist movements and a growing resistance to colonialism of every kind, many of the traditional faiths have experienced a remarkable reinvigoration. After Ceylon won its independence, for example, a significant number of Christian converts there reconverted to Buddhism. In India, Hindu traditionalist forces became strong enough to pass laws forbidding the entry of foreign missionaries. In Egypt, Nasser imprisoned or executed most of the leaders of the Communist Party.

In some instances, this reinvigoration resulted from reform movements within the religious group itself. Vatican Council II, for example, provided a powerful impetus to modernizers within the Roman Catholic Church in Latin America, giving the church renewed vigor in a number of countries, particularly in Chile.[21] Through professional religious leaders have been the most conspicuous proponents of traditionalism, they have usually had strong support from the old governing class, especially the large landowners. In fact, the rural population as a whole has generally supported them: it has not taken much imagination for these people to see that industrialization would make their labor unnecessary and their skills obsolete. For the same reasons, members of the old "professions"—for example, midwives, herbalists, and practitioners of traditional medicine—have been strong supporters of traditionalist ideologies and belief systems.

Ranged against people like these are individuals and groups who by virtue of educational, occupational, or other experience have been converted to the newer faiths. Early in a modernization movement, a disproportionate

---

[20] Halpern, p. 122.

[21] See, for example, Ivan Vallier, "Religious Elites: Differentiations and Developments in Roman Catholicism," in S. M. Lipset and Aldo Solari, *Elites in Latin America* (New York: Oxford University Press, 1967), pp. 190–232, or William V. D'Antonio and Frederick B. Pike (eds.), *Religion, Revolution, and Reform* (New York: Praeger, 1964).

number of the leaders are people who were won over to a new outlook during visits to industrialized societies, either as students or as workers.[22] Later, however, most of the leaders are people who were converted by experiences right in their own countries. Frequently they are children of members of the old governing class, gravitating, after conversion, to positions of leadership because of their superior training and other resources.

As we noted earlier, there are usually competing movements within the camp of modernizers, some advocating Western-style democracy, others the communist authoritarian model, still others some kind of hybrid system. The liberal Western model was the first to be tried in most industrializing agrarian nations. It has had its greatest support from the more prosperous segments of the new middle class—professional men, managers in new industries, and others with modern education. Socialist and communist movements were usually introduced next. Their support has been greatest among intellectuals, students, and the economically insecure—landless peasants, underemployed or unemployed urban workers, and the like.

The hybrid approach to modernization is the most recent and reflects the fact that many of the current generation of leaders have reacted negatively to both of the older models. Their idea is to synthesize not only liberalism and authoritarianism but modernism and traditionalism as well. Most of the nationalist ideologies that have flourished in the industrializing agrarian world since World War II have had a strong element of traditionalism. To some extent, nationalism is a reaction against colonialism, and crucial in the process of nationbuilding. This is especially true of countries that were under foreign control until recently.

There is more to modern nationalism than this, however: it is also an effort to reassert the importance of the cultural traditions of non-European peoples (in the case of Latin America, of peoples not in the Anglo-American tradition). This helps heal the breach between traditionalists and modernists by providing a position that is more or less acceptable to both. Moreover, it gives dignity to a nation's leaders in their relations with European (or Anglo-American) peoples. In this respect, the function of these nationalist movements is similar to that of the "black nationalist" movement in the United States, which seeks to increase the self-respect of blacks by emphasizing the worth of the black cultural tradition.

Unfortunately, the deliberate cultivation of nationalist sentiments easily leads to the hatred of other nations. Even when this is not a spontaneous development, leaders of industrializing nations may encourage it solely to divert criticism from themselves and their policies. It can be useful to blame "foreign devils" for all the defects and shortcomings, inevitable and otherwise, of one's

---

[22] For Latin America, see Robert E. Scott, "Political Elites and Political Modernization: The Crisis of Transition," in Lipset and Solari, p. 133.

own nation. A number of leaders in industrializing nations have succumbed to this temptation, but as the experiences of Sukarno in Indonesia and certain Arab leaders in the Middle East demonstrate, this polity is not without risks of its own.

INDUSTRIALIZING HORTICULTURAL SOCIETIES

Prior to the modern era, advanced horticultural societies were found in several locations in the New World, most of Africa south of the Sahara, and some parts of Southeast Asia. But during the last several centuries, more advanced societies conquered a number of these groups (among others, the Incas and Aztecs) and destroyed others by sociocultural assimilation (the fate of many backward hill tribes in India).[23]

In Africa south of the Sahara, however, things have been different. There, much of the traditional horticultural way of life has survived into the second half of the twentieth century, apparently because the period of European colonial rule was so brief and its impact on most of the native societies relatively limited. It is easy to forget that the period of European rule in most of sub-Saharan Africa did not begin until the last decades of the nineteenth century and ended early in the second half of the twentieth. Thus the process of institutional disintegration and transformation in these societies was just beginning. By contrast, many of the horticulturalists in the New World and Southeast Asia have been under alien control since the sixteenth century or longer. For this reason, the concept of industrializing horticultural societies is really applicable only in Africa south of the Sahara.

The problems of these societies are similar in a number of respects to those of industrializing agrarian societies. Both are confronted with a variety of radically new social and cultural elements introduced by diffusion from technologically more advanced societies. Both find that these new elements throw their traditional relations out of kilter and create serious tensions. Furthermore, both experience an almost continuous state of crisis because things are changing so fast.

At the same time, there are a number of important differences between them that reflect their horticultural and agrarian backgrounds and often cause them to react differently to the impact of industrialization. To avoid unnecessary repetition, we will focus mainly on these differences, referring only briefly to the points of similarity. Unless this is kept in mind, the differences between industrializing agrarian and industrializing horticultural societies may appear to be greater than they actually are.

---

[23] See, for example, F. G. Bailey, *Tribe, Caste, and Nation* (Manchester, England: Manchester University Press, 1960).

Technology, Productivity, and Demographic Patterns

Technologically, industrializing horticultural societies are much less advanced than industrializing agrarian, especially in their indigenous (native) technology. This is revealed in a number of ways. For one thing, they are much less urbanized: in one recent year, industrializing agrarian societies had an average of 27 per cent of their populations in cities of 20,000 or more, while industrializing horticultural societies had only 9 per cent in cities that large.[24] This is important, because the size of the urban population is a good measure of the growth of specialized crafts and trade and commerce.

Another indication of the technological and economic lag of horticultural societies is their low level of productivity. The extent of this lag is not usually revealed by the standard measures of productivity, such as per capita income. Using this measure, countries like Ghana, Liberia, Zaria, or Kenya appear to be at least as productive as China, India, and Burma and most of the other industrializing agrarian societies of Southeast Asia. But per capita measures of productivity fail to take into account the fact that agrarian technologies and economies are sustaining larger and denser populations. With these measures, we actually destroy much of the evidence of their technological superiority.

A better way to compare the technological development of societies that are still in the process of industrializing is by *per area* income. The question then becomes, How much can the society produce per square mile of territory? (There is some distortion even in this measure, because of the influence of large deserts and other unproductive territories, but while such things may appreciably affect the figures for a particular society, its effect on large groups of societies is not great.) Figures on gross national product show nearly a fivefold difference in the productivity of the two types of societies. In forty-nine industrializing agrarian nations, the median value of the gross national product was $10,400 per square mile; in sixteen industrializing horticultural nations, it was only $2,200.[25]

Despite its inferior technological development, the typical industrializing horticultural society has a standard of living roughly comparable to that of the typical industrializing agrarian society. Although its economy is only a fifth as productive, its population is only a fifth as dense.

This low density could turn out to be an extremely valuable asset. Modern methods of birth control are available to these societies at an earlier, more opportune point in their development than in the case of industrializing

---

[24] Calculations are based on United Nations, *Demographic Yearbook, 1970,* table 9. The figures provided here are medians for eleven industrializing horticultural societies and thirty-three industrializing agrarian societies.

[25] Calculations are based on GNP data in Russett et al., table 43, and area data are from *Statistical Abstract, 1966,* table 1287, and *The World Almanac, 1952,* pp. 289ff.

Figure 14.8 Harvesting in a cocoa grove, Ghana. Like many industrializing nations, Ghana is heavily dependent on a single crop; 60 per cent of its foreign exchange comes from cocoa.

agrarian societies. Thus, they do not have to become saddled, as most other developing nations are, with huge surplus populations that must be put to work even when their employment reduces the level of productive efficiency (as in the case of peasants working excessively subdivided farms). In the race to industrialize and modernize, most of the advantages—literacy, skilled manpower, commercial experience, urbanization, and so on—lie with industrializing agrarian nations. But low population density is one plus on the side of industrializing horticultural nations. Considering how serious the effects of overpopulation are, it is just possible that this single advantage could outweigh all the others.

Unhappily, the current demographic signs in sub-Saharan Africa are discouraging. Birthrates in most of its societies are running close to the human maximum (see Table 14.6). Death rates, meanwhile, have dropped considerably from the old equilibrium level: though there is little reliable evidence, they are estimated to be around 20 per 1,000. The average rate of increase, then, appears to be about 2.5 per cent per year—in other words, dangerously high.

Table 14.6 Crude birthrates in selected industrializing horticultural societies

Society	Crude Birthrate*
Niger	52.2
Rwanda	51.8
Togo	50.9
Dahomey	50.9
Madagascar	50.0
Nigeria	49.6
Upper Volta	49.4
Kenya	47.8
Guinea	47.2
Ghana	46.6
Ethiopia	45.6
Zaria	44.1
Uganda	43.2
Cameroon	43.1
Liberia	40.7

Sources: United Nations, *Demographic Yearbook, 1970,* table 13.

* Number of births per 1,000 population per year.

The Economy

Because the urban sector of the economy in horticultural societies is much less developed than in agrarian societies, the urban population has had even less experience with such fundamentals of modern life as money, trade and commerce, markets, occupational specialization, literacy, and bureaucracy. This makes it very difficult for modernizing governments and businesses to find skilled personnel to staff their organizations. The problem is especially serious in an era of nationalism (and nationalism is just as strong in these societies as in industrializing agrarian societies), because national pride often demands that businesses and government be staffed with native personnel, even at the expense of organizational efficiency.[26]

Data on literacy provide some idea of the relative magnitude of this problem for the two types of industrializing societies. In the late 1950s, 44 percent of the adult population in the average (median) industrializing agrarian society was literate; in industrializing horticultural societies the comparable figure was 7.5 per cent.[27] Assuming literacy as a minimum requirement for effec-

---

[26] See, for example, Gwendolen Carter (ed.), *African One-Party States* (Ithaca, N.Y.: Cornell, 1962), p. 371ff. and 461ff; Guy Hunter, *The New Societies of Africa* (New York: Oxford University Press, 1964), chap. 9, especially pp. 223ff.; International Bank for Reconstruction and Development, *The Economic Development of Uganda* (Baltimore: Johns Hopkins, 1962), pp. 23–24; or Ken Post, *The New States of West Africa* (Baltimore: Penguin, 1964), chap. 6.

[27] Calculations based on Russett et al., table 64. The figures are based on fifty-five industrializing agrarian and sixteen industrializing horticultural societies. Another indicator of literacy is the rate of newspaper circulation. This, too, varies greatly by societal type.

tive participation in modern economic life and assuming also that these nations will not be able to increase their rate of literacy any faster than other nations have, it will take industrializing agrarian societies at least fifty years to develop a fully qualified labor force and industrializing horticultural societies at least ninety.[28]

Horticultural societies face still other problems in economic development. We can see why when we consider the nature and meaning of work in traditional settings. Not long ago, the Inter-African Labour Institute characterized work traditions in horticultural Africa this way:

1. Work is viewed in its relation to the basic institution of family or clan; within the family, it is divided on the basis of age and sex.
2. Work is linked with religious rites.
3. Work activities are considered and evaluated in the light of a subsistence economy rather than a profit economy (i.e., one oriented to the production of the necessities of life rather than to the maximization of profits in a market economy).
4. Work requires neither foresight nor planning.
5. Time is largely irrelevant in work activities; no time-limits are set for most tasks.
6. There is little specialization.
7. For men, work is episodic; when a task has to be done, men often do it without a break, but intervals of inactivity are long and frequent.
8. Men hardly ever work alone; work activities (e.g., hunting parties and work parties) often resemble a collective leisure activity in modern industrial society.[29]

These traditions do little to prepare the members of these societies, especially the men, for work in a modern industrial society. A parallel list of the characteristics of work in industrial societies would, in fact, be an almost perfect contradiction.

One of the biggest problems is suggested by item 7. In analyzing horticultural societies, we saw how often farming is primarily women's work. The men's responsibility may be limited to the occasional clearing of new fields. Since women do the sustained, tedious chores—planting, cultivating, and

---

[28] Russett et al., table 65, provides data on the average annual increase in the rate of literacy for forty-three countries since about 1920. The median increase is 0.7 per cent per year; only nine of the forty-three countries had a rate in excess of 1 per cent.

[29] Based on Inter-African Labour Institute, *The Human Factors of Productivity in Africa,* as summarized in William H. Lewis (ed.), *French-Speaking Africa: The Search for Identity* (New York: Walker, 1965), p. 168. Many of these propositions were supported in papers presented to a recent conference on competing demands for labor in traditional African societies, cosponsored by the Joint Committee on African Studies of the Social Science Research Council, the American Council of Learned Societies, and the Agricultural Development Council. See William O. Jones, "Labor and Leisure in Traditional African Societies," *Social Science Research Council Items,* 22 (March 1968), pp. 1–6.

Figure 14.9 Medical laboratory, Louvanium University, Kinshasa, Zaria.

harvesting crops—men are free to do more interesting and exciting things—hunting, fighting, politicking, socializing, and participating in ceremonial activities. The disciplined, routinized forms of work so typical of an industrial economy are seldom encountered by men in these societies. In this respect, the peasant farmers of agrarian societies are far better prepared for industrialization. Yet even they have found the transition difficult.[30]

There is tremendous economic and social variation in sub-Saharan Africa today. At one extreme, a few tribes and villages remain virtually untouched by the influences of industrialization; at the other, the older patterns have been all but destroyed in cities like Dar es Salaam, for example.[31] In between is every conceivable combination of the old and the new—such as the woman in Nairobi who practiced witchcraft in order to earn the down payment on a truck so she could go into the trucking business.[32] (A more common pattern is for a person to work part-time in a factory while continuing to practice traditional horticulture.)

One observer reports that there have been four basic economic patterns in Africa in recent years.[33] The first, which is now extremely rare, is a pure subsistence economy in which the local village consumes only what it produces or obtains through barter with its neighbors. The second pattern he calls "taxed subsistence," which means that a village raises a cash crop or sends its young men out to work for cash so it can pay the taxes levied by the govern-

---

[30] See, for example, J. L. Hammond and Barbara Hammond, *The Town Labourer, 1760–1832* (London: Guild Books, 1949, first published 1917), especially chap. 2.

[31] On the latter, see, for example, J. A. K. Leslie's fascinating study, *A Survey of Dar es Salaam* (New York: Oxford University Press, 1963).

[32] Hunter, p. 85.

[33] Ibid., p. 94.

ment. The third might be called a mixed economy: villagers still rely on a subsistence economy for their basic necessities, but they simultaneously work for cash—not only because of taxes but so they can buy modern consumer goods. The fourth pattern is a predominantly cash economy in which even food is bought and laborers are hired to work on the farms.

These patterns, which typically follow one another in sequence, show how internal and external forces combine to transform a society's economy. On one side, there are the preferences and desires of the villagers themselves; on the other, the demands made, and attractions offered, by alien groups and institutions. It is easy to underestimate the power of the internal forces and interpret economic development as a process that is simply forced on reluctant villagers who want nothing more than to be left alone to live as their fathers did for centuries. But the problem is far more complex than this romanticized view suggests. Given a choice, most horticultural peoples prefer the industrial way of life—not knowing, it is true, all the implications and ramifications of their choice. Sometimes they adopt it *in toto,* like the family that migrates to the city; sometimes in part, like the couple who stay in the village but earn all the cash they can to buy modern tools, cloth, soap, a sewing machine, a radio, a bicycle, and the other products of an industrial economy.

The Polity

One of the striking features of sub-Saharan Africa is how young most of its societies are: almost without exception, they were established in the late nineteenth or the twentieth century. Most of them are the products of European colonialism, and their boundaries are largely the result of the rivalries of missions or colonial governments, the outcome of battles, the location of rivers, and a variety of other things that had little to do with the boundaries of the societies they replaced. Actually, the process was not too different from the one that produced most of the modern nations of Europe, Asia, and the New World.

Because of their newness, most African societies suffer from serious internal divisions that stem from traditional tribal loyalties. The colonial powers seldom destroyed the older tribal groups. On the contrary, in most cases they consciously preserved them as instruments of administrative control, allowing tribal rulers to serve as lower echelon officials in the new colonial societies. Colonial governments often pretended these groups were autonomous in order to put the burden, and the onus, of political control on their leaders. They also encouraged tribal rivalries, applying the ancient principle "Divide and rule." As a result, even after independence was won, there was a fundamental tension between tribal loyalties and national loyalties in most parts of Africa. This is one problem that few industrializing agrarian societies have had to contend with.

The consequences have been serious for sub-Saharan societies, however. In Zaria (formerly the Congo), tribal divisions nearly destroyed the new society in its first few years of independence. In Nigeria and Burundi, the fuse burned more slowly, but the results were even worse. In most other countries, tribalism remains an important divisive force, sometimes with the potential for civil war.[34] When they were still fighting for independence, many African lead-

Figure 14.10 Tribal chief on visit to Monrovia, capital of Liberia.

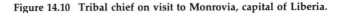

---

[34] See, for example, Aristide Zolberg, *One-Party Government in the Ivory Coast* (Princeton, N.J.: Princeton, 1964), pp. 202ff. and 286ff.; Hunter, pp. 286–298; or Lucy Mair, *New Nations* (Chicago: University of Chicago Press, 1963), pp. 114–122.

TRIBAL LAW VERSUS NATIONAL LAW:
THE CASE OF THE MARAKAWET ELDERS

On March 17, 1971, Kap sirir rap Koech, better known as Chelimo, a member of the Marakawet tribe in Kenya, had a quarrel with his wife and beat her to death. He then fled into the bush, but his brothers, following tribal custom, hunted him down and brought him before village elders, who, after deliberation, rendered the verdict of death, a judgment that was accepted by both of the families involved. Chelimo was then tied face down on the ground, and his older brother and the father of his murdered wife together brought large stones and smashed the back of his head. Word of their action came to government authorities, and Kibor, the brother, and Kirop, the father, were brought to trial under national law, which is based on English law, and were themselves condemned to death for murder.

In discussing the case, a reporter for the *Los Angeles Times* wrote, "In more developed countries like Britain and the United States, the law has evolved naturally, coming out of the folkways of the people. But in Africa, the law has been imported from an alien country and imposed upon a host of traditional laws of many different tribes.

"At independence, the new African leaders could have thrown out the colonial law and reverted to the old tribal laws. But they did not. Mainly because they feared chaos. The leaders want to create unified states, and unity would be held back if each small tribe practiced a law of its own.

"Selecting one tribal law and imposing it on all the others might even be more divisive. So the leaders decided to retain the foreign law that had become common to all tribes during colonial days.

"There was another reason. The new leaders consider themselves modern, educated men, and in their view much of traditional tribal law was not 'civilized.' They did not want justice governed by such law.

"But the use of European law has not been absolute. There has been an attempt, both in colonial days and now, to bend the European law to accommodate some of the traditional tribal law. In some cases, in fact, tribal law or, as it is called in the courts, 'customary law,' guides the decision of judges. If this were not the case, the legal system would be so alien that the people would attempt to ignore it.

"As a result, conflicts arise between the law of England and the law of the tribe. The case of the Marakawet elders illustrates this."

Excerpted from a story copyrighted 1972 by the
Los Angeles Times. Reprinted by permission.

ers (as well as their friends in the Western academic world) ignored or minimized the importance of these tribal loyalties, thinking that their countrymen valued them as little as they did and that the old ties were rapidly losing their vitality. Although this seems to be true in a few countries, it has proved a serious misjudgment in most.[35] Even in cities and towns, tribal loyalties are still meaningful to some degree.[36] In the light of American experience with ethnic loyalties, and considering the virtual absence of national institutions in Africa until recently, this is hardly surprising. With increasing urbanization, with the establishment of schools that indoctrinate children in a nationalistic outlook, and with the growth of the mass media to reinforce these early lessons, tribal loyalties will eventually disappear. But this will probably take decades, and in the meantime these allegiances will produce many bitter conflicts.

In other respects, the polities of industrializing horticultural societies have a lot in common with those of industrializing agrarian societies. Planning efforts, even basic administrative activities, are often hamstrung by the lack of trained personnel and by commitments to a rapid Africanization of the civil service. This is especially serious because most of these governments are also committed to programs of economic planning and development, a notoriously difficult and complex business.[37]

Another important similarity is the trend that one writer has referred to as "the erosion of democracy."[38] Prior to independence, most political leaders in these countries professed to be democrats in the West European sense, in other words, to believe in parliamentary government, a multiparty system, free elections, and so forth. Very soon, however—confronted by opposition that threatened to turn them out of office or by incipient chaos resulting from the tribalization of politics and the return to power of tribal chiefs and other proponents of traditionalism—most of them retreated to an advocacy of a one-party state with control largely or wholly in the hands of a strong executive (i.e., themselves). In a number of countries, civilian government was terminated and leadership assumed by the military.

Although many of the new governments have survived thus far, the pressures on them are often intense. One British observer has outlined the process that commonly develops in the wake of independence:

> As a new African government first assumes power, there seems to be much in its favor. There is enthusiasm, there are congratulations and good wishes from the world; many promotions to make, ambassadorships to be filled, national

---

[35] See, for example, Brian Weinstein, *Gabon: Nation-Building on the Ogooue* (Cambridge, Mass.: M.I.T., 1966).

[36] See Leslie, p. 32; or Merran Fraenkel, *Tribe and Class in Monrovia* (London: Oxford University Press, 1964), especially chap. 3.

[37] See Apter, *The Politics of Modernization*, pp. 130 and 328–330, or Hunter, p. 289.

[38] Mair, pp. 122ff.

development plans to occupy energies and give a sense of progress and achievement. Above all, it is an African government, it is "ours."

But there is a debit side. Naturally, the age-old frustrations of being governed were turned against the colonial power over years of agitation and electioneering. The anti-colonial struggle had aroused much expectation of greater freedom from restraint which is not compatible with the other goals of the nationalist movement. Nervous [foreigners] had often quoted the wilder expectations of the uneducated ("We shall print more bank notes"; "The Bank will be nationalized and forced to give us loans") and as caricature these stories are not important. But there is a more serious side. In rural areas there could be great impatience with continuing agricultural reform; and in the modern sector much expectation of a quick inheritance of opportunities and profits of expatriate trade [i.e., businesses owned by foreigners]. And there are other reversals. The Trade Unions, once a weapon of anti-colonialism, may seem to be sabotaging the national effort.[39]

He goes on to describe the problems national leaders face in their attempts to control the self-seekers within their party organizations and concludes that "The imposition of a standard of conduct and discipline is a trying task for a victorious party."

But these problems are all secondary compared with the really serious ones. Although they take different forms in different countries, these are common to most: "tribalism; the conflict between traditional and modern — the old authority and the new democratic forms; the whole control and status of land; the whole system of local administration; and ultimately, the moral standards and social norms which are to be established in society."[40] With the elimination of the colonial regime, all the hostilities are now focused on the new national governments — and this is sometimes more than they can cope with.

Social Stratification

Most of the new nations in sub-Saharan Africa profess socialist ideals. This does not mean, however, any real concern with the elimination of economic inequality. Rather, as one writer says, "quite often . . . the socialism of Africa is another name for nationalism. The common element of the various forms of [African] socialism . . . is the emphasis on development goals for which individuals must make sacrifices."[41] Another observer puts it even more strongly.

There is . . . little or no emphasis on the moral aspects of socialism, the gap between rich and poor. In Tropical Africa as a whole . . . the salaries and

---

[39] From *The New Societies of Africa*, pp. 286–287, by Guy Hunter, published by Oxford University Press under the auspices of the Institute of Race Relations. By permission of Oxford University Press.

[40] Ibid., p. 288.

[41] Apter, p. 329.

perquisties of the ruling group and of the whole professional and educated class are at or near the old [colonial] level, the profits of contractors and politicians are enormous, while very large sections of the economy remain at the old levels. Despite constant inquiry, we could find little evidence of "socialist" thinking in this moral sense, save among a few of the younger intellectuals in Lagos and Accra. . . .[42]

As in industrializing agrarian societies, patterns of stratification vary according to the relative political strength of the modernizing forces and the older forces of traditionalism. Where the latter are dominant, as in northern

Figure 14.11 Where modernizers are in control, the upper class is largely made up of the new political and intellectual elite: Jomo Kenyatta, first Prime Minister of Kenya, graduate of the London School of Economics, and author of the highly regarded ethnographic monograph, "Facing Mt. Kenya."

[42] From *The New Societies of Africa*, p. 289, by Guy Hunter, published by Oxford University Press under the auspices of the Institute of Race Relations. By permission of Oxford University Press. See also Daniel Bell, "Socialism," in *International Encyclopedia of the Social Sciences* (New York: Macmillan and Free Press, 1968), vol. 14, pp. 528–529.

Nigeria, the upper class is made up of the rulers of the old society: the chiefs, kings, or emirs, together with their ministers and retainers. Where the modernizers are in control, the more typical situation, the upper class is largely composed of the new political and intellectual elite and, in most countries, the new entrepreneurial elite.

Beneath the economically and politically dominant class, there are two fairly distinct systems of stratification. In the rural areas, where the traditional patterns prevail, an individual's status is largely a function of his own or his family's relation to traditional authorities (the village headman, the tribal chief, etc.). In urban areas, where the modern system of stratification is centered, education, occupation, income, and connections with the new political authorities become the crucial criteria.[43]

Cleavages and Conflict

By now it should be clear that industrializing horticultural societies are as badly divided as industrializing agrarian societies. They, too, are heir to nearly all the cleavages of traditional societies, and most of those of modern industrial societies as well. In one respect, however, their situation is even worse than the agrarian: because they are such young nations, they are still divided along tribal lines. This is a powerful divisive force, because it involves deep emotional commitments, always so difficult to control by rational, political procedures. But time is on the side of the advocates of national unity: with each passing year, the older loyalties weaken. Therefore, if civil war can be avoided for the next several decades, the problem will probably be resolved in most of these societies.

Religion and Ideology

The traditional religions of sub-Sahara Africa were relatively undeveloped, both organizationally and intellectually. There were no complex organizations of priests or monks, as there are in the major religions of the agrarian world, no body of sacred writings to serve as the core of a common faith, no tradition of religio-philosophical speculation, and, most important of all, no supranational faith uniting the members of different societies. As a result, these faiths could not easily defend themselves against the inroads of Islam and Christianity, especially when these were being introduced by peoples who were politically and economically stronger and whose way of life, therefore, seemed so obviously worthy of emulation.

Africans who still cling to the older tribal faiths are usually the residents

---

[43] Just as in industrial societies, status inconsistencies often develop. See, especially, Fraenkel, pp. 203–211. Their effects remain to be studied.

of the more isolated rural areas and the less educated residents of the towns. Since this describes the majority of the people in these societies, adherents of the older faiths are obviously still numerous. In Zaria, for example, only 30 per cent of the people are even nominally Christian or Muslim, in Zambia 13 per cent.[44] Among the modernizing elements of the urban population, however, the picture is very different. In Dar es Salaam, a city of 100,000 in Tanzania, 99.8 per cent of the population claim to be either Muslim or Christian—and this in a country still 60 per cent non-Muslim and non-Christian.[45] Similarly, in Monrovia, the capital of Liberia, 72 per cent regard themselves as either Christian or Muslim, although in the country as a whole, only 9 per cent do so.[46]

Conversions to Islam and Christianity are frequently for nonreligious reasons. For many, conversion is simply a status symbol, an effort to identify with modern ways and avoid being regarded as an ignorant, backward countryman. In Dar es Salaam, for example, many pagan tribesmen "on arrival in town call themselves Muslims—some few call themselves Christians—in order to conform, not to be conspicuous in a [community] where Islam is supreme and where to 'have no religion,' as people put it, is the mark of the uncivilized. Some go so far as to be circumcised and to be formally admitted to Islam: most merely use a Muslim name instead of a tribal one; some have two names, a Christian and a Muslim, to cover all eventualities."[47] Under the circumstances, it is hardly surprising to find that "the outward observances of religion are strikingly absent in Dar es Salaam: it is rare to see an African Muslim praying his daily prayers [and] in Ramadhan [the Muslim month of fasting] people may be seen anywhere eating and drinking publicly during the daily hours [a forbidden practice]," and the consumption of alcohol, also forbidden, is almost universal.[48] In Monrovia, where Christianity is dominant, the pattern is not quite so pronounced, but even here "the professing of Christianity remains a basic requirement of 'civilized' status," and "for a great many of the civilized, church membership has become largely a question of social status, and has little more significance than membership [in] other types of associations."[49] In many areas, both urban and rural, even those who have adopted Christianity or Islam continue traditional pagan practices.[50]

In the early years of colonial rule, Christian missions were an important force for modernization. This was primarily due to the mission schools, which

---

[44] Figures based on *Statesman's Yearbook, 1971–72.*

[45] The figure for Dar es Salaam is from Leslie, p. 210, and that for Tanzania from Russett et al., tables 74 and 75.

[46] Fraenkel, p. 154, and Russett et al., tables 74 and 75.

[47] From *A Survey of Dar es Salaam,* p. 211, by J. A. K. Leslie, published by Oxford University Press, 1963. By permission of Oxford University Press.

[48] Ibid., pp. 210–211.

[49] Fraenkel, pp. 158 and 162.

[50] Hunter, p. 74, provides numerous examples.

introduced literacy and elements of Western culture and, most important of all, opened up channels of communication with the larger world. As a result, the areas that came under Christian influence advanced more rapidly than those where paganism or Islam prevailed. In discussing Tanzania, one writer asserts:

> Mission schools and mission hospitals have been very important factors in changing tribal society, although their influence has been felt much more strongly in some areas than others. Very nearly a one-to-one correlation exists between mission influence, the cash-crop economy, fertile land, education, and the general desire for progress.[51]

Similarly, many visitors to Africa have commented on the singular success of the Christian Ibo of southeastern Nigeria compared with the Muslim and pagan tribes to the north.

With the rise of the independence movement after World War II, identification with Christianity became an ambiguous social attribute. Christianity was linked with colonialism, and colonialism was, by definition, a force detrimental to Africa. The missionaries came under heavy attack for dominating the churches and refusing to let native Christians assume positions of leadership. Furthermore, in an era of great social turmoil and insecurity, mission-brand Christianity often seemed too tame and too Western. In many areas, native leaders founded new sects, some basically Christian, others largely pagan, many a mixture of the two.[52] These sects usually have their greatest appeal for individuals who are in midpassage in the difficult transition from traditional culture to modern. Such people are subject to great insecurity, both economically and intellectually, and the sects often provide an element of reassurance. They also are popular because they accept polygyny and other traditional African practices condemned by the missionaries.

In sub-Saharan Africa, as in other industrializing areas, nontheistic faiths also compete with the older faiths. The most important of these is nationalism. In many cases, nationalism functions simply as a secular ideology. But sometimes, when it demands supreme loyalty, it assumes a truly religious character. In Ghana, for example, President Nkrumah assumed messianic titles, and his party (the Convention People's Party) took on quasi-religious functions.[53] This tendency is so marked that some students of the modernization process now speak of *political* religion in contrast to *church* religion.[54] Whether nationalism will survive in this extreme form no one can say. Its chances

---

[51] Carter, pp. 433–434. © 1962 by Cornell University. Used by permission of Cornell University Press.

[52] See, for example, Vittorio Lanternari, *The Religions of the Oppressed: A Study of Modern Messianic Cults,* trans. by Lisa Sergio (New York: Knopf, 1963), chap. 1, or Mair, pp. 171ff.

[53] The same has been true of Sékou Touré's Democratic Party in Guinea. See, for example, Apter, p. 299, n. 36.

[54] Ibid., chap. 8.

are probably linked with the new nations' efforts to modernize: the quicker and easier the modernization process, the poorer the chances for an extreme nationalism; the slower the change, and the more painful, the likelier it becomes.

Kinship and Family

In the traditional horticultural societies of precolonial Africa, extended family groups were extremely important. As one writer put it, in Africa "the [extended family] was the basic building block of society."[55] More than that, it was psychologically the center of the individual's world, establishing his identity and defining most of his basic rights and responsibilities.

Now the historical bases of power of the extended family are being destroyed. In the modern sector of the economy, the extended family no longer controls its members' access to the means of livelihood as it traditionally did through its control of the land. Similarly, family ties lose much of their political value when there is an increasingly impersonal governmental bureaucracy to be dealt with. Last but not least, the cult of the ancestors, centered in the extended family, declines in importance as Christianity and Islam grow.

Under the old system, most of the advantages of the extended family were enjoyed by the older generation, while the disadvantages fell disproportionately on the younger. Before the growth of cities and towns, young people had no choice but to accept the burdens and patiently await the day when they would become the privileged elders. Industrialization changed all this: at the very least, it offered youth a way to escape the authority of the elders, at best, a rise to fame and fortune beyond the wildest dreams of those who stayed in the villages.

We get some idea of this change from the following excerpt from a document written by an African townsman explaining to a European why Africans leave the villages. In it, he describes a typical conversation between two young villagers, one of whom says:

> Lucas, old boy, we have a very hard life here in the country; the authorities—I don't know if it is the chief or his assistants—have their knives into us. And as for Father and even Mother! . . . Listen, it was only the other day, you've seen the maize, cucumbers, and vegetables, all ripe? Well, this day hunger followed me around all day, I ran away from it but my feet wouldn't get me away, so I thought it best to go to our field and help myself to some cucumber. I admit I took one and swallowed it down without chewing. Then I got a mad desire to eat some maize and broke off three and went home to roast them. Presto, as the first was ready I began to eat it, then the second, when in come my parents from visiting. They see me and start straight in to abuse me, tell me

---

[55] L. A. Fallers (ed.), *The King's Men: Leadership and Status in Buganda on the Eve of Independence* (New York: Oxford University Press, 1964), p. 99.

Figure 14.12 The lure of the city: Lagos, capital of Nigeria.

never to darken their door again. That evening there was a big storm with lightning, one bolt of which struck a tree in that field and it fell and ruined a stretch of crops: then in the morning everyone said: Ah, yes, Juma ate unblessed food before we had sacrificed, that's why their field was destroyed. So the news spread and they sent me to expiate it, and when I got there the omens were against me and I was an outcast to the whole village. My father is an old man but he has no gratitude; since he was exempted from tax he has been to work for the chief only five times, every time it is his turn it's me that goes. . . .

I hate it here, better get a change of air—town air—even if it kills me. I am lucky enough to have borrowed the fare down, though I haven't enough to come back. But every day they sit on me, and now there is nothing for it but to disappear and give myself a break; in the town there are many people and many jobs, but here what job can a chap get? It's just the messenger coming in the morning, early, with a little bit of paper summoning me to the court; you get there and they tell you, you are charged by the agricultural inspector for not having a cassava field; if you ask who the inspector himself is, you're told, "That child over there." If you ask who is prosecuting and where he is they'll say, "So you are one of these bush lawyers are you? Do you suppose a full agricultural inspector will tell lies?"

Elders like this are not to be borne, in the end you may be had up for murder, better go to town where nobody knows me, and nobody will say what's that you're eating, what's that you're wearing, every man for himself and mind his own business: but here! You've only to cough and somebody ticks you off for getting your feet wet.

Last week I returned from safari with the dresser, carrying his loads, and only a little later they volunteered me again to carry the [District Commissioner's] loads, nothing but work, any time there's loads to be carried it's always me. . . . Well now, the rains are starting and lorries won't pass, off I go again. Soon I'll develop wheels and be a public service vehicle. Go to town any day.[56]

---

[56] From *A Survey of Dar es Salaam*, pp. 27–29, by J. A. K. Leslie, published by Oxford University Press. By permission of Oxford University Press.

Life in the extended family was obviously not the idyllic experience that those who romanticize simpler societies make it appear. For thousands of young Jumas, the choice is clear.

Actually, the break with the extended family is seldom as sharp as Juma's musings suggest. When they get to town, young men usually search out their kinsmen, who help them find employment and get settled. But in the long run the ties of the extended family are seriously weakened, and industrializing horticultural societies have not yet developed any real substitute for them.[57] This is a fairly serious source of social instability, yet the experience of industrial societies suggests it is inevitable.

Another problem confronting these societies is the shift from polygyny to monogamy. Polygyny was practiced in almost all the traditional horticultural societies of sub-Saharan Africa, while monogamy, as we have seen, is the rule in all modern industrial societies. Although the Christian missions fought polygyny vigorously, they had only limited success. Their opposition to it is, in fact, reputed to be one of the major reasons many Africans have been reluctant to be baptized. Eventually, however, the same forces responsible for monogamy in other industrial and industrializing societies will probably prevail here.

Considering the historical importance of kinship in horticultural Africa, such revolutionary changes are bound to be unsettling. Their effects will be felt at both the individual and the societal levels for a long time to come.

INDUSTRIALIZING SOCIETIES: PROSPECTS AND PROBLEMS

Not too many years ago, the prospects for industrializing societies looked bright and promising. All they had to do, apparently, was follow in the path blazed by the industrial nations of Western Europe and North America. In fact, by coming along later, they could profit from the others' experience, avoid many of their problems, and speed up the entire modernization process.

So it seemed.

A quarter of a century later, this prediction seems ludicrous. Far from occupying a favored position in history, industrializing societies today are in a singularly disadvantageous one. They are increasingly drawn into a global economic system in which industrial societies hold all the high cards. If they want to participate, they have to abide by rules the others lay down, and one of those rules is that they play the restrictive and hazardous role of supplier of raw materials, often of a single commodity. Thus they become economically dependent on countries that know little, and seem to care less, about the consequences of this dependency.

An economy evolving under these conditions is naturally going to develop differently than Europe's and the United States' economies did in the

---

[57] Ibid., pp. 60–61, or Fraenkel, pp. 127ff.

nineteenth century. Instead of starting out producing things like textiles, iron, coal, and machine tools, which led those nations to develop skilled labor forces and balanced economies, the nation industrializing today starts out by furnishing bananas or coffee, rubber or petroleum, in a highly competitive world market. And in most cases these things are not even produced by native firms, but by firms from industrial nations, firms whose interest in their host nation is restricted to its raw materials and its unskilled labor. Far from encouraging the development of a skilled labor force and a balanced economy, this simply fosters the growth of a depressed rural proletariat.

Then, as the developing nation tries to establish industries really its own, to build factories and branch out into something beyond raw materials, it

SON OF DOLLAR DIPLOMACY

As the Foreign Ministers of the Organization of American States wound up their annual meeting in Costa Rica last week, evidences of a new mood in Latin America were painfully abundant. Gone was the anti-*yanqui* rhetoric of the past—a rhetoric that indiscriminately blamed the U.S. for all of Latin America's woes. Instead, the Latins focused their attention on a single, overriding problem: the degree of economic power which the U.S. exerts in Latin America. . . .

These are not happy days for U.S. citizens living in Latin America. From the ambassador, living in virtual protective custody and surrounded by an army of bodyguards, to the housewife with her list of precautionary do's and don'ts—never take the children to school by the same route twice, vary the time of shopping trips to the supermarket—an American might perhaps be forgiven if he has begun to feel that he isn't welcome among his Latin neighbors. . . .

Behind the anger and bitterness that many Latin Americans feel today is a strongly held belief that, after all the rhetoric, money, and effort of the [Alliance for Progress], the main beneficiary has been the U.S. They point to the fact that between 1961 and 1966, Latin America received $6 billion in U.S. loans and investments, but paid back double that in debt payments, interest on loans and remitted profits. . . .

Opening a recent meeting of the Inter-American Development Bank in Buenos Aires, former Argentine President Roberto Levingston claimed that a "realistic analysis shows that not only has foreign aid been insufficient, but if the net movement of capital is taken into account, it becomes clear that it was Latin America which, paradoxically, contributed to the development of more advanced areas."

Excerpted from *Newsweek* story, May 3, 1971.
Copyright Newsweek, Inc., 1971, reprinted by permission.

is confronted by another hard fact: because most secondary industries are dominated by huge, immensely wealthy corporations based in industrial societies, small, new firms simply cannot compete. A single corporation, General Motors, has annual sales four times greater than *the entire gross national product* of a country the size of Peru (see Table 14.7). Because of the vast resources at their disposal, and because of the vast markets they control, such corporations can afford to adopt the latest technology as soon as it becomes available. Small firms with limited sales cannot: they must keep old equipment in use for a much longer period of time in order to write off their investment in it. This is, in effect, one more illustration of the way the market system favors larger units at the expense of smaller ones.

Meanwhile, the one real gift of advanced nations to their industrializing cousins has backfired. Modern methods of sanitation and preventive medicine have worked—too well. Death rates have dropped dramatically, but birthrates have not. As a result, populations in industrializing nations are growing alarmingly.

Like so many other problems of development, this one was not nearly so severe for societies that industrialized earlier. The reason is simply that no

Table 14.7 Nations and corporations: a comparison of the gross national products of selected industrializing nations and the annual sales of selected corporations, 1970, in billions of dollars

Nation or Corporation	GNP or Sales	Nation or Corporation	GNP or Sales
Argentina	$25.42	ITT	$6.36
GENERAL MOTORS	24.30	TEXACO	6.35
Pakistan	17.50	Peru	5.92
STANDARD OIL (N.J.)	16.55	WESTERN ELECTRIC	5.86
FORD MOTOR	14.98	Nigeria	5.80
Yugoslavia	14.02	Portugal	5.22
Indonesia	12.60	U.S. STEEL	4.81
ROYAL DUTCH/SHELL	10.80	Cuba	4.80
Philippines	10.23	VOLKSWAGENWERK	4.31
Iran	10.18	BRITISH PETROLEUM	4.06
Venezuela	9.58	BRITISH STEEL	3.50
Greece	9.54	NIPPON STEEL	3.40
GENERAL ELECTRIC	8.73	HITACHI	3.33
South Korea	8.21	South Vietnam	3.20
IBM	7.50	Ghana (1969)	2.28*
Chile	7.39	Burma (1968)	2.06*
CHRYSLER	7.00	Kenya	1.48*
UNILEVER	6.88	Tanzania	1.17*
Egypt	6.58	Costa Rica	0.94*
Thailand	6.51	Paraguay	0.60*

Sources: *The Washington Post*, Nov. 12, 1972, p. B-4, and United Nations, *Statistical Yearbook, 1971*, pp. 560–562.

* Gross domestic product.

Table 14.8 Average annual rates of population growth of industrializing societies in three periods

	Population growth rate 1815–1870			Population growth rate 1870–1925			Population growth rate 1963–1969
Great Britain	1.1	Romania	1.3	Philippines	3.5
Scandinavia	1.1	Poland	1.1	Iraq	3.5
Germany	1.0	Russia	1.1	Brazil	3.0
Netherlands	1.0	Balkans	0.8	Kenya	2.9
Belgium	0.9	Hungary	0.7	Ghana	2.7
Switzerland	0.8	Italy	0.6	India	2.5
France	0.4	Spain and Portugal	0.5	Indonesia	2.5
				United Arab Republic	2.5
				Pakistan	2.1
				China	1.4

Sources: The data for 1815–1925 were computed from Helmut Haufe, *Die Bevolkerung Europas* (Berlin, 1936) by Bert Hoselitz and are reported in "Advanced and Underdeveloped Countries: A Study in Development Contrasts," in William B. Hamilton (ed.), *The Transfer of Institutions* (Durham, N.C.: Duke, 1964), p. 39; the data for 1963–1969 are from United Nations, *Statistical Yearbook, 1970*, table 18.

one handed those societies any ready-made death preventives. In this area, as in others, there was a more coordinated pattern of development among the various parts of the sociocultural system. But the industrializing nation today has been given a powerful assist in increasing its population—without a comparable boost in other critical areas of development.

As Table 14.8 indicates, when the nations of Europe were in the process of industrializing, they had an average annual population growth rate of only 1 per cent. By contrast, most societies industrializing today are growing more than 2 per cent a year. This means, quite simply, that much of the potential for increased capital investment and for improvements in the standard of living is being swallowed up in the effort to feed, clothe, and house more and more people whose labor is not needed.

Runaway population growth also portends a serious food crisis for many of these countries, and in the not too distant future. Despite all the talk about a so-called "Green Revolution" based on new high-yield varieties of cereal grains, responsible commentators have repeatedly warned that it could do no more than provide a temporary respite—a brief period during which food production in the Third World would increase faster than population. Optimists have not wanted to believe this. But the fact is that for the Philippines, a country whose population growth rate is well over 3 per cent a year, the honeymoon is already over. For a few years, its shift to the new varieties of rice enabled that country to stop importing rice for the first time in half a century. But by 1971, the relentless growth of population forced a resumption of rice importation.[58]

---

[58] Similar reports are now coming from India, too. See *The Washington Post*, Nov. 27, 1972, p. A8.

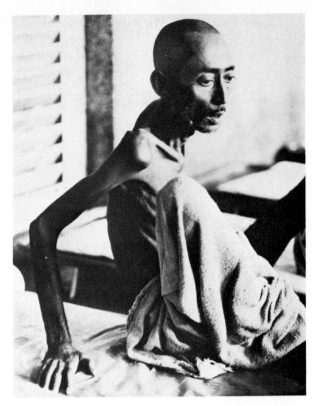

Figure 14.13 Man in Home for the Dying Destitute, Calcutta, India.

What, then, does the future hold for these societies? The overall prospects are certainly not good. A few of them may make the breakthrough to full-fledged industrialization, but it is extremely unlikely that most of them will manage it under the present world economic and political system.

The People's Republic of China has been trying an alternative route. Isolating itself as much as possible while it develops its own resources at its own pace, it avoids becoming dependent on more advanced societies for manufactured products. By sacrificing immediate advantages, China may thus be able to accumulate enough capital to build a broadly based industrial system of its own.

Whether this is feasible for China remains to be seen. It certainly would not be possible for any society that does not have large internal markets, substantial natural resources within its own boundaries, and a highly authoritarian government to check the natural tendency of its elite and middle classes to demand too much too soon.

For the majority of industrializing societies, the only real hope for rapid modernization lies in the formation of a new kind of world political system—some kind of world government with the authority to help those nations in a substantial way. Politically, this sounds utopian, but it is quite feasible technologically. We have already seen that, from the standpoint of transportation and communication, it would be easier to govern the entire world today than it was to govern the United States in George Washington's day (see Figure 4.1, page 77).

In the final analysis, the resolution of this enormous problem will depend on how the leaders of nations assess the relative costs and benefits of the various alternatives. Without substantially increased international cooperation, the eventual fate of many developing nations is not pleasant to contemplate.

CHAPTER FIFTEEN

Retrospect and Prospect

The study of societal evolution is much like the study of a giant mural. In both cases, we are easily overwhelmed by the many small details. If we hope to grasp the picture as a whole and develop some feeling for it, we have to step back from time to time and look at it in its entirety.

We began this volume with the larger view, but for the last nine chapters we have concentrated on different parts of the panorama. Now we must step back again for another look at the basic outlines and the overarching patterns. This time, however, we will try to discover the extent to which technological progress has been accompanied by progress toward man's other goals—freedom, justice, morality, and happiness.

We will also consider the fascinating and important question of the future. If sociology is to help us understand the societies we live in and depend on, it cannot limit its concern to those of the past and present. It must also try to see where the process of societal evolution is taking us. Because the rate of change promises to make tomorrow's world strikingly different from today's, predictions are risky. But that is not sufficient reason to avoid the subject. As one social scientist commented recently:

> we must try. . . . It is an intellectually and morally intolerable state of affairs that we plan twenty and thirty years ahead when we take a mortgage on a house . . . but pretend that in the matters of war and peace, or in the matters of the life and death of mankind, we can't see further ahead than two years at most.[1]

LOOKING BACK

A million years ago, the ancestors of modern man gave little indication that they were anything more than another variety of primate. There was nothing to suggest that this species would one day evolve into the dominant form of life, a creature capable of overcoming most of the limitations imposed on him by his environment and able to alter even the environment itself in major respects.

Today, we take all this for granted. With the wisdom of hindsight, we see that man was destined for a unique role. We see, moreover, that the key to

[1] From a statement by Karl Deutsch, as quoted in *Yale Alumni Magazine*, May 1967, p. 15.

his accomplishments lay in his ability to use symbols to mobilize information and energy. We also understand how he gradually escaped from the restraints of the genetic mode of adaptation and how sociocultural evolution finally replaced organic evolution as the dominant mode of human adaptation during the last 35,000 years.

The significance of this is hard to exaggerate. Sociocultural evolution, unlike organic evolution, has a natural tendency to snowball. Despite occasional reversals of relatively short duration, this tendency has persisted throughout man's history. As a result, we find ourselves today in the most revolutionary era of all, and change has become the central fact of life.

The use of symbols, the building of cultures, the whole process of sociocultural evolution—these are, by their very nature, social phenomena; and, as such, they presuppose the existence of societies. And long before there were men, primates lived in societies—which reminds us that societies were prerequisite to the development of *all* the more distinctly human qualities. Thus, the study of cultures and the study of human societies are inextricably intertwined.

Distortions

In our survey of human societies, certain distortions were unavoidably introduced. For example, because there is so little nontechnical evidence from the prehistoric era, our description may exaggerate the importance of subsistence activities in the daily life of Paleolithic societies. Similarly, because we took an evolutionary approach to the study of human societies and incorporated the whole span of human history into our analysis, we had to concentrate on the more basic patterns. Such a survey can never do justice to the human scene. However, we are all aware of the richness and complexity of human life, and its amazing variety. Not only is this part of our daily experience, but history and the arts continually remind us of it. For most of us, then, an overemphasis on the basic patterns comes as a badly needed corrective.

Progress Reconsidered

So far in our discussions of progress, we have carefully restricted its meaning to technological advance and its consequences. It is clear that progress so defined has occurred at the global level throughout virtually the whole of human history. The capacity of modern industrial societies to mobilize information and energy far surpasses that of the most advanced agrarian societies a thousand years ago, and their capacity was far above that of their most advanced predecessors of earlier eras.

Progress in this limited sense, however, has never been man's ultimate goal; and today, more than ever before, he is concerned with progress in the ethical sense and in terms of human happiness and freedom. This growing concern with the less utilitarian aspects of progress is, itself, interpretable in evolutionary terms: modern theories of motivation recognize that people's interests and concerns change as their conditions change.[2] As long as basic needs such as physical safety, food, and shelter are inadequately satisfied or their future satisfaction is uncertain, they tend to remain uppermost in our minds. But once these needs have been satisfied and we are confident they can be provided for in the future, then new needs and new concerns become dominant. Thus, the further a society advances technologically, the more it will care about, and actively pursue, progress in terms of freedom, justice, morality, and happiness.

Freedom   The high value that the affluent members of modern industrial societies attach to freedom is revealed in the growing challenge to all forms of authority, not only in the liberal democracies of the West but in the authoritarian nations of Eastern Europe as well. Even those who are not in the forefront of the libertarian movement are likely to consider the degree of freedom accorded the individual one of the basic measures of the attractiveness, and hence the progress, of a society, and they would deny that a technologically advanced, politically repressive society is truly progressive.

But human freedom is more than the absence of repressive social controls; it is also freedom from the restraints imposed by nature. People who must spend most of their waking hours in an exhausting struggle to produce the necessities of life are not truly "free"—even if there are few social restraints on what they do. A woman whose life is one long succession of pregnancies is not "free"—regardless of the kind of society she lives in. Disease, physical and mental handicaps, geographical barriers, and all the laws of nature restrict people and deny them freedom. For freedom does not exist where there is no alternative; and freedom can be measured only by the range of choices that are available. The fewer viable choices, the less freedom—and it matters little, from the standpoint of freedom, whether the restrictions are imposed by nature or by one's fellow men.[3]

Once we recognize this, it becomes clear that man's long struggle to advance technologically is not irrelevant to his desire for freedom. Every one of his technological innovations has resulted from his desire to overcome natural limitations on his actions. Thanks to this struggle, he is now free to talk across oceans or from a ship in space, free to travel faster than sound, free to live a longer life in better health while he enjoys a range of experiences far surpassing in richness and variety what was available to the greatest kings and emperors of the past.

---

[2] See especially A. H. Maslow, *Motivation and Personality* (New York: Harper, 1954), chap. 5, and p. 49 in this volume.

[3] Psychologically, it seems easier for people to accept restrictions imposed by impersonal physical forces than those imposed by other people, but this does not make the individual any more free.

There has been a price to pay, of course: technological progress has necessitated larger and more complex social systems. If we want the option of flying to another part of the country instead of walking there, or of watching the day's events on a screen in our home instead of hearing about them weeks later, we have to accept the social controls that are implied. The goods and services essential for such options can be produced only when there are organizations with rules and with sanctions to enforce the rules, and individuals with authority to exercise the sanctions. And these organizations can function efficiently only within the context of a society with rules to govern the relationships between them, and an authority system to enforce the rules. The only alternative is anarchy—and the loss of all the freedoms that modern technology affords.

Critics of modern society often say that the price has been too high, that the increased social restrictions outweigh the gains in freedom we derive from modern technology. They may be right—this is a matter each of us must decide for himself. In thinking about it, however, we need to beware of romanticizing the past. Before deciding that men are less free than they used to be, we should read the records of peasant life in agrarian societies and of the life of horticultural and hunting and gathering peoples. In doing this, we must resist the temptation to abstract the attractive features and ignore the appalling ones. We must remember that slavery and serfdom were not accidental characteristics of agrarian societies but reflections of basic, inescapable conditions of that way of life, as were the high mortality rate and short life span of many hunting and gathering peoples. Finally, we must keep in mind that the restraints in those societies were not all physical ones; there were often powerful social restrictions operating too.

Once we recognize the danger of comparing some rosy version of life in less advanced societies with the negative side of life in industrial societies, we are in a better position to consider whether freedom is a correlate of technological advance. We can say, first of all, that technological progress has clearly raised the *upper* level of freedom in human societies. People with the greatest measure of freedom in modern nations—that is, members of the upper classes—have a far wider range of choice than people with the greatest measure of freedom in less advanced societies. This is true with respect to everything from the individual's use of a leisure hour to his use of a lifetime. In this limited sense, then, there is a high positive correlation between technological progress and gains in human freedom.

The relation between technical progress and freedom for the *average* member of society is more complicated. If we compare the typical peasant in an agrarian society with a typical hunter and gatherer, it is not at all clear that there were any gains. In fact, the peasant had to live with a lot of new social controls, while gaining very little freedom from natural controls. Thus, during much of the course of evolutionary history—especially after the formation of the state—the average person probably experienced a decline in freedom. With

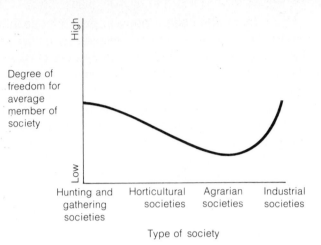

Degree of
freedom for
average
member of
society

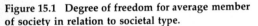

**Figure 15.1 Degree of freedom for average member
of society in relation to societal type.**

industrialization, however, the pattern changed: once the difficult period of transition is past, technological progress and freedom for the average person *do* begin to be positively related, as Figure 15.1 illustrates. Whether people in industrial societies have more freedom than hunters and gatherers is a moot point. Clearly they have more social restraints, but far fewer biophysical ones.

For the *least* free members of society, there appears to have been little change through the years. If we compare the least free members of modern societies—the inmates of many medical, mental, and penal institutions and the very poor—with the least free members of other societies, it is hard to see much difference: both are severely restricted. The chief difference is that in the more advanced societies the restrictions are more often imposed by society, in the simplest societies by nature.

Before leaving the subject of freedom, we should take note of the popular misconception that governmental activity necessarily results in a loss of freedom for the members of society. This is at best a half-truth. Laws do, of course, place restrictions on people, but often this is done in order to increase freedom, not reduce it. For example, when the United States established the death penalty for kidnapping in the 1930s, this restricted the freedom of a tiny predatory minority, but it increased the freedom of millions of children and parents. Similarly, the Pure Food and Drug Act was designed to restrict the freedom of businessmen who were willing to sell spoiled food and dangerous drugs for profit, but it increased the freedom of the rest of the population. Sometimes laws restrict everyone's freedom in one area—the freedom to proceed at will through a busy intersection, for example—in order to enlarge it in others. In short, most governmental regulations *redistribute freedom.*

The crucial question, therefore, is whether the gains outweigh the losses. With the growth of democracy, there have been efforts to increase the freedom of the less favored majority, and this often necessitates transferring some of it from historically favored groups and classes. In an effort to defend their privileges, such groups (e.g., the National Association of Manufacturers, the Chamber of Commerce, the American Medical Association) frequently argue that the new legislation is a threat to everyone's freedom—and they have been remarkably successful in this. What they fail to mention is that most modern social legislation, such as minimum wage laws or Medicare, has been adopted because the gains in freedom for those who benefit are judged to be more significant than the losses for others. This is, of course, only what we should expect in a democratic society. Admittedly, there is also a great deal of legislation that denies freedom to the majority in order to make those in office more secure or to benefit the elite. But in balance, the great growth in the power of government in modern democratic societies has increased freedom for the average person far more than it has restricted it.[4]

Morality Morality is a difficult subject. For one thing, it concerns so much of human life, ranging from personal behavior like sexual conduct to corporate acts of society like war. For another thing, judgments about what is good and what is evil have varied throughout history—not only from society to society but from group to group and individual to individual within the same society. Finally, the way we evaluate other moral codes is naturally influenced by our own. In order to simplify matters a bit, we will limit our discussion to a single, critical area, one in which a new moral consensus may be emerging—violence against other human beings. Among better-educated people in every industrial society, there seems to be a growing agreement that, except in self-defense, violence is wrong, and this provides a standard against which we can try to measure the historical trend. This ignores many other important dimensions of morality, of course, but we could not do justice to them all in this brief space.[5]

In the simplest human societies, hunting and gathering groups, the incidence of violence is strikingly low. Certainly in those which have survived into the modern era, warfare is uncommon. Fights and murders occur occasionally, but not often in most groups.

In horticultural societies, the situation is quite different. As we observed in Chapter 7, the cult of the warrior was prominent in many of them, with warfare encouraged and such violence as scalp taking, torture, and human sacrifice common. These were not the acts of deviant individuals, taken in defiance of group norms, but expressions of some of the most deeply held values of the entire society.

With the rise of agrarian societies, warfare became the concern of a specialized occupational group. The cult of the warrior declined in importance,

---

[4] The situation is not necessarily the same in nondemocratic societies. On the contrary, as in the case of Czechoslovakia, the increased power of government may be used to reduce the freedoms of the majority.

[5] The discussion of justice that follows touches on at least one other important dimension, economic morality.

human sacrifice gradually vanished, and the mutilation and torture of victims became, at best, tolerated acts, at worst, serious breaches of the moral code. But this does not mean that warfare became more humane: on the contrary, as the technological resources of armies increased, so did their devastation. The pillage and destruction of conquered towns and villages was commonplace, although the morality of these things was no longer unquestioned. Intragroup violence was also widespread in agrarian societies, and much of it was socially approved. The beating of women and children, for example, was often regarded as an essential part of the father's role, while masters could usually beat serfs and slaves with impunity for minor transgressions. Minor crimes were punished with death in many cases, and executions were regarded as public entertainment. And in the schools, physical punishment was considered the best stimulus to learning.

Since the rise of industrial societies, there has been a sharp decline in the incidence of socially approved violence within societies. For example, a gradual reduction in the number of crimes for which the death penalty could be given was followed by a decline in the frequency with which it was imposed even in these cases; and more recently there has been a widespread movement toward its total abolition. Within families and schools, violence against women and children no longer has public approval. And there is no longer physical abuse of the lower class by the elite. Even war has lost some of its respectability: skepticism about it is more widespread than ever before—not so widespread, obviously, as to prevent war entirely, but perhaps prevalent enough to make governments more cautious in undertaking military commitments. On the other hand, the destructive power of the modern military machine has grown even more awesome, as the horrors of Vietnam testify. And the ability of political leaders to sustain public support for a venture of this kind suggests that the change in popular thinking can easily be exaggerated.

Putting all this together, it seems that once again we have a curvilinear trend, with a declining standard of morality (as reflected by patterns of violence) after the hunting and gathering era but some reversal more recently. So far, however, the newer trend has been felt in intrasocietal relations more than in intersocietal.

Justice Basically, justice has to do with the fairness of a society in its treatment of its members. Although no one would quarrel with that as an objective, we run into trouble as soon as we try to define what "fairness" means. Should a society reward its members on the basis of how much they contribute to the common good, or according to their individual needs and capacities? Should the handicapped person, for example, be rewarded as generously as those who outproduce him? What about those unable to make any productive contribution at all? And what is a "fair" evaluation of the relative contributions of people in radically dissimilar activities—a symphony conductor, a bricklayer, a mother, a garbage collector, a student?

Questions like these point up the difficulty of measuring progress with respect to justice. An adequate treatment of the subject would require volumes. All we can hope to do here is call attention to basic trends and offer some tentative conclusions.

To begin with, as we observed in earlier chapters, social inequality became more pronounced as societies advanced technologically and status became increasingly dependent on the family into which one was born. The result of these developments was a weakening of the relationship between a person's efforts and his rewards. Whereas every boy in a hunting and gathering group had a chance of becoming the best hunter—and hence the more important man—in his society, a peasant's son could work to the limits of his strength and ability and be unable to advance even a notch above his father's social level.

The relationship between a person's natural ability and his rewards also declined with societal advance. For one thing, societies beyond the level of simple horticultural frequently excluded segments of their populations from access to rewards on the basis of religion or ethnicity, thereby denying many people the opportunity to use all their abilities. In addition, increasingly rigid stratification systems locked people into roles and situations where they could neither develop nor use their gifts, while those with few or none to use might occupy positions they were grossly unsuited for—even thrones. Societies also tended to hand out punishments the way they did rewards: on the basis of social status. This is especially evident in the criminal codes of many agrarian societies.

In general, then, it appears that societies became less just, less fair, as they developed technologically. However, there are signs of a reversal in this trend too. Industrialization has resulted in some decline in the level of social inequality. Industrial societies are more solicitous of their poor, their handicapped, and their minorities than the typical agrarian society. Criminal justice is less harsh: men are no longer hanged for stealing an egg, for example. And public education provides at least some chance for practically every child to develop his abilities. In short, after the long period of declining justice, there appears to be some movement in the other direction.

One further development deserves note: the long-term trend toward a more formal, less personal administration of criminal justice. In the simplest societies, everything was left to the injured individual and his kinsmen, who sought retribution by whatever means they judged appropriate. This commonly led to prolonged feuds and the multiplication of grievances. As more power was vested in rulers, the practice of blood vengeance was gradually replaced by judgments rendered on the basis of a code of laws, in courts administered by chiefs or kings or their ministers. This had several advantages. First, it introduced a greater element of rationality into the process: the decision no longer depended on the relative strengths of the contending parties. Second, it transferred responsibility for making the decision to a disinterested third party.

Finally, it placed the burden of carrying out the decision on a third party that was stronger than either of the contending parties, thus breaking the endless and often escalating cycle of the feud. On the whole, this development has probably contributed to the strengthening of the cause of justice.

Happiness Of all the possible measures of progress, happiness is the most elusive, for it depends so much—perhaps primarily—on the quality of interpersonal relations, whether there is love, mutual respect, cooperation, and so forth. And these things do not seem to depend on the level of technological development. Studies of modern hunting and gathering groups indicate that the most primitive people develop such qualities as often as members of modern industrial societies do.[6]

There are several respects, however, in which technological progress is definitely relevant to this kind of happiness. To begin with, some of life's greatest tragedies involve the premature death of a loved one—a cherished child, a father or mother, or a partner in a happy conjugal relation. We saw how common this was in most societies prior to the Industrial Revolution and can therefore appreciate what the recently expanded life-span has meant in terms of human happiness.

Health, too, contributes to happiness. When we are seriously ill, life may not seem worth living. Throughout most of history, man's understanding of disease was extremely limited, and it would be hard to argue that technological advance prior to the Industrial Revolution had any real impact on health. More recently, however, advances in sanitation and medicine have dramatically improved the physical well-being of the members of advanced societies. Unfortunately, modern medical technology has also had a negative effect: it has been used to keep alive individuals who, in simpler societies, would mercifully be allowed to die. Still, the net result has undeniably been positive.

Hunger, another cause of enormous human misery, has been drastically reduced in a large number of societies by industrialization. Table 15.1 shows two measures of the change that has occurred. Not only do the members of modern industrial societies have a high average caloric intake, but their diet is rich in fats and proteins, amazingly varied in content, and remarkably free from periodic shortages. As with health, it is easy to take these benefits for granted and lose sight of the link between technological advance and happiness.

The increased production of other kinds of goods and services, especially nonessential ones, has probably had much less effect on happiness. The absolute quantity of luxuries we enjoy is certainly not as important in this regard as how they compare with what people around us have. Thus the

[6] See, for example, Colin Turnbull, *The Forest People* (New York: Simon & Schuster, 1961); John Garvan, *The Negritos of the Philippines* (Vienna: Ferdinand Berger, 1964); or Kenneth MacLeish, "The Tasadays: Stone Age Men of the Philippines," *National Geographic,* 142 (1972), pp. 218–249.

Table 15.1 Fat content in diet and daily caloric intake per person, by society

Society	Fat*	Calories	Society	Fat*	Calories
United States	155	3240	Mexico	62	2600
Denmark	153	3180	Brazil	58	2700
New Zealand	148	3290	Japan	48	2460
France	144	3180	Peru	48	2300
United Kingdom	142	3180	Syria	48	2480
West Germany	136	2960	United Arab Republic	44	2960
Sweden	129	2880	Morocco	42	2180
Australia	129	3110	Nigeria	39	2170
Hungary	110	3140	Iran	37	1950
Israel	101	2930	Kenya	35	2240
Italy	98	2940	China	31	2050
Spain	89	2680	Philippines	30	2010
Yugoslavia	82	3200	India	24	1900
Soviet Union	74	3150	Indonesia	24	1870
South Africa	70	2870	Saudi Arabia	22	1830

Source: Food and Agriculture Organization of the United Nations, *Production Yearbook, 1969*, tables 136 and 138.

* Grams of fat per person per day.

headman in a simple horticultural society may be quite content with his few special possessions, because they are more than his neighbors own and as good as anything he knows about, while the middle-class American, surrounded with goods and services the headman never dreamed of, can feel terribly deprived when he compares himself with his more prosperous neighbors. In other words, insofar as happiness depends on material possessions, the degree of inequality is probably more important than anything else.

This suggests that in one respect, at least, technological advance has consistently lowered the level of human happiness; for although the growth in inequality has been halted since the start of the industrial era, the awareness of those better off and the opportunities for comparison have grown tremendously (especially since the advent of TV). To the extent that happiness depends on equality of possessions, therefore, we would expect to find less of it today than in prehistoric times.

Yet, when we take into account the advances in health, the greater abundance and improved quality of food, and the drastic reduction in premature deaths, it is clear that the Industrial Revolution has eliminated the sources of much of the misery of earlier eras. Putting it all together, we are again led to the tentative conclusion that the long-term trend for the average individual has been curvilinear, with a slow deterioration after the hunting and gathering era until the new technology of the modern period effected a sharp reversal.

Concluding thoughts In an earlier chapter we asked, in effect, why people have invested so much of themselves in the struggle for technical advance when it has not been more consistent in producing happiness and justice. We answered that people have always been more concerned with the immediate consequences of their choices and actions than with the long-term results and that the latter do not usually become evident until it is too late for society to reverse its course. We also said that people are rarely motivated by a desire for happiness and justice for mankind as a whole but concentrate their energies on achieving these things for themselves and those closest to them. Since what is advantageous for one group is so often achieved at the expense of others, the costs of progress have often outweighed the benefits for the total society or for mankind in general. Further, we noted how intersocietal selection, which favors the technically advanced, has helped ensure that technologically oriented societies survive, while those motivated more by a desire for happiness and justice have tended to disappear.

Idealists may well ask, therefore, whether technological advance has not, in fact, been a bitch goddess. Had human history come to an end a thousand years ago, one would have been forced to agree. But recent developments, especially those of the past hundred years, hold out the hope that technology may yet make a very positive contribution to the attainment of mankind's higher goals. There is nothing inevitable about this, of course, and it will certainly not occur automatically. But it does look as if technology is at least bringing into the realm of *the possible* a social order with more freedom, justice, morality, and happiness than any society has yet known.

Whatever our judgment about the wisdom of man's pursuit of technological advance, one thing is clear: it is only in terms of this technology and its consequences (the kind indicated on pages 82 and 83) that mankind as a whole has achieved fairly continuous and substantial progress. In short, the limitation we imposed on the meaning of progress early in this book still stands.

LOOKING AHEAD

For thousands of years, hoping for a glimpse into the future, men have turned to shamans and oracles, prophets and astrologers. Despite their sorry record, interest in the subject continues unabated, as indicated by the recent spate of books and articles on the future and by the revival of astrology.

The reason is clear: culture makes people aware of the relation between present events and future ones. This link is perceived far more clearly by man than by any other species, and his awareness of it has been heightened by the modern social revolution.

But despite our need of it, prediction remains a hazardous business. Only a hundred years ago, for example, Friedrich Engels wrote that warfare had reached the point where no significant advances in weapons could be expected. As he put it, "The era of evolution is therefore, in essentials, closed in this direction."[7]

We could cite so many equally unsuccessful efforts to foresee the future that prediction might appear to be entirely a matter of luck. Successful prediction does, in fact, involve an element of luck (and the more striking the prediction, the more luck is usually needed), because the future depends on the interaction of so many factors that no one can possibly assess them all correctly. Besides, the most critical factor in a situation may be so poorly understood that it upsets the most carefully reasoned analysis of the others. This is the case, for example, with certain aspects of the biophysical environment, on which all human life depends. We simply do not have the ability to predict such things as major shifts in climate or the appearance of new and deadly strains of bacteria or fungi. Thus, every prediction is automatically hedged with the tacit qualification that there be no significant change in the biophysical environment.

As we attempt to see what lies ahead for human societies, we will follow two basic guidelines. First, the shorter the time one tries to span, the greater one's chance of success. Setting predictions far in the future greatly increases the probability that some important but unforeseen factor will intervene and completely upset one's calculations. It also increases the chance that minor errors will be compounded, through repetition, into major ones. The safest predictions, therefore, concern the very near future. But these are also the least interesting and the least valuable. Because of this inverse relationship between accuracy and value, it makes sense to concentrate on predictions geared to an intermediate time span.

Second, the more thoroughly a prediction is grounded in an analysis of the past, the better its chance of success. This means we cannot simply extrapolate current trends into the future. Rather, we must know what conditions gave rise to a trend and what sustained it—or caused it to waver or accelerate—so that we can anticipate reversals and other shifts. For example, the birthrate in the United States dropped approximately one-third during a fifteen-year period, starting in the late 1950s; but it would be as irresponsible simply to project that trend to the end of the century as it would be to ignore it altogether. What we must do is identify important trends and understand their causes.

This kind of approach does not produce flat, unqualified predictions, the kind we would all like to see. Rather, we have to say that under conditions X, Y, and Z, outcome A is likelier than B, which in turn is likelier than C. The virtue of discussing the future this way is that it puts the assumptions on which our predictions are based out in the open where others can examine them and

---

[7] Friedrich Engels, *Herr Eugen Duehring's Revolution in Science (Anti-Duehring)* (New York: International Publishers, 1939, first published 1878), quoted by D. G. Brennan in "Weaponry," in Foreign Policy Association (ed.), *Toward the Year 2018* (New York: Cowles, 1968), p. 2.

challenge or modify them as new information or insights become available. Hopefully, this will lead to a progressive refinement and improvement of predictions.

Starting Points

If we apply the first of our two guidelines, we will focus on the next several decades. A shorter time span would be safer but less useful; a longer one would get us onto very thin ice. The period around 2000, the focus of most serious futurologists of recent years, takes us well beyond the point where we can simply say, "Things will be pretty much the way they are today," yet it does not get us into the realm of science fiction.

If we apply the second rule, we will build our predictions for societal evolution on the foundation provided by our analysis of human societies of the past and present. This means we will start with the fundamentals in our basic model of general evolution (see Figure 4.3, page 82). Before we try to make predictions about anything else, we must decide what we may reasonably expect with regard to the biophysical environment, man's genetic heritage, and technology. Only then can we safely move on to consider the future of the other elements in sociocultural systems.

Prospects: Environmental and Genetic Change

There will almost certainly be change in man's biophysical environment during the next quarter century, but most of it will probably be caused by feedback from his technology. If we can judge by the record of the last 10,000 years, there will be no significant independent, or autogenous, change. Not since the end of the last Ice Age has such a change had consequences for human life on a global scale. Even if important autogenous change does lie ahead, contemporary science cannot predict it.

The situation with respect to man's genetic heritage is much the same as that of the biophysical environment. There has been no major change in this *constant* aspect of population for more than 30,000 years. Even if some alteration should occur, past experience and our understanding of the principles of organic evolution both tell us it would occur so slowly that no appreciable effects would be felt before the year 2000—unless, perhaps, it were the result of man's own actions.

Thus, by a process of elimination, our attention is directed to technology as the prime initiator of change in the next several decades. We have to keep in mind, of course, that we are not starting with a world in equilibrium: a major revolution has been under way in human societies for years, and its effects will carry over into the future. The situation is something like that on a billiard table soon after a shot has been made: the balls are still bounding and rebounding, their total impact and ultimate resting places unknown. Thus, we cannot concentrate exclusively on the effects of future advances in technology; we must also watch for the still unregistered consequences of *past* advances.

Prospects: Technology

Benjamin Franklin once said that nothing is certain in this world but death and taxes. Were he alive today, he might add technological advance. A prediction of continuing advance at an accelerating rate does not depend simply on an extrapolation of the current trend. The basic factors responsible for the trend—the magnitude of the existing store of information, the great size of societal populations, and the amount of communication between societies— give every indication of providing even stronger impetus in the future than they do today. Furthermore, advanced industrial societies are engaging, for the first time in history, in a systematic, large-scale pursuit of new information. Investments in scientific and technological research and development have grown immensely, while computers and other devices that increase man's ability to acquire and analyze data add their own boost to the rate of change.

At present, only three things seem at all likely to halt this trend in the next few decades. First, a nuclear holocaust could destroy the fabric of modern industrial societies, in which event there would probably be a permanent reversion to the agrarian level. In a provocative volume entitled *The Challenge of Man's Future,* geophysicist Harrison Brown noted that the evolution of modern societies depended on a combination of circumstances that no longer exist, thus making a rebirth of industrial societies highly unlikely. Brown argues the case this way:

> Our ancestors had available large resources of high-grade ores and fuels that could be processed by the most primitive technology—crystals of copper and pieces of coal that lay on the surface of the earth, easily mined iron, and petroleum in generous pools reached by shallow drilling. Now we must dig huge caverns and follow seams ever further underground, drill oil wells thousands of feet deep, many of them under the bed of the ocean, and find ways of extracting elements from the leanest ores—procedures that are possible only because of our highly complex modern techniques, and practical only to an intricately mechanized culture which could not have been developed without the high-grade ore resources that are so rapidly vanishing.
>
> As our dependence shifts to such resources as low-grade ores, rock, seawater, and the sun, the conversion of energy into useful work will require ever more intricate technical activity, which would be impossible in the absence of a variety of complex machines and their products—all of which are the result of our intricate industrial civilization, and which would be impossible without it. Thus, if machine civilization were to stop functioning as the result of some catastrophe, it is difficult to see how man would again be able to start

along the path of industrialization with the resources that would then be available to him. . . .

Our present industrialization, itself the result of a combination of no longer existent circumstances, is the only foundation on which it seems possible that a future civilization capable of utilizing the vast resources of energy now hidden in rocks and seawater, and unutilized in the sun, can be built. If this foundation is destroyed, in all probability the human race has "had it." Perhaps there is possible a sort of halfway station [agrarian society?] in which retrogression stops short of a complete extinction of civilization, but even this is not pleasant to contemplate. . . .[8]

The second threat to a rising rate of innovation comes from the environmental crisis created by industrialization. Should a series of environmental disasters occur, as some environmentalists predict, advanced industrial societies might be forced to revert to a simpler way of life (something closer to the patterns of life in the nineteenth century), and the resources available for research and innovation might be reduced drastically. It seems unlikely, however, that the situation will deteriorate to that point by the end of the century. Rather, increasing efforts to find technological solutions to the environmental crisis will probably *step up* the rate of innovation.

The third development that might slow the rate of innovation is the attainment of a rate that proves psychologically or socially intolerable.[9] Even if this does not happen in the next quarter century, it will eventually, unless something else slows the rate first—or unless the effects of the changes can be made less disruptive. This could probably be accomplished if societies concentrated their innovative efforts in areas selected for their capacity to produce needed improvements with minimum repercussions. Intelligent planning would also emphasize innovations whose primary goal would be to simplify life. For example, high priority might be given to creating clean, dependable urban transportation systems to replace the millions of automobiles whose owners pay dearly—fighting traffic, weather, an inadequate maintenance system, and rising costs—and end up feeling guilty for contributing to pollution.

The possibilities for technological change that would entail a minimum of adjustment and a maximum of simplification are tremendous. But they presuppose a more rational ordering of national priorities than has been characteristic of industrial societies in recent decades.

The content of change Turning from the *rate* of future technological innovation to its *content*, we encounter a subject so vast and so technical that we can do no more than call attention to a few of the highlights. The authors of one of

[8] From *The Challenge of Man's Future*, by Harrison Brown, pp. 222–223. Copyright 1954 by Harrison Brown. Reprinted by permission of The Viking Press, Inc.

[9] For a discussion of this subject, see Alvin Toffler, *Future Shock* (New York: Random House, 1970).

the recent volumes that look ahead to the year 2000 listed 100 areas in which, in their judgment, important technological innovations are "very likely" during the last part of this century. They also noted 25 developments they consider "less likely, but important possibilities," and another 10 "far-out possibilities." Table 15.2 gives examples from all three categories.

Table 15.2 Examples of possible and probable technological innovations in the last third of the twentieth century, according to Herman Kahn and Anthony Wiener

Innovations rated as "very likely"

1. Multiple applications of lasers and masers for sensing, measuring, cutting, heating, welding, power transmission, communication, illumination, destructive (defensive), and other purposes
2. New or improved materials for equipment and appliances (plastics, glasses, alloys, ceramics, intermetallics, and cermets)
3. New sources of power for ground transportation (storage battery, fuel cell, propulsion or support by electromagnetic fields, jet engine, turbine, and the like)
4. Major reduction in hereditary and congenital defects
5. Extensive use of cyborg techniques (mechanical aids or substitutes for human organs, senses, limbs, or other components)
6. New or improved uses of the oceans (mining, extraction of minerals, controlled "farming," source of energy, and the like)
7. Three-dimensional photography, illustrations, movies, and television
8. Automated or more mechanized housekeeping and home maintenance
9. Extensive and intensive centralization (or automatic interconnection) of current and past personal and business information in high-speed data processors
10. Other new and possibly pervasive techniques for surveillance, monitoring, and control of individuals and organizations
11. Capacity to determine the sex of unborn children
12. More extensive use of transplantation of human organs
13. Chemical methods for improving memory and learning
14. Practical large-scale desalinization
15. Artificial moons and other methods for lighting large areas at night

"Less likely, but important possibilities"

1. Artificial growth of new limbs and organs (either in situ or for later transplantation)
2. Effective chemical or biological treatment for most mental illnesses
3. Chemical or biological control of character or intelligence
4. Conversion of mammals (humans?) to fluid breathers
5. Automated highways

"Far-out possibilities"

1. Life expectancy extended to substantially more than 150 years
2. Major modification of human species (no longer *Homo sapiens sapiens*)
3. Interstellar travel
4. Lifetime immunization against practically all diseases
5. Laboratory creation of artificial live plants and animals

Source: Adapted from Herman Kahn and Anthony Wiener, *The Year 2000: A Framework for Speculation on the Next Thirty-Three Years* (New York: Macmillan, 1967), tables XVIII–XX.

The 100 "very likely" developments are little more than an enumeration of fairly obvious applications of inventions and discoveries that have already been made. The first item, for example, simply involves the application of recently invented lasers and masers to a variety of tasks. All the details have not yet been worked out, but the important point is that the fundamental innovations—the laser and the maser—are accomplished facts. By 1967, almost every corporation and major university in the nation already had a laser for research purposes.[10] That same year more than 100 specific applications of lasers were being investigated, though only a handful had actually been adopted (e.g., "spotwelding" detached retinas).[11]

Several areas with exceptional promise for the next few decades involve fundamental innovations still so new that only a fraction of their potential has been explored. But equally important change is expected from major improvements in earlier inventions. Computers are a good example: in the fifteen years from the early 1950s to the middle 1960s, computer performance increased at least tenfold every two or three years.[12] Though we cannot expect this pace to continue indefinitely, computers will be able, by the end of the century, to handle a number of problems far beyond their present capacity.[13]

Not all innovations will be in the form of refinements and applications of existing information. New *fundamental* innovations are virtually certain, although it is extremely difficult to anticipate what they will be. We should not exaggerate their unpredictability, however, for we do know the areas where societies are investing the most money and effort, and we also know which areas seem to have been "mined out." If this information were properly analyzed, it might provide a basis for more effective long-range predictions of fundamental inventions. But for now, they are largely a matter of guesswork.

The gap between industrial and industrializing societies While we are on the subject of technology, we should note again the gap between the nations that are already industrialized and those still industrializing. This gap is apparent not only in the unequal production of goods and services and levels of national income but in the vast discrepancy in the consumption of the earth's resources by the two kinds of societies (e.g., the United States, with 6 per cent of the world's population, consumes about a third of the world's resources). There is little reason to expect that this gap will be reduced in this century and

---

[10] *The New York Times*, Jan. 15, 1967.

[11] Herman Kahn and Anthony Wiener, *The Year 2000: A Framework for Speculation on the Next Thirty-Three Years* (New York: Macmillan, 1967), p. 98.

[12] The measure of computer performance used here is the size of the memory space divided by the basic "add time" of the computer (which measures roughly a computer's ability both to hold and to process information). Kahn and Wiener, pp. 88–89.

[13] Ibid., p. 89.

some reason to expect that it may widen.[14] The best hope for bringing about a more equable situation lies, as we have said, in a single world government. If this seems improbable, alternative solutions are even more so.

Technology's feedback on the biophysical environment Over the course of evolutionary history, man's relation to the biophysical environment has changed dramatically. Hunting and gathering societies simply adapted to environmental conditions; there was little they could do to alter them. Following the horticultural revolution, men gradually began making changes on the earth's surface, clearing forests and planting gardens in their place. Although the balance of nature was affected wherever this happened, the impact was not great, for horticulturists usually had to move every few years, and their abandoned gardens reverted to wilderness. The agrarian revolution, however, ended all this. From this point on, men cultivated permanent fields and the land no longer reverted to forest.

But all the changes of the past were nothing compared with the impact of industrial societies. Modern technology has enabled man to rearrange the landscape and adjust the earth's natural features so drastically that entire areas that once teemed with life have been destroyed, while complex ecosystems that required millions of years to evolve have been damaged almost beyond hope in a matter of years, even months. Not even polar regions, oceans, or atmosphere have escaped the heavy hand of modern man.

Environmentalists have been warning us for years that our biophysical environment does not have an unlimited capacity for renewing itself. Some of the resources on which human societies depend, fossil fuels for example, are produced so slowly that for all practical purposes the supply can be considered nonreplenishable. Others, such as oxygen, are renewed much more rapidly but are nonetheless highly vulnerable. Yet, even as we have heard these warnings, our demands on the environment have risen at a fantastic rate. Between 1950 and 1970, an infinitesimal period of time by geological standards, the gross world product rose from just over $1 trillion to almost $3 trillion. If we consider what this represents in terms of the plunder of our planet, environmental crises of increasing number and severity should come as no surprise.

The simple fact is that the biophysical environment can sustain neither the infinite growth of its human population nor the endless demands of an advancing technology. There are limits to what it can provide for human societies. And for their part, human societies have a very limited repertoire of responses: they can control their numbers, and they can curtail their technol-

---

[14] See, for example, Kenneth Boulding, "The Gap between Developed and Developing Nations," in C. S. Wallia (ed.), *Toward Century 21* (New York: Basic Books, 1970), pp. 125–134, or L. J. Zimmerman, *Poor Lands, Rich Lands: The Widening Gap* (New York: Random House, 1965), chap. 7.

ONE VISTA: TWO VIEWS

Above Wheeling, West Virginia, the Ohio River flows past low forested bluffs and . . . on a hot summer day the smog from the steel factories and electric power plants hangs heavy over the river, obscuring the view of more smoke-stacks and more piles of coal farther upstream.

It is a vista industrialized America has come to abhor.

"What a beautiful sight," exclaimed Yeh Chih-hsiung [a newsman from the People's Republic of China], as we rounded a bend in the Ohio and saw two enormous chimneys belching white smoke. We stopped for a picture.

For China, eager to achieve total industrialization, it was an impressive spectacle, Mr. Yeh explained.

From Fox Butterfield, "Reporter's Notebook: Chinese on Tour,"
The New York Times, Sept. 3, 1972, p. 2. © by The New York Times Company. Reprinted by permission.

ogy. The more quickly they do one, the more leeway, relatively, they will have in the other. But at some point, societies will have to stop all growth—in numbers and in technological production—or the environment will do it for them, *its* way.

One thing that makes it extremely difficult to be optimistic about the environmental situation for the remainder of this century is the slow response of the major industrial nations. These are the nations that can best afford to apply pollution control devices and take the other steps necessary to protect their own environments and the air and water they share with the rest of the world's peoples. Because societies that are still industrializing can hardly be expected to invest in expensive pollution control devices when it is already so difficult for them to compete in the world market, it is imperative that industrial nations take the step first, and soon. But even if they do, it is doubtful that the year 2000 will find the problem less severe on the global level than it is now.

The limited steps industrial societies have taken to alleviate this problem do, at least, prove the situation is not hopeless. The British, adopting stringent legislation and applying new technologies, have almost eliminated London's deadly smogs, while the Thames abounds with fish for the first time in decades. This experience suggests that damage to the environment can be halted, even reversed, if the decision makers of industrial nations will only recognize the seriousness of the problem. Incidentally, Britain's solution serves as an ironic reminder of the part new technology will apparently play in solving problems brought on, in the first place, by technological advance.

A great deal of attention will have to be focused on recycling, as well, in the decades ahead. As John Ruskin noted a hundred years ago, industrialization is as productive of "illth" as of wealth. In the last half century, America's daily refuse increased sixfold.[15] At this rate, we will soon bury ourselves in our own depleted resources. Fortunately, the technological problems of recycling appear generally tractable, and this will probably be an important area of technological advance in the next few decades.

Technology's feedback on man's genetic heritage   In the distant past, technology apparently had a significant effect on population$_c$, or man's genetic heritage. As we noted in earlier chapters, most modern scholars agree that man's use of tools and his development of hunting techniques contributed, through natural selection, to the enlargement of his brain and to the development of the other parts of his physiology on which the use of symbols and the development of culture depend. It is also possible that technological advance subsequently affected man's genetic heritage by fostering the growth of some genetic strains at the expense of others. For example, advances in weaponry since the horticultural revolution may have favored the increase of more aggressive and violent individuals at the expense of the more pacific. But if this is so, we have no real evidence for it, and the logic behind it is hardly compelling. One might as plausibly argue that wars have led the most violent people to mutually exterminate one another.

But whatever technology's impact on population$_c$ was in the recent past, the fact is that it may be considerable in the near future, for we are now entering an era in which conscious, deliberate manipulation of man's genetic heritage will be possible. There are several ways this could occur. First, societies could deliberately control reproduction along the lines that eugenicists have advocated for years. For example, to ensure that only its healthier members reproduced, a government might require couples to be licensed to have children and levy heavy fines or other penalties for violations. Even if the requirement were not perfectly enforced, the genetic composition of a population could be substantially altered in only a few generations. A second, and far more drastic, potential for genetic manipulation lies in the process of "cloning." This is an asexual method of reproduction whereby an exact genetic copy of a plant or animal is generated from a single cell taken from any part of it. This makes it possible to produce literally thousands of exact replicas of a single specimen in a relatively short time. So far the process is confined to experimental laboratories, but it has already been applied to frogs.[16] And most scien-

---

[15] Stuart Chase, *The Most Probable Future* (New York: Harper & Row, 1968), pp. 13 and 67. Our figure is adjusted to cover the half century from 1922 to 1972 instead of Chase's 1915–1965 and to take account of the growth of population.

[16] Willard Gaylin, "The Frankenstein Myth Becomes Reality," *The New York Times Magazine,* Mar. 5, 1972, pp. 12ff.

tists are convinced there are no insurmountable barriers to cloning humans; all they need is time and money.

There are more immediate dangers for population$_c$ than cloning, however. Other products pouring out of the "cornucopia" of modern science include the still largely untried weapons of nuclear, biological, and chemical warfare, any of which might adversely affect man's genetic heritage. Although the politicians who finance these innovations and the scientists who produce them constantly reassure us that they have only the public interest at heart, a healthy degree of skepticism seems very much in order.

Fortunately, many scientists, too, are concerned, even alarmed, by the potentials inherent in advances such as these.[17] In addition to the obvious danger that they may be misused by authorities more interested in social control than in human welfare, there are the subtle dangers of unintended consequences. Consider, for example, the insurance factor built into the present genetic diversity of the human population. Should the biophysical environment change significantly at some time in the future, either through man's mistakes or through natural processes, genetic characteristics that are currently of little value, or even harmful (like the sickle-cell syndrome, for example), might suddenly become the difference between survival and extinction for the human race. As biologists have come to recognize, anything that reduces the genetic diversity of a population increases its risk of extinction. Thus, well-intentioned efforts to breed or clone a race of supermen could actually prove disastrous. A clear recognition of the dangers and implications of many of the newer innovations prior to their use is probably our best protection against their abuse.

Prospects: Population$_v$

If world population were to continue growing at its present fantastic rate, it would increase 8-fold in the next 100 years, 64-fold in the next 200, and over 500-fold in the next 300. Even if the earth could support such numbers—which it could not—life would hardly be attractive. Since cheap, efficient, and morally acceptable methods of birth control are now available,[18] the only question is when this rate of growth will begin to fall and how far it will drop.

As we have seen, the population problem is most acute in industrializing societies, where death rates have dropped dramatically but birthrates have declined hardly at all. There are several reasons for their difficulties. First,

---

[17] See, for example, Leon Kass, "The New Biology: What Price Relieving Man's Estate?" *Science,* 174 (1971), pp. 779–788; for a contrasting view, see Bernard Davis, "Prospects for Genetic Intervention in Man," *Science,* (1970), pp. 1279–1283.

[18] Pope Paul VI has reaffirmed the view of his predecessors Pius XI and Pius XII that modern methods of birth control are sinful, but opinion polls show that large numbers of Catholic priests and laymen no longer follow the Pope on this matter. For example, a recent Gallup poll found that more than half of American Catholics now regard abortion as a private matter between a woman and her physician (see *The Washington Post,* Aug. 25, 1972, p. A-2). It seems only a matter of time until church doctrine in this area is revised.

until recently most of their leaders were either unaware of, or indifferent to, un-controlled population growth and its consequences. In some cases, religious or political doctrines (e.g., Catholicism and orthodox Marxism) led leaders to deny that such a problem might exist. Second, even where there was recognition and concern, there appeared to be no solution: contraceptives were either too expensive or required more education than most people in those countries had. Third, because of the economic value of sons in rural areas and because of high death rates, most men resisted efforts to limit the number of their offspring. Finally, until quite recently the development programs sponsored by industrial societies focused almost exclusively on increasing production and ignored the economic implications of population growth. Now that, too, is changing, and the prospects for lower birthrates in these countries have improved somewhat.

Modest reductions in birthrates in the years immediately ahead will not be enough, however. Death rates in these countries are still fairly high (often 20 or more per 1,000 population), and improved sanitation and medicine will soon bring them down. Until they reach rock bottom (i.e., 8 or 9 per 1,000), the decline in death rates will simply offset much of the decline in birthrates. Since there appears to be little reason to believe that acceptance of either modern contraceptives or small families will occur more rapidly in these nations than it did in industrial nations, some of their governments will almost surely be forced to take a more active part in solving the population problem, if they hope to avert famine or other catastrophe.

Until now, most of these governments have restricted their role to such conservative efforts as establishing family planning centers. The next several decades will undoubtedly see these increase, along with state subsidization of contraceptives and abortions and programs like the current one in India, where men receive money and gifts in return for voluntary sterilization. Only time will tell whether any of these societies will choose, or be forced, to respond to population pressures with such measures as taxes on children or with more extreme, involuntary controls—licensing the right to have a child, for example, or compulsory sterilizations and abortions, or even the use of mass sterility agents administered, perhaps, through public water supplies.

Numbers are not a critical concern only in underdeveloped societies, however. In industrial nations that can easily feed their members, urban problems suggest that man resembles other animals in his reaction to the stress of crowding.[19] Animal behaviorists have observed for years that, under conditions of crowding, a wide variety of animal populations exhibit abnormal behavior—including suicide, fatal neglect or abuse of their young, gluttony, extreme hostility, withdrawal, and sexual aberrations.[20] Even if there is no biologi-

[19] See, for example, Stanley Milgram, "The Experience of Living in Cities," *Science,* 167 (1970), pp. 1461–1468.

[20] See, for example, John B. Calhoun, "Population Density and Social Pathology," *Scientific American,* 206 (1962), pp. 139–148.

cal explanation in man's case, the fact that crowding in human societies results in so many social ills is reason enough for population control.

It is probably premature to ask how far the world's birthrate will eventually fall, but it is interesting to speculate about it. At one point we suggested that a new equilibrium of births and deaths could be established somewhere in the neighborhood of 12 to 14 per 1,000 of each per year, which would mean an average life expectancy of seventy to eighty years *in a stable, or nonexpanding, population.* Although this may occur in some, perhaps all, of the more advanced industrial societies during the next generation, it is much less likely in industrializing societies, whose members constitute the majority of the world's population. For the world as a whole, then, the next twenty-five to fifty years will almost certainly see continued growth but at a declining rate, with the decline beginning in the very near future.

Looking further ahead, one can envision a day when societies decide that the great population growth of recent centuries resulted in more people than are really compatible with their values. They might then actually reduce their numbers through very stringent planning of births. This would be a dramatic departure in evolutionary history, but considering the growing concern with the *quality* of human life, it could very well occur—though hardly in this century.[21]

The population composition of many societies will almost certainly change in the near future. For one thing, the urban populations of industrializing societies will undoubtedly grow faster than the rural. The age composition of many societies will also change, with a relative increase in the number of middle-aged and elderly people. This is an inevitable consequence of declining birthrates, unless they are offset by equally sharp declines in infant mortality, or increases in adult mortality. Neither of these conditions is anticipated for the more advanced nations, though declines in infant mortality in developing nations could, in many cases, cancel the effects of declining birthrates. Where the proportion of older people does increase, the effects could be considerable: since youth is generally more predisposed toward change than age is, such a shift could act as a brake on the rising rate of social change.

Prospects: Social Structure

Scale of organization   So far, industrialization has meant larger societies, partly as a result of population growth within existing societies, partly as a result of their enlargement through merger and conquest. These trends have occurred in both industrial and industrializing societies, though conquest has

---

[21] Looking far into the future in one of his science-fiction novels, Fred Hoyle envisions a world in which the human population restricts its numbers to a few million, all of whom live in Mexico. The rest of the earth is left in a natural state and visited only during wilderness vacations.

been unimportant except in Africa's industrializing horticultural societies, where the European powers established the present set of nation-states during the colonial period.

With population growth almost certain to continue for some time, especially in the underdeveloped nations, and with merger and conquest also possible, if less certain, the small nation is rapidly becoming an economic and political anachronism. Economically, its home markets are too small to foster the growth of giant enterprises or provide the benefits of mass production. Politically, it is incapable of self-defense and smaller than any nation needs to be in this age of rapid transportation and communication.

In consequence, a number of multistate organizations have already formed, and, despite the resistance of many national leaders, there are almost certain to be more in the next several decades. The European Economic Community is the best-known example. Similar organizations would probably be advantageous for most of the peoples of Latin America, sub-Saharan Africa, the Middle East, and Southeast Asia.

Unfortunately, regional political unification—whatever its economic advantages—will not solve the problems of international competition and conflict. It might, in fact, intensify them by increasing the number of world powers of roughly equal strength. The best hope for eliminating the threat of war appears to lie in the formation of a single world government, but support for this is still extremely limited. Most political leaders continue to believe that peace can be preserved and their nations' interests protected within the framework of the present multination system. Probably nothing short of a near disaster—or the invention of some cheap and terribly destructive weapon that even small and poor nations could afford—could change enough minds to bring about global political unification. World unification could conceivably result from conquest by a single nation, but this, too, seems unlikely. The strong nationalistic feelings evident in so many parts of the world today, and widespread democratic and egalitarian tendencies, would make administration of a world empire extremely difficult. In short, prospects for world unification before 2000, by merger or by conquest, are remote.

Social and cultural differentiation   Even if there should be somewhat fewer societies by the end of the next several decades, as a result of some nations merging, there would probably be no real decrease in social and cultural differentiation. With machines doing more of the basic work, people will be able to devote more of their time and energy to the things they want to do. If our assumptions about the nature of man were correct, his derivative needs (page 29) are more varied than his basic ones. Therefore, as people increasingly turn their efforts to satisfying these needs, their activities are likely to become more diversified.

This tendency is already evident in all the more advanced industrial societies. Consider, for example, the need for entertainment: never before have there been so many different forms of it or such a variety of occupations in the field. The same diversity is found in most other fields—sometimes to such an extent that traditional job classifications are rendered obsolete. In a major university, for example, a faculty member often fills a unique niche. When he resigns or retires, no one is an exact replacement for him. Some of his responsibilities are assumed by colleagues, some are discontinued, and the person hired to replace him typically takes over part of his predecessor's duties and adds others. The old position, in effect, ceases to exist, and a new one is created to fit the new appointee. Although universities are extreme in this respect, many other organizations are moving in the same direction, and this custom tailoring of occupational roles is likely to become much more common in the years ahead.

Opportunities for differentiation and individuality are also growing outside the world of work. In highly productive societies, increased leisure and other resources allow people to develop and express their own distinctive abilities and personalities to an unprecedented degree. This growth in individuality seems almost certain to continue as technological advance provides both greater leisure and higher standards of living. The chief threat to the trend during the next quarter century is likely to come from ideologically motivated and repressive governments.

Social interaction   During the last hundred years, improved systems of transportation and communication have so revolutionized patterns of social interaction that the historical isolation of village populations has been virtually destroyed. It is hard to find the member of an industrial society whose life is still circumscribed by the boundary of his local community; even people who never travel have the world brought to them by the mass media. The same thing is happening in industrializing nations. Better roads and the spread of the mass media are knitting populations together, for the first time, in national networks of communication and interaction. These trends are bound to continue, barring a military or environmental catastrophe.

*Inter*societal interaction, too, has increased fantastically in recent years, largely through the growth of air transportation, which has carried unprecedented numbers of citizens from advanced industrial societies—young people in particular—to other countries. Many industrial and military personnel are stationed abroad; international tourism has become a major industry; and international trade has increased as the new technology has cut the costs of moving goods between nations. There is good reason to expect that these trends not only will continue but will accelerate, for the revolution in social interaction on an international scale is still in its early stage.

The polity   The most striking trend in the political realm during the last two centuries has been the growth of democratic forms and practices and the decline of monarchical ones. Although this has been especially marked in industrial societies, it has not been limited to them: democracy has also made some headway in industrializing societies. The first question, therefore, is whether this trend will continue.

In discussing the prospects for further democratization, we will have to consider separately (1) industrial societies that are already democratic, (2) East European nations, and (3) societies that are still industrializing. With respect to the first, we have already emphasized that even though we call them democracies, none has yet approached the democratic ideal of an equal voice for everyone. In most of them, the influence of the wealthy and the better educated is way out of proportion, and the influence of the poor is very limited despite their numbers. Even where this problem has been substantially overcome, as in the Scandinavian democracies, a minority of professional politicians and political activists still tend to dominate the political process.

Large numbers of citizens in democracies today are frustrated by their inability to make their voices heard or their influence felt. This discontent is not limited to the poor; it is shared by many others who, concerned by their government's slow response to society's most urgent problems, have generated their own growing pressure for greater democratization. The McCarthy movement in the 1968 presidential election and the McGovern movement in 1972 were both manifestations of this.[22]

If this discontent continues, which seems likely, it will probably focus on reform of the political process itself. One of its obvious targets would be the outdated mode of determining representation in legislative bodies: the eighteenth- and nineteenth-century principle of geographical representation is increasingly unsatisfactory, at least as the only basis. Thus, there may be efforts to add other bases of representation — such as occupation, wealth, ethnicity, sex, or age. An alternative reform, which would probably encounter less opposition, would be the establishment of public opinion polling organizations under the auspices of legislative bodies. Such polls could provide elected representatives with far more accurate, timely, and detailed information on the public's views than they can get from commercial pollsters like Gallup and Harris. With recent advances in electronics, there is no reason why the public should not soon be able to register its views in some new and more effective way. It is hard to believe the political process will linger forever in the horse-and-buggy era.

There is, of course, the possibility that democratic societies will move in the opposite direction — toward more control by political elites and less popular participation. However, democratic governments appear to be firmly established in all the advanced industrial societies outside the Communist bloc, and only once has an advanced industrial society abandoned democratic gov-

---

[22] On the Soviet Union, see Andrei D. Sakharov, *Progress, Coexistence and Intellectual Freedom* (New York: Norton, 1968), or Abraham Rothberg, *The Heirs of Stalin: Dissidence and the Soviet Regime, 1953–1970* (Ithaca, N.Y.: Cornell, 1972).

ernment as a result of internal forces (Germany in the 1930s). All other non-democratic regimes in advanced industrial societies came about either because industrialization occurred under a nondemocratic regime (as in the Soviet Union) or as a result of foreign conquest or its equivalent (as in Czechoslovakia in 1948 and again in 1968). Considering the stresses that most industrial nations have experienced—wars, depressions, racial and ethnic struggles, and so on—this is no small accomplishment. For the next few decades, the chief threats to democracy in these societies will probably be war and internal subversion. If either of these threatens societal survival, or if propaganda makes them *appear* to be threats, citizens may be persuaded to give up many of their political rights and concentrate power in the hands of some charismatic leader or totalitarian party. Happily, the chances of this do not appear great, but it would be a mistake to ignore them.

As for the nations of Eastern Europe, they offer the most striking testimony of all for the appeal of democracy. Events since the death of Stalin prove that despite a long, ruthless suppression, the desire for democracy was never extinguished. First in Yugoslavia, later in Poland and Hungary, more recently in Czechoslovakia and the Soviet Union itself, East Europeans have clearly expressed their wish for a greater voice in their governments.[23] And they have gotten results, too, despite some tragic repressions. Democratic elements are slowly being introduced into the political systems of most East European nations. A number of them, for example, now allow people who are not members of the Communist Party to run for public office. Some also provide a way for the electorate to reject candidates put up by Party officials, and this has actually been done on a number of occasions. Although democracy still exists in only rudimentary form, a trend is evident. The rate of change, however, remains painfully slow.

Finally, in societies that are still industrializing, the prospects for the growth of democracy are not too bright. If their serious economic difficulties persist and they cannot significantly improve their standards of living, authoritarian governments of both right and left will continue to flourish. In fact, there is a strong possibility that even countries like India and Chile, which have maintained democratic regimes in the face of the most serious economic crises, will be forced to a form of government that is better equipped to deal with economic problems and suppress political discontent. This somber prediction could be upset if industrialized societies took meaningful action to help these industrializing nations, but hopes for this are dim.

The economy   Continuing change in world economic institutions is inevitable. Increasing mechanization and automation virtually assure a progressive shift from primary and secondary industries to tertiary. The less advanced countries

---

[23] For a good review of events in the Soviet Union since Stalin's death, see Rothberg, op. cit.

will experience the greatest disruptive effects, since the collapse of the traditional rural economy is invariably traumatic. No nation has made the transition from an agrarian to an industrial economy without great suffering on the part of those who are forced off the land, and no one seems to be giving much thought to the problem of how to avoid it.

Past predictions that automation will lead to massive unemployment are unlikely to be realized. That the need for human labor remains immense is evident from a brief visit to almost any major city in the United States. Schools and hospitals are understaffed, public and private buildings are in need of maintenance and repair, streets are littered, parks are neglected and crime-ridden, and there is a general atmosphere of deterioration and neglect. If massive unemployment does ensue from automation, it will be because decision makers chose it, not because there is any lack of work to be done.

The next several decades will almost certainly see the governments of traditionally market-oriented societies play a growing role in their economies, although free-enterprise rhetoric will probably continue. But governments' increasing involvement in economic affairs will not ensure that the public interest is being protected. On the contrary, the experience of the United States in recent decades makes it painfully clear that governments can also intervene for the purpose of maximizing private profits. Although the members of democratic societies may have little control over the amount of government involvement, they will have a chance to determine whether it primarily benefits limited private interests or the population as a whole. The answer will hinge largely on the success of the democratizing efforts we just discussed.

At the global level, the trend toward increasing economic specialization seems likely to continue, especially for the underdeveloped nations, most of whom have no other way to acquire the capital they need to industrialize. Even if a less competitive system replaced the present dog-eat-dog pattern, economic specialization would still be advantageous. The chief difference would be that a more cooperative system would direct more of those advantages to the less industrialized nations.

Social stratification   So far, the Industrial Revolution has effected a modest reduction in the intrasocietal inequality of the agrarian era; and, hopefully, we have seen only the beginning of a trend. But it is extremely difficult to be sure: some contemporary developments suggest growing equality, some the reverse. Such accompaniments of industrialization as increasing educational opportunities, greater access to political information, the declining need for unskilled labor, and the democratic trend are among the factors favoring greater equality.

Meanwhile, the growing complexity of politics promises to make it increasingly difficult for people to understand the issues; the schools and the mass media offer ever greater opportunity for ideological manipulation; and the growing arsenal of "big brother" techniques and weapons, ranging from devices like electronic bugs and government data banks to still-on-the-drawing-board innovations (such as electronic brain manipulation, mind-bending drugs, and genetic engineering), provides means for monitoring and controlling society reminiscent of George Orwell's 1984.[24] Thus, we could be approaching an era of unparalleled inequality—an era in which a small, powerful elite mobilizes this remarkable new technology to dominate and control the rest of the population. Although this is unlikely for the remainder of the present century, it could become a very real possibility during the first quarter of the next.

Kinship Kin groups were traditionally the basic building blocks of societies. In addition to their role in reproduction and socialization, they played a vital part in political and economic life. In fact, in the simplest societies the kinship system was the basic force that held the group together.

Things are very different today, especially in industrial societies. Kin groups have lost many, perhaps most, of their historical functions, particularly in the important areas of politics and economics. Although some new functions have been added and some old ones retained, these are concentrated in areas of personal, rather than societal, importance. As a result, the preservation and protection of the kinship system is no longer the urgent matter for society that it once was.

When we look to the future, the extended family appears almost certain to continue its decline, largely as a result of increasing geographical mobility. It is extremely difficult, under such conditions, to maintain ties with all one's aunts, uncles, and cousins, to say nothing of second cousins once removed and great-aunts.

The future of the nuclear family is harder to predict. If the present trend continues, parents and children will see less of one another—especially in the early years, the one period when the traditional closeness is still usually preserved. Day-care centers are almost certain to expand and to enroll more, and younger, children. Although some people feel these centers introduce an unnatural practice, others counter that they are only an extension of an ancient practice. One writer has reminded us that "in the past, whenever human beings have acquired sufficient resources and power, as among aristocracies, they have put the burden of child-rearing on other shoulders" (i.e., those of slaves and servants).[25] He also points out that child rearing has traditionally been viewed as an arduous and even painful experience[26] and predicts that life in modern industrial societies will strengthen this view.

---

[24] See, for example, José Delgado, *Physical Control of the Mind: Toward a Psychocivilized Society* (New York: Harper & Row, 1969).

[25] Barrington Moore, Jr., "Thoughts on the Future of the Family," in *Political Power and Social Theory* (New York: Harper Torchbooks, 1965), pp. 172–173. See also Ralph Linton, *The Study of Man* (New York: Appleton-Century, 1936), p. 246.

[26] See, for example, the biblical account of David and his son Absalom or Jesus' parable of the prodigal son.

Ties between husband and wife will probably also be weakened, or at least strained, as a result of the increasing employment of married women. If women have fewer children and more education, their desire for careers, as opposed to mere jobs, is likely to increase. Counterbalancing this, however, is the deeply rooted need of both sexes for the intimate, intense, comprehensive, and sustained relationship that only marriage seems able to provide. In addition, the traditional family system of complementary skills—men more knowledgeable about mechanics and women about cooking, for example (or the reverse if they prefer it)—seems more rewarding than a system in which there is no division of labor and both partners are obliged to master the full range of skills. This has been one of the great disadvantages of single life according to many who have tried it.

It is these conflicting tendencies that make predictions so tenuous. Perhaps the most we can say is that the nuclear family seems certain to continue for a good many decades but that its survival will increasingly depend on individual choice rather than on economic and political necessity. Also, family patterns and life styles will probably become more varied, again reflecting the declining influence of necessity and the growing area of choice.

One important innovation that seems more likely all the time is the development of societal reproductive policies. Traditionally, such decisions were left to husbands and wives, though large families have sometimes been encouraged by financial subsidies (as in Nazi Germany, where they were encouraged because of their military value). Today, with the growing concern about overpopulation, governments, as we have seen, will probably become more active in their efforts to control birthrates. At the very least they can be expected to subsidize research in methods of birth control and programs to diffuse information. Many governments will probably make contraceptives, sterilization, and abortions available to those who cannot afford them and, if these methods are not enough, establish tax incentives to encourage small families.[27]

Prospects: Language

We began this book, you may recall, by noting how the unprecedented rate of change in the modern world is mirrored in our language: words and phrases are added, or their meanings altered, in response to change in other parts of the sociocultural system. Developments in science and technology, changes in social structure, new ideologies, and emerging social problems all contribute to the growth and change of language. The communications media have greatly sped up the process by which words and phrases are drawn from the specialized vocabularies of society's subgroups and incorporated into the common vocabulary. Unabridged dictionaries will undoubtedly be even bulkier by the year 2000.

---

[27] In other words, couples with more than two children may be subject to special taxes.

Balancing this growing variety at the societal level are trends at the global level; and they, too, are likely to continue into the next century. First, there is the growing use of English (and to a lesser extent French) as a second language in many of the nations of Europe, Africa, and Asia. If this trend continues long enough, it could cause a number of languages to go the way of Cornish or Gaelic. In language as in the free-enterprise system, there is a tendency for the rich to get richer and the poor poorer: the more powerful those who use a language, the more pressure on others to learn it. The political, economic, and educational leaders of small nations, such as Sweden, Ghana, and Cambodia, find so few foreigners fluent in their tongues that they must master French or English if they wish to move easily in international circles.

The linguistic diversity of the newer nations in Africa and Southeast Asia has also led to the spread of French and English. Not having a native tongue common to all its population, such a society typically takes the language of its former colonial power. Leaders settle on this solution (usually with reluctance) partly because they themselves are skilled in that language, partly because to choose one of the native languages would give one rival ethnic group an unfair political and economic advantage over the others.

A second trend involves the influence of the languages of dominant nations on other languages, through the process of social change. Since most innovations originate in these nations, new phenomena generally acquire their names there. Then, as these new elements—in everything from science to youth culture—spread to other countries, their original names are retained or only slightly modified. English words and phrases, in particular, have heavily permeated many languages this way—even in France some leaders complain about the spread of "Franglais," the contemporary vernacular with its heavy component of words and phrases derived from English.

Technological advance, which has produced our modern systems of transportation and communication and which is thus the ultimate cause of these trends in language, may someday see the elimination of man's linguistic diversity. This would be a tremendous boon to communication and greatly increase international understanding. On the other hand, it would make most of the great works of literature accessible only to trained specialists.[28] However, it could be argued that this is already true of the older works of every language. Most of Chaucer and some of Shakespeare, for example, are incomprehensible to modern English-speaking people without special aids or training.

Prospects: Ideology and the Higher Goals

Through most of history, man had little control over his future. It was largely shaped for him by an enormous complex of forces which he understood poorly

---

[28] Translations rarely do justice to the originals. Although a few translations become notable literary achievements in their own right—as in the case of Boris Pasternak's translation of Shakespeare into Russian—they invariably differ from the original in many basic respects. This is especially true of poetry.

or not at all and over which he had little or no control. In such a world, man did not *change* things nearly so much as he *adjusted to* things. And his ideologies were a basic mechanism in that process of adapting to the inevitable.

Gradually, but with rapidly increasing speed during the last 100 years, the situation changed. Man's store of information about the natural world grew, and, with it, the technical resources at his command. As a result of the changes he has made with his tremendous new power, man suddenly finds himself under great pressure: he may even be in a position where, if he is to avert disaster, he will have to bring the entire process of change under his rational control, making it more his servant and less his master. In short, man may finally have both the means and the motivation to assure him a major role in directing the course of history.

This is the evolution of evolution of which we spoke earlier (page 83)—fundamental change in the operation of the evolutionary process itself. If it should occur, one of the most significant consequences would involve the role of ideology. As ideology came to be less necessary in helping man adapt to the inevitabilities of his situation on this planet, it could become more important in helping him choose among the alternatives and options offered by modern technology. Thus, there would be a shift in the relative influences of ideology and technology in determining the kind of change that occurs in the years ahead.

Obviously, this does not imply any decline in the importance of technology. On the contrary, this new possibility is, itself, predicated upon technology—a highly advanced technology, a technology that would continue to define the limits of what is possible and determine the relative economic costs. More, it is the power of man's technology—neither good nor bad, simply powerful—which may make it both *possible* and *imperative* for him to take control of the entire process of societal evolution.

If man can somehow avoid the truly frightening pitfalls of the next few decades, he may enter an era in which peace, justice, and brotherhood will be viable alternatives for the first time since the forces of intersocietal selection began to make their ruthless and deadly influence felt. Let us hope he has the vision to recognize his opportunity and the wisdom to seize it.

Glossary

These definitions are not necessarily the only meanings of these words. Rather, they are the meanings used in this book and generally conform to standard sociological usage.

Achieved role A role that can legitimately be changed through the effort (or lack of effort) of the individual (e.g., occupation).

Adaptation The process of adjusting to, or adjusting, environmental conditions; hence, broadly, problem solving.

Aggregation A generic term referring to any collection of individuals; a population. The term is applicable to populations that constitute groups as well as to those that do not.

Agrarian era The period in history when there were no societies technologically more advanced than agrarian societies (c. 3000 B.C. to A.D. 1800).

Agrarian society A society in which agriculture is the primary means of subsistence. *Advanced* agrarian societies are differentiated from *simple* by the presence of iron tools and weapons.

Agriculture The cultivation of fields by use of the plow.

Alteration An innovation that involves a change in the form of some aspect of culture but no new information or new combination of existing information.

Analogue Something that is similar to something else; especially something that is *functionally* similar.

Anthropoid A member of the suborder of primates including man and the families most closely related to man.

Apparatchik A political functionary in the U.S.S.R.

or other East European society; a member of the Party or state apparatus.

Artisan A craftsman. The term is usually applied to craftsmen in agrarian or maritime societies.

Ascribed role A role that cannot legitimately be changed (such as age, sex, race, or ethnicity).

Association A formally organized secondary group that performs some relatively specialized function or set of functions.

Australopithecus The earliest hominid ancestor of man.

Autocracy Rule by one person.

Autogenous Self-generated; produced independently of external influences.

Autonomous Self-governing; not subject to the authority of others.

Band A nomadic community at the hunting and gathering level.

Biophysical environment The biological and physical components of the environment.

Bureaucracy (1) The administrative component of a government or other association; (2) a system of administration characterized by a highly formalized division of labor, a hierarchical system of authority, and action oriented to a complex and formalized system of rules.

Capitalism An economic system in which the basic problems of production and distribution are settled by means of the market system, with minimal governmental regulation or control (see *Market economy*).

Caste   A hereditary class with minimal opportunities for mobility into or out of the group.

Civilization   An advanced sociocultural system. The term is usually reserved for those with writing and urban communities.

Class   (1) An aggregation or group of people whose *overall* statuses are similar; (2) an aggregation or group of people who stand in similar positions with respect to some specific resource that affects their access to power, privilege, or prestige.

Command economy   An economy in which the basic questions of production and distribution are decided by political authorities (contrast with *Market economy*).

Communication   The exchange of information by means of signals or symbols.

Community   An informally organized group whose members are united either by a common place of residence or by a common subculture (see *Geographical community* and *Cultural community*).

Correlation   A measure of the degree of association between two variables. Correlation coefficients range from .0 when there is absolutely no relationship between the variables to ±1.0 when there is a perfect relationship (i.e., one value is a perfect function of the other).

Cultural community   A community whose members are united by ties of a common cultural tradition (e.g., a racial or ethnic group).

Culture   A society's symbol system and all the aspects of human life dependent on it.

Custom   A learned pattern of behavior which is at least moderately widespread in a society and which endures for a significant period of time.

Demography   The study of populations, their size, composition, and change.

Determinism   The assumption that chance plays no part in causal relations in the natural world and that all causal relations are therefore potentially predictable (contrast with *Probabilism*).

Diffusion   The transfer of cultural information from one group to another.

Discovery   An innovation that provides men with new information (compare with *Invention*).

Ecological community   A population of plants and animals of diverse species that occupy a given territory and are bound together by ties of mutual dependence.

Ecology   The science of the interrelationships of living things to each other and to their environment.

Economic surplus   Production that exceeds what is needed to keep the producers alive and productive.

Endogamy   The practice of marrying only within the group (whether society, tribe, community, or religious group).

Energy   The capacity for performing work.

Environment   Everything external to an organism or population that affects it in any way.

Era   A period of time during which a particular type of society is the most advanced in existence (e.g., the agrarian era).

Ethnography   The description of sociocultural systems, especially those of primitive peoples.

Evolution   A process of change in a definite direction, particularly from a simple to a more complex state.

Exogamy   The practice of marrying only outside one's group (contrast with *Endogamy*).

Extended family   A group of related persons, larger and more inclusive than the nuclear family, in which meaningful ties are maintained.

Family   See *Nuclear family* and *Extended family*.

Feedback The reversion of part of the effects of a given process to its source, modifying or reinforcing it (i.e., A influences B, thereby causing B to exert an influence back on A).

Fishing society A society in which fishing or fishing and gathering are the chief means of subsistence.

Fixed costs Costs of production that remain more or less constant regardless of the number of units produced (contrast with *Variable costs*).

Freedom The availability of alternative courses of action.

Frontier society An agrarian society that is expanding into the territory of less advanced neighboring societies.

Function (1) A characteristic activity of a person, thing, or institution, (2) a consequence of the actions of a person, thing, or institution, (3) a relationship in which changes in the magnitude of one variable are associated in a definite and determined way with changes in the magnitude of another variable.

Fundamental innovation An invention or discovery that either (1) opens the way for many other innovations or (2) alters the conditions of human life so that many other changes become either possible or necessary.

Gathering Collecting edible fruits and vegetables that grow wild.

Gene A segment of a chromosome with characteristic effects on the development of the individual bearing it; repository of a unit of heritable, biochemically coded information.

General evolution The evolution of human, societies throughout the world as a whole (see *Specific evolution*).

Genetic heritage of man All the genetically based attributes of man (compare with *Human nature*).

Genetics The branch of biology concerned with heredity.

Geographical community A community whose members are united primarily by ties of spatial proximity.

Governing class A largely hereditary class from which the political authorities of a society are recruited.

Gross domestic product Gross national product minus net income from abroad.

Gross national product The monetary value of the goods and services produced by a nation during a specific period (usually a year).

Group An aggregation whose members (1) act together in a common effort to satisfy common, or complementary, needs, (2) share common behavioral expectations, and (3) have a sense of common identity. The term may be applied to a society, an intersocietal unit, or an intrasocietal unit.

Guild A mutual aid association of merchants and artisans in the same trade (found in agrarian and maritime societies).

Headman The leader of a local community, usually in a preliterate society; one who leads rather than rules. The term is sometimes used (though not in this volume) to refer to the leader of a kinship group.

Herding society A society in which herding is the primary means of subsistence. *Advanced* herding societies are differentiated from *simple* by the use of horses or camels for transportation.

Hominid One of the Primate family Hominidae, including man and manlike creatures; specifically, Homo sapiens sapiens and his tool-making ancestors.

Homo erectus An early hominid ancestor of modern man.

Homo sapiens neanderthalensis Neanderthal man.

Homo sapiens sapiens Genetically modern man.

Horticultural era The period in history when there were no societies technologically more advanced than horticultural societies (c. 7000 B.C. to 3000 B.C.).

Horticultural society   A society in which horticulture is the primary means of subsistence. *Advanced* horticultural societies are differentiated from *simple* by the manufacture of metal tools and weapons.

Horticulture   The cultivation of small gardens using the hoe or digging stick as the chief tool. Horticulture is differentiated from agriculture by the absence of the plow.

Human nature   The behavioral consequences of mankind's common genetic heritage (compare with *Genetic heritage of man*).

Hunting and gathering era   The period in history when there were no societies more advanced than hunting and gathering (to c. 7000 B.C.).

Hunting and gathering society   A society in which hunting and gathering are the primary means of subsistence. *Simple* hunting and gathering societies lack the spear-thrower and the bow and arrow; *advanced* have one or both of these weapons.

Hybrid society   A society in which two or more of the basic modes of subsistence are substantially intermingled.

Ideology   A society's basic belief systems and their applications to daily life (made up of world views, values, and norms).

Industrial era   The period in history when industrial societies have been dominant (from c. A.D. 1800 to the present).

Industrialization   Increasing reliance on the newer inanimate sources of energy and the technological and economic consequences of this (compare with *Modernization*).

Industrial Revolution   The revolution in technology that began in England in the eighteenth century, has since spread to most of the world, and is still continuing.

Industrial society   A society in which industry has replaced agriculture as the chief means of subsistence and the newer sources of energy (coal, petroleum, etc.) are dominant; a society that consumes at least 2,000 kilograms of coal equivalent per person per year.

Information   A signal or symbol that is impressed on the memory system of an organism, population, or machine and influences its subsequent action.

Instinct   Genetically programmed responses or response sets.

Institution   A durable structure of interrelated customary practices.

Intelligentsia   Well-educated persons; the upper part of the nonmanual class in East European societies (occasionally used to refer to the entire nonmanual class).

Intersocietal selection   Spontaneous processes responsible for the survival of some societies and the extinction of others.

Intrasocietal selection   Processes, both spontaneous and deliberate, that are responsible for different rates of survival among elements of a sociocultural system.

Invention   An innovation that involves a useful new combination of existing information (compare with *Discovery*).

IQ or intelligence quotient   A measure of the combined effects of innate learning capacity and learning opportunities (particularly opportunities to learn test-relevant information); originally thought to be a measure of innate capacity alone.

Language   A system of symbols capable of transmitting and storing information.

Laws   Norms sanctioned by the state or society.

Learning   A process that manifests itself by changes in behavior (usually adaptive in nature) based on prior experience.

Legitimate   That which is morally or legally justified.

Legitimize   To make legitimate; to provide an ideological or legal justification for a practice that would otherwise be regarded as objectionable.

Maritime society A society in which overseas commercial activity is the primary means of subsistence.

Market economy An economy in which the basic problems of production and distribution are settled by means of the market system (see *Capitalism,* and contrast with *Command economy.*)

Mass media Communications media developed in industrial societies to reach the masses (especially TV, radio, newspapers, and movies).

Matrilineal kin group An extended family organized on the basis of common descent through the female line.

Matrilocality The practice of married couples living with or near the wife's female relatives.

Mean, arithmetic The quantity formed by dividing the sum of a set of numbers by the number of them.

Median The middle number in a series of numbers arranged in order from the highest to the lowest.

Mesolithic The Middle Stone Age (from c. 10,000 B.C. to 9000 B.C.).

Mobility, vertical See *Vertical mobility.*

Modernization All the long-term social and political changes that are associated with industrialization (compare with *Industrialization*).

Monopoly A commodity market with only a single seller.

Nation A multicommunity society governed by full-time political leaders (i.e., a society with more than minimal political development).

Natural selection Spontaneous processes resulting in differential rates of reproduction, and often in the eventual extinction of certain populations.

Neolithic The New Stone Age. This term is sometimes also used as an adjective to refer to horticultural societies.

Neophilia Love of the new, of change, or of novelty.

Nomad A member of a group that has no permanent settlement and moves about periodically (usually in a well-defined territory) in order to obtain food and other necessities.

Normative Of, or pertaining to, norms (i.e., having a moral and/or legal character).

Norms Behavioral prescriptions and proscriptions for the incumbents of specific roles in specific situations.

Nuclear family A man, his wife or wives, and their unmarried children living with them.

Oligarchy The rule of the few.

Oligopoly A commodity market dominated by a few sellers.

Organization A structured entity (see also *Social structure*).

Paleolithic The Old Stone Age (from c. 2,000,000 B.C. to 10,000 B.C.). The Paleolithic is divided into three parts: Lower (the earliest), Middle, and Upper (see *Pleistocene*).

Patrilineal kin group An extended family organized on the basis of common descent through the male line.

Patrilocality The practice of married couples living with or near the husband's male kinsmen.

Patrimony Property transmitted within a family from father to son.

Peasant An agricultural worker in an agrarian society.

Per capita income National income divided by population. (This measure is somewhat misleading as a measure of the standard of living of the average person, since a small number of people with very large incomes can pull the average far above the median).

Pleistocene The *geologic* era beginning about 1,000,000 years ago and ending about 10.000 years ago. The era was characterized by repeated expansion of glaciers (see *Paleolithic*).

Polity The political system of a group, especially of a society.

Polygyny   The marriage of a man to two or more wives simultaneously.

Population   (1) An aggregation of organisms; (2) the members of a society or other group considered collectively.

Population, constant aspect   The genetic heritage of mankind.

Population, variable aspects   Size, density, composition, distribution, and birth, death, and migration rates of a population.

Priest   A religious functionary believed to have supernatural powers that are bestowed on him by an organized religious group; one who mediates between God, or a god, and man. "Priest" is not to be equated with "shaman."

Primary group   A small group in which face-to-face relations of at least a fairly intimate and personal nature are maintained.

Primary industries   Industries that produce or extract raw materials (especially farming and mining).

Primates   An order of mammals that includes the prosimians (e.g., tarsiers and lemurs) and the anthropoids (e.g., baboons, chimpanzees, gorillas, and men).

Primogeniture   The right of the eldest surviving son to inherit all real estate.

Probabilism   The assumption that random events and chance factors (i.e., factors which are not predictable from a given theory) play a part in many causal relations in the natural world and that these relations, therefore, are *not* precisely predictable (contrast with *Determinism*).

Process   A series of related events with an identifiable outcome.

Progress   A series of changes that shows movement in a single direction (i.e., toward more, or less, of some quality such as size or complexity). The term is synonymous with *Evolution;* it does not imply increased goodness or happiness.

Religion   The world view of a group of people and the practices associated with that view (as used in this book, the term includes nontheistic religions, such as Communism and Humanism, as well as theistic religions, such as Christianity).

Retainer   An individual who owes service to a person or household of high status (usually found in horticultural and agrarian societies).

Role   A position which can be filled by an individual and to which distinctive behavioral expectations and requirements are attached. The term may also be used to refer to the part a group, institution, or other social unit plays in the life of a society.

Sanction   (1) A reward or punishment; (2) to reward or punish.

Secondary group   Any group that is larger and more impersonal than a primary group.

Secondary industries   Industries that process raw materials and turn out finished products.

Selection   See *Natural selection, Intersocietal selection,* and *Intrasocietal selection.*

Serf   A peasant farmer who is bound to the land and subject to the owner of the land.

Shaman   A person who is believed to enjoy special powers because of a distinctive relationship he has established with the spirit world; a medicine man. "Shaman" is not to be equated with "priest."

Signal   A genetically determined response to a stimulus and a means of transmitting information (see *Symbol*).

Social   Pertaining to the interaction of the members of a society.

Socialist society   A society in which there is little or no private ownership of the means of production (not applied to a society where the Socialist Party is in power if this condition is not met).

Socialization   The process by means of which a person acquires the culture of his society or group.

Social movement   A loose-knit group that seeks to change the social order.

Social organization   See *Social structure*.

Social structure   A network of relationships among people. The basic building blocks of social structures are *individuals* and *roles;* these are commonly organized into groups which are, themselves, the basic building blocks of a larger, more inclusive social structure. Synonymous with *social organization.*

Society   A territorially bounded and autonomous population of animals of a single species (e.g., men) maintaining ties of association and interdependence.

Sociocultural   Contraction of social and cultural.

Sociocultural evolution   Technological advance and its consequences (see also *General evolution* and *Specific evolution*).

Sociocultural system   The totality of characteristics of a group and its culture (includes population, language, technology, social structure, and ideology).

Sociology   The study of human societies.

Specific evolution   The evolution of an individual society (see *General evolution*).

Status   The relative rank of a person, role, or group, according to culturally defined standards.

Status group   A class made up of members of a racial, ethnic, or religious group (i.e., a class in which the resource involved is the individual's *membership in the group*).

Stratification   Class or status differentiation within a population.

Structure   The arrangement of the parts of an entity.

Subculture   The culture of a community.

Subsistence   The basic necessities of life; also the process by which they are obtained.

Surplus   See *Economic surplus*.

Symbiosis   A relationship of mutual interdependence of unlike organisms or populations.

Symbol   A culturally determined vehicle for the transmission of information (see *Signal*).

System   A more or less coordinated set of interrelationships among the parts or elements that form an entity. A system exists to the degree that the actions of the parts of an entity are coordinated both with one another and with the actions of the entity as a whole.

Systemic   Having the attributes of a system.

Technology   The information, techniques, and tools with which people utilize the material resources of their environment to satisfy their various needs and desires.

Technostasis   The absence of both technological advance and technological regression.

Tertiary industries   Industries that perform services (e.g., retail trade, government).

Theocracy   A society ruled by a priesthood in the name of some deity or by a ruler believed to be divine.

Tribe   A preliterate group whose members speak a common language or dialect, possess a common culture that distinguishes them from other peoples, and know themselves, or are known, by a distinctive name.

Unilinear theory of evolution   A theory which assumes that all societies follow exactly the same path of evolutionary development.

Urban community   A community whose inhabitants are wholly or largely freed from the necessity of producing their own food and fibers.

Values   The generalized moral beliefs to which the members of a group subscribe.

Variable   A concept in which the essential property is capable of varying in degree.

Variable costs   Costs of production that tend to vary in proportion to the number of units produced (contrast with *Fixed costs*).

Vertical mobility   Change of status, either upward or downward.

Working class   Those members of modern industrial societies who belong to families headed by manual workers.

World views   People's beliefs concerning the *ultimate* nature of reality; their interpretation of the totality of experience.

Picture Credits

The authors wish to acknowledge those who provided photographs and drawings used in this book.

Part I photo of *Man Walking Quickly under the Rain,* sculpture by Giacometti, by Herbert Matter. Courtesy of The Museum of Modern Art, New York.

1.2a Bruce Davidson, Magnum Photos, Inc.

1.2b Toni Angermayer, Photo Researchers, Inc.

1.2c Dennis Stock, Magnum Photos, Inc.

1.3 (left) By permission of Susan Johns
(right) Courtesy of The American Museum of Natural History

3.1 Louis Goldman, Rapho Guillumette Pictures

3.3 Peter Buckley, Photo Researchers, Inc.

3.4 Ed Fisher, by permission of the artist and *The Saturday Review*

3.8 Courtesy of The Bettmann Archive, Inc.

3.9 Ernst Haas, Magnum Photos, Inc.

4.2 By permission of Laurence K. Marshall, Peabody Museum, Harvard University

4.4 George Gerster, Rapho Guillumette Pictures

4.5 From Ellsworth Huntington, *Mainsprings of Civilization,* copyright © 1945 by John Wiley & Sons, Inc. By permission of Mrs. Rachel Brewer Huntington.

4.6 From Ellsworth Huntington, *Mainsprings of Civilization,* copyright © 1945 by John Wiley & Sons, Inc. By permission of Mrs. Rachel Brewer Huntington.

5.2 By permission of United Nations

Part II photo of *The Chariot,* sculpture by Giacometti, by Herbert Matter. Courtesy of The Museum of Modern Art, New York.

6.3 From Grahame Clark, *The Stone Age Hunters,* copyright © 1967 by Thames and Hudson Ltd., London. By permission of the publisher and the British Museum (Natural History)

6.5 Courtesy of Joffre Coe

6.7 From *Prehistoric Societies,* by John G. Clark and Stuart Piggott. Copyright © 1965 by Grahame Clark and Stuart Piggott. Reprinted by permission of Alfred A. Knopf, Inc.

6.8 From Hugo Obermaier, *Fossil Man in Spain,* copyright © 1925 by Yale University Press (plate XIV)

6.9 Courtesy of Joffre Coe

6.10 With permission from *Paleolithic Cave Art.* © Peter J. Ucko and Andree Rosenfeld, 1967. McGraw-Hill Book Company

6.11 From Grahame Clark, *The Stone Age Hunters,* copyright © 1967 by Thames and Hudson Ltd., London. By permission of the publisher.

6.12 By permission of the Smithsonian Office of Anthropology, Bureau of American Ethnology Collection

6.13 Laurence K. Marshall, Peabody-Harvard-Smithsonian Expeditions

6.14 Laurence K. Marshall, Peabody-Harvard-Smithsonian Expeditions

6.15 Laurence K. Marshall, Peabody-Harvard-Smithsonian Expeditions

6.16 Laurence K. Marshall, Peabody-Harvard-Smithsonian Expeditions

6.17 From Grahame Clark, *The Stone Age Hunters,* copyright © 1967 by Thames and Hudson Ltd., London. By permission of the publisher.

6.18 From Grahame Clark, *The Stone Age Hunters,* copyright © 1967 by Thames and Hudson Ltd., London. By permission of the publisher and Axel Poignant.

7.1 From Seton Lloyd and Fuad Safar, "Tell Hassuna," *Journal of Near Eastern Studies* (vol. 4, fig. 36). By permission of the University of Chicago Press.

7.2 From J. Mellaart, *Earliest Civilizations of the Near East,* copyright © 1966 by Thames and Hudson Ltd., London. By permission of the publisher.

7.3 Courtesy of The Metropolitan Museum of Art, Munsey Bequest, 1924

7.4 Courtesy of René Millon. All rights reserved.

7.5 Courtesy of The University Museum, University of Pennsylvania, Philadelphia

7.6 Reprinted with permission of the publisher from *The Ancient Maya,* third edition, by Sylvanus G. Morley: revised by George W. Brainerd (Stanford: Stanford University Press, 1956) plate 28, e, p. 187

7.7 By permission of Standard Oil Co. (N.J.)

7.8 By permission of Smithsonian Office of Anthropology

7.9 Courtesy of The American Museum of Natural History

7.10 By permission of Napoleon Chagnon, *Yanamamo:*

The Fierce People. Copyright © 1968 by Holt, Rinehart & Winston, New York

7.11 By permission of Napoleon Chagnon

7.12 By permission of Napoleon Chagnon (see his volume *Yanamamö: The Fierce People* for further details). Copyright © 1968 by Holt, Rinehart & Winston, New York

7.13 Courtesy of The American Museum of Natural History

7.14 United Nations

7.15 United Nations

7.16 United Nations

7.17 Courtesy of The American Museum of Natural History

8.1 Courtesy of The Metropolitan Museum of Art

8.2 Frontispiece from P. Delougaz, *The Temple Oval at Khafajah,* copyright © 1940 by University of Chicago Press. Courtesy of the Oriental Institute, University of Chicago

8.3 Courtesy of The Metropolitan Museum of Art

8.4 Courtesy of The Metropolitan Museum of Art. Museum Excavations, 1919–1920; Rogers Fund, supplemented by contribution of Edward S. Harkness

8.5 Courtesy of Department of Antiquities, Ashmolean Museum, Oxford

8.7 Standard Oil Co. (N.J.)

8.8 Standard Oil Co. (N.J.)

8.9 Standard Oil Co. (N.J.)

8.10 J. Allan Cash, Rapho Guillumette Pictures

8.11 Courtesy of The Metropolitan Museum of Art, Bashford Dean Memorial Collection, 1929

8.12 Courtesy of The Metropolitan Museum of Art, Rogers Fund, 1904

8.14 United Nations

8.15 United Nations

8.16 United Nations

8.17 United Nations

8.18 United Nations

8.19 United Nations

8.20 Standard Oil Co. (N.J.)

8.21 United Nations

8.22 Standard Oil Co. (N.J.)

8.23 Standard Oil Co. (N.J.)

8.24 Standard Oil Co. (N.J.)

8.25 United Nations

8.26 Standard Oil Co. (N.J.)

8.27 Courtesy of the Kunsthistorisches Museum, Vienna

9.1 United Nations

9.2 P. F. Mele, Photo Researchers, Inc.

9.3 Standard Oil Co. (N.J.)

9.4 By permission of Institut Français d'Archeologie, Beirut, Lebanon

9.5 Courtesy of The Metropolitan Museum of Art, Rogers Fund, 1906

Part III photo of *City Square,* sculpture by Giacometti, used by permission of Morton G. Neumann. John Mathieson, photographer.

10.1 The Smithsonian Institution

10.2 The Smithsonian Institution

10.3 The Bettmann Archive, Inc.

10.4 Wide World Photos, Inc.

10.5 Courtesy of *The Times,* London

10.6 Historical Picture Services, Chicago

10.7 F. W. Hoffman, U.S. Atomic Energy Commision

11.1 United Nations

11.2 René Burri, Magnum Photos, Inc.

11.4 Erich Hartmann, Magnum Photos, Inc.

11.5 Standard Oil Co. (N.J.)

11.6 United Nations

11.7 Courtesy of the New York Public Library

11.8 By permission of the Swedish Information Service

11.9 R. Capa, Magnum Photos, Inc.

12.1 Courtesy of the New York Public Library

12.2 Ian Berry, Magnum Photos, Inc.

12.3 Wide World Photos, Inc.

12.4 Wide World Photos, Inc.

12.5 Cornell Capa, Magnum Photos, Inc.

12.7 Yousuf Karsh, Rapho Guillumette Pictures

12.9 Bruce Davidson, Magnum Photos, Inc.

12.10 United Nations

12.11 By permission of CBS

12.12 United Nations

13.1 (Marx) Courtesy of the New York Public Library (Tillich) Burt Glinn, Magnum Photos, Inc. (Russell) Ian Berry, Magnum Photos, Inc.

13.2 Burk Uzzle, Magnum Photos, Inc.

13.4 Bill Brandt, Rapho Guillumette Pictures

13.5 Howard Harrison

13.6 Sandor Acs, Lincoln Center for the Performing Arts

14.1 United Nations

14.2 Standard Oil Co. (N.J.)

14.3a United Nations

14.3b United Press International

14.4 (Nasser) Burri, Magnum Photos, Inc. (Shah of Iran) Bruce Davidson, Magnum Photos, Inc. (Castro) Lee Lockwood, Black Star

14.5 Standard Oil Co. (N.J.)

14.6 United Nations

14.7 Standard Oil Co. (N.J.)

14.8 United Nations

14.9 United Nations

14.10 United Nations

14.11 Ian Berry, Magnum Photos, Inc.

14.12 United Nations

14.13 Wide World Photos, Inc.

Author Index

Subject Index